WHITE
PROTESTANT
NATION

WHITE PROTESTANT NATION

The Rise of the American
Conservative Movement

ALLAN J. LICHTMAN

Atlantic Monthly Press
New York

Published simultaneously in Canada
Printed in the United States of America

FIRST EDITION

ISBN-10: 0-87113-984-7
ISBN-13: 978-0-87113-984-9

Atlantic Monthly Press
an imprint of Grove/Atlantic, Inc.
841 Broadway
New York, NY 10003

Distributed by Publishers Group West

www.groveatlantic.com

08 09 10 11 12 13   10 9 8 7 6 5 4 3 2 1

To my mother and father, Gertrude and Emanuel Lichtman,
who kindled my interest in politics, and to my family,
Karyn Strickler, Kara Lichtman, and Samuel Lichtman.

CONTENTS

INTRODUCTION

On November 21, 2000, two weeks after Election Day, America still had no president-elect. The outcome of the election turned on an uncertain vote count in the state of Florida, with Republican George W. Bush clinging to a precarious lead over Democrat Al Gore. In Florida's largest jurisdiction, Miami-Dade County, a recount of slightly more than one-fifth of disputed ballots had netted Gore 157 votes. A full recount might add enough votes to his tally to swing Florida and the presidency to Gore.

The Bush campaign decided to stop cold the recount in Dade County. Its leadership in Austin, Texas, worked with leaders of the county's staunchly conservative Cuban-American community to muster 150 demonstrators, including forty to sixty out-of-state Republicans, to protest the Dade County recount on November 22. Gore's supporters were nowhere to be found; conservatives owned the streets that the left once controlled. Led by the activists flown into the state, including Ken Mehlman, national field director of the Bush campaign, and employees of GOP senators and congressmen, demonstrators stormed the county's election office, disrupted the ballot counting, and influenced an intimidated canvassing board to halt the recount permanently. Three weeks later the U.S. Supreme Court ended the recount across the state, with Bush ahead by 537 votes. But 150 zealous conservatives had already won the battle for Florida. They showed that at the turn of the twenty-first century, the right was better organized than the left, more passionate, and more devoted to winning control over government.

AN ENDURING LEGACY

The surge of the late-twentieth-century right can be understood only as part of a larger pattern of conservative politics. Although deeply rooted in earlier movements and traditions, conservatism assumed its distinctively modern form in the decade after World War I. American conservatism is as powerful and forward-looking as liberalism, although for conservatives the driving forces of American history are Christianity and private enterprise, not secular reason and social engineering. The right's political philosophy, organizing strategy, and grassroots appeal transcend its hostility to liberalism. Modern conservatism has a life, history, and logic of its own. It emerged not simply in opposition to the liberal state but alongside it, as an equally robust response to social and economic changes of the urban, industrial order.

Like liberalism, modern conservatism arose at a time of national crisis. For liberalism, that pivotal moment came with the Great Depression. For conservatism it came a decade earlier with the events surrounding America's involvement in World War I and the economic, social, and cultural upheavals that followed. The conservative consensus of the 1920s represented much more than an interlude of prosperity and reaction wedged between two eras of reform. It was more than one oscillation in an ever changing cycle of political activism and retrenchment. Despite the rise of the liberal state since the 1930s, conservatives have shaped American history no less profoundly than have liberals. Conservatives have put their stamp on policy and political culture and limited the rise of the liberal state primarily to the New Deal era from 1933 to 1938, the Great Society period from 1964 to 1966, and, more surprisingly, the Nixon years from 1969 to 1974.

The modern right arose out of a widespread concern that pluralistic, cosmopolitan forces threatened America's national identity. Those Americans most inclined to protect what they perceived as embattled traditional values came from all parts of the nation. They lived in every type of community, worked in numerous occupations, attended many different churches, or even lacked formal affiliation with a church. The vanguard of American conservatism in the 1920s, however, shared a common ethnic identity: they were white and Protestant and they had to fight to retain a once uncontested domination of American life.

At the core of right-wing politics in the 1920s and beyond was an anti-pluralistic ideal of America as a unified, white Protestant nation. Many factors, including race, religion, gender, nationality, and class, shaped America's anti-pluralist tradition. But the vitality of that tradition flows from an evolving cultural nationalism that combined these factors in different ways at different times. Positively, conservatives have insisted on upholding the values of America's Anglo-Saxon pioneers. Negatively, they have kept the country on edge as Cassandra's warning that pluralism would destroy the civilization that the pioneers had built. Virtually every dispute over radicalism, loyalty, reproduction, race, immigration, sexuality, crime, permissiveness, creationism, and school prayer had its forerunner in the '20s. So too did forms of right-wing political mobilization. These include the grassroots organizing of the Ku Klux Klan, the lobbying of patriotic and business associations, the defense of traditional womanhood by the DAR, the "scientific" case for white Anglo-Saxon superiority, and the radio evangelizing of fundamentalist preachers. Support for private enterprise complemented the anti-pluralist tradition in debates during the era over taxation, regulation, welfare, anticommunism, and labor relations.

The right has held together as a political movement since World War I through its core commitment to conserving white Protestant values and private enterprise, not free enterprise. American conservative politics is not about limited government, states' rights, individual freedom, or free markets. These are all dispensable ideas that the right has adjusted and re-adjusted to protect core principles. Conservatives have built their own versions of big government, carved out innumerable exceptions to free markets for business subsidies and friendly regulations, and restricted freedom in the interest of security. They have backed states' rights, for example, on racial issues, but not on alcohol and drug use, pornography, abortion, and gay marriage. In defense of core values, conservatives shifted from isolationists before Pearl Harbor to aggressive warriors against communism and terrorism. They have abandoned protectionism for free trade, public education for private school vouchers, and deficit control for "supply-side" tax cuts.

The moral aspirations of the modern American right have focused on the family, most conspicuously with the rise of a "pro-family" movement in the 1970s, but extending throughout the post–World War I period. Control over women's allegedly dangerous sexuality and autonomy is at the center of conservative politics. In this view, a morally ordered society requires a morally ordered family, with clear lines of divinely ordained masculine authority and the containment within it of women's erotic allure. Salacious, nonmotherly displays of female bodies, sex education in schools, abortion rights, easy divorces, and the tolerance of homosexuality and other forms of deviance undercut the reproduction and orderly progress of civilization. Feminist demands since the 1920s to upset manly and womanly distinctions and erode patriarchy de-feminizes women and feminizes men, opening the family and the nation to conquest (rape) and subversion (seduction). The history of failed civilizations, conservative physician Arabella Kenealy wrote in 1922, "shows one striking feature as having been common to most of these great decadences. In nearly every case, the dominance and [sexual] license of their women were conspicuous."[1]

The conservative tradition is white and Protestant in part because black Protestant culture has followed it own path to cultural pluralism and liberal politics. Both religion and race have mattered for conservatives who view nationhood as anchored in white, native-stock peoples and their distinctive culture. Since World War I, conservatives have been cultural, religious, and at times racial nationalists, dedicated to protecting America's superior civilization from racially or culturally inferior peoples, foreign ideologies, sexual deviance, ecumenical religion, or the encroachment of a so-called one-world government.

In the late twentieth century, however, white Protestants achieved a partial and uneasy rapprochement with white Catholics. Once older fears subsided, Protestant and Catholic conservatives found common ground on pro-family issues, communism, and militant Islam. This evolution on the right reflected a crucial double shift in American history: the decline of anti-Catholicism among white Protestants and the rise of a politically and theologically conservative Catholicism that put sexual morality, traditional gender roles, biblical truth, and the protection of Christianity above church teachings on labor, the death penalty, and social welfare. In an ironic but not surprising twist of history, white evangelical Protestants gave Catholic conservative candidate Patrick J. Buchanan his most enthusiastic support in the Republican presidential primaries of 1996 and the most devout Catholics preferred evangelical Protestant George W. Bush to Catholic John Kerry in the presidential election of 2004.

Within the conservative core, religion and enterprise contradict as well as reinforce each other. Corporations that follow economic self-interest may foster the opening of borders, the marketing of sin, and the breaching of national sovereignty. However, America's anti-pluralist tradition is fundamentally pro-capitalist. Anti-pluralist conservatives have cheered private enterprise as both efficient and virtuous. Even as Americans evolved from savers and craftsmen to producers and consumers, conservatives have sustained the linkage between virtue and enterprise. The business community has provided the right with indispensable expertise, influence, and resources. Anti-pluralism, in turn, gave the right a mass base and a passion that economic conservatism lacks.

Anti-pluralist conservatives have largely exempted capitalism from cultural corruption. This separation opened a space within which big capital could unite politically with ordinary shopkeepers, farmers, and workers, joining victims with their victimizers in the eyes of liberals. It also guided the formulation of state policy, with the first rule to do no harm either to individual virtues or to traditional institutions such as the church, the school, and the family. Conservatives have also turned to state power for revitalizing the culture. Still, the use of government to enforce moral standards has fluctuated over time and led to tension over conservative ambivalence about the state. After fading during the Great Depression and early Cold War era, the turn to government for moral compulsion gained new urgency and a broadened agenda after the tumult of the 1960s and battles over abortion, women's rights, and homosexuality in the 1970s.

Conservatives should not be confused with antigovernment libertarians. Unlike libertarians, conservatives care far more about the purposes to which government is put rather than its size, scope, or intrusiveness. Libertarians have overlapped conservatives in economic policies, but they also have overlapped liberals in social and foreign policies. "Conservatism is NOT Libertarianism," thundered conservative-turned-libertarian Karl Hess in 1968, because conservatism presumes that "in the choice between the rights of the state (society) and the rights of the individual that the rights of the state, of society, must come first." Unlike conservatives, libertarians are consummate pluralists who tolerate personal choices that conservatives would ban as deviant, disloyal, and immoral. Unlike conservatives, libertarians would stop government from backing business, mothball the CIA, and demote the military to a homeland garrison.

CONSERVATIVES AND THE BIG PICTURE OF HISTORY

Although a political movement in an open society contends with equally powerful rivals, defeat has not yet been final for either America's liberal or her conservative traditions. Conservatism, like liberalism, resides not only in the electorate, parties, and government but also in the schools and churches, mass media and the high arts, fraternal groups and corporations, and civic and trade associations. Conservative politics has had an enduring appeal to Americans seeking the clarity and comfort of absolute moral codes, clear standards of right and wrong, swift and certain penalties for transgressors, and established lines of authority in public and family life.

By the late twentieth century, as demonstrated by their victory in the fight over Florida votes in 2000, conservatives had gained an edge on liberals in critical aspects of political organizing and mobilization. The right led the left in tapping the resources of corporations and foundations and grassroots fund-raising through direct-mail solicitations. It used appeals to "family values" and "personal responsibility" to recapture the moral high ground that the left had occupied during the era of the civil rights struggle. It advanced the political uses of technology such as radio talk shows, television evangelism, and Internet blogs and Web sites to circumvent what was perceived to be a liberally biased media establishment. It outpaced the left in developing a richer network of partisan think tanks and advocacy groups outside the party structure. Conservatives also succeeded in carving out protected space for conservative scholarship that challenged mainstream ideas without the standard academic safeguards of open submissions and impartial peer review. And they have framed the language of politics to dictate terms of the national debates and put liberals on the defensive.

Ultimately conservatives have engaged in a struggle for control over American public life against a liberal tradition they have seen as not just wrong on issues but sinful, un-American, and corrosive of the institutions and traditions that made the nation great. To achieve their ambitious aims, conservatives have had to stay disciplined, mobilize their resources, and wage total war against liberals, with unconditional surrender as the only acceptable result.

By uniting Christianity and enterprise conservatives claimed to have protected Americans' pocketbooks and saved their souls. Since World War I conservatives claimed to have kept alive ideals of patriotism and virtue. They have questioned excesses of the modern state and defended the power of enterprise. Yet can conservatives serve both God and mammon? This age-old question intruded urgently on the right at the turn of the twenty-first century when an ascendant conservative movement tightly bonded with a capitalist order undergoing profound changes in the United States and worldwide. Critics across the spectrum questioned whether support for enterprise had become bought-and-sold government that serves rootless, amoral, and unaccountable enterprise across the world. They have worried that the rich are prospering at the expense of less affluent Americans. They have questioned whether the protection of virtue dissolved into coercive hypocrisy and defense of God and country into misguided imperial ventures, social engineering abroad, and the loss of constitutional restraints under a form of conservative big government at home. Even more than defeats in 1936 and 1964, conservative victories in 2000 and 2004 have raised the question of whether conservatism as it has evolved since World War I will endure as a powerful, coherent political movement in the United States.

1

THE BIRTH OF
THE MODERN RIGHT,
1920–1928

In 1920 the three leading Republican candidates for president, U.S. Army General Leonard Wood, Governor Frank Lowden of Illinois, and Senator Hiram Johnson of California, had hopelessly deadlocked the Republican nominating convention that convened in Chicago. Party leaders, purportedly after meeting in a smoke-filled room at the Blackstone Hotel, then turned to an unlikely compromise nominee, Senator Warren Harding of Ohio. In six undistinguished years in the Senate, the reliably conservative Harding had devoted far more energy to golf, poker, and womanizing than to matters of state. His speaking style, said journalist H. L. Mencken, "reminds me of a string of wet sponges." After Harding's nomination on the tenth ballot, the Republican National Committee paid to send his mistress on a world tour. The Republican-leaning *New York Times* said, "We must go back to Franklin Pierce if we would seek a president who measures down to his [Harding's] stature."[1]

Yet Harding quickly came to embody the sentiments of a conservative electorate in 1920. He promised a "return to normalcy" for Americans tired of liberal reform, war, and waves of Catholic and Jewish immigrants from southern and eastern Europe. He pledged to end "ineffective meddling" by government in business affairs and to govern as an "America First" president, who, mindful of "racial differences" among people, would open the nation's golden door to "only the immigrant who can be assimilated and thoroughly imbued with the American spirit."[2]

The incumbent Democratic president Woodrow Wilson was everything that Harding was not. Wilson was learned and erudite. He was a brilliant writer, an inspiring orator, and a master of statecraft. He had big ideas for leaving his mark on world history. But the future of America in the 1920s belonged to Harding's Republicans, not Wilson's Democrats.

In April 1917, a month after his second inauguration, Wilson led the nation into World War I. The president worried that war would imperil civil liberties and domestic reform and empower reactionary men of business. But he also nurtured plans for shaping a postwar international order based on self-determination, free trade, and collective security as alternatives to "atavistic imperialism and revolutionary socialism." If Wilson achieved these ambitious goals, he would likely become the first American president elected to a third term and establish his Democrats as America's enduring majority party. It didn't work out as planned for the president, the Democratic Party, the nation, or the world.

Modern conservativism took flight in response to the crisis that followed a brutal war and a failed peace. The war unleashed a wave of nationalism at home that brought on the government's repression of dissent and spread civil and racial strife across the nation. America sacrificed 118,000 young men to a savage war that annulled all standards of morality and restraint. Wilson's Democratic coalition first cracked in 1918, when Republicans recaptured the U.S. House and Senate, a week before Armistice Day, and congressional voting moved to the right. Then Wilson's peace plans collapsed amid the base ambitions of Europe's rulers, and bomb-throwing Bolsheviks replaced club-wielding Huns as the shadow falling on civilization. Although the president salvaged his plan for a League of Nations, the Senate rejected the treaty that established the League and Wilson suffered a debilitating stroke, which dashed his hopes for another presidential run. No matter. Failure abroad, social unrest and fears of radical subversion at home, and a postwar recession made 1920 a bad year for any Democratic candidate for president. On Election Day, voters cast their ballots overwhelmingly for a return to peacetime normalcy. Harding won the most decisive popular-vote victory in American history, with 60 percent of the poplar vote to 34 percent for Ohio governor James Cox, whom Democrats had nominated after forty-four ballots at their San Francisco convention.

By the 1920s a gulf had opened between Americans still devoted to a national identity defined by late-nineteenth-century Victorian values and those tied to the increasingly pluralistic cultural forces of the twentieth century. Anti-pluralists joined with leaders of business to forge a new conservative consensus in the 1920s that locked together support for private enterprise and white Protestant cultural values. The conservatives who dominated American politics in the 1920s established most of the enduring ideas and institutions that would ground the modern political right. Taken together, the prohibition of vice, anticommunism, conservative maternalism, evangelical Protestantism, business conservatism, racial science and containment, and the grassroots organizing of the Ku Klux Klan formed a stout defense of America's white Protestant, free enterprise civilization.

PROHIBITION POLITICS

For Wayne B. Wheeler of the Anti-Saloon League, the dark clouds of World War I had the silver lining of encouraging moral reform. "America has just two gigantic foes, kaiserism and the liquor traffic," Wheeler said, and he predicted victory over both these evils. Wheeler was right. In January 1919, two months after the war ended, the states ratified the Eighteenth Amendment prohibiting the manufacture, transport, and sale of alcohol. The successful campaign for prohibition showed that white Protestants, often led by women reformers, could successfully wage a bottom-up battle for their vision of moral conduct and a just society. Anti-alcohol campaigns had for many decades targeted working-class immigrants, most often Catholic, who patronized saloons and vice dens. In the South, prohibitionists argued that rum and whiskey had become symbols of freedom for blacks that led to social disharmony, crime, and the sexual violation of white women by black men.[3]

The Eighteenth Amendment was not the only "prohibition" for conservatives who sought moral renewal after the desolation of total war. By the mid-1920s America's broad program of state-sponsored morality had gained international attention. In 1925, British historian A. F. Pollard cited the United States as "the rising hope of stern and unbending Tories." American laws, he said, "were not so much a means of change as a method of putting on record moral aspirations, a liturgy rather than legislation; and the statutebook was less the fiat of the State than a book of common prayer."[4]

Prewar campaigns against vice and smut had fit comfortably with social reform. But modern conservatives shed commitments to improving housing or abolishing sweatshops. They focused instead on sexual permissiveness in an era of growing leisure time, mobility, privacy, unsupervised youth, assertive women, and defiance of law. The prewar increase in sexual experience before or outside of marriage accelerated during the 1920s. Skirts and bathing suits rose above the knee and popular versions of Freudian psychology proclaimed that sex was healthy and repression harmful. Sexuality paraded openly in the popular culture, while bawdier material fueled the underground trade in pulp novels, lurid memoirs, and pornographic magazines. Society was "assailed on all sides by a million erotic stimuli—in literature, in the theatre, and in life," wrote popular philosopher and historian Will Durant in 1929. "The sexual instinct escaped from the jail in which Puritanism had imprisoned it and ran amuck in the streets."[5]

For conservatives, moral decline afflicted not only America's great cities but also small cities and towns, where journalist Frank R. Kent uncovered a paradox of the Jazz Age. He discovered "the completeness with which all liberal thought has vanished, the astounding degree to which the country has become conservatized" in its politics. But Kent also found "the truly extraordinary extent to which the country is drenched with smut by the steadily increasing stream of pornographic periodicals and dirty fiction magazines." This "great bumper American smut crop," he said, posed "a greater menace to the future than any communistic, socialistic, or Bolshevistic propaganda." However, "the flood of sexual literature caters to a passion impossible to wholly curb or control." An undaunted Nellie B. Miller, literature chair of the General Federation of Women's Clubs, vowed that members would "fight against filth on Main Street." She proposed lawsuits, boycotts, and "the weapon which Main Street has employed from time immemorial in less worthy causes—social disapproval."[6]

Moral reformers struggled to scrub indecent and seditious material from the culture. In their view, smut thrived symbiotically with subversion, feminism, and the low morals of new immigrants from southern and eastern Europe. "The parlor Bolshevist in literary and art circles," wrote John S. Sumner, head of the New York Society for the Suppression of Vice, "are just as great a menace" as political agitators. "While the governmental authorities are struggling against foreign ideas and their advocates regarding political attack," he said, "we have had the same conflict with foreign ideas calculated and intended *to break down American standards of decency and morality.*" Sumner warned that "sex antagonism" brought on by "radical feminists" would "eventually break down the moral fiber of the nation." He said that America suffered from "racial indigestion" because "people in great numbers have come from countries where moral laxness is notorious." His society compiled statistics showing that "less than one-third of [obscenity] offenders were of real American stock." Moral guardians like Sumner, often backed by Protestant businessmen, also sought to sway public opinion, sometimes in concert with publishers worried about competition from small-time purveyors of smut. And some morals crusaders, such as white Protestant leaders of the Women's Christian Temperance Union, marketed their own uplifting material, with minimal success.[7]

The erotically charged society of the 1920s also led to fears that Americans, especially the young, were falling victim to deviant sexuality such as oral sex and homosexuality and to the scourge of venereal disease. After the war, however, efforts to prevent venereal disease through education and the administration of chemical prophylaxis that had been effective for American soldiers gave way to an emphasis on moral uplift and law enforcement. According to moral reformers of the era, preventative measures only encouraged prostitution and promiscuity. Their answers were to restore the moral integrity of society and rigorously prosecute prostitutes and other sex offenders. Congress failed to renew wartime appropriations for controlling venereal disease and state censorship boards banned as obscene films and other forms of anti-venereal propaganda. In 1926 the federal government eliminated federal aid to the states for preventing venereal disease and state appropriations for this purpose declined during the 1920s.[8]

Although Catholics opposed the campaign against alcohol, they often supported prohibitions not aimed at members of their faith. America's leading Catholic politician, New York's governor Al Smith, signed the 1927 Theater Padlock Law, which banned "obscene, indecent, immoral or impure" productions. The people, he said, "desire clean, moral public entertainment." In Boston, the renowned Ward and Watch Society, run by the city's Protestant establishment, had for decades attacked the entwined evils of degraded social conditions and impure culture. In the 1920s leaders of the society narrowed their concern to cultural purity as they made the transition from progressive to conservative. By the decade's end, however, initiative in the campaign for decency had passed from the Protestant establishment to Catholic leaders, who said that they were protecting ordinary citizens from greedy smut merchants and morally lax intellectuals and artists such as famed novelist Sinclair Lewis. A 1927 editorial in *The Pilot,* the official newspaper of the Archdiocese of Boston, condemned Lewis's portrayal of a wayward evangelist in *Elmer Gantry* for "possessing those two nauseating ingredients, sex appeal and religious skepticism, which apparently must be injected into the modern novel."[9]

After World War I, the Catholic Church crusaded worldwide for moral renewal, working through "Catholic Action" by the laity, papal edicts, suasion by the clergy, and sometimes alliances with government. In 1920 Pope Benedict XV warned that atrocities of war had led to "the diminution of conjugal fidelity and the diminution of respect for constituted authority. Licentious habits followed, even among young women." In 1930 his successor Pope Pius XI issued twelve rules to ensure that "feminine garb be based on modesty and their ornament be a defense of virtue."[10]

In Congress, disputes raged inconclusively over movie censorship and customs regulations of obscene materials. America needed to rescue a Jewish-dominated film industry "from the devil and the hands of 500 un-Christians," advised the Reverend Wilbur Fiske Crafts, one of America's first professional religious lobbyists. Since 1907, state and local censors had taken aim at movies, which they believed molded the character of everyday Americans untouched by highbrow culture. Although only federal regulators could effectively control the content and distribution of movies, many conservatives, including President Calvin Coolidge, balked at erecting a costly enforcement bureaucracy.[11]

To avert federal regulation and ease pressure from religious leaders and the movies' financiers, Hollywood adopted self-regulation. Presbyterian elder and former Republican Party chairman Will H. Hays headed a new professional association called the Motion Picture Producers and Distributors Association of America, which adopted a voluntary production code in 1930 (not put into full force until 1934) that ratified Christian morality and conservative politics. The code stated, "*Correct entertainment raises* the whole standard of a nation," whereas "*Wrong entertainment lowers* the whole living condition and moral ideals of a race." The code banned obscenity, nudity, drinking, sex outside of wedlock, suggestive dancing, drug use, homosexuality, prostitution, and amour between blacks and whites. Movies must not mention Jesus Christ, "except in reverence." They must not ridicule "good, innocence, morality or justice," "law, natural or divine," and "*ministers of religion*." They must never side "*with evil and against good*." The code tied "the Ten Commandments in with the newest and most widespread form of entertainment," recalled its author, Jesuit priest Daniel Lord. Without compulsory enforcement, however, filmmakers often circumvented the code.[12]

Efforts to restrain predatory drug addicts complemented the prohibition of alcohol. In 1914, Congress established federal control over opiates and cocaine, while states tightened their antinarcotics laws. A near panic over drug-induced crime that hit the United States during the 1920s led public officials and private reformers to declare America's first war on drugs. The nation closed its public drug treatment clinics and, as it had done with venereal disease, adopted a moral and law enforcement approach to narcotics. Addicts had no recourse other than illegal sources of supply. The decade's most energetic antinarcotics crusader, Richmond P. Hobson, head of the International Narcotic Education Association, claimed that "nine-tenths of the murders and robberies are now committed by addicts." He said that drugs are "a national calamity more devastating that the Black Death of the Middle Ages," and warned of more than a million drug addicts preying on America. For moral reformers, drug and alcohol use undermined the family and threatened the purity of American women. Even more than drink, however, enslavement to narcotics undercut discipline, self-mastery, and the free will needed to follow a godly life. In 1930 Congress established a Federal Bureau of Narcotics to enforce the drug laws and in 1937 began controlling marijuana through the Marihuana Tax Act.[13]

Despite a continued drug war, however, the nation's experiment with Prohibition crashed in the late 1920s. Prohibition exposed the tension between moral reformers and a business community opposed to government control over industry. The dynastic Du Pont family, which controlled the family chemical company and General Motors, took the lead in organizing the Association Against the Prohibition Amendment, which sought to turn public opinion against Prohibition. Although drinking declined during the 1920s, a continuing thirst for alcohol gave rise to a thriving underground market operated by organized criminal syndicates that waged bloody street battles for control of market share and paid off law enforcement officials to look the other way. The prisons swelled with felons convicted of violating the dry laws and collateral crimes. The cost of federal law enforcement quintupled during the '20s and intruded into the lives of ordinary Americans. Anyone looking for a drink could find a rural road-house, an urban saloon turned "restaurant" or "candy store," or a popular nightclub turned speakeasy where, for the first time, women could drink alongside men in an ambience of titillating sophistication. After 1925 the pretense of enforcing Prohibition evaporated in large cities. Even in rural Iowa, the state Republican chairman noted, "A great many of our people, who believe in temperance are coming to the conclusion that the Eigh-teenth Amendment and the Volstead Act do not contribute to the tem-perance or sobriety of the people."[14]

The failure of Prohibition marked one of the great political trans-formations in American history, the passing of the age when white Prot-estant cultural values sustained America's liberal reform tradition. From this point forward, liberalism would become inextricably connected to a pluralist vision of society. Eventually, the liberal tradition embraced full citizenship rights and constitutional liberties for all Americans along with toleration of diverse cultural values. Contrarily, anti-pluralist conserva-tives would return in later years to compulsory moral reform as a means for improving America's moral condition.

THE ANTICOMMUNIST CRUSADE

After the armistice that ended World War I, thousands of American troops remained abroad to fight Bolsheviks in the frozen Russian north—the first of many abortive efforts to roll back the communist frontier. But com-munism seemed to have stowed away on the ships that brought the troops home. Two American officials saw the reds coming: A. Mitchell Palmer, the forty-seven-year-old attorney general, and J. Edgar Hoover, the twenty-four-year-old head of the General Intelligence Division or "Radical Di-vision" of Palmer's Justice Department. Both men expected to achieve their life's goal by fighting reds in America. One was right.

Anticommunism, anchored in the antiradical traditions of the nine-teenth century, sustained America's modern political right. Anticommu-nism was not the sine qua non of conservative unity and success. Conservatism flourished in the 1920s when the communist threat was at a low ebb and thrived again in the post–Cold War era. Still, throughout most of the twentieth century, anticommunism remained the largest and most luminous planet orbiting the conservative sun. Anticommunism bonded elite economic conservatives with religious conservatives and middle- and working-class populists. It enabled members of immigrant and other ethnic groups to assert their identity as true Americans. It united Protestants and Catholics and gave the right an ever ready political club for bashing liberal ideals and policies. For conservatives, anticommunism became a gospel that could never be preached with too much fire and brimstone. For liberals, the flame of outrage did not burn with quite the same intensity, which left them continually vulnerable to attack.[15]

With Bolsheviks fomenting revolution and more than three million American workers on strike in 1919, a series of bombings and attempted bombings by alleged radicals led to a "red scare" at home. Raids organized by Attorney General Palmer, and synchronized by the fervently anticommunist Hoover, swept up thousands of mostly foreign-born suspected radicals between November 1919 and January 1920. The winding down of the red scare in 1920 doomed Palmer's hopes for a presidential nomination. He returned to private law practice in 1921, but in 1924 Hoover became director of the Justice Department's Bureau of Investigation (later renamed the Federal Bureau of Investigation). Until he died on the job forty-eight years later, Hoover pursued a central mission of countersubversion with the goal of eradicating communism, which he believed had special appeal to Jews and African Americans. By methodically expanding his bureaucratic power and molding the FBI to fit his Javert-like pursuit of subversives, Hoover provided legitimacy to nearly any anticommunist view that emanated from the political right for decades to come.[16]

Anticommunism pervaded government from top to bottom. Many states built on nineteenth-century precedents and adopted antisubversion laws. In 1919 twenty-four states passed laws against the flying of red flags. From 1917 to 1921 twenty-eight states enacted criminal sedition laws, which banned disloyal advocacy that ranged from advocating the forcible overthrow of government to any disloyal, profane, or abusive speech about government, the military, or the American flag. Conservatives applauded as the U.S. Supreme Court broadly construed these laws. Despite agreeing that the Bill of Rights applied to the states, the Court ruled in 1925 that state prosecutors need not wait "until the revolutionary utterances lead to actual disturbances of the public peace."[17]

Anticommunism independent of government took a leap forward in February 1919 when Theodore Roosevelt Jr. and other World War I veterans founded the American Legion. The legion quickly became the nation's largest veterans' organization. It signed up more than eight hundred thousand members in its first year, or one-fifth of all who had served in the military during the war. It made "one hundred percent Americanism" an organizing principle and began spearheading local countersubversive activities. One speaker at the legion's first national convention called for a "concrete plan to . . . wipe out every element of disloyalty in the nation." Legionnaires led attacks against allegedly radical unions and political movements. However, the legion relied mainly on persuasion. It published antiradical pamphlets and condemned pacifists, socialists, communists, and ordinary citizens who failed to see radicalism in a threatening light. During its 1921 convention, the legion resolved that expressions of "class consciousness and strife" were a "prostitution of free speech." It backed laws to "make the teaching of disloyalty in any school an offense punishable by fine or imprisonment," and urged members to monitor "all instances of disloyalty" in schools. Legionnaires shadowed and infiltrated suspected subversive organizations. Frank Cross, the legion's Americanism director, boasted in 1925 that his informers "work carefully, act normally, and absorb what information comes their way."[18]

The American Legion campaigned for veterans' benefits and promoted community service and civic activism. It further integrated two powerful, closely related traditions that had shaped the growth of American nationalism for decades. One was the lusty spirit of martial patriotism that flourished in the late nineteenth and early twentieth centuries, particularly through Civil War veterans' organizations such as the Grand Army of the Republic (GAR). The other was the spirit of reconciliation and reunion that developed through the GAR and its Confederate-remembrance counterpart in the South. By emphasizing the common bond of service and sacrifice on both sides during the Civil War, and deemphasizing bitter divisiveness, especially over issues of race, "reunionist" nationalism legitimized white supremacy, demonized Reconstruction, and fed into romantic images of an idealized southern past of racial harmony and goodwill. Although many thousands of black soldiers served in World War I, legion policy allowed southern members to create white-only posts.[19]

Anticommunism became both a business and a vocation in the 1920s. Fred Marvin, founder of Key Men of America, sold his *Daily Data Sheet* on subversive activities to businesses and patriotic groups. Harry Jung created the American Vigilante Intelligence Federation in 1927 to ferret out subversives among workers and union leaders. Jung sold lists of alleged reds and their sympathizers to employers, with priority attention to the Jews he believed had plotted the Bolshevik revolution and masterminded the American communist movement. Over three decades, Jung's files ballooned to some one million names, backing his claim to be the "nation's foremost authority on subversive forces."[20]

Prewar groups such as the National Security League, the American Defense Society, and the prestigious National Civic Federation turned to fighting Bolsheviks as part of the large but loosely organized Allied Patriotic Societies. In 1921 the Civic Federation warned that "Bolshevism and radicals" infested mainstream Protestant churches. It praised the Roman Catholic Church for upholding law and order, but admonished "priests whose viewpoints on social and economic questions meet with the hearty support and applause of radical and revolutionary elements in our country." Despite the Church's liberal teachings on many issues, its hierarchy and lay group, the Knights of Columbus, opposed godless communism. Edmund A. Walsh, Jesuit priest and founder of Georgetown University's School of Foreign Service, became a foremost scholarly critic of communism. He too saw Jews fomenting revolution, driven by "Jewish greed for gold and hatred of Christianity." However, fearful of fanning passions against Catholic immigrants and focused on building its own institutions, the Church less aggressively mobilized against communism than in later years.[21]

The Sentinels of the Republic, which called upon "every citizen" to become "a Sentinel" and "every home a sentry box," combined anticommunism with a broader conservative agenda. Although founded in 1922 by Republican Louis A. Coolidge (no relation to Calvin), former assistant secretary of the treasury, the Sentinels took flight after joining with business lobbies to block state ratification of a child labor amendment that Congress passed in 1924. This so-called Youth Control Amendment would enshrine "the socialistic theory that the citizen belongs to the state," the Sentinels said. The group warned that "those desiring social reforms" unwittingly aided "socialists and communists." Unless stopped, "the two elements will destroy the best governmental system—under which our people have achieved the greatest progress, prosperity, and happiness—that the world has ever known." Only "a perverted interpretation of the

General Welfare Clause of the Constitution" sanctioned misguided liberal reforms. A properly construed Constitution would bar "all Federal aid propositions, most regulations of business," and "superfluous" bureaucracies such as the Department of Labor's Children's Bureau. The Sentinels allied with the Catholic Church to block the formation of a federal Bureau of Education, splitting from some conservatives who sought federal support for public education and the teaching of English and patriotism in the schools. From 1925 to 1927, the Sentinels expanded modestly across America, recruiting some eight thousand members.[22]

As a coda to the red scare, Massachusetts courts in 1921 convicted two Italian anarchists, Nicola Sacco and Bartolomeo Vanzetti, of murder in conjunction with a payroll robbery. Their conviction became an international scandal for liberals and radicals who charged that government railroaded the men for their politics. The case prompted *Outlook* magazine to warn against both "the dangers of the Red Terror" and "the insidious prejudice and passions of the White Terror." However, by the time of Sacco and Vanzetti's execution in 1927, fears of both left-wing rebellion and right-wing repression had diminished in a safe and prosperous America.[23]

WOMEN CONSERVATIVES

"It takes women to fight women," said American Legion Auxiliary president and conservative activist Claire Oliphant, in 1925. Patriotic women stepped forward after the war to battle communists and their alleged fellow travelers among liberal women. "A liberal now is one who greases the tracks on the downward road to Communism," said Margaret Robinson of the Massachusetts Public Interests League.[24]

Conservative women drew on a maternalist ideology that affirmed inherent differences between the sexes and women's special role in rearing children as healthy, moral, and productive citizens. Conservative maternalists urged women of the new era not to slip the bonds of men and custom, but to reclaim their motherly responsibilities to rear courageous sons and domesticated daughters. They opposed reforms that confused sex roles, weakened families, or substituted state paternalism for parental responsibility. They worked to enforce Prohibition, clean up the movies, sterilize the unfit, restrict immigration, and above all crush subversion and sustain America's defenses, despite the lack of a credible external threat.[25]

Conservative women warned against radicals who would rip children from the home and rear them in nurseries run by the state. The radicals would end sexual restraint and manly competition. They would feminize men and coerce women into unnatural masculine roles through forced work and conscription. Conservative women found dangerous sex role reversals in women who embraced the unisex hedonism of the times: short skirts and bathing suits, bobbed hair, drinking, smoking, vigorous sports, necking and petting, and sensuous music and dancing. Jazz itself was "the accompaniment of the voodoo dancer, stimulating the half-crazed barbarian to the vilest deeds," wrote the music director of the General Federation of Women's Clubs. It was an "expression of protest against law and order, that Bolshevik element of license striving for expression in music." Patriotic mothers would uphold family morals and shun the competitive male spheres of business, politics, and war. Like women of Sparta, they would raise patriotic sons ready to risk their lives for the common defense.[26]

Conservative women worked mainly through independent single-sex groups, not electoral politics. Although active as publicists and organizers, they worried about "sex antagonism" and shunned competition for public office. "The Republican women of Massachusetts," conservative activist Elizabeth Putnam told President Harding in 1921, "do not consider that women have at present had sufficient training and experience to acquit themselves in public office in a manner which will add honor to their sex." Women of the right mobilized against the first federal welfare measure, the Sheppard-Towner bill of 1921, which provided aid to the states for the health care of mothers and infants. The law would weaken families, undercut traditional values, and advance paternalistic government, they argued. In the Sheppard-Towner fight, wrote editor Mary Kilbreth of the conservative *Woman Patriot*, "we have with us as allies the Constitution, and all the institutions on which . . . 'Western civilization is based.'"[27]

Conservative women united politically in the Woman's Patriotic Conference on National Defense (WPCND), a coalition with a peak membership of about forty patriotic and hereditary organizations, led by the 150,000-member DAR, the American Legion Auxiliary with more than 200,000 members, and the small but vocal Daughters of 1812. President Coolidge, Secretary of War John Weeks, Secretary of the Navy Curtis D. Wilbur, and Army Chief of Staff General John L. Hines addressed the 1925 inaugural conference. Conference closer Fred Marvin implored women to oppose "slackers, pinks, and pacifists." Claire Oliphant, the conference chair, assured America that "we are those women who are not afraid and were not afraid to raise our sons to be soldiers." Grace Brosseau, president-general of the DAR, opened the next Patriotic Conference in 1927 by applauding the woman behind the man: "she knows in her inmost heart that the right sort of men inherit the instincts of courage and self-preservation from the right kind of women." The WPCND upheld 100 percent Americanism, traditional family life, control over subversion, and preparedness for war. It denounced pacifism and internationalism, especially as espoused by liberal women. According to Flora Walker, head of the DAR's National Defense Committee, "To make an internationalist, you must destroy a citizen's loyalty to his country, and to attempt disarmament in a world of nations armed to the teeth is to court annihilation." Walker and Brosseau remade the once politically reticent DAR into a major player on the post-war right.[28]

To expose the threat posed by liberal and antiwar women's groups, Lucia Ramsey Maxwell, an employee in the War Department's Chemical Warfare Division headed by conservative General Amos Fries, spun in 1923 a widely circulated spiderweb chart, labeled "The Socialist-Pacifist Movement in America Is an Absolutely Fundamental and Integral Part of International Socialism." Former peace activist Haviland Lund published the chart in Henry Ford's magazine *The Dearborn Independent.* From two umbrella organizations—the Women's Joint Congressional Committee (a lobbying group) and the National Council for the Prevention of War—a web of subversion entwined fifteen groups, among them the League of Women Voters, the Federation of Business and Professional Women, the General Federation of Women's Clubs, the National Council of Jewish Women, and the Women's Christian Temperance Union. After protests from offended groups, the War Department promised to withdraw and destroy copies of the chart, but feminist leader Carrie Chapman Catt noted that "it is not easy to catch nor to stop a lie when it has once started on its course." Attacks from conservatives pushed to the right the giant General Federation of Women's Clubs and the prestigious Federation of Business and Professional Women.[29]

Most of the groups entangled in the so-called spiderweb chart espoused a liberal maternalism that shared conservative assumptions about sex differences, but sought to raise socially conscious children and apply principles of the household economy to social reform. These liberal maternalists who had led the fight for woman's suffrage were primarily middle- to upper-class white Protestants who embraced anti-pluralist Victorian values. The lobbying and grassroots campaign for suffrage drew its vitality from the ethnic, racial, and religious forces that backed Prohibition. Both white and black women fought for suffrage in the South and white suffragists had varying views on race. However, many claimed that votes for women would strengthen white supremacy by countering the few black males who voted. Northern suffrage leaders catered to both southern racism and anti-immigrant sentiment to win the backing needed to pass and ratify a constitutional amendment. Suffrage leaders excluded blacks from their organizations and endorsed immigration restriction and education requirements for voting. In twenty-seven suffrage and prohibition referenda held in northern states from 1906 to 1918, white, mostly evangelical Protestants overwhelmingly lined up behind both prohibition and suffrage, irrespective of their economic standing, literacy, occupation, and urban or rural residence. Fragmentary evidence from black city wards shows that African Americans usually stood apart from the prohibition crusade. The heavily white, Protestant, and evangelical composition of voting for Prohibition remained unchanged in state repeal referenda held during the 1920s.[30]

In 1919 the National American Woman Suffrage Association, which boasted two million members, formed the National League of Women Voters to press for post-suffrage reform. League women cut themselves off from alliances with racial or ethnic minorities and worked to maintain their Victorian respectability. "[We] did not want to form a woman's political party, and we are not 'feminists' in the embittered sense so often given to the word," said Illinois chapter president Mary Morrison. The league followed the precedent of the suffrage movement by proposing stricter naturalization laws, English as America's official language, and loyalty oaths and educational requirements for voting. League women still viewed voting as an individual decision by educated citizens, not as the mobilization of a worker, immigrant, or even a women's bloc. The league reinforced efforts to "Americanize" immigrant women and turn them into respectable mothers through training in citizenship, English, morals, nutrition, cleanliness, and family budgeting.[31]

The League of Women Voters pushed for enforcement of Prohibition, but not of the Fourteenth Amendment's guarantee of equal protection under the law or the Fifteenth Amendment's protection of voting rights for blacks. Its lily-white Negro Problems Committee ignored the boulder of racial disenfranchisement to kick away a few pebbles through "ballot marking classes for colored women" in "the states where the colored vote is a material and accepted fact"—bypassing the South. Two years later, the chair of the committee, renamed Inter-Racial Problems, said that she had "no report of meetings held or conferences conducted" but that she had worked to block legislation on racial issues that were "best considered outside of legislative halls."[32]

Liberal maternalists joined conservative women in opposition to an Equal Rights Amendment (ERA) proposed by Alice Paul's National Woman's Party to guarantee legal equality for women. Conservatives assailed what a *Chicago Tribune* editorial called the product "of thwarted sex" from a "professional feminism that has no sympathy from normal women who have too much respect for their sex to wish to be men." Liberal maternalists agreed. "Women cannot be made men by amending the constitution," reported a pamphlet of the National Consumers League. "Women will always need many laws different from those needed by men."[33]

Post-suffrage liberal women continued the Victorian tradition of petitioning men for reform rather than striving to become decision makers through election to office. In 1921, the new president of the League of Women Voters, Maud Wood Park, listed "Help to Men in Public Office," but not the election of women, as a "fundamental objective" for the league. Unlike conservative women, league members worried about the lack of women in public office. But the nonpartisan league declined to recruit, train, or finance women candidates. "It is a League for the political education of women like any other civic society," said the membership chair in 1922. In her 1924 farewell address, President Park said, "The fact that we should like to see more women of the right sort in public office, does not imply, however, that the League as an organization ought to start electioneering for women." Rather, the league would "help women make the best of themselves as voters" and advance "the human welfare side of government, in which women are particularly fit to be useful." The tiny Woman's Party occasionally endorsed candidates—almost always men—purportedly sympathetic to the ERA.[34]

Women had shifted gender boundaries by opening the gates of the parties after 1920, but men kept control of policy, nominations, elections, finance, and strategy. During the 1920s only one woman served in the U.S. Senate (for twenty-four hours, to fill a vacancy) and fewer than ten served in any session of the House of Representatives. Two women won governor's positions, one to replace her term-limited husband. In 1930 women held fewer than 2 percent of state legislative seats. A 1924 editorial in *Youth's Home Companion* rhetorically asked, "What would have happened if women had aspired to office? . . . It is noteworthy that they have not done that and the number who have displayed any marked political ambition is small—smaller than most persons anticipated when suffrage was conferred on them."[35]

After suffrage, women's groups pushed a Congress uncertain about the woman's vote to enact in 1921 the Sheppard-Towner bill for maternal and infant health care and in 1922 the Cable Act that granted independent citizenship for women. "Every Congressman had a distinct sense of faintness at the thought of having all the women in his district against him," said a lobbyist opposed to Sheppard-Towner. In 1924, however, the failure of the states to ratify a child labor amendment signaled the decline of a liberal women's movement that had lost the battle of the ballot to conservatives. In America's first gender gap, women concerned with upholding Prohibition and a stable social order surpassed men in voting for Republicans and conservatives. This liberal maternalist vision, moreover, failed to inspire armies of activists. Subscriptions to the League of Women Voters' magazine, *The Woman Citizen,* languished at what its managing director called a "pitiful" 15,000, while its membership plummeted during the 1920s from 200,000 to 80,000 mostly nominal members. "I know of no woman to-day who has any influence or political power because she is a woman. . . . I know of no politician who is afraid of the woman vote on any question under the sun," said Democratic leader Emily Newell Blair in 1925, a measure of how much had changed since Congress enacted Sheppard-Towner, which it declined to renew in 1927.[36]

Liberal women exacted a measure of revenge against the right late in the decade. In 1928, member Helen Tufts Bailie rocked the DAR with charges that its leadership had blacklisted as speakers 131 "undesirable" men, 87 women, and 306 groups. The blacklist named many of the nation's preeminent liberals, including Florence Allen, the first woman to serve on a state supreme court, and Mary Woolley, the president of Mount Holyoke College and a DAR member. It cited labor unions, the Federal Council of Churches, the NAACP, the YWCA, the American Association of University Women, and the National Catholic Welfare Conference. Bailie and fifteen other DAR sisters charged in a pamphlet entitled "Our Threatened Heritage" that red-hunter Fred Marvin had duped DAR officials into circulating a blacklist that insulated members from liberal opinion. The critics also blamed the "powerful influence of big industrialists and munitions manufacturers" for transforming the traditionally nonpolitical DAR into a conservative advocacy group. DAR president Grace Brosseau denied that the blacklist represented official policy and said that organization was patriotic, not political. She blamed the protest on "a few pacifists within our organization" and arranged for the DAR's governing board to expel Bailie for "disturbing the harmony of the society."[37]

Conservative women suffered another setback in a remarkable lawsuit that put to the test of legal testimony and cross-examination the right's political claim that liberalism reinforced communism. The case began in 1928 when DAR member Helen Brumley Baldwin filed a libel suit against the liberal Reverend William H. Bridge. She charged that Bridge had sullied her good name by writing that she had been lying about the connections between communists and liberals. Bridge called forth in his defense a parade of distinguished liberals who professed their opposition to communism. His expert witnesses included Oswald Garrison Villard, editor of *The Nation;* Jane Addams, the founder of Hull House; and Rabbi Stephen Wise, president of the American Jewish Congress—all named on the DAR blacklist. The *New York Times* reported that the three-day trial was a mini-Scopes case, "a public forum on communism, pacificism, socialism, and free speech," in which "Arthur Garfield Hays, President of the Civil Liberties Union and counsel for the Rev. Mr. Bridge defended the [liberal] doctrines of his witnesses and Joseph T. Cashman, attorney for Mrs. Baldwin defended the tenets of conservativism." After the judge dismissed Baldwin's claim, Bridge said, "The general policy of superpatriots in attempting to discredit all persons of liberal views by tying them up with Communist activities has received a death blow by the exposure this case has brought about." The DAR never fully recovered from these tribulations, which branded its leaders as stodgy relics, obsessed with hunting for reds in their chimneys and attics. A listing in the DAR's blacklist, like mention on

Richard Nixon's enemies list many years later, became a badge of honor on the left.[38]

The rise of conservative women's organizations backed by a robust women's vote had offered the right's male leadership a chance to tighten its hold over American politics. Women of the right were well organized and proud of their expertise on policy issues. Conservative men encouraged women to organize single-sex groups but also held to their vision of women's domestic role and failed to integrate women into their larger movement. Perhaps conservative women would have rejected a forward role. In any case, they had no such choice.

EVANGELICAL PROTESTANTISM

During the 1920s, fundamentalist Protestants spread the good news of the Gospel and challenged a religious modernism that in their view encouraged misguided secular reform and subordinated Christianity to flawed science, notably Darwinian evolution. The Reverend Curtis Lee Laws, editor of the national Baptist newspaper the *Watchman-Examiner,* coined the term "fundamentalist" in 1920 for Christians "who still cling to the great fundamentals and who mean to do battle royal for them." For fundamentalists, the Bible provided the only unified theory of material and spiritual life, fully compatible with the "facts" of God's natural world. Evolution, in their view, contradicted the Book of Genesis, conflated men with beasts, substituted theory for fact, and robbed human life of divine purpose and meaning.[39]

Despite deep historical roots, fundamentalism emerged as a self-conscious movement when British and American theologians, financed by California oil magnate Lyman Stewart and his brother Milton, published and widely circulated *The Fundamentals: A Testimony to the Truth,* twelve volumes of conservative theological writings dating from 1910 to 1915. Baptist minister William Bell Riley's World Christian Fundamentals Association gave fundamentalists visibility but failed to unify the movement. Wealthy businessmen seeking social peace, including the Rockefellers, sponsored the urban revivals of fundamentalist Billy Sunday, the premier evangelist of the early twentieth century. A former professional baseball player, Sunday patented an "aw shucks" appeal that drew multitudes down the "sawdust trail" to salvation and contributed to "the general toning up of the ethical standards and the revival of the spiritual life of the churches of the community," said Methodist Bishop Joseph F. Berry. Sunday said he didn't know much about theology, but he knew that religion led to both eternal life and happiness in the material world. And he knew that boot-leggers, profaners, Sabbath breakers, loose women, and radicals wrecked the country: "If they don't like our laws, there are ships sailing to Europe." He preached against "conflict between labor and capital" and urged em-ployees to give "honest work" for fair wages and reject "radical leaders who seem to be out to grab all they can regardless of the rights of Business or the Public."[40]

Fundamentalists militantly defended the literal truths of the Bible: that Jesus, the son of God, was born of a virgin mother, lived a sinless life, and performed miracles. In this view, Jesus died to atone for our sins, was bodily resurrected, ascended to heaven, and will return to pass final judg-ment on the saved and the damned. Salvation, moreover, required not just attending church or affirming proper doctrine but also accepting Jesus as personal savior—in effect, becoming born again in Christ. Many funda-mentalists also believed that mankind was coming to the end of times: a period of turmoil and tribulation prior to Christ's return, his thousand-year rule over earth, and ultimately his final judgment that would consign all souls to heaven or hell. Fundamentalists backed revivalist movements to spread the gospel worldwide but opposed ecumenical movements, which they said compromised theology and weakened moral standards in the quest to unify Christianity. Pentecostal Christians, known as "fundamen-talists with a difference," embraced strict doctrine but also emphasized the special gifts of the Holy Spirit such as speaking in tongues, prophecy, and faith healing. Black evangelical Protestants neither sought nor were offered alliances with their white counterparts.[41]

The era's conflict between fundamentalists and modernists reflected divisions between pluralists and anti-pluralists. "As sure as I know that the Bible was inspired of God, I know that Modernism is inspired by Satan," said the Reverend T. T. Shields, president of the Baptist Bible Union. Pres-byterian theologian J. Gresham Machen said modernism was "a different religion from Christianity." But modernist Presbyterian Dr. William Merrill insisted that the real quarrel within Christianity was "between the liberals who believe in tolerance and those clergy, who don't.... The fundamental-ists believe that all other viewpoints than their own should be excluded. We believe the more viewpoints in the Church the better. They want authority. We want liberty." For fundamentalists, however, liberty meant the free will to submit to God's word, not indiscriminant freedom of thought.[42]

Although often ridiculed as poor, uneducated, and bigoted rubes, fundamentalists had standing enough to challenge modernists for control over such mainstream denominations as the northern Presbyterians and Baptists. Although fundamentalists ultimately failed to win command of mainstream churches, their movement trounced modernist Protestants in dynamism and growth by proclaiming a single truth with no shades of gray as everyman's guide to life on earth and sojourn in heaven. In contrast, a dismayed modernist, in a widely cited *Atlantic Monthly* article, bemoaned modernism's "failure to bring to our struggling world either vision or courage for its salvation." The fundamentalism of the 1920s launched a broad, enduring evangelical movement that included many Protestants who did not self-identify in later years as fundamentalists.[43]

The evangelical ethos maintained a strong presence within mainstream churches, while explicitly evangelical churches grew far more rapidly than their rivals, none more so than the Southern Baptist Convention, which expanded from 3.2 million members in 1920 to 13.7 million in 1980, becoming America's largest Protestant denomination. Although modernist pastors struggled to fill empty pews in the twenties, evangelicals thrived within their own culture of Bible schools, conferences, summer camps, missionary ventures, Christian colleges, and independent "para-church" organizations. With new radio networks allotting free public service air time to the mainstream Federal Council of Churches (FCC), evangelicals pioneered the commercial use of radio in the 1920s—the "electronic church." Aimee Semple McPherson's broadcasts from her Four Square Gospel Church in Los Angeles, Paul Rader's radio sermons that reached across the Midwest, and Walter A. Maier's *The Lutheran Hour,* America's most widely heard religious program, created a national community of true-believing Christians and spread a mostly politically conservative ideology as well.[44]

Although fundamentalism was a spiritual movement, conservative theology correlated, if not perfectly, with conservative politics. "The Fundamentalist is as much of a Tory in social affairs as he is in theology," wrote modernist theologian Shailer Mathews in 1923. Eighty years later, the historian of fundamentalism George Marsden agreed, stating, "By the 1920s the one really unifying factor in fundamentalist political and social thought was the overwhelming predominance of political conservatism." Fundamentalists reacted against modernist reformers who sought perfection through social engineering that put science above scripture and social progress above saving souls. They believed that the Social Gospel movement that sought to apply Christian principles to social reform was a trap that led Christians to embrace secular rather than spiritual remedies for the ills of mankind and diverted their attention from the salvation of souls. Fundamentalists opposed programs of family regulation and welfare that interfered with parental authority, undercut personal responsibility, or upset the morality of reward and punishment. They believed in compassion and charity, but as delivered by individuals and communities of faith and not a distant secular bureaucracy.[45]

Although fundamentalists did not organize behind parties or candidates, they debated policy and issues. In their first political entanglement, fundamentalists opposed U.S. participation in the League of Nations. They challenged the League as social engineering run amok and the precedent for a one-world, secular government. Fundamentalists usually backed the control of sin, conservative policies on taxes, regulation, and immigration, and framed their movement as a combative faith led by manly pastors and church leaders. Women had other roles as participants in Bible conferences and institutes, Sunday school teachers, musicians, and youth workers. Still, the ubiquity of women pastors and their assertion of moral authority within the Pentecostal movement troubled fundamentalists from other traditions.[46]

In alliance with patriotic organizations and mainstream Protestants, fundamentalists entrenched religion within public schools, which became a contested ground of culture as high school enrollment doubled in the 1920s. In a break from the past, numerous states adopted laws and practices that fused education and religion. In the nineteenth century, only Massachusetts had required Bible reading in public schools. Led by the National Reform Association, a Protestant group dedicated to recognizing America as a Christian nation, eleven states and the District of Columbia required Bible reading during the 1910s and '20s and several others adopted Bible reading de facto. In these decades, thirty-four states provided released time during school hours for religious instruction by statute or practice and thirty-three authorized high school credit for outside Bible study. Although mandated by law in only a few states, nondenominational prayer in public schools became common practice as well.

A few states and many local school districts also prohibited the teaching of human evolution. Fundamentalists, however, lost the public relations battle with modernists in the 1925 trial of high school teacher John Scopes for violating Tennessee's law against teaching that man ascended from apes. The trial halted momentum for new anti-Darwin laws, but statutes and regulations stayed on the books in parts of the South and West, which stalled the teaching of evolution in many public schools across the country.[47]

After Scopes, fundamentalists began an unending argument about submerging religion within politics. Fundamentalist theologian E. Y. Mullins, president of the Baptist World Alliance, wrote to Billy Sunday that "one of the greatest dangers facing us now is that Christian people will be diverted from their task of saving souls into lobbying around legislators." He said, "It is contradictory to Protestant principles to get legislatures to interpret the Scriptures for us." Although teachers sometimes "abuse their opportunities and privileges and teach atheism and attack Christianity and the Bible," the remedy is not to inject "particular doctrines" into classrooms, but to pass "a law prohibiting attacks on religion." Sunday agreed: "We do have to watch the tendency to let the state interfere with religion. I like your statement that the best attack on Evolution is to let folks see it for what it is. . . . It hasn't a leg to stand on."[48]

BUSINESS CONSERVATIVES

For the Reverend A. B. Kendall of the United Society of Christian Endeavor, like many religious leaders of the period, America did not have to choose between God and mammon. "Material prosperity and godliness go hand in hand," he said in 1927. "The nation that sows morality and spirituality will reap peace and prosperity." The business of business pervaded white Protestant culture in the 1920s. Corporate spokesmen distanced modern enterprise from the robber barons of earlier times and extolled the ethos of service in the new consumer-oriented economy. Competitive enterprise provided affordable goods and services and the leisure needed for cultural pursuit. It encouraged self-reliance, sobriety, thrift, honor, and diligence, and punished sloth, dissolution, and arrogance. In turn, free enterprise required the discipline and virtues of religion; otherwise the economy would collapse under the weight of employer greed and worker apathy, leaving government to restore order by draconian means. According to journalist Edward Bok, writing in 1926:

> In fact the successful outcome of industry depends upon certain moral standards. Thrift, for instance, a higher standard of honor, the keeping of a man's word, steadiness, sobriety, a recognition of honorable dealings—all these Christian virtues have been brought directly into the life of civilized nations by Industrialism. The whole fabric of Business rests upon these moral forces.[49]

President Coolidge agreed that "material prosperity cannot be secured unless its rests upon spiritual realities. . . . If America is advancing economically, if it is the abiding place of justice and freedom, it is because of the deep religious convictions of its people." In 1930 Bible teacher and statistician William Ridgeway told the World Christian Fundamentals Association, "Every one of the 400 largest establishments of the United States is administered by Christian men. No great business success ever was attained by a corporation the founders and operators of which lacked faith in God." Some clergy worried about marrying Christianity and business, especially after ad man Bruce Barton published his best-selling *The Man Nobody Knows* (1925), which marketed Jesus as history's greatest salesman and CEO. Still, the religious press and prominent clerics usually blessed the union.[50]

Business lobbying reached new levels of integration, professionalism, and sophistication in the 1920s. Lobbying was nothing new. So many crude fixers worked the Capitol in the Gilded Age that the *Atlanta Constitution* quipped in 1885, "Why not abolish congress as a useless and expensive concern?" Lobbying, however, had changed from "the button-holing, gin-fizz drinking, and joke-telling type to the highly organized and specialized variety," wrote reporter L. C. Speers in 1929. The lobbyists traded on their expertise and personal contacts with public officials. They pressured decision makers from below through "spontaneous" letters and telegrams. Business lobbyists were especially active in state governments, where competition for economic development enhanced their power. They often worked with front groups like the American Taxpayers League or the League for Americanism.[51]

In addition to individual corporations and more than six thousand trade associations, business lobbied through two broad national organizations. The U.S. Chamber of Commerce, which represented mostly small enterprises, included thirteen hundred local chapters and trade associations by the mid-1920s. The National Association of Manufacturers (NAM) represented several thousand member companies, mostly from small and medium-sized enterprises. The NAM rallied enterprise behind an anti-union "American plan" that equated the open shop (in which employees did not have to join unions) with patriotism and labor organizing with disloyalty, a carryover from the red scare. Employers fought unions through spies, harassment, intimidation, strikebreaking, injunctions, and the firing and blacklisting of organizers. They also promoted a vision of social harmony through grievance procedures and company unions run by management. They put in place profit sharing and bonuses, athletic clubs, entertainment, health benefits, and insurance and pension plans. Thousands of middle-size to large firms patchily adopted such "welfare capitalism" to improve the lives of workers, reduce their independence, and strengthen their loyalties to employers.[52]

Business not only lobbied the government in the 1920s, in many cases it *was* the government. Magnate Andrew Mellon ran the U.S. Treasury from 1921 to 1931 and businessman Herbert Hoover guided the Commerce Department from 1921 until he ran for president in 1928. Wall Street lawyers Charles Evans Hughes and Henry Stimson headed the State Department during much of the decade. James J. Davis, secretary of labor throughout the twenties, began as a steelworker and union man but gained riches and business connections as director-general of the Loyal Order of the Moose. Charles Dawes, the first budget director, was a top banker and utility executive. Most senators and House members in the 1920s augmented their government salaries with privately earned income from business and law.[53]

Business joined with religious leaders in selling the idea that, in an open economy, bad character explained personal failure. They denied any class antagonism between bosses and workers, who were understood to be tycoons-in-waiting themselves. In a 1927 speech to the National Electric Light Association, David F. Houston, the vice president of AT&T, said, "Big corporations, formerly regarded as menacing to the masses, have been the channel through which the small investor has been furnished an easier opportunity to become a capitalist." Few economists offered dissenting views and no new generation of muckrakers replaced crusading journalists of the progressive era. Despite sick industries, widespread poverty and a large gap between rich and poor, real wages, home ownership, leisure time, and personal mobility increased during the 1920s. Consumer goods became affordable, especially with installment buying for durable products such as cars, radios, and washing machines. Advertisers didn't abandon but reshaped old virtues for a consumer economy: independent families purchased their own home; thrifty consumers bought goods on credit; responsible breadwinners kept their families healthy by buying refrigerators and packaged juices; and loving families listened to the radio together and vacationed in their automobiles.[54]

Even as conservative Republicans honed their free market rhetoric, they engaged with the private economy, "putting government behind rather than in business," Secretary of Commerce Hoover said in 1924. With the budget for Hoover's department more than tripling during the 1920s, government nurtured and protected enterprise through "associationalism"—a voluntary partnership between government and business, purportedly to serve the public good. Most of business welcomed this benevolent touch of government. "The commercialists stand for the policy of individualism or *laissez faire* in industry," Rinehart John Swenson observed in his 1924 political science text. Various forms of "government subsidies," however, "are not regarded as 'interference' by the industrial individualists."[55]

Under Republican presidents of the era, federal officials worked with trade associations, which the Supreme Court had authorized to share information without violating antitrust laws, to upgrade management practices, simplify industrial procedures, and standardize the specifications of tools, hardware, electrical products, and building materials. Republican administrations and Congresses also protected domestic industry, brought order to chaotic industries, promoted foreign trade and investment, and set up mechanisms to resolve labor-management disputes. Hoover led the push for Congress to regulate the struggling airline industry in 1926. He also backed the Railway Act of 1926, which supervised labor-management relationships in the industry and set a pattern for federal labor policy. On the seas, Congress extended subsidies to both shipbuilders and operators in the Merchant Marine Act of 1928. To impose order on the broadcast spectrum, Congress passed legislation in 1927 that established a Federal Radio Commission (later the Federal Communications Commission) and let broadcasters keep or sell their existing frequencies and block competitors from sharing airtime. This politically laden legislation required equal time for political candidates, prohibited aliens from owning radio stations, and banned indecent, obscene, and profane language.[56]

To run government like a business, Congress established in 1921 an executive Bureau of the Budget and a congressional General Accounting Office to audit spending. In response, the House Appropriations Committee reorganized into twelve subcommittees, one for each appropriation bill. Budget Director Dawes crafted budgets that cut spending from $5 billion in 1921 to $3 billion in 1924, which created a record $1 billion in surplus. In 1925 Secretary Mellon noted that 80 percent of the budget was "directly or indirectly attributable to war or national defense."[57]

In this environment, both employers and a labor movement dominated by craft unions of skilled workers under the American Federation of Labor (AFL) agreed that the American economic system had the potential to end poverty and create the leisure for a meaningful life. The number of strikes plummeted during the 1920s and labor union membership fell from 5 million in 1920 to 3.6 million in 1929, even as the labor force rose by 15 percent.

Foreign policy also reflected business priorities. As a creditor nation with the world's largest economy, the United States did not retreat from the world following World War I. Unlike Senator Robert M. La Follette of Wisconsin and other progressive Republicans who opposed America's entry into the war, the conservative Republicans who dominated government after the war were not isolationists seeking to keep America separate from the world. Rather, they were nationalists who opposed restricting American freedom of action through binding commitments abroad. Republican Congresses authorized the incorporation of investment trusts for international trade and suspension of antitrust laws for exporting associations. Government assisted private interests in gaining access to oil and other raw materials and developed plans for easing the burdens of Germany's reparation payments to the allies. However, Congress raised tariffs on behalf of domestic producers and resisted formal financial agreements among nations. This created openings for emerging multinational corporations, which established more than thirteen hundred foreign subsidiaries by 1929, and for private banks, which sent more capital abroad in the 1920s than lenders from all other nations combined. America also rejected participation in the League of Nations and commitments to combat aggression abroad or enforce international agreements.[58]

A small band of conservatives challenged modern industrial life through twelve essays published in 1930 under the pugnacious title *I'll Take My Stand.* These "Southern Agrarians" or "Young Confederates" indicted industrialism and collectivism for destroying Dixie's leisurely, spiritual, and cultivated style of life. Although none of the so-called agrarians farmed themselves, they said that only a society rooted in the soil, the family, and the community provided a fulfilling and uplifting life. The agrarian critique did not register with Jazz Age conservatives wedded to the capitalist order. In rural America, where auto ownership grew faster than it did in cities, mobility broke down isolation. Country folk could drive to church, family reunions, county fairs, and music festivals. Radio allowed rural people tune in to country music and gospel preachers. Gasoline-powered trucks and tractors cut the manpower needed for farm production, bus transport led to larger and better schools—which began teaching music and art—and electricity let people read at night. Rather than yearning for an agrarian utopia, conservatives lauded the robust and manly model of modernizing oil-rich Texas, which flexed its cultural muscles through the Dallas Little Theater, the *Southwest Review,* the University of Texas, and national broadcasts of David Guion's cowboy songs. Conservatives later rediscovered the agrarians and appropriated their Confederate nostalgia and defense of private property.[59]

Conservatives of the 1920s also rejected the views of progressive Republicans such as Senators La Follette, William Borah of Idaho, and George W. Norris of Nebraska. These transitional figures usually combined traditional views on cultural and social matters with a distrust of concentrated power, both in private corporations and in government bureaucracies. They assailed the Federal Reserve Board and other federal agencies for collusion with the "money power" of large banks and corporations at the expense of farmers and small producers. They opposed branch banking and chain stores and corporate mergers. Despite a base of fourteen U.S. senators, progressive Republicans had few allies in either party and failed to escape the dilemma of checking private power without expanding corruptible public power.[60]

RACIAL SCIENCE AND RACIAL CONTAINMENT

Some conservatives in the 1920s embraced an extreme variant of Darwinian science that theorized that inherited traits determined the capacities of individuals and races. Such thinkers might believe that every soul could be saved, but that not every person or race had the capacity for civilized achievement. Racial science and the related practical discipline of eugenics upheld the superiority of white Anglo-Saxon or "Nordic" Protestants from western Europe as compared to blacks, other colored peoples, and whites from southern and eastern Europe. Japanese and Chinese held a special status as inassimilable competitors to America's "great race."

Although not without dissenters, racial science was a vital transatlantic movement purportedly validated by studies of brain size and anatomy, comparative analyses of civilizations, IQ tests, and statistics on health, crime, and poverty. It became entrenched within prestigious American institutions such as the American Museum of Natural History, the Rockefeller Institute for Medical Research, the American Psychological Association, and the American Medical Association. Magazines, newspapers, and best-selling books such as Madison Grant's *The Passing of the Great Race* (1916) provided racial science with a popular reach. Racial science informed the related but distinct social program of eugenics, which would improve humanity by breeding superior stock (positive eugenics) and checking reproduction by the less fit (negative eugenics). The Eugenics Record Office, founded by genetics researcher Charles Davenport and directed by Harry Laughlin, promoted racial science and eugenics. Mary Harriman, the widow of railroad magnate E. H. Harriman, and the American Breeders Association—which paired biologists and animal breeders—backed the project. Proponents of eugenics disseminated their ideas through exhibits at museums and fairs, "fitter family contests," lectures, sermons, clubs, films, radio broadcasts, and widespread high school and college instruction.[61]

Racial science and eugenics might seem to sit uneasily with conservatives suspicious of social engineering and evolutionary theory. Indeed, some liberals, such as birth control pioneer Margaret Sanger, adopted elements of eugenics as a complement to social reform. Yet for conservative white Protestants, racial science tinged with eugenic ideas justified their privileges and politics. Like business ideology and evangelical religion, racial science severed the link between bad behavior and social conditions. It justified shutting America's doors to less fit peoples, strictly punishing crime, legally separating the races, and barring interracial marriage. It discredited social welfare measures, minimum wages, and rehabilitation programs. It complemented conservative maternalism by elevating motherhood as the duty of racially superior women. The fear of what Theodore Roosevelt had called "race suicide" again raised the specter of defeminized women, too independent and educated for motherly duties. "This contemplation of a career better than motherhood is merely a delusion," president emeritus Charles W. Eliot of Harvard warned the Harvard Dames in 1924.[62]

Racial science reached into street-level politics. In New York, State Senator Caleb Baumes defended against "mawkish sentimental" critics his 1926 "four strikes" law that put four-time felons away for life as incurable criminals. Other states followed his lead, with Kansas one-upping New York with a "three strikes" law. But New York City police official Gerhard Kuhne one-upped everyone by proposing to "kill off" incorrigible drug addicts.[63]

Racial science shaped other policies as well. In a 1922 book, *Eugenical Sterilization in the United States*, Laughlin proposed a "model" sterilization law that inspired legislation in American states and European nations, including Hitler's Germany—although the German statute was broader than American laws. Hitler wrote fan letters to American eugenicists and closely monitored what he saw as the pathbreaking refinement of eugenic practices in the United States. The Catholic Church, despite its dedication to strong families and maternal roles for women, resisted negative eugenics. The Church opposed interfering with reproduction and resented the anti-immigrant thrust of eugenic reformers. Still, by 1932 twenty-seven states had enacted sterilization laws for institutionalized persons, targeting the least powerful. Except for California, most states began widespread sterilizations only after the Supreme Court in 1927 upheld a Virginia law based on Laughlin's model. "It is better for all the world, if instead of waiting to execute degenerate offspring for crime, or to let them starve for their imbecility, society can prevent those who are manifestly unfit from continuing their kind," Oliver Wendell Holmes wrote for an eight-justice majority. "Three generations of imbeciles are enough."[64]

Immigration policy since 1903 had sought to protect America's racial stock by excluding the congenitally degenerate, psychopathic, and

feebleminded. In the 1920s, as Congress considered comprehensive legislation, Laughlin testified as "expert eugenics agent" for the House Immigration Committee that feeblemindedness and insanity abounded among
new immigrants. Congress brushed aside criticisms of Laughlin's methodology and in 1924 enacted the Johnson-Reed bill that limited European immigration to just over 150,000 per year with nationality quotas
based on the origins of the U.S. population, which heavily favored western and northern Europe, especially Britain. The act required entry visas,
with photographs—another facet of control—and largely excluded Asians.
It exempted most of the western hemisphere so that Mexico could continue supplying western farmers with cheap labor.[65]

Laughlin hailed the shift from an "economic basis for regulation" to
"biological principles" for "improving our heredity levels in physique,
intelligence and moral qualities." John Trevor, the head of the American
Coalition of Patriotic Societies, who helped develop the quota system, said
that the new law protected American interests and deprived "certain groups
of special advantages which they now possess." Opponents of restriction included liberal intellectuals, Jewish and Catholic members of Congress, and
black leaders who objected to reinforcing discrimination. A coalition of
prominent white opponents futilely urged President Coolidge to veto a bill
that "stimulates racial, national and religious hatreds and jealousies" and
"encourages one part of our population to arrogate to itself a sense of superiority and to classify another as one of inferiority." They cited the hypocrisy of exempting Latin Americans, who were no "more desirable or
assimilable than Italians, Poles, or Russians."[66]

By excluding blacks, Asians, Latinos, and American Indians from
calculations of America's national origins, immigration policy enshrined
whites as a privileged category, legally and culturally. The Supreme Court,
by strictly interpreting laws that limited naturalization to "free white persons" and those of African descent, fortified white privilege. In 1923 the
Supreme Court ruled in U.S. v. Thind that an immigrant from India, "a high
caste Hindu, although of the Caucasian or Aryan race, is not a white person within the meaning of the naturalization laws," which "were to be in-
terpreted in accordance with the understanding of the common man." The
Court recognized that, unlike Asians, "immigrants from Eastern, Southern and Middle Europe, among them the Slavs and the dark-eyed, swar-
thy people of Alpine and Mediterranean stock" would merge into the white

population "and lose the distinctive hallmarks of their European origin." Four years later, the Court ruled that Mississippi could classify a native-born child of Chinese ancestry as "colored" and consign her to segregated black schools. American society moved toward a polarity between whites and nonwhites as the "distinctive hallmarks" of new immigrants faded in the decades following. As the *Thind* court anticipated, however, race continued to be constructed and reconstructed, with opportunities for a decent life turning on both legal and de facto distinctions between whites and nonwhites.[67]

Both racial science and ingrained custom sustained practices aimed at containing racial minorities. About half a million African Americans and comparable numbers of southern white migrants flocked to jobs in northern cities during World War I. This Great Migration of both races continued after the war and inalterably transformed northern society, southernizing it, in a sense, by extending racial issues beyond southern boundaries. It brought black labor into competition with white workers, including many from the South. It ignited racial conflicts over housing, schools, public transportation, parks, and other accommodations and created a new bloc of voters in the ethnic crucible of urban politics. The main contours of modern racial conservatism took shape in the resistance to racial equality that grew in the decade after the war. Lynching, mob violence, and race riots exploded between 1917 and 1921. Violence erupted in northern cities where blacks began colliding with European immigrants and white southern migrants and in towns and cities below the Mason-Dixon Line where whites feared that racial control had eroded. This violence reflected not only social changes brought about by the Great Migration, but also resistance to white supremacy by black war veterans, black newspapers, and the NAACP, founded in 1909.[68]

The antiradical campaign after the war linked red scare and black scare. In 1920, Attorney General Palmer said, "Practically all the radical organizations in this country have looked upon the negroes as particularly fertile grounds for the spreading their doctrines. The radical organizations have endeavored to enlist negroes on their side, and in many respects have been successful." The even more militant J. Edgar Hoover viewed African-American demands for racial justice as equivalent to subversion. Through surveillance, informants, phone taps, break-ins, and intimidation, his Bureau targeted the NAACP and black newspaper editors. It also pursued those relatively few black leaders who actually participated in leftist or militant black politics, notably Jamaican immigrant Marcus Garvey, head of the Universal Negro Improvement Association, which claimed some two million dues-paying members worldwide. Garvey's paper, the *Negro World,* had a circulation of 200,000. Garvey preached race pride and power, unity of the black race across the world, collective self-help, racial separation and self-defense, and a back-to-Africa "Zionism." Garvey's views antagonized fearful whites, conventional black leaders, and the FBI, which hired its lone black agent to infiltrate Garvey's movement. Federal prosecutors convicted Garvey of mail fraud in 1923. President Coolidge eventually commuted his sentence and deported the race leader to Jamaica.[69]

Politically, African Americans found themselves caught between Democrats defending racial privilege in their traditional southern stronghold and Republicans chasing the votes of southern whites. The National Colored Republican Conference complained in 1924, "In the party's willingness to be fair, many have no confidence, and a change is imperative." The conference sought protection from lynching, "equal and the same rights of citizenship," revocation of "segregation rules in Federal Departments," the "appointment of colored Republicans to office," and "the enforcement of the entire constitution with the same vigilance and interest in every portion of it." In the 1924 election, Coolidge endorsed antilynching law but not the conference's other demands, and he refused to denounce the Ku Klux Klan by name.[70]

Racial containment extended to personal and private life. By 1948 thirty states had banned marriage between whites and nonwhites, variously defined. Local governments in the North kept schools and classrooms segregated by classifying students according to IQ scores (formulated to favor whites), manipulating district boundaries, pupil assignments, and the selection of sites for new construction. Governments limited the public services available in black neighborhoods and discrimination confined blacks to the lowest-paying jobs in government and industry and limited their admission to labor unions. "Neighborhood improvement" groups pressured city governments to contain black communities through zoning and other restrictions that protected white communities from tumbling property values. Real estate boards developed restrictive covenants in deeds that complemented less formal efforts to keep properties from transferring to blacks and minorities. Custom kept beaches, amusement parks, sports stadiums, and swimming pools largely segregated. Thus culture reinforced and reflected law and public policy, African Americans faced exclusion from public amusements of the Jazz Age, the camaraderie of rooting for hometown sports, or access to diverse city neighborhoods.[71]

Even sophisticated whites kept minorities contained as exotic others. Upper- and middle-class whites flocked to black Harlem in the roaring twenties. It was a place where anything went—bawdy shows, prostitution, drugs, and homoerotica—and nothing mattered once the revelers retreated to their white enclaves. The *New York Times* editorialized in March 1929, "What greater praise can there be for Harlem than to emphasize the delightful contrast it provides our white cognoscenti to the inhibitions of Main Street?" But whites overlooked "the terrific overcrowding, the outrageously excessive rents, the human toil with spade and pickaxe and washboard that goes to pay for these rents; the lack of playgrounds; the high tuberculosis and mortality rates; and the progress that is being made in spite of all these handicaps." When the stock market crashed seven months later, revelers left and progress stalled.[72]

In the West, anti-pluralists targeted other "nonwhites." California and other western states prohibited Asian immigrants from owning property and in some cases put their children in segregated schools. Federal officials used visa requirements to slow legal immigration from Mexico and a new border patrol cracked down on illegal entrants. These policies reinforced the idea of Mexicans as an "illegal" and troublesome presence, magnified by their alleged fecundity. "It is this high birth rate that makes Mexican peon immigration such a menace," California businessman Charles Goethe wrote to Harry Laughlin. "Peons multiply like rabbits." Although state laws did not formally segregate Latino children, officials used language deficiencies as a cover for assigning them to separate, underfunded schools that taught mostly vocational skills. Some California counties classified children of Mexican descent as Indians, who were legally subject to segregation.[73]

Aided by the League of United Latin American Citizens, Latino parents challenged informal school segregation in the 1920s and won in 1946. In *Mendez v. Westminster,* for which Thurgood Marshall of the NAACP submitted an amicus brief, plaintiffs drew on social science to contest racial stereotypes and expose defects of segregated education. Nearly all blacks and a majority of Latinos eventually found common ground in the Democratic Party, but not in a shared civil rights strategy, as most Latinos insisted on a white racial identity.[74]

GRASSROOTS CONSERVATISM: THE KU KLUX KLAN

From 1920 to 1925 the Ku Klux Klan grew more explosively than any political or social movement in U.S. history. In these few years the Klan recruited some three million to six million white Protestants from across America's working and middle classes, representing those who founded and "own this country," said Imperial Wizard Hiram Wesley Evans in 1923. Colonel William Joseph Simmons, son of an original Klansman of the Reconstruction era, founded what became known as America's second Ku Klux Klan in 1915. Klan leaders used modern marketing techniques to build thriving chapters in both cities and small towns. The Klan flourished not only in the South but also in Maryland, Indiana, Pennsylvania, California, Ohio, Michigan, New Jersey, Illinois, Oregon, Colorado, and Kansas. The Klan sometimes resorted to violence but more commonly participated in direct civic action and electoral politics. The incidence of lynching in the United States plummeted as the Klan grew in the 1920s. The Klan defended Nordic Americans and their traditional culture from Catholics, blacks, and Jews while also addressing economic issues.

The Klan occasionally challenged corporations that swallowed small businesses or put profits above morals, but it more persistently upheld the conservative consensus of the era by opposing un-American "class" legislation and strikes that it attributed to "foreign agitators." The Klan had an intensely local appeal as it worked to enforce traditional Protestant values by upholding Prohibition, fighting crime, and shutting down dance parlors, pool halls, and brothels. It backed public schools and hospitals and clean government but also boycotted Jewish- and Catholic-owned businesses. Klan members benefited from this strategy, which sustained their economic privileges as white Protestant Americans.[75]

Klan members donned white robes of purity, hid their identities under hoods, burned crosses, exchanged secret handshakes and greetings, and spawned a rich bestiary of leaders termed kleagles, wizards, goblins, and dragons. But underneath the lavish ritual lurked a serious political operation. The Klan elected thousands of endorsed candidates to school boards and local governments and extended its reach to state and national offices. Outside the solidly Democratic South, the Klan linked arms with anti-pluralist Republicans. Statistical analysis of all nonsouthern counties shows that white Protestants, both fundamentalist and mainstream, provided the base vote for Klan-sponsored candidates. Race and religion, not economic class or urban-rural residence, distinguished the Klan vote from support for other candidates. At its height in 1924 the Klan swept nearly every major election in which it had endorsed a candidate. Klan-backed Republican candidates—none of whom were incumbents—won governor's positions in Indiana, Kansas, Maine, and Colorado and U.S. Senate seats in Oklahoma, Colorado, and Kansas. VICTORIES BY KLAN FEATURE ELECTION noted a front-page headline in the *New York Times* on November 6, 1924.

Women joined the Women of the Ku Klux Klan to uphold the Christian family and stop crime and vice from ruining their communities. Women of the Klan, like other conservative women's groups, saw no contradiction between political activism and their defense of women's maternal roles. According to the Klan magazine *Fiery Cross* in 1923, women needed to protect the home from immigrants who "can live and make money where a white man would starve because they treat their women like cattle and their swarms of children like vermin, living without fear of God or regard for man." But women also needed to protect one another from philandering, abusive, or drunken husbands. They organized rallies and pageants and performed the daily rituals that unified the organization. They worked to cultivate white Protestant values in public schools and to eliminate unwholesome influences such as dance halls and consorting in automobiles. The women organized "whispering campaigns" against Jews and Catholics and anti-Klan candidates for public office. They led business boycotts and encouraged white Protestant women to vote. Like other conservative women, however, they refrained from seeking office themselves.[76]

In the summer of 1925, some 35,000 white-robed Klan members marched through the nation's capital as a quarter million onlookers gaped in wonder. However, the Klan was already in its supernova phase, a luminous star collapsing from within. In an article published in the prestigious *North American Review,* imperial wizard Hiram Wesley Evans sought to reverse the process by reaching out to mainstream Protestants. Evans offered a forward-looking program, built upon "a sane and progressive conservatism along national lines." It stood with the "plain people" and America's "pioneer stock" against a "Liberalism" that had "undermined their Constitution and their national customs and institutions" and "tried to destroy their God."

It was not the Klan, Evans said, but Negro, Catholic, and Jewish agitators who exploited race and religion, "because we are cutting into the profits they had been making in politics out of *their* races and *their* religions." The Klan had no quarrel with individual Catholics but opposed the organized church, with which it competed for the building of a national culture. Catholics ran corrupt city machines, promoted religious bloc voting, thwarted the Americanization of immigrants, undermined Prohibition, and sought "special and un-American privileges" for parochial schools. As for the Negro, he "is among us through no wish of his" and must be denied the power "to control our civilization," relieved from false "promises of social equality," and barred by law from polluting "sex relations" with superior whites. America must also close her doors to "low standard peoples" from abroad and ensure that "the American stock remains supreme." Evans distinguished the "Western Jew" of sound racial stock from "Eastern Jews of recent immigration. . . . not true Jews, but only Judaized Mongols—Chazars," who "unlike the true Hebrew" could not be assimilated.[77]

Evans failed to stop the Klan from massively losing members, street presence, and political clout. Although scandals exposed the hypocrisy and loose morals of its leaders, larger forces pushed the Klan from bright star to ashen core. The Klan's grievances dried up during the mid-1920s as social and economic tensions eased, America restricted immigration, unions declined, and white Protestant Republicans and southern Democrats ran the nation. By framing its appeal in overtly religious, ethnic, and racial terms the Klan had limited its potential for expansion and sparked a backlash that led to organized counterdemonstrations, condemnation in the press, and occasionally mob violence against Klansmen. Yet the Klan survived, more as a brand than as a movement. As generations of promoters on the fringes of the right proved, there was money and fame to be made in marketing hate, no less than other mass-produced goods.

Henry Ford, America's leading brand-name producer, abetted such anti-pluralism. Ford pioneered assembly-line methods for making cheap, reliable, and easy-to-operate cars. Although he crushed unions through espionage and intimidation and reduced work to repetitive tasks, Ford claimed to be advancing time-honored American values. He paid relatively high wages to dependable workers in traditional families—verified by investigators and staffers in Ford's so-called Sociological Department. He instituted the forty-hour, five-day workweek, creating the modern weekend as a period of leisure consistent with industrial demands. Henry Ford looms so large in the historical imagination that some analysts describe the period from World War I into the 1960s as the age of Fordism, marked by scientific management, mechanical production, repetitive labor, and mass marketing. Although progressive reformers had warned against the power of big companies to cut production and increase prices, Ford kept prices low and wages high through volume sales of reliable products. "Henry Ford has made the only real contribution to civilization in our lifetime," reflected industrialist and conservative activist Joseph Newton Pew in 1937. However, during the 1920s new forms of marketing geared to segmented groups of consumers and more differentiated products challenged Ford's one-style-fits-all approach.[78]

The "Jewish question" so obsessed Henry Ford that he published a four-volume set of books, collectively titled *The International Jew: The World's Foremost Problem,* based on articles printed from 1920 to 1922 in his *Dearborn Independent,* which Ford dealers distributed to some 700,000 readers. Ford and other conspiracy-minded conservatives relied heavily on a purported Jewish plot to dominate the world, as described in the *Protocols of the Elders of Zion,* a forged document that the Russian czar's secret police circulated in the early twentieth century to justify pogroms against Jews. The *Protocols* purportedly proved that Jews were the destructors of Christian civilization, preying on virtuous producers of real wealth and feeding on chaos such as the turmoil that followed World War I. British author Nesta Webster predated Ford in popularizing the *Protocols* and propagating conspiracy theories of history. Another influential woman theorist, Gertrude Coogan, wrote in her 1935 book *The Money Creators* that Jewish bankers manipulated financial systems to turn productive citizens into slaves to debt.[79]

Conspiracy theories endured as a staple of right-wing politics in the United States. They attributed the predicaments of modern life to a concrete enemy whose identify could be shifted from Jews and communists to international financiers, fanatical Muslims, or even the secret Society of the Illuminati, supposedly founded in the eighteenth century. Beyond fringe theories, conspiratorial thinking—often explicitly or implicitly directed at Jews—served to explain away failure on the right or turn the tables on its opposition. Charles Lindbergh blamed Jewish "influence in our motion pictures, our press, our radio, and our government" for pushing America into World War II. Republican Senator Robert Taft indicted media moguls, financiers, and businessmen "subject to New York influence" (a common euphemism for Jews) for stealing his presidential nomination in 1952. For decades, conservatives blamed a liberal cabal within the (heavily Jewish) academy for freezing conservatives out of scholarly journals and college faculties.

CULMINATION: THE PRESIDENTIAL ELECTIONS OF 1924 AND 1928

As journalist Frank Kent noted, America had become "conservatized" in the Jazz Age. Not until the early twenty-first century would conservatives approximate the power they held in the 1920s. The Republican Party, although not the only center of conservative politics, guarded the conservative consensus. The ability of political parties to unify and mobilize voters had weakened in the early twentieth century, but most politically active Americans still identified as Republicans or Democrats and partisan control of government still shaped policy.

Conservative Republicans solidified their control over government after withstanding the Teapot Dome scandals of 1923 in which high officials of the Harding administration profited from the illegal sale or use of government property, including federal oil reserves at Elk Hills, California, and Teapot Dome, Wyoming. Insiders speculated that the scandals would knock Harding out of politics, lead to a bloody succession struggle, and perhaps short-circuit the Republican era. After Harding died in August 1923, however, an untainted Vice President Coolidge stepped in as a popular president in a time of peace and prosperity.[80]

Coolidge triumphed in the presidential election of 1924 almost as decisively as Harding in 1920. His opposition included Republican Senator Robert M. La Follette, the candidate of a new Progressive Party sponsored by labor and farm groups. Democrats nominated corporate lawyer John W. Davis in a convention deadlocked for a record 103 ballots between

California Senator William Gibbs McAdoo and New York Governor Al Smith. The Davis campaign assailed Republican corruption, favoritism for the rich, and protective tariffs—a flashback to Grover Cleveland. As in 1920, Republicans outspent Democrats by three to one and Coolidge, mourning the death of his son Calvin Jr., ran what the *New York Times* called a "silent campaign," leaving most duties to other Republicans. The president outran both his competitors with 54 percent of the popular vote. La Follette polled 16.5 percent of the popular vote; his campaign of opposition to business monopolies never caught fire. The Democratic share sank to an historic low of 29 percent. The Democratic Party was "neither radical enough for the radicals nor conservative enough for the conservatives," said Thomas W. Hardwick, a former Democratic senator from Georgia.[81]

As in 1920, voter turnout in 1924, measured as a percentage of the adult population, fell well below levels of the late nineteenth century. Declining turnout reflected the weakening of party mobilization, personal registration laws and other legal barriers, women's suffrage, restrictions on southern black and lower-class voting, and rising numbers of legally disenfranchised aliens. Nonvoters in the 1920s were concentrated among racial and ethnic minorities, women, and less-affluent Americans. Yet voter turnout campaigns led by groups such as the League of Women Voters, the National Association of Manufacturers, the American Legion, and the National Civic Federation did not target typical nonvoters but focused on white, native-stock, middle-class Americans as ideal voters, shutting out allegedly less qualified "problem" voters.[82]

During Coolidge's term, Republicans completed their program for restricting immigration, raising tariffs, nurturing business, and cutting spending and taxes, with the rate for the top tax bracket falling from 73 percent to 25 percent. After Coolidge declined to run in 1928, leadership passed smoothly to his activist secretary of commerce, Herbert Hoover, an exponent of efficiency in government and business, who humanized his image and extended his renown by directing relief for victims of the great Mississippi flood of 1927. Conservatives and most progressive Republicans backed Hoover. Democrats nominated Al Smith, the first Catholic to head a major-party ticket. But beyond Smith's opposition to Prohibition, little of substance separated the candidates; Smith embodied the strivings of new-stock Americans to join, not challenge, the nation's prevailing culture.

Smith's nomination, however, led to a nationwide campaign among white Protestants to block the election of a Catholic president. Financier Bernard Baruch, the former director of Woodrow Wilson's War Industries Board, wrote to Winston Churchill of his surprise that "intolerance in the Land of the Brave and the Free would hold such sway." Baruch also predicted, however, that "in the very near future the world will blossom out into a great economic revival." Anti-pluralists pumped out inflammatory pamphlets, leaflets, handbills, and placards warning that Smith would sell out America to the pope. Even mainstream Protestants, including prominent church leaders and editors of the modernist *Christian Century,* argued that Catholic teachings and practices clashed with America's democratic principles. Smith attacked what he viewed as religious bigotry on hostile turf in Oklahoma City, but with little effect. Although Hoover personally avoided the religious issue, other Republicans and southern Democrats opposed to Smith's election did not. Wary Catholic leaders said only that a candidate's religion had no relevance in politics.[83]

The politics of race and religion merged in 1928 when Republicans implemented a "southern strategy" to breach the Democratic South by agitating against a wet, Catholic New York candidate; attempting to purge Negro leaders; and building "lily white" Republican machines. Pro-Smith Democrats countered by invoking their party's old-line defense of white supremacy in the South and chasing black votes in the North. ALABAMA TORN BETWEEN HATES IN THIS ELECTION headlined the *Chicago Tribune,* which reported on the struggles of southern white Protestants to choose "between papal domination and Negro domination." In the North, Smith cut into the Republican black vote but fell short of winning majority support. Hoover outperformed every prior Republican by sweeping the upper South, Florida, and Texas. Alabama stayed Democratic, barely.[84]

Hoover won 58 percent of the popular vote for the third consecutive Republican landslide. Although religions did not decide the election, Smith benefited from a pro-Catholic vote and Hoover from an anti-Catholic Protestant vote that was not limited to evangelicals, old-stock Americans, rural folk, or prohibitionists. About 75 percent of Protestants outside the South voted for Hoover and an equal percentage of northern Catholics for Smith. Voter turnout increased sharply in 1928, especially among women, who moved into near parity with men. Hoover won 58 percent of first-time voters, including most new women voters. Most of the increase in Democratic votes came from previous La Follette voters: 56 percent voted for Smith and 31 percent for Hoover. Although Smith sufficiently mollified business to achieve near parity in fund-raising, voters divided along class lines in 1928, with more affluent voters favoring Republicans. Class voting reflected the role of Republicans as guardians of the conservative consensus well before the New Deal era.[85]

Contrary to the notion that 1928 was a realigning or critical election that moved millions of urban, ethnic voters into the Democratic fold, data on party registration from five northern states show slight slippage for Democrats. In 1930, the Republican percentage of two party registrations inched upward from 65 percent in 1928 to 68 percent. In nine major cities, the Republican percentage rose from 61 percent to 64 percent. Franklin Roosevelt's election as governor of New York shone as a bright spot for Democrats in a dark age. However, Roosevelt conducted a postelection survey of Democratic leaders that revealed a demoralized and disorganized party, pessimistic about its future.[86]

"We have an opportunity to put the Republican Party in a position where it can remain in power without much trouble for the next twenty years," said Senator William Borah of Idaho. "We have a chance to build up a party in the South which will always make those states fighting ground." However, the weakness of Democrats in elections of the 1920s concealed the party's resilient strength. It is true that the Democrats' pluralism, which melded diverse voters from outside America's elite—whites in the South, working-class Catholics and new immigrants in the North, and reformers in the mountain states—had paralyzed the 1924 convention. But Democratic diversity also helped the party weather adversity, evolve with changing circumstance, and survive in contests for congressional and state offices. The Democrats' 1924 presidential candidate, John W. Davis, who loyally campaigned for Smith in 1928, said after the election, "I doubt whether a minority party can win as long as the country is in fairly prosperous condition. . . . Some day, I am sure, the tide will turn."[87]

2

CRYING IN THE WILDERNESS, 1929–1936

Herbert Hoover's landslide victory in 1928 inspired some of the least accurate predictions in the political history of the United States. "Continued prosperity," the *Chicago Tribune* reported after the election, was expected by "leaders of industry, business, and finance." The *Detroit Free Press* agreed that "voters have given the nation a new and powerful start along the broad high road of prosperity." The *Denver Post* added that "Prohibition is here to stay.... Never again will any great political party dare to try to ride into power on a beer keg or a whisky bottle."

Less than a year later a stock market crash began the nation's longest and deepest depression. America's Great Depression discredited the Hoover presidency, gave liberal Democrats a chance to govern the nation, and ended the national experiment with Prohibition. After Franklin Roosevelt defeated Hoover in 1932, the conservative remnant fought to hold the moral high ground against a liberal order that threatened to poison America with noxious foreign doctrines. In 1934 the Republican National Committee (RNC) warned, "American institutions and American civilization are in greater danger today than at any time since the foundation of the Republic."[1]

THE AGONY OF HERBERT HOOVER

On April 30, 1930, six months after Wall Street crashed, the U.S. Chamber of Commerce reassured Americans that business had heeded President Hoover's call to sustain production, jobs, and wages. "The forces both of government and private business have joined hands in a nation-wide effort to reduce the severity of the depression and shorten its duration," the Chamber of Commerce reported. A day later the president responded,

"I am convinced we have now passed the worst and with continued unity of effort we shall rapidly recover."[2]

As demonstrated by his record as secretary of commerce, Hoover had more faith in government intervention in the economy than did his predecessor Calvin Coolidge. Beyond exhortations to business, Hoover acted energetically to expand public works and purchase surplus farm goods with federal funds. He reduced immigration to keep American jobs for Americans only and ensure the "fitness of the immigrant as to physique, character, training and our need for service." By executive order in September 1930 he cut immigration from European countries to about 15 percent of quota levels and slashed by nearly 90 percent visas issued for Canada and Mexico. The president incited controversy only when he ratified conservative protectionism by signing the Hawley-Smoot Tariff Act in 1930, which squeezed the world's economy by restricting the flow of American capital abroad. As the 1930 elections approached, Hoover knew that his remedies had failed and his optimism was misplaced. "It seems to me that any hope of industrial recovery between now and winter is rapidly vanishing and that we will need to face a very serious problem of unemployment," he confided to his secretary of commerce.[3]

With no deference to the president or concern for keeping the peace between elections, Democrats waged war against a wounded administration. To sustain the new perpetual campaign, Democratic Party chair John J. Raskob for the first time established the Democratic National Committee as a permanent organization with a national headquarters staffed by professionals. Their barrage of anti-Hoover propaganda staggered an administration unprepared for politics as war. Patrick Hurley, who served as both secretary of war and political adviser, lamented, "We cannot fight . . . if we continue to have our political opponents tell the story and then point out here and there the defects in their story, we are on the defensive." The backpedaling Republicans lost fifty-two House and eight Senate seats in 1930, as well as six governors' mansions, with conservatives suffering most of the losses. "Any party which takes credit for the rain must not be surprised if its opponents blame it for the drought," said banker and diplomat Dwight Morrow, one of the few successful Republican Senate candidates. Still, conservatives hoped that a revived economy would restore voters to sanity and Republicans to power in 1932.[4]

THE REPUBLICANS' CIVIL WAR

Civil war between the GOP's conservative majority and progressive senators shed more Republican blood. A few months before the midterm elections, Senate progressives confounded the president and right-wing Republicans by joining with Democrats to defeat Herbert Hoover's first nominee to the Supreme Court, John J. Parker of North Carolina. The debate over Parker, the only High Court nominee that the Senate rejected between McKinley and Nixon, was explicitly ideological. Organized labor and the NAACP charged Parker with putting "property rights" over "human rights" and opposing political equality for African Americans. Parker's defeat undermined Hoover's plan to build a white Republican Party in the South. It marked a drift of public sentiment away from deference to property and capital, in addition to the political emergence of African Americans. It widened the rift between conservative Republicans, who voted for Parker 28 to 4, and progressive Republicans, who rejected him 13 to 1.[5]

The conservatives struck back in the 1930 primaries by ambushing progressive Republican senator George W. Norris of Nebraska, "a cancer in the Republican Party that must be cut out," said Scott Lucas, the Republican National Committee's executive director. The conservatives recruited a grocer whose name was also George W. Norris to run against Senator Norris and sow confusion on the ballot. They fabricated a sham Republican organization, the Loyal Republican Club, which charged that Norris had sold out to wets, Catholics, and Tammany Hall by supporting Al Smith in 1928. With grocer Norris failing to qualify for the ballot, Senator Norris survived. But warfare between Republican factions led the press to speculate about a third-party movement or a realignment of major parties along liberal and conservative lines. Senator Norris, however, emerged from a conference of progressive Republican leaders in March of 1931, pessimistic about either retaking control of the GOP or forming a viable third party. Absent a "national primary" or a "political revolution" within the Republican Party, he noted, "no progressive could be nominated in a party with its machinery—from precinct organizations to the National Committee—controlled by conservatives." A third-party alternative to Republicans and Democrats would "cost an immense amount of money . . . require an army of missionaries," and could not "be a success" at the polls.[6]

Much was at stake in the struggle between conservatives and progressives at a time when parties financed candidates, recruited volunteers, and guided campaigns. Party bosses, not primary voters, selected most delegates to the national conventions that nominated presidents and wrote party rules and platforms. "My how the insurgents are yelling," Hoover adviser James MacLafferty wrote in his diary in 1930. "Maybe it means a split in the party. There had better be a split than to have the insurgents eventually capture the Republican Party."[7]

INTO THE MAELSTROM

Historian Charles A. Beard probed discord within the GOP in a 1931 *New Republic* article titled "Conservatism Hits Bottom." Yet neither the economy nor conservatism would hit bottom for another two years. From 1929 to 1933, real per capita Gross Domestic Product (GDP) plunged by a third and unemployment soared from the low single digits to 25 percent. Average weekly earnings in manufacturing fell by a third, total farm income declined by nearly 60 percent, and investment in plant and equipment by businesses plunged 90 percent. Although the president encouraged private giving, charitable contributions, excluding bequests, fell by a third during his term. The welfare capitalism of the 1920s languished as corporations put their survival above employee benefit programs. Federal Reserve Board governor Eugene Meyer famously quipped to tourists in 1932 that he governed "the state of bankruptcy."[8]

For home owners, the depression's grim reaper arrived in the envelopes that held property tax bills. With property assessments falling less rapidly than income, property taxes consumed a growing share of home owners' earnings. Property tax delinquencies in cities with populations of over 50,000 ballooned from 10 percent in 1930 to 26 percent in 1933, before declining as recovery took hold. Residents of mostly white neighborhoods formed several thousand small tax-resistance groups during the Hoover years. The resisters, although not unified nationally, claimed to defend productive citizens from parasitic bureaucrats. "Now that the taxpayers finally have become acutely tax conscious," reported the New York *Daily News*, "they demand that all sources of waste, graft, and official extravagance be dried up." Both the Hoover administration and business groups ignored the tax revolt even as it reached flood tide in the election year of 1932. Falling federal revenues and rising costs left no latitude for tax relief from a president who, like most contemporaries, dreaded budget deficits. After a public outcry killed proposals for a national sales tax in 1932, Hoover pushed through Congress the largest percentage income tax hike in peacetime, erasing most reductions of the 1920s and raising the top bracket rate from 25 percent to 63 percent.[9]

HOOVER'S WARS

Herbert Hoover fought a two-front war during his last two years in the presidency, battling both the lingering depression and "the illusion that the Federal Government is a remedy for everything." Although touted as a technician, Hoover was a moralist steeped in Protestant cultural values. In a remarkable speech delivered in 1930 at the King's Mountain Revolutionary War battlefield, Hoover said that America's "principles and ideals grew largely out of the religious origins and spiritual aspirations of our people." He warned that foreign ideologies such as "Socialism, or its violent brother, Bolshevism" would destroy "the nation's spiritual heritage" and "deny religion and seek to expel it. I cannot conceive of a wholesome social order or a sound economic system that does not have its roots in religious faith." Religion grounded a beneficent economic system and an industrious, thrifty, morally responsible, and resourceful people—prerequisites for "our vast economic development." Even in hard times, conservatives yet had a mission to uphold the world's premier Christian civilization.[10]

In January 1932, with Americans howling for relief, Hoover reluctantly turned to government. During the next two hundred days he won passage of legislation to ease mortgage debt, increase banking reserves, and expand credit for farmers and developers. He signed a bill sponsored by his antagonist, Senator Norris, to protect labor from court injunctions and "yellow dog" contracts that barred workers from joining unions. He assented to the formation of a Reconstruction Finance Corporation that made low interest loans to banks, railroads, and insurance companies. But he opposed federal regulation of business and finance and vetoed legislation enacted by Democrats and progressive Republicans in Congress for direct aid to individuals and families—the so-called federal dole. "Never before has so dangerous a suggestion been seriously made to our country," he wrote in his veto message.[11]

Hoover's conversion to activism, like Galileo's rejection of science, convinced none of his enemies. Independent liberals such as the editors of the *Nation* and the *New Republic* demanded tighter regulations and more generous spending on public works and relief. Governor Franklin Roosevelt of New York decried "top down" policies that ignored "the forgotten man at the bottom of the economic pyramid." Even Republican allies warned about the appearance of favoritism to the rich. Hoover confidant John H. Bartlett wrote, "They will give him some credit for the Two Billion Dollar Reconstruction Corporation and its aid, but they are bound to feel that that is more to aid the corporations and that he is neglecting the people."[12]

In 1928 Hoover had campaigned with backing from the right and left wings of his party. Four years later he retained only the right; just two of the Senate's fourteen progressive Republicans stumped for him. Despite rising public opposition to Prohibition and personal doubts about enforcement, Hoover kept the faith with cultural conservatives and opposed efforts by northern Republicans to insert a repeal plank in the party platform.[13]

Governor Roosevelt overcame the opposition of conservative Democrats, led by John Raskob and Al Smith, to win a fourth-ballot presidential nomination after offering the second spot to favorite son John Nance Garner of Texas. Conservative Democrats backed the ticket after the convention adopted a moderate platform. Still, Hoover charged that Democrats "bring forth a philosophy of government which would destroy the whole American system on which we have built the greatest nation of one-hundred and fifty years."[14]

Many business leaders, despite declining fortunes and frayed relations with Hoover, shared the president's mistrust of Roosevelt's call for a New Deal based on "bold, persistent experimentation." The heavily favored Democrats nearly matched Republicans in total financial contributions for 1932, but a few extraordinarily large donations skewed Democratic receipts. Donors of $1,000 or more favored Republicans nearly two to one. Democrats also charged bosses with abusing their power by warning employees that the election of Roosevelt would jeopardize their jobs. Former GOP chair Senator Simeon Fess of Ohio responded, "To say that a manager responsible for the employment of labor has no right to call his men in and say to them what he thinks would be wise for them, leaving them with the liberty to do as they please, is un-American." It was controversy without consequence. As Coolidge's aide Edward Tracey Clark told the former president, "There is not today one Republican leader in banking or industry whose support would not bring out jeers of derision. . . . They are all either discredited or have received such favors from the Government that what they say is without actual effect."[15]

Hoover had responded more forcefully to hard times than any prior president. Yet for most suffering Americans he seemed unequal to the crisis of his times. His wooden manner and political missteps, such as forcibly evicting veterans who had encamped in Washington to demand payment of their World War I bonuses, made him appear insensitive as well. Hoover won less than 40 percent of the popular vote and just six northeastern states; the gains he made in the South during 1928 slipped away. With working majorities in Congress, Democrats had achieved unified control of national government for the first time since 1918. No third party made an impact. Statistical analysis of all counties outside the South demonstrated that northern white Protestants and more affluent voters again made up the Republican base. Since 1928, however, the president had lost ground among voters hurt most by the economic slide and Protestant ethnics who had resisted voting for a Catholic Democrat in 1928. The only bright spots for the Republicans were women and blacks. Women continued to vote more conservatively than men and most African Americans returned to their Republican roots. "There is one consolation in the size of the majority," wrote Hoover spokesman Ted Joslin. "Namely it is so large that nothing would have changed the result."[16]

The fall of the House of Hoover began a two-stage realignment of party loyalty, policy making, and political power. During the first "depression stage," from 1930 to 1932, voters rejected a failed administration. They gave Democrats control of the government and an opportunity to change national policy, recruit new voters, and convert disaffected Republicans. Realignment remained incomplete in 1932 as the GOP narrowly held on as the majority party outside the South. However, the yellowing Republican playbook lacked strategy for opposition politics. Republicans blamed their losses on the bad luck of holding office during a worldwide depression that did not respond to sound remedies in time for vindication at the polls. They stopped their ears even to friendly voices urging adjustment to changed times. J. L. Matthews, Republican campaign director for southern California, warned his party in a confidential memo during FDR's first year:

Recent change in this country was caused by the coming to a head of a great national sore—the perpetuation of business and financial methods that belonged in the nineteenth century, and which, when arbitrarily retained, came into disastrous collision with a country in the throes of profound economic, social, and industrial change. . . . The younger men and women who are nominally Republican will not be aroused to conformity on the basis of pre-panic days.[17]

Most Republicans, like buggy makers in 1900, believed their time would come again when the competition's rickety contraptions failed. Hoover adviser James MacLafferty reflected in his diary that "vindication can only come" for Hoover "if the [dire] prophecies he made in his campaign speeches come true and God forbid that they should for their fulfillment will mean untold disaster to this country and to everybody in it, including myself." What was bad for the nation was now good for conservatives and vice versa.[18]

A RAW DEAL FOR CONSERVATIVES

Hoover was out of power in 1933, but not out of politics. The former president became a relentless critic of the new administration and set out to control the Republican Party with an eye toward possible vindication in 1936. The next chairman of the Republican National Committee, MacLafferty said, must be someone "who was loyal to [Hoover] and that by loyalty I meant devotion; someone that truly preferred his, Hoover's interests to his own." However, a faction led by Charles Hilles, the veteran RNC member from New York, opposed harnessing the Republican future to a devalued ex-president. This was no ideological feud but a raw struggle for power between Hoover and no less conservative rivals. The *Literary Digest* noted that the GOP included "Hoover conservatives, the National Committee Conservatives (popularly denominated the 'Old Guard' under Mr. Hilles) [and] a slight sprinkling of Liberals."[19]

Hilles was the consummate Republican insider: the power behind the powerful. A suave and successful insurance executive, Hilles cultivated connections with Wall Street and sat on the boards of several corporations. He never sought public office or front-page glory but, like a Republican Richelieu, he wielded hidden power through his fund-raising prowess, tireless correspondence, and thirty years of trading favors. He was both an unremitting conservative and a shrewdly pragmatic politician who built coalitions not for personal power or financial gain but to protect right-wing principles of the GOP. For Hilles and his allies, conservatism was their passion, the Republican Party their anodyne. These right-wing activists would give ground neither to Democrats nor to progressive Republicans, who they kept frozen in a ninth circle of party hell. "The only useful purpose of the Republican Party," Hilles wrote in 1934, "is a resolute resistance to economic heresies and the offer of substitute proposals that are sound and constructive." More than any other American of the 1930s, Hilles sustained conservative control of his party.[20]

The impasse between Hoover and Hilles ended in 1934, when party factions reached a compromise that allowed Henry P. Fletcher, a former ambassador to Italy and an admirer of Mussolini, to become the new head of the RNC. "The new chairman is all right," wrote Hilles. "He is just as sound and orthodox as you and I." Fletcher had no illusions about the diminished party he had inherited. The problem for Republicans was simple but vexing: as the economy began to recover in 1933, President Roosevelt emerged as one of the most resourceful political leaders and policy innovators in American history. "I am inclined to think we are living in a fool's paradise, and that Mr. Roosevelt has caught the imagination of the average man quite as truly as Theodore Roosevelt and Andrew Jackson and Thomas Jefferson," lamented James Beck, the solicitor general for Harding and Coolidge.[21]

Scholars have aptly noted that FDR's reforms were incremental, modestly funded, and designed to rescue the capitalist economy. Nonetheless, Roosevelt's New Deal was a transforming moment in American life. It challenged old structures of power, threw up new ones, and created new social roles and opportunities for millions of Americans who worked for government, labored in offices and factories, or farmed for a living. It advanced American pluralism by offering jobs and power to Catholics and Jews and a few African Americans without disrupting local traditions or challenging the anti-pluralist values of many who benefited from its programs. The New Deal reversed prior insular and protective international economic policies by taking America off the gold standard and reducing trade barriers. It shifted the center of American politics by taking on responsibility for steering the economy, promoting social welfare, regulating labor relations, and curbing the abuses of business. Henceforth,

Americans would expect their government to ensure prosperous times, good jobs, and high wages and to aid those unable to fend for themselves.

Still, paradoxes lurked within the new paradigm. Although Americans expected tangible benefits from government, they also clung to traditions of self-help, limited government, states' rights, and fiscal responsibility. In 1937, the first year of extensive and sophisticated surveys, polls showed overwhelming public support for federally guaranteed health care, minimum wage laws, and government work programs. But Americans opposed the trend toward government regulation and centralized power. They favored cutting back on spending for relief and the general functions of government. People's expectations of prosperity also made government vulnerable to big business's willingness to invest, hire, and produce. But the New Deal state had considerable autonomy to implement its vision of the policies needed to restore prosperity, given its liberal ideology and an electoral base that was largely independent of business.[22]

In 1933, as FDR enacted his New Deal program and sold it on the radio in his fireside chats, conservatives railed against a president who they said combined fascist repression and communist collectivism. Roosevelt was seizing "complete power of Fascism," Senator Fess of Ohio wrote, "in order that he may inaugurate the Soviet recommendations that are emanating from his inner cabinet of professors who are steeped in socialism." Hubert Work, a former GOP chair, warned that a remnant of conservative leaders was all that he could see "standing between this nation and the wrecking of its institutions of government." Hoover said that the administration "violated principles which reach to the very foundation of our nation and race."[23]

THE RIGHT STRIKES BACK

In 1934 the right stopped mourning bitter fortune and, like Democrats under Hoover, declared war on the president. The Republican National Committee rejected pleas from the Younger Republican League for fresh ideas and ratified instead a "Statement of Principles" drafted by a committee of unyielding conservatives led by the ubiquitous Hilles. The manifesto eschewed policy analysis for a morally charged, anti-pluralist critique of the New Deal. "We must not see destroyed in four years a civilization which has been centuries in building," the manifesto stated. New Deal liberals, "in place of individual initiative, seek to substitute complete government control of all agricultural production, of all business activity." The drafters invoked the word "American" three times in half a sentence, advocating "American democracy, working along American lines, in accordance with the spirit of American institutions." It was a baby step from this manifesto to a one-line platform that a local activist proposed: "One God, one country, one religion, one law, one finance, one public school, one language, one vote, one ticket."[24]

Most ominous for the administration was growing opposition from most politically active business leaders and organizations. Some sixty heads of major corporations, all male and white, served on a Business Advisory Council lodged within the Department of Commerce. These executives envisioned that business would govern itself under the National Recovery Administration (NRA), which Congress empowered to set industry codes on prices, wages, production, and labor relations. By mid-1934, however, challenges from aggressive bureaucrats and militant workers, conflicts between small and large firms, and the tribulations of setting and enforcing codes for a sprawling economy killed the dream of business self-government. Instead, a growing alliance between Democrats and labor threatened to make the NRA a lever for shifting power from bosses to workers.[25]

Men of enterprise, wistful for obliging government, felt the sting of an administration that in their view disparaged business and encouraged class warfare. "The case against business is being tried on the front page of the newspapers," said A. W. Robertson, chairman of the board of Westinghouse Electric, in his 1934 keynote address to the U.S. Chamber of Commerce. "Business has been charged with being solely responsible for all our troubles. . . . Surely business cannot have been 100 percent wrong and equally surely government cannot be 100 percent right." Ruly Carpenter, a Du Pont in-law and a director of the family corporation, believed that business was 100 percent right and government 100 percent wrong, especially with a president ruled by "[Felix] Frankfurter and his thirty-eight hot dogs—a gang of fanatical and communistic Jew professors." Fears that radical Jews wielded excessive power in Washington spread widely among conservative men of business. Frank W. Buxton, editor of the *Boston Herald*, wrote privately about "substantial men who sympathized with anti-Semitism . . . I was amazed at the intensity with which highly intelligent men argued that the Jews were controlling the President."[26]

Ruly persuaded fellow Du Pont director and conservative Democrat John J. Raskob to join with the Du Pont brothers, Irénée, Pierre, and Lammot, to challenge the New Deal through a new organization eventually dubbed the American Liberty League. Former Democratic presidential candidates Al Smith and John W. Davis helped plan the league along with industrialists such as Alfred P. Sloan Jr., president of General Motors, in which the Du Ponts held a controlling interest; Ernest T. Weir, president of National Steel; J. Howard Pew, president of Sun Oil; and E. F. Hutton, chairman of General Foods. The founders decided that the league would neither shelter a coalition of conservative groups nor recruit grassroots activists. Raskob and the Du Ponts would save America from the top down.[27]

The founders considered naming their organization the "National Property League" or the "Association Asserting the Rights of Property," but as influential General Motors executive Donaldson Brown noted, "Any organization which was known to be directly interested primarily in the defense of established property rights" would lack public support. The root of evil in America, he warned, was not economic but moral: "What this nation really is facing is a condition in which public morality has broken down," where "all rights are a matter of the moment and the majority can change them at will." In response, the league launched a broad crusade for conservative ideals that advanced the maturation of an interest-group politics not tied to a particular issue or constituency. Organizations like the Anti-Saloon League, the Association Against the Prohibition Amendment, and the American Birth Control League focused on single issues. Other groups, for example the National Association for the Advancement of Colored People, the League of Women Voters, and the National Association of Manufacturers, represented specific constituencies. Never before had a richly funded interest group advanced a sweeping political ideology, implemented a nationwide campaign of education, and addressed a broad spectrum of issues.[28]

Men of business, led by the Du Ponts, General Motors executives, and heads of family enterprises such as Weir and Pew, ruled the Liberty League. It had a sprinkling of academics, but only token representation from labor, farmers' organizations, citizens' associations, or public officials. No Democratic officeholders or party officials and only two notable

Republicans, Representative James Wadsworth of New York and Senator David A. Reed of Pennsylvania, joined the league, which failed to achieve star power when America's hero Charles Lindbergh rejected its presidency. Still, the league's insular leadership wagered that Americans would follow tutelage from the best men of enterprise. With the league delaying its official debut until after the 1934 midterm elections, its directors marked time by hosting opulent dinners and dunning the rich for contributions.

The National Association of Manufacturers (NAM), which hemorrhaged members during the early depression years, recovered after Roosevelt's election. Led by conservative corporate presidents who called themselves the "brass hats," in reference to the military discipline they hoped to impose on business, the NAM launched a successful membership drive and set opposition strategy against labor and the New Deal. From 1931 to 1940, NAM's active membership shot up from fewer than one thousand to nearly five thousand firms, as business responded to the stresses of economic depression and liberal reformers in Washington. Although about two-thirds of member firms employed fewer than five hundred workers, major corporations dominated NAM's board and policy committees. The NAM still hoped to thwart independent unions, discourage strikes, discipline workers, and forestall federal programs that loosened workers' dependence on their bosses. But employers could not succeed without a revamped strategy adapted to the loss of business prestige after 1929 and citizens' changed expectations of government.

The new business strategy emerged in a 1934 memo by the NAM's Employment Relations Committee, which formulated covert and indirect methods for stifling labor power and liberal reform: "The plan here proposed has for its immediate object the curtailment of the power of [independent] craft unions, and ultimately to destroy them." Otherwise, "there might follow an organization that would make the present craft unions seem like a blessing." Although "collective bargaining is here to stay," in the hands of independent unions, "it is a vicious menace even when it is not evil in effect." However, "in the hands of employers and their own workers it's the most effective tool for preventing strikes and labor troubles that ever has been invented. If craft unions are torn down some machinery must be set up in its place. This would be what is now called the company union."[29]

By openly opposing collective bargaining, executives would appear reactionary and self-serving. Instead, NAM advised indirect opposition through "publicity engineering, which means using publicity as a tool and not an end in itself." Shrewd employers would publicly back collective bargaining rights but with enough qualifiers to defeat or enfeeble specific proposals. "Manufacturers should make public declaration that they believe in collective bargaining," but include such prohibitive conditions as disclosure of union finances and limitations on strikes and picketing. Employers should launch an "intensive publicity campaign on union finances" and tell "the dramatic story of unfair strikes to gratify an agitator's greed, of graft, of intimidation, of blackmail, even murder . . . with the overlords of unions standing for it." Surrogates should generate this publicity: "Little of it would go forth under the Association's sponsorship. All the Association should do is to declare in favor of a constructive program." Similarly, "the Association has no choice but to appear to favor unemployment insurance in principle if it wants to make any fight against it." Instead, industrialists should carp on detail, "assaulting every working plan proposed, for they are all vulnerable." Effective opposition to unemployment insurance and other liberal reforms "is possible only if the Association is on record as favoring some plan to protect the workers."

After consulting with social psychologists, NAM launched an energetic public relations campaign to stymie the New Deal and "to sell free enterprise"—a term that NAM claimed to have "taken out of the category of technical phrases used only by economists" and made "part of the American vocabulary." To promote free enterprise and the harmony of interests between labor and capital, NAM expanded its public relations budget from $36,500 in 1933 to $467,759 in 1936. The association established a National Industrial Information Committee to coordinate public relations and a Church-Industry Committee to educate ministers on economics. In tandem with such companies as Ford, General Motors, Du Pont, and Texaco, the NAM entered show business by threading pro-business themes into programs it sponsored on radio.[30]

Under adversity, conservative men of business had devised lasting strategy for engineering opinion as they shifted from coercion to persuasion and from obstruction to misdirection. Proud businessmen did not always welcome this strategy. "I don't think any of us have been aggressive enough to think we could go down there [to the White House] and demand this or demand the other thing," NAM chairman Robert Lund privately told fellow executives in 1934. "What we are doing instead is attempting to adjust ourselves and modify or change or meet half-way, the situation." Although Lund "wouldn't want to have what I am saying repeated . . . the strong position for us to take is for us to stand for what we know is sound in the way of social insurance." Still, the new approach of misdirection guided business's strategy for achieving its goals. Businessmen would neither initiate liberal state programs nor blunder into opposition and "be branded as a selfish reactionary unworthy of any consideration," the NAM memo warned. They would pay lip service to reform while working to kill liberal programs or shape them in their interest. They continued efforts to adopt favorable subsidies and regulations and "capture" public interest regulators and turn them into patrons of industry.[31]

In 1935, Congress passed the Wagner National Labor Relations Act, which protected collective bargaining through federally supervised and certified union elections and prohibited unions run by companies and unfair labor practices. Instead of demanding repeal, NAM called for amendments that served "the welfare of the public" by balancing union and employer rights. As Lewis Carroll's Humpty Dumpty famously said, however, a word "means just what I choose it to mean, neither more nor less." For business, the words "public interest" or "public welfare" meant the interests of enterprise, which, in turn, it was argued, served the public. NAM's proposals were dead on arrival in a Democratic Congress, but pollster George Gallup reported in 1937 that "Congress will eventually meet the regulation issue face to face unless labor succeeds in selling its case to the public." His polling showed that two-thirds of Americans agreed with NAM proposals for strict government regulation of unions.[32]

New strategies did not mean, however, that companies set aside stern measures to break unions. Although lacking support from the Roosevelt administration, companies turned to local police forces to subdue unruly strikers and private firms to infiltrate and spy on unions, intimidate organizers, and battle picketing workers. Testimony before a Senate investigating committee in the mid-1930s showed that industry had purchased more tear and nauseating gas than all American law enforcement agencies combined and had stockpiled arsenals of machine guns, rifles, pistols, and shotguns. Members of the American Legion joined in strike-breaking efforts. The legion grew rapidly during the early depression years as it worked to expand benefits for veterans and protect the American way of life. For many legionnaires, the wave of strikes that followed the election of Franklin Roosevelt threatened the Americanism they pledged to uphold. Despite misgivings by some legion officials, thousands of legion vigilantes engaged in often violent and sometimes deadly strike-breaking efforts.[33]

THE THIN RED LINE

Republicans in 1934 anticipated that, as in every midterm election since the Civil War era, the party locked out of the White House would gain congressional seats. But prophecy proved to be the font of error as worried candidates vacillated between the National Committee's hard line and the dissenting views of GOP progressives. Republican progressive Senator Gerald P. Nye of North Dakota said the party "must lay out a program that is progressive, and not a program that says 'sit still and don't rock the boat.'" Conservative House Minority Leader Bertrand Snell of New York, however, said the campaign was "between those who believe in the philosophy of Thomas Jefferson and Abraham Lincoln and those who believe in the Russian philosophy of Lenin and Trotsky." With Americans still voting against Herbert Hoover and his depression, the GOP lost thirteen House and nine Senate seats, nearly all of them held by conservatives. Voters dismissed Senators Fess of Ohio and Liberty Leaguer Reed of Pennsylvania. In Missouri, Republican senator Roscoe Patterson lost to an obscure Democrat named Harry Truman.[34]

These midterm results continued realigning party loyalties as Democrats made headway in converting Republicans and recruiting first-time and newly eligible voters. The Republican percentage of the two-party registration slipped in five states from 59 percent in 1932 to 52 percent in 1934. In nine major cities, the percentage of registered Republicans tumbled from 52 percent to 42 percent. For the first time in a national election, Democrats won a majority of African-American voters. In Chicago, Arthur Mitchell became the first black Democrat elected to Congress, defeating Oscar De Priest, the last remaining black Republican.

Progressive Republicans blamed the party's conservatives for its midterm setbacks and called for rebuilding popular support by emulating Democrats. "Unless the Republican Party is delivered from its reactionary leadership and reorganized in accordance with its one time liberal principles, it will die like the Whig party of sheer political cowardice," warned Senator William Borah of Idaho. But the conservatives insisted on keeping the GOP ideologically pure and saving it for the day that the New Deal died. "Personally, I am pretty well fed up with a lot of our Republicans talking liberalization of the party," former Senator Walter Edge of New Jersey wrote. "I believe the future of the Republican Party lies in maintaining a critical attitude toward every one of the New Deal experiments. . . . Sooner or later the American electorate will tire of these experiments. . . . but if the Republicans wriggle and pussyfoot all around the lot, trying to out-liberalize our opponents, we will become just a mass of broken pottery." Fletcher assured him that "as long as I am Chairman of this Committee, Republican principles are not going to be bargained for temporary, elusive, vote-catching expedience."[35]

The conservatives worried that Borah's remedy would backfire by unilaterally disarming the GOP. Republicans relied on an investment strategy for winning elections by outspending Democrats through contributions from business. Despite their disappointment with lagging donations in 1934, GOP strategists expected future riches if they continued to honor conservative ideals. A "me-too" party, they said, would find itself rattling a tin cup for small change and shouting to be heard above the din of liberal Democrats. "Certainly we can't out-radical them," wrote Representative Wadsworth. "[If we] offer compromises we shall lose the respect of all thinking men and as a party we shall perish." Business donations were vital in the new big government era, "to offset the sinister activities of the publicity agents of the Democrats, masquerading as government employees," wrote influential Republican National Committee member M. L. Requa of California. With federal programs and payrolls boosting Democrats, whatever Republicans might spend was "an insignificant sum in comparison with the hundreds of millions, perhaps billions, which have been deliberately spent by the Democratic Party for the purpose of solidifying their own position and making it impregnable."[36]

After Chairman Fletcher and fellow conservatives rejected liberalization, Chase Mellen, the reform-minded chair of Manhattan's Republicans, lashed back. He asked rhetorically whether the people viewed Roosevelt or the Du Ponts as the "protector of the masses." Could Republicans win in 1936 with "the same policies which characterized the most recent Republican administration?" Mellen challenged Fletcher to call a party meeting "directed at how best we may 'humanize,' if you find the word 'liberal' repugnant to you." Fletcher and the rising star within the party, John D. M. Hamilton of Kansas, the RNC's general counsel who would succeed Fletcher as chair in 1936, called the GOP together in 1935, not to "humanize" the party but to reaffirm its conservative birthright. Hamilton convened several regional "grassroots" conventions, the largest of which brought thousands of activists from midwestern and Plains states to Springfield, Illinois. "I believe the mid-west is more conservative today than New York," Hilles said.[37]

The Republican Party realigned regionally during the 1930s. Senator Borah and other western GOP progressives were social conservatives. They supported immigration restriction, prohibition, and antiobscenity laws, but they opposed big business and finance and sought to eliminate sweatshop labor, monopoly pricing, and foreclosures of family farms. The next generation of western Republicans, however, came of age after the Progressive era and upheld the conservative consensus on both social and economic issues. In turn, a new generation of less conservative Republicans rose in the East, in response to the growing urban and ethnic voting blocs of their region. With the West moving right and the East moving left, the ideological center of the Republican Party remained similar, but the conservative base of the party shifted from the East to the West.

CRUSADING CONSERVATIVES

Independent groups on the right, unaffiliated with the political parties, informally aligned with the GOP to mobilize manpower, brainpower, and money power against FDR. Victory over Roosevelt was not the most important thing for the right in 1936—it was the only thing. Most politically active businessmen, including those affiliated with the NAM, the Chamber of Commerce, and corporate trade associations, opposed the New Deal's ambitious post-1934 agenda. They turned their thumbs down on the stringent regulation of utility companies, a more powerful Federal Reserve System, tighter supervision of financial markets, aid to farmers, and "soak the rich" taxation. They opposed federal labor protections and work programs for the unemployed. A few business leaders were more sympathetic to Social Security legislation that established direct aid to the elderly in addition to old-age pensions, unemployment compensation, and

aid to the disabled and mothers with dependent children. The vast majority of politically active business leaders and associations, however, opposed
Social Security, although following NAM's strategy they recognized its
unstoppable momentum and sought to keep costs down and protect private insurance plans.[38]

Management had particular scorn for the Wagner National Labor
Relations Act. A survey by the Associated Business Papers found that "virtually every industry served by its 125 publications opposed the Wagner
Act." Business leaders likewise condemned the Works Progress Administration, which placed millions of the unemployed in government jobs. For
conservatives, "WPAism" symbolized the New Deal's many fallacies. A
readers' survey by the investor's journal *Dow Theory Comment* found more
than 90 percent opposition to the WPA. Roosevelt's approval rating among
its readers fell from 38 percent in 1932 to 15 percent in 1936. A membership survey by the U.S. Chamber of Commerce found that 97 percent
opposed the philosophy of the New Deal and, out of thousands of prominent executives, the Democratic National Committee managed to piece
together a list of only thirty-five mostly obscure businessmen who backed
Roosevelt's reelection.[39]

Roosevelt's first term was a unique moment in history. It was the only
time that American politics generated such far-reaching policy change over
concerted opposition from business. Even FDR's in-house executives on
the Business Advisory Council rejected most of his economic program, and
several of his severest critics resigned. The council poured out its opposition in confidential memos that analyzed proposed legislation. The Wagner
Act, "if enacted into law, would strike one of the severest blows at the public
interest which the country has ever suffered." The administration's farm
program needed "fundamental changes." Stringent regulations of financial markets were "extremely detrimental to the public interest" and proposals for curtailing utility holding companies needed drastic amendment.
Roosevelt should not expand Federal Reserve powers or push his progressive tax bill—"a half-baked measure conceived in politics [that] would
produce unfortunate results." He should broadly cut welfare spending and
balance the budget.[40]

Although businessmen, big and small, opposed regulations that raised
costs, empowered labor, or hampered their autonomy, they still sought out
federal subsidies and regulations that boosted profits, limited competition,

or stabilized markets. Banks and industrial firms benefited from billions in loans and stock purchases from the Reconstruction Finance Corporation, trade liberalization, and the Export-Import Bank's financing of exports. The government underwrote the housing industry by subsidizing mortgage lending and boosted business productivity through public investments in roads, highways, harbors, airports, bridges, and electricity. After the Texas oil boom dropped prices to twenty-five cents for a barrel of crude, big oil companies gained the passage of state quota laws that limited production in order to stabilize prices. At the federal level, in 1935, big oil interests secured the Connally Hot Oil Act that bolstered these laws by prohibiting the interstate shipment of so-called hot oil produced in violation of state quotas. Major coal producers, in cooperation with the United Mine Workers, gained the Guffey Act, which limited competition by setting minimum prices for the sale of coal. Producers of brand-name products and small retailers gained the Miller-Tydings Act, which authorized states to enact "fair trade" laws that set minimum prices for the resale of brand-name goods. Independent grocers and other competitors of chain retailers won enactment of the Robinson-Patman Act, which prohibited price discrimination by sellers. Big trucking companies gained the Motor Carrier Act of 1935, which limited competition on interstate routes. Major agricultural producers secured renewed price supports and protection from foreign competition.

The American Liberty League awakened after the 1934 midterms and began spending big money on a campaign of public education against the New Deal. The league claimed 125,000 (mostly inactive) members and 27,000 contributors, although the Du Ponts and executives from family-controlled firms accounted for most revenue. The league's largest public solicitation raised a meager $32,000. A disheartened E. F. Hutton urged businessmen to stop "shirking their duties" and to "stand up and fight [the] radicals and demagogues who have built up class distinction and class hatred [and] pull down the men of competence to the basis of the man of incompetence." He urged managers to recognize interests "beyond matters of finance, production, distribution, accounting, and reports" and to rally millions of stockholders and small investors against the "demagogic attack on business" and efforts to create a "social order in which the individual is entirely subordinate to the State." But businessmen failed to heed his call for open rebellion against the liberals in Washington. Time and again, the Liberty League failed to extract contributions from men of means loath to risk exposure as contributors. Two celebrity donors, movie producer Hal Roach of Metro-Goldwyn-Mayer and automobile innovator Walter Chrysler, reneged on pledges of $20,000. These capitalists, with an eye on protecting their enterprises, feared antagonizing the party in power. League founder Raskob lamented, "The most discouraging thing to me is the way men in our walk of life, who should stand forth fearlessly and lead, are being cowed down by threats of being cracked down if they stick their necks out."[41]

Unwanted publicity from congressional investigators also stung the league. After Roosevelt's election Democrats and progressive Republicans used congressional investigations to stir up a "brown scare" that tied the right to predatory business and fascist sympathizers. In 1934 Senator Gerald Nye, a progressive Republican and isolationist, held public hearings on the munitions industry that damned the Du Ponts as "merchants of death." In 1935 Representative Samuel Dickstein, Democrat from New York, convened the special committee he co-chaired on Nazi activities in the United States to hear retired General Smedley Darlington Butler testify that agents for titans of enterprise, including Liberty League founders, had pressured him to recruit veterans led by the American Legion for a citizen army to overthrow the Roosevelt administration and put the nation under martial law. The committee concluded that "attempts to establish a fascist organization in the United States . . . were discussed, were planned, and might have been placed in execution when and if the financial backers deemed it expedient." Details of the supposed plot, however, sank into the muck of accusation and denial.[42]

The Liberty League shook off unwelcome publicity to commence the most ambitious marketing of conservative ideas in American history. In 1935 and 1936 it published and disseminated more than 135 pamphlets to members, newspapers, libraries, universities, and public officials. The league published a monthly bulletin of news and opinion, sponsored radio broadcasts, recruited students for chapters at colleges and universities, and assembled its own brain trust of conservative professors. In an appeal to anti-pluralists, Raskob warned that liberals "seem intent even on destroying religion," which, in turn, "will destroy Capitalism, the foundation of our whole business and social order." The league provided both a substantive and constitutional defense of private enterprise. Its Lawyer's

Committee, headed by Raoul Desvernine, general counsel for the U.S. Steel Corporation, claimed that New Deal legislation was unconstitutional— and by implication need not be obeyed. League leaders also backed restrictions on voting by allegedly unfit citizens and opened lines of communication with white supremacists. Raskob and Pierre Du Pont sought to strike "undesirables" from the voter rolls. League Secretary William H. Stayton lamented that "we have been breeding stupid and antisocial people faster than we have good citizens." Pierre Du Pont corresponded with the Klan's Hiram Evans about uniting to fight America's "Red menace." The league struck no deal with the Klan, although the Du Ponts kept prodding the imperial wizard to oppose the New Deal. A slew of Liberty Leaguers backed the quixotic 1936 presidential primary campaign of Georgia's racist governor Democrat Eugene Talmadge.[43]

The Liberty League found that the New Deal did not come tumbling down when it trumpeted conservative ideas. Despite their expertise in marketing, Liberty Leaguers persuaded few Americans to restore the gods that had failed in 1929. Policy and philosophy killed the league, not language and rhetoric. As Chase Mellen warned, conservatives simply were working the wrong side of the tracks for common folk who paid no income taxes, didn't care about construing the Constitution, and trusted FDR more than they did the Du Ponts. Other conservative groups faced similar challenges. In New York, Ogden Mills founded the Republican Builders to counter Roosevelt's "forgotten man," with "the 'forgotten' Republicans whose voice has not counted because of their inability to devote to politics their time and effort." Mills pried contributions from such celebrity tycoons as Andrew Mellon and J. Paul Getty. He united the Morgan and Rockefeller interests with donations from Morgan partner Thomas W. Lamont and family patriarch John D. Rockefeller Jr., who laundered his $2,500 through an intermediary to maintain the family's policy of avoiding contributions to groups that they did not control. But Mills's builders failed to rally forgotten Republicans. From Ohio, Robert A. Taft, an ambitious state senator and son of a president, wrote, "I have not made any headway in starting in Ohio an organization similar to the National Republican Builders." Mills, who had hoped to recruit thousands of former Republican postmasters, responded that "our organization is more or less marking time."[44]

A vanguard of businessmen led by the irrepressible E. F. Hutton converted the Crusaders, an anti-Prohibition group, into a lesser cousin of the

Liberty League. It called for a spiritual revival in America and pledged "to fight vigorously any attempts to have the majority of Americans ruled by organized minorities seeking special advantages." It sponsored *The Radio Voice of the Crusaders,* heard on some eighty stations around the country. The group published pamphlets and a book, *The Crusader,* which rallied "the sound, constructive and patriotic elements of our great country against the New Deal's political racketeers and preachers of class hatred." Major corporations, including General Mills, Du Pont, Sun Oil, General Motors, Heinz, Nabisco, and Standard Oil of Indiana, financed the Crusaders.[45]

Merwin Hart organized his more enduring but controversial New York State Economic Council (later renamed the National Economic Council) with contributions from Sloan, the Du Ponts, President J. H. Alystone of Otis Elevators, and James Rand of Remington Rand. The council served mainly as a vehicle for Hart's one-man lobbying for conservative causes and his personally written, widely circulated Economic Council letter, which dissected issues such as economy in government, immigration, and the left-wing infiltration of schools and churches. Hart became best known for passionate anti-Zionism (which led to charges of anti-Semitism that he denied) and for promoting anticommunist, authoritarian regimes in Spain and Portugal.[46]

Raymond Pitcairn, president of the Pittsburgh Plate Glass Company, revitalized the Sentinels of the Republic in early 1935 with an $85,000 contribution to a group that had raised precisely $15,378.74 since 1931. The revived Sentinels had the singular distinction of vanquishing the New Deal in a straight-up legislative battle by winning repeal of a federal law that required those filing federal income taxes (about 7 percent of the population) to submit a publicly accessible form printed on pink paper that listed the taxpayer's gross income, deductions, net income, and tax liability. By contrast, utility lobbies had failed to defeat regulation of the industry, despite a lobbying budget of $3.5 million and guidance from the best minds in public relations. The Sentinel's underdog victory offered a model for conservative success. The Sentinels had bombarded members of Congress with letters, telegrams, and facsimiles of the so-called Pink Slip stamped with the slogan "I Protest Against this Outrageous Invasion of my Right of Privacy," which also appeared on stickers that taxpayers pasted on their federal tax returns. The Sentinels inspired genuine public outrage, not the contrived populism of the utility industry that had coerced employees into signing letters and petitions and forged fictitious names on thousands of mass-produced telegrams protesting federal regulations.[47]

The Pink Slip victory fired a shot of adrenaline through the arteries of the right. The *Philadelphia Daily News* enthused, "The Sentinels of the Republic achieved a great victory because they started the fight alone. They were unselfish. They were patriotic. They were militant. They had a just cause. Because of these things the people rallied behind them." The Sentinels followed this triumph with an innovative campaign of satire and ridicule through a "Pro-Constitution, Anti-Bureaucracy Show" that debuted in Philadelphia in 1935 to some thirty thousand visitors and then hit the road. The show featured political cartoons, flashing lights and gongs that marked the ballooning public debt, and an animated motion picture— *The Amateur Fire Brigade: A Fable of the New Deal*—billed as "the first successful adaptation of the political cartoonists' art to the motion picture screen." The film showed the president driving a derelict New Deal fire engine and riding backward on a donkey that kicks his 1932 platform to splinters. It featured the "Brain Trust Ballyhoo Boys" playing games of "soak the rich" and "public funds poker" and building a house of alphabet blocks for Uncle Sam that burns down when the New Deal's amateur fire brigade arrives too late to save it. Funding constraints and clashes with state censors kept the show from catching on nationwide.[48]

Other organizations included the Southern States Industrial Council, formed in 1933, which shined among regional groups. It eventually recruited more than seven thousand small businesses in defense of regional wage differentials, nonunion employment, business autonomy, and access to cheap black labor. The Brookings Institution tilted its intellectual weight to the right under Harold G. Moulton, its president from 1927 until his retirement in 1952. Moulton directed studies that validated his market ideology and impugned the New Deal for setting class against class, spending beyond its means, and choosing "centralized authority [over] what is left of free competitive enterprise."[49]

Opposition to the New Deal launched Joseph Newton Pew Jr. and J. Howard Pew, the brothers who controlled Sun Oil (later Sunoco), on their three-decade run as preeminent financiers of the right. Although born to privilege, the Pews were also high achievers who enriched their inherited company while pursuing public affairs. The Pews pumped millions of dollars into the Republican Party and millions more into sponsoring patriotic

Christian leadership. Joseph Pew, like Charles Hilles, was a partisan warrior who fought to empower the GOP and keep it safe for conservatism. Forget coalition building or third-party schemes. Southern Democrats and other conservatives should join the Republican Party to avoid the European mistake of chaotic multiparty politics. "The two-party system and the loyalty of all people to their party affiliations [are] the foundation and the only foundation of our Republic," Pew wrote. He also believed that "only the Anglo-Saxon people are conditioned for representative government which basicly [*sic*] requires sportsmanship and a sense of fair play to maintain." With the support of family members, Pew bought tacit control over the Pennsylvania state party and influence in national Republican circles. Like Hilles, he chose to exercise and not flaunt power, shunning publicity, officeholding, and special pleading for his company. Joseph Pew believed that tycoons should speak softy and carry a big purse. In the 1930s the Pews led all American families in generosity to the GOP, including the Rockefellers.[50]

The devoutly evangelical Protestant J. Howard Pew, with Cromwellian faith and ardor, fought on a wider front than his brother against what he saw as the secular heresies and high tyranny of the liberal state. Beyond writing checks, he avoided entanglement in Republican politics, preferring to work outside the party system. J. Howard Pew financed right-wing advocacy groups, business associations, religious organizations, books, magazines, newspapers, films, radio broadcasts, and conferences. "For 20 years I have been convinced we never would accomplish anything worth while by merely changing the party in power," Pew reflected in the 1950s. "If we want to save America, we must do it by changing the minds and hearts of our people." In the 1930s Pew helped sustain the Liberty League and the Crusaders. He became chairman of the board and chief benefactor of Grove City College, which he molded into a source of conservative Christian leadership and a model for other institutions. He contributed five-figure sums to Spiritual Mobilization, which merged Christian piety and conservative politics, and he directed the United Presbyterian Foundation, which opposed religious modernism and the church's backing of secular reform.[51]

In 1935 the Pews bought the *Farm Journal* magazine to help bring "the truth, which is something all the politicians most assiduously steer away from," to rural America, "the real sane and thoughtful background of our whole social order." As acknowledged by publisher Graham

Patterson, the Pews controlled "final decisions of the *Farm Journal,* including editorial." Although the *Journal*'s circulation initially fell behind the Pews' goal of two million, it passed that mark during the 1940s and turned a six-figure yearly profit, becoming the leading journal of opinion in rural America.[52]

J. Howard Pew and his circle of politically active, anti-pluralist industrialists, including Du Pont executive Jasper Crane and Chrysler vice president B. E. Hutchinson, did not just throw money at conservatives but carefully screened every supplicant. "When somebody offers me a plan in which I can see some hope for the future, I will give it my enthusiastic support," Pew said. These self-styled business intellectuals read deeply, corresponded voluminously, and reviewed drafts of books and articles. They studied politics and markets, wrote reports, and addressed civic, business, and religious functions. They funded anti-pluralist Protestant groups and played church politics to demonstrate, in J. Howard's words, "that Christianity and freedom are inexorably tied together" and that "New Dealism, Socialism, and Communism are substantially the same thing—and all of them are the very antithesis of Christianity."[53]

A remnant of old-line Democrats joined the anti–New Deal coalition. These so-called Jeffersonian Democrats clung to the party's ancient traditions of states' rights, limited government, and frugal spending. Led by Bainbridge Colby—Woodrow Wilson's secretary of state—their number included such notable "formers" as Joseph Ely, former governor of Massachusetts, and James Reed, former senator from Missouri. The Jeffersonians did not believe they had left the Democratic Party; the New Deal party had left them. "The Democratic Party of today is only a so-called Democratic Party," Colby said. "It bears little resemblance, if any, to the party which carried the 1932 election." It was time to choose between "loyalty to party organization or duty to country." Colby proposed that conservative Democrats meet privately to plan opposition strategy, whether an internal revolt, a third party, or alliance with Republicans. However, the Jeffersonians, like the Liberty Leaguers, failed to recruit conservative southern Democrats, who held real power in the party. "My feeling is that we will get little help in the final stages of any independent movement from men who are in the mainstream of office-holder careers, or those who expect and earnestly hope at one time to hold office," Colby lamented. The southern conservatives "are good men but they are not the type who will ever pursue the line of independence in politics." The disheartened Colby delayed plans for ambushing the New Deal until 1936.[54]

THE OUTER BANKS OF THE RIGHT

On the edges of the right dwelt demagogues of so-called shirt movements, the men who branded an extreme version of anti-pluralist ideology. Modeled on Mussolini's black shirts in Italy and Hitler's brown shirts in Germany, shirt movements grew worldwide during the depression years, with blue shirts in Canada, Portugal, and Ireland; gray shirts in Cuba; red shirts in India and the Middle East; and gold shirts in Mexico. America's most prominent shirt leader, William Dudley Pelley, commanded the Silver Shirts, which may have recruited as many as twenty-five thousand members nationwide at its peak in 1933. Gerald Winrod of Kansas, the "Jayhawk Nazi," published a newspaper, *The Defender,* with a circulation of a hundred thousand, and won 21 percent of the vote in the 1938 Kansas Republican primary for U.S. Senate. Other shirt leaders included George Deatherage of West Virginia, head of the Knights of the White Camelia; George W. Christians, of the Tennessee-based Crusader White Shirts; Art J. Smith of Philadelphia's Khaki Shirts; and Joseph McWilliams, organizer of the Christian Mobilizers in New York City. Virgil Effinger, a former Klansman, ran Detroit's violent Black Legion. Remnants of the Klan mutated into virulent anti-Jewish groups and more than a hundred other small anti-Semitic groups formed between 1933 and 1941. Anti-Semites fed into prevailing opinion by warning that Jewish refugees from Nazi persecution would inundate the United States and by charging that Jews controlled America's media and banks. According to polls from the late 1930s, about half of the public thought Jews excessively influenced business and finance and nearly two-thirds held Jews at least partially responsible for their persecution in Europe. Shirt groups embraced authoritarian leadership, militarism, mystical nationalism, and sometimes mob violence. Their leaders strutted and fretted on the national stage. They gained headlines and worried legislators and prosecutors but ultimately signified little within the larger conservative movement.[55]

Pro-fascist politics, however, gained traction among some American ethnic groups. In 1933 an American branch of the German Nazi party organized the Friends of the New Germany, which recruited some five thousand members but took a beating in the press for its overt ties to Hitler's government. Berlin severed formal relations with the American Friends in 1935, but the group reemerged as the ostensibly independent German-American Bund, led by Fritz Kuhn. This naturalized U.S. citizen who had earned an Iron Cross as a German infantry officer in World War I fancied himself the American führer. But the German government pulled the puppet strings on the Bund, which distributed Nazi propaganda, harbored German spies, and mimicked Hitler's martial enthusiasm, leader worship, and Aryan solidarity. It even blundered into the 1936 presidential election, endorsing Republican Alf Landon to counter what it said was the Jewish New Deal of "President Rosenfeld." The Bund never gained mass membership but it inspired tens of thousands of sympathizers and held high-profile rallies, which backfired by stoking anti-Nazi sentiment. In 1939, shortly before New York detectives arrested Kuhn for stealing funds from his Bund, Mayor Fiorello La Guardia and the Manhattan district attorney Thomas Dewey, both Republicans, exchanged letters about prosecuting Kuhn.

> La Guardia: "Dear Tom: You can have him."
> Dewey: "I don't want him either. I guess the ashcan is the best place for him."[56]

Among other nationality groups, Ukrainians founded an American branch of the European pro-Nazi Organization for the Rebirth of the Ukraine, which became a center of Nazi propaganda in the United States. Italian fascism, however, emerged as the largest and most prestigious movement of the far right. Inspired by Mussolini, pro-fascist sentiment swept such patriotic societies as the Sons of Italy, the Federation of Italian War Veterans, and the Dante Alighieri Society, all of which had ties to the Lictor Federation, which Mussolini's government organized to promote Italian fascism in the United States. The Italian-American press overwhelmingly backed Mussolini, as did most of the American Catholic Church's leadership, impressed by a dictator who had signed a concordat with the Vatican in 1929. Until Mussolini's war against Ethiopia in 1935–36, Italian fascism escaped the opprobrium of its Nazi counterpart. In 1933 Harold Lord Varney, manager of the Italian Historical Society, sought conservative support for "launching a Fascist Party of America." Italian Americans, however, stayed loyal to the Democratic Party and ultimately backed FDR's foreign policies.[57]

Political theorist Lawrence Dennis gave a sophisticated twist to right-wing thought in *The Coming American Fascism* (1936), which argued that an Italian- or German-style corporate state was preferable to an otherwise certain communist takeover of the United States. He said that the United States had better prepare for fascism and make sure that the "right people" ran the new order. The technocratic movement that swept across America in the early 1930s, with appeal to both the right and the left, also influenced Dennis's work. The technocrats preached that with expert planning and direction America could efficiently utilize resources and labor to end the depression and create abundance. Dennis claimed to have analyzed social trends dispassionately, but the very title of his book made him a notorious figure.

RIGHT RELIGION, RIGHT POLITICS

"Bad bankers, rather than bad banking; bad investors, rather than bad investments; bad politicians, rather than bad politics; bad citizenry, rather than bad legislation" had brought on the Great Depression, wrote the Reverend Louis S. Bauman of the Church of the Brethren in 1933. Although Bauman and other evangelical leaders of the period did not usually endorse candidates, join campaigns, or donate to partisan causes, they entered debates over policy and political philosophy, primarily through evangelical newspapers and magazines. Evangelicals backed some liberal programs, such as the Civilian Conservation Corps, and a few denounced greedy businessmen in the early days of the New Deal. However, evangelicals with a public profile usually faulted the New Deal's secular activism, its relativistic ethics, and its collectivist measures. Redemption from economic calamity could not be found in a liberal state that "leaves out God and leaves out sin," warned the *Sunday School Times*. Calamitous times demanded the revival of the Holy Spirit, which redeemed people's souls and inspired them to live moral, productive lives. "The Gospel of Christ is an individual message to the individual heart," declared *The Teacher*. "There is no gospel to men in the mass." In the *Moody Monthly*, published by the prestigious Moody Bible Institute of Chicago, the Reverend James Edward Congdon disparaged the idea that "the elevation of the race will be the product of reformatory and regulatory legislation [that] overlooks or rejects the fact of a fallen humanity."[58]

Evangelicals argued that the New Deal discouraged the Christian virtues of self-help, thrift, and charity, and instead encouraged sloth, dissolution, and dependence. Liberal programs ignored the corruption of liquor, prostitution, and gambling, while hobbling the private enterprise system that rewarded disciplined virtue through freedom of choice. *The Teacher* assailed "wrong track" government policies that offered secular solutions to spiritual problems and were "penalizing industry, thrift, economy, self denial, for the benefit of the shiftless and wasters." Some evangelicals denounced radicals who had infiltrated government, the media, schools, and churches, shaping the secular reform programs of mainstream denominations. "It claims to be guided by Christ," the editor of the *Christian Advocate* said of the Methodist Foundation for Social Service, "though others think that Karl Marx is its real Messiah." Elzoe Prindle Stead of Georgia's Women's Christian Temperance Union took aim at the materialist editors and educators who "offer[ed] Humanism as a religion." Presbyterian minister Daniel Russell denounced "the delusion that the church is outmoded, and that the trend is toward some sort of humanism or scientific philosophy." Instead, "a steady emphasis must be put on the fact that there is no morality without the aid of the church."[59]

Four figures led the merger of conservative politics and religion. In 1934 John R. Rice, a defector from the Southern Baptist Convention, founded the independent newspaper *Sword of the Lord*. Rice built the *Sword*'s circulation to a robust 250,000 and made it the most influential fundamentalist paper in America. He ultimately published more than two hundred books and pamphlets that circulated in the tens of millions. Rice opposed liberal welfare and regulatory measures, urging good Christians to "free America from the hateful, immoral, unchristian New Deal which threatens to throttle private enterprise."[60]

After breaking with the Presbyterian Church in the mid-1930s, the Reverend Carl McIntire founded the fundamentalist Bible Presbyterian Church, dedicated to "militant Christianity patterned after the original Presbyterians." McIntire published a weekly newspaper, the *Christian Beacon*, and later began a radio program, *The Twentieth Century Reformation Hour*. In 1941 he founded the American Council of Christian Churches as a counterpoint to the mainstream Federal Council of Churches.[61]

Manufacturer R. G. LeTourneau, America's leading producer of earth-moving equipment, formed the Christian Business Men's Association to propagate the gospel and counter liberal activism. LeTourneau hired chaplains for his workers, began a religious radio program, and published an in-house journal of religion that expanded to a free circulation of 600,000 worldwide. "I deem it necessary to carry on such an extensive religious program," he said, "because I believe God wants me to do it." In a reverse of usual tithing, LeTourneau claimed that he gave 90 percent of his income to Christian causes.[62]

In 1935 Dr. James W. Fifield, a Los Angeles minister, joined with leading industrialists to found Spiritual Mobilization, a precursor of later Christian right groups. Spiritual Mobilization sought to mobilize "Protestant pastors" to uphold the pre-crash fusion of Christian principle and business practice at a time when "government was placing controls and restrictions on many areas of life" and "secular religions were offered to replace the genuine faiths." Spiritual Mobilization did not openly endorse candidates or parties. But by insisting that religion inform all matters of policy, it carved out a wider public space than focused religious lobbies such as the Anti-Saloon League or the National Reform Association. Spiritual Mobilization put a higher priority on conserving private enterprise than on stamping out drinking, gambling, or prostitution. It made "the religious case for individual liberty" and opposed liberal programs that usurped man's "inalienable rights and responsibilities." It called upon "the Church and clergy to champion those rights and the spiritual, Capital 'F' Freedom upon which they depend." It opposed the "pagan collectivism [that] lies at the heart of communism, socialism, the Welfare State, and all varieties of the planned economy." America could not rest on "mere recommendations for new political machinery [or] mere economic palliatives." Solutions must be pursued at "the level of religion and theology."[63]

During the 1930s, Spiritual Mobilization published a monthly journal, numerous brochures, and a bimonthly magazine mailed free to ministers. It produced a radio program heard on some six hundred stations nationwide, held regional conferences, and recruited clergy to receive materials and spread its political message. Spiritual Mobilization avoided a specific theology and claimed to be nondenominational. However, its staff and advisers were all white Protestants with business connections, including Donald J. Cowling, president of Carleton College, and celebrity preacher Norman Vincent Peale. Businessmen who believed that the right politics followed from the right religion bankrolled Spiritual Mobilization. They hoped to inspire ordinary Americans, like peasants after the French Revolution, to demand religion and the old regime. According to a 1948 compilation by J. Howard Pew, "the list of those who have been contributing $5,000 a year to Spiritual Mobilization" included fifteen of the nation's largest companies. Contributors included Carnation, Chrysler, Firestone, General Motors, Gulf Oil, Sun Oil, U.S. Steel, Colgate, and Standard Oil. Spiritual Mobilization was officially nonpartisan, with donations tax deductible to individuals and, eventually, corporations. However, Reverend Fifield, speaking "as an individual citizen," delivered a radio address in 1940 that endorsed Roosevelt's opponent Wendell Willkie to protect religion and freedom "by continuing the no-third-term principle and by electing a leader who has proved his concern for moral ideals."[64]

Other Christian conservative initiatives focused on cultural and social issues. Evangelical Protestants strengthened their critique of evolution through a new science called "creationism," which was designed to harmonize the Bible and modern science. In 1935 evangelical ministers and amateur scientists founded the Religion and Science Association, followed in 1937 by the Deluge Geology Society, devoted to proving that God created the earth in a literal six days. In 1941 creationists formed the more enduring and intellectually formidable American Scientific Affiliation. However, it too grappled with the conundrum of using science to affirm religion.[65]

Both Protestants and Catholics who were concerned with purifying the culture pushed successfully for tighter censorship of the movies. In 1934 Hollywood moved from voluntary to compulsory enforcement of the production code it had adopted in 1930. The movie industry established a formal Production Code Administration with censorship powers, directed by conservative Catholic journalist Joseph Breen. Two years earlier, Breen had blasted voluntary regulation by Jewish producers and directors: "It may be that Hays thought these lousy Jews out here would abide by the Code's provisions but if he did then he should be censured for his lack of knowledge of the breed." Production companies embraced formal self-regulation under pressure from financiers, conservative Protestants, and the Legion of Decency, a mass-membership Catholic organization run by American bishops. As always, it also sought to avoid federal regulation. Hollywood's in-house watchdogs did not seek to ban films but to move them onto the screen in acceptable form and so keep revenues flowing. Movies approved by the Code Administration almost always passed muster with the Legion of Decency and state censorship boards. State boards, however, vetoed movies not reviewed by Hollywood, including documentaries on venereal disease and the Spanish Civil War.[66]

The Christian conservative ethos of the 1930s, if harsh and punitive for holy warriors such as Rice and McIntire, promised more than a negation of secular reform. Christian conservatives joined in a dialogue with liberals over the causes and meaning of human suffering, the path to fulfillment, and people's moral obligations. Their morally charged message may not have resonated with people's struggles to find and hold jobs, hang on to their land, or meet the family budget. But the affirmation of moral living by Christian conservatives struck a chord with the satisfaction people drew from hard work, solid accomplishment, and devotion to the simple virtues of daily life. Their critique of character-killing handouts and boondoggles spoke to people's daily struggle against temptation and their resentment of shiftless neighbors living off the work of others. Their attack on bureaucrats and tax collectors reflected people's distrust of greedy, meddling, bossy strangers. Their strict rules and group enforcement drew on people's struggles to fulfill obligations to their families and communities and avoid backsliding into sin. And their defense of wholesome entertainment, biblical teachings on creation, school prayer, and Bible reading drew upon the comfort people found in familiar ways of life and communion with those who shared their values.[67]

CRUSADING WOMEN

In 1934 investment consultant Cathrine Curtis dreamed of recruiting an army of conservative women to defeat the New Deal. "One lone woman crying in the wilderness—raising her voice in protest—makes no impression on our legislature," she said. "But the raised voice of one hundred thousand women would be capable of blasting the ordinary Senator or Congressman right out of his seat in Congress." Curtis failed to raise her army of women; hard times had diminished women's conservative activism. The *Woman Patriot* closed shop in 1932 and the DAR, faced with falling membership, stepped back from politics. The Liberty League and the Crusaders made ill-fated efforts to form women's auxiliaries. Curtis and a few other enterprising women stepped into the conservative breach.

Briefly, Curtis gained a larger audience than any conservative woman of the era. From early 1934 until February 1935, Curtis delivered "women and money" radio talks on the American Broadcasting System. In a reversal of liberal maternalism, Curtis said that women who managed the household budget could thrive on Wall Street, but New Deal taxes and regulations blocked their path to riches. Among her broadcasts on "Stock Market Hints for Women," Curtis tucked in programs on "Americanism," "Current Events," and "The New Deal in Wall Street." "Women have more time on their hands than have men," she said, "and they can spend this time in no better way than spreading the doctrines of Americanism." In 1935, after American Broadcasting decided to terminate Curtis's politically controversial broadcasts, she founded Women's Investors in America to help women gain financial independence. Curtis claimed an inflated membership of nearly 300,000 for the group and crusaded against the New Deal, which she said interfered with women's efforts to succeed in private enterprise. In 1936 she sent Congress a new "Declaration of Independence" that called for slashing taxes, cracking down on aliens "who swarm on our relief rolls," and ending the New Deal spending that "built a giant political machine."[68]

Suburban homemaker Elizabeth Dilling became a celebrity voice for anticommunism in the 1930s. In 1932 Dilling joined with conservative Chicago industrialist and author Edwin Marshall Hadley to form the Paul Reveres, based on the premise that America was not founded as a democracy but as a republic, with deference to "wise and just" representatives "free from public passions and prejudices." The Paul Reveres blasted the New Deal for inciting popular passions "with the inevitable result that . . . a small but powerful minority takes charge and the people become enslaved under a dictatorship." Although these ideas endured on the right, the Paul Reveres disappeared and Dilling found her true calling in anticommunism. After a trip to the Soviet Union in which she found shuttered churches and souls without salvation, Dilling returned home rallying women "who fight for the protection of the young" to defeat the communist threat to Christianity.[69]

Dilling privately published two widely circulated books—*The Red Network* (1934) and *The Roosevelt Red Record* (1936)—that drew on the files of Harry Jung's American Vigilante Intelligence Federation to impugn hundreds of organizations allegedly aligned with "the Red movement" and

thirteen hundred individual "reds" or "pinks." Her targets recalled the
DAR's blacklist from the 1920s. They included the YMCA, ACLU, and
NACCP along with Eleanor Roosevelt, Walter Lippmann, H. L. Mencken,
and William Borah. The reds worked with fellow travelers in the United
States, especially the radical "Jewish element," Dilling said, to control the
New Deal and upset divinely balanced hierarchies of race and gender.
"Neither the races nor the sexes can ever be equal," she wrote. "They
will always be different and have distinctive functions to perform in life."
Government programs, Dilling said, "forced work" upon women, ousted
them from the home, and stranded them in a hostile marketplace.[70]

To enliven her grim message, Dilling drew upon forms of entertainment familiar to women. Her political bulletins featured intimate, chatty
news about the Dilling family. She amused her subscribers with bits of pro-
Christian and anticommunist doggerel and led her lecture audiences in
songfests that skewered subversives to the tune of "Clementine" or "Take
Me Out to the Ball Game." Dilling won followers across the spectrum of
the right. Shirt leaders distributed her books and Hans Diebel sold copies
at his Aryan Bookstore in Los Angeles. The FBI, local police officials,
members of patriotic societies, and congressional investigators used her
research to expose radicals. *Chicago Tribune* publisher Robert McCormick
and Florence Hague Becker, chair of the DAR's National Defense Committee, endorsed Dilling's work. Becker's endorsement roiled the DAR and
prompted moderate opposition to her election to the organization's national presidency in 1935. Becker moved the DAR back into politics, with
a primary mission to combat subversion in the schools. Dilling's boosters
included nationally prominent evangelical pastors J. Frank Norris and Arno
C. Gaebelein, and William Bell Riley of the Christian Fundamentals Association. The *Moody Monthly* recommended Dilling's *The Red Network* to
"every true patriot and fundamentalist minister."[71]

Dilling outraged the left by equating liberalism with treason, a thesis
that journalist Eugene Lyons amplified in his 1941 book *The Red Decade:
The Stalinist Penetration of America,* which, unlike Dilling's works, gained
attention and in some cases favorable reviews from mainstream intellectuals. Historians have documented the communist influence on American politics and culture during the 1930s when the Communist Party
sought to expand its power and combat the right through a "popular
front" alliance with socialists and liberals in the United States and Europe.

But the American Communist Party remained under Soviet control. Its leaders took orders and money from Moscow, recruited spies, and set up espionage rings that targeted both government and industry. Communist-controlled labor unions accounted for about a quarter of union membership by 1940. Still, communists did not dominate left-wing culture or politics of the era and lacked the influence needed to shape the policies of government.[72]

With Dilling, Curtis, and other women still locked out of mainstream conservative leadership, women continued to work through single-sex groups like Curtis's Women's Investors. Women's groups comprised about half of the organizations under the umbrella of the American Coalition of Patriotic Societies, and the Woman's Patriotic Conference on National Defense continued meeting, although without the fire of earlier years. A women's group named Pro America—begun by members of a garden club in Seattle, Washington—tied itself to the Republican Party. It recruited about twelve hundred members in Oregon and a scattered few elsewhere. In 1940 it ranked among the top ten independent contributors to the Republican presidential campaign. Marguerite Snow Morrison and her rich husband, A. Cressy Morrison, launched American Women Against Communism, which warned that the reds planned to conquer America with Negro shock troops, whom they would pay off with a "Negro Republic" in the South's "black belt." No woman of the 1930s, however, gained a leadership role in conservative politics beyond these women's organizations, none of which attracted a mass following or much attention from the mainstream press.[73]

THE CONSERVATIVE ARMADA

In 1936, after enduring three years of liberal reform, a mighty armada of the right set sail against the New Deal. The main battle fleet included the Republican Party, the Liberty League, the NAM, and the Chamber of Commerce. Around these vessels swarmed lesser warships such as the Jeffersonian Democrats, Sentinels, Crusaders, Pro America, and Spiritual Mobilization. Editorials in most nonsouthern newspapers cheered the progress of the fleet, led by Robert McCormick's widely read *Chicago Tribune*. There was less, however, to conservative power than met the eye. With the development of political action committees still nearly a decade in the future, opposition conservatives lacked the capacity to endorse and finance candidates, pay for political ads, or deploy volunteers to knock on doors, distribute literature, and muster voters to the polls. Conservative organizations, like retail businesses, relied on marketing techniques to sell ideas and policies to the public. Their messages, however, were not targeted to particular audiences or tested for their influence on the choices made by voters.

As the 1936 election approached, charges of anti-Semitism and racism again distracted the right. Implicit quotas continued to restrict Jewish admission to colleges, universities, and professional schools. Much of Christian social life remained closed to Jews, who also faced ongoing discrimination in employment. But an investigation of lobbying activities by the liberal Senator Hugo Black of Alabama uncovered politically damaging overt anti-Semitism in the mainstream right, implicating Alexander Lincoln, president of the Sentinels. Black released a letter by one of Lincoln's correspondents warning of the "Jewish brigade that Roosevelt took to Washington," and Lincoln's response that "I am doing what I can as an officer of the Sentinels. I think, as you say, that the Jewish threat is a real one." Lincoln pleaded not guilty to anti-Semitism and mustered Jewish testimony on his behalf, but his conservative allies inadvertently blew the sparks of scandal into flame. Sentinel official Thomas Cadwalader denied that "the Jews as a race or religion were trying to pull down civilization," but added that "many conspicuous Jews in the world are engaged in that effort." Outspoken conservative Henry Joy, president of Packard Motors, joined the debate, ineptly writing, "There is decidedly too much Jewish influence in power in our government by presidential appointment and approval." The controversy forced Lincoln to resign his presidency and tainted both the Sentinels and the conservative movement.[74]

In 1936 Democrats identified the Liberty League as the softest target on the right and, according to Democratic publicist Edward L. Roddan, decided to parade the league's "directorate before the people [and] blame them for everything." When the right knocked the New Deal as radical and un-American, Democrats struck back against "economic royalists" whose greed had ruined the economy in 1929. Liberals refused to concede the defense of freedom to conservatives and seized the moral high ground with pleas for economic justice and rights for labor. Directors of the Liberty League, reeling from these counterpunches, contemplated disbanding and "removing from the campaign an element which would prove embarrassing to those who hope for the defeat of the present administration." But the league fought on to avoid "acknowledging failure" and discouraging other groups that "have endeavored to protest against the undermining of American institutions. ... Our demise would be ballyhooed to the skies as a New Deal victory." The Republican Party was careful, however, to avoid the appearance of collaboration with the Liberty League.[75]

HITTING ROCK BOTTOM

In seeking a candidate to face FDR in 1936, Republican kingmakers looked westward, where they found Governor Alf Landon of Kansas, Senator Arthur Vandenberg of Michigan, and Frank Knox, publisher of the *Chicago Daily News*. Setbacks in recent elections had deprived the party's eastern wing of its most prominent leaders, and a candidate from the West seemed more welcome to Main Street than a New Yorker or a Bostonian. Front-runner Landon was the lone Republican governor to have won re-election in 1934. He had roots in the party's progressive past, but the right found him sufficiently pliable for their purposes. His lack of national experience and stature might have mattered in a year of bright party prospects, but not in 1936. With Vandenberg looking to 1940 and Knox fading, the seventy-year-old progressive senator William Borah of Idaho emerged as Landon's main rival.

Borah's backers included progressives mingled with a few conservatives, led by newspaper magnate Frank Gannett. The publisher touted Borah as the only Republican with a chance to beat President Roosevelt. For Gannett, any Republican was preferable to FDR, whose policies "might be called Fascism, Nazism, or Communism. It all amounts to the same thing." The president's "castigation of the Liberty League and the big interests," Gannett told Borah, "makes it pretty difficult for the Republicans to consider a candidate representative of that class. ... You are the only candidate in the field who is immune to this attack." Borah's backers argued that "the main issue in the next Presidential Campaign will undoubtedly revolve around the Supreme Court." They warned that if the Court were "packed by the present Executive ... socialism would be wrapped around our neck for 25 years." The conservatives behind Borah admired his social and cultural views and believed his opposition to concentrated power would incline him to appoint Supreme Court justices skeptical of bureaucratic expansion. But Borah refused to repudiate his support for tariff reduction, generous aid to the needy, the dissolution of corporate monopolies, and other progressive policies that alienated most of the GOP's economic conservatives. In a letter to Frank Gannett, he wrote, "The price [demanded by economic conservatives] is entirely too high for their support or even the presidency. . . . I am not buying the Presidency, Gannett, by surrendering my convictions upon public questions." Borah kept his integrity and Landon won the presidential nomination.[76]

Conservatives had hoped that Huey Long, Louisiana's charismatic senator, who outdid the New Deal with his Share the Wealth plan for leveling wealth and incomes, would run a third-party campaign that drained votes from FDR in 1936. After Long's assassination in September 1935, however, Dr. Francis Townsend, the champion of generous old-age pensions, and the "radio priest" Father Charles Coughlin initiated an insurgent movement that melded liberal economics with anti-pluralist conservatism. Coughlin had gained a weekly radio audience of some thirty million listeners and said that six million had joined his National Union of Social Justice. Ex-minister Gerald L. K. Smith, a Long associate, joined their campaign. "As part of the Communism he thinks the Roosevelt administration is taking us into, Smith sees religion menaced," wrote journalist Mark Sullivan. But the allies lacked campaign experience, a political organization, funding, or a nationally known candidate. Ultimately, they chose as their candidate for president an obscure progressive Republican representative, William "Liberty Bell" Lemke of North Dakota, a champion of debt relief for farmers.[77]

Jeffersonian Democrats still hoped to trade an endorsement of Landon for input on the Republican platform or even a cabinet appointment. But Republicans ignored these geriatric Democrats with big dreams and small followings. The self-exiled Jeffersonians called their own Democratic convention to drum President Roosevelt out of the party. The forty delegates who assembled in Detroit in August included no Democrat of standing, but they enacted a platform that blasted the administration for promoting "a collectivist state [that replaced] the doctrine of democracy with the tenets and teachings of a blended communism and socialism." Al Smith and other leading Jeffersonians endorsed Landon and campaigned on his behalf. But the Jeffersonian Democrats formed no permanent organization, impressed no bloc of voters, and disappeared after 1936.[78]

Like Hoover in 1932, Landon ran with backing only from the Republican right. In 1936, however, a business community desperate to defeat FDR opened its purses. After barely outspending Democrats in 1932, Republicans led the heavily favored incumbent party by $8.9 million to $5.2 million in 1936. The GOP led Democrats by more than four to one in contributions of $1,000 or more. Republicans led by nearly seven to one among manufacturers and fourteen to one among bankers and brokers. Studies of contributions by members of wealthy families and top corporate executives in 1936 found that about 80 percent of contributors donated only to the Republican campaign, including most members of Roosevelt's Business Advisory Council. Brewers and distillers, southern businessmen, and Jewish entrepreneurs uncomfortable with the cultural nationalism of the GOP accounted for the few exceptions to solid business support for Republicans. Otherwise, the pro-Republican bias prevailed broadly across industrial sectors. The *Chicago Tribune*'s McCormick spent more than $50,000 in unreported funds for pro-Landon canvassers in the Chicago area, making him the largest benefactor of either campaign.[79]

John Hamilton, the new RNC chair, formed an Industrial Division under entrepreneur Sterling Morton to enlist employers to stuff pay envelopes with leaflets warning that workers would lose wages and jobs if Roosevelt returned to the White House. The Industrial Division informed heads of industry that it was their duty "to tell those whose employment is in your hands, how YOU regard the future." Thousands of employers cooperated in distributing to six million workers some sixty-nine million pieces of anti–New Deal literature. Nearly a quarter century later, an aged Morton ruefully noted, "This Industrial Division was unique in that to my knowledge it is the only political committee which got 100 percent results. . . . Every state we worked in went solidly against our candidate."[80]

Unified conservative support netted Landon only 37 percent of the popular vote in November. Lemke limped in with 2 percent. As Roosevelt's campaign chair Jim Farley had famously predicted, Republicans won only Maine and Vermont. Postelection poll data showed that a majority of African Americans backed Roosevelt in 1936, as did three-quarters of Jews and Catholics. The GOP still polled better among women than men, but for the first time since suffrage a majority of women voted Democratic. White northern Protestants evenly split their votes, while the most affluent 20 percent of voters backed Landon.

Not even the spending, organizing, and educating of the right could overcome the real world of 1936. Roosevelt and his programs were popular with voters—businessmen were not. Most Americans were better off than they had been four years before, no scandal or foreign policy disaster undercut FDR, and Landon lacked the fire to inspire voters. "I don't think it would have made any difference what kind of campaign I made as far as stopping this avalanche," Landon said. Federal programs that dispensed jobs and benefits also changed the dynamics of politics, binding people's destiny to the government. Jeffersonian Democrat James Reed lamented that given "persons on relief, plus the 8,600,000 drawing direct pay from the government, plus the contractors who have been growing fat on government work, plus the farmers whose itching palms were stretched out for government checks, we have an army of mercenaries so great that it fully accounts for the result."[81]

In part, Roosevelt overrode business opposition, enacted his program, and won reelection by respecting the social conservatism of his time. The New Deal reforms that transformed the nation on so many different levels were, in fact, a function of the political support of millions of mostly immigrant northern industrial workers and southern working-class whites who, in the 1930s and for some time to come, never wanted or needed to distance themselves from their own attachments to anti-pluralist conservatism. New Deal reforms helped redefine the standing of many Americans once perceived as outsiders and set the stage for later civil rights initiatives. Yet reformers hesitated to jeopardize their economic programs by igniting social issues like rights for blacks and women or liberalized immigration.

The revival of government activism, the participation of African Americans in New Deal programs, and a few high-profile appointments of blacks to government agencies turned a majority of black voters from Republicans to Democrats by 1936. But a president loath to agitate the passions of race or upset his alliance with the white South allowed Jim Crow—the racial caste system that privileged whites—to rule below the Mason-Dixon line. In turn, white southerners who controlled most committees in Congress backed the New Deal and delivered their bloc votes to Democrats. While FDR zipped his lips, 88 percent of Republicans voted to bring an antilynching law to the Senate floor, compared to 53 percent of northern and 11 percent of southern Democrats. In a 1935 memo Will

Alexander, an administration adviser on race relations, listed nine reasons why "Negroes feel disappointed in the administration," including discrimination in federal programs, the displacement of black tenant farmers and sharecroppers, and inaction on antilynching law. During the 1936 campaign Alf Landon, not Franklin Roosevelt, met with civil rights leaders and endorsed antilynching legislation.[82]

The New Deal was a good deal for the South, which pulled in far more in federal aid than it returned through federal taxes. But southern Democrats shaped New Deal programs to protect Jim Crow. They did not carve racial distinctions into federal law but they kept the results of discrimination intact through superficially nonracial provisions that were incorporated within New Deal legislation. Southerners ensured that state governments, not bureaucrats in Washington, administered federal programs such as Aid to Dependent Children, thereby empowering white local officials to rule on eligibility and benefit levels. By insisting on the exclusion of domestic and agricultural labor, southerners fenced out about 60 percent of black workers in their region from eligibility for old-age pensions and unemployment insurance under the Social Security Act. Similar provisions kept most black workers from coverage under the Wagner Labor Relations Act, and federal farm payments flowed to white landowners who could profit by evicting black tenant farmers and sharecroppers. The Federal Housing Authority routinely rejected black applicants for loans and contributed to white migration from cities to suburbs.[83]

New Deal liberals clung to the family breadwinner model, which justified programs that privileged men. The Civilian Conservation Corps excluded women and only a handful of women landed federal relief work, with most laboring in sewing circles and other customary low-paying, low-status pursuits. About one-fourth of the codes under the National Recovery Administration authorized lower minimum wages for women than for men. The National Labor Relations Act largely bypassed women, who rarely held union membership. New Deal job training programs benefited mostly men, while unemployment compensation and old-age insurance flowed mainly to long-term male wage earners working outside of agriculture and domestic service. The Aid to Dependent Children program presumed that the primary role for women was to raise children; state authority to set eligibility standards gave priority to white widows with children.[84]

Restrictive immigration and refugee policies and racial constructions of Americanism endured through the New Deal years. Despite criticism from Columbia University anthropologist Franz Boas and other scholars, racial science remained entrenched in the academy and popular culture. Through 1936, Boas failed to win American scholarly agreement for a statement repudiating scientific racism, even as practiced in Nazi Germany. "[Those] who are of the opinion that racial descent and character are closely correlated," Boas complained, "have not a shadow of proof for their contentions." In the popular culture and even in New Deal murals, statues, monuments, posters, and photographs, the American ideal was almost always represented by white Anglo-Saxons. Legalized sterilization by state authorities soared during the 1930s to some twenty-two thousand institutionalized persons, compared to half that number during the previous twenty-five years. A 1937 Gallup Poll found 84 percent support for sterilizing "habitual criminals and the hopelessly insane."[85]

In 1936, after losing badly in four consecutive presidential and midterm elections, Republicans seemed nearly as obsolete as the Whigs they had displaced in 1854. Since 1928 the party had lost 178 House seats, 40 Senate seats, and 19 governor's mansions. The GOP retained in the new Congress a meager 89 House members and 16 senators. After losing New Jersey in 1937, the party held seven governorships with a combined population less than that of New York State. As Democrats completed the realignment of party loyalties, they recruited new voters and converted Republicans. From 1928 to 1936 the GOP's share of the two-party registration fell from 65 percent to 45 percent in five northern states with registration statistics and from 61 percent to 35 percent in major cities. Participation in Republican primaries fell from 78 percent to 46 percent.[86]

Nineteen thirty-six was the year in which conservatism finally hit rock bottom. The right now had to think about the unthinkable: four more years of Franklin Roosevelt and a Democratic Congress. Unless conservatives could conjure strength from weakness, they would continue to battle uphill against a swollen bureaucracy, militant unions, and boondoggle programs, all sustaining liberal Democratic control of government in the United States.

3

UP FROM THE ASHES, 1936–1945

In December 1936, as Americans prepared for the brightest holiday season since 1928, the Republican National Committee met to address what Representative Hamilton Fish of New York called a "greater crisis than ever before in the history of the Republican party." The GOP had to "adapt or die." It could not subsist on ideas "over a quarter of a century behind the times" and linked "with the employers of labor, with special privilege, and wealth, and reaction." Representative Everett Dirksen of Illinois agreed that Republicans were "too content, too narrow, too idle, too prone to be satisfied with the existing order of things, when we know that there is a different spirit in America today." To catch up to the times, reformers urged the dismissal of John Hamilton as party chair. The siren call for party reform, however, sounded no sweeter in 1936 than it had in 1934; the committee voted 74 to 2 to retain Hamilton. Conservative policies were good enough for most Republicans, who anticipated a rebirth when liberal follies brought on the next great crash. For the duration, Republicans needed to hold the barricades for private enterprise and Christian values.[1]

THE PHOENIX RISES

Sixteen days after becoming the first president to be inaugurated on January 20, Franklin Roosevelt pumped life into embalmed conservatives by proposing legislation to expand the size of the Supreme Court. His plan authorized the president to nominate an additional justice for every justice that declined to retire after seventy years and six months of age, a criterion that covered six sitting justices in 1937. FDR was seeking to control a court that had struck down the National Recovery Act and seemed poised to repeal his New Deal by toppling the Social Security Act and the

Wagner National Labor Relations Act. The conservative Supreme Court, Roosevelt said, was functioning "not as a judicial body, but as a policymaking body . . . reading into the Constitution words and implications which are not there, and which were never intended to be there." Policy making by courts was nothing new. Judges had broadly construed the Fourteenth Amendment to sweep away laws that set minimum wages, banned employers from punishing workers for joining unions, or limited antiunion injunctions. Following Napoleon's maxim of never interrupting your enemy when he is making a mistake, Republican leaders let disgruntled Democrats carry the fight against so-called court packing. One such Democrat, Representative Samuel Pettengill of Indiana, noted that Republicans "are lying low so as to not hurt the cause by forcing the Democrats to defend the proposal as a party measure. For once they are acting smart."[2]

Publisher Frank Gannett put up $49,000 of his own money to challenge court packing through a National Committee to Uphold Constitutional Government. "The president now dominates Congress," Gannett warned. "To have him also dominate the Supreme Court would give him complete control of the government. This means the end of our democracy." The committee's guiding hand, executive director Edward Rumely, avoided affiliation with Republicans. Instead, he culled his anti-Roosevelt material from defecting Democrats and disillusioned progressives. Rumely refined the art of direct mail to the point where he reached "about one million men and women, one of every twenty-five families, who give leadership to this nation's thinking." The committee added to this ground game "a great bombardment by air;" some three hundred radio stations aired talks prerecorded by committee spokesmen. Rumely also pioneered the use of direct-mail fund-raising. He followed an "inflexible rule [that] not a single mailing was sent without subscription blanks" for donations. The resulting flow of small contributions from ordinary citizens, the committee claimed, distinguished their group from "the Liberty Leaguers, the Crusaders, and other economic royalists." After Interior Secretary Harold Ickes denounced the committee's "mail order government," it turned this slur into a slogan, boasting that "'Mail order government' is good government," even "more powerful than lobbies or bureaucrats." Such hubris earned the committee congressional investigations and subpoenas to produce financial records, which Rumely successfully resisted to the jubilation of conservatives.[3]

The committee's white Christian leadership targeted racial and religious minorities by saying that their civil liberties depended on judicial independence. Again, however, conservatives did not apply their defense of the Constitution to the protection of minority rights in the Fourteenth and Fifteenth Amendments. As a constituent wrote to Democratic senator James Byrnes of South Carolina, who backed FDR on court packing: "If I got up tomorrow and advocated rigid adherence to the 14th and 15th [Amendments] of the Constitution, the same folks who are yelling 'Constitution' loudly now would fight among themselves for priority in applying the tar and feathers." Evangelical ministers Theodore Graebner and Ralph Nollner encouraged fellow pastors to denounce court packing in their sermons and recruited ten clergymen of diverse creeds to testify that tampering with the Supreme Court would subordinate religion to politics. Nollner printed their testimony in his magazine *America Forward*, which upheld private enterprise, the profit motive, and other "elements which have made the American system succeed."[4]

Shrewd conservatives recognized that they might win a battle against FDR but not the war over the Court. In 1937 the Supreme Court upheld the Wagner Act and the Social Security Act, leveling constitutional barriers to federal welfare and regulatory laws. Journalist Ray Tucker wrote, "The Court's record remains 100 percent New Deal since the day the 'packing' proposal was introduced. The biggest shell game on record is working to perfection ... the opposition is still too dazzled by the spectacular but phony issue to realize that the White House prestidigitator is quietly raking in all the chips that count." Ultimately FDR would put his stamp on the Supreme Court the old-fashioned way, by appointing nine justices, more than any president since George Washington. Conservative support for the Supreme Court declined and liberal support increased with each decision upholding a liberal program or expanding minority rights.[5]

Conservatives also confronted the rising power of labor, as NAM had anticipated in 1934. In 1936 the newly formed Congress of Industrial Organizations (CIO) began efforts to organize America's mass industrial workforce, not just the skilled workers covered by craft unions. It challenged major corporations through the new tactic of the sit-down strike. Instead of walking out, workers occupied plants, blocked production, and fought off efforts to remove them. The sit-down strike succeeded against both General Motors and Chrysler, with little violence as neither Roosevelt nor the Democratic governor of Michigan Frank Murphy deployed government forces against the strikers. "Labor is moving into a position of dominance politically and industrially," wrote an analyst for the *Farm Journal.* "General Motors is no longer run by its board or its officers. . . . What they do will depend a lot on what labor wants and what labor tells them to do."[6]

When U.S. Steel capitulated without a fight to the CIO's demands for recognition, industrial unionism spread quickly and, for the most part, peacefully across industrial corporations. Unlike Britain's Conservative Party government, which enacted stringent labor regulations after a general strike in 1926, Congress and the Roosevelt administration did not reign in unions. The Wagner Labor Relations Act provided labor unions legitimacy and protection, but it also made labor dependent on the political balance of power in Washington. Still, with Democrats running government, unions became entrenched in basic industries. Membership soared from three million in 1933 (11 percent of nonagricultural labor) to fifteen million (35 percent) in 1945, six million of whom were enrolled by the CIO. Labor became a key political player, allied with Democrats and a foil for conservatives. John Bricker, the conservative Republican candidate for governor of Ohio in 1938, was not alone in campaigning against sit-down strikes and union bosses. Mention the name of CIO leader John L. Lewis in small-town and rural Ohio, the *Cleveland Plain Dealer* observed, and "women and children would hide in storm cellars and farmers would grab pitchforks and muskets." A nationwide Gallup Poll conducted in 1938 found that by more than four to one, voters would oppose CIO-endorsed candidates.[7]

CONSERVATIVES ON PATROL

The twin curse of losing the Supreme Court as well as the fight to contain unions prompted a new round of mobilization on the right. Gannett's committee evolved into what a board member called "a sort of Liberty League or permanent Anti-Roosevelt organization." The committee opposed "collectivism," communism, "labor monopolists," and "special privilege" for minorities. So did the new Church League of America, formed in 1937 by Henry P. Crowell, chairman of the board of Quaker Oats and the Moody Bible Institute; ad man G. W. Robnett; and lawyer Frank Loesch. The league recruited both clerical and lay members to deliver its message that

Christian teaching "elevates and dignifies human personality in contrast to the so-called 'Collectivist' or Marxian doctrines." As the census of 1940 drew near, the league, which claimed a hundred thousand members, lashed out against prying bureaucrats. Loesch said he would refuse to disclose his income to "a census enumerator who is a politician and a deserving Democrat" and urged others to resist census snoops.[8]

On the more distant right, the Constitutional Educational League, directed by Joseph P. Kamp, formerly editor of the far-right journal the *Awakener,* targeted the CIO. His league, with offices in four states, published the anti-Semitic newspaper *Headlines and What's Behind Them* and claimed to have distributed more than two million copies of Kamp's pamphlet "Join the CIO—and help build a SOVIET AMERICA." John Trevor's American Coalition of Patriotic Societies, working with Walter Steele, publisher of the right-wing magazine *National Republic,* broadened its call "to keep America American" by severing diplomatic relations with Russia, suspending immigration, and deporting undesirable aliens.[9]

Radio priest Father Charles Coughlin returned to politics in 1937 as a militant social conservative. He founded a right-wing paramilitary, anti-Semitic group known as the Christian Front, which urged patriots to "act, buy and vote Christian," and his sermons and magazine, *Social Justice,* became overtly pro-Nazi. Although Coughlin's radio audience shriveled in the late 1930s, he still had a sizable following that included Irish, Italian, and Polish Catholics anxious to prove their pro-Christian Americanism by enlisting in an anticommunist crusade that was also laced with attacks on Jews—as American as apple pie. The Catholic Church's top media star, Bishop Fulton J. Sheen of *The Catholic Hour* on NBC, backed the Christian Front. So did the church's most outspoken editor, Father Patrick Scanlon, of the widely circulated *Brooklyn Tablet.* Like Coughlin, Scanlon thought Jews had too much "influence, affluence, and power—and so often use it against Christians." The nation's leading prelate, Archbishop Francis J. Spellman of New York, ignored pleas to denounce the Christian Front. Father James Gillis, another radio priest, who also edited the *Catholic World,* wrote a syndicated column, and contributed to *The Catholic Hour,* joined Coughlin in opposing Roosevelt's foreign and domestic policies. In 1940 the FBI arrested seventeen Christian Front thugs for sedition. But Coughlin's standing with anticommunist churchmen insulated him from attack. Congress declined to investigate the Christian Front and FBI

Director Hoover said, incredibly, that "the Rev. Charles E. Coughlin, radio priest, had no connection with the Christian Front." Not until 1942 did the Church force Coughlin out of politics, the same year that NBC dismissed Gillis.[10]

Conservatives also challenged the left for control over the schools. The American Legion, the DAR, the NAM, the American Federation of Business, the Guardians of American Education, and the Hearst newspaper chain targeted best-selling social studies texts by progressive educator Harold Rugg of Columbia University's Teachers College. Rugg's texts explored social tensions and class conflict and praised government planning, welfare, and regulation. His critics said that he slighted American heroes, denigrated patriots and rugged individuals, and favored foreign collectivist ideals. An article on Rugg in the *American Legion Magazine,* "Treason in the Classroom," warned, "'Catch 'em young'! That's the motto of the radical and communistic textbook writers who all too evidently have been in control of the field." By the mid-1940s sales of Rugg's texts slid 90 percent from their 1930s peak. But the legion failed to persuade school boards to adopt a patriotic textbook of American history, called *The Story of our People,* which it had commissioned and funded.[11]

UNITING WHITE PROTESTANT AMERICA

In 1937, after four years of bullying by FDR, Republicans revived Hoover's dream of breaking up the solidly Democratic South and uniting white conservatives across America. Republican fusionists hoped to create a nationwide conservative majority of white Protestants to vanquish the liberal opposition of African Americans, Catholics, Jews, and unbelievers. Party chair John Hamilton welcomed Democratic votes but disdained cross-party initiatives as a distraction from rebuilding the GOP. Others disagreed. The party's 1936 vice presidential nominee Frank Knox commended "the sound strategy of coalition" and anticipated that a "bitter internecine struggle between the conservative Democrats and the New Deal Democrats [would] leave the party rent asunder." Knox proposed that conservatives should establish parties of Constitutional Democrats in the South and Constitutional Republicans in the North, with the two eventually merging into a united national party. Senator Arthur Vandenberg confided to Alf Landon, who was the titular head of the GOP after losing to FDR in 1936, "I continue to believe that some sort of a fusion or coalition or union ticket may be necessary." Landon agreed that Republicans should attempt to "gather under one banner all the elements of opposition that disbelieve in the Roosevelt theories of government."[12]

Frank Gannett also had big ideas about "bringing under one tent all those who . . . want to defeat the New Deal." Thirty years before Richard Nixon's "silent majority" and forty years before Jerry Falwell's "moral majority," Gannett envisioned forming "a great middle-class bloc" committed to "the Constitution and the enterprise system." Gannett's new majority of "thrifty, frugal, hard-working, self-respecting and God-fearing men and women who built America" would oppose the New Deal's constituency of "the slackers, the shirkers, the incompetent, and the unfortunate." Conservative Democrat Samuel Pettengill, who retired from Congress in 1938, contracted with Gannett's group for lectures, articles, and broadcasts "anchored to the point of view of the middle class American . . . who believes in the American Constitution and the King James version of the Bible."[13]

A new political coalition, however, remained out of reach for conservatives. After Congress rejected court packing, Republican leaders decided to rally their own troops rather than pursue futile schemes for realigning the parties. Democrats from the one-party South predictably refused to sacrifice their secure public offices and seniority in Congress for the promise of a new party in the sky. When Gallup asked in November of 1937—with the wounds of court packing still raw—"which party best represents your viewpoint," 58 percent of respondents nationwide cited the Democrats and 32 percent the Republicans. Only 19 percent said it was time to "form a new party of anti–New Deal Democrats and Republicans"; 63 percent approved of Roosevelt's leadership.

An unbridgeable gulf of policy also separated Republicans and southern Democrats. Republicans voted far more often than northern Democrats against southern interests on free trade and agricultural assistance, which were life and death issues for the rural, export-dependent South. Civil rights proposals isolated southerners from northern Democrats, but also from Republicans. In December 1937, the so-called conservative coalition made a fleeting appearance in Congress; 80 percent of southern Democrats and 93 percent of House Republicans voted to kill legislation establishing minimum wages and maximum hours, outvoting 78 percent of northern Democrats. This coalition in which a majority of Republicans and southern Democrats voted against a majority of northern Democrats did not reappear in force until the wartime Congresses. From 1937 to 1942, southern Democrats voted much more like northern Democrats than Republicans.[14]

Even the appearance of unity eluded conservatives in 1937 when their leaders in Congress failed to unite on a "Conservative Manifesto" drafted by Senator Vandenberg for the GOP and Senator Josiah Bailey of South Carolina for the Democrats. Conservative Democrats balked at defying their president. Republicans, said Minority Leader Charles McNary, worried that "anyone who signs that thing is going to have a Liberty League tag put on him." But the manifesto took on a life of its own. After the press published a leaked copy, business trade associations distributed some two million reprints across the nation.[15]

As the right struggled for unity, the administration challenged conservative Democrats. Although FDR had already entrenched New Deal programs within the federal budget and bureaucracy, he wanted a more uniformly liberal Democratic Party to extend reform and control the nominating convention and party committees. After Senate Majority Leader Joseph Robinson died in July 1937, Roosevelt broke precedent and interceded on behalf of Alben Barkley of Kentucky, who beat the conservatives' choice for leader, Patrick Harrison of Mississippi, by one vote. "The Great Divide of the Democratic Party was the selection of the Majority leader," wrote Roosevelt confidant Ernest Cuneo, "both sides and both men had to have it, [after which] the power of the Democratic Committee was now in the White House." In 1938 FDR urged Democratic primary voters to reject several conservative southern senators and House Rules Committee chairman John J. O'Connor of New York. This effort, to separate liberal "sheep" from conservative "goats," ended in failure. O'Connor lost his primary and reemerged as head of the American Democratic Committee, a Republican front group, but every targeted senator won renomination. The purge was "a bust," said Democratic Party chair James Farley.[16]

RETRIBUTION FOR LIBERALS

The most serious problem for Democrats in the midterm election year of 1938 was not internal strife but a disappointing economy. In 1937–38, America suffered the economic affliction that conservatives knew the vengeful gods of the market would eventually visit upon the New Deal. In the summer of 1937, after four years of recovery, the economy hit a skid that continued into the following year. Industrial and farm production declined from 1937 to 1938 and unemployment surged from 14 percent to 19 percent. Liberals, who blamed the downturn on predatory corporations and stingy fiscal and monetary policy, prescribed an eclectic mix of bottom-up reform and recovery. To jump-start the private economy, liberals called for more unemployment relief, farm benefit programs, and higher spending on federal projects. To repair structural flaws, they urged new curbs on business abuse, antitrust litigation, and minimum wage and maximum hour legislation. Through these proposals, liberals hoped to achieve a mixed system of public and private initiative that smoothed out cycles of boom and bust, regulated business on behalf of consumers, and maintained welfare programs that buoyed purchasing power and eased the harsh consequences of market competition.

For conservatives, including some within the administration, meddlesome government was the problem, not the solution. In their view, liberal tinkering had killed the enthusiasm to invest, hire workers, and take risks for future profits. Conservatives proposed to ease regulations and lower taxes and spending. They would stop government from competing with private enterprise or stifling management's prerogatives. This unbinding of enterprise would spark an economic revival that would wipe out unemployment, raise living standards, and despite—or because of—tax reductions flood the treasury with the revenue needed to balance the budget.

According to the GOP's 1936 nominee for vice president, Frank Knox, "This present depression is entirely home made and of a political origin. Business confidence has been undermined by the political policies pursued in Washington, including the intolerable tax burden and staggering debt . . . the way into a dictatorship may lie along the route of unbearable taxes and unpayable debt." At the 1938 meeting of the Chamber of Commerce, Democratic senator Edward R. Burke of Nebraska—soon to turn Republican—indicted government as "Public Enemy Number One." The chamber agreed. It passed resolutions that called for removing "unnecessary regulations" and "freeing initiative in enterprises," which would "raise revenues for the government while reducing the burdens of taxation [and] make possible an earlier balancing of the budget." Clarence Francis, vice chairman of the Business Council, recommended "modifying recently enacted legislation of a nature which obviously is depressing business—such as labor relations, tax and securities control laws," and avoiding new "farm and wage and hour legislation." NAM opposed wage and hour laws but "thought that it was unwise to oppose it openly" and debated "how it might be properly castrated, without admitting to the public that the purpose was clean cut emasculation."[17]

The president and Congress responded in 1938 with remedial bills that reflected conservative input but tilted to the left. Congress raised spending moderately, enacted a new farm program, and passed the landmark Fair Labor Standards Act that set minimum wages, maximum hours, and limits on child labor. It strengthened the Securities and Exchange Commission and authorized the Federal Trade Commission to protect consumers from fraud. Conservatives won concessions on reducing taxes on capital gains and profits that corporations did not distribute to shareholders. They also killed the administration's plan for reorganizing the government to expand executive power, institutionalize New Deal reforms, and support the centralized planning of federal intervention in the economy. The conservative press hailed this defeat as "a personal Waterloo for the President," a "stunning rebuke to the president's dictatorial ambitions," and "evidence of the fear of the executive which has grown so amazingly since the 1936 landslide."[18]

Yet Roosevelt had already retreated from ambitious proposals for government reorganization and economic planning that had emerged from Congress and his own advisory committee. Beyond some special cases, the administration did not resurrect the efforts of the National Recovery Administration to set codes for industry. It proposed no major antitrust legislation and failed to press the progressive case that large-scale corporate enterprise dangerously concentrated economic and political power. Polls from the late 1930s showed that federal relief and work programs, banking reforms, minimum wage laws, and regulation of business abuses were highly popular with the public. But bold measures to rearrange the private economy or centrally guide decisions about production, prices, wages, and employment lacked public support or proven success.[19]

Conservatives gradually learned that Americans backed limited government and private enterprise in principle but also expected benefits from the state. The right could not expect politicians to sacrifice their careers by depriving constituents of pensions, relief payments, minimum wages, consumer protection, unemployment compensation, farm subsidies, and government jobs. In April 1938, at a three-day confidential meeting between the Business Advisory Council and corporate guests the council chairman W. Averell Harriman preached a sermon on practical politics. He said that business leaders "have assumed that the President and Congress would oppose public trends that we [corporate executives] did not like." But politicians who cut popular programs would "in all probability have sacrificed their political careers. They have been blamed by business for putting their careers ahead of public duty, and yet we would not advocate that a business firm, in order to perform a patriotic service, should court bankruptcy."[20]

Still, the ailing economy primed Republicans for a comeback in 1938 without having to abandon conservative ideas. "If business conditions continue to get worse Mr. Roosevelt will be on the toboggan, regardless of Republican principles or the absence thereof," wrote GOP senator Frederick Steiwer of Oregon. The GOP leadership worried that plans for a midterm party convention—pushed by Herbert Hoover—would spark needless controversy and put the former president in the spotlight. Instead of holding a convention, the Republican National Committee set up a grassroots Program Committee headed by Dr. Glenn Frank, former president of the University of Wisconsin. The last such GOP committee, organized in 1920, consisted almost entirely of white, male, and middle- to upper-class Protestants, with very few black or Catholic participants. This time the Republicans guaranteed diversity through the first explicit racial and religious quota system imposed by a major political party in the United States. The party required that precisely eight blacks, sixteen Jews, and thirty Catholics serve on the 273-member Program Committee. The RNC instructed Chairman Frank to solicit the views of Republicans nationwide and report back to the party only after the 1938 elections. Among the proposals submitted to the committee was Hebert Hoover's eleven-point program to restore a "system of free men and private enterprise" and reestablish the "common morals" appropriate "in a Christian country."[21]

To further expand the GOP base, Hamilton tapped Marion Martin, the National Committeewoman from Maine, to run a new National Federation of Women's Republican Clubs (later the National Federation of Republican Women), which quickly achieved a membership of nearly one hundred thousand. The federation followed a disciplined party line and did not challenge the political authority of men and made no effort to recruit, train, or assist women candidates.[22]

In 1938 the GOP nearly doubled its contingent in the House, picking up eighty-one seats along with eight Senate seats and fourteen governorships, although Democrats retained 60 percent of House and 70 percent of Senate seats. Thomas Dewey, Manhattan's precocious gang-busting district attorney, became a celebrity in defeat, after almost deposing FDR's friend, the incumbent New York governor Herbert Lehman. Ohio added two stars to the darkened Republican galaxy: Senator Robert Taft and Governor John Bricker. These were not surprising results. The economy was barely recovering in late 1938 from the recession within the depression. Most voters were worse off economically than in 1936, when many Democrats had precariously won election in Republican-leaning states and congressional districts.

The election of 1938 halted the realignment of voters that had strengthened Democrats since 1930 and ended the prolific era of New Deal reform. For the next twenty-five years, conservatives would largely contain any major domestic expansion of the liberal state. But conservatives learned that liberalism was not a spent force when they tried to enact their priorities or roll back the New Deal. A 1939 study by Gannett's Constitutionalists found, "*Republicans in Congress thus far have made little headway in undermining confidence in the major objectives of the New Deal.*" Although Congress checked liberal ambitions, it failed to repeal or revamp a single important New Deal program or enact legislation favored by conservatives. President Roosevelt remained the defender of the economy, the champion of the common man, and the foe of greedy tycoons. Robert P. Burroughs, RNC member from New Hampshire, said, "The general public has been convinced by Roosevelt and the others in the New Deal that the business men are the corrupt people and that in comparison the politicians are disciples of high-mindedness, clean living, and straight shootings."[23]

CONSERVATIVES AGAINST WAR

In September 1939, the outbreak of World War II shifted the tectonic plates of politics, putting Republicans on wobbly ground for regaining the White House and Congress or overtaking Democrats in the party loyalties of

voters. The menace of fascism in Germany and Japan for a time reconciled the president with restive southern Democrats and recast him as the
indispensable guardian of freedom and security worldwide. Conservatives
feared that a wartime president would expand executive power, squeeze
industry, and keep Americans addicted to liberal government. "What
Roosevelt has in mind is to insist that money which heretofore has gone
for boondoggling and political purposes, is necessary for national defense,"
wrote John Callan O'Laughlin, publisher of the *Army Navy Journal.* "Our
participation in another world war," said Senator Vandenberg, "would
swiftly and necessarily force our government into the strait-jacket of an
American dictatorship."[24]

FDR's policies of preparedness for war, sanctions against fascist ag-
gressors, and aid to allied nations incensed conservatives who supplied the
force and passion, the most jolting rhetoric and stinging arguments against
involvement abroad. Nearly all Republican officeholders and independent
conservatives were noninterventionists who rebuked the president for
pushing America into the wrong war, at the wrong time, against the wrong
enemy. For these self-proclaimed "America First" nationalists, the peril
to white Christian civilization came not from Nazi Germany but from
Communist Russia and nonwhite heathens from the East.

Charles Lindbergh, who had accepted honors from Hitler's government in 1938, articulated such fears. Tens of millions listened to his
speeches on the radio, read press transcripts, or followed his arguments
in news stories. Two weeks after war began in Europe, Lindbergh called
it "not wars in which our civilization is defending itself against some Asiatic intruder [but] simply one more of those age-old struggles within our
own family of nations." A month later, he added, "Our bond with Europe is a bond of race. . . . If the white race is ever seriously threatened,
it may be our time to take our part in its protection to fight side by side
with the English, French, and Germans, but not with one against the other
for our mutual destruction." Ironically, the Nazis claimed that Germany
was saving the white race and needed help from Americans who had
pioneered segregation and other barriers to "racial bastardization." Many
black American leaders opposed intervention in what they viewed as a
white man's imperialist war. When Germany invaded Russia in 1941,
Lindbergh said, "I would a hundred times rather see my country ally
herself with England, or even with Germany, with all her faults, than the

cruelty, the godlessness, and the barbarism that exists in Soviet Russia."
Lindbergh admired Germans sufficiently to father three children with a
German woman after the war, a secret that he kept from his wife and six
children at home.[25]

In 1939 Roosevelt achieved the first of many embattled victories for
his foreign policies when Congress revised America's Neutrality Laws by
repealing the embargo against arms sales to belligerents. The House came
close to killing the measure and changing the course of American and world
history. Republicans voted two to one against repeal in the Senate and nearly
unanimously in the House; overwhelming majorities of northern and southern Democrats in both chambers voted for repeal. After Germany conquered
France in mid-1940, Roosevelt pushed the first peacetime draft through
Congress, again in the teeth of Republican opposition. On his own initiative, the president sent fifty aging American destroyers to Britain in exchange
for basing rights. He banned the export of scrap metal, iron, and aviation
gasoline to Japan, which was pursuing a lengthy war of conquest in China.

In response, R. Douglas Stuart, a student at Yale Law School,
formed a committee that, although not pacifist in philosophy, would
oppose America's involvement in war "even if England is on the verge
of defeat." Stuart's father was executive vice president of the Quaker Oats
company, a stronghold of evangelical conservative politics. In September
1940, Stuart became director of the America First Committee, chaired by
the prestigious retired general Robert E. Wood, chairman of the board of
Sears, Roebuck. Wood had backed Roosevelt through 1936 but lost faith
during the second term. America First pitched a big enough tent to shelter a diverse throng of old-line progressives, apostate liberals, legal scholars, pacifists, socialists, and even communists—until Germany invaded
Russia in 1941 and the party line changed. However, conservatives financed
and ran the group and provided its grassroots base. The committee integrated both fear of war and the New Deal into its literature, which warned
that war would bring on a "New American Order," a virulent form of government control over enterprise worldwide. "If America goes into this war,
the NEW ORDER will come overnight. No part of our vast business machine will escape the most minute and comprehensive regimentation by an
army of bureaucrats in Washington." The "NEW AMERICAN ORDER
[means] four things—TAXES, DEBT, SPENDING, AND REGIMEN-
TATION, but on a scale hitherto undreamed of."[26]

Corporate America had a complex response to World War II. Even after France fell, some conservative executives continued to oppose the administration for mongering war as a part of a renewed liberal grab for the power to regiment business. In August 1940 Edgar Queeny, the CEO of Monsanto Chemical, wrote that liberals were plotting "to continue themselves in power, and that then there will be no need to defend ourselves from totalitarianism because we will already have it." By that time a split had developed within enterprise. Although most business leaders worried about wartime controls, they also doubted that enterprise could survive a Nazi victory. Most business publications and corporate heads came to back a business–government partnership for America's rearmament and aid to foreign allies, even at the risk of fomenting war and fortifying presidential power. Wall Street and multinational business, working through the Rockefeller-supported Council on Foreign Relations, proposed an aggressive foreign policy with generous aid to Britain and China and punitive sanctions against Japan. Most holdouts against intervention either ran or owned domestic-oriented and family-based businesses, among them Wood and Queeny, Sterling Morton, and Henry Ford. Prominent noninterventionists included meatpacker Jay Hormel; U.S. Chamber of Commerce president James S. Kemper; textile magnate William H. Regnery; H. Smith Richardson of the Vick Chemical company; E. T. Weir, president of the American Iron and Steel Institute; and publishers Robert McCormick, Frank Gannett, William Randolph Hearst, and J. M. Patterson of the New York *Daily News*.[27]

Dozens of major multinational firms, however, including General Motors, IBM, Du Pont, Ford, Alcoa, and Standard Oil, had contractual and other business arrangements with German companies and cartels. Most contracts predated Hitler's rise to power but continued under his rule. In some cases, deals survived Pearl Harbor. Business arrangements with the Nazis helped Hitler build his war machine and impeded America's access to materials and technology. According to an explanation offered by Alfred Sloan, president of General Motors, "An international business operating throughout the world, should conduct its operations in strictly business terms, without regard to the political beliefs of its management, or the political beliefs of the country in which it is operating."[28]

Conservative leaders of the America First movement were not isolationists, dedicated to separation from the world, but disengaged nationalists who believed that American should act unilaterally to protect and advance its exceptional civilization and not tie its destiny to foreign regimes. Before Pearl Harbor, however, policies of disengaged nationalists and isolationists ran on parallel tracks. The nationalists never acknowledged a moral imperative for defeating Hitler, or a relationship between American interests and the fate of peoples abroad. Despite calling for an impregnable continental defense, the nationalists usually opposed measures to project American power beyond the hemisphere. They opposed drafting soldiers and some argued that a strengthened military could encourage acts of war. America First spawned hundreds of local chapters and claimed eight hundred thousand members. Yet anti-interventionists failed to defeat policies that the president certified as essential for the security of the country and the defense of good against evil.

Republican leaders of the House and Senate joined the conservative opposition to programs of aid and preparedness. House Minority Leader Joseph Martin privately admitted that "I believe it essential for the Allies to win," but balked at pumping up the power of a president who "failed at home and abused the power granted him." The pragmatic Martin believed he could maintain "a united Republican Party in Congress" only by deference to the party's overwhelming noninterventionist majority. Ten weeks before Pearl Harbor, maverick Republican representative Charles Plumley of Vermont ripped into Martin for losing his "New England backbone" and giving in to isolationism. "In war time there is only *one* state of mind. That is *to win*," Plumley warned. "The day of eye-opening will be a sad one for the Republican party."[29]

Gerald L. K. Smith's Committee of One Million, formed in 1937 to save Christian America from communists and unions, joined the anti-interventionist campaign. Smith organized protest rallies, petitioned Congress, distributed mass mailings, and delivered radio addresses. Despite Smith's association with anti-Semites—he would become openly anti-Semitic after Pearl Harbor—conservatives in Congress spoke at Smith rallies, placed his speeches in the *Congressional Record,* and arranged for him to testify before Congress. Smith attracted a large public following. He claimed that more than a million Americans signed his petition to stay out of war and hundreds of thousands attended his meetings, made a donation to his committee, or signed membership forms. "To millions I am a racketeer, crackpot, and lunatic," Smith said in 1942. "To other millions I am a crusader, a lover of truth, and a devotee of those vital principles on which our whole civilization depends."[30]

Although the America First Committee repudiated extremists, it could not stop Nazi propagandists from promoting its work or followers of shirt leaders from booing the president at their rallies. It didn't help that America First stayed mum about Nazi atrocities, occasionally let slip positive comments about Hitler's Germany, and sponsored speaking tours by pro-Nazi aviator Laura Ingalls. A more militant group with some overlapping leadership, the Citizens Keep America Out of War Committee, called for President Roosevelt's impeachment. Interventionists seized on this agitation to ignite another "brown scare" that rippled through the government and popular culture by 1940, abetted by British intelligence and the exposure of Nazi agents within the United States. Congress investigated organizations ranging from Gannett's Constitutionalists to the German-American Bund, ignoring distinctions between the center and outer fringe of the right. Newsreels, radio broadcasts, documentaries, and briskly selling books echoed dire warnings from President Roosevelt and the Navy Department about the "Trojan Horse" of a Nazi fifth column operating within the United States. Captain America, Batman, and Superman defeated Nazi spies and saboteurs in Marvel and DC Comics. New watchdog groups arranged antifascist rallies and publicity campaigns.[31]

Conservatives never opposed fascism with the same passion and resolve as their crusade against communism. Responses to Russia's invasion of Finland in late 1939 underscored this dual standard. Anti-interventionist Republicans such as Herbert Hoover, Arthur Vandenberg, and Hamilton Fish, all of whom opposed spending pennies on Britain, called for sending millions to Finland. Legislation that authorized a U.S. loan to Finland passed the House by voice vote and the Senate by nearly two to one, with support from both interventionists and their opponents. Hoover organized a private fund to assist the Finns, with contributions from Father Coughlin and other fiercely anti-interventionist figures. Jasper Crane, chairman of Finnish relief in Delaware, explained that conservative backing for "the Finnish resistance to the Russian invasion has killed Communism in this Country as 'dead as tripe.' I can't broadcast this point, but Mr. Hoover told me how widespread this reaction is to the Finnish Relief Fund."[32]

The brown scare competed with another red scare. In 1938 Democratic representative Samuel Dickstein of New York proposed a permanent committee to investigate domestic fascism—the Special House Committee for the Investigation of Un-American Activities (HUAC). But the House kept Dickstein off the committee, which, led by conservative Texas Democrat Martin Dies, paid less heed to fascism than communism and an ill-defined lot of "fellow travelers." Ironically, later research uncovered that Dickstein had been on Moscow's payroll, although he apparently provided nothing of value. HUAC exposed communists in the Federal Writers and Theater Projects, which Congress closed down in 1939. It probed the left-wing infiltration of unions, Hollywood, and the munitions industry. But conflicts between the Dies committee and the FBI, the buffoonery of its chair, its bumbling disregard for civil liberties, and its Dilling-like harrying of improbable reds discredited the committee. J. Edgar Hoover, however, continued to entrench anticommunism within an expanding FBI, especially after he gained broad presidential authority to investigate subversives, including wiretap surveillance without a court warrant. State legislatures authorized commissions and committees to investigate subversion, usually on the left. Most of these "little HUACs" disappeared during World War II but they returned in the early Cold War.[33]

Conservative women, despite backing preparedness for war in the 1920s, became noninterventionists in the late 1930s. These women also viewed communism, not fascism, as America's real enemy and worried about warmongering Jews and radicals. Cathrine Curtis, the founder of Women Investors in America, warned that communists colluded with Jewish Wall Street investors in fomenting a war to supplant the British empire with rule by commissars and financiers. She formed the Women's National Committee to Keep the U.S. Out of War. Famed anticommunist author Elizabeth Dilling joined with Lyrl Clark Van Hyning, a wealthy conservative activist from Chicago, to form an organization called We, the Mothers Mobilize for America. Dilling led a band of mothers to demonstrate in Washington against the Lend-Lease program of American aid to the allies fighting Germany and Japan. In scenes reminiscent of the suffrage era, white middle- and upper-class women in long dresses, fur coats, stylish hats, and heeled shoes circled the Senate chamber until dispersed by police. They organized a sit-down strike that led to Dilling's arrest. Controversy over the march—which Curtis opposed—led Dilling to resign from We, the Mothers, which faded under Van Hyning's less creative leadership.

Most antiwar women activists joined the National Legion of Mothers of America. After the vast Hearst newspaper chain urged women to join the group in late 1939, the legion assumed a life of its own, with funding from conservative businessmen and enthusiastic responses from conservative white, Christian women across America. Best-selling novelist Kathleen Norris, who served on America First's board, became president of the National Legion, which plausibly claimed a membership of several million women. In June 1940, more than a million women voted by mail to approve overwhelmingly a resolution forbidding the president to send troops abroad without a national plebiscite vote by the American people. The National Legion published a weekly newsletter dedicated to a "True Americanism" that combined anti-interventionism with anticommunism, white supremacy, evangelical Christianity, opposition to the New Deal, and eventually anti-Semitism. When the Senate debated the military draft in late 1940, legion mothers gathered at the Capitol to burn in effigy Roosevelt's ally Senator Claude Pepper of Florida and hold a "death vigil." They dressed in black and shrouded their faces with dark veils. The legion disintegrated as America united behind the war, although Norris's successor Cathrine Curtis kept the group nominally alive.[34]

The antiwar mothers tapped into conservative women's fears that the New Dealer's war would destroy families by forcing mothers to work and consigning children to day-care centers run by bureaucrats. The mothers said that a heartless president would needlessly sacrifice America's sons in the killing fields abroad and break the family budget with wartime taxes. His foreign alliances would weaken Christian values, bring refugee hordes to America, and encourage alien subversives at home. Again, the mothers urged women to enter the public sphere and do what men could not do: in this case, defeat the warmongers. The mothers' groups activated far more opponents of intervention than the America First Committee and reached more women than any movement since suffrage, with the potential to profoundly influence American foreign policy and expand mass support for conservative politics. Male leaders of the conservative movement, however, again declined to rally women to their cause.

In prewar debates, conservatives forfeited to liberals the moral high ground they had fought to hold during the New Deal. Unlike interventionists, who argued that good must defeat evil, or pacifists who rejected war on principle, conservatives had no inspirational moral defense of their position. Falling victim to the moral relativism they had charged against liberals, conservatives proposed that Americans learn to live amid the contaminants of a fascist-ridden world. With civilization in peril across Europe and Asia, conservatives declined to embrace America's moral responsibility to scale national barriers and defend human freedom. Looking inward, they denied that America's destiny was intertwined with other nations or that its vital interests extended beyond its borders. "If we conserved instead of spending the three hundred billion necessary to defeat Hitler," wrote conservative Democrat and Notre Dame Law School dean Clarence "Pat" Manion, "we will have established a complete insurance against any conceivable post-war economic problem, and at the same time, we will have saved the lives of several million American boys." More grandly, former progressive Republican Amos Pinchot wrote that America First "sternly rejects the destructive and silly notion that America should go forth over the world and dominate it, fight its wars, write its peace, and from that point proceed to reform all the peoples of the world, democratizing them and guaranteeing them a millennium of justice and happiness, world without end. Amen."[35]

THREE TIMES CURSED

The mission to deny President Roosevelt an unprecedented third term in 1940 seemed like rolling a boulder uphill. A 1939 nationwide Gallup Poll found that respondents preferred Roosevelt to any challenger, although most said that they would have backed a Republican candidate in the absence of war abroad. Texas conservatives promoted Vice President John Nance Garner as an alternative to FDR, but no Democrat could compete with the president, who dropped Garner from his ticket in favor of liberal visionary Henry A. Wallace, his secretary of agriculture. When the Republican Convention convened on June 24, just two days after Nazi troops marched into Paris, delegates hoped for salvation from George Washington's two-term tradition. The retired but still astute RNC member Charles Hilles wrote, "The campaign will boil down to two issues, the international and the third term. But for the third term it would be difficult to beat Roosevelt. But for the world crisis Roosevelt would fade from the scene."[36]

Among GOP contenders, Robert Taft of Ohio in just two years as a senator had become FDR's most incisive critic. However, like Senator

Arthur Vandenberg, Taft lacked popular appeal and lagged in the polls. Already journalists had labeled Taft with the three words that would haunt his every bid for the presidency: "Taft can't win." Frank Gannett stroked his rich man's vanity with a long-shot campaign. Thomas Dewey had a certain romantic allure and swept the party primaries. But the thirty-eight-year-old New York crime fighter had never held public office above county prosecutor and was a risky candidate in perilous times. His once lofty standing in the polls declined as the convention neared. With no candidate breaking clear of the pack, dark horse Wendell Willkie outraced the field. Although a utility executive, Willkie was an internationalist, a civil libertarian, and a Democrat until 1939. Yet Willkie earned conservative stripes as a warrior for private enterprise. He benefited from a skillful publicity campaign guided by industrialists, bankers, and publishers who opposed the New Deal but favored preparedness and aid to Britain. "The election of Willkie will result in no diminution of assistance to the British," Columbia University alumnus George A. Ellis assured his alma mater's president, Nicholas Murray Butler, during the campaign. "Roosevelt's reelection will almost certainly precipitate this country into a war for which it is in no way prepared, and the result of which may be disastrous rather than beneficial to the British."[37]

Conservative Republicans closed ranks "to win with Willkie." Journalist Frank Kent wrote to Mrs. Taft that he "would rather have Bob president than Willkie. I did get myself convinced that Willkie was the only man who could win—and I still feel that way." Gerald L. K. Smith, Fathers Coughlin and Gillis, and Kathleen Norris endorsed Willkie. Dilling declared it "a Christian's duty" to ignore the moderate Republican's me-too campaign and "protest at the polls against New Deal dictatorship, Red treason and war, by voting for Willkie." Willkie did not oppose the draft or the substance of Roosevelt's destroyers-for-bases deal. However, Willkie eventually caught up with disengaged nationalists by accusing the president of plotting America's entry into the war. FDR responded by pledging to the "mothers and fathers" of America that "your boys are not going to be sent into any foreign wars." He summoned home Joseph Kennedy, his ambassador to Britain, to assure Catholic voters of the president's peaceful intent.[38]

Some conservative religious groups openly opposed FDR in 1940. In May, two thousand delegates to the World Christian Fundamentals

Association, which had declined since the 1920s but still claimed to speak for a million true believers, denounced the administration for supporting the "lawless sit down strike," attempting "to destroy the constitution" through court packing, and pushing "to involve us in the European war for the express purpose of perpetuating their unconstitutional regime." The real fifth column, the association claimed, consisted of "third termites who seek to sacrifice youth on a foreign battlefield in order to advance their greed for political power." Politically conservative minister Norman Vincent Peale, who had served on the board of Spiritual Mobilization, urged ministers to work for FDR's defeat. The *United States Baptist*, the leading independent Baptist journal, slammed Roosevelt as a president who "has led this nation into a moral toboggan."[39]

The Willkie campaign, plus new fund-raising rules, loosened the Republican National Committee's hold on presidential politics. Hundreds of independent Willkie Clubs weakened party discipline but strengthened outreach to voters and donors. The Hatch Act of 1939 had limited contributions by individuals to $5,000 (exempting state and local committees) and fund-raising by political committees to $3 million. Despite complaints by RNC treasurer C. B. Goodspeed that "we will not have as much as Wrigley has got to present his chewing gum," the GOP outspent Democrats by raising funds through state parties and independent groups. GOP committees and Willkie Clubs spent a record $14.8 million, dwarfing the $5.9 million spent by the Democrats. The Committee to Uphold Constitutional Government led independent groups with a $400,000 anti–third term campaign.[40]

Republicans secured a greater share of the business dollar in 1940 than in 1936, with some Jewish businessmen finding Willkie acceptable on foreign policy and preferable on economic issues. Republican Committees received 732 donations of $1,000 or more compared to 193 for their Democratic counterparts. Brokers, bankers, and manufacturers contributed eleven times more to Republicans than to Democrats. Some of the nation's wealthiest families, including the Rockefellers, the Pews, and the Du Ponts, dispersed six-figure contributions among party committees. The largest contributors to Democrats were federal appointees, none of whom chipped in more than $10,000. Richard J. Reynolds, however, of the North Carolina tobacco company, loaned $300,000 to Democratic state committees.[41]

Cultural issues remained muted in 1940. In 1938 President Roosevelt had aggravated the sore spot of race when he suggested eliminating the poll tax as a requirement for voting. But the president quickly retreated to his customary silence on race. Walter White, secretary of the NAACP, wrote to FDR in 1939 that although "Negroes generally are grateful to you and Mrs. Roosevelt for the attitude which you have shown, the status of the Negro is so desperate that they are naturally disturbed about the many things which could have been done but which have not been done by the present administration." In 1940 the GOP again took a more advanced position on civil rights than the Democrats. Black Republican Henry Patterson asked why the party of traditional morality could not win back "the Negroes [who] are naturally among our most religious and conservative people?"[42]

The administration continued to duck other social issues. Polls showed most Americans believed that married women should not work, that women shouldn't wear shorts in public, and that a qualified woman was unacceptable as a presidential candidate. FDR slowed his first-term appointments of women, allowed exploited domestic workers to be excluded from wage and hours legislation, and stayed silent on the Equal Rights Amendment that Republicans inserted in their 1940 platform. Roosevelt's America also kept its doors open only a crack to refugees. In 1940, Congress enacted and Roosevelt signed the Smith Act, sponsored by conservative Democrat Howard W. Smith of Virginia, which required the registration and fingerprinting of aliens, eased deportation rules, and made it a crime to advocate the violent overthrow of the government.

Wendell Willkie ran a credible campaign but still won only about 45 percent of the popular vote, while Democrats retained 69 percent of the Senate and 61 percent of House. With war neutralizing opposition to FDR's third term, voters lacked incentives for rejecting the party in power. The economy briskly recovered from the double-dip depression, the administration avoided major scandal, and no foreign enemy struck the homeland. Postelection polling showed that, like Landon, Willkie did best in small towns and farm communities, among women, professionals and upper-income earners, and white Protestants outside the South. African Americans narrowly stayed with the Democrats in 1940, with most defections coming from German and Irish Americans unhappy with the president's pro-British policies.

In the election returns, dismayed Republicans found proof that Democrats had become America's majority party. "Victory for Willkie was nearly impossible," wrote former Liberty Leaguer James Wadsworth.

"A veritable army is arrayed against us. Nearly all of industrial labor ... everybody out of a job or on relief who looks to Roosevelt as to Santa Claus. ... The large foreign elements think they are going to get something out of Roosevelt. Then comes your solid South. ... The sum total of these elements is enormous." Add in the conversion of African Americans by the Democrats and the deficit facing Republicans grew larger yet. Every poll taken in 1940 and 1941 confirmed what party registration data showed: Republicans had fallen to second place nationwide, trailing Democrats in voter loyalty by 5 to 10 percent.[43]

A UNITED AMERICA?

During the thirteen months between the election and Pearl Harbor, Willkie disavowed his campaign rhetoric and became a one-man chorus of praise for an aggressive foreign policy. But the disengaged nationalists in Willkie's party left him behind. They hatched the myth that eastern commercial and international business interests had stolen the nomination from Taft, the grassroots favorite—a prelude to the right's postwar assault on a so-called eastern establishment of moderate Republicans and liberal Democrats. Yet Taft lost in 1940 because he failed to inspire the Republican masses, winning only 16 percent of the primary vote and between 10 and 20 percent support in preconvention polls of Republicans.

After the election, most Republicans continued to war against FDR's policies, including a plan to lend or lease weapons and supplies to nations resisting German and Japanese aggression. Disengaged nationalists denounced Lend-Lease as "a war dictatorship bill" that would prolong the fighting in Europe, strip bare our homeland defense, and eventually drag America into war. But most Americans viewed aiding the allies as a preferable alternative to joining in the war. Lend-Lease cruised through Congress in early 1941, backed by 99 percent of House Democrats but only 15 percent of Republicans. In the Senate, 79 percent of Democrats backed the bill, compared to 37 percent of Republicans. A few noninterventionists believed that America was more likely to become embroiled in the Asian than the European theater of war. America First leader William R. Castle, a former ambassador to Japan, warned that by denying Japan vital raw materials the United States was provoking a needless war in the Pacific.[44]

After losing on Lend-Lease, the America First Committee offered its chairmanship to Charles Lindbergh, who declined but still became the committee's featured speaker. Attesting to Lindbergh's remarkable profile, polls showed that most Americans knew where he stood on foreign policy. But few agreed with the once unassailable hero whom the Roosevelt administration tagged as ringmaster of the pro-fascist fifth column. In a September 1941 speech, a beleaguered Lindbergh charged that "leaders of both the British and Jewish races, for reasons which are understandable from their viewpoint as they are inadvisable from ours, for reasons which are not American, wish to involve us in the war." He opined that America's tolerance of Jews could not survive the tensions of war and that "their greatest danger in this country lies in their large ownership and influence in our motion pictures, our press, our radio, and our government."

America First's leadership puzzled over the hue and cry that followed what field director Page Hufty called "a very temperate, kindly put, statement of fact." Lindbergh's statement "needed to be said, and the Chapter reaction has been nearly unanimously in favor." The committee officially blamed the "interventionists" for distorting Lindbergh's remarks and injecting "the race issue into the discussion of war or peace." Lindbergh, however, had played into FDR's hands by seeming to confirm that anti-Semitism infected his movement. Conservatives had blundered into controversies over the Jewish question before Lindbergh and would do so again, but never on so large a stage with so much at stake. "He personally has become the heart of our fight," Hufty wrote. "It is therefore impossible to criticize him without criticizing the whole cause." Criticism of Lindbergh and America First filled the media, and a Gallup Poll showed that public approval of his foreign policy had thudded to a low of 15 percent. But the *Christian Century* noted the irony that "One hundred clubs and hotel foyers rang with denouncement of Lindbergh on the morning after his Des Moines speech—clubs and hotels barring their doors to Jews."[45]

Pearl Harbor finished off America First but elicited no remorse from its leaders. "Our principles were right," said General Wood. "Had they been followed, war could have been avoided." According to Lindbergh, "The final judgment of our policies must be left to the future and to more objective times; but in this final judgment I have complete confidence." Herbert Hoover wrote, "I have not approved the policies towards Japan

and have felt that this constant sticking of pins in rattlesnakes would produce just such a result. . . . If this had not been done, Japan, from her own
internal exhaustion, would have totally collapsed without the loss of a single
American life." In the four days between Pearl Harbor and Germany's declaration of war against the United States, Hoover hoped that "we can even
yet limit the area of the war." America First contemplated "supporting the
war effort against Japan" while continuing "opposition to entering the
European war." But the committee voted to dissolve rather than execute
earlier plans to enter electoral politics. The time had not passed, wrote
Sterling Morton, "for a vigorous and vigilant group to see that the interests of our country come first," but the tarnished America First Committee was "not the proper vehicle for that purpose."[46]

WAR AND REACTION

At a meeting of the Republican National Committee in April 1942, supporters of a united war effort overruled dissenters and sought to scrub away
the lingering stain of isolationism by resolving that "after this war the responsibilities of the nation will not be circumscribed within the territorial
limits of the United States." For the first time in eight years, Republican
Party resolutions spared liberal domestic policies. The Roosevelt administration cooperated with Republicans in Congress on plans for postwar
international organizations. But the administration unilaterally and secretly
set policy on the future of eastern Europe, China, and the former Axis
powers.[47]

Some antiwar activists expanded Castle's prewar warning by accusing FDR of leading America into war through a "back door" by baiting
Japan into attacking a battleship fleet deliberately bottled up in Pearl Harbor. In this view, war with Japan served the interests of a Soviet Union
pressed by Germans in the West and wary of a Japanese attack from the
East. Conservatives critiqued FDR's demand for Germany's unconditional
surrender, which they said discouraged internal resistance to Hitler, prolonged the war, and opened Europe to communist penetration from the
East. After the war, such revisionist scholarship on these issues became
standard wisdom among some on the right.[48]

If conservatives correctly predicted the advent of war, they mistak-
enly expected that business would be the first casualty. Business did not

in fact confront crushing regulations, labor empowerment, punitive taxation, and competition from government. Instead, leaders of enterprise gained concessions from government to produce the matériel of war. Businessmen helped make and implement federal policy and profited from building war plants and filling defense contracts. Labor lost its quest to share in wartime production decisions and agreed to a no-strike pledge and limitations on wage increases while gaining maintenance of membership clauses that required workers who were union members to remain in the union as a condition of employment. Major corporations locked up most contracts, but small business also profited by serving home front needs. Congress hiked corporate taxes but created loopholes that favored business. More than ten thousand business executives worked in wartime agencies, limiting the authority of bureaucrats over industry. The businessmen forged relationships with the military and gained inside influence, information, and expertise. As the war progressed, a president who had pledged to drive the money changers from the temple ordained some of the most agile among them into the priesthood. By war's end businessmen headed the Departments of State, Navy, and Commerce, the Lend-Lease Administration, the Office of Economic Warfare, and the Office of War Mobilization.

Business capitalized on its contributions to the war. NAM sponsored *This Nation at War,* a weekly radio program aired on ninety stations. It organized talks on "postwar jobs for soldiers" and Soldier's of Production rallies to show that what was good for business was good for the war effort. The Chamber of Commerce set up a lobbying office in Washington and eight hundred local committees to spread the gospel of business. Moderate business leaders from the Business Council founded a new organization in 1942, the Committee for Economic Development (CED), to plan for a postwar conversion that protected enterprise but also preserved a "constructive" role for labor and government. Advertising agencies formed the War Advertising Council to rally public opinion behind the war, the advertising industry, and its corporate clients. The council assisted business in crafting ads that conflated industry and its products with patriotic backing for the war.[49]

In July 1942 the Roosevelt administration for the first time deployed its police powers against the right. About six weeks after federal agents captured a team of German saboteurs in the United States, prosecutors indicted for sedition twenty-eight German agents, Bund members, and far-right activists including Elizabeth Dilling of the mothers' movement and shirt leaders Gerald Winrod and Joseph Pelley. The indictment named the America First Committee and antiwar mothers' groups but no left-wing opponents of war. The trial began in 1944 under new indictments that dropped the antiwar groups and added the alleged pro-fascist Lawrence Dennis. Prosecutors charged defendants with violating the Smith Act of 1940 by conspiring with Nazi agents to overthrow the U.S. government. The trial dragged on through eight inconclusive months and the death of the presiding judge. In 1946 a new judge dismissed all charges, ruling that a new trial would be a "travesty on justice."

Conservatives charged the president with chilling free speech and tarring his political opposition as anti-Semitic and pro-fascist. "The crackpots in the so-called sedition trial," Sterling Morton wrote to Alf Landon, "were the victims of just what the New Dealers would have liked to subject you, Bob Wood, Lindbergh, myself and others to if they hadn't felt that we had too many friends, too much standing, and too many resources to make it worth while." Father Coughlin and the charismatic anti-interventionist Gerald L. K. Smith remained untouched. Isolationist historian and civil libertarian Harry Elmer Barnes wrote to Roger Baldwin of the American Civil Liberties Union:

> There is surely some immediate and ironical satisfaction is seeing some of these "birds" get a dose of their own medicine—in seeing Betty Dilling get the Red Network converted into a Brown network and in beholding some of the notorious anti-Semites have the Forged Protocols of Zion revived in reverse and turned upon them. . . . However, we should be especially solicitous about defending the liberties of those whom we personally despise. Illegal methods used against our enemies may later be turned against us and our friends.[50]

Author John T. Flynn claimed, in a pamphlet funded by the men who backed America First, that an anticonservative "Smear Bund" directed by the Anti-Defamation League of B'nai Brith (ADL) used "for terroristic and defamatory purposes" information on "the private lives of public men" that was "perhaps more extensive than any government or police bureau." The ADL and co-conspirators, he wrote, forged chains of guilt by association that entwined "everyone who disagrees with the Smear Bund as 'Nazi' or

'Fascist.' . . . Anybody who knows him or reads a speech by him or writes him a letter is also anti-Semitic and, of course, Nazi." But Flynn's charges had no ripple beyond conservative circles.[51]

For the 1942 midterms, Samuel Pettengill turned full circle and signed on as finance director for the Republican Party. The Reverend Norman Vincent Peale assumed the leadership of his old group, renamed the Committee for Constitutional Government. In the elections, Republicans picked up enough seats to control 48 percent of the House and 39 percent of the Senate. However, the GOP continued to endorse at least a version of postwar internationalism, led by born-again internationalist Senator Vandenberg, the GOP's leading advocate of bipartisan foreign policy. But Vandenberg's internationalism had its limits. The senator said in 1943 that he would preserve "a totally sovereign country," America's right to "make all of our decisions for ourselves," and "American interests as well as American responsibilities."[52]

Rather than gutting the president's emergency powers or challenging his conduct of the war, congressional critics waged a guerrilla campaign through investigations, criticism, and harassing legislation—what some called the "war within the war." Conservatives passed a binding antistrike bill over the president's veto and terminated FDR's New Deal work programs, including the Works Progress Administration and the Civilian Conservation Corps. However, Congress also voted to withhold taxes at the source of income and, by lowering the minimum income subject to taxation, expanded the number of taxpayers from 3.9 million in 1939 to 42.6 million in 1945. It made taxes more steeply progressive than any time in American history but overrode Roosevelt's veto and cut his requested tax increases for 1944. When the president's National Resources Planning Board proposed ambitious liberal reforms, Congress abolished the board, although planning continued in other government venues.

The State Department's Advisory Committee on Postwar Foreign Policy, led by members of the Council on Foreign Relations, sought epochal changes in America's foreign policy, with the United States taking command of a peaceful and interdependent world open to democratic values and capitalist enterprise. According to Isaiah Bowman, a leader of the Advisory Committee, America had to "think of world-organization in a fresh way" and accept "world responsibility. . . . The measure of our victory will be the measure of our domination after victory."[53]

In 1944 Congress enacted the National Resources Planning Board's recommendations for benefits to veterans, although the board and the Roosevelt administration did not envision a veterans' only welfare program. The American Legion repackaged the program as a generous and politically impregnable "G.I. Bill of Rights" that provided unemployment and educational assistance for veterans and loans for investments in businesses, farms, and homes. It established hiring preferences for veterans, and later amendments added medical benefits. These benefits flowed disproportionately to white males. Few women served in the armed forces and black and other minority-group veterans confronted racial bias in the bill's local administration as well as ongoing discrimination in employment, education, and lending practices. The law also privileged heterosexual citizenship by excluding soldiers discharged for homosexuality. The G.I. Bill expanded the middle class, fueled the growth of suburbs, added to America's professional expertise, and contributed to traditional marriage and rising birthrates. It also widened gaps in higher education and income between whites and blacks. From 1943 to 1947 federal veterans spending rose more than tenfold and by the latter year consumed about a fifth of the budget.[54]

Southern and northern Democrats clashed in 1944 over whether the federal government or the states should administer voting by troops stationed overseas. With Republican backing (polls showed that the solider vote strongly favored FDR), southerners won the battle to keep military voting in the hands of the states, with their suffrage restrictions and cumbersome procedures. Still, the dispute alienated many Dixie Democrats from their party. "The list of Southern grievances is long," observed *Time* magazine in 1943, "'coddling' of the Negro, 'coddling' of labor, attacks on the poll tax, upping of Southern pay scales, failure to redress discriminatory freight rates, the 1938 Purge [of southern conservatives]." In 1945 southern Democrats added another grievance when the Roosevelt-packed Supreme Court struck down the all-white primary election. Southern Democrats in Congress veered to the right during the war when they moved into a middle ground between Republicans and northern Democrats and became part of a durable "conservative coalition" that often outvoted northern Democrats.[55]

THE WARTIME CHRISTIAN RIGHT

In 1941 fundamentalist Carl McIntire organized an association of Bible-believing Christians repulsed by the political and religious liberalism of the Federal Council of Churches. McIntire cannily named his group the American Council of Christian Churches, suggesting a national scope broader than his following of a few hundred thousand fundamentalists. By baiting liberals and pushing the edges of conservative rhetoric, McIntire gained national attention for his fusion of fundamentalism and private enterprise. His American Council claimed that America "has been a Protestant country" and should follow "the Bible as the infallible Word of God" and recognize "Jesus Christ as a personal Saviour from sin and death and hell." America must reject, he said, the Federal Council's striving for a sterile "ecumenical unity of Christendom." McIntire's group denounced the Federal Council for its pacifism and social doctrines, which were "hardly to be distinguished from Communism." His Council said that "the presuppositions of capitalism are in the Bible" and promised that "when the Federal Council issues its socialist pronouncements on Labor Day, we will issue one telling Labor to get saved, to put its faith in Christ." Despite rebuking mainstream Protestants for "dabbling in politics and economics," the American Council established its own political lobbying and public relations operation funded largely by Merwin Hart of the National Economic Council. "Things are beginning to break the right way in regards to the petitions and our activity in behalf of proper labor legislation, etc.," the council's lobbyist told McIntire in 1946. "Many who formerly questioned such activity recognize now the propriety of such activity."[56]

In 1943 a more inclusive group of white, Protestant evangelicals than McIntire's fundamentalists formed the National Association of Evangelicals (NAE) under the spiritual guidance of Harold John Ockenga, pastor of Boston's Park Street Church, and the executive leadership of J. Elwin Wright, head of a New England association of evangelicals. The NAE, like the American Council, styled itself an alternative to the Federal Council of Churches, which it said lacked "a positive stand on the essential doctrines of the Christian faith" and espoused "programs and institutions which are nonevangelical or apostate." The NAE shared both McIntire's theology and his mission to move American politics to the right, but they rejected McIntire's contentious style and his decision to limit his group's membership only to fundamentalist churches. The NAE sought to reach a broad audience with its conservative views on religion, culture, and politics by representing a "third group," the "neo-evangelists ... a great unvoiced multitude of Christian people" standing between what it saw as the Federal Council's modernists and McIntire's "contentious radicals." Unlike McIntire's council, the NAE welcomed members of Holiness or Pentecostal churches and evangelical Protestants who belonged to mainstream denominations.[57]

Prominent radio preachers Charles Fuller and Walter Maier helped launch the NAE. In turn, the NAE formed the National Religious Broadcasters to gain airtime for evangelicals, which was largely allocated as free network time to the Federal Council of Churches. The evangelicals and fundamentalists dominated the market for paid religious broadcasts, but their programs aired mainly on local stations.

The NAE's initial membership of about 300,000 expanded to 1.3 million by 1950. It solicited members "regardless of race or nationality" but in practice recruited only white evangelicals and initially limited membership to men, relegating women to an auxiliary group. The NAE published a monthly news bulletin, sponsored radio broadcasts by affiliated preachers, and held annual conventions, Bible conferences, and adult education programs. It would not "speak for its constituency on controversial issues except when expressly authorized by them to do so." Despite this caution, by 1950 the NAE gained financial backing from conservative businessmen and began to align itself with the Christian right. The NAE's 1950 convention called for "participation by Christians in political affairs and training of Christian young people for government." The convention opposed "all forms of communism, regardless of the name it masquerades under." It endorsed "competitive free enterprise and private ownership" and said that social progress could come only by focusing on "man's condition as a sinner. ... Good things come out of a man's heart only when cleansed (regenerated) by the saving faith in Christ and not out of a good council, a good planning board, nor a good tax." The NAE opposed national health insurance, civil rights laws, and federal aid to education. It called for a balanced budget and curbs on ads for liquor. It urged control over anti-Christian and radical textbooks in public schools and "breaches of Christian principles of accepted Biblical morality and good taste" on television. It opposed ecumenical movements that corrupted true belief and paved the way for one-world government.[58]

The NAE, however, fell short of its dream to mobilize God's army of tens of millions of evangelicals. "Evangelicals have themselves, principally, to blame," Elwin Wright said. Like fainthearted men of business, "many churches and organizations sit on the sidelines, too timid, too complacent, too egotistical, too cynical, or too indifferent to join their hands with those who have dared to hope, dream and sacrifice to bring about an effective united front." By 1970, after twenty-five years, the NAE had enrolled only 2.5 million members, counting church congregations and individuals.[59]

The American Council and the NAE assailed godless secular humanists but battled most passionately for supremacy within Christianity. Beyond their disputes with modernist Protestants, both groups, with equal vehemence, denounced the Catholic Church. Their quarrels with Catholics were both theological and political. Catholics, they said, propagated the heresies of papal authority, priestly powers, worship of saints and relics, and salvation only within the Catholic Church. Misguided Catholic teachings also undercut capitalism, coddled criminals, sustained the welfare state, and pandered to labor. In his keynote address to the NAE's 1945 convention, Dr. Ockenga indicted the anticommunist Catholic Church as "a greater menace than Communism itself, [which was] now reaching for control of the government." He warned of political pressures to "transform a fundamentally Protestant culture to a fundamentally Roman Catholic culture in the United States," replete with the "autocracy, monopoly, and undemocracy [that] now prevails by Roman Catholic dominion in South America." McIntire's council agreed that "Romanism's hatred of Protestantism is as intense as its hatred of communism" and urged "a vigorous, united, and unrelenting resistance to Romanist totalitarianism on the national, state, and local levels."[60]

The neoevangelicals brought the gospel to wayward youth in 1945 when Pastor Torrey Johnson, radio host Percy Crawford, and former jazz band leader Jack Wyrtzen founded Youth for Christ, International. This unlikely trio hoped to win young people to Christ by spicing up evangelism with Christian music and movies, personal testimonies, Bible games, vaudeville acts, and discussion groups. Rallies featured sports stars, repentant hoodlums, and even a pious horse that kneeled at the cross and stomped its foot three times to worship the Trinity. Teens could join the legion of the saved, redeem their country, and have good clean fun. The group's first professional organizer, a charismatic young evangelist named Billy Graham, helped attract an estimated one million young people to rallies in 1946. Youth for Christ leaders denied any interest in politics but, like other white evangelical Protestants, fostered a conservative political culture wary of radical subversion, secularism, and delinquency.

Youth for Christ's organizers encouraged wholesome entertainment and also insulated youth from such temptations as dancing, drinking, smoking, gambling, bebop music, and commercial films or plays. The movement's leaders targeted white youth and made minimal outreach to blacks or Latinos, who they viewed as dangerously radical, lawless, and promiscuous. Youth for Christ scorned secular reforms. According to Graham, America needed to be saved through "a spiritual reawakening. If we don't have it, we are done for." Branches of the Christian Business Men's Association funded the group and provided local contacts, as did the Kiwanis, Elks, Rotary Clubs, and other fraternal lodges. A 1946 report of the ecumenical International Council of Religious Education warned, "The movement is largely adult controlled and is not a real youth movement."[61]

George Benson, a former Protestant missionary and president of Harding College in Arkansas, became the first wartime Christian right entrepreneur to parlay fund-raising skill and a compelling political message into national prominence. Benson made Harding College the center of what he called the National Education Program that would "move public opinion at the grassroots in the direction of godliness and patriotism." After impressing conservatives with his 1941 congressional testimony on economy in government, he expanded the program nationwide. Benson crisscrossed the land, speaking at fraternal lodges, chambers of commerce, trade associations, and civic clubs. He decried punitive taxes and regulation, immoral and wasteful boondoggles, and the "combined threats of inflation and its political corollaries—socialism, revolution, and dictatorship." Benson's sincere advocacy earned him time on broadcast networks, a radio program, and a syndicated column distributed to some twenty-five hundred small-town newspapers and reprinted in corporate publications. J. Howard Pew, Sterling Morton, and George Pepperdine, founder of Western Auto Supply stores, backed his efforts to "re-educate the masses to the value of free enterprise and constitutional government." So did General Motors, Standard Oil, U.S. Steel, Du Pont, and Quaker Oats.[62]

Conservative business leaders initiated their own projects that fused religion and politics. In 1944 radio personality Lowell Thomas joined with corporate executives to bring into the home a Christian conservative message for "the vast multitudes who do not go to church," and women who "have always kept alive our most sacred traditions of religious, spiritual, and ethical values." The group recruited the conservative Reverend Peale to edit an inspirational magazine called *Guideposts*. According to Eddie Rickenbacker, World War I flying ace, president of Eastern Airlines, and dedicated conservative, this weekly publication would feature "simple, non-churchy stories of how outstanding men make practical, personal use of religious faith." The payoff for Rickenbacker and his friends in business was getting "America back on its religious foundations . . . the best hope we have. The religion of today is the patriotism of tomorrow." Peale promised to checkmate "the philosophy of materialism and collectivism" by "creating a new and spiritual counterforce, to reach public thinking on a nation-wide scale." In addition to Rickenbacker, *Guideposts* was backed by J. Howard Pew, Stanley Kresge, head of the retail chain later called KMart, and legendary baseball executive Branch Rickey. Reverend Peale told donors that, "This money will be used to excellent advantage in helping the cause in which we have a common interest." *Guideposts* soared to a paid circulation of several hundred thousand within five years.[63]

The expanded scope of the Christian right during the 1940s signified a rough divide within American Protestantism between theologically conservative evangelicals—whether fundamentalist or neoevangelical—and theologically modern liberals, each with its own para-church and quasi-religious institutions. Mainstream Protestants self-identified about three to two as Republicans in the 1940s and '50s. Although politically active evangelicals upheld conservative ideals, most of the heavily southern evangelical community, including Billy Graham, identified as conservative Democrats until the political upheavals of the late twentieth century.

SECULAR COMPETITION FOR MINDS AND HEARTS

In 1940 Samuel Pettengill made a breakthrough for conservatives by taking the liberal idea of the "right to work"—the right to a job—and turning it into the right to work without meddling by bureaucrats and union bosses. Contracts that required employers to hire only union workers (the "closed shop") or workers to join unions or pay dues once hired (the "union shop") violated the right to work, as did most regulation of business. Before long, Pettengill wrote, "Individuals will have no right to decide what hours they shall work, what pay they shall receive for their labor, or in fact at what task they shall toil." Antiunion groups grasped the transforming power of Pettengill's argument. In 1936 southern conservative Vance Muse had organized the Christian American Association to "preserve Christian democracy" and oppose the CIO's plot to "totally communize America." In the 1940s his association lobbied for right to work amendments to state constitutions, antitrust prosecutions of unions, and a national constitutional convention to "guarantee the God-given right to work and earn a living." In 1943 the *Nation* warned that "the Christian Americans ... are winning by default. Their strength is being underestimated, their intentions judged too charitably."[64]

Business regrouped after the demise of the Liberty League, although with a lighter touch. In 1937 corporate presidents Alfred Sloan of General Motors, William S. Farish of Standard Oil of New Jersey, and Lewis H. Brown of Johns-Manville—America's largest asbestos producer—launched the nonpartisan Tax Foundation to challenge liberal fiscal policies by providing information to the public about excessive taxation and wasteful spending. The American Economic Foundation, a brainchild of Fred G. Clark, the former "Voice of the Crusaders," unraveled the mysteries of capitalism for everyday Americans. Clark tapped the same financiers as the Crusaders had to get on the radio with his *Wake Up, America* series beginning in 1941. Clark's National Schools Committee conducted teacher training and distributed instructional materials on "sound values and proven economic principles" for elementary and secondary schools. His foundation sponsored studies on the distribution of income, which found that workers consumed the lion's share of revenue that business produced.[65]

In 1943 the Pew brothers expanded their influence into rural America when they purchased *Pathfinder,* a biweekly small-town journal. With control over both the *Farm Journal* and *Pathfinder,* the brothers blanketed the countryside with a conservative, pro-Republican message. The Pews consolidated the financing and production of the two magazines to unify their ideology and subsidize the losses of *Pathfinder* with the profits of the *Farm*

Journal. By 1946 the Pew publications were as ubiquitous in country homes as family Bibles, with a circulation of 3.7 million. According to publisher Graham Patterson, with "the two magazines . . . we should be in a position to wield a tremendous influence with small town and rural America."[66]

The Pew brothers and Henry Regnery, a member of the family that bankrolled America First, also financed a plan by journalist Frank Hanighen and former journalist and Haverford College president Felix Morley for a "weekly analysis, factual and editorial, of those national and international developments which are manifestly of outstanding significance." Their brainchild, a magazine called *Human Events,* would oppose "despotic bureaucracy at home [and] entanglement in a new variation of the ill-fated 'Holy Alliance' abroad." It would uphold "the Christian principles which have made us great" and fight "the threat to the American heritage that is the more insidious because it comes to a large extent from within." In addition to the magazine, the management of *Human Events* established a foundation that could receive tax-deductible contributions.[67]

Morley and Hanighen launched *Human Events* in early 1944. The journal defended private enterprise against collectivism and upheld the disengaged nationalism of America's prewar right. In the 1950s it followed the right in shifting to aggressive anticommunism. *Human Events* and a later pamphlet series on current affairs found a readership within sophisticated conservative circles. It subsisted on a minimal budget and a few thousand paid subscribers and failed to become the hoped-for opinion leader that would counter liberal publications such as the *Nation* and the *New Republic.*[68]

In their own eyes, politically active leaders of industry and commerce such as Frank Gannett, Alfred Sloan, E. F. Hutton, and the Pew brothers selflessly served the public, not their personal interests. Such conservative men of enterprise assumed that business would thrive if Republicans recaptured government, although they hardly suffered under the Democrats. These magnates entered politics, however, not to win special benefits for their firms but to improve their country. They backed organizations that worked to develop and articulate conservative principles, not to pad the bottom line of particular companies. In the language of social theorists, the business crusaders were after hegemony—insinuation of their values and priorities into American culture, institutions, and leadership. Except for the terminology, conservative business leaders would not have disagreed, but they would have added that their activism put their personal interests at risk from vindictive liberals in government. General Motors executive William S. Knudsen observed of the Liberty League, "Most of the moves that were made by the League reverberated back here, and made our job considerably harder than it was to begin with. In fact, I think the General Motors Corporation was singled out more than any other Corporation through the connection of its officers in the Liberty League."[69]

THE WHITE BACKLASH

For a decade New Deal policy makers had kept liberal programs from becoming perceived as minority programs. That effort began to unravel during World War II with the white backlash in America's cities against rising aspirations of African Americans for decent jobs and healthy places to live. A decade earlier, white city dwellers had rallied for taxpayer rights. Now, they defended white people's right to associate with "their own kind," in opposition to wartime government programs that in their view foisted shiftless and dangerous blacks on their neighborhoods, schools, and workplaces.

The war had complex racial effects. The shock and horror of Pearl Harbor revived fears of a "yellow peril." The federal government uprooted more than 110,000 West Coast residents of Japanese heritage—two-thirds of whom were American-born citizens—and interned them for the war's duration. The brutal Pacific war became openly racist. Both official propaganda and camp talk among soldiers transmuted the Japanese into swarms of vermin to be exterminated on the battlefield or in their homeland. Blacks, Hispanics, and Native Americans entered a segregated military that consigned dark-skinned men to the same menial work that most of them performed in civilian life. Black soldiers missed out on the bonding that white troops experienced on ships and in battlefields, and racial tension flared in the military. According to an internal army study by editor Andrew Goodfriend of the *Stars and Stripes*, "Instead of abating the racial tensions which endanger American internal security, war seems to have aggravated them." The Negro soldier was "the target of rumor and report which minimize his bravery, honesty, and loyalty. If there has been a gasoline shortage, it has been the 'nigger' or 'jigg' who sold it for personal profit. If supplies have disappeared, if cowardice has been manifested, if a portion of American society has proved itself unworthy of sharing in the glory and fruits of victory, rumor declares the Negro guilty." In southern and border state communities where Negro troops mingled with white residents, the army fielded endless reports of pushing, jostling, and angry words along with sporadic episodes of serious violence. "There is more racial feeling than I have ever experienced in the past twenty-three years," reported Michael J. Curley, archbishop of Baltimore and Washington, D.C.[70]

Racial discord struck northern cities as well. In 1941, under the threat of mass protests by black leaders, President Roosevelt signed an executive order that banned racial discrimination in defense industries and government and established a Fair Employment Practice Committee. Government policy and manpower shortages opened doors for blacks in war industries; more than half a million African Americans left the South for northern cities. As African Americans moved into segregated industries, polls showed that only about a third of white Americans favored laws to guarantee racial equality in the workplace. In some cities, whites rioted to protest public housing projects and organized "hate strikes" to show their outrage at being forced to labor side by side with blacks. In Philadelphia, white workers shut down the transit system for a week to protest the hiring of African Americans as streetcar operators. In Baltimore, the army had to put down a strike at Western Electric by white workers demanding segregated toilets. In 1943 the bloodiest race riot since Reconstruction erupted in Detroit, leaving thirty-four dead. Racial violence exploded in some forty-seven cities that year, with whites attacking Latinos as well as blacks. During the so-called zoot suit riots in Los Angeles, white soldiers and sailors beat and stripped Latinos who wore the distinctive loose-fitting outfit to show their defiance of the square, white world.

Racial tension turned political as whites formed civic associations to protect their neighborhoods from the crime, debauchery, and falling property values they attributed to racial mixing. In a 1944 Roper Poll, 69 percent of whites objected to having a hypothetical black family move in next door. In Detroit from 1943 to 1965, whites founded nearly two hundred groups to protect the racial integrity of their neighborhoods. In Detroit's mayoral elections of 1943, Mayor Edward Jeffries's backers charged that blacks would ruin white neighborhoods and schools and molest white women on city streets if his liberal opponent prevailed. Business interests, conservative Republicans and Democratic politicians in the South abetted the white backlash. They drew upon well-honed rhetoric crafted in the 1920s and '30s that assailed "special privilege" for minorities to oppose state-level antidiscrimination bills as "quotas laws" that would inflame racial discord and discriminate against whites.[71]

In 1943 an alarmed Elmo Roper warned of a white backlash against black demands for equal rights and opportunities. His surveys showed that "not less than 10 percent of the northern whites" were "violently anti-negro," while "another quarter . . . avowedly and openly want complete, not just partial segregation." He feared that if "the negro, militantly . . . demands his rights" it would spark "open antagonism and even violence" among the most hostile 10 percent. It would solidify the next 25 percent "in their fear of, distrust of, and antipathy for, the negro." And it would cause many of the remaining whites who were "neither particularly friendly or unfriendly toward the negro to begin to wonder whether or not there weren't such a thing as 'a black menace.'"[72]

PEANUT POLITICS

In a postelection study of the 1942 midterms, the Republican National Committee optimistically concluded, "Definitely the Republicans have reached a position where they can, with intelligent leadership, hope to win a complete victory in 1944." Maverick political analyst Lawrence Dennis disagreed in a more insightful postelection memo he prepared for General Wood. Dennis scorned the conventional wisdom that the war was not an issue for the next presidential election. The war was "the only American issue, now or during this generation," he wrote, and not a good one for conservatives or Republicans. "Kibitzing the administration's conduct of the war is peanut politics," Dennis said. As in 1920, Republicans could regain power only by "riding in on a post-war wave of anti-war and anti-foreign-intervention reaction." But the GOP was rent by "contradictions between a nationalistic, isolationist tariff and immigration policy on the one hand and an internationalistic Wall Street, foreign loans, intervention and world peace set of policies and ideas on the other hand." Internationalism indefinitely prolonged the war "in the form of a world crusade for peace and plenty for everybody, everywhere . . . insuring a permanent Democratic regime to carry on the Crusade. . . . If the American people continue to fear foreign evil as they now fear Hitler and Japan and as they feared the South after the Civil War, our international crusade will go on and the Democrats will stay in power as did the Republicans after the Civil War."[73]

Dennis warned that eventually it would not matter whether Democrats or Republicans controlled the government. To fight "Communist sin," America had to build a bigger and more invasive government than ever before contemplated in its history. Such a big government regime would strive to master the world and placate America's masses at home with "New Deal boons." You couldn't "plump for W.P.A. projects for foreigners and none for the home folks," he wrote. A postwar crusade would keep Democrats in power for a while, but soon party would become irrelevant. Neither Democrats nor Republicans could escape the iron logic of the leviathan state. The anticommunist campaign would be of "such cosmic magnitude and such indefinite duration that the national undertaking could only be rationally carried out by a single and necessarily, self-perpetuating regime." Moreover, postwar government would have to deal with the contradiction between lingering imperialism abroad and Jim Crow at home. "You can't tell either Americans or Indians that we are fighting to preserve the British Empire. . . . You can't tell the Chinese that we are fighting to put the British back in Hong Kong." You couldn't plunk for freedom abroad and keep "colored people in their place" at home.

General Wood hoped to escape Dennis's grim prognosis through the charismatic leadership of conservative war hero General Douglas MacArthur—"the only man the Republican party can put up who is sure of defeating Mr. Roosevelt." MacArthur, he believed, would launch a "holy war" against liberal sin. Wood and Senator Vandenberg began an "undercover movement" to nominate MacArthur in 1944. Vandenberg, who was hardly nonpartisan in his politics, said, "We *must* beat the 4th Term. It is the 'last round-up' for the American way of life." Frank Gannett, former GOP chair John Hamilton, and first-term GOP representative from Connecticut Clare Boothe Luce joined the draft-MacArthur movement. Luce—a playwright and the glamorous wife of Henry R. Luce, publisher of *Time, Life,* and *Fortune* magazines—was one of America's first celebrity politicians. Although not predictably conservative, Luce had a romanticized view of generals, especially MacArthur. "I would give willingly, and happily, a year of my life to spend a month out there with you now," Luce wrote to MacArthur at his Australian headquarters in 1943. Vandenberg had a romanticized view of Luce. After spending a late-night hour reading a book on Saint Paul that Luce had sent him, Vandenberg wrote, "I should have preferred to spend it [the hour] with you. And that 'goes' whether 'wholly conquered by my spiritual side or not.' See you soon—I hope, I hope."[74]

MacArthur was "the easiest man in the world to elect, and the hardest to nominate," Luce said, as she surveyed a field packed with front-runner Thomas Dewey, Wendell Willkie, and John Bricker. MacArthur's backers, who called themselves the "board of directors," packaged him as the hero who stood above politics but who would accept a presidential nomination if drafted by the people. Luce advised the general to continue "to deny all interest, keep your magnificently dignified silence." Although most enthusiasm for MacArthur came from the America First crowd, the directors had reason for hope. A Gallup Poll in September 1943 showed MacArthur with 42 percent of the vote against FDR, a point better than Willkie and just three points behind Dewey. Republican House members rated MacArthur a surprising second to Dewey as the candidate most likely to defeat FDR. But Dewey became unbeatable when Bricker's campaign stalled in Ohio and Willkie withdrew after losing in Wisconsin. The MacArthur boomlet burst when GOP representative A. L. Miller of Nebraska released letters in which MacArthur endorsed harsh attacks on the New Deal. "I shall never understand why the MacArthur letters were written in the first place [or] the tragic ineptness of the Nebraska Congressman in turning them loose," Vandenberg wrote. "And so our great adventure ends!"[75]

Republicans nominated the moderate Dewey on the first ballot and for balance chose the conservative Governor Bricker of Ohio for vice president. As Dennis predicted, Dewey ran a self-professed campaign of "competence against incompetent bungling." He refused to dredge up what Representative Luce had identified in 1943 as conservatives' deepest fears: that if the liberal Roosevelt government won the war, it would "lose the peace first by destroying the 'free enterprise system' at home, and secondly by an unrealistic attempt abroad to institute WPA-ism (globaloney)"—a term that Luce had coined to disparage the plans of liberals for a global postwar New Deal. In turn, Roosevelt refrained from raising what Luce called the inner fears of liberals, that conservatives "would lose the peace by returning the government to the Hooverite apostles of Depression, Toryism, etc." and "the economic and military 'isolationism' of the '20s, which would make the next world war inevitable." The nation thus avoided Luce's nightmare scenario of a "political civil war" within the United States that would not be "as bloody," but would be "more bitter than the war against the Axis." This political war over ideology, however, would erupt in the postwar years.[76]

In 1944 Republican campaign committees outspent their Democratic rivals by $13.2 million to $7.4 million, even with Democrats exploiting Roosevelt's One Thousand Club, which promised access to administration officials for a $1,000 contribution. Democrats also tapped the financial power of Hollywood liberals. Donors who worked in "amusements and the arts" contributed $8,500 to Republican committees, compared to $128,750 to Democratic groups. A Hollywood Democratic Committee raked in another $136,000. Excluding Hollywood, twelve times as many donors who earned $75,000 or more from corporations contributed to Republicans than to Democrats. To get around legislation banning unions from direct spending on federal campaigns, the CIO formed an independent political action committee that was exempt from contribution limits. The CIO-PAC and other labor committees raised $2 million and mobilized volunteers for Democrats. Robert Lucas, a former executive director of the RNC, said shortly after the election, "An organization should have been launched, nation-wide, last July (when I urged it) to parallel Hillman's P.A.C. . . . I believe in publicity and plenty of it but without vigorous, hard-fighting organization work to back it up the effort and money is wasted." Lucas concluded, "I have little hope that anything much will be attempted."[77]

Dewey's peanut politics earned him no more than Willkie's 45 percent of the popular vote. Republicans lost eighteen House seats and picked up one in the Senate, which left Democrats with better than 55 percent majorities in each chamber. The war had decisively ended the depression, kept the Democrats in power, and disarmed the opposition. Still, conservatives believed that the president was too ill to survive his full term and expected better times when their nemesis gave way to his pedestrian vice president. Truman "would not be influenced to any substantial degree by his former undesirable associates," Sterling Morton wrote. "Above all, I believe he has no delusions of grandeur, nor a desire to be president of the world." But former GOP chair John Hamilton warned, "The politician does not understand that we are in the throes of a social transition, but is willing to content himself with the thought that this is a passing phase which centers around the President's charm, and, when Mr. Roosevelt has played out his score, we shall revert to political normalcy."[78]

4

THE BEST AND
THE WORST YEARS
FOR CONSERVATIVES,
1945–1952

Christian right advocate George Benson became so valuable to the conservative cause by 1947 that backers insured his life for a million dollars. Benson established the grassroots appeal and fund-raising power of a message that upheld both private enterprise and white Protestant values. As part of his well-funded National Education Program, Benson brought thousands of business executives to his Harding College in Arkansas "to learn about the American way of life" at Freedom Forums. He organized workshops for ministers, a speaker's bureau, and summer youth seminars. Benson extended his radio broadcasts to 362 stations, syndicated his column in 150 local newspapers, and produced a television program called *The American Adventure*. He established a patriotic American Studies program at Harding College as a model for Christian education and published a monthly newsletter with a circulation of about forty thousand. Benson broke new ground with his creative anticommunist cartoons and films, including *The Truth About Communism,* which Ronald Reagan narrated. His films, which warned that communists had infiltrated American government and culture, attracted millions of viewers and found their way into schools, civic groups, and military education programs. Hundreds of corporations distributed his materials to employees. When critics charged that Benson's enterprises had turned Harding College into a propaganda mill for the extreme right-wing, he defended its Christian right patriotism as "the rock on which we have built our way of life."[1]

THE WAR THAT FOLLOWED THE WAR

By 1944 the National Association of Manufacturers had armed itself to fight a "war of ideas and opinions" for freeing private enterprise of unwanted controls once the shooting stopped. NAM sought to prove that business knew better than government how to meet Americans' expectations for "more jobs, higher living standards, and greater security." NAM recognized that it had to improve its image for a public that "has not yet forgotten 1929," when business failed to address the nation's economic and social problems and "it was government—and government only—which volunteered to take decisive action."[2]

In an internal strategy memo, NAM noted that without "a conscious decision by the public to re-establish an economy of freedom and individual initiative, public opinion will allow government controls to be extended indefinitely into peace," sending America "down the same road of collectivism that is being taken by almost every other civilized country." To show that industry "operates as much in the public interest as the private interest," NAM hiked its public relations budget, doubled its staff, and assigned its National Industrial Information Committee (NIIC), chaired by J. Howard Pew, to craft an effective public message. It targeted workers, women, farmers, teachers and students, clergy, and patriotic groups. As in the 1930s, NAM relied on "extensive utilization of the 'indirect method' of influencing public opinion." Industrialists should avoid "negative positions [that] create the impression that we favor the status quo" and promote business as "the most sincere sponsor and the most reliable protagonist of social progress." They should make "constructive recommendations [or] at least should interpret our opposition in terms of the public's welfare rather than our own."[3]

Business also needed to downplay its self-interested departures from free enterprise. Despite our "preaching of the *philosophy* of free enterprise," the NIIC's executive director wrote, "even businessmen, when faced with the hard, cold facts of their immediate self-interest, will endorse 'exceptions' to any commonly-accepted definition of the function of competition." Examples abounded, he said.

> The Coal Industry would feel very hurt if it was charged with not believing in free enterprise and competition, yet an important segment of it wants the Guffey Act, which is the very negation of competition.

Drug manufacturers and the producers of other types of branded merchandise will always cheer for free enterprise and competition, yet they can rationalize a system of price maintenance laws.

The automobile industry, which many of us accept as an outstanding example of competition, contains many people who argue in behalf of non-competitive price-fixing on used cars.[4]

A labor management conference that President Truman convened three months after defeating Japan gave business its first reality check. As striking workers demanded wage hikes they had deferred during the war, NAM rallied employers to end wartime controls over production, pricing, and hiring decisions. They sought to hold the line on wages and check union demands for gaining increased bargaining power by organizing supervisors and opening corporate books to inspection by union leaders. In developing its conference strategy, NAM deflected mild pressure for conciliation from Eric Johnston, the moderate president of the U.S. Chamber of Commerce. The Committee for Economic Development avoided the conference but kept up its research and lobbying. With labor divided, President Truman standing aside, and NAM defending the interests of business, managers defeated labor's most threatening demands.[5]

Like Alexander after Thebes, business kept piling up victories. In 1945 Republicans and conservative Democrats voted together to cut personal and corporate taxes. With NAM again in the lead, the business community's expensive media and lobbying campaign killed off most wage and price controls during 1946. That year Congress also abolished the wartime Fair Employment Practices Committee, which freed management from another constraint on its authority. Southern executives and local officials checked the CIO's Operation Dixie campaign to unionize the employer-friendly South. Conservatives thereby thwarted labor's plans to consolidate power nationwide, advance liberal politics in Dixie, and deter firms from fleeing south to avoid unionization. Opposition from business and congressional conservatives kept liberal Democrats from writing full employment guarantees into federal law, which the right saw as WPAism run amok. The compromise Employment Act of 1946 made "maximum employment" a goal, not a mandate. Conservatives also successfully opposed President Truman's program for national health insurance, federal housing programs, and civil rights laws. In addition conservatives, who privileged congressional power during an era of Democratic presidents, backed bipartisan laws enacted in 1946 to strengthen congressional oversight of the executive.[6]

THE NEW POSTWAR ORDER

After Congress repealed wartime regulations, business delivered on its promise of prosperity, though it benefited mightily from federal investments in infrastructure, technological innovations of the war, low-cost purchases of government plants, and plentiful cheap oil. By 1947 real GNP was about 50 percent higher than in 1940, unemployment had nearly disappeared, and 95 percent of workers toiled in the civilian economy. The United States controlled half the world's industrial capacity, held half of the world's gold and currency reserves, and accounted for most of the world's direct foreign investments. Many conservatives, however, watched in dismay as internationalist financiers and industrialists joined with liberal Democrats to implement the "New American Order" that the America First Committee had warned about in 1941. With backing from the eastern media, Ivy League professors, Wall Street lawyers, Hollywood, and mainstream clergy, these new allies put aside old quarrels over domestic policy and built upon wartime relationships to achieve a stunning extension of government that nationalized and even internationalized American policy. Their aim was not to expand welfare and regulation at home but to promote business expansion and economic development worldwide, battle communism, and keep the peace through collective security arrangements among free nations.

The postwar internationalist era began in 1944 with two international conferences. At Dumbarton Oaks in Washington, D.C., the United States, the Soviet Union, Great Britain, and China formulated plans for the United Nations and at Bretton Woods, New Hampshire, delegates from forty-four countries negotiated economic agreements that, in effect, pegged the free world's economy to an American dollar, convertible to gold. American dollars primarily funded an International Monetary Fund (IMF) to keep currencies stable and a World Bank to underwrite development and infrastructure projects in western Europe and, later, in the less-developed world. The United States strengthened the Export-Import Bank to grant overseas loans for purchasing American goods. The bank bolstered American foreign policy goals and *Business Week* noted that it helped "private banks in gradually reviving a formerly lucrative business" of foreign loans. Under broad negotiating authority that Congress granted the president in the Reciprocal Trade Agreements Act of 1945, the United States joined twenty-three nations in 1947 and reduced trade barriers through the General Agreement on Trade and Tariffs.[7]

Overall, this "American program" of open markets and "international economic collaboration," wrote Jacob Viner of the Council on Foreign Relations, "makes it economically possible for most countries, even if small, poor and weak, to live free and with chances of prosperity." Otherwise, "expect a return of the economic warfare which prevailed in the 1930s, with its political tensions, its economic wastefulness, and its favorable setting for the emergence of desperate countries with ambitions fatal for themselves, or for others, or for the world at large."[8]

Disengaged nationalists and domestically oriented business leaders, however, opposed policies that they believed exported the New Deal worldwide, coddled ungrateful foreigners, threatened American sovereignty, and smoothed the path to world government. J. Howard Pew sounded an early warning in November 1944.

> Within the next two years, either through the medium of treaties or legislation, America will determine whether our children are to live in a Republic or under National Socialism; and the present Administration are definitely committed to the latter course. . . . Our government in cooperation with the English Government, are trying to accomplish these purposes through the medium of treaties . . . of which the Dumbarton Oaks Conference and Bretton Woods Conference form a part.[9]

In 1945 and 1946, a majority of Senate Republicans, nearly all of them conservatives, voted for Senator Taft's amendment to kill by delay America's participation in the IMF and World Bank. In both Houses, conservative Republicans voted against reciprocal trade agreements, the Bretton Woods arrangements, and a $3.75 billion loan for British recovery. As government spending, presidential authority, and worldwide obligations expanded in the Cold War, conservatives warned of a dangerous enlargement of government and executive power, of entangling alliances with unreliable foreign powers, and of threats to the liberties of Americans at home. Yet the right lost every key vote in the Democratic Congress, which continued a losing streak on foreign affairs dating to votes on the revision of America's neutrality laws in 1939.[10]

By 1950 the combination of New Deal programs, wartime taxation, veterans' benefits, defense spending, business subsidies, and global commitments had vastly expanded government's role in the economy. From 1927 to 1950 total government spending more than doubled as a share of Gross Domestic Product (GDP), rising from 12 percent to 25 percent. Most of the increase came in federal spending, which quintupled from 3 percent to 15 percent of GDP, reversing the once large lead in spending held by state and local governments. Most federal dollars fueled warfare not welfare. In 1950 defense, veterans' benefits, intelligence, and military-related debt payments consumed two-thirds of the federal budget. The new mixed private–government economy meant more than rising expenditures by government. Government also underwrote much of the private sector. Defense budgets financed civilian construction projects, research and development, and industries such as aerospace. The federal government subsidized education and health care through the G.I. Bill and housing by guaranteeing and insuring mortgages, assisting construction, providing home owner tax breaks, and creating a secondary market for mortgages. It financed exports with the Export-Import Bank and opened American corporate access to foreign resources and labor through IMF and World Bank loans. It funded vast irrigation projects in the West and continued providing mining and grazing interests access to public lands at below market costs. It sponsored atomic energy development, began building a national highway system in the late 1950s, and continued to subsidize agriculture.[11]

In the new economy, executives came to Washington for a piece of the action and often turned for assistance to a new breed of lobbyists. Former idealists who had designed liberal programs to keep business under heel made handsome profits by selling their expertise and inside contacts to wealthy corporate interests. In 1941 FDR's aide Thomas "Tommy the Cork" Corcoran became the first pivotal New Deal figure to turn from reformer to lawyer-lobbyist. Corcoran gained lucrative fees from executives who learned during the war that big government meant big profits. After the war, a slew of New Deal liberals followed his lead.[12]

The advent of insider lobbyists—for decades mostly Democrats—had profound political implications that blurred distinctions between right and left. The new operatives made the Democratic Party less dependent on grassroots mobilization and more beholden to financing from business. They opened a revolving door between public service and private employment and tightened the knot that tied business to government. Earle R. Muir, president of the Louisville Trust Company, wrote in 1950 that business "demands that the government get out of business, and at the same time asks for government aid through loans, grants, and subsidies." With government loans "growing from a few million to more than 20 billion dollars" a year, he said, even his fellow bankers were "going socialist." A few years later, journalist Frank Chodorov reflected that the "current crop of industrial leaders . . . became accustomed to doing business with the government, and adjusted their thinking accordingly; to put it bluntly, they learned to equate business with lobbying."[13]

HAD ENOUGH?

In the first postwar election, held in 1946, the GOP's new slogan HAD ENOUGH? evoked scarcity, high prices, and labor strife under Democratic rule in Washington. The erratic Truman, who sponsored liberal programs but also scolded labor and fired holdover New Dealers, failed to inspire Democrats. With many Democratic voters staying home in 1946, Republicans won control over Congress for the first time since 1930. To the Senate voters elected conservative Republicans such as Joseph McCarthy of Wisconsin, William Knowland of California, William Jenner of Indiana, Harry Cain of Washington, and John Bricker of Ohio. Commentators later dubbed these high-profile conservatives the "Class of '46." House freshmen included two young pragmatists, Republican Richard M. Nixon of California and Democrat John F. Kennedy of Massachusetts.

In postwar Britain, voters defeated Winston Churchill and his conservative majority in Parliament. Americans, however, could not dispatch the Democrats in a single blow. The midterm elections of 1946 issued no policy mandate to Republicans in Congress, who had to confront a president armed with veto power, the bully pulpit, and the initiative in foreign affairs. According to Clarence Brown, the GOP's campaign director, "Many people who voted in the last election were not voting particularly for the Republican Party. . . . They were voting their protest [against Democrats].

. . . The victory of 1946 was simply the winning of a skirmish, and the real battle that has been going on is still going on between those who believe in two different political philosophies."[14]

Republicans and conservative Democrats in the new Congress reveled in their power not just to block but also to enact legislation. With President Truman standing against them, however, the right won only scattered victories. NAM and other business groups spent more than $3 million on public relations and lobbying in support of revising the Wagner Labor Relations Act. The resulting Taft-Hartley Act rewrote for the first time a sacred New Deal text and underscored labor's dependence on government. It incorporated many if not all of business's highest priorities. It banned closed shops, which required firms to hire only union members. The act empowered the president to seek court injunctions to halt for eighty days strikes that "imperiled the national health or safety" and gave employers free speech rights to oppose unions. It required union officers seeking protection under the labor laws to file financial reports and noncommunist affidavits. It excluded supervisory and managerial personnel and "independent contractors" from Wagner Act coverage. After Taft-Hartley, the Wagner Act covered only half of the workforce. Taft-Hartley restricted unfair labor practices by unions such as strikes and boycotts that were called to pressure another employer or influence the outcome of a jurisdictional quarrel among unions. It delegated to states the authority to enact so-called right-to-work laws banning union shops, which required hired workers to join a union or pay dues. By 1957 eighteen states, all in the South and West, had adopted such laws.[15]

President Truman vetoed the Taft-Hartley Act, which the CIO had damned as a "slave labor bill." But Republicans and southern Democrats mustered enough votes to override the veto, even though 85 percent of northern Democrats in Congress backed the president. By opposing Taft-Hartley Truman had succeeded in repairing relations with labor and flaying conservatives. The president's strategy was "entirely different than if there were any real point to bargaining and compromise," wrote presidential aide Clark Clifford in a strategy memo first drafted by veteran New Dealer James Rowe. The memo advised the president to rally liberals and union members by refusing "to bargain with the Republicans" or "to accept any compromises." Truman likewise refused to compromise with conservatives on slashing taxes by 20 percent. Like Franklin Roosevelt in 1938, he rejected the conservative claim that low taxes would sustain an economic boom that increased federal revenue and pared the national debt. Twice Congress passed tax-cutting bills; both times enough southern Democrats voted with the president to sustain his vetoes. Conservatives settled for a diluted tax cut that kicked in just in time to perk up a sluggish election-year economy.[16]

Both Truman and his adversaries knew that the late 1940s differed from the conservative era that had followed World War I. The Democratic base vote, which had four times elected FDR, could readily elect another liberal president in a contest three years removed from the tensions of war. Senator Robert Taft of Ohio, the right's tacit leader, recognized that it would be "political suicide" to attempt to undo New Deal benefit programs, and instead embraced a Rooseveltian "obligation to the people of the United States to see that everyone has at least a floor under his income; under his medical care; under his education; and under his shelter." Even more: "I do not think it can be done by private enterprise, and it has not been done by private enterprise." But unlike "socialistic" Democrats, Taft would bypass centralized authority and deliver "aid to states and localities, which preserves individual liberty and the independence of the States and local communities while undertaking to prevent hardship and poverty in every possible way." With an eye on realigning the South, Taft said, "My program for assistance to health, education and housing is based on raising the standard in the poorer States, most of which are in the South."[17]

THE WAR AGAINST "COMMUNIST SIN"

President Truman rebounded from the midterm election disaster by re-igniting America's crusade against evil abroad. By 1947 negotiations over the unification of Germany had broken down and the Soviet Union had imposed its rule on most of eastern Europe. Soviet dictator Joseph Stalin was backing communist parties in western Europe and a left-wing insurgency in Greece. He was pressuring Turkey for joint control of the Dardanelles Straits, which is part of the connection from the Mediterranean to Russia's Black Sea. When Great Britain informed the United States that it could no longer afford to aid Greece and Turkey, the United States stepped into the breach. In March 1947 President Truman asked Congress to ratify a policy of containment that obliged America to keep the reds from engulfing new territory across the globe. His Truman Doctrine called for military and economic assistance to Greece and Turkey but it also broadly declared that "It must be the obligation of the United States to support free peoples who are resisting attempted subjugation by armed minorities or by outside pressures." The Republicans' leader on foreign policy, Senator Arthur Vandenberg, backed the president, reportedly advising him to "scare the hell" out of Republicans in Congress. "Senator Vandenberg has become the captive of all the errors committed in the name of a so-called 'United' American foreign policy," complained conservative GOP representative Ralph W. Gwinn of New York. "He rejects even the idea of a Republican world policy."[18]

Disengaged nationalists like Representative Gwinn balked at joining another Democratic-inspired crusade, even against sinful reds. Republican financier Sterling Morton marveled:

> In the predictions our group [America First] made, we could not imagine the insane extravagance with which the war was conducted, the cynical bartering of the territory of the formerly free and friendly nations, the revival of the slave trade, the revengeful destruction of the industrial heart of the European economy or the post-war necessity for a global WPA! Nor could we imagine that the destruction of Hitler would give rise to a much more ruthless and powerful dictator— one who kills and imprisons on a wholesale scale while Hitler did so on a retail scale.

America should have let Hitler and Stalin "cut each other's throats on the plains of Russia," he said. "After that, neither could have been a threat to the Anglo-Saxon nations." GOP Representative Howard Buffett of Nebraska confessed, "I would rather put a fully loaded machine gun in the hands of a delinquent than more opportunities for international destruction in the hands of our State Department." His party colleague John Vorys of Ohio concluded, "If we fought for world peace, security and freedom, either we lost the war or it is still going on." Disengaged nationalists again fell on the losing side of a moral divide and the bill to aid Greece and Turkey passed easily, although neither country fit the model of a free democratic state.[19]

Maverick conservative analyst Lawrence Dennis saw his 1942 predictions of Democratic victory and a leviathan state fulfilled in the Truman

Doctrine. "Truman should win in a walk in 1948," he wrote. "The Republicans, having accepted the internationalist doctrine in the bi-partisan foreign policy, now lack a basis for a successful opposition. . . . Accepting the Truman doctrine for a holy war on communist sin all over the world commits America to a permanent war emergency. . . . The executive has unlimited discretion to wage undeclared war anywhere, anytime he considers our national security requires a blow to be struck for good agin sin." Why start with Greece and Turkey? "Answer: the Standard Oil monopolies in mid-east oil."[20]

On cue, Truman pushed through Congress the National Security Act of 1947 that (with amendments) established a Department of Defense, a Joint Chiefs of Staff, a National Security Council within the executive office of the president, and a Central Intelligence Agency primed for both covert operations and intelligence gathering and analysis. He pushed for a massive European aid program (with a smaller allocation to Japan) proposed by war hero and secretary of state George C. Marshall. Conservatives played on fears of inflation and bankruptcy to challenge the aid programs that they saw as extending New Deal liberalism to foreign affairs. "Not even this nation, as rich and powerful as we are," Senator Knowland of California said, can "run an international WPA." Republican governor Frank Carlson of Kansas warned, "Our United States Treasury is not the world's money pot. . . . The Democrat policy of spending American dollars to meet the threat of communism appears to me a losing battle." Frank Gannett asked, "Will the begging never end? . . . We can raise these staggering sums from only two sources; from additional levies upon the overburdened taxpayers, or by running the printing press, causing inflation and reducing the value of the dollar."[21]

Conservative opposition to the Marshall Plan melted away after communists seized control of Czechoslovakia, the last bastion of democracy in eastern Europe. Senator Taft's motion to reduce funding levels failed by twenty-five votes in the Senate and the final aid bill easily passed both houses of the Republican Congress. Truman also negotiated a military alliance with European democracies that culminated in the formation of the North Atlantic Treaty Organization (NATO) in 1949.

The right still lacked a positive, morally uplifting alternative to Truman's containment policies abroad. Postwar conservatives lurched between withdrawing from the world and marching to Armageddon. Many conservatives had condemned Truman's decision to use the atomic bomb against Japan. By the late 1940s, however, prominent conservatives contemplated the use of ultimate weapons against the reds. "Either get out and let the Slavs overrun Europe and Asia, which will probably cause the break up of the U.S.S.R. by indigestion," Sterling Morton wrote, "or drop a few atom bombs on the Kremlin. We can't plead morality as a deterrent—not after Hiroshima." Republican Representative Vorys contemplated "the ghastly, staggering and tantalizing question of whether using the atomic bomb to try to end this tension is a duty—or just a temptation." Conservative intellectual James Burnham prophesied that total war with the Soviets was imminent, which meant that the United States must be prepared "to strike an immediate paralyzing blow with atomic weapons." The cautious Senator Taft favored capital-intensive investments in a home-based air force, to hold down government spending, balance the budget, make room for tax cuts, and limit the temptation to intervene in foreign conflicts. But he failed to articulate a strategy of his own for advancing American interests abroad. "Our Party has no foreign policy," GOP Representative Ralph Gwinn of New York wrote in 1949 to Hugh Scott, chairman of the Republican National Committee.[22]

Moreover, containment was not a static Maginot Line of defense, but an active policy to bust left-leaning unions abroad, rig foreign elections, overthrow anti-American governments, export American values, and disrupt the red empire. The CIA conducted psychological and cultural warfare through front organizations, media outlets, business corporations, student groups, academics, artists, journalists, political movements, and private foundations. It covertly financed Radio Free Europe and Radio Liberty, which broadcast into red territory with the credibility and flexibility of privately run operations. The CIA also backed the Crusade for Freedom, a private organization that raised funds for these two broadcasting operations and promoted anticommunism within the United States. General Dwight Eisenhower launched the Crusade with a speech on Labor Day 1950 that pictured America as waging a "battle for the truth" against a soulless enemy determined to deny humanity God's gift of liberty and freedom.[23]

Simultaneously, the United States worked not just to contain the spread of communism but also to liberate peoples under communist control. The Truman administration secretly pursued this so-called rollback strategy by infiltrating communist-controlled territory to conduct guerrilla warfare, sabotage infrastructure, and instigate rebellion. These capers, however, invariably failed. Communist spies compromised many missions and U.S. intelligence agencies failed to solve the problem of how to conduct operations within suspicious, closed, and repressive regimes. The covert U.S. operations also depended upon an unstable and amateur mix of unreliable émigrés, soldiers of fortune, former fascists, and partisans of departed regimes. In 1952 Frank Lindsay, the CIA's once enthusiastic director of rollback in eastern Europe, conceded in a classified memo, "The instruments currently advocated to reduce Soviet power are both inadequate and ineffective against the Soviet political system." Four years later, Time-Life vice president C. D. Jackson, who had previously served as President Dwight Eisenhower's adviser on psychological warfare, wrote, "International psychological activity must have within it, like raisins in a cake, little bits of cold, hard action. . . . We desperately need a raisin or two—the detachment of Albania, a successful large-scale raid on the Mainland of China. . . . But are we today capable of this kind of thing?"[24]

THE ENEMY WITHIN

Although liberals led the fight against communism abroad, conservatives seized the initiative in fighting subversion at home, where they had the backing of two powerful arms of the government—the FBI and the House Un-American Activities Committee (HUAC). The FBI, which had swelled from fewer than one thousand employees in 1939 to about five thousand in 1946, energetically investigated (legally and illegally) suspected subversives. It infiltrated the Communist Party and fed intelligence to congressional investigators, friendly journalists and intellectuals, and private red hunters. It worked the media to play up the communist threat and in 1950 reactivated a wartime American Legion contact program that had recruited sixty thousand legionnaires to inform on the left. Director Hoover personally used his access to confidential information about Supreme Court nominees, including transcripts obtained from the wiretapping of political figures, to influence the appointment and confirmation of justices to favor conservatives.[25]

State and local governments revived "little HUACS," conducted surveillance and investigations, adopted loyalty oaths, outlawed the Communist Party, and required subversive groups to register with the government. Urban police forces in cities such as Chicago, Los Angeles, New York, and Philadelphia formed "red squads" to investigate, infiltrate, harass, and intimidate subversives. The red squads shared information with corporations, government agencies, and selected journalists and politicians. In Chicago the police kept dossiers on some eight hundred "subversive" organizations including the League of Women Voters, the NAACP, Planned Parenthood, the Chicago Council on Foreign Relations, and the Federal Council of Churches.[26]

Testimony from defecting Soviet cipher clerk Igor Gouzenko; Elizabeth Bentley, who had served as a courier for Soviet espionage networks within the United States; and Louis Budenz, former editor of the Communist Party's *Daily Worker,* confirmed suspicions that wartime America swarmed with communist spies. Although such exposure prompted the Soviets to dismantle their American spy rings, Hoover testified to Congress in 1947 about the continuing menace of "the enemy within," which he did not limit to card-carrying communists. "I do fear for the liberal and progressive who has been hoodwinked and duped into joining hands with the communists," he said. He worried that "communists are able to secure ministers of the gospel to promote their evil work," and he warned that "communists and fellow travelers, under the guise of academic freedom, can teach our youth a way of life that eventually will destroy the sanctity of the home, that undermines faith in God, that causes them to scorn respect for constituted authority and sabotage our revered Constitution." In keeping with this elastic definition of subversion, the right broadly targeted Hollywood, churches, and schools.[27]

Hollywood's studio heads—most of them Jewish, anxious to prove their Americanism, and pressured by competition from foreign films and the nascent television industry—joined the antiradical campaign. Aided by organized crime, which gained power as radicalism declined, these executives crushed an allegedly communist-infiltrated union of production workers and took control over movie sets. With government's help, they tightened control over films' content. In 1947 HUAC probed how reds beat the Production Code to insinuate into films what actor Adolph Menjou called "sly, subtle, un-American class-struggle propaganda." Stars such as Robert Taylor, Gary Cooper, and Screen Actor's Guild president Ronald Reagan confirmed that communists abided in their midst. Reagan's encounters with radicals in Hollywood began moving this New Deal Democrat toward the right and prompted him to quietly pass names of suspected subversives to the FBI.[28]

Congress cited for contempt ten Hollywood personalities—six of them Jewish—who refused to answer the question: "Are you now, or have you ever been, a member of the Communist Party?" The Justice Department prosecuted these members of the so-called Hollywood 10. Studio heads fired the offenders and voted to refuse employment to communists, launching a fifteen-year blacklist that had the backing of conservative organizations.[29]

Conservatives also targeted alleged left-wing influence in Protestant churches. The Layman's Council of Carl McIntire's American Council of Christian Churches widely circulated its pamphlet "How Red Is the Federal Council of Churches," a spider chart of allegedly subversive council leaders. "Christian Americans must act vigorously and promptly," the laymen warned, "or their churches will become no more than wings of the Communist-Socialist movement." Author John T. Flynn seconded this warning in his book *The Road Ahead* (1949), which sold more than a million copies and another four million in a *Reader's Digest* condensation. This conservative critique prompted the Presbyterian church to warn about confusing "treason and dissent," putting falsehood over fact for "propaganda value," and equating one's politics with God's will. Two years later, in 1951, Cincinnati layman Myers G. Lowman formed the Circuit Riders to fight "socialism and communism and all anti-American teaching in the Methodist Church." In 1956 the Circuit Riders disseminated a pamphlet alleging that 2,109 Methodist clergymen had ties to communist front organizations.[30]

For conservatives, the Federal Council of Churches exposed its red underbelly in 1948 by joining a new World Council of Churches. The Federal Council hailed "unity among Christians," but conservatives said that religious pluralism adulterated Christian doctrine, propagated left-wing ideas, and promoted world government. The World Council enraged conservatives when it issued a report that rebuked not just communism but also "laissez-faire capitalism." Federal Council president Charles P. Taft— Senator Taft's brother but a moderate Republican—added the modifier "laissez-faire." This caveat did not cool the right's anger over the World Council's charges that unbridled capitalism failed to "meet human needs," produced "serious inequalities," and exalted "success in making money."

Only by challenging "economic injustice and racial discrimination," the council said, could churches reverse "conditions favourable to the growth of Communism." Reverend McIntire responded by forming the International Council of Churches, which existed mainly on paper but gained attention with a lofty title and provocative right-wing positions.[31]

Within the academy, conservative critics reproached progressive educators for fixating on experiential learning, critical thinking, and civic activism. They called upon schools to reward excellence and teach basic skills, patriotic U.S. history, the best of Western civilization, and timeless religious principles. In 1950 women of the conservative group Pro-America rallied angry parents in Pasadena, California, to pressure the school board into firing their nationally prominent superintendent of schools Willard E. Goslin. They charged that Goslin followed a "Columbia cult of progressive educators" and indoctrinated "children on the collapse of our way of life." Allen Zoll, a veteran of Father Coughlin's Christian Front, led insurgencies against red-tinged educators. Protesters across the nation distributed his pamphlets: "Progressive Education Increases Juvenile Delinquency," "They Want Your Child!," and "How Red are the Schools?" The "only answer" to the education crisis, stated the Talmadge family's *Southern Conservative* newspaper, was "the election of real Americans to school boards." Although the National Education Association warned at its 1951 convention of right-wing "attacks on the public schools," conservatives lacked the means for controlling America's school boards.[32]

Conservative publicist Lucille Cardin Crain joined the struggle for the student mind after roiling women's groups in 1948 with her coauthored pamphlet "Packaged Thinking for Women," published by the National Industrial Conference Board, which J. Howard Pew largely financed. Crain arraigned "socialist planners" in Washington for packaging and disseminating a pink propaganda line to women's groups. In 1949 she launched the *Educational Reviewer* to judge whether textbooks stood "for or against our basic American social and political philosophy." She found that "wrongly slanted views" imposed by liberal bureaucrats pervaded texts in economics, political science, and history. The *Reviewer* "has been attacked so often," Crain said, "that it is apparent that there is a concerted drive on by the bureaucracy of the National Education Association to stamp out all criticism of anything the left-wingers in education choose to do."[33]

Oilman William F. Buckley Sr. spent more than $20,000 to float the *Reviewer,* which lacked paying subscribers or sponsors. "I have reached the point where I think that if capital is not interested in upholding our institutions," Buckley told Crain, "it is too much of a task for the rest of us to do the whole job." John T. Flynn agreed: "It horrifies me when I see the vast sums of money that pour out from foundations established by wealthy men into the hands not merely of socialists, but actually into the hands of Reds," whereas "dedicated men and women like Mrs. Crain go through agonies to meet pitiful little budgets." But "damning bad textbooks, as most of us do, has little value," conservative organizer Leonard Read said. "Writing new ones, good ones, to replace the bad ones is the only practical solution." After 1953 the *Reviewer* lived on as an empty shell, valuable only for its tax exemption.[34]

Crain inspired women to join the Minute Women of the U.S.A., founded in 1949 by sculptor Suzanne Silvercruys Stevenson and business executive Vivian Kellems, the organizer of the antitax Liberty Belles. The Minute Women defended the "inspired Americanism" that protected their sex. "In every country where freedoms are lost it is the women who pay the price," its newsletter warned. "Does anyone think for a minute that the Russian women under Soviet rule want to dig ditches" or that women would choose "the separation from family and the indignities and hardships of Communal living in Red China. Don't presume that 'it can't happen here.'"[35]

The nonpartisan Minute Women, in a departure from the past practice of conservative women's groups, encouraged Republican and southern Democratic women to seek public office. The group called upon parents to protect their children by flushing radicals from the schools and urged government to follow "just plain 'good housekeeping'" by cutting taxes, spending, and bureaucracy. It stayed "loosely organized and flexible, thereby giving maximum freedom of operation with minimum opportunity of infiltration." President Suzanne Stevenson appointed all officers and operated free of bylaws. Members circulated a newsletter, mailed out chain letters, and used telephone networks to call meetings and lobby officials. Stevenson left the Minute Women in 1952 to form a new political party, the Constitution Party, which she soon disavowed in a row over its anti-Semitism. Several hundred thousand mostly middle-class white women likely participated in Minute Women activities during the 1950s. To win back the schools, the women wrote letters, distributed Zoll's pamphlets, bought radio time, and ran for local office, often concealing their organizational ties. Their newsletter asked members to challenge schools that were teaching "'one worldism,' 'internationalism,' and exploiting the idea of a purely worldly 'brotherhood of man.'" In Houston, the Minute Women elected several school board members, who instigated the firing of the deputy superintendent of schools. Racked by internal strife and ignored by conservative men, the movement faded away during the 1960s.[36]

In higher education, conservatives hoped to reassert orthodoxy in economics and culture by replacing academic freedom with the corporate model of control by managers and board members. "The Board of Directors lays down the policy in a corporation," wrote J. Howard Pew. "In a college, the Board of Trustees should lay down the policy and all the members of the faculty should carry out that policy." At his personally financed Grove City College, Pew said, "Chapel is compulsory, Bible is taught; academic freedom as practiced is not tolerated." Princeton alumnus and industrialist J. P. Seiberling joined other executives in urging universities to cease the "teaching of socialism under the protection of so-called 'academic freedom,'" and to "begin to educate young people into American concepts and American ideas" that were not "watered down by foreign isms, including internationalism."[37]

This critique of academic freedom gained prominence through *God and Man at Yale* (1951) by the precocious William F. Buckley Jr., a recent Yale graduate whose father had bankrolled Crain. Buckley claimed to have uncovered "one of the most extraordinary incongruities of our time: the institution [Yale] that derives its moral and financial support from Christian individualists and then addresses itself to the task of persuading the sons of these supporters to be atheistic socialists." Buckley argued that a few elite liberals suppressed the values of a conservative majority among alumni and trustees. He called for "value orthodoxy" to uphold the Christian and capitalist traditions to which the vast majority of trustees and alumni subscribed. A counterattack by the Yale establishment gave Buckley instant celebrity and launched the first conservative star since Charles Lindbergh. Later, Buckley extended his critique to all secular thought that subjugated humanity to scientific control. He wrote, "The profound crisis of our era is, in essence, the conflict between the Social Engineers, who seek to adjust mankind to conform with 'scientifically'-calculated utopias, and the disciples of Truth, who defend the organic moral order."[38]

THE CONSERVATIVE BRIGADE

After World War II, established organizations of the right continued their campaigns to oppose communism and defend private enterprise and white Protestant values. Examples included George Benson's Harding College operation and revived versions of the Church League of America, the Committee for Constitutional Government, American Women Against Communism, the Daughters of the American Revolution, and the American Legion.

New players also joined the conservative brigade. Chinese textile importer Alfred Kohlberg became a fierce advocate for Chiang Kai-shek's anticommunist Nationalists in China and an early proponent of the domino theory, which warned that unchecked communism in Asia would eventually reach America's coastline. Kohlberg charged that America's most important think tank on Asian issues, the Institute for Pacific Relations, served as a red front. In 1946 he launched and funded his own organization, the American China Policy Association, adorned with a letterhead of prominent conservatives and backed by Chiang's government. Unlike the Institute for Pacific Relations, Kohlberg's group did not sponsor scholarship, but it did issue press releases that analyzed Asian events and American policy from his perspective. Kohlberg also claimed to have founded the largely symbolic China Lobby, which was not a formal organization but a loose coalition of former military officers, Christian missionaries, members of Congress, academics, and independent anticommunist leaders (including some liberals) who militantly opposed communism in Asia. Although larger forces drove American policy in Asia, pressure from the more conservative backers of the China Lobby helped discredit State Department and Foreign Service officials who suggested accommodation with communists in Asia.[39]

Kohlberg also fought communism at home. In 1946, with funding from J. Howard Pew and Jasper Crane, Kohlberg revived the conservative periodical *Plain Talk* to promote his anticommunist beliefs. The following year, he funded American Business Consultants, a private company that was run by three former FBI agents to expose subversives, including those "who disguise themselves as liberals." Following Harry Jung's model, the firm rummaged for radicals in publications, membership rolls, fundraising lists, and petitions. In 1950 American Business Consultants extended Hollywood's blacklist to the broadcast media. Its publication *Red Channels* listed 151 alleged communists and sympathizers in radio and television, including such well-known performers and writers as Edward G. Robinson, Orson Welles, Leonard Bernstein, Dorothy Parker, and Lillian Hellman. Even stripper Gypsy Rose Lee made the list. In 1948 Kohlberg founded the American Jewish League Against Communism to prove that Jews could clean their own house of sedition. According to board member and conservative political commentator George Sokolsky, however, the league was Jewish in name only and had more support from Christians than from Jews.[40]

The anticommunist movement united conservative Protestants with Catholics. Cardinal Francis Spellman of New York, auxiliary bishop Fulton Sheen of New York, and editor Patrick Scanlon of the *Brooklyn Tablet* crusaded against communism as a more dire threat to Christianity than fascism. Father John Cronin of the National Catholic Welfare Conference wrote an influential internal report on American communism for U.S. bishops in 1945. It drew on unverified information from raw FBI files that Bureau officials had released to the author. Cronin later worked in secret as the primary speechwriter for Vice President Richard Nixon. Bishop Sheen became the most widely viewed television preacher in the 1950s, drawing audiences as large as thirty million per week for his program *Life Is Worth Living*. He marketed anticommunism as proof that Catholicism and loyal Americanism fit together and gained recognition for converting notable Americans to Catholicism and conservative politics. Sheen's prominent converts included former communists editor Louis Budenz and attorney Bella V. Dodd, socialist journalist Heywood Broun, Henry Ford II, and Clare Boothe Luce. Grassroots Catholic groups pitched in to fight the reds, including the Catholic Daughters of the Americas, Catholic War Veterans, and the Blue Army of Our Lady of Fatima, which was dedicated to the Fatima prophecy that devotion and prayer would liberate Russia from communism. The Knights of Columbus sponsored anticommunist groups and the Association of Catholic Trade Unionists fought to purify the unions. The Catholic hierarchy mobilized priests to expose subversion in their communities, distribute patriotic literature, and teach anticommunism in parochial schools and youth organizations.[41]

Anticommunism, however, did not turn Catholics into Republicans. The first National Election Study in 1948 found that 65 percent of white Catholics but only 43 percent of white Protestants voted for President Truman. Neither did it mollify conservative Protestants who opposed liberal Catholic teachings on labor and welfare. "We are glad to see the Roman Catholic Church using its great influence against communism," said Jasper Crane. "It would be far better to work with [Catholics] and try to enlighten them further about the advantages of freedom." At its 1950 convention, the National Association of Evangelicals continued to criticize the "militant and aggressive tactics of the Roman Catholic hierarchy." It slipped derogatory references to Catholics into nearly every policy resolution. Fair employment laws, for example, "will open every business to the inroads of Communism and Roman Catholicism."[42]

Superrich Texas oilman and real estate investor H. L. Hunt joined the conservative movement in 1951. Although a gambler and multiple bigamist, this anti-pluralist ideologue preached evangelical piety and government-enforced morality. He backed Senator McCarthy and opposed unions, welfare programs, and the regulation of business. In 1951 Hunt formed the tax-exempt Facts Forum to fight radicalism by helping people to choose for themselves the "right" side of political issues. The forum's counselors included former America First leader Hanford MacNider, actor John Wayne, and retired generals Robert Wood and Albert Wedemeyer. Facts Forum organized discussion groups, sponsored debates, and circulated books. It aired a regular program on more than three hundred radio and several dozen television stations in which forum director Dan Smoot— a former FBI red hunter—summarized the conservative and liberal sides of controversial issues, but always with more verve for the conservative position. The forum broadcast Smoot's yearly "Hope of the World" sermon calling for national redemption through Christian faith and began issuing conservative editorials in December 1954. After Smoot left the Facts Forum in 1955, he gained a substantial following through his own television and radio broadcasts and his newsletter, the *Dan Smoot Report*.[43]

THE LEFT RESPONDS

President Truman joined the anticommunism crusade that burned through America during his first term. In 1947 he initiated a federal program to screen the loyalty of federal employees and list subversive organizations. For the first time, federal employment became explicitly conditional on political opinion. A year later, the Justice Department prosecuted leaders of the diminished and infiltrated Communist Party for sedition. Louis Budenz, testifying as an expert witness for the government, explained that reds turned words inside out through "Aesopian language, based on the well known writer of fables, Aesop" that had an innocent meaning for outsiders but also contained a hidden message for communist conspirators. The administration cosponsored a "Freedom Train" exhibit on patriotic Americanism. From late 1947 through January 1949, the train drew more than three million visitors as it rolled across thirty-five thousand miles of track and made three hundred stops in all forty-eight states.[44]

The postwar right found that, like the mythical soldiers who sprang from kernels of corn, warriors of the left kept on coming. Liberals endorsed anticommunism by forming Americans for Democratic Action (ADA) in 1947. The ADA upheld what historian and cofounder Arthur Schlesinger Jr. called a "vital center" liberalism to contain communism, achieve liberal reform, and elect Democrats. When conservatives said that religion sustained freedom, the ADA responded by saying that poverty bred communism and freedom flourished in economically secure, open societies. Although the ADA's membership hovered at below fifty thousand during its first fifteen years, it exploited an extensive network of scholars, journalists, public officials, union leaders, and political activists. Liberals successfully defused anticommunism as an issue through the 1948 elections; polls rated both parties equally in handling the internal communist threat.[45]

Conservatives, however, believed that communists exploited the freedom available in American society. Like liberals during the Nazi era, conservatives argued that it was better to tread the edges of civil liberties than let subversives erode American liberty and security. Conservative columnist David Lawrence, the founder of *U.S. News & World Report*, compared "the tactics used in ferreting out the subversives" to "bombing military targets—it is too bad if some of the civilians near the military installations get hurt, but they have no business being there . . . no business getting mixed up with subversive groups at all." Moreover, liberals who had propagated the brown scare in the 1940s voiced "not a single criticism at precisely the same type of congressional inquiries . . . when the New Deal was benefiting from those investigations politically."[46]

In the best-selling *The Road Ahead* (1949), journalist John T. Flynn warned, "If every Communist in America were rounded up and liquidated, the great menace to our form of social organization would still be with us." Flynn popularized the term "creeping socialism" to describe the intentions of liberals who never "pronounce in public the word socialism" but were copying "the plan by which England was sneaked into socialism." Although American liberals rejected European-style labor parties and social democracy, Truman's Democrats advocated national health insurance, antidiscrimination laws, housing programs, and federal aid to education. Republican strategist Arthur Summerfield agreed that Truman was following "exactly the pattern of the Fabian Socialists in Britain who forty years ago deliberately mapped a campaign to introduce socialism in Britain piece by piece, not under socialist labels (because they knew the British people did not want socialism) but, as in America today, in the guise of reform." Senator Taft warned, "Most people do not realize what Truman's program would actually mean. . . . We would have a socialist government, even more extreme than that in England." The Southern States Industrial Council began a "Socialism vs. Freedom" campaign to detach preachers and educators from the "British-style socialism of the Democratic Party." In a rare transatlantic gesture, Merwin Hart of the National Economic Council imported British author Cecil Palmer for a lecture tour to give Americans his "exceedingly grim account of nearly 4 years of Socialism in practice [and] to show that a good Christian and a good socialist don't add up."[47]

THE BRAINS OF THE RIGHT

In 1944 economist Friedrich A. Hayek's book *The Road to Serfdom*, an everyman's version of Austrian school free market economics, became a surprise best seller, heralding a wave of conservative scholarship. Like the National Association of Manufacturers in the 1930s, Hayek extolled the virtues of free enterprise. He argued that government intervention could not correct imperfections in markets. Any government control over spontaneous, free competition sent nations down "the road to serfdom" that ended in fascism or communism. The book's economics would have seemed commonplace to Adam Smith, and its politics to Calvin Coolidge, but its huge success showed that conservatives could best liberals on their home turf— the battlefield of the mind. Yet Hayek resisted efforts to brand him as a conservative, which he identified (incorrectly) with the defense of the status quo. As a believer in the creative, transforming power of markets, he preferred to identify with nineteenth-century liberals.

After the war, Henry Regnery formed a publishing company for conservative authors who were rebuffed by mainstream houses. Like communists who "used books as a part of their propaganda," Regnery would "use books to woo and win the 'masses' as part of our Cold War program." He hoped to reach "the small minority who control the communication of ideas . . . the people who, in a sense, 'run the world.'" Regnery published William F. Buckley Jr., Russell Kirk, Willmoore Kendall, Richard Weaver, Whittaker Chambers, Felix Morley, and Louis Budenz. "Regnery is doing a yeoman job in publishing books of the kind we like," said Sterling Morton. Other conservative publishers included Devin-Adair and Caxton Press. Intellectual historian Richard Weaver's 1948 book *Ideas Have Consequences,* a complement to Hayek's celebration of markets, impressed conservatives with its defense of Western traditions and eternal values.[48]

Russell Kirk's 1953 book *The Conservative Mind* gave conservative ideology a historical sweep and intellectual grandeur. Kirk was not the right's creative Dr. Johnson, but rather its Boswell—the man who brought conservative ideas into mainstream thought. Kirk proposed "six canons of conservative thought" that tacitly fused Hayek and Weaver, although he discussed neither man's work in his book. Conservatives, he said, believed in divine rule, the connection between private property and freedom, and the value of order, tradition, and classes. Conservatives opposed social engineering, efforts to achieve "equality of condition," and the supposition that all change was positive. According to Chrysler executive B. E. Hutchinson, business conservatives recognized that Kirk lacked economic expertise, but they still endorsed "the moral and spiritual principles to which he subscribes [as] those which furnished the foundations upon which our capitalistic system was built." These principles, Hutchinson said, are "disregarded in all the collectivistic philosophy which undergirds Communism, Socialism, Fascism, and, last but not least, our own 'New Deal.'"[49]

With less fanfare, conservative thinkers also produced weighty scholarly works that influenced the right for decades to come. For example, *The New Science of Politics* that political philosopher Eric Voegelin published in 1952 rejected the idea that political science could model itself on natural sciences such as physics and chemistry. Voegelin upheld instead the importance of spiritual life for human communities and attacked the philosophical roots of secular social engineering and its extreme expression in revolutionary movements. A year later, pioneering sociologist Robert A. Nisbet published *The Quest for Community: A Study in the Ethics of Order and Freedom.* It called for a restoration of community, social order, and voluntary associations such as the family, the church, and civic groups, which he argued were eroding because of dependence on the state.

In 1946 Leonard Read, former general manager of the Los Angeles Chamber of Commerce, launched the Foundation for Economic Education (FEE) to educate opinion makers on the merits of free market economics and Christian morality. The FEE opposed minimum wages, social security, labor legislation, protective tariffs, and foreign policies such as the Marshall Plan that expanded the size and scope of government. In one of its first publications, a pamphlet called "Roofs or Ceilings?," future Nobel laureates Milton Friedman and George J. Stigler skewered the practice of rent control. Most of the nearly $300,000 that FEE spent during its first five years came from tax-deductible contributions by electric utilities, extractive industries (including Pew's Sun Oil), and steel and automotive companies. The FEE evoked Christian principles and economic efficiency in defense of free markets. Read agreed with board member Jasper Crane that "we are going to be beaten if we rely entirely on the argument of dollars and cents." Instead they needed to "extol liberty as a spiritual thing." Read added that freedom necessarily derived from a "spiritual premise." The Reverend Edmund A. Opitz, a former staff member of Spiritual Mobilization who wrote essays for FEE that challenged social gospel theology, said, "Such political freedom as we know, or have known, stems from Christianity."[50]

To remedy the right's parochialism, Friedrich Hayek formed an international organization in 1947 known as the Mont Pelerin Society (the society's leaders named it after the site of their first meeting in the Swiss Alps). Scholars, businessmen, and a few policy makers attended its annual meetings. The society promoted both "absolute moral standards" and "private property and the competitive market." It advocated the deregulation of industry and finance, the privatization of state functions, and free trade as a means for liberating the market economy, promoting the common good, and avoiding dictatorship. The Mont Pelerin Society sponsored studies showing that resistance to communism in free nations weakened as labor and left-wing reformers gained power. American members included Leonard Read, J. Howard Pew and Jasper Crane, Milton Friedman and George Stigler, James Ingebretsen of Spiritual Mobilization, Howard Kershner of the Christian Freedom Foundation, and several officials of the Volker Fund. Yet the society did not hold its first American meeting until 1958, in part because it lacked funds to cover the expenses of European members. Crane took the lead in raising from his business contacts the funds needed to hold the American meeting.[51]

Ironically, in the midst of this intellectual ferment, literary critic Lionel Trilling wrote in 1950 that conservatives did not "express themselves in ideas but only in action or in irritable mental gestures which seek to resemble ideas." Remarkably, some scholars have cited this unfounded observation to prove the supposed feebleness of the postwar right. Also in the 1950s, sociologist Daniel Bell and historian Richard Hofstadter belittled the right in their book *The New American Right* (1955) by contending that America's grass roots swarmed with paranoid and irrational "pseudo-conservatives" out of step with modern life. Although this work influenced interpretations of the right for a generation, it missed the right's positive agenda, its broad popular appeal and intellectual heft, and its directorship by many of the nation's accomplished leaders of business, religion, and politics.[52]

THE STRUGGLE FOR POLITICAL ACTION

After World War II General Robert Wood proposed to remedy the lack of political action groups on the right. He founded American Action, through which he would lead America First veterans into the breach again to "defeat the announced plan of the radical minority groups to capture and control the 1946 Congress." This activist organization would not depend on "a group of men in New York, Chicago, or Boston" to churn out publicity. It would "originate in grass roots" and achieve "local organization in fifty congressional districts" to influence elections. American Action failed in its quest for grassroots support. The group struggled against charges of isolationism and extremism, lagged in fund-raising and recruitment, made no mark on the 1946 elections, and disappeared.[53]

William Anderson, the head of the American Christian Alliance, proposed more boldly to Republican leaders and financiers in 1946 that the party should formulate plans for mobilizing "the Protestant Church 'constituency'" behind Republican candidates. He argued that the "blindness and folly" of the GOP in failing to rally this natural voting bloc for the party of anticommunism, private enterprise, and traditional values would "lose it a victory in 1948 which ought to be easy." Anderson proposed a "broad, permanent, educational project" that would rally churchgoers to register and vote. Republicans should not "run the risk of 'betting' that the party can win without stirring up the support of this church element." RNC chair B. Carroll Reece endorsed the plan, but Anderson lacked the credibility and connections to win over the moneymen. After Republicans lost the 1948 elections, Anderson claimed vindication for his ideas and said that the party would return to glory only when it ceased to treat the church constituency "with indifference and contempt."[54]

The experience of Spiritual Mobilization showed the difficulties of mobilizing ministers for political action. An internal report found that ministers responded positively to the group's message that "a loss of faith in God and individual salvation" had led to both communist dictatorships and the fallacies of secular liberal reform in the United States. But the report lamented the lack of "strong and able ministers" to deliver the message. "The dearth is particularly in QUANTITY, but also in QUALITY." Most of the group's two thousand collaborating ministers "have done little or nothing for the program." Spiritual Mobilization faced "a tremendous challenge [in] awakening ministers to their task and responsibility [because] many ministers in America are enamored of humanistic purposes and objectives, and have an inadequate understanding of the true nature of our business and labor and other economic problems." Moreover, "Spiritual Mobilization as a movement is mistrusted by most of the ministers as a possible fascist movement, using the church as a front behind which to save the entrenched employer interests, and BIG BUSINESS." Spiritual Mobilization survived as an organization for nearly thirty years after its founding in 1935. However, it faded in the late 1950s and disappeared unnoticed in the early 1960s.[55]

In turn, businessmen feared that a contribution to Spiritual Mobilization was "sure to be dubbed 'propaganda' and business will be charged to have ulterior motives in attempting to sell the American Way of Life though Ministers," said Don Mitchell, president of Sylvania Electric Products. B. E. Hutchinson plumbed more deeply, writing to Pew, "Our only real hope for salvation lies in a spiritual regeneration of our society, in a 'revival.'" But "we are 'executives' at heart and naturally turn to the tools of our trade. We try to hire someone, a Fifield, a Kiroak, a Peale to expertise the job as professionals in the field of spiritual activity." Yet "what we seek to accomplish is not susceptible to organizational treatment because it is the most intensely personal individual thing there is—the relationship of a man himself with his God."[56]

Reverend Peale's magazine *Guideposts* took a less transparently political approach. In a fund-raising letter, Peale said that with the advent of Cold War, "No business will be worth anything if Christian civilization is not maintained . . . the issue is Christianity or catastrophe—Christianity or Communism." Donors responded positively and the magazine's circulation soared to three hundred thousand by 1950. Eventually its circulation reached five million, topping all religious magazines. It is unclear, however, whether its stories of personal inspiration—a *Reader's Digest* of the Christian right—met the political objectives of its corporate sponsors.[57]

THE SURPRISE ELECTION

In 1948 conservatives yearned for a candidate worthy of a presidency they would surely inherit after deposing the unpopular Truman. "The Republican Party must win [in 1948] or I fear that America is lost," wrote Ohio senator John Bricker. With conservatives' perennial favorite Senator Robert Taft languishing in the preprimary presidential polls, some on the right turned again to the enigmatic white knight General Douglas MacArthur. "We may win in 1948 under our present leadership, but I doubt it," former RNC chair John Hamilton wrote. MacArthur, however, was different. "I sense and believe, as do thousands of Americans, that in General MacArthur's heart he is fighting a Holy War—that he leads a modern crusade." MacArthur Clubs sprang up around the country and President Truman took the general's Caesarian potential seriously enough to write that if MacArthur made "a Roman Triumphal return to the U.S. a short time before the Republican Convention" he would retire and offer the Democratic nomination to another general: Dwight Eisenhower. MacArthur's admirers waited in vain for their Godot. The general spurned his own advice that "the first principle of politics, as of war, is to win" and refused to leave his command post in Japan and become an announced presidential candidate unless he received "a mandate from a large section of the American people."[58]

The Republican nomination turned on a few primaries, which went poorly for conservatives. Former Minnesota governor Harold Stassen defeated the absentee MacArthur in the general's home state of Wisconsin, ending a campaign that never began. Taft lost to Stassen in Nebraska and barely beat him in Ohio, another reminder of the conventional wisdom that "Taft can't win." Stassen lost to the 1944 nominee Tom Dewey in Oregon. When Republicans convened in June, only Dewey's résumé included strong poll numbers, credible primary results, and national campaign experience. He won a third ballot nomination and then spurned the right's choice for vice president—House Majority Leader Charles Halleck of Indiana—to fashion a dream ticket of two governors: Dewey of New York and Earl Warren of California.

The most divisive issue in 1948 was not communism but race, which divided Democrats of the North and South. The smoldering discontent of southern Democrats flamed into revolt after President Truman's message to Congress in February 1948 proposed the most ambitious civil rights program in the history of the Democratic Party. Later that year, Truman issued executive orders that desegregated the armed forces and the federal civilian workforce. Clark Clifford's strategy memo for the 1948 campaign had advised the president to counter Republican efforts to win back the black vote. He said that the resulting "difficulty with our Southern friends . . . is the lesser of two evils." The South would not likely vote Republican, and populous northern states, which had large numbers of black and white liberal voters, were far more important to the president's reelection than smaller states of the South.[59]

Southern Democrats charged Truman with breaking the compact that let white supremacists rule Dixie in return for delivering bloc votes to Democrats. Georgia senator Richard Russell, their tacit leader, warned against tampering with "States' rights and white supremacy," which were the basis of "Southern devotion to the Democratic Party." He added that a "federal Gestapo" was poised to deploy "every power of the Federal Government . . . to destroy segregation and compel intermingling and miscegenation of the races in the South." The Democratic Convention rejected Russell's last-minute candidacy for president after delegates had replaced a bland compromise plank on civil rights with a bold declaration proposed by the Minneapolis mayor Hubert Humphrey. Yet Russell and most of his southern congressional colleagues declined to desert their party. They knew that after 1948 they would either dominate a new Democratic Congress or reshape a party out of power.[60]

Local politicians, led by governors Fielding L. Wright of Mississippi, Ben T. Laney of Arkansas, and J. Strom Thurmond of South Carolina, organized the campaign to challenge Truman's Democrats. Shortly after the Democratic Convention concluded in July, an informal convention of six thousand self-selected states' rights Democrats nominated Thurmond as the presidential candidate of a newly formed States' Rights Party, which the press dubbed "Dixiecrats" over Thurmond's objection. Across the South, crowds waving Confederate flags heralded another regional revolt. Although known as a moderate, Thurmond led a white supremacist campaign to preserve "the racial integrity and purity of the White and Negro races." Yet Thurmond, who had concealed a mixed-race daughter he had fathered in 1925, knew better than most that segregation was a porous barrier to interracial sex. Rather than advocating open racism, however, Thurmond focused instead on states' rights, although locals in South Carolina noted the contradiction with his support for Prohibition, federal aid to education, and federal projects in his state.[61]

Thurmond's campaign, even spiced with a familiar conservative scolding of reds, pinks, and labor racketeers, gripped only the South. Steep barriers to ballot access by third parties kept voters from punching the Thurmond ticket except in North Dakota and southern states. Thurmond won 2.5 percent of the popular vote and electoral votes from four Deep South states where Dixiecrats ran the Democratic machine.

Truman also faced an insurgency from his left, led by Henry Wallace, who he had fired as secretary of commerce. In a campaign that Truman and ADA liberals damned as communist-controlled, Wallace vowed to discard America's "militarist and imperialist" foreign policy. He urged the United States to stop propping up foreign dictators, to support international control of atomic energy, and to cooperate economically with the Soviet Union. But Wallace won only 2.5 percent of the popular vote, below the threshold needed to turn urban states against the president or to demonstrate public enthusiasm for his foreign policy views.

Convinced that he could fly on autopilot to victory, Dewey replayed his "peanut politics" of 1944. Many Republicans objected post hoc, but not

E. F. Hutton, who urged Dewey in late September to "take off the kid gloves and start to slug." Hutton advised, "Against a man armed with brass knuckles, well schooled in the art of eye-gouging, biting, and kicking, it is a poor judgment to defend oneself with a powder-puff. The time has come to nail the lies, refute the slander and hit back." Dewey brushed aside such truculence, secure in the assurance of the pollsters and pundits that he was a certain winner in November. When early returns confirmed expectations by favoring Dewey, the headlines of several newspapers echoed the page-one banner of the *Chicago Tribune:* DEWEY DEFEATS TRUMAN. Americans awoke to a different reality, however. Truman took 49.5 percent to Dewey's 45.1 percent in the popular vote and won nearly 60 percent of the Electoral College. Democrats also regained control of Congress; the party gained seventy-five House and nine Senate seats, enough to give the Democrats control of 60 percent of House seats and 56 percent of Senate seats. Every piece of the mosaic designed by Truman's advisers fell into place. Truman reactivated the Roosevelt coalition, retaining 89 percent of FDR's 1944 vote, according to the National Election Study. Except for Thurmond's four states, Truman swept the South and garnered most of the national black vote, which provided the margin he needed for paper-thin victories in Illinois and Ohio. Truman lost New York but won California, confounding Dewey's dream ticket.[62]

When Thurmond's followers awoke from their sugarplum dreams of unmaking the president and remaking the South, they stumbled back into politics as usual. The states' rights movement neither bonded with northern conservatives nor made Dixie the fulcrum of power between the major parties. Southern Democrats in Congress slid back into committee chairs and Thurmond walked out of the dying States' Rights Party and back into his Democratic home, winning a Senate seat on a write-in vote in 1954. The Dixiecrat revolt, however, heightened the siege mentality of the white South, making defense of the color line a patriotic duty. In 1950 voters dismissed the Senate's most liberal southerners: Claude Pepper of Florida and Frank Graham of North Carolina. A young radio reporter named Jesse Helms helped white supremacist challenger Willis Smith defeat Graham in the Democratic primary. Helms's campaign work earned him time in Washington as Smith's administrative assistant. Dixiecrat sentiments reemerged nationwide in what the *Washington Post* headlined in 1951 as "Dixie mania," symbolized by a craze for the Confederate flag and culture. "The growing popularity of the Confederate Flag throughout the Nation is amazing," Thurmond wrote in a local paper that year. The flag represented "not only the lofty and high principles for which the South fought the War Between the States, but is also an emblem of resentment to the socialistic trend of Truman and his cohorts."[63]

Although northern conservatives declined to lose with Thurmond, they still opposed civil rights measures, especially a federal Fair Employment Practices Commission (FEPC) with binding enforcement powers. Conservatives warned against federal programs that granted special privileges for minorities, imposed burdens on business, and helped the reds by intensifying racial tension in the United States. Merwin Hart of the National Economic Council advised "personal conversation, and the quiet use of personal Christian influence" on race matters. "Bills like the FEPC and the anti-discrimination laws are of communist origin," he said. George Washington Robnett of the Church League of America decried "minorityism" as "a new national disease that has grown of New Deal Marxism," pitting "race against race—and group against group." Publisher Henry Regnery said that civil rights bills were "intended only to create trouble. It is high time that politicians, in seeking votes, give attention to the 80 percent or more of the voters rather than to the 10 percent or 15 percent of organized minorities." Sterling Morton objected to "forcing Negroes into a factory against the wishes and protests of persons employed there." If Negroes and Jews "would spend half as much time improving their manners as they do in complaining of discrimination, they would have much less discrimination to complain of."[64]

Journalist George Schuyler, America's most noted black conservative, opposed coercive civil rights laws that he said played into the hands of communists. He trusted African-American progress to the workings of the market economy and the nation's traditions "of individual initiative and decentralized authority." Already, he said, blacks had made "unprecedented economic, social, and educational progress" in the United States. Schulyer delivered these remarks to the 1950 Congress of Cultural Freedom in Berlin, which the CIA financed to showcase anticommunist intellectuals. The *Congressional Quarterly,* the *Freeman,* the *Christian Science Monitor,* and *Reader's Digest* reprinted his speech. Schuyler later opposed civil rights legislation of the 1960s.[65]

Conservative Republican politicians joined the chorus of opposition to civil rights initiatives that burdened their business allies. "I am in favor of working toward the elimination of racial discrimination," said GOP senator Karl Mundt of South Dakota, "but I am not in favor of the particular bill for an F.E.P.C. That was a sly New Deal trick to set up a new political bureau and give it control over every employer in America." George Hansen, chair of the Republican Party's Subcommittee on Civil Rights, reported in 1949, "We have not tried to establish any policies as to civil rights. . . . I question whether legislation is going to be the effective way of determining civil rights." Senator Taft, who had backed laws to end lynching and poll taxes, said, "I have always been opposed to the F.E.P.C. because it would impose a complete government regulation on all employment. . . . The fundamental issue between the Parties is whether more and more totalitarian control shall be centered in Washington, or whether liberty shall be restored the individual and his local government." Taft opposed "compulsory federal action, which, I think, in the end will do more harm than good to the Negro race." Within the states, Republicans in positions of power often blocked the passage of fair employment practices legislation.[66]

SNATCHING BACK VICTORY

"The result of the [1948] election is a tragedy," Taft wrote to Charles Paul, who had managed his 1948 primary campaign in Washington State. "Now we have to begin all over again and the New Deal has taken on a new crusading spirit." Corporate leaders lamented that their spending on opinion engineering had failed its sternest test. Business seemed more skilled in selling chewing gum than in selling itself to a public skeptical of self-serving claims. According to a 1949 Roper Poll, 77 percent of Americans agreed that big corporations usually understated their profits to fool the public. Dean James E. McCarthy of Notre Dame University's College of Commerce said that the business community's "dull" propaganda failed "to dispel the fog of suspicion and distrust in which he has been forced to operate." Management consultant Peter Drucker wrote of botched efforts at "changing the thinking of the employee." E. F. Hutton scorned business publicity for its "conference room language" rather than "words that bounce along the sidewalk." Former NAM president Robert Lund lamented "that the believers in free enterprise have such poor success in informing the public. The wild-eyed radicals leave us badly in the dust." Undaunted, business would continue its salesmanship and attempt to sharpen its marketing techniques.[67]

Rather than pondering the paradox of losing both northern blacks and southern whites in 1948, Republicans contrived the myth of the sleeping conservative voter. The Dewey campaign "gave a sleeping pill to Republican voters. It was a campaign lacking in courage and calculated only to arouse indifference," said GOP leader Clarence Budington Kelland. "Truman won by default of an expected 6 to 8 million not showing up," agreed Marrs McLean, vice chair of the Republican Finance Committee. Taft vowed to awaken the right in the next presidential election by vanquishing what adviser Tom Curtis termed "the 'liberal' internationalist establishment," and its "me-too" candidates who defeated "the true liberals to whom I suppose the word conservative would more aptly apply these days."[68]

Political analyst J. Harvie Williams circulated a memo among Republican activists in 1950 that exploded the myth of sleeping conservative voters by showing that low turnout in recent national elections correlated with areas of Democratic not Republican strength. It showed that the GOP could reign again as America's majority party only by uniting conservatives North and South. Otherwise, it would remain "a *national-minority party*" because even in the North it held sway only "outside the big cities." Republicans could not make opposites attract with both the conservative countryside and the liberal cities in the North. Instead, Republicans could become the nation's majority party again only by cementing their "informal alliance" with southern Democrats. "The whole future of the United States," he said, depended on efforts to convert conservative white southern Democrats into Republicans.[69]

After reading Williams's memo, Senator Mundt of South Dakota vowed to "curb the growing trend toward socialism by bringing together the people of the North and the South who think alike on so many issues." He worried that Democrats would continue to win elections by combining "electoral votes that they need from the South on the basis of tradition, habit, and prejudice" with northern votes from "corrupt political machines, labor unions and left-wing pressure groups." If that happened, the country would "follow Britain into Fabian socialism." In 1951 Mundt recruited women of Pro-America to canvass the South and published a newsletter targeted to southern Democrats. He launched a media blitz and recruited Republican and Democratic conservatives for a Committee to Explore Political Realignment. Former conservative Democrat Samuel

Pettengill hailed Mundt's antidote to "the suicidal policy of the GOP high command in constantly sticking harpoons into the South to appease minority groups in northern states, which they have generally lost any way."[70]

Mundt's committee, however, included no southern Democrats and missed the point made by former governor of Texas Dan Moody, who said that the GOP would fail in its efforts to convert southern Democrats because "all contests for local offices are settled in the Democratic primary elections" and no politician would voluntarily surrender power. The committee closed shop before the 1952 primaries. Its conservative leadership feared that efforts to win over southern Democrats might help the moderate Dwight Eisenhower, who was popular in the South, defeat their preferred candidate, Senator Taft. "I have always thought it was an appalling mistake to close up that 'realignment committee,'" *Human Events* editor Frank Hanighen said. "His backers were afraid it would compromise Taft's chances of getting the Southern delegates in the convention."[71]

Republican moderates countered Mundt by again calling for a liberalized party. In 1949 so-called young Turks in the Senate challenged the leadership of Senator Taft—"the symbol of reaction"—in the words of Senator Irving Ives of New York. Their failure did not discourage *Fortune* editor Russell W. Davenport from launching the Republican Advance, a "middle way" educational organization of liberal and moderate Republicans whose aim was to "*combine* the goals of what has come to be known as the Welfare State with the goals of ethical individualism." For Davenport, the European experience warned not of creeping socialism but of dangerously polarized politics. "Nothing could be more politically bankrupt than the Republican attitude, that whatever the Democrats propose must be opposed, regardless of its merits," Davenport wrote to moderate Republican senator John Sherman Cooper of Kentucky. Rather, "the genius of our political system lies in the fact that on *most* issues *both* parties *agree*. Were this not so we should be torn apart by fundamental political differences; or driven into a state of political trauma like that of France." However, middle way politics lacked the fire needed to convert voters of either the left or the right. Davenport's boss, publisher Henry Luce, told Davenport that his group of "liberal Republicans" had failed to come up with ideas that caught "my eye, ear or imagination." Davenport's nascent movement collapsed into the Eisenhower for president campaign in 1952; if the middle way could not sell itself, perhaps a war hero could do so. Davenport advised Eisenhower: "I do think that it is perhaps unnecessary, from now on, to use the words 'Right' and 'Left' very much. Let's do away with these 'ideologies' and get down to brass tacks of doing things the way Americans do them."[72]

RESTORING AN INDEPENDENT RIGHT

After Truman's victory, conservative financier and Du Pont executive Jasper Crane began raising funds for creating the long-sought "high caliber journal of opinion" for conservatives. Herbert Hoover endorsed the project as "necessary if the kind of American civilization that we cherish is to survive." Crane worked on fund-raising with Alfred Kohlberg. They secured $150,000 in capital, a $100,000 pledge from J. Howard Pew, and backing from Inland Steel, Quaker Oats, and Sears, Roebuck. The new publication was named the *Freeman*, after a journal edited by classical liberal Albert Jay Nock from 1920 to 1924. It debuted in 1950 as a biweekly magazine with a base of five thousand subscriptions that Kohlberg transferred from his failed anticommunist publication *Plain Talk*. The editors of the *Freeman* pledged to uphold "the moral autonomy of the individual" and "economic liberty" while battling "communists, socialists, government planners, and other collectivists." They backed foreign peoples who opposed communism but not the "machinery of world organization." The *Freeman* disappointed conservatives. It put anticommunism above economics and suffered from internal dissension, editorial turnover, and lagging circulation. It lacked advertising revenue from an indifferent business community. In 1954 trustees sold the *Freeman* to the Foundation for Economic Education, which published the magazine monthly, with limited circulation.[73]

The right gained a toehold on American campuses in 1952 through the Intercollegiate Society of Individualists (ISI)—a conservative version of the Intercollegiate Society of Socialists. Frank Chodorov served as president and William F. Buckley Jr. as vice president. The Foundation for Economic Education and J. Howard Pew donated start-up funds, aided by Jasper Crane, the Volker Fund, and Spiritual Mobilization. ISI established a lecture bureau, organized discussion groups, and distributed conservative literature. Like the Foundation for Economic Education, the new society combined capitalist economics with Christian teachings. "Libertarianism divorced from basic Christian philosophy is inadequate to return America to its original course," wrote executive director E. Victor Milione. "I am thoroughly in accord with both." Rather than a vibrant on-campus presence, ISI became a one-man band run by Milione, who reported to Crane in 1959 that the group had only "eight fairly active chapters." It functioned mostly as a distribution center for literature sent to an eighty-five-hundred-person mailing list—the names on which Milione claimed as members. But Milione acknowledged to the financier, "I fear that conservatives, myself included, are in danger, at times, of succumbing to their own public relations releases, regarding their strength in numbers. . . . Considering that there are over 2,000 colleges in the nation with an enrollment of over 3,500,000 students and that the faculties of these schools are overwhelmingly 'liberal,' we are little more than a gnat on the backside of a horse."[74]

Evangelical Christianity reached secular campuses in 1951 when seminary student Bill Bright and his wife, Vonette Zachary Bright, founded a group called Campus Crusade for Christ. The Brights aimed to bring the gospel to places where "there were no waiting lines for preachers." The couple signed a "Contract with God" promising to be Christ's servants and began crusading at UCLA to convert "the world's leaders of the future." Bill Bright instructed Crusade workers not just to win souls for Christ but also to turn every initiate into a recruiter. The Crusade targeted male athletes and coaches in order to prove that Christianity was a manly, winning religion. Legendary Oklahoma football coach Bud Wilkinson told a thousand guests at a 1957 Crusade banquet, "The team that prays together plays together." In 1966 the Crusade formed Athletes in Action, a more activist version of the independent Fellowship of Christian Athletes, as a subsidiary organization. By then, the Campus Crusade had a hundred staffers working on forty campuses.[75]

Bright had big dreams of regenerating the nation and evangelizing the world. In 1956 he boiled down his message to the Four Spiritual Laws: that "God loves you and offers a wonderful plan for your life," that "man is sinful and separated from God," that "Jesus Christ is God's only provision for man's sins," and that "we must individually receive Jesus Christ as Savior and Lord." By revitalizing the faith, Bright expected to fight communism, defend marriage and private enterprise, and uphold traditional moral standards. By the early twenty-first century the Campus

Crusade claimed to have more than twenty-five thousand paid staff members serving in most countries worldwide. It also reported that its movie on the life of Christ, *The Jesus Film,* was viewed more than six billion times, thus apparently making it the most-watched movie in history.[76]

In 1949 E. F. Hutton put his money behind his ideology to found a group he called Freedoms Foundation, located at a property he owned in Valley Forge, Pennsylvania. Through this educational foundation, which Dwight Eisenhower and Herbert Hoover graced as honorary chair and president, respectively, Hutton hoped to combat what he called the "deodorized Communism" that left-wing educators taught from the grade schools to the colleges. Freedoms Foundation sponsored conferences and seminars and supported the work of patriotic scholars. But it devoted most of its resources to saving America the old-fashioned way, with cash doled out as awards to schoolchildren and ordinary citizens who demonstrated "a zeal for personal responsibility, and understanding, and belief in liberty." During the foundation's first fifteen years, it recognized some twelve thousand individuals, organizations, and communities out of a million-plus applicants for its awards.[77]

J. Howard Pew sustained a host of postwar enterprises. He made substantial contributions to *Plain Talk,* the *Freeman,* Spiritual Mobilization, the Intercollegiate Society of Individuals, the Foundation for Economic Education, and other conservative groups. He paid to produce and disseminate conservative literature and, in a rare gesture for a man of the right, he sustained a women's group, pouring some $20,000 into Cathrine Curtis's Women's Investors Research Institute. Pew financed books on American history and current affairs and scripts for the Protestant Film Commission, whose goal was to "make the influence of Protestant Christianity felt through the medium of the film." He funded a project of the National Industrial Conference Board for "an authoritative treatise [to] define liberty in spiritual terms as stemming from the teachings of Jesus." Most enterprises faltered, however, and Pew bemoaned the quality of products he had paid for and their failure to inspire everyday folk.[78]

Still, Pew waxed upbeat about financing a Christian right group, the Christian Freedom Foundation, which he founded in 1950 in collaboration with the Reverend Norman Vincent Peale. The foundation sought to reach "as large a number of ministers as possible who will subscribe to the general concept of freedom in all its parts, which of course comprehends economic freedom as well as the others." Howard Kershner, a conservative journalist, became its first president. Anti-pluralist white Protestant clergymen held every board position. The foundation's biweekly magazine *Christian Economics* stood for "free enterprise—the economic system with the least amount of government and the greatest amount of Christianity." Pew and his family paid to distribute *Christian Economics* to nearly a hundred thousand Protestant clergymen, few of whom paid the yearly voluntary fee of one dollar. At its peak in the early 1960s, the magazine also had a circulation of about an equal number of laypersons. The Pews covered most of the foundation's $430,000 first-year deficit and kept it breathing for more than twenty years with average annual donations of about $300,000. Pew monitored the contents of *Christian Economics*, sometimes disputing Kershner's views. Like Spiritual Mobilization, the Christian Freedom Foundation avoided theology, but combined "economic analysis [and] the relationship of that science to moral principles." Like Leonard Read, Kershner said, "The message of Jesus applies to economic law as well as to moral law—they both are God's law."[79]

VALIDATING ANTICOMMUNISM

In August 1949 the reds shattered containment and added half a billion people to their domain when Mao Tse-tung's armies defeated forces of the American-backed government of Chiang Kai-shek in China's civil war. Chiang evacuated his army and government to the offshore island of Taiwan. A month later, President Truman announced that Russia had broken America's monopoly on atomic weapons. By early 1950, 70 percent of American poll respondents agreed that Russia sought "to rule the world" and 52 percent expected another world war within ten years. More than 80 percent believed it was very important for the United States to contain communism.

For conservatives, these setbacks proved that lax or compromised Democratic governments had let the reds shape America's foreign policy and steal its secrets. "The Russians undoubtedly gained three to five years in producing the atomic bomb," said former FBI agent and Republican representative from Illinois Harold H. Velde. "American government for the last 15 years has had the official attitude, from the White House down, of being highly tolerant of and at times even sympathetic to the view of

Communists and fellow travelers." Further proof came in January 1950 when a jury convicted Alger Hiss of perjury, after the statute of limitations had expired on espionage. In 1948 ex-communist Whittaker Chambers had implicated Hiss as a Soviet spy during the 1930s. Hiss was the president of the Carnegie Endowment for International Peace. He was a graduate of Harvard Law School and a former State Department official who had accompanied FDR in 1945 to the Yalta Conference of allied leaders, which right-wing critics charged had sold out eastern Europe to the Soviets. Conservatives said that Hiss's conviction validated anticommunist investigations and established a link between domestic radicalism and Soviet expansionism. By making the Hiss case a personal vendetta, House Republican Richard M. Nixon became a national figure. In California's 1950 Senate election, Nixon defeated Democrat Helen Gahagan Douglas, the so-called pink lady, who he accused of appeasing communists.[80]

In February 1950, a month after Hiss's conviction, Senator McCarthy upped the ante of partisan anticommunism. In a speech delivered to the Republican Women's Club of Wheeling, West Virginia, McCarthy claimed that the American State Department was riddled with communists (although the precise number he cited remains a matter of dispute) who were passing secret information to the Soviet Union and undercutting American foreign policy. The "traitorous actions" of communists within American government, he said, were causing America to lose the "final, all-out battle between communistic atheism and Christianity." The traitors did not arise from among "the less fortunate or members of minority groups" but rather from the establishment of Wall Street, the Ivy League, and the big foundations. Like Hiss, these men "have had all the benefits that the wealthiest nation on earth has had to offer." McCarthy collaborated with Albert Kohlberg, conservative reporters and commentators, and newspaper barons such as Robert McCormick and William Randolph Hearst. The Catholic senator won the support of Cardinal Francis Spellman of New York, editor Patrick Scanlon of the *Brooklyn Tablet,* the Knights of Columbus, and most Catholic newspapers. A Gallup Poll in March 1950 found that Americans who believed McCarthy outnumbered those who thought he was "playing politics" by 50 percent to 29 percent.[81]

With Democrats in power, McCarthy served the interests of Republicans. Senator Taft advised McCarthy that "if one case didn't work . . . bring up another." Senator John Bricker of Ohio told McCarthy, "Joe, you're a dirty son of a bitch, but there are times when you've got to have a son of a bitch around, and this is one of them." McCarthy also had allies among leading conservative Democrats such as Representative John Rankin of Mississippi and Senator Pat McCarran of Nevada, both of whom had crusaded against alleged subversives within their own party long before McCarthy appeared on the scene.[82]

McCarran used his standing as chair of the Senate Internal Security Subcommittee to investigate subversives and steer antiradical laws through Congress. In 1950 Congress overrode Truman's veto and enacted the McCarran Internal Security Act, which required communist groups to register with the government, and authorized the president to intern suspected subversives during a national emergency. In response, FBI director Hoover compiled a list of some fourteen thousand potential detainees that included both Communist Party members and those with "anarchist or revolutionary beliefs" or former associations with communists. McCarran also won passage over Truman's veto of the McCarran-Walter Immigration and Nationality Act of 1952. The act authorized the exclusion or deportation of immigrant and visitor aliens with ideologies that purportedly threatened national security. It retained the quota system with preferences for western Europeans, but also established token quotas for Asians, defined by race and not nationality, and reserved slots for skilled workers and the immediate families of permanent alien residents. Most Republicans and southern Democrats in both Houses voted for the two bills, while most northern Democrats backed the president.[83]

Ironically, while McCarthy was charging the Truman administration as soft on communism, a special study group, chaired by Paul Nitze, the State Department's director of policy planning, was drafting National Security Council Report 68, which it delivered to the president in April 1950. NSC-68 called for stern and costly measures to counter the Soviet threat to America's national security. It did not rule out the possibility of "deliberate resort to war by the Soviet Union" and warned that the United States must attain military superiority, even at the cost of "significant domestic financial and economic adjustments." A study group of the Council on Foreign Relations similarly concluded: "We and our friends can make the Soviets respect our peaceful intent and moral purposes only by rapidly producing powerful military forces." Winning the Cold War, the group said, was worth the price of "definite recessions in our standard of living through payment of taxes, longer work hours, and military service" and at least a temporary "sacrifice of individual liberties."[84]

Two months after the completion of NSC-68, the armies of Communist North Korea invaded the American-backed South Korea. For President Truman, the conflict in Korea was not a civil war but Soviet imperialism that tested America's resolve to contain communism. Without authorization from Congress, but with the support of a UN Security Council Resolution, Truman dispatched American troops to bolster the retreating armies of South Korea. North Korean forces came close to winning their war of conquest when they drove the American and South Korean armies into a small defensive perimeter in the southeast corner of the Korean peninsula. After a daring amphibious landing behind enemy lines by General Douglas MacArthur freed a reinforced allied army to take the offensive, Truman revived the dream of rolling back communism by authorizing American forces to cross into North Korea. This incursion provoked the intervention of Chinese Communist troops, which pushed the allied forces back into South Korea. The combatants eventually fought to a standstill along the border between the two Koreas, at a cost of nearly fifty-five thousand American lives and likely millions of Asian lives.

In the 1950 midterm election, McCarthy stumped for Republicans in fifteen states. He joined other campaigners in blasting left-wing Democrats; bipartisan foreign policy became a victim of the campaign. Elizabeth Farrington, president of an increasingly conservative Federation of Republican Women, rallied women against the "Communist effort to destroy our Christian civilization." The American Medical Association (AMA) amassed a $3.6 million war chest to defeat Truman's plan for national health insurance, which its president, Dr. Elmer L. Henderson, called the "spearhead of socialism." The AMA ran ads on 353 radio stations, thirty magazines, and in every daily and weekly newspaper in America. Republicans cut the Democratic majority to thirty-six House members and two senators. President Truman said after the election, "We have got a peculiar situation in the Congress, a purported Democratic majority, yet we haven't got it." His aides identified eleven "Regressive Democrats" in the new Senate, nine from the South and two from the West, who "voted wrong more often than right." They identified thirty-three regressive House Democrats, all southerners. Only eight Senate and eleven House "Progressive Republicans" offset these defectors.[85]

The press credited McCarthy with defeating several Democratic senators, including Majority Leader Scott Lucas of Illinois, who lost to future Republican leader Everett Dirksen, and conservative Democrat Millard Tydings of Maryland, who chaired a subcommittee that called McCarthy's charges about communists in government "a fraud and a hoax." The *New York Times* noted that in the new Congress "McCarthyism is simply today a very considerable force . . . and it seems to be here to stay."[86]

In early 1951 a chastened president rejected General MacArthur's advice to abandon limited war and deploy American airpower against military bases in Communist China, blockade the Chinese coast, and unleash the armies of Chiang Kai-shek against southern China. Contrary to presidential directives, MacArthur publicly aired his views on both war strategy and foreign policy. On April 5, 1951, Republican House Minority Leader Joe Martin released nonconfidential correspondence from MacArthur that recommended following the "conventional pattern of meeting force with maximum counter-force" in Asia, where America was selflessly fighting "Europe's war. . . . If we lose the war in Asia the fall of Europe is inevitable."[87]

A week later President Truman fired MacArthur for insubordination and the general finally made his triumphal return home. Although conservatives still in transition from disengaged nationalism had yet to settle on fighting to victory anywhere in the world and MacArthur was a better general than he was a policy advocate, they presented him as living proof that liberal Democrats in Washington were too naive and compromised to thrash the reds. "After the tragic dismissal of General MacArthur," the Republican senator Harry Cain of Washington wrote, "the war was run, not by the heroic leaders who brought World War II to a victorious end but by the incompetent clique of presidential cronies and communist sympathizers who had so completely lost the peace." Senator Dirksen of Illinois added, "Never has anything so stirred the country as this inept dismissal of a big soldier by a little President." The National Association of Evangelicals commended MacArthur for his "example of Christian citizenship and moral and spiritual alertness." It praised "his understanding and insight of Communism . . . while others in high places have displayed their lack of understanding by their record of appeasement." Senator McCarthy ventured into swifter waters by charging Secretary of State Dean Acheson and Secretary of Defense George Marshall with complicity in a "great conspiracy" directed from Moscow: "A conspiracy on a scale so immense as to dwarf any previous such venture in the history of man."[88]

Contrarian thinker Lawrence Dennis belittled the idea that "Korea proves that FDR and Truman did not know how to handle Russia and were too much influenced by pinks on the inside." The Korean tragedy had deeper roots, he said. It "could not have been avoided once we were committed to unconditional surrender and the general ideology of religious war." Dennis's call for disengagement had some purchase among conservatives still wavering between retreat and apocalypse. Norman Thomas, an antiwar activist and former socialist candidate for president, observed that his onetime Republican allies in the America First Committee displayed "a curious reasoning that probably we should not have gone to war in Korea at all but that now we should have a war with China which somehow we can win by atom bombs and Chiang's troops." During the "great debate" over America's overseas obligations that took place in the winter of 1950–51, conservatives unsuccessfully opposed Truman's plan to reinforce American troop strength in Europe. Despite polls showing that most Americans put a higher priority on stopping communism in Europe than in Asia, conservatives dubious about presidential power challenged Truman's authority to commit American forces abroad. They questioned the costs of deployment and the wisdom of propping up foreigners reluctant to pay for their own defense.[89]

Still, in Senator McCarthy, conservatives had a champion who moved voters and frustrated liberals. Even mild Republican criticism of the senator stilled as the 1952 elections loomed. In a March 1952 poll, 54 percent of respondents agreed that infiltration of communists "into important government positions" was a strong reason for voting Republican. In September 74 percent agreed that America needed to "do a great deal more to clean out communists in the government."

VOTERS LIKE IKE

Dwight Eisenhower viewed his campaign for president in 1952 as another crusade for freedom. The general was not crusading against Democrats but against fellow Republican Robert Taft. Ike viewed a Taft presidency as a catastrophe that would undo the collective security measures that contained communism and deterred a third world war.

Taft and other disengaged Republican nationalists terrified Eisenhower and his advisers. Their mistakes included prewar isolationism and later opposition to the IMF and the World Bank, NATO, trade pacts, foreign loans, military and economic aid, and international troop commitments. In 1950 the GOP senator Henry Cabot Lodge Jr. of Massachusetts—later Eisenhower's campaign chair—had advised the general, "The neutralist and defeatist influence in the Republican Party might get so strong that it would be your duty to enter politics in order to prevent one of our great two Parties from adopting a course which could lead to national suicide." A year later, Lodge reiterated, "The arguments which were persuasive then are a great deal more persuasive now." An Eisenhower campaign memo titled "Demolish the Enemy" noted, "If Taft had been president, we wouldn't have to worry about bringing Gen. Eisenhower back from Europe—Europe would have fallen long ago to the Communists without Marshall Plan, etc." Eisenhower mused about discarding Taft Republicans and "getting the Progressive Southern Democrats and the Progressive Northern Republicans together."[90]

Taft also embarked on a crusade, but his was against Democrats masquerading as Republicans. "The Eisenhower Movement is a small clique," warned Taft staffer George Smith, "almost alien to the basic principles of the Republican Party—which is determined to put their candidate over on the party as was done with Willkie in 1940." Senator Homer Capehart of Indiana said, "The nomination of General Eisenhower would mean the end of the Republican Party." Taft wrote in his private, handwritten notes about the Eisenhower campaign, "E. guided by me-too-ers. . . . No attack on new deal—or T-A [Truman-Acheson] foreign policy. . . . No cuts in foreign spending means no cuts at home. E has gone along with whole foreign policy." Eisenhower would bring "Democrats into Republican primaries" in an "attempt by new deal to take over the Rep. Party and avail themselves of a name military hero for that purpose."[91]

Conservative Republicans united behind Taft only after overcoming misgivings about his popular appeal and ideology. "When he [Taft] repeats his old unqualified ideas of Liberty and then advocates, even in the same paragraph, socialist programs wholly inconsistent with the principles of Liberty," Representative Ralph Gwinn wrote in 1950, "it brings home fearfully the moral collapse that besets us." Taft complained, "My views are misunderstood and often deliberately misrepresented," especially "by the labor unions and by the extreme conservatives." It was Taft or bust, however, for the right. Senator Vandenberg had died in 1951 and General MacArthur had passed his seventieth birthday without gaining wisdom about politics. Even MacArthur's acolyte Robert Wood said of Taft, "We cannot desert the man who had no hesitation in putting his name on the Taft-Hartley Act, the man who fought unlimited government controls, the man who fought communism in government, the man who fought for our kind of America."[92]

The 1952 campaign drove a wedge between the GOP's conservative activists who favored Taft and everyday Republicans who preferred Eisenhower. A June Gallup Poll showed Taft trailing Eisenhower by seven points among all Republicans, but leading two to one among GOP county chairs. "The Old Guard still is pretty much in control of the Party," wrote Representative Walter Judd of Minnesota. "They feel they have carried the Party through all the dark years when it was doldrums, and they are determined not to let any other groups, newcomers or otherwise, gain the ascendancy." H. L. Hunt, however, was a diehard MacArthur booster in 1952, reportedly spending $150,000 to promote the general's noncandidacy and writing to Taft that he should yield to MacArthur if the convention deadlocked.[93]

The nomination ultimately turned on contests over delegates' credentials, notably in Texas, where Eisenhower had lured Democrats into Republican caucuses. Ike's backers claimed to have created the expanded coalition needed to beat the Democrats. Taft's allies said that Eisenhower had weakened the GOP and violated its rules, even though Texans did not register by party and Eisenhower's caucus voters had signed a Republican loyalty oath. "The Democrats tried to move in on the Republican Party in Texas contrary to law, decency and every moral concept of the two-party system," wrote former party chair B. Carroll Reece. Taft backers in the Texas state party tossed out the caucus results and appointed a pro-Taft slate of delegates. But Eisenhower outmaneuvered Taft when the party convention adopted Ike's "fair play" resolution that excluded contested delegates from voting in credentials contests. The convention seated most Eisenhower delegates, which rankled conservatives for years thereafter.[94]

Eisenhower won a first-ballot nomination and chose to run with the precocious anticommunist star Senator Richard Nixon of California. But Nixon was a dry bone for conservatives, who saw him as more of an opportunist than ideological kin. Nixon himself became a campaign issue when critics charged that wealthy Californians had set up a secret slush fund to support the senator's political activities. In his famous "Checkers speech," which attracted the largest television audience to that point in history, Nixon rebutted charges of wrongdoing by mixing sentimental appeals with explanations that he had used the fund only for legitimate political purposes and had delivered no special favors to contributors. His little dog Checkers, Nixon said, was a gift to his daughter that she would keep.

Taft left the Republican Convention convinced that the same eastern establishment that had pushed America into war and unwise postwar commitments had stolen his nomination. He blamed "the New York financial interests and a large number of businessmen subject to New York influence . . . and four fifths of the influential newspapers." Yet conservatives, not liberals and moderates, controlled the GOP convention. Taft had succumbed to his own lackluster appeal and the misfortune of facing a phenomenon of history in Eisenhower, who led Taft in polls of Republicans and matched up far better against Democrats. After meeting with Eisenhower in September, Taft hopped on the general's bandwagon and beckoned conservatives to come aboard. Senator McCarthy had already said that he would campaign for the Eisenhower-Nixon ticket.[95]

Ike reciprocated with a generally conservative campaign. Eisenhower charged that communism had "reached into government itself" and blamed Democrats for the loss of China, the Korean War, and tensions in Berlin. To pry ethnic voters away from the Democrats, Ike promised new efforts to liberate Russia's "enslaved" satellite states. He said that the Truman administration "lives on deficits," takes "everything we have got in taxes," and "cheapens your money." Ike delivered his most inspirational message in five words—"I shall go to Korea"—his pledge to settle that mess of a war. Conservatives lined up behind Ike rather than the Democratic candidate—not President Truman but his anointed successor, Adlai Stevenson, the liberal and intellectual "egghead" governor of Illinois. Eisenhower, who like Taft opposed compulsory laws against employment discrimination, was the first Republican presidential candidate to campaign in the South. Although, editorially, the northern press usually favored Republicans, Eisenhower fared better than any candidate in twenty years: he won endorsements from 67 percent of daily newspapers, including a majority of southern papers, compared to 15 percent nationwide for Stevenson.[96]

From Richard Nixon's Checkers speech to twenty-second "Eisenhower Answers America" TV spots and a one-hour broadcast on election eve called *Crusade in America*, Republicans pioneered the modern television campaign. "You sell your candidates and your programs the way a business sells its products," said Republican Party chairman Gus Hall. Democrats joined the television campaign but lacked the funding and PR expertise to match the GOP. In a mishap that symbolized the new television wars Eisenhower, who had fought World War II unscathed, suffered a slight injury when a television studio clock fell on his head. About a third of the TV spots aired by both parties negatively assailed the opposition. Television hiked the costs of campaigns and elevated the role of consultants to plan, produce, and market advertising.[97]

Eisenhower won 55 percent of the popular vote and thirty-nine states, including four in the upper South. His party recaptured control of Congress by winning a narrow majority of both Senate and House seats. For the first time since 1930, Republicans had gained unified control of the national government. In Arizona, underdog Republican Barry Goldwater toppled Senate Majority Leader Ernest McFarland. The election of 1952, however, was a sign not so much that the Republicans' time had come as that the Democrats' had, for the moment, gone. To become a majority party again, Republicans would need to retain control of the national government and slice into the Democrats' lead in the party loyalties of voters.

5

STRANGERS IN
A MODERN
REPUBLICAN LAND,
1952–1960

Joseph Mazzei, an unassuming man who managed a movie theater near Pittsburgh, was one of the FBI's most productive undercover informants on the American Communist Party. In 1953 his testimony helped convict five Pittsburgh communists of plotting to overthrow the American government and revealed a communist plan to conquer the United States and assassinate the reds' number one enemy: Senator Joseph McCarthy. According to information that Mazzei provided to McCarthy's Subcommittee on Investigations, the communists had launched a bogus "peace offensive [as the] last stage in the program of administering a 'sedative' to the American people before the hammer of war falls on Continental United States." By preaching peace, the reds had hoped to build a "clamour for tax reduction" that would sap America's military budget. The Kremlin had instructed party members in the United States to subvert "schools, churches, and children" and target Senator McCarthy "for liquidation or murder—an American agent [is] assigned to the job." Three years later, federal officials admitted that Mazzei was an unreliable witness who had fabricated the communist plot to attack the United States and assassinate Senator McCarthy. The Supreme Court ordered a new trial for the men convicted of sedition by his testimony and the government dropped the case.[1]

By 1953 the right was swinging full circle from disengaged nationalism to a nationalism engaged with battling the global "communist conspiracy." After Korea, conservatives viewed the world with a Manichean clarity that had eluded them during the Nazi era. McCarthy and other conservatives seized upon Mazzei's information and similar evidence to prove the urgency of a communist threat, which, they asserted, liberal Democrats and the moderate Eisenhower administration ignored. But the right's reliance on dubious evidence and methods would discredit their anticommunist crusade. Conservatives would also confront the dilemma of how to defeat the reds while clamoring for tax cuts, balanced budgets, curbs on executive power, states' rights, and small government.

MIDDLE WAY REPUBLICANISM

Conservatives remained strangers in a strange land during a "modern Republican" presidency that navigated between right and left. President Eisenhower said that his middle way philosophy weaved "between conflicting arguments advanced by extremists on both sides of almost every economic, political, and international problem that arises." Eisenhower's highest priority was to balance the federal budget and control inflation, which suited his middle- to upper-class constituents. He believed in protecting the private economy from government meddling, but he also said, "Should any political party attempt to abolish social security, unemployment insurance, and eliminate labor laws and farm programs, you would not hear of that party again in our political history." Ike ratified Truman's approach to collective security and pledged to "put ourselves on the side of individual right and liberty as well as on the side of fighting Communism to the death."[2]

Eisenhower established a center/right presidency, governing to the left of conservative Republicans but well to the right of most Democrats. He rejected liberal proposals for national health insurance, urban renewal, and fair employment practices legislation. He made business-friendly appointments to regulatory agencies and reversed prior policy by turning over to the states mineral rights in a three-mile band of oil-rich ocean "tidelands" bordering the American coast. Still, conservatives fumed over moderate appointees and a settlement in Korea during his first year that did not include concessions from the communists. Many conservatives agreed with General James Van Fleet, the former American army commander in Korea, who said in June 1953, "All we have to do is start on all-out effort in Korea and the Reds will come begging to us." Although Secretary of Agriculture Ezra Taft Benson shined as a

conservative beacon in the cabinet, conservatives from farm states resisted Benson's free market proposals to cut agricultural supports. Conservatives in Congress, led by Taft until his premature death in July 1953,
balked at defying their president. In his first two years Ike secured a
moderate legislative harvest that included a newly created Department
of Health, Education and Welfare, higher minimum wages, and expanded
social security benefits.[3]

America did not demobilize after the Korean War. In 1955 total
defense-related spending remained at about 85 percent of its wartime
peak and consumed about three-quarters of the federal budget. Eisenhower
worried that excessive federal spending would generate damaging inflation, debase the currency, ignite class conflict, and discourage Americans from saving, producing, and investing. He believed that the leader
of the free world had a duty to manage his country's economy properly
and sought to tamp down spending while deterring communist aggression. Eisenhower's "new look" defense policy included covert operations,
economic assistance to developing countries, aid to local forces resisting communism, and investment in cost-efficient airpower and nuclear
weaponry. To keep the reds guessing, the administration threatened
"massive retaliation" against unprovoked aggression. Still, Eisenhower
recognized that even an American surprise attack would not destroy
Soviet military capacities. He prepared for a protracted global struggle
that was "not merely a military one . . . its other phases—economic, social, and political—are far more threatening than the military."[4]

Eisenhower backed international alliances and expanded the cultural offensive against communism. He authorized the CIA to topple
leftist governments in Guatemala and Iran—in his view, a dose of prevention against communism—but rejected as dangerous and impractical schemes for rolling back Soviet power. He pursued arms-control
agreements with the Soviets, despite opposition from conservatives, and
resisted pressure for military intervention in Vietnam in 1954 to save
French colonial forces from defeat by the nationalistic Marxist leader
Ho Chi Minh. Eisenhower said that if Indochina fell to communism, other
nations could fall "like a row of dominoes." But he believed that "A proper
political foundation for any military action was essential. Since we could
not bring it about (although we prodded and argued for almost two years),
I gave not even a tentative approval for any plan for massive intervention."

The United States retained its influence by backing a pro-American government in South Vietnam that was headed, not accidentally, by a Christian, the Roman Catholic Ngo Dinh Diem.[5]

In a 1954 critique that resonated for years on the right, B. E. Hutchinson of J. Howard Pew's circle of business conservatives derided Ike's "middle-of-the-road philosophy" that did not "exactly embrace socialism [or] make substantive overtures to freedom." The result was "continued grand spending with consequent deficits and inevitable continued inflation," which led to the irony "that socialism may make more strides under the party which has been traditionally conservative than it made under our more openly left-wing rival."[6]

TAMING THE LIBERAL STATE

To curb the liberal state, conservatives proposed constitutional revisions to constrain the president and limit the capacities of government to redistribute wealth and power. In a last gasp of disengaged nationalism, conservatives backed an amendment that Senator John Bricker of Ohio proposed in 1953–54 to protect American sovereignty and thwart proponents of world government. The Bricker amendment would give to Congress a veto over international negotiations by requiring legislation to put into effect provisions of treaties or executive agreements with foreign nations. Henry Cabot Lodge told Eisenhower that the amendment was a win-win proposition for conservatives, who would either "have cut down the powers of the Presidency" or created a grievance to nurse against the administration. Bricker and other conservatives sought to guard against America's adoption of UN conventions on human rights and genocide that they felt made backdoor domestic policy by subjecting Americans to foreign tribunals, limiting the international arms trade, and pushing socialized medicine, desegregation, and compulsory unionization on the United States. "Should such treaties as the human rights covenants or the draft statute for an international criminal court be adopted by UN members, we would have world government in fact if not in name," Bricker said.[7]

The DAR and Minute Women fired up their telephone networks to form the Vigilant Women for the Bricker Amendment. The women collected more than two hundred thousand petition signatures for the amendment, which a six-hundred-member delegation presented to the senator in bundles tied with red, white, and blue ribbons. Young conservative activist Phyllis Schlafly joined the group to support "the most important and necessary legislation that the present Congress can pass." Women like Schlafly again defied stereotypes by outorganizing men; male leaders again largely ignored the women activists.

The failure of the Bricker amendment and a weakened substitute extended the right's losing streak on foreign policy and spawned a conservative martyr in Pat Manion, a right-wing Democrat and Eisenhower supporter. After Ike fired him from his position as chairman of the Commission on Intergovernmental Relations for backing the Bricker amendment, Manion turned misfortune into opportunity by launching America's first conservative radio talk show, the *Manion Forum*. In the *Forum*'s first four years, Manion hosted more than fifty white male luminaries of the right: Samuel Pettengill, William F. Buckley Jr., General MacArthur, and senators Bricker, Goldwater, Jenner, Knowland, and McCarthy. These leaders "love the United States as it flourished before International Socialism dimmed its luster," Manion said.[8]

Some conservatives also proposed constitutional amendments to curtail the liberal state's funding and its role in the private economy. Retired industrialist Paul K. Morgenthaler founded the Organization for the Repeal of Federal Income Taxes (ORFIT), which was dedicated to "cutting off the money supply, which enables the Socialists and Internationalists to control our government." Willis F. Stone, an industrial engineer, started the American Progress Foundation, which pushed a "23rd Amendment" that would restrict the federal government to delivering the mail. By axing the Federal Employment Service, the Federal Housing Authority, the national parks, and scores of other government enterprises, Stone promised to get "bureaucratic empires out of competition with private enterprise." His amendment would also help Republicans by freeing voters from their dependence on government.[9]

Morgenthaler and Stone soldiered on until 1956, when their groups merged under the leadership of food company owner D. B. Lewis and proposed a single "Liberty amendment" that would close the books on both income taxes and government enterprises. Striking down government's "illegal business," Lewis claimed, would "produce sufficient savings to eliminate all of the income and inheritance taxes and leave more than Four Billion Dollars in the Treasury to reduce the national debt. *It is as simple as that.*" The alliance produced more internal strife than external success. Business balked at sacrificing government contracts or benefits and nationalists worried that a slimmed-down government would be a pushover for the reds.[10]

Beginning in 1955, a group that called itself the Campaign for the 48 States advocated wider, if less drastic, constitutional reforms. With loans from J. Howard Pew, J. C. Penney, and Ralph Gwinn, veteran conservatives Robert Snowden, Albert Hawkes, and Robert Dresser launched a campaign to combat "the enormous power of the left-wing conspirators." They would circumvent Congress by persuading thirty-two states to call a constitutional convention for the purpose of enacting five amendments "which will control forever the power of ANY group to use the Federal Government as a tool to establish its private ideas of Utopia." In addition to the Bricker amendment, the campaign proposed amendments to reform the Electoral College, balance the federal budget, restrict taxing power, and authorize states to amend the Constitution independent of Congress— a turnabout from earlier conservative efforts to deter amendments. Leaders of the campaign hoped to "arouse and frighten the parents of this nation to the extent that tyranny could—and will—happen to our children when our financial structure collapses or explodes because of inflation, more socialism, and Big Government." Few parents were buying. In 1958 Snowden told Pew that their campaign "is a 'dead dodo.'" Pew responded that "A properly developed program" required "(1) wide popular support, (2) constructive policies advanced in an affirmative manner, and (3) a large budget involving many millions of dollars." In addition, "much work at the grass roots must be done in order to create a nucleus on which to build."[11]

CHALLENGING THE ESTABLISHMENT

In the new Republican Congress that convened in 1953, Representative B. Carroll Reece of Tennessee, a former head of the Republican National Committee, used his power as chair of a special investigating committee to follow liberal money to its source by investigating tax-exempt foundations, notably the three pillars of the establishment, Rockefeller, Carnegie, and Ford. The committee's majority report rebuked the federal government for funding the liberal state through tax exemptions to foundations dedicated to "moral relativity" and "social engineering" by "elites" who scorned the traditions and values of ordinary citizens. Foundations used their money, influence, and prestige to "the detriment of our basic moral, religious and governmental principles." They advanced "socialism and collectivist ideas," "world government," and the "derogation of American 'nationalism.'"[12]

The foundations made no secret of backing ambitious programs of social engineering. In 1950, for example, Rockefeller's trustees proposed "support for the biological sciences . . . to gain, for the animate universe, an understanding and a capacity to guide and control which is comparable to what we have gained for the physical universe." They said, "The gap between our sciences and our morals is primarily a gap between the capacity with which we control the physical forces of nature and the wisdom with which we control ourselves." Science would uncover "the essential nature of living things" and lead to a "general science of order." Criticism came both from conservatives, who charged that the foundations were using scientific methods to override America's religious and moral values, and from liberals, who said that foundations were attempting to clamp corporate control on the world.[13]

Reece's investigators passed over the small foundations that sustained the right: the William Volker Fund, and the Alfred P. Sloan, Fleming, Earhardt, Harnischfleger, and Relm foundations. The Pew Memorial Foundation (later the Pew Charitable Trusts), set up in 1948, also escaped scrutiny. In spending its foundation's money, the Pew family deliberately sought to avoid investigation, federal regulation, and charges of political bias. "All foundations throughout this Country are in a difficult position," J. Howard Pew said. "Because the money of some foundations has been used for subversive purposes, all foundations face legislation which may be disastrous. . . . All of us who are interested in the control of foundations must exercise the greatest care in seeing to it that the money is properly used." The Pew Foundation financed patriotic schools such as Alma College in Michigan and Grove City College in Pennsylvania and evangelical groups like the Billy Graham Evangelistic Association. However, J. Howard Pew "opposed giving any of our Foundation money to propaganda purposes. If we can give our Foundation money in advocacy of sound economic and social procedures, then the Ford and Rockefeller Foundations can justify the giving of their money for the advocacy of socialistic measures. The latter must be stopped."[14]

Senator McCarthy's continued needling of the establishment exasperated the Eisenhower administration. McCarthy's Subcommittee on Investigations held more than 150 public and closed-door hearings that targeted the State Department, the Voice of America, the Government Printing Office, General Electric, Alliss-Chalmers, and, most explosively, the U.S. Army. "The reactionary fringe of the Republican Party that hates and despises everything for which I stand," Eisenhower wrote, "are so anxious to seize on every possible embarrassment for the Administration that they support him. . . . Old Guardism and McCarthyism have become synonymous in the public mind." Former campaign chair Henry Cabot Lodge advised the president, "Investigation of the Army, while ostensibly aimed at making sure that the Army is secure against communist penetration, is actually part of an attempt to destroy you politically." From April through June 1954, the U.S. Senate held nationally televised hearings on McCarthy's spat with the army. After the hearings, viewed at least in part by eighty million Americans, McCarthy's approval rating in the Gallup Poll plunged from 50 percent to 30 percent and the Senate appointed a special committee to consider his censure. McCarthy's troubles, however, did not deter liberal or conservative members of Congress from uniting to outlaw the Communist Party in the Communist Control Act, which President Eisenhower signed in August 1954.[15]

Alfred Kohlberg's China Lobby assumed concrete form in the early Eisenhower years as the Committee for One Million Against the Admission of Red China to the United Nations. Public relations consultant Marvin Liebman, another lapsed Marxist turned conservative, organized, promoted, and raised funds for the committee. Republican representative Walter Judd of Minnesota, a former medical missionary to China, gave the committee cachet on Capitol Hill and recruited a few Democrats to deflect criticism from the left. The committee existed as a letterhead, not a membership organization. After getting some one million Americans to sign its petition against admitting Red China to the UN in 1954, it became the Committee *of* One Million.

Right-wing organizer Liebman had learned from the left "a perfectly simple pattern" for creating political organizations:

1. Enlist a prestigious, preferably nonpartisan leadership figure.
2. Compile a list of prominent individuals interested in your project regardless of differences on other matters.

3. Get the leader to invite figures on your list to sign a statement of purpose and serve on an "advisory board" that required neither time nor effort.

4. Print a letterhead with the well-known names. Get an affluent business leader to raise corporate money. Print the group's statement as an advertisement and a mailer for soliciting funds.

5. Set up a rubber stamp executive committee board, give yourself a title, and get on monthly retainer. Develop a stable of figureheads willing to put their names on other letterheads.

By following these easy steps conservatives could create letterhead organizations overnight.[16]

CIVIL RELIGION

Mainstream Protestant groups worked with the Advertising Council and the American Legion in the 1950s to advance "spiritual values in both personal and community life." Protestant and Catholic churches boomed after World War II. Protestant church membership rose from 27 percent of Americans in 1940 to 36 percent in 1960, and Catholic membership from 17 to 23 percent. Polls from the 1950s found that churches had become America's most trusted institutions, that 99 percent of Americans professed to believe in God, 90 percent recognized the divinity of Christ, and only 18 percent said they would vote for a well-qualified atheist candidate for president.[17]

For evangelical critics, however, mainstream Protestant activity was the gray flannel piety of a conformist age. According to evangelical magazine editor L. Nelson Bell, mainstream Protestants emphasized "organizational matters, programs, and social reform rather than soul redemption." Real Christians were "primarily concerned that the *message* be kept true to the Bible and that it be preached, taught, and lived that others too may come to know Christ as Savior." Such evangelicals propagated the holy word worldwide, led by William Cameron Townsend's Wycliffe Bible Translators. J. Howard Pew and the Pew Charitable Trusts generously funded Townsend's group and Bell lent his prestige. In foreign arenas, Christian missionaries, international business, conservative anticommunists and military leaders, and the social engineers of American government shared common goals. The missionary work contributed to breaking down indigenous cultures, opening their lands to the global economy, blunting leftist appeals, and instilling a Protestant work ethic.[18]

Eisenhower incorporated into his presidency a form of civil religion that rallied the American people behind nonsectarian spiritual values that he believed promoted such virtues as thrift, courage, hard work, and patriotism. "Our government makes no sense unless it is founded on deeply felt religious faith—and I don't care what [religion] it is," Ike said, although his piety had a decided Christian tilt. Eisenhower belonged to no formal church but he became the first president to attend a preinaugural church service—at the Reverend Edward L. R. Elson's National Presbyterian Church. A month later, Eisenhower joined Elson's congregation, which included J. Edgar Hoover, among other Washington luminaries. After taking his oath of office with two open Bibles, Eisenhower recited a personally composed prayer, which the GOP distributed as a pamphlet.[19]

Eisenhower began cabinet meetings with a silent prayer and promoted the National Day of Prayer that Congress had established in 1952. In 1953 he became the first president to attend the weekly Christian prayer breakfast held in the Capitol, saying, "Prayer is just simply a necessity." Ike's presence led to the tradition of an annual Presidential Prayer Breakfast (later renamed the National Prayer Breakfast) attended by senators, members of Congress, Supreme Court justices, cabinet officers, ambassadors, military commanders, business and labor leaders, and foreign dignitaries. The president backed the Knights of Columbus's proposal to insert "under God" into the Pledge of Allegiance, which Congress enshrined by statute on Flag Day, June 14, 1954. The administration issued a 1954 stamp bearing the motto "In God We Trust" as an international "postal ambassador." A year later, Eisenhower approved adding the motto to U.S. currency. He spoke on radio and television to support the American Legion's "Back to God" program. In his reelection year of 1956, he appointed the first presidential assistant on religious affairs and spoke of a "nation founded on religious faith."[20]

The right sought to shape civil religion by working within the National Council of Churches, a successor to the Federal Council of Churches. In 1951 the council's founders, eying J. Howard Pew's wallet, made him chair of a National Laymen's Committee that was salted with other business leaders. In a letter to Pew, fellow magnate Sterling Morton pointed out that the clergy who "have consistently attacked business and industry are now making a great campaign to get contributions from the corporations they have so excoriated. Don't you get the rather sardonic pleasure I get out of this situation?" Pew entered a marriage of convenience to move organized Protestantism to the right by "working from the inside" to ensure that the National Council's pronouncements were "economically sound" and to challenge its "left-wing representation." "No activity is so important as that of working with the ministers," Pew wrote. "If we would save our freedom, we must get the ministers back." Pew fell short of his goal. "My influence with the National Council of Churches is almost nil," he admitted in 1953. "I had hoped that working from the inside I could accomplish something worthwhile; but all I have succeeded in doing was getting some of their material held up and other material watered down a little." The council refused to modify its 1954 statement on economic issues with Pew's language "that the over-expanded power of the state . . . is the road to slavery" and free enterprise was "the only Christian economic system." Instead, it voted to terminate Pew's committee as of 1955.[21]

Pew fired back with a report that rejected the authority of a "corporate church" body to speak for pastors or worshippers. Churches should hew to their cosmic mission of saving souls, shunning "economic or political controversy" that lacked "moral or ethical content" and distracted from working for "the Redemption of all Mankind." National Council president Charles Taft rejected such self-censorship. In a letter to Pew, he lectured: "Economics, politics, and social relationships are inextricably mixed with each other and with matters of ethical and moral principle. The Christian Church throughout history has never admitted any such limitation." Pew later responded, "There is ample evidence to show that the National Council of Churches, its Board and the departments, divisions and committees which it has set up constitute the most powerful subversive force in the United States." Other conservatives agreed. Utility executive William Mullendore wrote to retired Du Pont executive Jasper Crane, "Those who are determined to continue down the road of collectivism, statism and socialism are in control of most of the avenues of expression in most of the policy-making bodies in business, in politics, in education, and, as your Report reveals, in the religious field also."[22]

Business leaders contributed directly to civil religion. Led again by the big-spending National Association of Manufacturers, business continued weaving together America's religious heritage and material achievements. NAM advanced an American identity based on faith, freedom, patriotism, and personal responsibility for one's own destiny. In an internal 1952 memo on "Building a Better America," NAM noted, "A better America must include a growing support of religion and high moral principles based on religious convictions. It can only come from unwavering faith—from dedication to the belief that God, in creating man, meant him to retain his individual dignity all through life, with freedom from regimentation and exploitation by government or any group." While companies focused on employees, NAM pounded home its message across America through its Peabody Award–winning television program *Industry on Parade* and pamphlets distributed to women's clubs, fraternal groups, teachers, clergymen, and civic organizations. It launched a "Jobs—Freedom—Opportunity!" campaign with paid ads and "suggested" news stories.[23]

In contrast to the more vehement antiradicalism of small business groups like the National Federation of Independent Business, the cultural message of big business centered on images of ingenious managers, industrious workers, consumers with full shopping baskets, and contented families. This harmony of interests, stated NAM, made life "easier, more enjoyable" and safer from "disease and dictators alike." As this last phrase suggests, a current of fear ran through business leaders who worried that political culture remained secular, collectivist, scornful of enterprise, and heavily influenced by the labor movement. Even in the relatively secure big business sector, few firms welcomed unionization. In the words of a speaker at a 1957 meeting of the Industrial Relations Research Association, "If American management upon retiring for the night were assured that by the next morning the unions with which they dealt would have disappeared, more management people than not would experience the happiest sleep of their lives." Major nonunion firms adapted the "welfare capitalism" of the 1920s to the post–World War II era. Firms such as Sears, Kodak, Du Pont, McCormick and Company, National Cash Register, and Standard Oil provided packages of benefits to employees and drew on insights from the behavioral sciences to develop management practices that secured the loyalty of workers. In addition, union and nonunion firms sought to sway the opinions of their workers, their customers, and the public against unions and to lobby for restrictions on labor beyond Taft-Hartley.[24]

Companies could also take stern measures against unions as illustrated by the response to the strike that the United Auto Workers launched in 1954 against the family-owned Kohler plumbing company. The company refused to accede to demands for higher wages and benefits. It hired strikebreakers and detective agencies to infiltrate the union ranks. Labor responded with picket-line violence and a national effort to boycott the company's products. The strike dragged on for six years until the National Labor Relations Board ruled in 1960 that Kohler had engaged in unfair labor practices. Meanwhile, conservatives, including Senator Barry Goldwater, used the Kohler srike to sustain their claims that unions were violent and lawless and validate their call for new government regulations. Although business leaders continued to work on improving their educational campaign and fine-tuning its targeting to particular groups, by the mid-1950s, union membership was beginning a long-term decline in the United States.[25]

THE RELIGIOUS RIGHT

In the 1950s the Reverend Carl McIntire built a robust Christian right to counter mainstream church groups and propagate his theologically and politically conservative message. Reverend McIntire's enterprises included his American and International Councils of Christian Churches, his political lobbying organization, his monthly publication *Christian Beacon,* and his radio show, *The Twentieth Century Reformation Hour,* which premiered in 1955 and eventually aired on more than six hundred stations. McIntire brought new figures into conservative politics and sustained the political activism of fundamentalists in mid-century America.[26]

Evangelical preacher Billy James Hargis had been beating the backwoods for his Christian Crusade until the early 1950s when McIntire brought the young minister into his domain. Hargis, who called his benefactor "the Martin Luther of our day," soon rose to prominence on balloons. He directed McIntire's project that flew helium balloons fitted with mini Bibles into Soviet territory, where the "spiritually starved captives of Communism" would eagerly retrieve them. In 1956 Hargis claimed that his balloons had inspired the Hungarian people to revolt against their Soviet masters. Hargis built the Christian Crusade into an empire that included a *Christian Crusade Magazine,* books, pamphlets, lectures, radio and television broadcasts, and training schools for Christian conservatives.

Hargis targeted not only communists but also alleged labor racketeers and proponents of sex education, ecumenism, world government, peaceful coexistence with the reds, and civil rights. Hargis excelled in the solicitation of direct-mail donations. By the late 1960s his operations were raking in more than a million dollars a year and Hargis's broadcasts were airing on five hundred radio and two hundred fifty television stations. In the 1970s his enterprises would crumble after he admitted having sexual relations with male and female students at a college that he'd founded.[27]

In 1953 McIntire brought to America an Australian physician, lay preacher, and self-taught expert on communism named Fred Schwarz. The doctor stayed on to organize his own Christian Anti-Communism Crusade, which used a mix of evangelism and popular science to show how communists bred and slaughtered people like cattle. Schwarz taught of the "historical link between liberal theology, Modernism and Communism." He denied allegations of anti-Semitism, but also claimed, "The best way to enlist anti-Communist fighters is to enlist them in the army of Jesus." Dr. Schwarz crisscrossed America with a traveling anticommunism school that boasted such conservative celebrities as counterspy Herbert Philbrick, the retired admiral Chester Ward, and Dr. Edward Teller, the father of the H-bomb. He made headlines in 1961 when he capped his Southern California School by packing twelve thousand cheering followers into the Hollywood Bowl for a rally with stars Ronald Reagan, John Wayne, Jimmy Stewart, and George Murphy—who later became the first movie star elected to the Senate. Another several million watched on television courtesy of Richfield Oil, Schick, and Technicolor. The companies sponsored the rally's broadcast on thirty-three television stations in six states. The crusade's revenue rose from $367,000 in 1960 to $1.2 million in 1961, although it never again approached that peak-year performance.[28]

McIntire also mentored a young minister named Francis Schaeffer, whose writings and lectures would inspire leaders of the Christian right in the 1970s. Schaeffer served as foreign secretary for the American Council of Christian Churches until breaking with McIntire in 1956. Schaeffer propagated the message that freedom followed the Bible across the world. "Bible-believing Christians are the true liberals," he said. "The Modernists are the reactionaries. It is the Bible-believing Christian who is continuing to insist upon individual freedom all over the world, and equally all over the world it is the Modernists who are casting away our freedom . . . so that their socialistically planned economy can come into effect."[29]

Other religiously based movements thrived in the 1950s. Edgar Bundy, a former air force officer and nonpracticing minister, revived the Church League of America to "rekindle the spirit of valiant Christian Americanism." Bundy quadrupled the league's funding from $50,000 in 1958 to nearly $200,000 in 1961. He published E. Merrill Root's *Brainwashing in the High Schools* and his own book, *Collectivism in the Churches.* He distributed films, including *Ronald Reagan on the Welfare State,* "a hard-hitting expose of the drive to substitute State Welfarism for the traditional system of individual liberty." Bundy testified before Congress and spiced up the league's newsletter with provocative exposés such as "Abusing the Girl Scouts," "Communism on the Campuses," and "Moscow and the American Negro." He accumulated a vast library that included "one whole section built around John Dewey, whose philosophy of pragmatism softened many intellectuals in America for their acceptance of communism." For ten bucks, donors received Bundy's reports on subversives, which were based on files that covered three million organizations and persons "attacking or ridiculing a major doctrine of the Christian faith or the American way of life," including the Ford Foundation, the National PTA, the ACLU, and the Girl Scouts. The league acquired records from the former research director of the House Un-American Activities Committee and used undercover agents who "sat in on Communist and leftist meetings and brought out miniature tape recordings of the proceedings." It shared files with the Wackenhut detective agency, founded by George Wackenhut, a conservative former FBI agent, in order to conduct background checks for business. Bundy continued his tireless advocacy until 1982, when he resigned amid accusations that he had sexually molested young male volunteers.[30]

After folding Facts Forum in 1956, H. L. Hunt founded LIFE LINE (which he always capitalized) two years later as an explicit Christian right advocacy group that linked "business and patriotism" with "Christianity and Americanism." LIFE LINE published a newsletter, ran a book club, and conducted seminars across America. It featured a "6-day a week radio commentary and sermon" by Pastor Wayne Poucher, who had run Strom Thurmond's write-in campaign for the Senate in 1954. In a letter to General Albert Wedemeyer, Hunt lamented "the timidity of business in fear of putting up its own defense." He hoped that "forthright business concerns" would sponsor LIFE LINE and recruited a letterhead board of familiar conservatives. But Hunt mostly self-funded an organization whose annual budget topped $1 million by 1963. LIFE LINE's first radio broadcast rebuked the Supreme Court for coddling communists and defended the Bible as a guide to modern life. By the 1960s LIFE LINE had extended its reach to television and its radio broadcasts aired on some five hundred stations in forty-seven states.[31]

Some conservatives admired a movement called Moral Re-armament that had emerged in 1938 from the evangelical Oxford Group in Britain, which also spawned Alcoholics Anonymous. Moral Re-armament's founder, the Pennsylvania-born Reverend Frank N. D. Buchman, said that his movement would make communism obsolete. "First you must have new men. New nations will follow naturally and logically. . . . God's plan for the world is infinitely greater and more perfect than any imposed by a government on its people. It is the Dictatorship of the Holy Spirit." Buchman feared communism more than he did fascism. In a 1936 radio address, he had said, "I thank heaven for a man like Adolf Hitler who built a front line of defense against the anti-Christ of Communism." In 1955 a who's who of conservative Senate and House members joined GOP senator Arthur Watkins of Utah in praising Moral Re-armament for "doing a great deal of good in the world." But the movement declined in the United States after Buchman's death in 1961.[32]

The prayer breakfast movement, begun in Seattle during 1935 by Methodist minister and Goodwill Industries executive Abraham Vereide in collaboration with local businessmen, had a long, influential life. Vereide's National Committee for Christian Leadership put together "an informal association of men in positions of responsibility who are finding . . . the WAY, the TRUTH and the LIFE" through total dedication to Christ. The group blamed early military setbacks in World War II on America's moral dereliction—"the failure at home to do right and to trust God." During the Cold War, as the prayer breakfast movement advanced in the United States and abroad, executive secretary Wallace Haines said, "The power of Christ in the minds, hearts, and wills of leaders is the best hope that the free world will be strong enough and magnetic enough to command the loyalty of men everywhere."[33]

In 1944 Vereide's group renamed itself the International Christian Leadership (ICL), moved its headquarters to Washington, D.C., and became more active politically. It sponsored weekly congressional prayer breakfasts and began organizing prayer groups sponsored by governors, mayors, and state legislators across America. It established branches in foreign nations and sent representatives abroad to meet with world leaders. It worked with the CIA to produce an anticommunist propaganda film called *Militant Liberty* and sponsored anticommunist lectures in the United States by officers, board members, and supporters. The ICL sponsored and paid for the annual Presidential Prayer Breakfast that Eisenhower had launched in 1953. Invitations came from "Members of the Congress of the United States of America," which added to the impression that the breakfast was an official government function. "The new evangelism," Vereide said in 1955, was not limited to spiritual conversion. It had to "express itself in governmental affairs, in the legislative assemblies and in the political arena. Rebels against the Divine order must be firmly eliminated from positions of responsibility and leadership." That year, at the ICL's annual meeting, its chairman, Frank Carlson, Republican senator from Kansas, said that the group's mission was a "worldwide spiritual offensive" that would vanquish communism and bring the rule of Jesus Christ to peoples across the globe.[34]

During the Eisenhower years, the ICL became one of the most influential, if least known, operations in Washington. By 1961 it claimed to have organized eighteen small prayer groups in Washington, D.C., two hundred more across the nation, and foreign groups in more than thirty counties. It had nine full-time paid staff and an annual budget of $150,000, mostly from a few secretive wealthy backers—the group did not solicit public donations. Members of the Senate and House as well as mayors, governors, and state legislators across the nation cooperated with Vereide's group in holding quasi-official prayer breakfasts. Vereide's all-male inner circle during the 1950s included Billy Graham, Bill Bright of the Campus Crusade for Christ, wealthy businessmen such as hotelier Conrad Hilton, Senator Carlson, and more than twenty other members of Congress—all of them Republicans or southern Democrats.[35]

BATTLING "NEANDERTHALS"

A month before the 1954 midterm elections, despite Eisenhower's 52 percent approval rating, Democrats led Republicans by a record 53 percent to

27 percent in national party identification, according to a Gallup survey. Disappointments at the polls would embolden right-wing critics, Eisenhower's advisers warned. "The Neanderthal Men are laying the groundwork for reassertion of party control if things don't go right in November," said adviser Gabriel Hauge. "You saved the Republican party from these men once. I am confident you will keep it that way. . . . For this Neanderthal Wing I do not propose the course proscribed by the Fifth Commandment [do not kill]. But that is not to say I would object to euthanasia."[36]

Ike's belated campaign tour on behalf of fellow Republicans did not stop the party from losing both houses of Congress. According to political adviser Bryce Harlow, Democrats had branded Republicans as "the Party of Big Business—the Party which cares more for the dollar than for human beings." The party's official analysis noted "labor's outstanding organizational and propaganda influence in behalf of Democrats." In February 1955, labor consolidated its power when the CIO and AFL merged as the AFL-CIO, with the Committee on Public Education (COPE) as its political arm. Conservatives lacked a similar grassroots base, especially as anticommunist fervor cooled with the death of Stalin, the end of the Korean War, and federal legislation to check subversion. Shortly after the midterm elections of 1954, the Senate censured Senator Joseph McCarthy, which destroyed his political influence and discredited his methods. In the 1956 case *Pennsylvania v. Nelson*, the Supreme Court disabled state sedition laws by ruling that federal law superseded state statutes. Four other decisions issued by the Supreme Court on June 17, 1957—a day that conservatives christened "Red Monday"—limited the power of the federal government to investigate and prosecute alleged subversives. A year later, a bill to reverse the *Nelson* ruling failed by one vote in the Senate.[37]

During the period of McCarthyism, from the senator's West Virginia speech in 1950 through his censure in 1954, communist spies plied their trade in movies like *Security Risk*, *I Married a Communist*, and *Pickup on South Street*. But investigators uncovered not a single surviving spy ring in the United States or one communist holding a consequential position in government. Presidents Truman and Eisenhower knew that Russia had dismantled its American spy rings after World War II. In 1939 the United States had cracked the Soviet diplomatic code, although the government would not begin releasing decrypted cables (code-named Venona) to the public until 1995.[38]

McCarthy unsettled Americans, including many anticommunists, because he pushed Cold War culture to its edge. He obliterated distinctions between external and internal threats. He opened a gulf between the self and the suspicious other, and between the orthodox and the deviant. For McCarthy and his backers, security threats came from both the privileged elite and those on the American margins. Homosexuals posed a special danger as America's "closeted" other—they gathered in hidden places, spoke in special (Aesopian) codes, engaged in dangerous role reversal, and lived in fear of being outed. McCarthy targeted homosexuals with the help of aide Roy Cohn—a closeted homosexual—and even McCarthy's critics pursued "sexual perverts" as security risks.[39]

FBI Director Hoover refused to let the antiradical crusade die of natural causes. From 1956 through its public exposure in 1971, Hoover initiated domestic covert action programs, known as COINTELPROs— an acronym for Counter Intelligence Programs—that he directed mainly against the left. Through more than two thousand secret operations, the Bureau spied on and harassed both violent and nonviolent groups. In the 1950s COINTELPROs targeted the Communist Party, but by 1960 Hoover had expanded their coverage to fellow-traveling groups. The program reflected Hoover's obsession with alleged black radicals. It targeted Martin Luther King Jr. and other civil rights leaders as part of an effort to discredit the movement for racial equality.[40]

After all but one member of the GOP's Senate leadership voted against censuring McCarthy, Eisenhower vowed to cleanse right-wingers from his party. Yet the Herculean task of party reform started slowly and faltered after Ike's heart attack in September 1955. "When the '54 results were in, Ike realized two things," wrote adviser C. D. Jackson: "(A) His dear Republicans hadn't learned a damn thing; (B) he had wasted two years." Party reform "did not actually begin until the spring of '55. Then, in the fall came the heart attack.... So out of four years, less than one was spent *working* at the problem of putting up the right kind of Republican candidates."[41]

THE RISE OF ENGAGED NATIONALISM

During the Eisenhower years the right completed a transition from disengaged nationalism to an engaged nationalism dedicated to winning the Cold War. Engaged nationalists updated "America First" ideology to uphold America's moral authority as an exceptional civilization empowered to protect its interests and values unilaterally by means of its own choosing across the globe. Under changed circumstances, the task of the right was no longer to isolate America from foreign contagion but to defeat the reds without bowing to feckless allies, arrogant neutrals, or a left-leaning UN. The United States should refuse diplomatic recognition of the Soviet bloc, aid only firmly anticommunist allies, and aggressively roll back the red frontier. It should keep open all responses to red aggression and subversion, including nuclear retaliation, and follow MacArthur's doctrine of fighting wars to win.

As analyst Lawrence Dennis had predicted in 1942, the crusade against "Communist sin" meant adjusting conservative ideas to accommodate big government. An early warning came in 1952 from rising conservative star William F. Buckley Jr. "We have to accept Big Government for the duration," he wrote, "for neither an offensive nor defensive war can be waged, given our present government skills, except through the instrument of a totalitarian bureaucracy within our shores." Conservatives had no choice but to embrace "the extensive and productive tax laws that are needed to support a vigorous anti-Communist foreign policy." Moreover, "if [conservatives] deem Soviet power a menace to our freedom (as I happen to), they will have to support large armies and air forces, atomic energy, central intelligence, war production boards, and the attendant of centralization of power in Washington." Editors of the *Freeman* agreed. "We are being forced to spend billions and to arm and to tax and to interfere with the freedom of the market for one reason alone, and that reason is Kremlin Joe's overriding purpose to subvert the world." In 1954 Buckley concluded, "We will have a fighting chance in a future war against the state," but no "chance to save ourselves from Soviet tyranny if we pursue Eisenhower's foreign policy." Ironically, defeating the Soviets would prove easier than defeating big government.[42]

By 1954 leading politicians of the right embraced engaged nationalism. GOP senate leader William Knowland charged that Eisenhower's policies of "coexistence and atomic stalemate will result in ultimate communist victory. [Under] 'peaceful coexistence' . . . the United States or other free nations of the world will be allowed to exist only until communism is able to subvert them from within or destroy them by aggression from without." He argued that the president should warn the Soviets that either military aggression or subversion of the free world risked nuclear retaliation by the United States on the Russian homeland. Engaged nationalism swept so quickly through conservative Republican ranks that by late 1954 William S. White of the *New York Times* wrote that Knowland's "cold war views command a greater degree of support among Senate Republicans than do those of the President." Knowland called for an American blockade of Communist China and for free nations of Asia to retake the mainland. Former America First leader and American Legion commander Hanford MacNider said, more provocatively, in 1955, "Let's go over there, put a blockade on their coast, and bomb them off the map." Eisenhower ignored such talk and to the chagrin of conservatives met Russian premier Nikita Khrushchev at a 1955 summit conference in Geneva.[43]

Eisenhower scorned conservatives who, he said, would replace "security through strength, alertness and allies" with the policy of "the so-called 'preventive war'—that is, choose the most favorable moment and move to attack." Democratic diplomat Chester Bowles, a former America First member, agreed. "The five Republicans next in importance to Eisenhower (i.e., Nixon; Knowland, Senate Republican Leader; Bridges, Chairman Republican Policy Committee; Martin, House Leader; and Hall, National Chairman) have isolationist records and a peculiar weakness for preventive war," said Bowles. By the late 1950s even domestically oriented business leaders turned to engaged nationalism, including the leadership of the National Association of Manufacturers, which reversed course and began to advocate substantial federal spending on defense and budget cuts only for domestic programs.[44]

CONSERVATIVE IDEOLOGY: THE CORE HOLDS

Readjustments of secondary ideas during the 1950s did not unravel the right's core principles of conserving private enterprise and traditional Protestant values. Disputes among conservative anticommunists, libertarians, and traditionalists roiled some intellectuals but had little practical effect on conservative politics. All conservatives were anticommunists, differing only in tactics and degree. Conservatives usually confined libertarian ideas to economic policy, often with exceptions for business subsidies and friendly regulations. Otherwise, conservatives backed a government big and intrusive enough to repel foreign enemies, quash subversion, and curtail corruption of the culture. Few conservatives agreed with libertarians on tolerating disloyalty, perversion, and pornography or standing down America's defenses and learning to live and let live with communists. Samuel Pettengill said that for "persons *not loyal* to this country" or for "lurid sex literature . . . the right of society should prevail over any supposed right of the individual." Buckley agreed, saying, "I am for the kind of individualism . . . consistent with a Christian sense of community." David Franke, codirector of the National Student Committee for the Loyalty Oath, wrote in a magazine ironically called the *Individualist* that "moral standards and absolutes" trumped "freedom of belief." On contested issues of loyalty oaths, artistic expression, investigation and prosecution of radicals, sexual deviance, and academic freedom, conservatives, including those who voted in Congress and state legislatures, invariably chose moral standards over libertarian license.[45]

Conservative intellectual James Burnham devised his own political litmus test for sifting out conservatives from liberals. In each case, his test had conservatives opposing and liberals favoring libertarian propositions, such as the following:

> "Any interference with free speech and free assembly is wrong."
> "There should be no interference with academic freedom."
> "We always ought to respect the religious beliefs of others."
> "Everyone is entitled to political and social rights without distinction of any kind, such as race, color, sex, language, religion, political or other opinion, national or social origin, property, birth or other status."
> "A dictatorship is always wrong."
> "Everyone has the right to freedom of opinion and expression."[46]

Conservatives also assailed "anti-anticommunists" who found the cure of repression worse than the disease of subversion. In the words of the Republican senator Styles Bridges of New Hampshire, "A person who contends that the regulation and investigation of communists is a violation of individual civil liberties must be classed as an anti-anticommunist. . . . He would rather give up his liberty and freedom to the Soviet threat than give way on his concept of what our individual civil liberties allow." Anti-anticommunists, Bridges said, doubted that "the threat of international communism to our government and our American way of life is a real one" and believed that laws to regulate it were "neither necessary nor desirable and that the repression of the activities of communists is a violation of individual civil liberties."[47]

Like the battle against communism, traditional religious values united the right, including the self-professed libertarians who led or funded the Foundation for Economic Education and the Intercollegiate Society of Individualists. As tycoon Jasper Crane explained, "We libertarians . . . seek spiritual ends and believe primarily in evangelism as the means for promoting the growth of the Kingdom." Leonard Read, founder of the Foundation for Economic Education, agreed. "The current flight from integrity may otherwise be described as a shifting of personal allegiance on an enormous scale from God to Democracy." His colleague Edmund Opitz wrote of "two opposing philosophers facing each other in battle. . . . There is, on the one side, the God concept" and, on the other side, "cosmic materialism," which banished God from the world. The libertarians behind the Foundation for Economic Education, the Intercollegiate Society of Individualists, and the *Freeman* also backed the Christian Freedom Foundation and Spiritual Mobilization. Even conservatives lacking in genuine faith bowed at the altar of religion. Conservative academic Russell Kirk observed, "Chodorov, an atheist, now tosses in an occasional condescending reference to God, in the hope of pleasing Mr. J. Howard Pew."[48]

Although conservatives had often described themselves as libertarians in contrast to activist liberals, only a few marginal figures on the right such as economists Murray Rothbard and Robert LeFevre and best-selling novelist Ayn Rand embraced a broad libertarian agenda. Rand scorned those she saw as phony libertarians on the right who tainted individualism with religious faith—"the worst curse of mankind, as the exact antithesis and enemy of thought." Rand gained a large personal following—the so-called Randians—who included self-help guru Nathaniel Branden, philosopher Leonard Peikoff, and Alan Greenspan, legendary chair of the Federal Reserve Board from 1987 to 2006. In 1950 Rand complained to Jasper Crane that, among conservatives, "those who are opposed to it [big government] have been given no voice, no leadership, no chance to express their opposition." Four years later, J. Howard Pew wondered in a letter to Leonard Read if conservatives "should continue to use the word 'libertarian.'"[49]

Political disputes on the right centered not on conflict between traditionalists and marginalized libertarian purists but on conservatives' ambiguous relationship to the state. As illustrated by responses to proposals that would eliminate income taxes and government enterprises, conservatives who advocated low taxes and free markets clashed with those putting a higher priority on national security and with business leaders who sought special benefits from government.

THE THINKING PERSON'S RIGHT

William J. Baroody, a Catholic son of a Lebanese immigrant who became an economist for the U.S. Chamber of Commerce, sought to win for conservatives what Winston Churchill called the "empire of the future . . . the empire of the mind." After rising to vice president of the American Enterprise Association in 1954, Baroody's passion and organizing genius turned this struggling organization into the premier think tank of the right. Three ideas guided Baroody's advocacy for his association. First, the right's public relations campaigns addressed symptoms not causes. Second, by forfeit, the left had won the competition for the mind. Third, his think tank could restore intellectual parity for the right by making sure that "sound thinkers in academic, political, ecclesiastical, and public information circles [were] supported, encouraged, and given through the *intelligent* use of available resources, the kind of opportunities which the leftists give" for injecting ideas "into the mainstream of the nation's intellectual life." Baroody persuasively marketed this narrative to donors for the next quarter century.[50]

Baroody moved the association from New York to Washington, upgraded the quality of its research and analysis, and recruited an advisory board of such able scholars as economists Paul McCracken and Milton Friedman and legal scholar Roscoe Pound. The refurbished think tank analyzed legislation and issues such as trade, taxation, defense, and foreign policy. It gained the attention of politicians and journalists. It recruited outside scholars for research but stayed independent by rejecting contract work for particular clients. Baroody launched a corporate fund-raising drive that increased the association's income from $115,000 in 1954 to $266,000 in 1960. Major contributors included General Motors, U.S. Steel, Allen-Bradley, General Dynamics, Johns-Manville, General Electric, Socony Mobil Oil, and Eli Lilly. Baroody also coaxed large donations from

J. Howard Pew and Sarah Mellon Scaife, an heir to the Mellon family fortune, and persuaded leading business executives to serve on the think tank's board of trustees. In 1962, after moving up to the presidency, Baroody renamed his group the American Enterprise Institute—known as AEI—to distinguish it from a membership association beholding to a particular constituency.[51]

The tax-exempt AEI pledged to balance intellectual debates through analysis in which "the facts and the implications of policy issues are brought out in objective and non-partisan fashion." But why should corporations pay for impartial studies, with the chips falling where they may? The answer was that the right scholars, chosen for the right projects, would produce the right answers. As AEI board member William L. McGrath, president of the Williamson Heater Company, explained, "The general theory of AEI is that if any piece of legislation is analyzed factually and on the basis of the principles involved, the answer to the question will usually come up on the conservative side." If liberals proposed weakening the Taft-Hartley Act, for example, "I would like to suggest that we try and have the AEI make an analysis of such a proposal, which, in my opinion, would work out very satisfactorily as far as our interests are concerned."[52]

By the early 1960s Baroody sat atop a conservative "empire of the mind." AEI formed the Institute for Social Science Research in 1956 to probe big issues and helped found the Georgetown Center for Strategic and International Studies in 1962 (CSIS) to explore "strategies by which free societies can utilize their total strength to preserve and further develop the values underlying Western civilization." AEI overlapped with the independent Hoover Institution on War, Revolution, and Peace in personnel and ideology. Herbert Hoover had founded the institution in 1919 as a library of primary historical sources, but by the 1950s it had evolved into a conservative research center. Baroody served on Hoover's board and his deputy W. Glenn Campbell became Hoover's director in 1959.[53]

The right still struggled, however, to turn ideas into political action. General Robert Wood, the former chairman of the America First Committee, rose again in 1954 to fill this gap by starting For America, which he called "a Right Wing ADA [Americans for Democratic Action]." With Pat Manion and former MacArthur aide General Bonner Fellers as co-chairs, Wood hoped to unite "existing patriotic and civic organizations."

For America did not lobby or endorse candidates but, like the Liberty League, chose to market educational programs for "Americanism as embraced in God, Country, limited Constitutional Government, and States Rights" and against "super-internationalism, world-federalism, or one-worldism." Initial funding came from Texas oilman Robert M. Harriss and the organization's letterhead gleamed with retired brass, including General Fellers, Admiral Ben Moreell and Generals Mark W. Clark and Albert C. Wedemeyer. For America lacked the liberal ADA's brainpower or relationships with journalists, intellectuals, party leaders, and officeholders. As another top-down marketing enterprise, it recruited no foot soldiers to distribute literature, ring doorbells, or sign petitions. Former representative Hamilton Fish, a founding member, complained that "prohibiting political activity and setting For America up virtually as an educational foundation nullifies and repudiates completely the original plans, principles and policies."[54]

We, The People!, another Chicago-based organization, began in 1955 as a "federation of all conservative patriotic organizations, to save Constitutional government and personal freedom." Founder Harry T. Everingham, a veteran conservative organizer, wanted to elect conservatives and persuade officeholders to "oppose all attempts to substitute atheism, alien ideologies or anti-Christian traditions in place of our Christian concepts." Its directors included commentator Dan Smoot, Willis Stone of the Liberty Foundation, and Merwin Hart of the National Economic Council. Like For America, however, We, The People! became what Stone called "another so-called national organization run at the top, by the top and apparently for the top, with the Directors and members given solely the opportunity of conforming or quitting."[55]

GOD'S WILL IN PRINT, PART I: *NATIONAL REVIEW*

William F. Buckley Sr. envisioned a political career for his brilliant son by which he would "take an independent stand within the Republican party," and "raise cain [*sic*] with the Connecticut machine, Republican foreign policy, McMahon's atomic record, and the Young Republic Club (which I understand is dominated by radicals, mostly Jews)." But the son chose instead to save conservativism with his pen. In 1955 Buckley Jr. teamed with *Time* magazine writer Willi Schlamm to raise funds for the right's holy grail—the weekly journal of opinion. If their proposed weekly magazine had existed earlier, their prospectus said, it would have shredded the myth that "Taft could not win if nominated." It would have exposed the "manipulated arguments of the Left" against McCarthy and the Bricker amendment, and bolstered the Reece committee's denunciation of foundations that advanced "world federalism and socialism." To avoid death by dissension, the twenty-nine-year-old Buckley served as CEO and held all voting stock. Buckley and Schlamm recruited cerebral journalists James Burnham and Frank Meyer. Buckley was Catholic. Schlamm, Burnham, and Meyer were Jews by heritage and former Marxists. After failing to purchase the *Freeman* or *Human Events,* they began anew, with a project perpetually short of cash, despite a $100,000 loan from Buckley's father and donations from Sterling Morton, Eastern Airlines CEO Eddie Rickenbacker, General Electric executive Lemuel Boulware, candy manufacturer Robert Welch, textile magnate Roger Milliken, oilman Henry Salvatori, and industrialist Charles Edison.[56]

Buckley launched the *National Review* (*NR*) as a biweekly magazine in late 1955; two years later, Schlamm left and Republican operative William Rusher joined *NR* as publisher. Buckley attempted to cover the magazine's deficits by soliciting tax-exempt donations to nonprofit groups that he then rerouted into his magazine. What Buckley called his "captive tax exempts" included the American Jewish League Against Communism, the Intercollegiate Society of Individualists, the Educational Reviewer, and the Foundation for Social Research, run by James Ingebretsen of Spiritual Mobilization.[57]

Buckley trailed only Ronald Reagan in advancing postwar conservatism. He became a prolific organizer, a media star, a responsible cop on the conservative beat, and an inspiration for young conservatives. Buckley sought to vanquish the left in close intellectual and literary combat and convert the "opinion makers" who "control *the elected*" to his ideology. The never modest editor sold his project to donors as "the most important conceivable enterprise for conservatives in this country." According to publisher Rusher, *NR* was a "radical operation [to] redesign the intellectual premises of the modern world in the same way that the liberals . . . redesigned the premises in their day and turned them into the weapons of materialism, and positivism, and relativism with which they have conquered and denatured and all but destroyed the West."[58]

Unlike gutter fighters like Joe McCarthy, grim doomsayers like Carl McIntire, or rustics like Karl Mundt, Buckley was witty and urbane. He understood that American politics was theater and became a national celebrity, with media interviews, public debates and lectures, a syndicated column, and a television show. Under Buckley, the *National Review*'s circulation hit twenty-five thousand in 1958 and seventy thousand by 1962, surpassing rivals on the left. In his "Publisher's Statement," Buckley wrote that *National Review* "stands athwart history, yelling Stop," which implied not only that America was on the wrong track but also that his magazine was beginning Year One of a respectable conservative movement, disassociated from the Ku Klux Klan, the Liberty League, and the America First Committee.[59]

CONSERVATIVE CATHOLICS

Despite the eclectic religious heritage of its editors, *NR* followed Buckley's Christian ideology. The prominence of Catholics such as Buckley, McCarthy, Baroody, and Manion in the midcentury right paralleled the rise of a politically conservative Catholicism that put anticommunism, defense of property, and Victorian morals above church teachings on poverty, labor, war and peace, and the death penalty. Pope Pius XII in Rome and Cardinal Spellman in the United States led this conservative movement, bolstered by the Knights of Malta and Opus Dei. The Knights, founded during the Crusades, survived as the only sovereign order within the Roman Catholic Church, enjoying special access to the pope and diplomatic privileges. Although ostensibly devoted to charity, the modern Knights united prestigious and powerful conservative figures across the Atlantic. European nobility, many tied to fascist and monarchist movements, had led the Knights between the wars and recruited conservative American businessmen to leadership roles, including John J. Raskob. After World War II, Cardinal Spellman became the Knights' "grand protector" in the United States and conservative Democrat J. Peter Grace, president of W. R. Grace and Company, its lay leader.[60]

Pope Pius XII's church, which towered over the debris of postwar Europe, worked with American agents to check the reds and open the world to Christianity and capitalism—higher priorities for the Vatican and Washington immediately after the war than settling scores with Nazis. Church officials assisted the CIA in aiding anticommunist parties in western Europe and recruiting former Nazis and collaborators for covert operations, intelligence, and scientific work. The Knights of Malta aided these operations with their diplomatic privileges and financial resources. In 1948 the Knights awarded their highest honor to Reinhard Gehlen, the former chief of Hitler's intelligence on the Eastern Front, who the CIA recruited to run its station in West Germany. Key American intelligence officials became Knights, including General William "Wild Bill" Donovan, head of America's wartime intelligence agency, the Office of Strategic Services; John McCone, director of the CIA under President John F. Kennedy; James Jesus Angleton, the CIA's counterintelligence chief from 1954 to 1974; and William J. Casey, President Ronald Reagan's CIA director. Grand Protector Spellman and lay leader Grace worked with U.S. intelligence to resettle hundreds of German scientists, many with Nazi affiliations, to work on U.S. defense projects in government and private industry.[61]

The Spanish priest Josemaría Escrivá de Balaguer founded Opus Dei—God's Work—in 1928 to "place Jesus at the summit of all human activity throughout the world." Opus Dei leaders guided disciples to godly perfection in all phases of life. Its leadership recruited members from the worlds of business, finance, the academy, journalism, and government. Women had a subordinate and largely domestic role. Opus Dei wielded power through its mentoring of well-placed members, influence in the Vatican, and tacit control over banks, businesses, schools, publishing houses, and broadcast facilities. After World War II, Opus Dei thrived in Spain under General Francisco Franco, with members holding key government posts. Although lacking an explicit political program, it espoused a conservative philosophy that condemned moral transgressions, equality for women, and left-of-center movements that threatened private enterprise. In 1982 Pope John Paul II made Opus Dei the Church's only "personal prelature," which gave it the privilege of operating across geographic boundaries without supervision from bishops. After Opus Dei established an American branch in 1949, nearly every prominent U.S. citizen associated with Opus Dei was conservative, both theologically and politically. According to a study of Opus Dei in the United States and abroad by journalist John L. Allen Jr., "The evidence seems overwhelming that most Opus Dei members, in matters of secular politics are conservative. . . . What Opus Dei adds, perhaps, is a doctrinal formulation that gives people more confidence in advancing these positions publicly, and a greater sense of personal obligation to be coherent in their choices."[62]

The values and politics of conservative Protestants and Catholics flowed into a common stream during the 1950s. Both upheld the supernatural mysteries of Christianity, the literal truth of scripture, and the bringing of Christ to all humanity. For both conservative pastors and priests, freedom was the gift of choosing to live within God's love and according to his holy word. A just society, Buckley and J. Howard Pew agreed, taught Christian morality in schools, encouraged traditional marriage and discouraged divorce, prohibited deviant sexuality, protected private property, and controlled subversion and pornography. In public, Buckley said, "*National Review* rejects the current belief that truth is arrived at in public opinion polls. It insists, rather, in an organic moral law and in enduring truths." Privately, he wrote more grandly.

> I happen to believe that the kind of conservatism I identify myself with is the best worldly expression of the Christian position, but I normally go out of my way not to express that view, because I do not want the temporal arrangements I advocate to suffer from the refusal of many to accept the existence of a divine order.

Buckley was a Knight of Malta and a former CIA agent with close ties to Opus Dei in Spain. Buckley so loyally backed the Franco regime that it offered him official honors to recognize "gratefulness from the Government of Spain." Buckley responded that everyone at *NR* was "an ardent friend of Spain" but that he could be "of maximum service to you and to Spain" without "any official recognition of whatever small services I have been in a position to make."[63]

Conservative American Catholics, however, stopped short of advocating the formal subordination of the state to the church. Their goal was not to promote the power of Rome but to suffuse the state and culture with Christian principles. According to Rusher, *NR*'s Protestant publisher, Catholics and Protestants in *NR* "believe that an event of world significance occurred in Western history 2,000 years ago [the birth of Christ] and that Western civilization is the vehicle by which the significance of that event has been and continues to be transmitted to subsequent generations." In the early 1950s, conservative Protestants had cheered Pat Manion's book on America's religious heritage *The Key to Peace*. J. Howard

Pew enthused, "I shall support Dean Manion in almost anything he wants to do, short of acting as a propaganda agent for the Catholic Church," which neither Manion nor Buckley demanded of conservatives. Buckley even challenged papal authority for political ends. The *National Review* ridiculed as "a venture in triviality" Pope John XXIII's 1961 encyclical *Mater et Magistra,* which called upon governments to meet people's material needs and protect the rights of women, minorities, and workers. Albert J. Nevins, president of the Catholic Press Association, responded, "The extreme right refuses to admit the 'social doctrine' of the church" and believed that "Bill Buckley carries more weight than the Pope."[64]

Conservative Catholics found another home in the Cardinal Mindszenty Foundation, named for a Hungarian prelate whom communists had imprisoned in Budapest since 1949. Mindszenty was an ultra-conservative prelate who had opposed the extension of democracy to Hungary and backed the restoration of the Hapsburg monarchy. The Reverend C. Stephen Dunker, a missionary expelled from China, and Eleanor Schlafly, an anticommunist activist who had worked for Radio Liberty, began the foundation in 1958. Eleanor's sister-in-law Phyllis Schlafly served as political director.

The foundation would fight communism and promote "faith, family, and freedom." It took a hard-line approach to internal subversion and foreign policy. It rejected much of Catholic social teaching, opposed welfare and civil rights as communist-inspired plots, and charged that liberals were aiding the growth of communism. It said that communists had penetrated the highest levels of American government, including the Departments of State and Defense, the CIA, and the Supreme Court. The foundation published a newsletter, the *Mindszenty Report,* produced a syndicated radio program called *The Dangers of Apathy,* and distributed films on the plight of Christian clerics in communist lands. The foundation formulated its own version of FDR's Four Freedoms: "freedom to keep our religious heritage, freedom from obscenity, freedom from criminal attacks, and freedom from Communist conspiracy." The foundation's conspiratorial thinking, its rejection of negotiations with the Soviets, its assault on liberals, and its denunciation of civil rights and welfare put it at odds with most American bishops, despite a shared opposition to communism.[65]

GOD'S WILL IN PRINT, PART II: *CHRISTIANITY TODAY*

After failing to remake the National Council of Churches in his conservative image, J. Howard Pew lit his lamp in search of the "spiritual revival" needed to "arrest the plunge of our Country toward self-destruction." He found what he was looking for when he met L. Nelson Bell, the father-in-law of Billy Graham, and other neoevangelical revivalists. In 1955 he wrote to his friend B. E. Hutchinson, "Dr. Bell, Billy Graham and their group impress me as having the only tenable answer to the fundamental problem which our country faces." In Graham's words, "Before there can be a changed society there must be changed people to make up that society, otherwise we are trying to make Non-Christians act like Christians. . . . Personal salvation must come before social reformation." Pew and Graham formed an alliance with profound impact on American political history. "God has given to me the ear of millions," Graham wrote to Pew. "He has given to you large sums of money. It seems to me that if we can put these two gifts of God together, we could reach the world with the message of Christ."[66]

Pew gave generously to the Billy Graham crusades and collaborated with the evangelist to found a theologically and politically conservative, but also widely respected, journal of opinion. Graham assured the oilman that the proposed magazine, *Christianity Today,* could "change the entire course of the American Protestant Church. . . . Instead of being liberal, like so many are, it will be conservative, evangelical, and anti-Communist. I sincerely believe it is the greatest possible investment an American businessman can make in the Kingdom of God at this moment."[67]

Graham's charisma and Pew's money lured preeminent neoevangelicals to *Christianity Today:* Carl F. H. Henry as editor and Bell—a leader of the Christian Amendment movement to make Christianity America's official religion—as executive editor. President Eisenhower's pastor, the Reverend Edward L. R. Elson, joined as an associate editor. Harold Ockenga, first president of the National Association of Evangelicals, headed a board of directors that included Pew and Graham, who was a silent member in order to keep up a facade of independence. Pew pledged $150,000 for *Christianity Today* and assured founders, "As to the finances, I would say that I am prepared to underwrite the costs for the first year—so

that in any event there will be no problem as to the organization expenses."
To avert charges of big business control, Pew funneled contributions through
Ockenga's Park Street Church, which transferred funds in its name to the
magazine. Other backers included the Billy Graham Evangelistic Association (another means for routing Pew money into the magazine), the Volker
Fund, the Fleming Foundation, and Maxey Jarman, CEO of the Genesco
apparel company.[68]

The magazine debuted in October 1956. It aimed "primarily to reach
ministers, particularly to win liberals to the evangelical position." The editors mailed copies to some 160,000 ministers, mostly free of charge, and secured some 27,000 paid subscribers, which rose to about 40,000 in two years,
equally divided between ministers and laypersons. It reached a politically
conservative audience, as evidenced by a 1956 reader's poll that showed an
eight to one preference for Eisenhower in his rematch with Adlai Stevenson.
An in-house survey by Opinion Research Corporation found that four-fifths
of ministers read the magazine, far outpacing ten other religious publications. It quickly became the most intellectually challenging, best edited, and
most influential publication of evangelical Christians. By the early 1960s the
paid circulation hit 150,000, well ahead of *National Review* and *Human Events*.
In a 1962 article, "Conservatism Today," *Time* magazine observed that *Christianity Today* was "indispensable—if often irritating reading—in manses and
seminaries across the U. S. . . . It preaches a kind of literate, highbrow fundamentalism. Strongly conservative in its economic and political views,
strongly Biblical in its theology, it is a byproduct of the one-man refurbish-
ing job done on the U.S. Protestant church by Billy Graham."[69]

The magazine's founders believed in the synergy between conservative theology and "conservatism in economics and sociology," Pew wrote.
"I have never known a minister who was conservative in his theology, who
was not at the same time sound in his social and economic philosophy."
Graham agreed. "Faith in the Scriptures and the centrality of the cross . . .
also affects the political and social outlook tremendously." In a January
1959 meeting Ockenga assured board members that the editors were "always keeping in mind the close inter-relation between socio-economic
issues and theological beliefs. . . . Liberalism in theology almost inevitably
leads to liberal socio-economic philosophies." Pew, Graham, and the editors agreed that unlike the National Council of Churches, *Christianity Today*
was a voluntary association, free in editor Henry's words to address issues

without "making political pronouncements in the *name of the Church*." Pew asserted, "You cannot take life and divide it into separate compartments—one for your Christianity, another for your economics, another for your social relations, etc." Graham assured the tycoon that the editors were not "going to allow anything to appear in the magazine that will conflict with our views on economics and socialism" or contradict "our basic policies" hammered out at board meetings. Henry agreed: "We are sure that at bottom our politico-economic ideals are so largely one."[70]

VOTERS STILL LIKED IKE, BUT NOT REPUBLICANS

After Eisenhower suffered a heart attack in September of 1955, Senate Minority Leader Knowland, in another gesture of right-wing defiance, tossed his hat halfway into the ring, saying he would run for president if ill health kept Eisenhower on the shelf. In February a recuperated president spiked all rival campaigns, although some moderate Republicans lobbied Ike to dump Nixon. Although the president contemplated forming a centrist coalition by picking a moderate Democrat, he once again declined to shake up his party. The president retained Nixon and backed all GOP candidates. A disgruntled Pat Manion, however, rallied northern conservatives from For America and segregationists from southern "states' rights" organizations behind the insurgent third-party campaign of former IRS commissioner T. Coleman Andrews. The candidate ran, ironically, against the income tax "that has financed every boondoggling usurpation of the rights of the states and every something-for-nothing fraud against the people." Andrews pledged to protect the states from federal encroachment and to end America's "drift toward socialism."[71]

In the election year, Ike won passage of the Federal Highway Act, which authorized the construction of an interstate highway system financed largely by new federal taxes on fuels, tires, and commercial vehicles. Still, foreign crises dominated the rematch against Adlai Stevenson. When a revolt in Hungary led to a new nationalist regime, which Soviet tanks and troops crushed just days before the 1956 election, the U.S. had neither the means nor the will to act. America had offered only rhetoric and broadcasts from Radio Free Europe, which raised expectations about American aid that the administration never intended to provide. A November survey, however, found that only 23 percent of respondents believed that the United States "should have done more to help Hungary win freedom from Russia." In the Middle East, after the Egyptian president Gamal Abdel Nasser seized control of the Suez Canal, a military force led by Britain, France, and Israel invaded Egypt to both "liberate" the canal and overthrow Nasser's regime. On the eve of the election, the invaders agreed to Eisenhower's demand, reinforced by a UN resolution, for a cease-fire. "You cannot resort to force in international relationships because of your fear of what might happen in the future," Ike wrote.[72]

Eisenhower won 57 percent of the popular vote and forty-one states. Andrews's third-party campaign netted less than 1 percent. Ike matched Hoover's 1928 performance in the South by carrying seven states, and he became the first Republican to win a majority of the white southern vote— 51 percent, according to the National Election Study. Yet the Democrats retained their narrow margin in both the Senate and House. Eisenhower's modern Republicanism was neither converting Democrats nor luring new voters to the GOP.[73]

SECOND-TERM BLUES

A year after Eisenhower cracked the South, the RNC's southern strategist I. Lee Potter wrote that the party had lost momentum in the region and alienated potential recruits. Republicans slipped backward in the South when events forced President Eisenhower to enforce the Supreme Court's 1954 decision *Brown v. Board of Education,* which outlawed legally segregated schools. In September 1957 the president dispatched federal troops to Little Rock, Arkansas, to protect black children entering the city's previously all-white Central High School. By making it clear that he was merely acting to enforce a court order and not putting the moral weight of his presidency behind integration, Eisenhower managed to please neither segregationists nor civil rights activists.[74]

The Little Rock crisis was part of a triple whammy in the fall of 1957 that signified a troubled second term. A tight monetary policy by the Federal Reserve Board and a drop in private investment led to a recession that lasted into the midterm election year. A month after Little Rock, the Soviets launched Sputnik—humankind's first orbiting vehicle in space—and gave Russia a propaganda triumph that threw into question America's technical and scientific superiority. After Sputnik, journalists, political leaders, military officials, and a leaked top-secret report of an administration study group warned of an emerging "missile gap" that left America vulnerable to Soviet attack.[75]

The right sought to frame the 1958 midterm elections as a choice between worker freedom and bondage to unions. Conservatives secured the petition signatures needed to place "right-to-work" referenda to eliminate union shops on the ballot in six states, notably Ohio and California. A National Right to Work Committee led by former New Jersey representative Fred A. Hartley, cosponsor of the Taft-Hartley Act, and financed mostly by small business, joined with NAM and the U.S. Chamber of Commerce in claiming that a middle-class "silent vote" would counter labor opposition. In California, Senator Knowland abandoned his seat to run for governor and position himself for a presidential bid.

Voters rebuked Republicans, conservatives, and right-to-work amendments. The GOP dropped forty-seven seats in the House, thirteen in the Senate, and five governorships. After the election Democrats controlled 65 percent of the seats in both chambers of Congress. The voters also upheld the union shop in five of six states, including Ohio and California. Voters dismissed Senator Bricker in Ohio and in California, Democrat Edmund G. "Pat" Brown killed Knowland's dream of a governorship and potential presidency. In Utah maverick conservative politics cost the GOP another seat when former governor J. Bracken Lee's independent campaign split the conservative vote and doomed the incumbent senator Arthur Watkins. Not a single member of the famous conservative Senate "Class of '46" remained in office after the election. Nelson Rockefeller emerged as the nation's leading moderate Republican after beating incumbent governor Averell Harriman in New York. Conservative columnist James J. Kilpatrick quipped after the election, "My impulsive answer to the question, where do conservatives go from here is down to Paddy's Grill to get falling down drunk."[76]

After the dismaying election, business redoubled its salesmanship and became more openly political. General Electric, the nation's second largest employer, led the way with its "Syracuse plan," which set up education programs and incentives for fifteen thousand managers and supervisors to engage in politics. GE organized a "citizen education" campaign to promote a "better business climate." The company's vice president, Lemuel Ricketts Boulware, pioneered an aggressive approach to labor relations that critics dubbed Boulwarism. Rather than bargaining with union leaders, Boulware presented them with a "fair" and nonnegotiable "final" offer. GE bypassed labor leaders and sought to convert workers to management's point of view through company newspapers, magazines, and book clubs. It employed Ronald Reagan from 1954 to 1962 to host its weekly television show *General Electric Theater* and sell the company's conservative ideology in speaking tours of GE plants and business, charitable, and fraternal groups. During his GE years, Reagan completed his odyssey to the right. He learned how to take a hard line on labor and pitch his political appeals directly to the people.[77]

Other companies moved into politics, including Gulf Oil, which claimed, "If we are to survive, labor's political power must now be opposed by a matching force—among the corporations that make up American business." The Chamber of Commerce produced a training text called *Action Course in Practical Politics* that it sold to many of the nation's major corporations. Corporate executives set up a national association, the Effective Citizens Organization, to coordinate political action.[78]

Even in a Democratic Congress business gained in its top priority of regulating labor through the Landrum-Griffin Act of 1959 that controlled union racketeering and corruption. Both President Eisenhower and conservative Democratic senator John McClellan of Arkansas backed the campaign for Landrum-Griffin. For three years McClellan conducted hearings on labor's financial misdeeds and strong-arm tactics, burning into the public consciousness the alleged evils of union bosses.[79]

THE RIGHT REORGANIZES

After the midterm debacle of 1958 the Republican leadership in both houses of Congress, prompted by Senator Karl Mundt of South Dakota, secretly met to build a workable political organization that would maintain the facade of independence from the GOP. Senator Owen Brewster of Maine said, "They kept their participation quiet in order to avoid embarrassment among their associates and misunderstanding by others." Their new organization, Americans for Constitutional Action (ACA), would strive to help elect members of Congress "who will work for strengthening the Opportunity State—against the tyrannical 'welfare state.'" ACA contributed money and expertise to candidates and compiled an index of congressional voting that gauged support for "the God-given dignity of the individual" and opposition to "'Group Morality' and a socialized economy." Retired U.S. Navy admiral Ben Moreell, chairman of the board of Jones and Laughlin Steel corporation, headed a board of industrialists that also included Herbert Hoover, Felix Morley, and Edgar Eisenhower (the president's conservative brother). In 1955 Moreell had written, "We are now locked in the grip of Armageddon . . . which will determine when man can learn to obey God's laws in time to avoid destruction" from "a decadent group morality, imposed on mankind by the force of secular law." The ACA's voting index proved useful for conservatives, but its influence waned after it failed to tilt the 1960 elections to the right.[80]

The Janus-faced Liberty Lobby, founded by author and organizer Willis Carto in 1957, was both a lobbying operation and a hate group. Carto pledged to liberate Washington from occupation by "an aggressive coalition of minority special interest pressure groups." By 1962 his Liberty Lobby had a Washington office run by Curtis Dall, Franklin Roosevelt's former son-in-law. The lobby presented testimony to Congress on proposed legislation and published a monthly *Liberty Letter* that urged conservatives to shift "their activity from the unproductive non-political and educational to the political." The letter analyzed legislation and instructed readers in how to influence the votes of their representatives in Congress. The lobby gained national attention in 1964 with two controversial pamphlets that circulated in the millions. "LBJ: A Political Biography" exposed Lyndon B. Johnson's unsavory past and "The Ev and Charlie Show" scorned mainstream GOP leaders Everett Dirksen in the Senate and Charles Halleck in the House as "sellouts, more dangerous than some of the more blatant and admitted leftists in Washington." After the election, the lobby published another pamphlet, called "Looking Forward," which urged conservatives to build cadres within the Republican Party to ensure "the survival of the Western World" and postpone any decision about forming a new party of their own. By the late 1960s the Liberty Lobby claimed two hundred thousand subscribers to its *Liberty Letter,* which surpassed all other political publications of the right or the left.[81]

The Liberty Lobby also propagated Carto's racist vision of the world, which he had earlier elaborated in a four- to six-page monthly bulletin called *Right.* Carto's thought combined anti-Semitism, extreme anticommunism, and white supremacy. He warned that human destiny would be decided by a grinding struggle between "the white and the colored races of the world, of which Russia is lord." His demonology, guided by neo-Nazi visionary Francis Parker Yockey, blamed Jews for instigating World War II and deceiving Americans into fighting the Nazis—"the only real anti-communists forces which have ever existed and perhaps doomed the entire West." In the postwar era, he argued that a "ruling elite in Washington," under Jewish influence, was retreating "before an aroused, armed Russian-Asiatic threat." Carto embraced racial science to prove the superiority of Nordic peoples, opposed racial integration, and called for the repatriation of blacks to Africa. Directors of the Liberty Lobby promoted these ideas in limited-circulation publications, such as the biweekly newsletter *Washington Observer* and the intellectual journal *Western Destiny*, edited by white supremacist Roger Pearson.[82]

The American Security Council (ASC) that General Wood, other industrialists, and former FBI agents founded in 1955 at first specialized in identifying subversives within the United States. ASC president John M. Fisher, the security director for Sears, Roebuck, raised seed money from Sears, Marshall Field, and Motorola. He billed ASC as an arm of industry that screened employees and job applicants. After taking over the files of Harry Jung's American Vigilante group, the ASC claimed in 1958 to have some two million card files on persons affiliated with "Communist and other statist movements" and a membership of 175 companies. By the 1960s ASC had broadened its goals to shaping foreign and military policy. Its use of Liebman's letterhead technique to acquire prominent names such as H-bomb scientist Dr. Edward Teller, Dr. Stefan Possony of the Hoover Institution, Generals Mark Clark and Curtis LeMay, and Admiral Ben Moreell led critics to label ASC "the voice of the military-industrial complex."[83]

Also in 1958, NAM board member Robert Welch founded the John Birch Society. Its goal was to battle communists who had "already gone at least one-fourth of the ways towards . . . taking over this country" because of a "collapse of the rock of faith on which our morality was built." The society was an offshoot of industry's long-standing war on the left. Welch wrote to retired Chrysler executive B. E. Hutchinson that "only the American business community still has the combination of financial strength, traditional morality, and common sense to make the truth known to enough of the American people." Welch launched his group a month after NAM had warned in a recruitment letter, "Our free enterprise system is slipping away from us. . . . If the present trend continues, we will have a government dominated by well-organized minorities." For his seventeen-member founding council he reached into NAM for three former presidents and one former vice president. Other prominent industrialists joined the council, as did talk show host Pat Manion, former third-party presidential candidate T. Coleman Andrews, and China Lobby founder Alfred Kohlberg. Welch named his society for a U.S. intelligence officer killed in 1945 by communists in China, "probably the first American casualty in that third world war, between Communists and the ever-shrinking 'free world.'" But the American commander in China, General Albert Wedemeyer, told Welch that Birch's own folly had led to his death.[84]

To battle the vast communist conspiracy in the United States, Welch demanded "unshakable loyalty" from Birch Society members who worked in small groups across the nation. Like communists, Birchers churned out front groups, whether to impeach Chief Justice Earl Warren or to get America out of the UN. John Birch groups subdivided when they reached twenty or more members, enabling conservatives to rally around community issues.[85]

Local groups took Welch's conspiratorial thinking a step further to warn that government was fluoridating water "to soften the brains of the American people and make them pushovers for communism" and setting up a vast mental health asylum in Alaska as a "place of exile, communist-fashion, where all who disagreed with 'liberal' concepts could be quietly put away." Others charged that urban planners were plotting to impose on American communities "Soviet-type central communications, and demagogic executive and administrative control." These charges pushed to a far edge the conservative critique of a society that exploited science to control the lives of Americans and erode patriotism, religion, and tradition.[86]

MASSIVE RESISTANCE

Democratic senator Harry F. Byrd of Virginia coined the term "massive resistance" in 1956 shortly before 101 southern senators and representatives issued a manifesto denouncing the Supreme Court's decision in *Brown* as a "clear abuse of judicial power" and urging opposition to integration short of "disorder and lawless acts." In the largest movement on the right during the 1950s, southerners again mixed white supremacy with stock conservative themes. They charged that forced integration threatened private property, religion, public safety and morals, and states' rights. They linked integration with communist subversion, union racketeering, and the loss of American sovereignty. To counter the liberal case that Jim Crow hurt America's global standing, resisters argued that disorderly black soldiers abroad discredited the United States.

White Citizens' Councils defended segregation, beginning in 1954 when state judge Thomas Pickens Brady and local businessmen formed the Citizens' Council of Indianola, Mississippi—for citizens who "wouldn't join a Ku Klux" but would defend "the God-given right to keep his blood white and pure." The FBI estimated in 1956 that "41 [council] organizations for which figures are available reflect a total membership of 116,000." Council leaders like Judge Brady and fellow Mississippian W. J. Simmons sought to unify the movement within the South and extend its reach to conservatives nationwide by arguing that southern resisters were fighting America's war against collectivism and communism. Judge Brady, in an address to the Commonwealth Club of California, expressed the hope that "all constitutional, liberty-loving citizens in this country will rise up in our defense and join hands with us in waging our lonely fight to preserve America from Godless Communism."[87]

Despite such outreach, the councils remained mostly southern and locally based, with mostly middle-class members—small-town officials, shopkeepers, lawyers, doctors, and farmers. Some moderates tied to corporate interests said that massive resistance discouraged the investments and government contracts needed in the South. But they failed to halt massive resistance, which unlike Thurmond's 1948 campaign had the backing of the South's leading politicians. A far more violent Ku Klux Klan than the 1920s version also defended the old order through mayhem and murder. Perpetrators escaped retribution from the South's all-white justice system until federal officials overcame J. Edgar Hoover's resistance and began prosecutions in the late 1960s under civil rights laws.

State governments deployed their coercive power to maintain segregation, led by Mississippi's Sovereignty Commission, which spied on and harassed blacks and sympathetic whites. The commission also launched a national lobbying and propaganda campaign to block civil rights legislation. These agencies, along with southern chairs of Senate and House committees, and J. Edgar Hoover, again linked red scare and black scare. They warned that communists manipulated the civil rights movement for their own ends. Southern governments also filed lawsuits to block and delay integration, outlawed the NAACP, closed integrated schools, aided all-white private academies, and mandated "nonracial" pupil assignment that replicated segregation.

Segregationist propaganda drew on history, law, science, and biblical scholarship. Several academics, including Wesley Critz George, former chair of the Anatomy Department at the University of North Carolina, and Henry E. Garrett, a past president of the American Psychological Association, lent their prestige to the claim that inborn intellectual and cultural deficiencies of African Americans justified segregation. Amateur anthropologist Carlton Putnam popularized the same ideas in his widely read book *Race and Reason* (1961), which became a classic on the right. Putnam charged that an "equalitarian conspiracy" of minority groups "willing to destroy Anglo-Saxon civilization because of real or fancied grievances" had imposed a curtain of silence on racial science. Crude versions of scientific racism filtered down into Citizens' Council propaganda: "Professors Admit Integration Fails to Smarten Negroes," "Integration Means Degeneration," "Prolific Negresses Bleed Whites White." In 1959 southern segregationists joined with proponents of Nordic superiority from the Northeast—both academics and political activists—in the International Association for the Advancement of Ethnology and Eugenics, which propagated racial science through its journal *Mankind Quarterly*. Association scientists entered the federal courts in the 1960s as expert witnesses in lawsuits that sought to overturn *Brown* by challenging scientific testimony on the effects of segregation.[88]

Massive resistance gained significant financial backing in the North from textile heir Wickliffe Preston Draper, who had founded the Pioneer Fund in 1937 to promote research "into the problems of race betterment" and breeding by children of America's pioneer stock. Eugenics researcher and promoter Harry Laughlin served as the fund's first president. Draper more generously backed massive resistance in the South than any other figure. He donated $215,000 in cash and stocks to the Mississippi State Sovereignty Commission. He also contributed to the white citizens' councils, segregated Christian academies, and exponents of scientific racism.[89]

Massive resistance coexisted uneasily with religion. Academically trained ministers and mainstream Protestant leaders often counseled compliance with the law. Still, most evangelical ministers from segregated southern churches equated integration with liberalism in religion and invoked biblical sanction for segregation. A Jewish pamphleteer urged "Northern Jewry to settle their own labor problems, dishonesty, racketeering, communism, bossism, graft, corruption," and leave the South in peace.[90]

For about a decade, from 1954 through 1963, massive resistance delayed and disrupted school integration before succumbing to federal court rulings, changing public attitudes, and tougher civil rights laws. Although council leader Simmons boasted that southern resisters had sparked a "conservative revolt through the country," even sympathetic conservatives outside the South declined to join a movement that northern opinion tied to the "Lost Cause of the Confederacy."[91]

Nonetheless, northern conservatives opposed the *Brown* decision and compulsory civil rights laws, forfeiting to liberals the moral high ground on race. Senator Barry Goldwater denounced the "fire-eating talk ... among Negroes and those whites who would use them only a means to gain power." The DAR opposed integration and We, The People! resolved, "States must have the sole power to regulate such matters as (1) conduct of their schools, (2) racial problems, (3) voting qualifications."[92]

Most prominent voices on the mainstream right, including *Christianity Today* and *National Review,* also opposed government programs to outlaw segregation and discrimination. In its one detailed statement on racial integration, *Christianity Today* published "Segregation and the Kingdom of God" by E. Earle Ellis, an assistant professor of religion at Aurora College in Illinois. Ellis flogged Christians who ignored "the evil implicit in a consistent integrationist philosophy" that puts the equality of groups above the liberty of individuals. He defended the South's right "to preserve its European racial and cultural heritage," ripped "Christian integrationists [as] one cause of the worsening race relations in the South," and pronounced integration a failure in the North. The same bad theology, Ellis said, seduced Christians into backing integration, "Christian socialism," and "world government and world citizenship." The magazine's own editorial in the same issue tread a fine line on race relations. The editors condemned race prejudice and called upon the churches to promote "neighbor-love from every human being." However, they also repeated the familiar conservative argument against civil rights measures, saying that "forced integration is as contrary to Christian principles as forced segregation."[93]

In several editorials, the *National Review* condemned civil rights for upsetting social order and prerogatives of a superior white race. A 1956 *NR* editorial denounced the *Brown* desegregation decision as "one of the most brazen acts of judicial usurpation in our history, patently counter to the intent of the Constitution, shoddy and illegal in analysis, and invalid as sociology." A 1957 editorial, "Why the South Must Prevail," stated that the southern "white community" justifiably prohibited voting by Negroes because "for the time being, it is the advanced race." Restating scientific racism in their own idiom, the editors wrote, "It is not easy, and it is unpleasant, to adduce statistics evidencing the cultural superiority of White over Negro: but it is a fact that obtrudes, one that cannot be hidden by ever-so-busy egalitarians and anthropologists." In 1959 conservative theorist Richard Weaver published a defense of the segregationist South in *NR* and two years later privately lauded Buckley for having the courage to say "The doctrinaire position on integration is untenable, either in theory or practice."[94]

In private, Buckley expanded on his belief in black inferiority, writing in late 1961, "I pray every Negro will not be given the vote in South Carolina tomorrow. The day after, he would lose that repose through which, slowly but one hopes surely, some of the decent instincts of the white man go to work, fuse with his own myths and habits of mind, and make him a better and better instructed man, and hence a man more likely to know God." Like the founders of the Liberty League, Buckley said, "Democracy is not one of my absolutes. . . . The point I insist upon is the essential competence of civilized man to judge what is and what is not pointed in the direction of enlightenment." Buckley's racial views did not stop at the water's edge. He traveled to apartheid South Africa at its government's expense, disseminated South African propaganda in the United States, and accepted expensive gifts from South African officials, who steered private funds from their country to his magazine. He teamed up with Marvin Liebman to found the American Afro-Asian Education Exchange, which aimed at presenting "the views of the South African Government." In a signed article, Buckley edged close to endorsing apartheid publicly. "I cannot say, 'I approve of Apartheid'—its ways are alien to my temperament. But I know now it is a sincere peoples' effort to fashion the land of peace they want so badly." Most American conservative leaders in the 1950s and '60s doubted that Africans had the capacity to govern themselves and backed white settler regimes in South Africa and Rhodesia and colonial governments in Angola and Mozambique as essential bulwarks against communism.[95]

By the end of the Eisenhower years, the right still lacked political action committees or a means for mobilizing voters comparable to labor unions on the left. Still, a vibrant conservative culture was flourishing across America. According to a Gallup Poll taken in July 1960, more Americans would have supported a conservative than a liberal political party. Yet the mainstream press paid little heed to the right. Even the provocative John Birch Society failed to gain media attention. For two years after its founding in November 1958, not a single reference to the society appeared in the *New York Times, Washington Post, Chicago Tribune,* or *Los Angeles Times.*

THE NEW FACE OF THE RIGHT

During Ike's first term, Senator Barry Goldwater of Arizona had been a good soldier for his party. In the second term, however, Goldwater seized his chance to lead the GOP's right-wing faction. Goldwater blasted Ike's $72 billion budget for fiscal 1958 and declared that modern Republicanism was inclined "to bow to the siren song of socialism." Goldwater's once robust support for the president's position on legislation fell to less than 50 percent, second to last among Senate Republicans. "Senator Goldwater has really hit hard and the response has been terrific," cheered Senator William Jenner of Indiana. "I told Barry he has now removed himself from the 'faint hope' class to an 'irreconcilable.'"[96]

Goldwater bashed labor bosses and won a tough reelection battle amid the conservative wreckage of 1958. "Goldwater made not one particle of compromise with the 'liberal' line," noted the *Indianapolis Star.* "If Republicans across the country want to know how to recoup their losses and win for a change, let them call in Barry Goldwater." His Senate peers made the call and reelected Goldwater in 1959 as Republican Senate campaign chair. *Human Events,* in a July 1959 editorial, proposed Goldwater for president.[97]

Goldwater, the rugged westerner with the Jewish name, had become the conservative hero. In 1960, at the prompting of talk show host Pat Manion, Goldwater contracted L. Brent Bozell to ghostwrite a brief but blunt manifesto, *The Conscience of a Conservative,* a right-wing twist on Mao's *Little Red Book. Conscience* eventually sold some 3.5 million copies. Its pages crackled with the tension on the right between opposition to the liberal state and the need for state power to crush permissiveness and communism. Although Goldwater refused to tilt against windmills by opposing Vice President Nixon's nomination in 1960, he did not repudiate a grassroots "Goldwater for President" campaign. When Nixon journeyed to New York to negotiate with Governor Rockefeller on modifications in the Republican platform, Goldwater denounced this "Compact of Fifth Avenue" as the "Munich of the Republican Party" and let supporters place his name in nomination at the convention. His convention speech called for unity behind Nixon, but also for conservatives to "grow up" and "take this party back" from moderates. Nixon, however, chose to run with former senator Henry Cabot Lodge Jr., Ike's moderate campaign chair from 1952. More salt in conservative wounds.[98]

For some conservatives, the Republican Party, like Israel under Ahab, had strayed too far for redemption. The far right's 1950s power couple, Kent and Phoebe Courtney of Louisiana, called for a third party, or a "second party," because "the candidates of both parties stand for the same old New Deal." The Courtneys published the *Independent American* newspaper as a compendium of conservative writing with a claimed circulation of nine thousand. They self-published books, disseminated what they called "Tax Fax" pamphlets on issues, and founded the Conservative Society of America—a grandiose name for their mom-and-pop operation. However, the couple had the swagger to convene five hundred activists for a new party convention in October 1959. Speakers included Robert Welch, Dan Smoot, J. Bracken Lee, and William F. Buckley Jr. Without the resources for a viable party, however, the convention could only praise Goldwater and hope to bury Nixon.[99]

At the *National Review*, editor Frank Meyer said that Nixon's nomination meant "nothing better than a mild decrease in our rate of growth towards collectivism at home and our surrender to collectivism abroad." He urged a "principled boycott of the 1960 Presidential campaign" that could lead in 1964 to "a possibility of conservative victory, whether through recapture of the Republican Party or through creation of a new alignment of forces." Fellow editor James Burnham, however, backed Nixon because Kennedy represented what "*NR* is not merely against, but recognizes as its primary targets." These included "disintegrative leftist ideologues ... the most dangerous and ruthless of the trade union bureaucracy; the appeasers and collaborationists; the most extreme secularists (ironically enough!), including the most Jewish Jews; the city lumpenproletariat; the socialists, fellow-travelers and communists." Rusher would oppose Nixon "as a first step toward breaking away from the Republican Party altogether —toward a third party, to be formed when the moment is ripe." *NR* ultimately took Meyer's position; it would remain agnostic in 1960 and fight again in 1964.[100]

ANOTHER CATHOLIC DEMOCRAT

Nixon confronted another prodigy in John F. Kennedy, the junior senator from Massachusetts. Knowing that the South was contested territory, Kennedy took the unusual step of selecting one of his rivals, Senator Lyndon Johnson of Texas, for the vice presidential nomination. Kennedy positioned himself as the leader for a new generation poised to embark on a "new frontier" of domestic reform and Cold War activism. He struck the theme of a nation in decline and called for sacrifice in the service of country. Kennedy's Catholicism sparked another religious debate, less strident than when Al Smith ran for president in 1928 but with the issues little changed. Billy Graham honored his rule by staying officially nonpartisan, but he signaled his preference for Nixon by delivering the invocation at a Nixon-Lodge rally. *Christianity Today* stayed officially neutral to retain its tax exemption, but the magazine published an open letter to Senator Kennedy on the issue of religion, written by Charles Clayton Morrison, former editor of the *Christian Century,* a magazine that opposed Al Smith in 1928. Editor L. Nelson Bell and board chair Harold John Ockenga joined with Norman Vincent Peale and the National Association of Evangelicals in warning against electing a Catholic president. Like Smith, Kennedy confronted critics on enemy turf. At a meeting of the Greater Houston Ministerial Association, he said, "I believe in an America where the separation of church and state is absolute—where no Catholic prelate would tell the President (should he be Catholic) how to act, and no Protestant minister would tell his parishioners for whom to vote."[101]

Vice President Nixon scrupulously avoided the religious issue. He urged voters to put aside party and ideology and select the better-prepared candidate. But Kennedy shattered this rationale by performing well in the nation's first televised presidential debates. More critically, Nixon was defending a dying regime that was plagued with a mild election-year recession and discontent at home. America was playing catch-up in the space race, and Eisenhower's negotiations with Khrushchev ended in disaster when prior to a 1960 summit meeting in Paris the Soviets shot down an American U-2 reconnaissance plane and captured its pilot. In Cuba, Fidel Castro, leader of the Cuban revolution, expropriated American property and began moving his nation into the Soviet orbit. Nixon implored Eisenhower to hike spending and prime the election-year economy, but the fiscally conservative president refused to put aside his principles. Ike had earlier told his cabinet that "the true problem that faces Western civilization is this: can free government, faced by the thrust of a single-controlled economy, continue to exist, in view of the many demands made by special interests, softness, and the indulgence of selfish motives?"[102]

Nixon nearly tasted the sweet grapes of victory. He lost to Kennedy by 100,000 votes out of more than sixty-eight million cast, though he lost in the Electoral College 303 to 219. The National Election Study found that Kennedy had won the votes cast by 34 percent of white Protestants, 83 percent of Catholics, 89 percent of Jews, and 71 percent of blacks. Outside the South, he won 29 percent of the white Protestant vote, compared to Smith's 25 percent. Kennedy did not win because Protestants became reconciled to a Catholic president. He won because blacks had become Democrats since 1928 and white Protestants were a smaller share of the electorate. Kennedy's campaign also pointed to the future of American politics with its creative use of television, polling, personal organization, and image making. These innovations diminished the role of party organizations in presidential elections and led to the more costly media-driven campaigns.

Kennedy's narrow margins of victory in Illinois and Texas prompted Republicans to challenge the vote count in court despite an official disavowal from the ambitious Nixon, who wanted no part of sour grapes because he planned to fight again on the same battlefield of presidential politics. GOP representative and former missionary Walter Judd preached a sermon on voter fraud that Republicans would heed in 1964 and for decades to come. "A party can still lose an election if it is not sufficiently alert and tough in policing registrations and voting booths and counting procedures to make certain that only legitimate votes are cast and all votes legitimately cast are honestly counted."[103]

CONSERVATIVES FALL, RISE, AND FALL AGAIN, 1960–1968

Senator Barry Goldwater was no bigot. He had joined an Arizona branch of the NAACP and worked for the integration of the Arizona National Guard. But he knew that his future as a conservative Republican depended upon uniting northern conservatives with white Protestant defenders of Jim Crow in the South. On November 18, 1961, Goldwater told a GOP meeting in Atlanta that he opposed measures "to enforce integration of the schools." The Republicans, he said, could not "out-promise the Democrats" in competition for black votes. The party needed to "go hunting where the ducks are." According to South Carolina journalist George McMillan, "Not since Sen. Strom Thurmond have southern segregationists had a presidential candidate who talked their language that plainly." Goldwater's political strategy helped him defeat the GOP's eastern establishment and win the Republican presidential nomination in 1964 with support from 97 percent of southern convention delegates. Goldwater swept the Deep South in the general election, but his devastating defeat nationwide would for a time open the floodgates of liberal reform and revive the political fortunes of pragmatic Republican Richard Nixon.

CAUTION IN THE WHITE HOUSE

John F. Kennedy spoke boldly but governed cautiously. He reached into the establishment for moderate cabinet appointees and his modest domestic proposals for medical assistance to the elderly and federal aid to education died in a stand-pat Congress, although he gained authority to reduce tariff barriers and expand international trade. Kennedy's moderation did not deter Senator Goldwater from charging in early 1962 that Kennedy "the wagon master, is riding on the left wheel all the time." From the far right came the urgent warning that under the guise of a military exercise in Georgia called Operation Water Moccasin, which trained American and foreign troops in counterinsurgency warfare, the administration was preparing UN forces for an invasion of the United States.[1]

In foreign affairs, Kennedy suffered an early setback when an American-sponsored exile invasion of Cuba at the Bay of Pigs ended in disaster. Kennedy approved the operation, which the CIA had planned during the Eisenhower administration as a last chance to dislodge Castro. Kennedy salvaged his public approval by taking personal responsibility for the fiasco, which heightened his suspicion of expert advice and hasty action in foreign arenas that America did not fully understand and could not easily control. Kennedy had greater success in Europe, where he coolly stared down threats by the Soviet premier Nikita Khrushchev to abrogate Western rights in Berlin. His administration completed the triad system of nuclear deterrence—manned bombers, land-based missiles, and missiles fired from submarines—while seeking to develop more flexible capacities for responding to guerrilla-style "wars of liberation."

In the developing world, Kennedy embraced the liberal anticommunist program of modernizing backward states by encouraging market economies, democracy, and human rights. His showpiece, the "Alliance for Progress" in Latin America, failed to meet expectations for achieving these reforms. This forced Kennedy, like Eisenhower, to rely on covert action and backing for pro-American regimes. In Southeast Asia, Laos and South Vietnam faced communist-led insurgencies. During Kennedy's transition to the White House, a Rand Corporation study had warned that the administration's greatest challenges would come in the less developed world, where "the US may well find that its limited war forces have neither an appropriate terrain nor opportunity for deployment." In Laos, Kennedy resisted pressure from advisers for military operations and brokered the negotiation of a neutralist regime. In Vietnam, as in China under Chiang Kai-shek, communist pressure was crumbling a weak, corrupt government. Again, Kennedy rejected military intervention in force. However, lacking a diplomatic solution, he expanded the presence of American military advisers in Vietnam to some seventeen thousand by 1963 and approved a military coup against the failed regime of President

Ngo Diem, who South Vietnamese generals would assassinate on November 2, 1963. By then, Kennedy was working on a plan that contemplated withdrawing one thousand troops initially and extracting most American forces by 1965. Kennedy kept the plan under wraps to forestall conservative charges of appeasement during his reelection campaign.[2]

Conflict with business interests, followed by a rapprochement, marked the first of two turning points for the Kennedy administration. Like Democrats before him, Kennedy worked with the Business Council to secure business confidence, even after the council broke with the Commerce Department to become a private organization in July 1961. Walter Heller, chairman of the President's Council of Economic Advisers, told Kennedy, "Let's not antagonize them or contribute to the image of a Kennedy administration *versus* business." Adviser Ted Sorensen demurred: "Most big businessmen are, by conviction, habit, and association inherently opposed to this administration and its policies." He said. "No program could eliminate their opposition or 'lack of confidence' to the extent that it is emotional, illogical, political, and inevitable." Kennedy challenged business by successfully opposing price increases by steel companies who had defied his voluntary wage-price guidelines in the spring of 1962.[3]

After the stock market tumbled in 1962, Kennedy became the first American president to embrace an openly Keynesian approach to managing the economy by adjusting fiscal and monetary policy to achieve full employment and low inflation. Rather than investing in social programs, however, he lined up with the Committee for Economic Development, the National Association of Manufacturers, and the U.S. Chamber of Commerce behind a conservatively packaged tax cut. With these actions, Kennedy won the minds, if not the hearts, of the skeptical business community. Procter and Gamble economist Wilson Wright noted, "An important part of corporate management now subscribes to the idea that taxes should be reduced even when government expenditure is increased."[4]

For the moderate Committee on Economic Development, Kennedy's cautious Keynesian program was the culmination of a twenty-year quest to achieve an economic balance that cut taxes, maintained existing social programs, and relied on private sector growth to achieve prosperity, not government planning and regulation. Although comprehensive tax cuts stalled in Congress, Kennedy won passage in 1962 of tax breaks for business investment and depreciation. The Kennedy administration began a four-decade turnabout in tax policy in which the federal government would take a smaller share of revenue from progressive corporate and personal income taxes and a greater share from regressive payroll taxes paid mostly by middle-class workers. From 1962 to 1972, corporate income taxes fell from 21 percent to 16 percent of federal receipts, while payroll taxes rose from 17 to 25 percent. "In a much shorter time than expected," concluded an internal report of the Committee on Economic Development, "CED policy statements have influenced major policies of the new administration to an extent that we cannot properly advertise."[5]

A second turning point came in October 1962, when U.S. spy planes detected the Soviets deploying offensive nuclear missiles in Cuba. Determined not to repeat the hasty decision making that resulted in the Bay of Pigs failure or blindly follow expert advice, Kennedy rejected any military action or diplomacy that lacked teeth. He initiated a successful naval blockade of Soviet supply ships and cut a deal with Premier Khrushchev. Russia would remove the missiles from Cuba. The United States would secretly withdraw missiles from Turkey and agree informally not to dislodge Castro by force. The crisis stiffened Kennedy's resolve to think independently and ease global tensions. Ten months after their confrontation in the Caribbean, Kennedy and Khrushchev signed a treaty banning nuclear tests in the atmosphere and the oceans, the Cold War's first nuclear pact.[6]

For conservatives, Kennedy had not defused a threat to peace in the missile crisis, but emasculated American foreign policy by again selling out Cuba to Fidel Castro. Veteran organizer Marvin Liebman teamed up with William F. Buckley Jr. to create another letterhead organization, the Committee for the Monroe Doctrine, to defend America's right to intervene militarily in Western Hemisphere nations, notably Cuba. The committee's chairman, Eddie Rickenbacker, said, "Cuba will, without forcible interference by the United States, be permitted to remain as a Communist colony and therefore as a base for the continued political and psychological subversion of other nations in this hemisphere." If America was "afraid to do anything about Communism in Cuba," Rickenbacker warned, "what chance do we have to do anything about Communism in Berlin, Vietnam, Eastern Europe, or in South America?" Another Buckley-Liebman creation, the National Committee Against the Treaty of Moscow, futilely opposed ratification of the Test Ban Treaty.[7]

Kennedy's cautious approach to touchy domestic issues and his deft handling of foreign affairs paid off in the midterm elections of 1962. The Democrats lost four House seats and picked up four in the Senate: an unusually strong showing for a party that controlled the White House. But Republicans won four new House seats in the South, their first gains in the region since 1954. The GOP's southern political director, I. Lee Potter, said, "I like to fish when the tide's coming in. . . . And the tide's coming in now in the South."[8]

THE RAMPAGEOUS RIGHT

The media discovered the right during the Kennedy years when the dam of anonymity burst on the John Birch Society. After two years of silence, in just eleven months, from February to December 1961, more than seven hundred articles on the society flooded the *Washington Post, New York Times, Los Angeles Times,* and *Chicago Tribune.* The media's negative, even alarmist, coverage of the right was reminiscent of the prewar brown scare. "The John Birch Society has been brought out of hiding," said a *New York Times* exposé after an insider leaked Robert Welch's privately published tract *The Politician.* In this work, Welch had outdone McCarthy by branding President Eisenhower "a dedicated, conscious agent of the Communist conspiracy." An unrepentant Welch blamed the reds for his bad press, claiming that a "mother article" planted by communists had set in motion "tirades against the Society."[9]

The Birch Society's secrecy and fantastic claim that communists had "a minimum of *forty percent* of total control" of American life in the early 1960s contributed to its dubious reputation. If you thought Earl Warren was a red, the Council on Foreign Relations a nest of traitors, and the civil rights movement a plot to make the South a "Soviet-controlled Negro Republic," the Birch Society was for you. Most members, however, cared more mundanely about tax collectors picking their pockets, predators stalking their streets, pinks subverting their schools and churches, and brainwashed soldiers defecting to the communists. A 1961 report by California's attorney general, Democrat Stanley Mosk, found that "businessmen, retired military officers," and, memorably, "little old ladies in tennis shoes" joined the society. Later studies found that members were younger and better educated than expected, with large contingents of evangelical Protestants, Catholics, homemakers, and professional and white-collar workers.[10]

The society's chilling message, devoted leadership, and shrewd use of paid and volunteer organizers made it the most effective grassroots group on the right since the Klan of the 1920s. Organizer Marvin Liebman wrote, "Much of the public action I can evoke through the various committees with which I work comes from John Birch Society members." Senator Goldwater said, "I am impressed by the type of people in it. They are the kind we need in politics." Later, he hedged his bets, saying, "I see no reason to take a stand against any organization just because they're using their constitutional prerogatives even though I disagree with most of them." In early 1964, a nationwide poll by Opinion Research Corporation found an astonishing 65 percent name recognition for the John Birch Society, compared to 42 percent for the venerable National Association of Manufacturers and just 21 percent for Americans for Constitutional Action. By a ratio of twelve to one, respondents said the society's endorsement would make them less likely to vote for a candidate.[11]

According to its audited financial statement for 1964, the John Birch Society had revenues of $1.7 million, which topped all conservative groups. It collected $537,000 in dues from perhaps thirty to fifty thousand members and inspired a much greater following of local activists. It spent most of its budget on paid staffers and coordinators and recruited numerous volunteer organizers. It erected billboards urging the impeachment of Earl Warren and showing Martin Luther King Jr. at what the society alleged was a communist training school. It published *American Opinion* magazine and organized campaigns to "Support Your Local Police Force," "Expose the 'Civil Rights' Fraud," and boycott merchants selling Soviet bloc goods.[12]

The controversies that Welch provoked, however, alarmed his leadership council. Pat Manion demanded that Welch resign to counter the "'Smearbund,' which is out to beat the organization with the old argumentum ad hominem. . . . It is truly terrible that in order to keep the Society together you must now get out of the limelight." Manion added that this was "what every member of the Council to whom I have spoken has recommended." Barry Goldwater agreed. "The best thing Bob Welch could do at the present moment would be to resign his leadership of the Birch Society, and failing that, the Birch Society should disband and reorganize under another name." Welch survived to lead his society for two more decades.[13]

The brown scare spread to the military when the press reported that General Edwin Walker, commander of the federal troops that intervened in Little Rock, had indoctrinated his soldiers with John Birch Society propaganda. Although this was hardly the first case of proselytizing by right-wing officers, the Pentagon orally "admonished" Walker, a relatively light punishment. But to avoid future tiffs it also banned all "political advocacy" by military officers. Some conservatives viewed Walker as a martyr of the communist conspiracy—a new MacArthur. Senator Thurmond charged that the Kennedy administration had turned Walker into "an example of what would happen to any officer who candidly taught his troops about the total nature of communism."[14]

The military trod lightly on General Walker—who fizzled as a conservative leader—because it hoped to keep the lid nailed on the Pandora's box of politics in the military. When the Walker controversy erupted, however, rebellious generals in France were caught plotting to overthrow the republic and murder President Charles de Gaulle, raising the specter of a military coup in the United States. More soberly, the incident recalled President Eisenhower's farewell warning of a military-industrial complex with "economic, political, even spiritual" influence and "the potential for the disastrous rise of misplaced power." General Walker was one of many dedicated conservatives in a military establishment that had more sway over American and international opinion than any other agency of government. Uniformed officers addressed politically charged issues through Armed Forces Radio, educational programs, speeches and lectures, and exchange programs with foreign nations. The military molded domestic opinion through a Defense Orientation Course for educators, lawyers, and executives and through summer classes for reserve officers at the National War College. The American Legion and other veterans groups, defense contractors, the Navy League, the Association of the Army, and the Reserve Officer's Association presented a military slant on public affairs. Although military leaders did not speak with one voice, they typically distrusted liberals, fretted over internal subversion, and viewed the Cold War as a military struggle against an implacable Soviet enemy. As the century progressed, the percentage of U.S. military officers identifying as Democrats or liberals plunged to single digits.[15]

The military's conservative politics resonated in communities sustained by defense contracts and the subsidized migration of skilled defense workers to mostly southern and western localities. According to a study by historian Lisa McGirr of grassroots conservative activism in defense-heavy Orange County, California, an epicenter of the right,

> Conservatives in Orange County enjoyed the fruits of worldly success, often worked in high-tech industries, shared in the burgeoning consumer culture, and participated in the bureaucratized world of post–World War II America. Their mobilization, then, was not a rural "remnant" of the displaced and maladapted but a gathering around principles that were found to be relevant in the most modern of communities.

Although resentful of handouts to "welfare cheats" and "special privileges" for minorities, much of the conservative base depended on "military socialism" or the "warfare state"—the government's mobilization of Cold War capital, labor, and expertise. If conservatives had pulled the plug on big government, the lights would have winked off in ranch homes across suburban America.[16]

Another Birch Society member, Robert Bolivar DePugh, gained attention in the 1960s with his Minutemen, a band of perhaps three hundred to four hundred patriots who armed themselves to repel a communist invasion. If Welch outdid McCarthy, DePugh outdid Welch. He warned, "Within a very few years, perhaps even months, our nation could be conquered and enslaved by the Communists." He asked, "When murdering Communist bands come roaming through your community . . . will you wear a soldier's pack or a slave's chains?" DePugh claimed to represent twenty-five thousand warriors. He instructed patriots on fashioning homemade machine guns and high explosives from ammonium nitrate, "a common fertilizer used on farms throughout the United States." His newsletter, *On Target*, warned liberal members of Congress, "Traitors beware! Even now the cross hairs are on the back of your necks." Federal prosecutors eventually convicted DePugh of firearms violations, which terminated his group, but not the presence of extremist right-wing militias on American soil.[17]

THE RESPONSIBLE RIGHT

The *National Review* crowd worried that the likes of Welch, DePugh, and Willis Carto of the Liberty Lobby would consign all conservatives to lunatic hell.

Buckley and his circle fancied themselves as the philosopher kings of conservatism who proclaimed eternal truths from the mountaintop and rallied the masses below. *NR* was not just "the intellectual leader of the American Right," publisher William Rusher remarked but, more grandly, of the "Western Right." The philosopher kings would function as "movement conservatives," in the mode of Charles Hilles and J. Howard Pew, seeking to win elections and build conservative institutions and culture.[18]

In confidential memos, Frank Meyer, *NR*'s leading theorist, set as their goal "the establishment of responsible leadership . . . uniting a properly directed conservative movement" by steadying both "opportunistic politicians" and "instinctive" conservatives who were too often swayed by "'know-nothing' leaders." Responsible conservatives needed to tame but not abandon the "hard right," Meyer said. They needed "the continuing, uncompromising instinctive opposition to the whole kit and kaboodle of the Roosevelt revolution, which has supplied a large proportion of the troops in every right-wing movement from the days of the Liberty League and America First through the Taft campaigns, the McCarthy days, and today." *NR* and its allies would build a robust but "respectable movement" that gained authority over these "vital forces of the hard right." Meyer concluded, "Our problem here bluntly, is to negate the influence of 'know-nothing' leaders while maintaining connections and potential influence over their followers." Publisher Rusher, however, said pessimistically, "The real problem is our own dog-in-the-manger attitude. . . . We are unable to organize America's conservatives ourselves, and unwilling to let anybody else do it."[19]

Responsible conservatives understood that liberals threatened America more than a tattered Communist Party. They knew that the right would languish unless it repudiated overt anti-Semitism, racism, and lurid conspiracy theories. Buckley drew anti-Semites out of his circle by denouncing the *American Mercury* magazine for what had become its open anti-Semitism by the late 1950s. "Nothing is more tiresome than the charge that every member of the American Right is ex officio anti-Semitic," Buckley wrote. "The typical Rightest is something quite different: he is, or tends to be, pro-Christian." Beginning in 1962, *NR* editorials took aim at Buckley's former friend Robert Welch of the John Birch Society, at first separating the leader from his followers but later dropping that distinction. In the 1960s, *NR* continued to denounce the *Brown* decision on school integration and joined all other conservative publications in opposing civil rights laws. But it no longer wrote about the racial inferiority of blacks.[20]

To promote their sanitized right, the *NR* crowd launched Young Americans for Freedom (YAF) at a 1960 meeting of nearly a hundred young activists, mostly male and all white, at the Buckley estate in Sharon, Connecticut. YAF rejected both left-wing and consensus politics. Its founding manifesto, the "Sharon Statement," written largely by the precocious twenty-six-year-old M. Stanton Evans, editor of the *Indianapolis News,* stated, "It is the responsibility of the youth of America to affirm certain eternal truths." These included the "individual's use of his God-given free will" and the dependence of "political freedom" upon "economic freedom." It proposed confining government to "the preservation of internal order, the provision of national defense, and the administration of justice," but also stressed "victory [over communism] rather than coexistence." The statement endured as definitive, if contested, doctrine.[21]

Unlike the Intercollegiate Society of Individualists—an office, a mailing list, and Victor Milione—YAF had a living, if small, presence on more than two hundred campuses. According to a 1962 survey by Opinion Research Corporation of colleges with conservative clubs, these organizations recruited less than 1 percent of student enrollment. As compared to members of the left-wing Students for a Democratic Society YAF members were slightly less likely to come from an upper-middle-class family, but they were far more likely to identify their religious affiliation as Catholic or Protestant, rather than Jewish or "nonreligious."[22]

Guided by Marvin Liebman's public relations skills and sustained by an annual budget of about $200,000, raised primarily through dues-paying members and solicitations to conservative businessmen, YAF gained coverage from media listening for a conservative heartbeat in America's youth. Members challenged the National Student Association, a nationwide confederation of college and university student governments, as a left-wing front. They wrote letters and editorials, campaigned for right-wing candidates, picketed the White House, sponsored speakers, established student newspapers, and assailed firms that traded with the Soviet bloc. In their most celebrated initiative, YAF packed Madison Square Garden in March 1962 for a rally that featured Barry Goldwater, their enthusiastic choice for president. After the 1964 election, a YAF protest convinced Firestone to scrub plans for a synthetic rubber plant in Communist Romania.[23]

For its adult midwives, YAF represented responsible conservatism. James Burnham noted that the "decent and responsible" YAFers were "the ones who are going to have to defend and save this country," not "that crowd of cowards, traitors and dupes" on the left. "YAF is not at all 'far Right,' [but] has essentially the same political views as *National Review*." However, the senior *NR* crew learned that, unlike their letterhead fronts, they could not control the internal politics of a flesh-and-blood membership group. The adults made the mistake, Rusher said, of treating YAF "as another Committee of One Million, only this time with teen-agers on its letterhead." Factional strife erupted from YAF's first days, limiting its impact and stunting its growth; membership likely peaked at far fewer than its claimed fifty thousand. Still, Buckley, Rusher, and Liebman had pulled off another grand illusion. "It would be easy to overrate" what YAF and "similar groups have already done," Rusher wrote. "I know the YAF story from the inside, and it is considerably less impressive than the public façade that Marvin has so ably created." Nonetheless, "when all appropriate discounts have been made for exaggeration," these organizations were representative "of a growing urge on the part of conservatives to Do Something."[24]

To "Do Something" about pushing Republican Party politics to the right, Buckley had suggested to financiers at a 1957 meeting that they launch a conservative party in New York as a "counterpart to the Liberal Party," the state's well-established third party of the left. The Conservative Party would "endorse all Republican nominees *with the exception of the one or two most objectionable from a conservative point of view*." It would establish "the size of the hard conservative vote," which "would be a formidable weapon to level at the Republican Party in future nominating conventions." In their prospectus, delayed until 1961 because of the death of designated organizer Eli Zrake, the founders said, "The conservative political movement cannot place its ultimate faith in a third party, but must instead seek its ultimate political realization through the Republican Party." Yet conservatives could not "bring real influence to bear upon the Republican Party unless, at the margin, there exists the possibility of organized conservative dissent." The new state party would "bring down the liberal Republican *apparat* in New York State" and "provide a model and inspiration for conservatives in other states who are oppressed by a monolithic liberal control of both major political parties."[25]

In 1962 the Conservative Party recruited David Jaquith, a Syracuse manufacturer, to take on Governor Nelson Rockefeller. Jaquith blasted Rockefeller for presuming that "increased State government activity is the solution to every human or personal problem" and for fabricating a "special benefit program of some kind for everyone except the taxpayer." Jaquith won 3 percent of the vote, enough to guarantee the Conservative Party a place on the ballot for the next election. He also wounded Rockefeller by holding him below his previous margin of victory. The Conservative Party became a fixture in New York State, slating mostly Republican candidates but also sponsoring nominees of its own. The party did not exactly turn Empire State Republicans into *NR* subscribers but it nudged them slightly toward the conservative center of the GOP.[26]

The "responsible" conservatives, however, could not halt agitation against the right from the media or the Democrats. In a November 1961 speech at a Democratic fund-raising dinner in Hollywood, President Kennedy echoed FDR's warning about a fifth column of right-wing "fanatics" who "find treason in our finest churches, and in our highest court and even in the treatment of our water." The president ridiculed the right for suggesting that "the sell-out at Yalta" rather than "the presence of Soviet troops in Eastern Europe drove it to Communism" and that "treason in high places" rather than "a civil war removed China from the free world." Soon after, union leaders Walter and Victor Reuther and liberal attorney Joseph Rauh Jr. delivered a memo that Attorney General Robert Kennedy had requested on the "radical right," which they said ranged from Goldwater on the "left" to Welch on the "right." The authors said that radical right groups were "probably stronger and almost certainly better organized than at any time in recent history" and threatened "the President's program at home and abroad." Their memo called for disciplining radical military officers, listing far-right groups as subversive organizations, and suppressing the Minutemen. It urged reigning in J. Edgar Hoover, who "exaggerates the domestic communist menace," and damming "the flow of big money to the radical right" by challenging the tax exemptions of conservative groups.[27]

The administration responded with an Ideological Operations Project that targeted twenty-two conservative organizations for IRS scrutiny. The Democratic National Committee complemented this effort with a campaign to silence radio broadcasts of the right. The committee called upon the Federal Communications Commission to enforce the fairness doctrine, which required the balanced presentation of opposing views. In its most consequential ruling, the commission revoked Carl McIntire's license to operate radio station WXUR in Philadelphia and his appeal died in the federal courts. The McIntire case had a chilling effect on right-wing radio broadcasting and fueled conservative efforts to repeal the fairness doctrine as a restriction on the free market of ideas, although conservatives continued to back restraints on disloyal and profane speech.[28]

Kennedy's strategy, William Rusher admitted, was "devastatingly effective" in slathering tar on conservatives. "Substantially all of the mass-based organizations through which the Right has attempted to mobilize itself for effective political action have been lumped together in one ball of wax and lustily smeared by everybody from Kennedy and the Liberals through the Luce publications. . . . The Liberals have succeeded in narrowing almost to the vanishing point the area of what might be called Permissible Dissent in this country." Conservative intellectual Willmoore Kendall echoed John T. Flynn's complaint about the "smear bund" of the 1940s. He said that for liberal propagandists, "It is a brief step from Conservative to Right, another brief step from Right to Extreme Right, and another from Extreme Right to Fascist." Despite modest success with the YAF, Rusher lamented in a letter to Buckley that *NR* had failed "to found, or at least find, somewhere in this broad country, a mass-based organization to which we can give allegiance and support." The richest, most active right-wing groups—the John Birch Society, LIFE LINE, the Christian Crusade, the Liberty Lobby, the Christian Anti-Communism Crusade, and the enterprises of Carl McIntire and Dan Smoot—failed the "responsibility" test. Worse yet, in the early to mid-1960s, the mainstream media usually put the *National Review* crowd into the same category as these far-right groups.[29]

Still, White House aide Meyer Feldman reported to the president in 1963 that the right remained alive and well, spending "as much as $25 million annually," airing "programs on at least 1,000 radio stations," and producing "an enormous amount of direct mail literature, newspaper advertising, and speeches." He reported, "The same names are found in many of the right-wing organizations and the same foundations, corporations and individuals contribute to many of them." Although $25 million seemed formidable to critics, a motivated business community could have financed conservative causes far more richly. Admiral Ben Moreell said he was "fed up to here" with leaders of enterprise whose love of profit left "no time or energy left to fight for the system that made their business possible." He denounced those "who support socialist projects of short-range advantage to themselves [or] who 'play ball' with the political apparatus in power when there is a potential 'payoff' in government largess."[30]

BOARDING GOLDWATER'S CANOE

Despite these frustrations, a self-styled syndicate of conservative opera-tives who had pushed the Young Republicans to the right during the 1950s took aim at adult Republican politics. In October 1961 three syndicate veterans—*NR* publisher Bill Rusher, political organizer F. Clifton White, and Representative John Ashbrook of Ohio—met with nineteen other right-wing activists and financiers in Chicago to form "a brand-new and highly professional [conservative] faction in the national Republican pic-ture." With White as full-time organizer, the group resolved to board "the only relatively empty canoe on the lake" by offering Senator Goldwater the "professional organization . . . he desperately needs." They sought ei-ther Goldwater's "nomination in 1964, or—failing that (which is a real possibility)—a firm grip on the conservative wing of the GOP." They operated below the horizon and asked of Goldwater only that "if questioned about our activities, he refrain from repudiating us."[31]

While moderates slept, White met with party activists to line up convention delegates for what would become an independent "draft Goldwater" operation. Goldwater confessed self-doubts. "I have never been much of a leader, but more of a pusher, and I think I can do more in that role than I can by stepping out in front." It was a keen self-assessment. Goldwater was engaging, sincere, and willing to go where timid pols feared to tread—good for a pusher. But he was also erratic, shallow, and tempera-mental—bad for a leader. A decade later, Goldwater confided to Rusher, "You remarked at one time that in my modesty I would admit that I was probably not mentally equipped to be President and I still would cling to that idea. It's really the major reason why I didn't immediately embrace your efforts." In Goldwater, however, conservatives had a champion with more starch than Taft. "Goldwater seems to me to be possessed of a con-sistency that Taft never attained," wrote old warhorse B. E. Hutchinson.

"Taft's integrity was unassailable, but there were inconsistencies in his political position."[32]

Goldwater's followers did not execute a conservative coup against the Republican Party; the GOP was already solidly conservative in its activist core. Rather, White's efforts to win over local party leaders brought together newly minted southern Republicans with the entrenched conservative activists that Charles Hilles had nurtured in the 1930s, Robert Taft had inspired in 1952, and Eisenhower had failed to purge during the next eight years. These long-suffering loyalists toiled in the precincts and climbed the party ladder to become county chairs, members and chairs of state committees, and convention delegates. They cheered as Republicans made a staunch conservative—the New York representative William Miller—chairman of the Republican National Committee. An analysis prepared for the Republican Congressional Campaign Committee concluded that Goldwater supporters "feel intellectually and emotionally that at last the Republican Party has a 'real Republican.'... Many of them were frustrated by Taft's loss to Eisenhower in 1952 and have waited all these years to find someone else they can support." Even as Goldwater's standing among all Republicans fluctuated in the polls, he easily topped surveys of GOP county chairs and 1960 delegates to the Republican Convention. Goldwater supporters controlled the board of directors of the Federation of Republican Women and the Young Republicans, still under the syndicate's spell, elected Goldwater supporter and U.S. House staffer Donald "Buz" Lukens as its national chair in June 1963. Lukens became a conservative star who won election to the U.S. House and the Ohio State Senate until an Ohio jury convicted him in 1989 of paying a female minor for sex.[33]

THE GREAT REPUBLICAN ISSUE

By 1961 moderate New York governor Nelson Rockefeller had come to believe that he would eventually face off against Barry Goldwater for the GOP's presidential nomination. In December 1961 Rockefeller's adviser George Hinman told his boss that race was "the Great Republican Issue." He added that the racist sentiment within the GOP was increasingly focusing on Goldwater and "Barry has been falling increasingly for it." With an ascendant civil rights movement battling segregation and discrimination, race most clearly marked the divide between Goldwater and the Rockefeller Republicans—symbolically, strategically, and substantively.[34]

Moderate Republicans watched in dismay as segregationist leaders such as state chair Wirt Yerger of Mississippi, gubernatorial candidate Charlton H. Lyons of Louisiana, and Senate candidate William Workman of South Carolina refurbished lily-white party organizations in the South. The South Carolina state party reported, "In 1962 and 1964 not a single Negro showed any interest in participating in the statutory party reorganization or its activities. . . . This was welcomed by new Party leaders as victory in the South at any level could never be achieved by a Negro dominated party." Katherine K. Neuberger, a Republican party official from New Jersey, wrote to Lyons: "The only thing that bothers Republicans in the North is that the new Republican Party in the South has been created by former Democrats who were more Segregationist in nature than the philosophy of the Democratic Party in the South and who are using the Republicans as an instrument to further these philosophies."[35]

The Republican National Committee shrugged off such carping and urged southerners to replace Democrats with "MORE conservative" Republicans. The GOP scrapped its minority-outreach division and launched an organizing drive among white southerners, ironically called Operation Dixie. In 1963 Black Republican Grant Reynolds, the party's consultant on minority issues, pleaded in vain for "a real program to recapture the Negro vote—a program which is at least equal in intensity to 'Operation Dixie.'" The conservative Republican appeal to the white South had a class as well as a racial component. An expanding middle class in the "right to work" South embraced militant anticommunism, antiunion policies, and opposition to the welfare state.[36]

For Rockefeller Republicans, Goldwater's southern strategy represented bad morals and worse politics. With Rockefeller taking a hard line to match Goldwater's conservative positions on defense and economic policy, relatively little of substance beyond a chasm on civil rights separated the two candidates. "Their theory," Hinman told Rockefeller, "is that by becoming more reactionary than even the Southern Democratic Party, the Republican Party can attract Southern conservatives who have been Democrats, and by consolidating them with the conservative strength in the Middle West and Far West, the Republicans can offset the liberalism of the Northeast and finally prevail." This approach, Hinman said, "is unsound politically, as well as morally." According to the *Advance Magazine Newsletter,* the self-styled "flaming moderate" voice of the GOP, the "election will be decided in the metropolitan North, Midwest, and West," where Goldwater's policies "will alienate millions in both races." Rockefeller warned the GOP not to "write off the Negro vote of the big cities [nor to] erect its political power on the outlawed and immoral base of segregation."[37]

Yet the southern strategy also had a northern component, which was based on the belief that a white backlash against black demands for jobs, housing, and government assistance would pay political dividends in 1964. The racial backlash that Elmo Roper had detected in his polling data during World War II continued through the postwar era of white flight to the suburbs. Relatively high home prices and a lack of public transportation fenced off many suburbs to African Americans. So did racial steering by realtors, racially restrictive covenants (which the Supreme Court outlawed in 1948), discriminatory lending practices, and the reluctance of owners and developers to sell homes to minorities. Within the cities, realtors engaged in "block busting" practices by selling to an African American in a white neighborhood, then buying homes cheaply from fearful whites and profitably reselling to black buyers. Urban renewal programs concentrated minorities in segregated public projects or neighborhoods that whites had abandoned. From 1940 to 1970 the black population of America's cities with a population of fifty thousand or more soared from less than 10 percent to nearly 25 percent.[38]

The white backlash emerged locally in the early 1960s. In 1961 city manager Joseph Mitchell of Newburgh, New York, won acclaim from conservatives, including Goldwater, when he defied federal and state law with regulations to slash welfare payments, force recipients to work, discourage illegitimate births, and deter the migration of poor (black) families to his city. FAMOUS OVERNIGHT: JOSEPH MCDOWELL MITCHELL, announced a headline in the *New York Times* on June 24, 1961. In Boston, school committee member Louise Day Hicks won a landslide reelection in 1963 after denying that de facto racial segregation existed in city schools. In Detroit that year, a council of white home owner's associations secured enough signatures to place on the ballot a Homeowners Rights Ordinance exempting property owners from antidiscrimination laws and regulations. The ordinance echoed a Property Owners Bill of Rights that the National Association of Real Estate Boards had adopted in the same year.[39]

After listening to "backroom chats" at a 1963 meeting of the Republican National Committee, Rowland Evans and Robert Novak reported, "Substantial numbers of Republican Party leaders from both North and South see rich political dividends flowing from the Negrophobia of many white Americans." The surprising strength of segregationist governor George C. Wallace of Alabama in Democratic primaries in 1964 seemed to validate this presumption. Wallace polled 30 percent in Indiana, 34 percent in Wisconsin, and 43 percent in Maryland, where he won a majority of the white vote. "If it hadn't been for the nigger bloc vote, we'd have won it all," Wallace snarled—the one time he used that word within earshot of reporters.[40]

In response to civil rights demonstrations and violent responses by southern officials, Kennedy ended two years of hesitation, put his prestige behind the struggle for racial justice, and drafted comprehensive civil rights legislation in 1963. But polls showed that white Americans thought he was moving too fast on minority rights and Kennedy's approval rating fell from nearly 70 percent in the summer of 1963 to the mid-50s in the fall. Conservatives saw their southern strategy snapping into place. In June 1963, a week after Kennedy addressed the nation on civil rights, Goldwater privately assured adviser Denison Kitchel that he opposed most of Kennedy's civil rights bill. On voting, Goldwater wrote, "I believe it does damage to states' rights." On equal accommodations: "I am completely opposed to this as being obtained through legislation." On employment discrimination: "I am in agreement with this, but it must come from voluntarism and not compulsion."[41]

THE REPUBLICAN END GAME

In 1963, with a Goldwater nomination no longer a distant hope, his conservative backers worried that the GOP's moderate eastern wing would again impose its will on the party's choice of a presidential candidate. Although Nelson Rockefeller's divorce and remarriage to a socialite nicknamed Happy tarnished his reputation, moderates lined up behind the New York governor who warned that the GOP risked becoming "a party of extremism, a party of sectionalism, a party of racism." According to Senator Karl Mundt of South Dakota, "The east wing of the Republican Party which reflects the highly urbanized thinking in this country has really opened up its guns against Goldwater using Rockefeller as its first line of attack." The moderates' "main purpose is to prevent Goldwater or any other conservative from becoming the titular head of the Party and/or becoming President. This is an unfortunate attitude which this group has manifested ever since the days of the Philadelphia Convention when they succeeded in planting Willkie on the party." Earlier, Goldwater Republican Robert Sprinkel of California had warned that conservatives were "playing big stakes when we play with Mr. Luce [publisher of *Time* and *Life*] and Mr. Eisenhower and Wall Street and Mr. Rockefeller."[42]

Politics in America changed after Kennedy's assassination on November 22, 1963, and the succession of a southerner, Lyndon Johnson of Texas. Johnson pledged to redeem Kennedy's unfinished legacy, but as a disciple of Franklin Roosevelt he also planned to implement an ambitious liberal agenda. In early 1964 he began international negotiations that substantially reduced U.S. and international tariffs and in February won enactment of Kennedy's proposed income tax cuts for individuals and corporations. In July, Johnson signed the Civil Rights Act of 1964. It banned discrimination by race or sex in employment, ended the era of legal segregation in the South, and prohibited segregation in public accommodations owned by private parties. During his first year, Johnson added to these holdover initiatives a "war on poverty" designed to provide the skills, work experience, and community solidarity needed for self-help by the poor. Led by JFK's brother-in-law R. Sargent Shriver, a new Office of Economic Opportunity administered the war on poverty. Johnson saw no distinction between the economic liberalism of his war on poverty and the civil rights liberalism of the Civil Rights Act that cleared the way for minorities to share in American prosperity.[43]

In a May 1964 address Johnson articulated his vision of a "Great Society" that would complete Franklin Roosevelt's mission of domestic reform. At the same time, he secretly considered plans to escalate the war in Vietnam after the election. In August 1964, after alleged but not fully verified attacks on American destroyers operating off the Vietnam coast, Johnson easily pushed through Congress the Gulf of Tonkin Resolution, which authorized him to use American military power in Vietnam.

The Supreme Court, led by Chief Justice Earl Warren, also stirred social change. The Warren Court expanded the rights of women, minorities, welfare recipients, and the criminally accused. It banned prayer and

Bible reading in public schools and required legislatures to draw election districts of roughly equal population to conform with the principle of one-person, one vote. Opinion on the Court turned full circle from the New Deal years. Liberals defended the Court's broad reading of the Constitution and conservatives demanded "strict construction." The movement to impeach Earl Warren was but the deepest end of an ocean of right-wing discontent. Goldwater complained, "The Constitution is now widely held to mean only what those who hold power for the moment choose to say it means." Like FDR, conservative leaders hatched plans for taming judges, including a proposed constitutional amendment that would authorize Congress to overturn Supreme Court rulings by a two-thirds vote.[44]

Despite the prospect of a difficult race against a popular president who hailed from the South, Goldwater declared his candidacy for president in early 1964. He then cast aside White and his syndicate for a more familiar but less experienced "Arizona mafia" led by three lawyer/operatives: Denison Kitchel, Dean Burch, and Richard Kleindiest. His new team, however, could not control Goldwater's loose lips. Goldwater called America's missile force "undependable" and suggested that NATO commanders should have discretion to use tactical nuclear shells and rockets on a European battlefield. He advocated removing Castro, perhaps through a second foray by rearmed Cuban exiles. He opposed farm and antipoverty programs and controls on business abuse. He mused about making Social Security voluntary and selling off the Tennessee Valley Authority, a federally owned corporation set up during the New Deal to provide electric power and development aid for the Tennessee Valley region. As a senator, Goldwater's contrarian positions made him a moral force, but as a prospective president they made him, in the word of the day, "extreme." Publisher William Rusher wrote, "The idealized Goldwater of last summer, who was not yet a candidate could serve more comfortably than the flesh-and-blood candidate of 1964 as a handy object upon which frustrated conservatives could project a fantasy of unresisted and immaculate victory."[45]

Goldwater's musing on nukes signified more than the chatter of an unruly candidate. As an engaged nationalist, Goldwater yearned to open up a war on the reds that he believed the establishment had avoided out of fear and out of greed for sustaining Cold War profits. Like former senator William Knowland, Goldwater would repudiate peaceful coexistence and pressure the Soviets through all necessary means, including the threatened use of conventional or nuclear weapons. "The real isolationists are the men in this Administration," Goldwater said, "who talk and talk, but fear to act, who can only mumble when the American flag is torn down, trampled on, and spat upon." The administration "shrugs off the responsibilities of world leadership," "disarms this nation," and "watches our free world alliances crumble, as is the case with NATO." Such bellicose rhetoric prompted more than a hundred thousand scientists to organize against Goldwater, including thirty-three of America's forty Nobel laureates. MIT chemist John Sheehan noted that scientists weren't "only against him as being trigger-happy with nuclear weapons." They also opposed "his general concept of the use of force in all parts of the world to settle our problems."[46]

After placing third in New Hampshire—behind runner-up Richard Nixon and upset winner Henry Cabot Lodge, Nixon's 1960 running mate—Goldwater's standing among Republicans nationwide plunged to less than 20 percent in some polls. An ordinary candidate would have just disappeared, but Goldwater had a movement behind him and a solid bloc of southern delegates. Still, to lock in the nomination, Goldwater had to win a major contested primary with first-class opposition. His chance came in California's June primary, which opened up as a clean contest against Rockefeller after Lodge and Nixon withdrew. Rockefeller had a fat budget, led in the polls, and enjoyed the backing of the state's party establishment and most newspapers. Meanwhile, Goldwater wandered back into the nuclear battlefield, suggesting, "Defoliation of the forests [in Vietnam] by low-yield atomic weapons could well be done." But when Happy Rockefeller gave birth to a son, Nelson Jr., a week before the primary, it rekindled memories of Nelson Sr.'s messy divorce and remarriage. California's vibrant conservative group United Republicans of California backed Goldwater, as did an army of volunteers inspired by his conservative cause. Goldwater won California by a single percentage point and virtually sealed the nomination. He was the first conservative Republican to beat the unbeatable establishment of the Rockefellers, Eisenhower, Henry Luce, and Wall Street.[47]

A week later, moderate governor William Scranton of Pennsylvania backed into the presidential race when Goldwater broke with the Republican leadership to vote against the Civil Rights Act. "Scranton is going to head the liberal wing of the Republican Party," quipped comedy writer Robert Orben. "A unique kind of wing—it's never been able to get off the ground." Scranton blasted Goldwater's "extremism" but moved few delegate votes, which foreshadowed later events. A convention dominated by enthusiastic conservatives booed Rockefeller when he rose in defense of a plank condemning extremist groups and awarded Goldwater an easy first-ballot victory, anchored by support from 97 percent of southern delegates. Rather than appeasing moderates, Goldwater picked a conservative soul mate, party chair and New York congressman William Miller, for his running mate. Worse yet, Goldwater proclaimed in his acceptance speech, "Extremism in the defense of liberty is no vice. . . . Moderation in the pursuit of justice is no virtue."[48]

"To extol extremism," Rockefeller said in a postconvention statement, "is dangerous, irresponsible and frightening." The *New York Times* called Goldwater "a disaster for the Republican Party [and] a threat to the country . . . a man whose foreign policy is unthinkable and whose domestic policy is unbelievable." After Nixon publicly implored him "to clear the air once and for all" on extremism, Goldwater drafted a response saying, "I neither correct nor modify my choice of words; I repeat and reiterate them." But in a revised public version he said that he had meant only that "wholehearted devotion to liberty is unassailable and that half-hearted devotion to justice is indefensible." Speechwriter Harry Jaffa, author of the infamous line, said that it meant, "Very simply, that nothing is either good or bad because it is extreme. Extreme generosity, extreme tolerance, extreme fairness, are all qualities which we do, or at least should admire."[49]

With the nomination came the prize of the Republican National Committee, which Goldwater stocked with loyalists. He appointed his Arizona associate Dean Burch as chair, snubbing Clif White once more, and he tapped William Baroody, who had taken a leave from the American Enterprise Institute, as a strategist and chief policy adviser. The campaign kept its distance from Buckley and the *National Review* crowd, who the *New York Times* had said represented "the forces who occupy the supposedly narrow territory to the right of the Arizona Senator." Baroody's associate W. Glenn Campbell, head of the Hoover Institution, did not formally join the campaign, but had said, "I am doing everything within my limited powers to assist in nominating and electing Senator Goldwater."[50]

Mindful of the close and contested vote in 1960, the GOP rolled out a ballot security plan in 1964, dubbed Operation Eagle Eye after a similar effort in Arizona. The party planned to station one hundred thousand "eagle eyes" at polling places to discourage fraudulent voters. With Eagle Eye targeted at minority neighborhoods in thirty-six cities, critics called it a transparent ploy to reduce turnout by Democrats. In Houston, handbills circulated in black neighborhoods warned that authorities could arrest voters who had an outstanding parking ticket or traffic conviction.[51]

Goldwater's campaign combined a law and order theme with a thinly disguised assault on the Civil Rights Act. According to a confidential campaign memo: "Johnson has failed to exert leadership or to take action in curbing the increase in crime (occurring throughout the country), arresting the trend toward riots, looting, and vandalism as a way of life, halting the widespread breakdown in law and order, or reversing the decline in morality and increase in disrespect for the value of human life." Conservatives attributed the dissolution of an orderly society to liberal permissiveness, the expulsion of God from public life, and social programs that battered the family and rewarded bad habits. They used carefully coded language to tap into white fear of black crime and sexuality, without directly stirring racial antagonism. Every element of the breakdown of public order, the memo urged, should "be treated as a prong of a single fork—a fork labeled 'moral crisis' [and] jabbed relentlessly from now until election day."[52]

On the campaign trail, Goldwater charged, "The moral fiber of the American people is beset by rot and decay. . . . Is this the time in our nation's history for our Federal Government to ban Almighty God from our school rooms?" He said, "It is on our streets that we see the final, terrible proof of a sickness which not all the social theories of a thousand social experiments has even begun to touch. Crime grows faster than population, while those who break the law are accorded more consideration than those who try to enforce the law."[53]

In addressing civil rights, Goldwater dropped the constitutional justifications for his vote against the Civil Rights Act and took aim at the white southern gut. "The fundamental issue of our day—the new area into which the act of 1964 dangerously treads—is the issue of unfair discrimination in the private affairs of men." He lamented the use of "racial quotas as a substitute for the principle of equal opportunity in every aspect of social life." He added, "Our aim, as I understand it, is neither to establish a segregated society nor an integrated society. Our aim is to preserve freedom." He slammed the Warren Court for wielding "raw and naked power" and departing from "judicial restraint." He promised to appoint justices "who will support the Constitution, not scoff at it." Senator Thurmond, who became the first big-name southern Democrat to turn Republican, roared his assent: "The Democratic Party has rammed through Congress unconstitutional, impractical, unworkable, and oppressive legislation which invades inalienable personal and property rights [and] has encouraged lawless, civil unrest, and mob actions." Goldwater did place limits on the agitation of racial issues. He mutually agreed with President Johnson not to exploit racial unrest in America's cities during the "long hot summer" of 1964, and he vetoed the airing of an openly racist film on social disorder, called *Choice,* produced by Clif White and California conservative activist Rus Walton.[54]

Economically, Goldwater was a debt hawk who voted against the Kennedy-Johnson tax cuts. He voted against reducing the capital gains tax and for an automatic increase in taxes if the federal budget should top $100 billion. Goldwater belittled the Johnson tax cut as "impulsive, massive, politically motivated tax-cut gimmickry . . . designed to drug the economy into an artificial boom." Yet Goldwater also pledged—reportedly under the tutelage of economist Milton Friedman—"to find ways to keep more money in [voters'] pockets" with a 25 percent, phased-in tax cut. With Goldwater also urging higher defense spending, Johnson's ticket mate, Senator Hubert Humphrey of Minnesota, asked how he could "increase spending, reduce revenues and balance the budget at the same time?"[55]

Business entered electoral politics in 1964 through BIPAC, the Business-Industry Political Action Committee, founded primarily by CEOs of mid-level companies. BIPAC would counter "labor's power at the polls" with resources that "only the national business community has the political potential to provide." NAM president Werner P. Gullander acknowledged that business had lagged "in doing the things which are necessary if sound economics are to find expression in government actions." The *Washington Post* noted, "The only surprising thing about the creation of the Business-Industry Political Action Committee is that it has been so long in coming. . . . It would be most unfortunate if candidates had to choose between competing special interests for financial assistance to make a campaign for congress possible." BIPAC shunned the Johnson-Goldwater contest to focus on Congress. It distributed about $200,000 to eighty-six House and twelve Senate candidates, mostly Republicans, with a few conservative southern Democrats tossed in. Although most BIPAC-endorsed candidates lost in a bad Republican year, BIPAC endured and inspired kindred groups. Corporations also continued their training and public relations programs. By 1964 U.S. firms had trained more than half a million employees, most of whom quietly contributed to compatible candidates. Business interests were learning how to influence politics without losing friends.[56]

Goldwater reaped few benefits from big business. He had the backing of a few leading executives and many conservative activists from mid-level companies such as textile entrepreneur Roger Millikin and oilman Henry Salvatori, who also financed *National Review*. Still, in the words of historian of government-business relations Kim McQuaid, he "scared most big business leaders to death." Corporations had prospered under Kennedy and Johnson and their cautious CEOs worried about Goldwater's votes against tax cuts and his erratic policy talk. President Johnson promised that America could have it all: low taxes, aid for the poor and elderly, and fat contracts for business, all floated by a rising tide of economic growth. Several dozen corporate leaders, mostly Republicans, formed a National Independent Committee for the Johnson ticket and other executives quietly backed the president. Republicans countered by raising small sums through direct mail from 650,000 donors, compared to fewer than 50,000 in 1960. Democrats relied heavily on big-ticket contributors and organized labor. Prior to 1964, contributions from Business Council members had flowed overwhelmingly to Republicans. In 1956 and 1960 members had contributed a combined $550,000 to Eisenhower and Nixon and just $39,000 to Stevenson and Kennedy. In a dramatic reversal of precedent, members contributed $140,000 to Johnson and $90,000 to Goldwater in 1964. Vice presidential nominee William Miller charged that Johnson had forged the kind of "dangerous alliance" of big government, big business, and big labor that "came to life in Germany three decades ago when Adolf Hitler offered the people a welfare state program, with promises to build everything they needed."[57]

The Goldwater campaign lacked seasoned leadership and failed to cultivate a press that his managers dismissed as hopelessly biased against conservatives. It little mattered. Goldwater had won the California primary despite a chaotic effort, and according to the National Election Study Republicans contacted more voters (20 percent) for the general election than Democrats (15.5 percent). The problem for Goldwater was competing against a popular incumbent president with a record of policy accomplishment during peaceful and prosperous times. Even the sporadic racial violence that erupted in cities such as New York and Philadelphia during the summer of 1964 did not stir voter fears of widespread disorder. In a bid to bury the right and validate his domestic program, Johnson pressed his inherent advantages by vilifying Goldwater as a radical eager to kill off Social Security and mash the nuclear button. Goldwater, however, blamed his problems on fellow Republicans. "My defeat was insured," Goldwater said in 1965, "by the stiletto job Rockefeller and Scranton and others had done on me."[58]

Johnson won a record 61 percent of the popular vote and 90 percent of the Electoral College. His Democrats gained better than two-thirds majorities in both houses of Congress. Goldwater's southern strategy was successful not in the new suburban South, but in the Deep South, heart of Jim Crow, where support for Strom Thurmond's Dixiecrat campaign had been strongest in 1948 and where defense of the color line remained most firmly entrenched. Goldwater swept all five Deep South states, four of which had not voted Republican since Reconstruction, but won no other southern states. He captured three of four Deep South counties, compared to fewer than a fifth won by Eisenhower in his 1956 landslide. Earlier, in the summer of 1964, when the president signed the Civil Rights Act, Johnson had mused to aide Bill Moyers, "I think we have just delivered the South to the Republican Party." The Republican Party's executive director John Grenier said, "History will not be concerned with motives of the Southern vote" but only with the fact of its conversion to the GOP.[59]

ANOTHER ROCK BOTTOM

Conservatism did not die in 1964, but Goldwater's defeat undercut the position of conservatives within the Republican Party, discredited Goldwater's ideas as irresponsible extremism, and opened the way for Lyndon Johnson to extend the liberal state. Postelection polls found that 45 percent of voters tabbed Goldwater not as conservative but "radical;" 52 percent said that extremism had a "great deal" or a "fair amount" of influence on their vote.

Even the election of a Republican president in 1968 would not revive the Goldwater agenda. The right would not recover from its near death in 1964 until conservatives rebuilt their political infrastructure in the 1970s, gained a nationally appealing leader in Ronald Reagan, and exploited liberalism's failures under President Jimmy Carter and Democratic Congresses.

A week after the election, Eddie Rickenbacker said that conservatives should not fall into despair. "The election proved there are 27 million American men and women who are willing to work for a living against 42 million who prefer to be slaves of a Johnson welfare state. . . . It cannot last and most of them will find this out before many years pass." But conservatives could not rewrite the grim arithmetic of post-Goldwater politics. An historic low 25 percent of Americans called themselves Republicans after the election and the GOP lost ground in Congress and state governments, with conservatives suffering most of the erosion. Only 16 percent of Goldwater voters thought that the senator and his followers should control the GOP. The percentage of voters contacted by Republicans fell from 20 percent to 15 percent during the next decade and under 30 percent of Americans called themselves Republicans even in the aftermath of Richard Nixon's landslide victory in 1972.[60]

The conservative United Republicans of America said that despite the many activists inspired by Goldwater, the outlook for the future was "dismal." The right had to rectify its failure "to organize politically" and could "no longer afford the luxury of non-political Conservative activity." The *California Statesman,* a conservative monthly magazine, presciently advised conservatives to "dig in with a long-term practical program for the future [and reject] dreamland shortcuts that only consummate in additional defeats." The right had to begin "the hard task of laying a sound foundation" on its anti-pluralist base, not relying on economic issues "because too many people fear the effect of the potential withdrawal of government subsidies. . . . The salable issues are morality, and protection of the public from Negro violence and favoritism under the civil rights program. . . . Economic liberals, union members, pensioners, and others who reject economic conservatism still believe in God, and in the protection of their families, jobs, and homes from Negro pressure and violence."[61]

In 1964, unlike 1936, Republicans dismissed their conservative party chair; a humbled Goldwater agreed to replace Burch with the nonideological political operative Ray Bliss of Ohio, who firmly opposed Goldwater's idea of realigning the parties along ideological lines. Like Rockefeller and moderate Michigan governor George Romney, Bliss favored a "big tent" GOP. He said, "If the Democratic Party is big enough for Harry Byrd and Hubert Humphrey, then the Republican Party is big enough for Jack Javits and Barry Goldwater." Race, above all, still separated Goldwater from the moderates. Romney privately chided Goldwater for having "never effectively deviated from the Southern-rural-white orientation." Robert Taft Jr., who lost a bid to follow his father as senator from Ohio, agreed that "the issue of civil rights . . . was more than any other factor, a dead cat hung around the elephant's neck that did devastating damage in all areas except the South." He urged a "total recommitment of the Party to an effective Federal civil rights program." The Republican Governor's Association rejected "all forms of narrow political radicalism, whether of the right and the left" and endorsed "all necessary action, public or private, to root out discrimination and the effects of discrimination throughout the United States." The most liberal Republicans joined the Ripon Society, founded in 1962, "to fight for the middle ground of American politics."[62]

As Johnson had anticipated, however, the demise of legalized segregation cleared the way for an eventual North-South alliance of white Protestant Americans within the Republican Party. No longer did the Democratic Party represent the last line of defense against integration and racial mixing. Without sacrificing moderate support, northern Republicans could ally with southerners, especially those of middle to upper class, who were dedicated to protecting racial privilege, private enterprise, and white Protestant values. Conservatives could even recapture the long-lost moral high ground on race by arguing for a "colorblind society" in place of the liberal's so-called racial spoils systems, which set racial quotas for minorities and discriminated against whites. Through such language, Republicans won the battle to frame racial issues in the late twentieth century and could oppose civil rights measures without appearing to be racist or opposed to minority progress. The power of incumbency and local organizations, the pull of history, Republican scandals of the 1970s, and the increase in black voters from 4 percent of the electorate in the 1950s to 22 percent in the 1980s slowed but did not stop realignment in the South.[63]

Conservative Republicans on both sides of the Mason-Dixon Line claimed that racial discrimination was a blight of the past, kept alive only by self-serving race leaders. As in earlier years, conservatives labeled virtually every civil rights initiative after 1964, whether it involved affirmative action or not, as a quota law. "The Democrat and Negro leadership," wrote Sherman T. Rock, chairman of the North Carolina Alliance of Conservative Republicans, in 1966, "represent segregation in reverse, special privileges for negroes at the expense of others who bear no sense of shame or guilt for whatever crimes or misdemeanors their former oppressors, and present comrades, committed against them." He added, "The Negro leaders say they want equality. This is exactly what the Republican party offers. No more, no less." Simultaneously, conservative Republicans also took advantage of white fears of black lawlessness and disorder to inspire opposition not only to civil rights measures but also to a broad range of liberal tax, spending, and regulatory initiatives.[64]

Colorblind ideology did not erase the color line or white privilege. Rather, it protected the prerogatives of race with a legitimacy that the overt racism of Jim Crow lacked. A colorblind America froze in place the effects of past and ongoing discrimination. It ignored the effects on minorities of ostensibly nonracial policies such as investment and lending patterns that bypassed minority communities, seniority preferences in employment, local funding of education, gerrymandered legislative districts, and the special access of alumni children to higher learning. In 1967, when William F. Buckley Jr. ran unsuccessfully for the governing board of Yale, he challenged affirmative action on minority admissions as "egalitarian hocus-pocus" and said that Yale should defer to "the older families—the members of what the English, in tones increasingly hushed, refer to as 'the governing class.'"[65]

THE STRUGGLE FOR RELEVANCE

Conservatives struggled to capitalize on Goldwater's grassroots appeal. In early 1965 Goldwater's Arizona operatives founded the Free Society Association (FSA) to educate Americans about the conservative principles of his campaign while avoiding charges of extremism. "Let's move on this—much interest," Goldwater appended to a note that ceded to the FSA "any and all surplus funds of the Citizens for Goldwater-Miller Committee." According to Charles Lichenstein, an FSA founder and the editor of its newsletter, "The Republican Party is the true home, the only home, of responsible conservatism." Even Goldwater's blessing, however, could not kindle enthusiasm for yet another nonpartisan educational organization like the Liberty League or For America that did not engage in political action and drained funds from Republican organizations. FSA closed its doors in 1969 without making much of an impact on American politics.[66]

Insiders at *National Review* created the more successful and enduring American Conservative Union (ACU) in late 1964 as another purported Americans for Democratic Action (ADA) of the right. Youthful Republican congressmen Donald C. Bruce of Indiana and John Ashbrook of Ohio, both syndicate veterans, chaired the ACU. Robert Bauman, president of Young Americans for Freedom, served as secretary. The *NR* crowd was involved: Frank Meyer as treasurer, William F. Buckley Jr. and Brent Bozell as members of the board, and William Rusher as political action director. Following a familiar model, the founders created "a separate but cooperating educational group," the American Public Affairs Educational Fund, to garner tax-deductible and corporate contributions that were forbidden to ACU "because of possible political and lobbying activity."[67]

ACU's founding letter asked, "How did the ADA, small in numbers, provide the manpower to take over the intellectual political and economic leadership of the United States?" It did so by mustering "the intellectual and political resources of the liberal movement toward the single ultimate objective of achieving political power." It "banded together to help other Liberals achieve positions of power and influence in government, the press, radio and TV, and private foundations to work for a socialist America." ACU's founders emulated both ADA's strategy and its aversion to extremists. No John Bircher could serve as an ACU officer, director, or adviser. After enduring a transition marred by dissension and financial distress, ACU became a major inside player on the right, although not a force for mobilizing masses of conservative voters.[68]

The ACU published a magazine, *Battle Line,* and developed a scorecard of voting on key issues by members of the Senate and the House. The ACU rating quickly become the gold standard by which conservatives measured political leanings in Congress. ACU affiliated with the Conservative Club of Chicago, a notable forum for the discussion of conservative ideas. It gained financial independence through direct-mail solicitations from lists of conservative activists that the White-Rusher group had compiled during the 1964 campaign. In 1969 ACU founded the Conservative Victory

Fund (CVF) to fund right-wing candidates for Congress, and in 1974 it held its first annual Conservative Political Action Conference (CPAC), the largest and most prestigious assemblage of the right to date. The CVF contributed $160,000 to candidates in 1970 and $110,000 in 1972.[69]

Pragmatic journalists and politicians led the ACU, not magnates like the Du Ponts and the Pews, soldiers like Ben Moreell and Albert Wedemeyer, or lawyers like Denison Kitchel and Richard Kleindienst. ACU specialized in head-butting politics. It analyzed how turncoat Republicans in Congress gave Johnson the margin of victory for his programs. It chided the "Wednesday Group" of liberal House Republicans, begun by John Lindsay of Manhattan, for missing "no opportunity to promote their views, justify their party irregularity, and attempt to sway their conservative GOP colleagues to their point of view." It reprised a 1950s-era assault on liberal foundations, ironically berating their exploitation of "federal 'tax exemption' laws." ACU weighed in on race and extremism, warning, "No matter how many times Republicans denounce extremism, the Klan, the Birch Society, and white supremacy, the Ripon Society will continue to accuse responsible conservatives of having sympathy with extremists." It echoed Goldwater's argument that the black vote was lost to the GOP and the party should welcome southern whites into its fold.[70]

Conservative book clubs and organizations kept ideas churning on the right. This included the work of former Volker Fund director Richard C. Cornuelle, who gave a sharply political and partisan twist to the scholarship of sociologists such as Robert A. Nisbet, who analyzed small communities and voluntary associations. Cornuelle argued that voluntary groups could be more effective than government in solving problems and could restore the vitality of local neighborhoods and communities. "The success of the Republican political position depends only incidentally on politics," Cornuelle explained. The GOP needed to provide "detailed blueprints for private action, and state and local action, on public problems. Then we must produce results, not just gripe at the government for trying to." Cornuelle's ideas—bankers running student aid programs, parent associations forming schools, businesses taking over antipoverty programs, and church groups rehabbing drug addicts—had a lasting impact on both conservative Republicans and libertarians.[71]

In defense and foreign affairs, the American Security Council raised its public profile. It aired a daily radio program on a thousand stations by decade's end and published attention-getting reports. Patrick J. Frawley, the Schick razor magnate, incensed by Castro's appropriation of his company's properties in Cuba, financed council projects. In the early 1960s Frawley succeeded J. Howard Pew as the leading financial angel of the right; he spent an estimated $1 million a year during the decade on conservative causes. Beyond contributing about $250,000 annually to the American Security Council, Frawley bankrolled the Christian Anti-Communist Crusade, the Cardinal Mindszenty Foundation, and the Billy Graham Crusade. He funded a $100,000 conservative essay contest, television specials, and radio broadcasts. He set up a publishing company for the work of Father Daniel Lyons, formerly a columnist for the Catholic weekly newsmagazine *Our Sunday Visitor,* edited by John Birch Society council member Richard Ginder. Frawley financed television ads for the Goldwater-Miller ticket in 1964, helped launch Ronald Reagan's political career, and contributed generously to other California conservatives.[72]

Buckley sought to sustain the conservative élan of the Goldwater movement by descending into the valley of electoral politics as the Conservative Party candidate for mayor of New York in 1965. He challenged John Lindsay, the liberal Republican superstar, who had been "hand picked by the Rockefeller-Scranton-Javits minority of the Republican Party as their instrument to reconquer the GOP and wipe out the hard-won gains made by conservatives in 1964," according to Buckley's brother and campaign manager, James Buckley. "This will not be a local campaign," James Buckley told the press. "The issues involved affect every city in the nation." With nothing to lose, Buckley used his debating skills to wound Lindsay, sell conservative ideas, and expose what he charged was a corrupt bargain between the Democrats and liberal Republicans who controlled New York.[73]

Buckley accused both parties of catering to "voting blocs" rather than to individuals. He would deprive "the voting blocs of their corporate advantages" and create a government "devoted to dismantling, rather than establishing, artificial privileges of the kind New York has been establishing for years, following the lead of Washington DC." He would stiffen criminal penalties, give police more authority, abolish union monopolies and minimum wage laws, dismantle welfare programs, and raze public housing projects. He called New Yorkers who protested the Vietnam War "young slobs" and charged baseball legend and black Republican Jackie

Robinson with inciting Negroes to riot when Robinson called upon African Americans to band together in self-defense against racial bigots. In a confidential memo to Conservative Party members, Buckley wrote, "On [my campaign] the future hopes of the national Republican Party may very well depend; from which it may follow on its success, the future of the country may well depend." His 13 percent of the vote did not defeat Lindsay or save America, but it showed that agitation of social and racial issues could win for conservatives votes from traditionally Democratic, white ethnic voters within America's cities.[74]

The Goldwater campaign, however, had created three conservative stars: Ronald Reagan, Richard Viguerie, and Phyllis Schlafly. Reagan became a political celebrity and an appealing face for conservatives after making an acclaimed speech for Barry Goldwater, entitled "A Time for Choosing," which Frawley paid to have televised nationwide and local Republican committees replayed across the country. Richard Viguerie, just thirty-one years old in 1964, understood that direct-mail fund-raising from small donors was the philosopher's stone that transmuted copper into gold. Viguerie formed a pioneering direct-mail company after the election, which he initially based on the names of 12,500 Goldwater donors. Schlafly's book *A Choice Not an Echo,* published in 1964, foreshadowed a campaign slogan and sold several million copies. It fed into the right's conspiratorial thinking by posing Goldwater as the heroic opponent of an establishment allegedly controlled by the international Bilderberg Group and its junior partner in the United States, the Council on Foreign Relations. The Bilderbergers were a group of bankers, businessmen, intellectuals, and policy makers from Europe and the United States who met secretly each year since being convened in 1954 by Prince Bernhard of the Netherlands at the Bilderberg Hotel in his home country. For Schlafly, the Bilderbergers were a "shadow government" whose American minion Lyndon Johnson would "abolish our Army, our Navy, our Air Force and our nuclear weapons, and make us subject to a United Nations Peace Force." Although Schlafly won election as vice president of the Federation of Republican Women, in another blow to conservatives she failed in her 1967 bid for its presidency. But Schlafly followed an independent path to influence, publishing the *Phyllis Schlafly Report* and fund-raising through her tax-exempt Eagle Trust Fund.[75]

THE LIBERAL MOMENT

This post-Goldwater bustle on the right did not deter President Johnson from seizing his moment. As in 1933, conservatives could only watch in dismay as a Democratic president steered liberal programs through a willing Congress. Unlike in the 1930s, a business community relieved to escape Goldwater's eccentricities posed little opposition to a liberal president who cultivated and organized executives who were enjoying lower taxes and higher profits. Johnson also configured policies to meet the needs of business. For example, the Food Stamp program subsidized large agricultural interests and aid to the elderly let Blue Cross insurers shed high-risk subscribers.[76]

Johnson embedded the struggle for minority rights within the liberal agenda and in another departure from the New Deal he targeted needs—housing, health care, nutrition, and education—rather than groups such as the elderly or the unemployed. New reform movements, drawing on the civil rights model but grounded in America's growing middle class, propelled federal regulations into new realms, which would prove unfamiliar and costly to business. In 1962 Rachel Carson's landmark best seller *Silent Spring* exposed the hazards of the pesticide DDT and inspired the rise of an environmental movement. In 1963, Betty Friedan's *The Feminine Mystique* helped launch a new wave of feminism, which she solidified by joining with other feminists to form the National Organization for Women (NOW) in 1966. The "second wave" feminists demanded equal opportunity in education and employment, reproductive freedom, positive cultural images of women, and rights for homosexuals. Antipoverty activists, inspired by socialist intellectual Michael Harrington's 1962 book *The Other America,* demanded programs to empower the less affluent to transform their lives.

Ralph Nader, the author of *Unsafe at Any Speed* (1965), which assailed the auto industry for putting profits above safety, spearheaded a new consumer rights movement. Young activists known as Nader's raiders flocked to Washington to expose and fight abuse and corruption in industry and government. In 1969 Nader founded the Center for the Study of Responsive Law, the first of some forty nonprofit groups that implemented his vision of "the public interest." Rather than targeting particular industries that could "capture" regulators, the new reformers won popular support for what scholars called "post-material" regulations on the environment, rights for minorities and women, consumer protections, and worker safety, with business bearing the costs.[77]

Johnson guided legislation through Congress that established medical care for the elderly (Medicare) and for the poor (Medicaid). He gained an upgraded Food Stamp Program, federal aid for housing and education, and a model cities program that bypassed mayors and councils to assist inner-city residents in setting up self-improvement programs. The president entrenched liberal programs in the bureaucracy with a National Endowment for the Arts and Humanities and new cabinet departments of Transportation and Housing and Urban Development. Congress enacted laws to curb water and air pollution, the Wholesome Meat Act, the Fair Packaging and Labeling Act, and both the National Traffic Safety Act and the Highway Safety Act. Johnson established a federally funded legal services program for the poor and reluctantly signed the Freedom of Information Act that expanded public access to federal records.

Johnson advanced the liberal civil rights agenda by winning passage of the Voting Rights Act of 1965. The act outlawed literacy tests and authorized the federal government to ensure minority registration and voting. Along with the Twenty-fourth Amendment to the Constitution, which banned the poll tax in federal elections, it opened the ballot box to millions of disenfranchised blacks throughout the South. The act outlawed political systems that denied minorities the opportunity to participate fully in the political process and elect candidates of their choice. Civil rights attorneys used this provision of the act to invalidate electoral districts and at-large election systems in both the North and the South that excluded minorities from electing their preferred candidates to office. In the decade following passage of the Voting Rights Act, the number of black elected officials in the United States rose from just a handful to some four thousand, nearly all Democrats. By executive order in 1965, the president established the first federal affirmative action program for minorities that required federal contractors "to take affirmative action" to ensure minority opportunity in hiring and employment. In 1967 he extended affirmative action to cover women. An Equal Employment Opportunity Commission began enforcing prohibitions against racial and sex discrimination.

A new immigration law enacted in 1965 eliminated nationality quotas and opened immigration equally to peoples worldwide. Organizations on the right rushed to lobby against the bill, including the American Coalition of Patriotic Societies, revived by a $35,000 contribution from Wickliffe Preston Draper, financier of the Pioneer Fund, which supported work on racial science. In the *National Review*, sociologist Ernest van den Haag—an immigrant from Holland—made the conservative case for nationality quotas. "Patriotism is not racism," he wrote. "The wish to preserve one's identity and the identity of one's nation requires no justification—and no belief in superiority." He argued that we should consider the United States "settled territory" and "stop encouraging immigration altogether."[78]

Johnson, the Democratic Congress, and the Warren Court had rebuilt liberalism on the rubble of the Goldwater defeat. Like Humpty Dumpty after the fall, all the right's horses and all the right's men couldn't put the Goldwater agenda together again. Predictions by conservatives since 1936 that the nation was passing the point of no return seemed accurate by 1966. The time seemed to have passed to bridle the redistributive power of government, halt Keynesian management and unwanted regulations of business, or end special privileges for women and minorities. Practical conservatives recognized the difficulty of privatizing Social Security, slashing welfare, restricting immigration, or keeping social engineers from tinkering with traditional institutions. Equally remote were prospects for restoring religion to the public square and achieving moral reform. Conservatives could forget about curtailing foreign aid, rebuffing arms control, pulling America out of the UN, or withdrawing recognition of the Soviet Union. In 1967 the seventy-five-year-old Jasper Crane wrote to the eighty-five-year-old J. Howard Pew, "We have a tougher fight against socialism and the improper use of force than we realized thirty or more years ago. I still believe that we will win, but it may take a long time."[79]

To the chagrin of conservative Catholics, liberal reform even swept through the musty chambers of the Vatican when Pope John XXIII convened the Second Vatican Council "to throw open the windows of the Church." In four sessions through 1965, held primarily under John XXIII's successor, Pope Paul VI, the council blew away ideas and practices that had moldered in the Church for centuries. Vatican II emphasized the pastoral duties of the Church and the need for greater relevance to a world challenged by poverty, racism, human rights violations, and threats of nuclear annihilation. The council decentralized authority within the

Church and allowed for expanded freedom of thought and conscience by individual Catholics. It extended lay participation in church affairs and called upon Catholics to advance social justice across the globe. It adopted a less magisterial liturgy that allowed the celebration of mass in vernacular languages, reached out ecumenically to non-Catholics, backed freedom of religion, and absolved Jews from responsibility for the death of Christ.

LOSING THE CULTURE

Trends in the American culture dismayed conservatives. Leaders on the right worried that scruffy, drug-taking, and promiscuous hippies, not clean-cut members of the YAF and the Young Republicans, were setting the trends for young Americans and the broader culture. "The hippies are the anti-Christ," warned the Christian Heritage Center. "They are the creatures Christ predicted, for with their long hair and beards and filthy poverty, they are loathsome creatures of the Lord." Crime and social disorder escalated after 1960 and a sexual revolution swept the country, certified in a 1964 *Time* cover story that reported, "The U.S. seems to be undergoing a revolution of mores and an erosion of morals that is turning it into . . . a 'sex-affirming culture.'" Some 39 percent of women who turned fifteen between 1964 and 1973 had premarital sex by age eighteen, compared to just 26 percent for those turning fifteen a decade earlier. Women and homosexuals, not just straight men, demanded and practiced sexual freedom, while sex education became commonplace in public schools.[80]

Unlike in the 1920s the postwar generation of conservatives had not yet mobilized to control the arts and popular culture. Beginning in the 1950s courts and legislatures had toppled legal barriers to free expression and Hollywood replaced its production code with a permissive film-rating system in 1968. Hit songs celebrated sex and drugs and, in 1970, a sex manual, *Everything You Always Wanted to Know About Sex But Were Afraid to Ask*, topped the best-seller list. Even television was loosening up its portrayal of sex, race, and politics. Journalist and Republican Women's Club official Martha Rountree told the General Federation of Women's Clubs in 1970, "Everywhere we look and turn or look and read, we are finding smut, dirt, filth, vulgarity, perversion, homosexuality, abuses of every kind, crime, sadism, immorality, and destruction of property and human values."[81]

In 1965 media consultant Robert Salter warned conservatives that they were losing the battle for the culture. The right could not match the novels of Gore Vidal and James Baldwin, the plays of Bertolt Brecht, or movies like *Dr. Strangelove.* It had not countered "the subtle impressions in television and films that writers and directors slip in because of their own liberal convictions." These media turned the businessman into "a crook or a fool," patriotism into "a joke," and military leaders into "bumbling idiots." In competing with hip culture, the square right only parodied itself, as illustrated by the marketing of Janet Greene as the "pro-American folksinger." According to her sponsors in the Christian Anti-Communist Crusade Greene was a "new and effective anti-Communist weapon." Greene sang warnings: "Be careful of the Commie lies. Swallow them and freedom dies." She sang the blues for conservatives smeared as fascists: "Which organization can it be? That is what perplexes me." Best of all, wrote conservative columnist Woolsey Teller, "She looks like a girl. Not many female protest singers can say that." So, if you were "tired of the folk singers who whimper, weep and wail at everything the United States does, but cheer the Viet Cong . . . Janet Greene's songs are a welcome relief from that slop."[82]

For conservatives, the government contributed to cultural decline by violating their rule of doing no harm. It sanctioned permissive sex education and banished religion from public life. As dozens of states debated sex education in the late 1960s, conservatives charged that progressive educators had established in schools the faux religion of secular humanism. According to columnist John Steinbacher of Anaheim, California, sex education "interlocked with the affirmation of the so-called New Morality and the doctrine of permissive sex found in the so-called sexual revolution . . . all three movements, again, are allied with the doctrine of Humanism." Anaheim had gained national attention for its battles over sex education. Nationally, Gordon Drake of the Christian Crusade emerged as the Allen Zoll of the movement against sex education. His widely circulated booklet, *Is the School House the Proper Place to Teach Raw Sex?,* warned of children succumbing to Marxism, promiscuity, hedonism, nihilism, and venereal disease. Organizations creatively named POSE (Parents Opposed to Sex Education), MOMS (Mothers for Moral Stability), and SOS (Sanity on Sex) used Drake's material to prove that children needed only abstinence, strong families, and parental guidance.[83]

Court decisions of the 1960s banning religious observances in schools undermined a singular achievement of conservatives in the 1920s. The real issue, noted editors of the *Wall Street Journal*, "is much broader than prayers. There is a push to eradicate all traces of religion from all public life, even to the barring of any Christmas observances in schools and communities." This secularism represented "a hopeless misunderstanding of our culture" and "the wildest kind of discrimination, not least against the children it would deprive of pleasure and spiritual profit." Conservative members of Congress introduced numerous versions of a constitutional amendment to reverse court rulings on prayer and Bible reading. The House held hearings during 1964 and Christian right leader Carl McIntire organized prayer rallies, a post card campaign, and a petition drive that secured a million signatures. Prominent evangelical Protestants and conservative Catholic leaders denounced the Court's decisions, including Billy Graham, Norman Vincent Peale, Bishop Fulton J. Sheen, and Cardinal Francis J. Spellman. Most mainstream religious groups, however, accepted the decoupling of religion and public education. An amendment to restore prayer in schools gained 167 House cosponsors in 1964, but liberals killed it in committee. The Senate roundly defeated a prayer amendment in 1966, although every senator with a right of center voting record, except Democrat Sam Ervin of North Carolina, voted aye.[84]

THE LIBERAL MALAISE

Franklin Roosevelt's New Deal endured for six years, until the midterm elections of 1938. Lyndon Johnson's Great Society survived for only three years, until the midterm elections of 1966, when voters registered their discontent with the failing war in Vietnam and the limits of Johnson's programs to affect social change. Two days after Johnson's inauguration, ambassador Maxwell Taylor had cabled from Vietnam, "We are presently on a losing track and must risk a change. . . . To take no positive action now is to accept defeat in the fairly near future. Furthermore, the action required goes beyond any mere improvement. . . . The game needs to be opened up." The president had three options: all-out war ("blow them out of the water in ten days," Johnson said), limited war through measured air strikes and ground operations, or negotiated withdrawal. Reluctantly, Johnson chose the middle course. He would not display unmanly personal and national weakness, encourage communist aggression, damage America's credibility, and risk losing the electoral mandate of 1964 by running from a fight. Total war lacked public support and risked nuclear confrontation or a major land war in Asia. But Johnson did not expect military victory through limited war. Rather, he hoped to force a negotiated settlement by raising the costs of war for the North Vietnamese. In June 1965 Johnson told his cabinet, "Our objective is just that: it is to convince them that they can't win there. We think we can achieve this objective by moving toward a stalemate, convincing them that the situation in the south will not lead to a military victory." Johnson took his nation to war with a goal that dared not speak its name in public: stalemate. How could he ask Americans to risk their lives to tie one for the Gipper? By the end of 1966 Johnson had dispatched some 385,000 American troops to Vietnam.[85]

Rising casualties and stalled progress in Vietnam were not the only precipitants of a public unease that boosted Republicans. Explosive social issues that Democrats had so long suppressed disrupted liberalism's advance, even as the economy continued growing and unemployment remained low. Johnson's prodigious efforts in fighting discrimination and poverty raised unreachable expectations among African Americans both in the ghettoes of American cities and in smaller towns and suburbs. In 1965 black frustration in the Watts section of Los Angeles erupted into a week of violence that left thirty-four dead, more than a thousand injured, and millions of dollars in property damage. Urban riots, along with the formation in 1966 of the Black Panther Party—depicted by government and the media as a violent vanguard of black revolution—spurred fears of racial insurrection. After championing black progress, Johnson's Democratic Party found its majority threatened by racial issues. "The civil rights program and all of the welfare programs to help the Negro have backfired," Albert S. Porter, Democratic National Committeeman from Ohio, wrote to Vice President Humphrey in 1966. "We give them Head Start, Demonstration Cities, Economic Opportunity, A.D.C.... So what do we get in return? Riots, Molotov Cocktails, picket lines, insurrection, demonstrations." At a 1967 cabinet meeting, Labor Secretary W. Willard Wirtz said, "Looking at the riots, I worry that we might be reaching the wrong kids, not the hard core. The statistics merely indicate success with youngsters susceptible to reason and within the reach of persuasion—not the rioters deep in the ghettoes."[86]

In jeopardy from the draft and disillusioned with broken promises of a just society, students began militant protests as part of a "new politics" or "new left" movement, a reverse mirror image of Goldwater's anti-establishment crusade. Inspired by the pivotal free speech movement at the University of California's Berkeley campus in 1964, which demanded that the university administration allow students to engage in political activities on campus and freely express their opinions, and rallied by left-wing groups like Students for a Democratic Society, students battled racism, repression, militarism, and poverty. The House Un-American Activities Committee had put Berkeley on the national map with its widely viewed 1960 film *Operation Abolition,* which showed apparently disorderly students protesting a committee hearing in San Francisco, spliced with footage of alleged communists subpoenaed for testimony. Beyond politics, some dissidents sought to achieve communal earth-friendly living, to adopt non-Western spirituality, to engage freely in sex and mind-altering drugs, and to reject the illusory materialistic world. "Nothing is real and nothing to get hung about," sang John Lennon. Among African Americans, a black power campaign reminiscent of Marcus Garvey's back-to-Africa movement of the 1920s touted racial pride, militant self-defense, and freedom from domination by whites. Like conservative whites, black power advocates demanded control of their local communities. Feminists declared that the "personal is political," charging that women's personal grievances reflected systematic oppression by a male-dominated patriarchy and required political solutions.[87]

In the 1966 midterms, Republicans picked up eight governorships, some seven hundred state legislative seats, three Senate, and forty-seven House seats, although Democrats still held 64 percent of Senate seats and 57 percent of House seats. A Democratic Party analysis suggested that the white backlash might have come a little too late for Goldwater. "The single issue which appeared to be critical . . . was that of race rioting and the pace of Negro advances in our society." The AFL-CIO pointed to "widespread unease over Vietnam" and the "apathy" of "Negroes who, two years after passage of the Civil Rights Act, have not improved their position as much as they had hoped." The union group warned that "the white backlash was an issue affecting our own membership" and "the white population generally, including union members, will increasingly live in suburbs, outside the sphere of either party or union political organization." Still, the AFL-CIO reported, the elections were "a repudiation of Barry Goldwater," because the GOP "worked hard and very successfully in 1966 to build a new image." Conservative voting scores by Republicans in Congress hit a twentieth-century low in 1967–68 and did not rise again for another decade.[88]

In California, however, Ronald Reagan defeated Governor Pat Brown, the conqueror of Knowland in 1958 and Nixon in 1962. With a deftness that had eluded Taft and Goldwater, Reagan presented a genial, optimistic face to voters. He skillfully marketed conservative themes, distanced himself from extremist leaders but not their followers, and played upon the social unrest and fears of African-American rebellion that drove voters to reject the Democratic Party. Reagan also secretly collaborated with FBI Director Hoover to suppress radicalism, centered at Berkeley. "Agitators on other campuses take their lead from activities which occur at Berkeley," Hoover wrote in a confidential memo. Curbing agitation at Berkeley "could set up a chain reaction which will result in the curtailment of such activities on other campuses throughout the United States."[89]

THE COLOSSUS FALLS

In looking ahead to a reelection campaign in 1968, Johnson worried most about new politics radicals. "Even if the Peacenik-Black Power effort is *not* strong enough to cause us to lose any of these key industrial states," warned an unsigned internal memo in July 1967, "it continues to be a serious threat to our national unity. . . . Riots, bloodshed, demonstrations, property destruction, and other forms of civil disobedience confuse and weaken our nation when we must be strong." The rift between new politics or modernist liberals and the practical men or custodial liberals behind Johnson was "philosophical and psychological as well as political," noted a study by the liberal National Committee for an Effective Congress. "The real argument is over who is in touch with reality and who is in touch with mythology—the custodian who sees reality in term of specific interests, or the modernists who hold that intangible moral questions are today's reality."[90]

In the 1966 midterm election year, with Johnson's assent, the FBI expanded its COINTELPRO program to spy on and disrupt the "Black Nationalist-Hate Group" and the "New Left Group." Unlike the "White

Hate" program, which the FBI had confined to violent groups such as the KKK and the Nazi Party, the "Black Nationalist" program swept in civil rights organizations such as Martin Luther King Jr.'s Southern Christian Leadership Conference. The "New Left" program was an equally elastic politically charged effort "designed to neutralize the New Left and the Key Activists," according to a memo by assistant FBI director Charles Brennan.[91]

Under pressure from the administration to probe foreign influence on domestic protest, the CIA illegally spied on domestic dissidents. It infiltrated black activist and antiwar organizations, gleaned data from police departments and other local authorities, and submitted thousands of reports to the FBI and other agencies. The CIA intercepted and opened the international mail of domestic war critics and scanned conversations recorded by the National Security Agency. These programs continued until their exposure by the press and congressional investigators in the mid-1970s. Yet the failure to link domestic dissidents with foreign provocateurs disappointed both Johnson and his successor Richard Nixon.[92]

Losses in the 1966 midterm elections pushed Johnson no closer to resolving the war in Vietnam. In 1967 the president pleaded with his generals to "search for imaginative ideas to put pressure to bring this war to a conclusion"—not just "more men or that we drop the Atom bomb." The military had no other answers and American troop strength ballooned to a peak of 550,000 in 1968. That winter, the North Vietnamese and the Viet Cong guerrillas launched a surprise offensive during Vietnam's Tet (New Year) holiday. American and South Vietnamese troops technically "won" the Tet engagement, but the intensity of the attack made continued predictions of victory sound hollow, widening Johnson's credibility gap with the public. In March 1968, Johnson's new secretary of defense, Clark Clifford, warned, "The major concern of the [American] people is that they do not see victory ahead . . . more men go in and are chewed up in a bottomless pit."[93]

The war and domestic unrest divided the Democratic Party and left Johnson an isolated president, struggling to deliver the "guns and butter" he had promised the American people. Johnson's honeymoon with leaders of enterprise soured when he refused to pare down the Great Society and made them swallow tax hikes and new regulations. As Johnson's advisers had predicted, it was not conservative critics who imperiled his presidency but antiwar liberals within the Democratic Party. A peace candidate,

Senator Eugene McCarthy of Minnesota, won a surprising 41 percent against Johnson in the New Hampshire primary, with votes from both doves and hawks who were distressed about stalemate in Vietnam. After New Hampshire, Senator Robert Kennedy of New York emerged as a more formidable challenger. "Of the two doves," White House adviser Fred Panzer said, "Bobby is the one with the claws." Beyond opposing the war, Kennedy offered an ambitious program of liberal reform to cure poverty and promote social justice. On March 31, a dispirited and exhausted president told a national television audience that rather than seek reelection he would work on bringing peace to Vietnam.[94]

Robert Kennedy's assassination after his potentially decisive win in the California primary secured the nomination for Vice President Humphrey, who entered the race too late for the primaries but wrapped up delegates selected by party bosses. The 1968 Democratic Convention symbolized the era's turmoil—police and demonstrators battled on the streets of Democratic mayor Richard Daley's Chicago. Although Humphrey turned to the center in picking Senator Edmund Muskie of Maine as his vice presidential nominee, he appeased New Politics Democrats by authorizing a commission to reform the party's nominating process, headed by liberal senator George McGovern of South Dakota.

Mark M. Jones, who had taken over the National Economic Council after Merwin Hart's death, enumerated conservative grievances against Democrats in the September 1968 edition of his group's newsletter. The Johnson administration had "undermined and sabotaged the credit of the United States" and collaborated with "Communism, Socialism, and Internationalism." Johnson had "built up a Frankenstein of domestic Socialism." His administration had "promoted and incited racial turmoil and riots" and implanted "the social cancer of welfarism by building up a parasitic mob of nonproducers." The Democrats coddled criminals and pornographers, accepted "known perverts as leaders," hijacked education, and engaged in the "systematic and widespread undermining and weakening of the family." More than anticommunism, Jones's indictment centered on social issues related to race, sexuality, education, pornography, and the family.

Yet the post-Goldwater Republicans offered no ray of hope. The "biparty liberal movement," Jones said, diluted ideological differences. The professionals who ran the GOP had forsaken conservative ideals for "personal prestige and private profit." The "unlimited tenure of political ficeholders" led officials of both parties "to feel that their office becomes their tool." The "growth and development of a thought-control system," including "the press, radio, TV, movies, book publishing, and education" kept either party from challenging the liberal state. Echoing conservative analyst Lawrence Dennis's warnings from the 1940s, Jones wrote that neither party could resist the lure of leviathan government. He wrote that if Republicans won in 1968, with "$200 billion a year to blow, with no real accountability," they too would exploit "not only the power, but the money of the Federal Government."[95]

William Baroody, president of the American Enterprise Institute, offered a similarly grim prognosis. He said that even if a liberal malaise swept Democrats from office, conservatives still lacked the ideas and infrastructure needed to turn electoral success into policy change. Conservative reform "requires a well thought out set of ideas concerning policy if it is to achieve its purpose." Instead, conservative thinkers were "a lonely lot, supported by only a few.... The alliance with men of affairs must be made now." For Richard Ware of the Relm Foundation, which provided financial assistance to conservative scholars, conservatives had to use their resources to "change the tone of academic orthodoxy" through a long-term process that "prepares a climate of thought, ultimately, in which the election of 1980 may be, for a change, uphill-going for the left."[96]

THE PRODIGAL SON RETURNS

Some on the right who believed that Americans preferred smiling to snarling conservatives sought salvation in 1968 with Governor Reagan. But after less than two years in office, Reagan was not ready to leave the cocoon of California politics. Following a plan designed by former Goldwater strategist F. Clifton White, Reagan ran as a stealth candidate for president. His lack of interest in the office, some said, was the best acting job of his career. Like MacArthur, he hoped to become the savior of a deadlocked convention.

Richard Nixon's triumphant return foiled Reagan's underground campaign. Barry Goldwater began Nixon's recovery by preemptively endorsing him in early 1965, followed by Buckley in 1967. Other conservative leaders fell in line, including Strom Thurmond, who helped deliver the South. With Reagan still untested outside California, conservatives saw

Nixon as their best insurance policy against moderates Nelson Rockefeller or George Romney. Obligingly, Romney wrecked his campaign when he attributed his earlier support for the Vietnam War to "brainwashing" by American generals and diplomats. Reagan's boosters placed the governor's name on the ballot in selected primary contests, but the stealth candidate won only as the favorite son in California. An indecisive Rockefeller entered the race at the end of April, too late for a serious campaign. Nixon's lack of a fixed ideological compass, his long service in government, and his campaigning for Republicans in 1966 reconciled all party factions.

Although Reagan became the available man at the GOP convention, his coyness left him without world enough or time to woo delegates. The delegates balloted only once, giving Nixon a narrow majority before Reagan shrewdly moved for Nixon's unanimous nomination. For second place on his ticket, Nixon chose Governor Spiro T. Agnew of Maryland—a borderline southerner and a moderate who veered to the right on social issues.[97]

Nixon, however, could not stifle the insurgent third-party campaign of George Wallace, who mocked the major parties as "tweedledee and tweedledum." Like King Lear's jester, however, Wallace had purpose behind his comic act. He eventually hoped to win enough southern states to deadlock the Electoral College and force an election by voting in the House of Representatives, with each state holding one vote. Wallace anticipated bartering his southern loyalists for "a solemn compact" with the winner, which, like the Compromise of 1876 that ended Reconstruction, would pledge to curb federal interference in southern race relations. Wallace further hoped to gain the following needed to capture the Democratic Party nomination in 1972. He planned to rally a conservative populist majority of southerners, patriotic union families, and northern ethnic voters worried about crime, lax morals, and government meddling in their lives. This coalition would represent the hardworking, productive Americans squeezed between parasitic bureaucrats and their shiftless clients on the welfare rolls. Although a hastily assembled American Independent Party nominated Wallace in 1968, he was a genuine independent, not a party builder.

Wallace invoked familiar conservative themes of antiradicalism and fidelity to God and country. He avoided overt racial appeals and instead focused on upholding law and order, achieving victory against communism, and the relationship between these two goals. "Those people who advocate a breakdown of law and order eventually wind up in Havana and Hanoi and Moscow," he said. Unlike Goldwater, who staggered into Johnson's left hooks, Wallace jabbed, struck, and danced away. He struck at "pseudo-intellectuals" like the "bearded professor who thinks he knows how to settle the Vietnam War when he hasn't the sense to park his bicycle straight." He struck at the "select elite group" of bureaucrats and judges who looked "down their noses at the average man in the street," the victim of activist judges and intrusive government. He danced around a hostile media to organize rallies and speak before business and fraternal groups. He became the first presidential candidate to frequent the new medium of talk shows. He responded to charges of racism by decrying "reverse discrimination" against whites and saying, "The biggest bigots in the world are—they're the ones who call others bigots." Every Wallace appearance, ad, or pamphlet included an appeal for donations. More than $9 million poured in during 1967–68, mostly from small contributors, although surviving White Citizens' Councils passed on laundered donations, John Wayne chipped in $30,000, and Nelson Bunker Hunt, H.L.'s equally conservative son, donated as much as $300,000—in the southern cash-only tradition. John Birch Society members quietly led the campaign in a dozen states, mostly in the West.[98]

Wallace's literature compared his firm resolution to the waffling of Nixon and Humphrey. Wallace supported "law and order" while Nixon gave political "lip service" to crime and Humphrey "weakly" blamed crime on poverty. Wallace would "crush riots with a swift blow" while Nixon stood silent and Humphrey supported "anarchy and riots." Wallace opposed "black racism." Nixon said that "black racists only are O.K." and Humphrey favored "black against white." Wallace opposed "welfare cheaters," which Nixon and Humphrey supported. Wallace opposed "supreme court dictatorship." Nixon offered "apologies for Earl Warren" and Humphrey the "criminal lover" defended "LBJ-crony Justice Abe 'Fixer' Fortas." Wallace wanted "a military victory" in Vietnam or would "get the U.S. out." Nixon and Humphrey offered only "double talk." Wallace promised "firm and determined opposition to Communist world domination." Nixon took "the appeasement line" and Humphrey was an "appeaser—soft on communism."[99]

Wallace avoided Goldwater's mistake of threatening popular programs or igniting fears of nuclear war. His platform courted working-class voters with planks for higher Social Security and Medicare benefits, new job training programs, and public works for the unemployed. It urged a stronger defense but not tactical nuclear warfare in Vietnam. Mainstream conservatives deplored Wallace for disrupting the GOP's southern strategy and, like Father Coughlin, embracing both crude racism and activist government. A *Human Events* poll of "two hundred prominent conservatives" found that none backed Wallace. Buckley argued that, stripped of his racial policies, the real Wallace was a Humphrey-style liberal. For some on the right, however, so-called respectable conservatives protested too much. "The disarray of the conservative respectables in the face of the Wallace surge would make an interesting psychological study," wrote Buckley's friend Neil McCaffrey, the founder of the Conservative Book Club. "Here is a man who takes conservative issues and conservative concerns, scorns euphemisms, and goes right for the gut. . . . What troubles me most deeply about this split in conservative ranks is the superciliousness with which the respectables view the Wallace followers and their genuine concerns." Conservative third-party advocate Kent Courtney said, "William F. Buckley can clown his way through a New York mayoralty campaign and everyone is supposed to be amused but when a political powerhouse like George Wallace appears on the scene he is accused of being a demagogue and a populist."[100]

Wallace eventually regretted his choice of trigger-happy retired air force general Curtis LeMay as a running mate. His problem on Election Day, however, was not LeMay but voters' reluctance to "waste" their ballot on a supposedly unelectable third-party candidate. Wallace slid from 23 percent in the polls to 13.5 percent of the actual vote. He survived as a regional candidate, winning 29 percent of the southern vote, compared to just 8 percent in the North. He won five Deep South states but failed to reach 15 percent in any northern state. Rather than inspiring a revolt of alienated lower- and middle-class voters, Wallace performed about equally well across income groups and slightly better in union than nonunion households, according to the National Election Study.

The Nixon campaign emulated Wallace. Agnew blasted the Democrats as "soft on inflation, soft on Communism, and soft on law and order." He ripped the "self-appointed elitists" who thought their "educations give them the right to decide which laws to obey and which to disregard." He belittled demonstrators as "spoiled brats" who "take their tactics from Castro and their money from Daddy." Nixon promised to end the Vietnam War but declined to discuss specifics of his plan and through a back channel pressured the South Vietnamese government to resist any peace deal until after the election. Nixon charged that crime would double within a year if the "soft-on-criminals" Democrats retained the presidency. He said that the Warren Court favored "the criminal forces over the peace forces" and pledged to appoint "strict constructionist" judges "who saw their duty as interpreting law and not making law."[101]

Nixon edged out Humphrey 43.4 percent to 42.7 percent in the popular vote and won the Electoral College by 301 to 191. The Democrats easily held on to both houses of Congress, including their southern seats. But conservative candidates united most white Protestants, North and South. Nixon (60 percent) and Wallace (14 percent) together won very nearly three-quarters of the national white Protestant vote, according to the National Election Study. Humphrey's meager 26 percent left him eight points behind the Catholic Kennedy in 1960. Fifty-five percent of Catholics backed Humphrey, 84 percent of Jews, 97 percent of blacks, and 52 percent of religious "others" and the unaffiliated.

GOP analyst Kevin Phillips argued in an influential 1969 book, *The Emerging Republican Majority,* that the election portended a Republican realignment emerging from the growing states of the southern and western Sun Belt. Phillips proved correct in identifying the Sun Belt as a source of Republican strength but was wrong about an imminent realignment. The war in Vietnam had elected Richard Nixon by splitting the Democrats, driving President Johnson into retirement, burdening his party with a foreign-policy disaster, and sparking social unrest. Still, the GOP had not cut deeply into Democratic majorities in Congress or the Democrats' hold on party loyalties. In the South, elected officials remained solidly Democratic.

THE RIGHT REBUILDS IN ADVERSITY, 1969–1976

After becoming president, the always suspicious Richard Nixon planted spies at meetings of both conservative and moderate Republicans. Just ten months after inauguration day, one of his spies reported that conservatives were already thinking about dumping a president who talked like Goldwater but, as Mark Jones of the National Economic Council had predicted, governed like Johnson. At a 1969 meeting of the influential Philadelphia Society, founded in 1964 for private discussions of weighty matters such as "Religion and the Crisis of the Twentieth Century," Nixon's informant reported "considerable dissatisfaction" with "a 'rubber president' who bends to the left too easily." One conservative thought that Nixon "could be unseated from the Right just as Johnson was from the Left" and pointed to Ronald Reagan as a liberator "on the Right who can build a national movement a la Gene McCarthy." Ironically, according to another Nixon spy, moderate Republicans were also "knocking the administration." A president who had adopted the slogan "bring us together" had managed to repel both factions of his party.[1]

BUYER'S REMORSE ON THE RIGHT

Like Eisenhower, Nixon stocked his cabinet with pragmatists and governed more moderately than he campaigned. "Our peerless leader in the White House may not be a true-blue conservative," said columnist James J. Kilpatrick, but "he is as conservative a President as we had any hope of electing, and we are lucky to have him." Other conservatives publicly disagreed. The American Conservative Union lamented that even many conservatives in Congress had "adopted what has now become the president's own standard operating procedure; they talk conservative, but go along with the liberalism that the President has been espousing." For Brent Bozell, Buckley's smarter brother-in-law who left *NR* to found *Triumph,* a right-wing Catholic journal, Nixon was the result of years of squandered opportunities. Even with liberals reeling from crime and disorder, a failed war, and disappointing policies, the right had failed to step into the breech of history. "Secular liberalism has fallen," Bozell told fellow conservatives. "Yet no one reaches out to you for support. . . . The conservative program was trounced in Goldwater's moment, and had been forgotten by Nixon's."[2]

In Nixon's first year, good news for the right came improbably from New York City where conservative John Marchi defeated Mayor John Lindsay in the Republican mayoral primary. Lindsay was the future of Rockefeller Republicanism, Apollonian in appearance, courtly in manner, and unabashedly liberal. "The capture of the New York City GOP by conservative Republicans is a permanent blow to the Dewey-Rockefeller Eastern Liberal Establishment coalition," cheered Pat Buchanan, Nixon's conservative speechwriter. "The Bastille has fallen."[3]

The president pleased conservatives by opposing the busing of school-children to achieve integration and appointing two right-leaning southerners to the Supreme Court, Circuit Court Judge Clement Haynsworth Jr. of South Carolina and Circuit Court Judge G. Harrold Carswell of Florida, although neither won confirmation. He embraced strict anticrime measures and declared a "war on drugs," which he enforced through the Controlled Substance Act of 1970. Also in 1970, an inspired Elvis Presley asked Nixon to appoint him "Federal Agent at Large" in order to penetrate the "drug culture" through his entrée to "the hippie elements, the SDS, Black Panthers, etc." Elvis did not get his appointment but he did score a meeting with the president and a souvenir narcotics agent badge.[4]

Nixon, however, also understood that people expected benefits from government and veered to the left in most of his policy proposals. He introduced a program to share federal revenue with the states, a Family Assistance Plan (FAP) to replace welfare programs with guaranteed minimum incomes for all families, and a federal medical insurance program. During his first term he signed legislation that expanded Social Security benefits, tied payment levels to the cost of living, and established the Supplemental Security Income Program for Americans who lacked the means to meet basic needs for food, shelter, and clothing. He signed laws that established the Environmental Protection Agency and the Occupational Health and Safety

Administration. In a blow to states' rights, he worked with Congress to expand the federal regulation of state governments on matters such as pollution control, civil rights, and health care. He enforced guidelines for integrating public schools and instituted the "Philadelphia Plan," the first specific affirmative-action plan for minority hiring by federal contractors. Although Attorney General John Mitchell proposed diluting the Voting Rights Act, Nixon signed a renewal in 1970 that strengthened the law. His IRS threatened the tax exemptions of segregated private academies in the South that enrolled several hundred thousand white students.

Yet Nixon's private musings disclose a man no less obsessed than Phyllis Schlafly with an establishment of big businessmen and financiers, journalists, Wall Street lawyers, and graduates of Ivy League colleges. He told his staff that they were engaged in a "deadly battle" with the establishment and needed to appoint only loyalists to federal positions. "No one in ivy league schools to be hired for a year—we need balance—trustworthy ones are the dumb ones." Jews were especially "untrustworthy . . . Look at the Justice Department. It's full of Jews." Few business leaders "stood up" for the administration "except Main Street biz." The Business Council was "not worth a damn." He wanted to focus on winning over "the non-elite biz men—they produce, they are with us." Nixon brooded over his enemies in the press—"75% of those guys hate my guts"—and complained about needing to "keep some incompetent blacks" in the administration. "I have the greatest affection for them, but I know they ain't gonna make it for 500 years." Like Theodore Roosevelt, he brooded over the "suicide" of the white race, saying, "When births decline, nations decline." In twenty years, America would be "40 percent Black, Mexican, etc. Those who have fewest [children] should have the most." Homosexuality loomed as another threat. "I don't mind the homosexuality, I understand it," Nixon said. "Nevertheless, goddamn, I don't think you glorify it on public television, homosexuality, even more than you glorify whores. . . . You know what happened to the Greeks! Homosexuality destroyed them . . . homosexuality, dope, and immorality are the enemies of strong societies."[5]

ENTER NEOCONS . . . EXIT LIBERTARIANS

In the late 1960s a loosely connected group of ex-liberal and radical intellectuals, most of them Jewish and based in New York City, had begun making contributions to conservative politics. By the mid-1970s they were known nationally as "neoconservatives." The group included such distinguished public intellectuals as historian Gertrude Himmelfarb; sociologists Nathan Glazer, Daniel Bell, Peter Berger, and Seymour Martin Lipset; political scientists Jeane Kirkpatrick, Richard Scammon, and James Q. Wilson; and political analysts Ben Wattenberg, and Norman Podhoretz and his spouse, Midge Decter. Their circle included Christian theologians Michael Novak and Richard John Neuhaus, as well as the polymorphic Daniel Patrick Moynihan. The movement's "Godfather," Irving Kristol, earned only a BA degree but held university professorships. He published no books but became one of America's most influential political thinkers. A neoconservative, Kristol famously quipped, was a liberal who had been "mugged by reality."[6]

Some conservatives looked askance at formerly left-wing Jewish intellectuals sifting into their ranks. But neocons offered the right fresh thinking and bright academic credentials. They blamed many ills of modern life on a "new class" of liberal intellectuals and bureaucrats who encouraged dependence on government and disparaged capitalism, traditional culture, religion, and patriotism. As square superachievers, the neocons despised self-indulgent hippies who turned the privilege of a college education into a four-year turn-on. "If there is any one thing that neoconservatives are unanimous about, it is their dislike of the 'counter-culture,'" Kristol said. The neocons could uniquely challenge liberals from inside the intelligentsia, with entrée to prestigious magazines and peer-reviewed journals. They also founded their own publications. *Public Interest,* started by Kristol and Daniel Bell in 1965, battled liberals on their own empirical turf. It published analyses showing the negative consequences of social engineering programs designed to empower the poor, end de facto segregation, or clean up the slums. Its contributors argued that the cultivation of virtue and character was essential to the success of any social policy. Later, the *National Interest,* founded by Kristol in 1985, assailed what it viewed as the naive foreign policy of the left and urged the sweeping use of American power to advance its interests and spread its ideology abroad. The neocons engaged the public through their signature journal of opinion, *Commentary* (edited by Podhoretz), and a profusion of popular books, magazine articles, opinion pieces, and media appearances.[7]

Neocons defended the morality and efficiency of capitalism. They extolled traditional American culture, assailed debased standards of higher education, and challenged affirmative action, which Kristol compared to slavery. With a few exceptions, neocons mirrored traditional conservatives in blaming decadence not on the capitalist economy but on the decay of religion, the celebration of the unrestrained self, and the decline of authority. They backed well-run, carefully targeted social programs "for the temporary relief of competent people," as management professor Peter Drucker wrote in a 1969 *Public Interest* article. But they opposed programs that undercut self-reliance and character, especially among "the Negro masses." Neocons promoted engaged nationalism, anticommunism, and support for Israel as a pro-American outpost of democracy in a hostile Middle East. For neocons, liberalism had flinched at communist evil, denigrated traditional American values and culture, and embraced flawed systems of social engineering.

A second generation of neoconservatives did not rival the founding generation's intellectual depth, its passion for empirical study, or its concern with domestic and cultural issues. Second-generation neocons plunged into Republican Party politics as unabashedly partisan opinion and policy makers, especially on national defense and foreign affairs. And they demonstrated little of the first generation's support for well-designed social programs. Many joined the administrations of Ronald Reagan and both presidents Bush. Prominent second-generation figures included William Kristol (Irving's son), John Podhoretz (Norman Podhoretz's and Midge Decter's son), Elliot Abrams (Norman and Midge's son-in-law), Michael Ledeen, Robert Kagan, Kenneth Adelman, Eliot Cohen, Richard Perle, Daniel Pipes, Paul Wolfowitz, Dov Zakheim, Douglas Feith, Charles Krauthammer, and I. Lewis "Scooter" Libby. Among neoconservatives, only Daniel Moynihan entered electoral politics. However, after winning election as Democratic senator from New York in 1976 Moynihan voted well to the left of center.

The neoconservatives were not monolithic in their ideas. But their thought closely paralleled the pioneering work of political philosopher Leo Strauss and national security analyst Albert Wohlstetter. Strauss, a Jewish-German émigré and a professor at the University of Chicago from 1949 to 1969, probed ancient texts for esoteric meanings and inspired a larger, more prestigious following in the United States than any other conservative scholar. So-called Straussians became the most notable body of conservatives outside of economics, business, and law to emerge as a force on college campuses. Strauss challenged the pluralism of the twentieth century that made all cultures and values equal and rejected the absolute principles of religion. He attributed social chaos and violence, deteriorating culture and community life, and the rise of dictators to an overweening secular liberalism that sealed off the sacred from the profane and neglected the moral principles that protect freedom from tyranny. "Oblivion of eternity," he wrote, "is the price which modern man had to pay, from the very beginning, for attempting to be absolutely sovereign, to become the master and owner of nature, to conquer chance."[8]

Modern secular thought, with everything provisional and relative, lacked standards in either natural rights or religion for untangling good from evil or elevating civilization above barbarism. Only recovery of the sacred could restore individual virtue, establish a just and culturally unified society, and turn the barbaric communists and fascists from the gates of civilization. Unlike true-believing Christians, however, Strauss made no commitment to the truth of dogma. He believed that the hidden secret of the premodern philosophers was that humanity possesses no regnant truth, no perfect virtue, only philosophers whose principles bound society together and leaders who carried out their ideas. This formulation explains how Jewish intellectuals could become high priests in a movement of Christian soldiers. Neoconservatives often talked about religion but almost never about theology or their own lived faith.[9]

In the 1950s and '60s, Albert Wohlstetter formulated ideas for using the weaponry and strategy of war not just to keep the peace but also to defeat communism and advance America's position in the world. He deprecated the idea that America should maintain the minimum military force needed to deter Soviet aggression. He argued instead that effective deterrence depended on a capacity for massive and certain retaliation after a Soviet first strike. Given that all deterrence was uncertain, however, the United States needed to be able to win a sustained nuclear war and protect its civilian population. Wohlstetter rejected massive retaliation as a sufficient response to communist aggression. He argued that the American military must be powerful and flexible enough to fight limited wars in peripheral areas by using antiguerrilla forces, conventional armies, and possibly tactical nuclear weapons. The use of "smart" weapons such as cruise missiles would allow America to prosecute such wars while minimizing collateral damage. A versatile, fully budgeted and unfettered military, antiballistic missiles, and civil defense programs would deter nuclear attack, limit the carnage if deterrence failed, and yield victory in a sustained nuclear war. These policies would put pressure on a weak Soviet economy to compete militarily. They would raise the costs of sponsoring "wars of liberation" in developing regions and enable the United States to apply military power for diplomatic ends. *"Large increases in Soviet defense budgets are very much more painful than increases in Western defense budgets,"* Wohlstetter wrote in 1959.[10]

As neocons entered politics, a small libertarian contingent established its own movement, with the distinctive core values of a voluntary "live and let live" society. Libertarians would radically deregulate economic and social life, dismantle most of government, and confine the military to border defense. Economists Murray Rothbard and Robert LeFevre crafted intellectual rationales for the libertarians. Former Goldwater speechwriter Karl Hess became their bearded, bead-wearing public face. A libertarian uprising at Young Americans for Freedom (YAF) in 1969 led its honorary chairman Ronald Reagan to worry that "under the guise of 'libertarianism' . . . there are those who would try to destroy YAF as an effective and powerful force among our young people." Although national chair David Keene purged the "very small group of pseudo-anarchists in YAF who are not in accord with our organization's beliefs," some libertarians still roiled local chapters.[11]

Libertarians called their movement the "new right"—a counterpart to the "new left"—which likewise opposed the draft, regulation of personal behavior, the military-industrial complex, and the war in Vietnam. David Nolan, formerly with Willis Stone's Liberty Amendment Committee, cooked up the idea for a Libertarian Party at a meeting in his Denver, Colorado, kitchen in December 1971. Nolan wondered "why people like us agreed with conservatives on a lot of things, but obviously had fundamental disagreements with conservatives on a lot of other issues. And there were areas where we could see that liberals made sense."[12]

William F. Buckley Jr. publicly denounced libertarianism as a "kind of anarchy." He said, "The ideological licentiousness that rages through America today makes anarchy attractive to the simple-minded." The newsletter of the fledgling Libertarian Party, in turn, charged that ballyhooed efforts by the *National Review* crowd to achieve a so-called "fusion" of libertarian ideas with traditional moral concerns produced only "a potpourri of anti-Communist interventionist bromides in the foreign policy area and pro-economic-freedom stands mixed with anti-civil-liberties stands on domestic issues. . . . Almost always conservatives wound up on the side of the big-budget, anti-free-speech forces in any debate." Libertarian organizer Ed Crane said that fusion was a rhetorical device that gave conservatives license "to harness the power of the state to serve their particular brand of intervention into voluntary human action." Columnist Donald Feder agreed that conservatives lacked "a consistent freedom philosophy. [They say] 'I believe in laissez-faire capitalism too. I also want to burn your dirty books, force my personal morality upon you, and send you off to strange and exotic climes to die for the Flag.'"[13]

Libertarianism became a much discussed ideology in the late twentieth century, but it never caught fire as a political movement. The libertarians barely dented the voter base for Republicans, failed to hold the balance of power between parties, and quarreled over ideological purity versus practical politics. The libertarians lured no key figures away from major parties, gained a peak of 1 percent for their presidential candidates, and elected only a handful of local officials. In 1973, the Libertarian Party developed its own congressional ratings. Senators averaged only 35 percent and House members 40 percent.[14]

SOWING DISCORD

The bloodshed that continued in Vietnam under Nixon prompted campus demonstrations and antiwar marches. In May 1970, for the only time in American history, respondents to a national survey cited campus unrest as the most important problem facing the country. Many Americans believed that the protesters, rioters, hippies, radical feminists, and black-power militants kept decent citizens from educating their children or benefiting from their hard-wrought labors. Americans for Constitutional Action damned "the terrorists on our campuses" for committing "acts of barbarisms equaled only by the Huns, Vandals, and Goths who wiped out civilization and learning in the last dying days of ancient Rome." As illustrated by the mail received by Republican congressmen John N. "Happy" Camp and Page Belcher of Oklahoma, ordinary citizens poured out their anguish in letters to Congress. One constituent wrote, "Close all colleges and universities for one year. Maybe that would cause the 'silent majority' of students to stand up and be counted." Another asked, "Is my life to be in vain, because of the ungodly, un-American action of the small numbers of unbelievers, cowards, hippies, yippies, and such ilk?" Some demanded stern remedies. "Put down the rioting even if we have to shoot to kill. . . . If it takes guns, bring on the guns." After the killing of student protesters in May 1970 by National Guard forces at Kent State in Ohio and police officials at Jackson State in Mississippi, another constituent wrote, "A few more killings of students will no doubt help the situation."[15]

The Nixon White House saw in this backlash a rare chance for the presidential party to win a midterm election. "We need to get our whole crew thinking in attack terms," wrote Nixon's chief of staff, H. R. (Bob) Haldeman. Part of their strategy was to contrive outrage and manipulate protest. "The President feels that we are doing too good a job of keeping the demonstrators out of the halls," wrote aide Dwight Chapin in an internal campaign memo. "The President's whole pitch is built around having a few demonstrators in the hall heckling him so that he can refer to them and their 'obscenities.' We have a new role now. Once the hall is three-quarters full, we can let in fifty to a hundred demonstrators. . . . This should give the President the opportunity to strike out at them should he desire to do so."[16]

Nixon tightly controlled the midterm elections. He directed fund-raising through the White House and campaigned only for select Republican candidates. Vice President Agnew led the GOP's attack strategy. He denounced the "radical-liberals" who represented "a whimpering isolationism in foreign policy, a mulish obstructionism in domestic policy and a pusillanimous pussyfooting on the critical issue of law and order." He pilloried demonstrators as "misfits" and "garbage" but reserved special scorn for the "liberally biased" media's "effete corps of impudent snobs." Nixon's strategists choreographed Agnew's performance to discredit and intimidate media and win over fed-up voters, North and South. "Our real game plan," wrote political adviser Lyn Nofziger, "[is] making our own point in our own time and in our own ways that the press is liberal, pro-Democratic and biased."[17]

With much media attention focused on Nixon's "Southern strategy" to capture Dixie, George Wallace's backers charged that Republicans were cynically trying "to 'out-Wallace' George C. Wallace [by] pursuing the hard-hitting get tough approach." Nixon and Agnew, they charged, were an "insult to the people of the South. [Their] mouths speak one way while their records tell a different story." Senator Edmund Muskie of Maine led a Democratic counterattack in 1970, accusing the GOP of pandering to fear and assuring voters of his party's commitment to law and order. The clash proved inconclusive; the GOP lost a modest nine House seats and gained two in the Senate. The Democrats, however, picked up eleven governorships and gained in state legislatures. To the delight of Wallace's backers the GOP fizzled in the South.[18]

Nixon hoped to win reelection in 1972 not just through a Southern strategy but by utilizing a national strategy to mobilize those voters who neoconservatives Richard Scammon and Benjamin Wattenberg identified in their book *The Real Majority* (1970) as "the middle-income, middle-aged, middle-educated, and white" center of the electorate. "Let the press squeal about a 'Southern Strategy,'" wrote White House aide John R. Brown. "In addition to adding Southern Protestants by the tens of thousands to the New Majority, we are making it a national one by adding as many Northern Catholics." Nixon assigned young conservative staffers to a Middle America Committee, headed by Harry Dent, a former aide to Senator Thurmond, and charged it with wooing white, middle-class voters who were "deeply troubled primarily over the erosion of what they consider to be their values." This "silent majority" of Americans believed that "as individuals they have lost control of a complicated and impersonal society which oppresses them with high taxes, spiraling inflation and enforced integration while rewarding the very poor and very rich." The administration would woo the silent majority with the "'old values' of patriotism, hard work, morality and respect for law and order."[19]

Conservative rhetoric was not enough for the young Turks on Dent's committee who yearned to change policy. "The futility of our effort and the rigidity of our mandate should be apparent," wrote Tom Charles Huston, former head of the YAF. "Politics is policy and policy is politics," but administration policies were "a blue-print for an expanded welfare state." Yet Nixon and his senior strategists saw their future not as hard right but "center/right" to "center/left." Nixon's domestic policy adviser John D. Ehrlichman said, "*The Social Issue strategy is a centrist strategy,* not a liberal or conservative strategy." The administration's "non-conservative initiatives [were] deliberately designed to furnish some zigs to go with our conservative zags. . . . As we can, consistent with the Social Issue concept, we will try to co-opt the opposition's issues."[20]

In domestic policy, presentation mattered most. On his Family Assistance Plan to reform welfare, Nixon's advisers warned, "A public abandonment of the posture on FAP could be very devastating on credibility issue. . . . If we have to push FAP hard to get it and do so, we will not only lose right wing support but perhaps lose the grass roots and Republican small *c* conservatives." To counterbalance the FAP, Nixon vetoed comprehensive child care legislation "as an opportunity to pay homage to the right," according to his conservative adviser Charles W. "Chuck" Colson. On civil rights, Nixon emulated William Howard Taft, who busted more trusts than Theodore Roosevelt but bragged less. He said, "Where helpful, we should assert that more desegregation has resulted during our administration than during our predecessor's, but without flaming rhetoric." Having lost and then won two of the closest presidential elections in U.S. history, Nixon hoarded every vote for 1972. We "can't exclude *anyone*," he said. He denied that "all is lost" regarding the union vote, especially among Teamsters and "hard hat" construction workers who backed the war and middle American values. The Teamsters endorsed Nixon in 1971 after he pardoned their imprisoned leader Jimmy Hoffa. The administration would "pay attention" to blacks, "keep some around [to] avoid Goldwater problem." As for Jews, they "won't get many, but don't write them off." Nixon said they should quietly woo Jewish and black support by meeting with leaders, but should "avoid speaking publicly to groups."[21]

Such calculation was too much for Pat Buchanan. "Neither liberal nor conservative, neither fish nor fowl, the Nixon Administration . . . is a hybrid whose zigging and zagging has succeeding in winning the enthusiasm and loyalty of neither the left nor the right, but the suspicion and distrust of both," he wrote in 1971. "The President is no longer a credible custodian of the conservative political tradition of the GOP." The president and his strategists sought no such responsibility; they anticipated racing to victory in 1972 without the drag of conservative principle. "The right wing would rather lose than give up one iota as far as principle is concerned," Nixon told Buchanan. Only left wingers were "always willing to compromise their principles in order to get power because they know without power they cannot put their principles to work." Ironically, the right had given up many of its principles to back Nixon in 1968.[22]

RECONSTRUCTING THE PRESIDENCY

No political strategy could reelect a president ground between the mill-stones of a hopeless war and a stagnant economy. In the most remarkable turnaround in U.S. history, Nixon ensured his reelection by igniting an economic boom, defusing the controversy over Vietnam, and remaking the Cold War. The politician who forgot nothing would not repeat the mistake of 1960, when Eisenhower chose principle over the expediency of rousing the election-year economy. Nixon knew that principle was no defense for a president who failed to deliver the prosperous full-employment economy that people expected of government, reasonably or not.

In 1971 Nixon shattered and rebuilt his presidency. Announcing that "I am now a Keynesian," the president and his new treasury secretary and protégé, former Democratic governor of Texas John Connally, checkmated critics with a "new economic policy" that packaged deficit spending and tax cuts to create jobs and spur growth with wage and price controls to curb inflation. To reduce the trade deficit and relieve foreign pressure on the dwindling gold reserve, the president imposed a 10 percent surcharge on imports and ended the era of Bretton Woods by suspending the convertibility of the dollar into gold. Henceforth, market forces set the value of currencies, which led to an explosion of international financial transactions that the administration encouraged by cutting taxes on U.S. purchases of foreign securities and raising foreign lending and investment ceilings. With no outflow of gold, America could tolerate large budget and balance of payments deficits paid for by foreigners with their surplus dollars. From 1974 to 2000, the value of foreign-owned United States securities rose from $67 billion to $3.6 trillion.[23]

The administration worked with Congress to cut business taxes and raise Social Security levies. This policy mix continued to shift the tax burden from corporations to workers. From 1972 to 1981 payroll taxes rose from 25 percent to 31 percent of federal revenues, while corporate income taxes fell from 16 percent to 10 percent. The president also instructed officials to spend every dollar they could scrape together. "Whatever it costs, Cap, to get the jobs Cap, get them," Nixon told his deputy budget director Caspar Weinberger. "I don't care about the budget. I don't care about inflation or anything else. Get the jobs." AFL-CIO president George Meany put aside his agreement with Nixon on Vietnam to blast the president for "trickle down" economics, "based on the idea that if you make the fat cats a little fatter, somewhere along the line the poor simpletons are going to profit." Conservatives charged Nixon with heresy for his economic controls and warned that "sooner or later" pent-up inflation would wreck the economy. Nixon cared only that sooner came later than Election Day. And he got his jobs—three million in 1972—as real growth climbed by 5.3 percent.[24]

In Vietnam, Nixon slashed American ground forces. He ended the draft to still domestic unrest. The withdrawal reflected Nixon's policy of "Vietnamization," which assigned increasing responsibility for the war to the South Vietnamese, and fit within a broader Nixon doctrine that placed the burden for resisting aggression on local forces, with U.S. assistance. American casualties fell to fewer than seven hundred in the election year. Simultaneously, Nixon escalated American air strikes and mined Haiphong Harbor in North Vietnam to avoid withdrawal legislation and ensure a "decent interval" before the likely collapse of the South. "I look at the tide of history out there, South Vietnam probably can never even survive anyway," Nixon confided to his national security adviser Henry Kissinger. In the midst of negotiations with North Vietnam, Kissinger prematurely but dramatically announced two weeks before the election, "Peace is at hand."[25]

Nixon dreamt of making history by reordering international structures of power to ease communist pressure on the United States and defuse the tensions of a troubled world. Nixon disappointed conservatives by refusing to isolate and pressure communist powers. Instead, Nixon and Kissinger mapped out a pragmatic strategy to achieve relaxed tensions, or détente, with the Soviet Union and simultaneously to engage with Red China and play off this rising power against the Russians. Nixon's new China policy led to the seating of Communist China in the UN, the expulsion of the Nationalist Chinese (which the administration opposed but knew was inevitable), and eventually to American recognition of the communist government.

The China "opening" increased pressure on the Soviets for agreements with the United States. After becoming the first American president to visit Russia since World War II, Nixon returned with agreements to ensure that neither superpower would upset the balance of terror that kept the peace. The ABM treaty restricted the deployment of antiballistic missile systems and the SALT treaty limited strategic weaponry. The new spirit of détente also yielded a commercial pact and America's recognition of the boundaries of Russia's satellite states in return for mutual pledges to respect human rights that were formalized in the Helsinki Accords of 1975. Nearly three decades after the onset of the Cold War, the United States had formally abandoned its goal of rolling back communism in eastern Europe. However, the declaration on human rights inspired dissidents behind the Iron Curtain and gave the West ammunition for pressuring the Soviets. Nixon's foreign policies scored with a public that trusted its famously anticommunist president not to appease the reds. An August 1972 survey found that, by six to one, Americans believed Nixon would more effectively deal with China and Russia than his Democratic opponent, South Dakota senator George McGovern.

For movement conservatives, Nixon compounded misguided economic and foreign policies by supporting the Equal Rights Amendment; affirmative action; the Endangered Species Act; environmental, consumer, and worker protection laws; and a strengthened Voting Rights Act. He ran up more debt than LBJ and prepared the first federal budget since World War II in which social spending exceeded military spending. "An increasing number of conservatives are beginning to think . . . that a Nixon defeat in 1972 might not be so catastrophic after all," *Human Events* reported. "It will take more than gestures, more than sops, more than words and phrases to gain back the conservative support he has lost," wrote the now chastened columnist James Kilpatrick.[26]

In a thirty-one-page memo that he circulated among conservative insiders, journalist M. Stanton Evans indicted Nixon for making "impressive strides toward the political liquidation of American conservatism," even though the 1968 election had administered "a stinging repudiation of the liberal way of doing things in Washington." With his program of wage and price controls and other liberal initiatives, the turncoat president had acted "not merely to continue but to expand upon the social and economic policies of his Democratic predecessors." Instead of cutting off federal dollars to the left ("defunding the left"), he salvaged "such Kennedy-Johnson programs as OEO, Model Cities, radical legal agitation, and other policies which are fronts for leftward politics." In defiance of "Nixon's statements across the years and many specific pledges made in 1968, he acted—in Southeast Asia, China, and Russia—as though Communist intransigence could be overcome through concessions—the working axiom of Democratic predecessors. . . . The Nixon regime itself bears heavy responsibility for the continued deterioration of American military strength."

A Humphrey administration, Evans wrote, "likely would not have been much worse and in some respects might have been a great deal better. For Nixon is able to move left on crucial issues with much less public opposition than would have confronted Humphrey." With both parties "suddenly wedded to liberal assumptions . . . the liberals win the point of principle by default, and the only area of controversy remaining is a haggle over details."[27]

Conservatives representing *Human Events,* the Southern States Industrial Council, *National Review,* and Buckley spin-offs like the YAF and ACU—dubbed the "Manhattan Twelve" after their meeting place— formally suspended their support for the president in July 1971. Yet as one critic quipped, "You fellows seem to be always late—about two to four years!" The Twelve's political consultant, Jerry Harkins Jr., agreed that "organizationally, conservatism as a political force both within and without the Republican Party has diminished substantially since 1968." Still, they recruited the Republican representative John Ashbrook of Ohio to compete in the 1972 presidential primaries so that liberals could not define Nixon as marking the outer boundary of a respectable right.[28]

Unrest on the right never panicked a president who "makes the point that we don't need to worry too much about the right-wing nuts," Haldeman wrote, in reference to Buckley and Reagan. Nixon tried to mollify Buckley with a symbolic appointment to the Advisory Commission on Information of the United States Information Agency and won Reagan's assurance that he would lead a pro-Nixon California delegation to the Republican Convention. "We've just got to keep Reagan from jumping off the reservation," Nixon told Haldeman.[29]

As Democrats once said of Grover Cleveland, conservatives could love Nixon for the enemies he made—liberals scorned his conservative zags as catastrophe and his liberal zigs as "Tricky Dick" deception. For liberals, Nixon was both a ruthless partisan warrior and a visceral conservative who backed liberal initiatives only to confound the left and appease voters. Scholars have continued to debate whether the substance of policy under Nixon constitutes a liberal legacy independent of his conservative rhetoric; divisive politics; prejudices against women, gays, Jews, and racial minorities; and his overweening personal ambition. In 1972, however, Nixon managed to simultaneously back liberal programs and maintain his conservative image. Congressman Ashbrook's primary campaign melted in the first thaw of spring and, in an April Gallup Poll, 51 percent of respondents described Nixon as conservative, 25 percent as moderate, and 15 percent as liberal.[30]

A BLOWOUT ELECTION

As the presidential election approached, Nixon speculated about joining with conservative Democrat John Connally to form a new majority party, not anchored on the right but cutting an arc from "Rockefeller to Reagan." Mostly, however, Nixon fretted about his reelection and his legacy. The Committee to Re-elect the President (CREEP) neither backed independent political groups favorable to Republicans nor worked with congressional leaders to elect Republicans.[31]

CREEP worked to manage public opinion. It guided federal grants and loans to influence "key states and major voting bloc groups." In order to keep "the President and White House dissociated with the program in the event of a leak . . . all information about the program would be transmitted verbally." The vice president continued to pummel the media and the administration planted articles and "citizen" letters in newspapers. The administration secretly cajoled and pressured America's leading pollsters, Gallup and Harris, for advance tips on their findings and influence over topics, questions, and spin control. CREEP worked with the gifted young organizer Karl Rove, executive director of the College Republicans, to win the votes of eighteen- to twenty-year-olds, newly enfranchised by the Twenty-sixth Amendment. Rove rigged mock presidential elections held on campuses "to obtain favorable publicity for our candidate" and achieve "the demoralization of the opposition [who] thought they had the youth vote." After each campus victory, a college Republican was supposed to call the press "posing as an impartial citizen." To tie the opposition to social unrest, Nixon told Ehrlichman during the 1971 May Day demonstrations in the capital to "be sure police are hurt tomorrow; they tagged me with Birch Society so be sure McGovern et al. can't avoid these demonstrators."[32]

The Nixon campaign collected a record $61 million, far more than the amount raised by its Democratic opposition. It accepted illegal corporate and cash donations and in some cases arranged government favors in return. It put more pressure on the IRS than previous presidents to inves-

These alleged subversives were deported from the United States during the Red Scare of 1919–1920. The Red Scare launched the fifty-year career of J. Edgar Hoover as America's leading anticommunist and established anticommunism as a key issue for conservatives. *Genealogy Images of History*

Republican President Warren Harding (right), whose landslide victory in 1920 began the conservative era of the 1920s, on a camping trip with Thomas A. Edison (center) and Henry Ford (left). *Genealogy Images of History*

These three men were the leading lights of conservative government during the 1920s: (from left to right) President Calvin Coolidge, Secretary of the Treasury Andrew Mellon, and Secretary of Commerce (and future president) Herbert Hoover. *Library of Congress*

The back-room power broker Charles Hilles (bottom left), who kept the flame of conservatism alive in the Republican Party during the New Deal years, is shown with other members of the Republican National Committee in the 1920s. *Genealogy Images of History*

Left: Hiram Wesley Evans, the Grand Wizard of the Ku Klux Klan, leads a march through Washington, D.C., in 1925. The Klan grew to several million members in the early 1920s, but Evans failed to halt its decline later in the decade. *Library of Congress*

Right: Paul Rader, a pioneer of radio evangelizing, promises to join with businessmen to uplift Chicago by saving souls. Business leaders became key financiers of the Christian Right in the 1930s. *Billy Graham Archives*

Conservatives assailed President Roosevelt's "court-packing" as a thinly disguised effort to destroy the independence of the Supreme Court. Although Roosevelt failed to win passage of his court-packing proposal, he eventually put his stamp on the Court with nine appointments. *Franklin Roosevelt Presidential Library*

Conservatives struck a law-and-order theme in the 1930s, charging that radical agitators and labor leaders promoted riots and violent strikes. *Rightwing Collection of the University of Iowa Libraries*

GET THE LEADERS. YOU'LL FIND THEM WAY BACK IN THE REAR!

Many conservatives backed Elizabeth Dilling's claim that the administration of Franklin Roosevelt was riddled with subversives.

Movie censor Will Hays (second from right), a former chairman of the Republican National Committee, confers with star Carole Lombard. Control over movie content was an important priority for conservatives in the early twentieth century. *Indiana Historical Society*

From left to right, isolationist Democratic Senator Burton K. Wheeler of Montana, Charles Lindbergh, Kathleen Norris (president of the National Legion of Mothers of America League), and socialist leader Norman Thomas attend an America First rally. As America First's most prominent spokesperson, Lindbergh would taint the anti-interventionist movement with anti-Semitism when he charged that Jews were pushing America into war. *Library of Congress*

Elizabeth Dilling was arrested while protesting President Roosevelt's interventionist policies prior to Pearl Harbor. Dilling, Kathleen Norris, and other conservative women rallied millions of women to oppose Roosevelt's foreign policies, but male conservative leaders largely ignored their robust move-ment. *Library of Congress*

The conservative power couple of the 1940s: Republican Congresswoman Clare Booth Luce and husband Henry Luce, the publisher of *Time* and *Life*. Henry Luce was a leader of the so-called "eastern establishment" of Republican bankers, industrialists, and media moguls. *Library of Congress*

The married Republican Senator Arthur Vandenberg of Michigan wrote this romantic letter to Clare Booth Luce during their unsuccessful campaign to nominate Douglas MacArthur in 1944. *Library of Congress*

The charismatic Billy Graham first made a name for himself as an evangelist for Youth for Christ in the 1940s, one of the many postwar organizations of evangelical Protestants. In the 1950s Graham joined with conservative financier J. Howard Pew to launch the influential conservative, evangelical magazine, *Christianity Today. Billy Graham Archives*

Anticommunist Senators William Jenner (R-Indiana, at left) and Pat McCarran (D-Nevada) traveled together to Canada to question Soviet defector Igor Gouzenko. The testimony of former communists revealed the activities of Soviet spies in America during World War II and helped convince the Kremlin to close down its spy rings in the United States. Domestic subversion, however, remained a key issue for conservatives in the 1940s and '50s. *Library of Congress*

In 1948 Democratic Governor J. Strom Thurmond of South Carolina (with paper in hand) and other southern governors presented their grievances against President Harry S. Truman's civil rights program to Senator J. Howard McGrath, chairman of the Democratic National Committee. Later that year Thurmond ran as the States' Rights candidate for president. *Library of Congress*

Many veterans attended this 1949 convention of the American Legion, a bastion of anticommunism since its founding after World War I. *Wisconsin Historical Society*

Left: Conservatives charged that President Truman let Asia become consumed by communism by firing General Douglas MacArthur during the Korean War. *Library of Congress*

Right: Conservative Republican Senator Robert Taft of Ohio, shown here campaigning, was never able to shake the charge that in presidential elections, "Taft can't win." *Wisconsin Historical Society*

Dwight D. Eisenhower won the Republican presidential nomination in 1952 when the convention seated his Texas delegates rather than a competing delegation pledged to Taft. This so-called "Texas steal" rankled conservatives for decades and prompted Taft to charge that "businessmen subject to New York influence" had stolen the nomination from him. *Library of Congress*

Chief Justice Earl Warren administered the oath of office to Eisenhower in 1956. On the left is Republican Senate leader William Knowland of California, a conservative critic of Eisenhower's foreign policy who led the transformation of conservatives from disengaged to engaged nationalists, dedicated to fighting the Cold War to victory. *Library of Congress*

Republican Senator Joseph McCarthy of Wisconsin, America's most prominent and controversial anticommunist crusader, makes a point at the Army-McCarthy hearings that led to his political demise. *Wisconsin Historical Society*

Conservative activists, financiers, and oil tycoons H. L. Hunt (left) and J. Howard Pew (center) conferred with Walter Hallanan, the chairman of the National Petroleum Council, at the 1954 convention of their trade association, the American Petroleum Institute. Hunt founded Facts Forum and LIFE LINES and Pew backed the Republican Party and many conservative leaders, publications, and organizations. *Corbis*

This anticommunist palm card from the 1950s equates communism with one-world government, a persistent theme of conservatives since World War I. *Wisconsin Historical Society*

Strike a Blow for Human Liberty!

Help stamp out the baboon slave State of one Communist Worldism

FOR GOD AND COUNTRY

FIGHT

CommUNISM

SAVE OUR CONSTITUTION

Join in the fight to rid our American Republic of these enemies of civilization and human dignity.

The work of intellectual Russell Kirk influenced three generations of conservatives. He presented a grand historical synthesis of conservatives' ideas. *Intercollegiate Studies Institute*

Support for conservative presidential candidate Barry Goldwater in 1964 was not considered respectable within mainstream Republican circles. Despite bitter opposition from Governor Nelson Rockefeller of New York and moderate "Rockefeller Republicans," Goldwater won the nomination in 1964 at a convention dominated by conservative delegates. *Ed Valtman, University of Southern Mississippi, cartoon collection*

William F. Buckley Jr. won 13 percent of the vote in his independent campaign for mayor of New York City in 1965. He showed that conservatives could use social issues to win support from ethnic voters such as the Italians and the Irish. *Library of Congress*

Moderates regained the initiative within the Republican Party after Goldwater's landslide defeat. In 1967, moderate Gladys O'Donnell (left) defeated conservative Phyllis Schlafly (right) for the presidency of the National Federation of Republican Women. Schlafly recovered to become a preeminent leader of conservative women in the 1970s and '80s. *Library of Congress*

A new and effective Anti-communist Weapon

The communists have been using FOLK-SINGING FOR YEARS

Now the tables have been turned; a clear message, a rich voice, wonderful music.

Ideal for young people.

A RECORDING OF THESE SONGS NOW AVAILABLE

JANET GREENE *SINGS*

Fascist Threat
and
Commie Lies

45 RPM

THE FASCIST THREAT

I've heard it said and it makes me fret,
America has a fascist threat.
Which organization can it be?
This is what perplexes me.

BE CAREFUL OF THE COMMIE LIES

When I was young, it seemed to me
The whole wide world would soon be free,
But communism is on the rise,
And Satan has a new disguise.

Conservatives found it difficult in the 1960s to compete for influence within the popular culture. This was demonstrated by the failed effort to market Janet Greene as the anticommunist folk singer. *Rightwing Collection of the University of Iowa Libraries*

Richard Nixon is shown at the 1969 National Prayer Breakfast with behind-the-scenes operative Abraham Vereide, founder of the influential prayer breakfast movement. Vereide's successor, Douglas Coe, shown with Billy Graham (left) and Republican Senator Frank Carlson of Kansas (right) in the 1970s, turned Vereide's organization into the secretive group known as "The Family," which has come closer than any other movement to establishing Christianity as a semi-official American religion. *Billy Graham Archives*

Since the 1930s conservatives had argued that communists and fellow-traveling liberals were subverting America's schools. This theme is illustrated by a LIFE LINES cartoon from 1959 and by publications for sale at the bookstore of the John Birch Society in 1970. *Rightwing Collection of the University of Iowa Libraries*

Cartoons from the Liberty Lobby's "Liberty Letter" in the 1970s suggest that two-faced liberals opposed the Vietnam War but favored aid to Israel and that international bankers manipulated the foreign policies of the United States. *Rightwing Collection of the University of Iowa Libraries*

Reverend Sun Myung Moon, head of a self-made Unification Church, met with Nixon in 1974 after he said that God told him to forgive the president for Watergate. From the 1970s through the end of the Cold War, Moon's church spent far more in the United States on anticommunist and conservative causes than any other organization. *National Archives and Records Service*

Ronald Reagan fell just short of winning the delegates needed to defeat President Gerald Ford for the Republican presidential nomination in 1976. In an unsuccessful effort to win over moderate delegates, Reagan surprisingly announced that liberal Republican Senator Richard Schweiker would be his presumptive ticket mate. It would not be the last time that Reagan confounded conservatives. *Karl Hubenthal, Ed Valtman, University of Southern Mississippi cartoon collection*

Ronald Reagan and his chief advisors rejected advice from conservatives that they run an ideological campaign in 1984 and build a foundation for governing from the right in the second term. Instead, Reagan and Vice President George H. W. Bush ran on the record of the first term. *Library of Congress*

```
11/24/86   (HILL)  1640
           S-CH (R/O of NSPG) was the damndest meeting. Pdx
                  started saying objectives are          P
                  - new kind of Iran                     VP
                  - end war                              S
                  - discourage terrorism                 Cap
                  - see hostage out                      Pdx
                                                         Casey
                                                         DR
                                                         Cave
                                                         Meese

           Then Casey gave assessment of CIA assets. [The
           rest of this may be classified and is in any event
           immaterial.]

           Meese said nothing. Pdx  Is all about our policy
           toward Iran, how we right and will keep going.  I
           stopped him and gave him a diff. view.  Made no
           impact whatever.  P untouched.  What we sold had
           no impact.  P defiant.  "Understand me and get off
           my back kind of view."

           So, Pdx said now time for discussion.  (1) Send
           emissary around to explain our goals.  (2) how to
           work the channel that still in operation.

           P very hot under the collar and determined he is
           totally right.
```

Secretary of State George Schultz kept careful notes of a top-level administration meeting on November 24, 1986, dealing with press reports that the United States had sold arms to the terrorist state of Iran to gain the release of American hostages held by Islamic militants. The notes show that President Reagan firmly supported the policy and was angry only about the press leaks. *Library of Congress*

President Reagan and Chief of Staff Donald Regan at a summit meeting with Soviet leader Mikhail Gorbachev in Geneva, Switzerland, in 1985. Negotiations between Reagan and Gorbachev prefigured the end of the Cold War, nearly resulted in drastic reductions in nuclear arsenals, and produced a treaty that eliminated intermediate-range nuclear missiles in Europe. Conservatives opposed the treaty, but Reagan sold it to the public and the Senate. *Library of Congress*

November 1, 1993

Memorandum for: Republicans
From: Dick Armey
Re: "The Moral Equivalent of War": How Republicans Can Win the Health
                  Debate and Enact True Health Reform

      With the ceremonial unveiling of President Clinton's 1,342-page "Health Security Act," America enters the most important domestic policy debate of the past half-century -- a debate that is, in effect, the Battle of the Bulge of big-government liberalism.

      Even as the whole world rejects statism, American Democrats are launching a final desperate gambit to win the permanent loyalty of the great middle class through dependency on a massive new government entitlement. On the outcome of this gambit hangs the future, not only of the Republican party, but of every American citizen.

President Bill Clinton became embroiled during his first two years in conflicts over gays in the military and his plan to provide health care to all Americans. In his November 1993 memo, "The Moral Equivalent of War," Republican Representative Dick Armey of Texas proposed how to defeat the president's health care program, advance conservative ideas, and establish Republicans as America's majority party. *Carl Albert Center*

SOURCES OF HARD CURRENCY FOR DEMOCRAT PARTY	HOW TO CUT THE FLOW OF CASH
UNIONS (AFL-CIO's $6 billion in dues, 10% for politics =$600 million	Free trade; Enforce *Beck* decision; repeal *Davis Bacon Act*, repeal *Jones Act*
TRIAL LAWYERS $24.2 million ($103.4 million '89-95) $700,000 to Clinton/Gore and $2 million to DNC by spring '96)	Tort reform, Product liability
LAW/LOBBYING FIRMS $1.89 million (1997-98)	Hire more Republicans; Republican leadership refuses to meet with Dems
TRADE ASSOCIATIONS $6.54 million (1997-98)	Hire more Republicans; Republican leadership refuses to meet with Dems; make Fortune 500 firms aware of whom they are hiring to represent them in Washington
NEA (2.5 million members) $2.9 million	School choice

After the midterm elections of 1998, Republicans sought to cut off sources of funding and support for the Democratic Party. As illustrated by this excerpt from a 1999 strategy memo, the initiative included measures to weaken the AFL-CIO, trial lawyers, and the National Education Association. It also included an expansion of the "K Street Project" that Texas Representative Tom DeLay and activist Grover Norquist had launched to reward lobbying firms for hiring Republicans and punishing the firms that hired Democrats. *Carl Albert Center*

Pat Robertson (right), president of the Christian Coalition, and Executive Director Ralph Reed (left) took the lead in reviving the Christian Right after the demise of Jerry Falwell's flagship Moral Majority in 1989. *Corbis*

Governor George W. Bush of Texas worked closely with adviser Karl Rove, who later guided Bush to victory in the presidential elections of 2000 and 2004 and served as the president's chief political strategist. Rove's strategy primarily involved rallying the conservative base rather than attempting to build coalitions with other voter groups. *Corbis*

tigate the president's "enemies." Roughly based on a plan developed by Tom Huston of the Middle America Committee, CREEP subjected opponents to espionage, harassment, surveillance, and "dirty tricks," such as forging letters on an opponent's letterhead, planting false stories in the media, and spreading rumors about candidates' personal lives. The IRS probed such mainstream left-to-center groups as Americans for Democratic Action, the Urban League, and the National Council of Churches. After defense department analyst Daniel Ellsberg released to the *New York Times* the so-called Pentagon Papers, the CIA's critical analysis of the war in Vietnam, Nixon set up a covert "plumbers" unit to plug leaks. He ordered the wiretapping of newspaper reporters and federal employees. Campaign operatives bugged the Democratic National Headquarters in the Watergate building in Washington, D.C. On June 17, 1972, police arrested five men employed by the campaign after they broke into the Watergate headquarters to replace a defective listening device. Federal authorities later arrested two former White House aides—G. Gordon Liddy and E. Howard Hunt—for complicity in the break-in.

The Democratic presidential field ranged ideologically between George Wallace on the right and George McGovern on the left. Each George hoped to woo voters who were alienated from a corrupt establishment. McGovern espoused the "new politics" that challenged America's alleged militarism, materialism, and racism. He rebuked the "establishment center," which insisted on "seeing the planet as engaged in a gigantic struggle to death between the free world and the Communist world." The establishment led America "into the stupidest and cruelest war in all history" and created a "military monster [that] inflates our economy, picks our pockets and starves other areas of our national life." His rival George Wallace complained that McGovern is "stealing my thunder," posing as "an anti-establishment candidate."[33]

Under rules drafted by the Democratic Party Commission on Delegate Selection chaired by Senator McGovern, the 1972 Democratic nomination campaign was the first that required candidates to compete for delegates in primaries and caucuses nationwide. McGovern picked up delegates in states where other candidates had failed to prepare for an open contest. After coming surprisingly close to defeating the heavily favored Senator Muskie in the New Hampshire primary, McGovern used his antiwar policies to build a grassroots movement and win the nomination after staving off a late challenge from Hubert Humphrey. Wallace won several southern primaries before a would-be assassin's bullet left him paralyzed from the waist down and effectively ended his campaign. Nixon's surrogates took a page from the Johnson campaign and branded McGovern as a radical candidate of "Amnesty, Acid, and Abortion."

With the economy pumping out jobs, the war winding down, and McGovern lacking the evidence to connect Watergate to the president, Nixon won nearly 61 percent of the popular vote and forty-nine states. A far-right candidate, John Schmitz, won 1.4 percent. A hastily assembled libertarian campaign netted only a few thousand votes for philosophy professor John Hospers. But a Republican elector in Virginia voted for Hospers because Nixon had "moved the government toward ever greater control over the lives of us all." The GOP regained momentum in the South, picking up three Senate seats, seven House seats, and one governor's mansion. However, the political realignment anticipated after 1968 remained stalled. Democrats kept control of Congress; Republicans lost two seats in the Senate nationwide and gained only twelve in the House.[34]

After the election Democrats who felt alienated from McGovern's new politics formed the Coalition for a Democratic Majority (CDM). Founders included Humphrey, Senator Henry Jackson of Washington, and leaders of the AFL-CIO. Guided by neoconservatives, the CDM sought to move the Democratic Party to the center and regain control of the Cold War and traditional Americanism from the disengaged and countercultural McGovernites. In the words of Norman Podhoretz and Midge Decter, the CDM sought to restore the party's "great tradition" by refuting the canards that "American society is sick and guilty, morally bankrupt and inherently corrupt" and that the elite "knows what is best for others." The party had to oppose quotas established in accordance with "birth and group origin" and reverse its "cavalier attitude toward the tens of millions of Americans who are genuinely and correctly concerned about public safety and respect for law." Democrats needed to reject "the idea that the United States must withdraw from its international responsibilities and affect a serious diminution of its own power." Neoconservative intellectual Ben Wattenberg chaired the CDM and Penn Kemble, a political organizer for the AFL-CIO, ran day-to-day operations. Neoconservative stars Decter, Jeane Kirkpatrick, and Seymour Martin Lipset served as cochairs.[35]

IMPOTENT POWER

In his second term, a president barred from seeking reelection planned to wield the power of his office to punish his enemies, build his establishment, and centrally control the Republican Party. He planned to bring the federal budget and bureaucracy under heel by refusing to spend funds appropriated by Congress, reorganizing government to expand presidential power, and appointing aggressive young conservative Howard Phillips to dismantle the Office of Economic Opportunity set up by Lyndon Johnson to administer antipoverty programs. Morton Blackwell, an official of the Young Republicans, compiled the résumés of a thousand youthful conservatives who he hoped to place in government jobs. But revelations that top administration officials had directed the Watergate break-in and pressured defendants into silence engulfed the second term in scandal. By the summer of 1973 White House counsel John Dean and top staffers Ehrlichman and Haldeman had resigned and the attorney general had appointed Harvard Law professor Archibald Cox as a special prosecutor on Watergate-related crimes. A special Senate Committee began uncovering the crimes and transgressions that Nixon had hoped to keep hidden by covering up the Watergate break-in. By early 1974 even some fellow Republicans were fed up with Nixon. Edward Brooke, a moderate Republican senator from Massachusetts, complained, "Too many Republicans have defined that dread word 'Watergate' too narrowly. It is not just the stupid, unprofitable, break-in attempt. . . . It is perjury. Obstruction of justice. The solicitation and acceptance of hundred of thousands of dollars in illegal campaign contributions. It is a pattern of arrogance, illegality and lies which ought to shock the conscience of every Republican."[36]

In the midst of the Watergate investigations, Spiro Agnew became the first vice president since John C. Calhoun in 1832 to resign the office. The isolated Agnew had no part in the high crimes of Watergate, but as governor of Maryland he had committed the low crimes of pocketing bribes and kickbacks from contractors doing business with the government. The president let an expendable and obviously guilty vice president avoid jail time by pleading no contest to a single count of income-tax evasion. Agnew resigned on October 10, 1973, and disappeared from public life. Under the Twenty-fifth Amendment, ratified in 1967, President Nixon, with the approval of both houses of Congress, appointed Agnew's successor. The president passed over his first choice, the former treasury secretary John Connally, who had converted from Democrat to Republican in 1973, and chose a little-known but confirmable candidate who presumably would stand aside for Connally in 1976. In December 1973, House Minority Leader Gerald Ford of Michigan became America's first appointed vice president.

The Watergate scandal splintered conservatives. Some refused to give ground to liberals by abandoning Nixon. Into the summer of 1974 Senator Goldwater remained loyal and said Nixon "had done nothing wrong." Some suspended judgment, agreeing with *National Review*'s William Rusher that "the proof should precede the penalty." Others, like Mike Djordjevich, former chair of the Young Republicans of California, blamed the mess on "wishy washy" conservative leaders who contrived to "have the press and others make Nixon a conservative and indirectly degrade the entire conservative cause by association." Howard Phillips, who left the administration when Nixon failed to slash liberal programs, agreed that conservatives who had "long provided Richard Nixon with his most dependable support . . . should now play the decisive part in requiring his departure from public life." He insisted that "liberals, far more than conservatives, benefit from Richard Nixon's continuation in office." Conservatives "badly misplaced" their faith in a politician whose "*betrayal* of conservative values, rather than the image of his *adherence* to them, deservedly contributed to his tragic downfall." Under Nixon, "our ideological opportunity has been squandered, our loyalties have been unreciprocated, and our party's reputation for integrity has been virtually destroyed."[37]

The Korean-born Reverend Sun Myung Moon, head of the self-made Unification Church, knew with prophetic certainty that America should forgive President Nixon, because God had told him so. Moon believed that God had anointed him to complete the failed missions of Adam and Jesus to achieve perfect marriages, procreate pure children, and found a sinless paradise on earth. Adam failed because of Eve's relations with Satan. Jesus failed because the crucifixion prematurely disrupted his mission to marry and procreate. The church demanded the complete devotion of its followers—self-designated as "Moonies"—including control over their labor, worldly goods, and marriage. Moon presided over the mass marriages of hundreds, even thousands, of couples. During the Watergate investigation, Moonies prayed, fasted, and marched in front of the White House as part of a campaign to "Forgive, Love, and Unite" behind a cleansed president rededicated to fighting communism and moral decline. In February 1974 Nixon summoned Moon to the White House, where the messiah told him, "Don't knuckle under to pressure. Stand up for your convictions." Moon's pro-Nixon campaign and a rally that packed Madison Square Garden made him a national celebrity.[38]

Although Nixon fired Cox as the Watergate prosecutor, his successor Leon Jaworski won a Supreme Court decision on July 24, 1974, that gave him access to recordings of White House conversations. Soon after tape transcripts implicated Nixon in criminal acts for covering up the Watergate break-in, Senator Goldwater joined with other GOP leaders to warn the president of an unstoppable impeachment by the House and conviction in the Senate. Bowing to the inevitable, Nixon resigned on August 9, 1974. He had presided over an era that marked the last great expansion of America's liberal state. Legislative initiatives of the Nixon years came not only from the president but also from the Democratic Congress, sometimes with the president's reluctant agreement and occasionally despite his opposition. Nixon also moved the Supreme Court to the right with his 1971 appointment of William Rehnquist, Barry Goldwater's legal adviser in the 1964 campaign, who would become chief justice in 1986. Nonetheless, a comprehensive scholarly study of federal legislation ratified the conservative complaint that "the state-enhancing thrust of the 1960s toward greater expenditure and regulation continued with great force in the 1970s" until slowing down later in the decade.[39]

Gerald Ford became president of the United States without having stood for election in a constituency larger than a congressional district in Grand Rapids, Michigan. Ford instantly antagonized the right by appointing Nelson Rockefeller as vice president. He also took uncharacteristically bold action to end the "long national nightmare of Watergate" by issuing a full pardon of Richard Nixon. No less damaging to Ford than the acid rain of Watergate was fallout from a troubled economy. In 1973 an oil embargo imposed by the Organization of Petroleum Exporting Countries (OPEC) added to the inflation produced by growing federal expenditures—unchecked by withdrawal from Vietnam—rising wages, and falling productivity. The economy began suffering from a new affliction called "stagflation"—an improbable mix of lagging growth and high unemployment and inflation. Ford proposed spending cuts and a tax surcharge on incomes and corporate profits, which neither cured the ailing economy nor pleased the left or the right. In the 1974 midterm elections, the GOP lost forty-three House seats, four Senate seats, and five governorships. The Democrats advanced in the suburbs and rebounded in the South.

A decade after Republicans had cheered Goldwater in San Francisco, conservatism hit rock bottom again. The right still lacked effective political action groups. The leading conservative journals, *National Review* and *Human Events,* had lost circulation since each peaked at more than one hundred thousand in the 1960s. Buckley and his circle had created most of America's respectable conservative organizations—ACU, YAF, and the New York State Conservative Party—but none of them had achieved mass membership or presence in the South and the West. After the 1974 midterms Republicans held but 33 percent of the House and 38 percent of the Senate, with conservatives suffering most of the losses. Republicans controlled the governor's mansion and both legislative houses only in the state of Kansas, compared to twenty-seven Democratic-controlled states. In bellwether California, Democrats held the governorship and both Senate seats. According to polls, only 20 percent of Americans called themselves Republicans.

"If you ask me what the Republican Party stands for today, I'd have to say I honestly don't know," the Republican senator Bill Brock of Tennessee confessed to an audience of Young Republicans in early 1975. "The GOP can be called a 'major party' today only by courtesy," Clare Boothe Luce bluntly wrote. "It isn't dead yet, but it isn't exactly alive either." The problem for this "zombie party" was that "as a *party,* it stands for about zilch."[40]

UP FROM THE BOTTOM

Even so, America's resilient conservative tradition was poised for resurrection. The Democratic "Watergate babies" in Congress invested most of their political capital in reforming government, not in doling out benefits. These "procedural liberals" limited Congress's seniority system, checked the power of committee chairs, killed off the House Un-American Activities Committee, and reduced the votes needed to end a Senate filibuster from two-thirds to three-fifths. They curbed the president's war-making powers and expanded congressional input on the budget. Even before the 1974 elections, the Democratic Congress limited candidate donations and spending, established a Federal Election Commission, and publicly funded presidential elections. However, a Supreme Court decision that struck down spending limits as a violation of free speech but upheld restraints on contributions inadvertently created a flood of unrestricted "soft-money" donations to parties and an explosion of independent and corporate Political Action Committees. These PACs could make unlimited independent expenditures in campaigns and contribute $5,000 to candidates in primary and general elections. The number of corporate PACs exploded from 139 in 1975 to 1,710 in 1985, while labor PACs inched upward from 226 to 388. Independent PACs, which numbered 110 when first tallied in 1977, rose to 1,003 in 1985. "An unprecedented opportunity was created for the Republican Party by the 1974 Federal Elections Campaign Act," Republican operative Lee Atwater later wrote. "This has been a very significant source of funding for the GOP ever since."[41]

In August 1971, a wake-up call to business came from an unexpected source. Two months before President Nixon appointed him to the Supreme Court, corporate lawyer Lewis Powell wrote a lengthy memo to the U.S. Chamber of Commerce warning that business faced an imminent threat to its survival. Powell argued that corporate America could no longer peacefully coexist with a liberal movement that was undercutting the country's private enterprise system and the culture that sustained it. This "broad attack" on enterprise, Powell said, was coming not just from "extremists of the left," but also "from the college campus, the pulpit, the media, the intellectual and literary journals, the arts and sciences, and from politicians."

Powell marveled at how "the enterprise system tolerates, if not participates in, its own destruction" by sustaining a left-wing press and academy. Ralph Nader and his band of "respectable liberals and social reformers" topped his enemies list. Nader's consumer crusades and the civil rights, women's, and environmental movements had brought on an onerous regulatory regime different in kind from the more tolerable industry-specific New Deal. Since the mid-1960s government had adopted sweeping new laws and regulations that cut across industry to limit pollution, control energy production, advance minority and consumer rights, and protect worker health and safety. Although scholars dubbed such reforms "post-material," Powell said that they plunged daggers into the heart of enterprise, driving up costs, diverting investment in unproductive directions, cutting the productivity of workers, and hobbling executives and owners. Business "responded—if at all—by appeasement, ineptitude, and ignoring the problem. . . . The day is long past when the chief executive officer of a major corporation discharges his responsibility by maintaining a satisfactory growth of profits." Instead, "top management must be equally concerned with protecting and preserving the system itself."

According to Powell, business leaders should promote only scholars and teachers who "believe in the system." They should insist on revision of leftist textbooks, monitor the media for liberal bias, and demand equal time for conservative views. They should offer incentives for work by sympathetic scholars and devote resources to media advertising. Businessmen should seize and use political power "aggressively and with determination—without embarrassment and without the reluctance which has been so characteristic of American business." Business should fund legal action and mobilize stockholders as a political force. "There should be no hesitation to attack the Naders, the Marcuses and others who openly seek destruction of the system. There should not be the slightest hesitation to press vigorously in all political arenas for support of the enterprise system. Nor should there be reluctance to penalize politically those who oppose it." In sum, business needed to use its financial might to capture the centers of power that shaped policy and public opinion: the political parties, the academy, the media, the legal system, and the popular culture. The Powell memo did not immediately unite business and conservative activists or let loose a flow of corporate dollars into conservative causes. But it did catalyze a quarter of a century of rebuilding on the right.[42]

In 1973 the American Conservative Union had similar advice for conservatives. It said that the right needed a "comprehensive agenda for conservative political action which has been sorely needed but conspicuously missing for the better part of a generation." Conservatives had to replace the "prevailing liberal mentality" that defined the problems facing America and instead focus political debate on their own ideas. They should draw on scholarship demonstrating "that the major difficulties in American life" were the result of "*liberalism itself*." Otherwise, "the conservative interest is defeated before it offers battle." The right should formulate a positive "conservative legislative agenda" consistent with its commitments to patriotic Christian values and private enterprise. It should cultivate "friendly media" and develop "think tanks to turn out the kind of research available to liberals." It was past time for conservatives to reverse a political process that left them with no options other than to whittle away at liberal proposals.[43]

The conservative revival that followed these critiques came about because of the passion that surged within activists who built infrastructure, revised strategy, and found prolific new sources of funding. Generous top-down funding came not primarily from corporations but, for the most part, from a new generation of foundations established and controlled by family entrepreneurs. Notable examples included:

- The John M. Olin Foundation, funded by the eponymous family chemical and munitions business.
- The Lynde and Harry Bradley Foundation, begun by the founders of a manufacturing firm based in Milwaukee.
- The Smith Richardson Foundation, financed by the family company that sold Vicks VapoRub.
- The Lilly Endowment, begun by three family members through donations of stock from their pharmaceutical business, Eli Lilly and Company.
- The Koch Family Foundations, founded by David and Charles Koch, who controlled Koch Industries, the second largest privately owned company in America.
- The Adolph Coors Foundation, run by Colorado brewer Joseph Coors.
- The Scaife Family Foundations, controlled by Richard Mellon Scaife, heir to the Mellon fortune.

By 1980 foundations had transformed the right by funneling some $20 million a year to conservative groups. The top fund-raiser was Scaife—the J. Howard Pew of his time. Unlike Pew, Scaife wrote little, rarely spoke in public, and formed no circle of business intellectuals. However, according to a *Washington Post* analysis, from 1960 to 1999, "Scaife and his family's charitable entities have given at least $340 million to conservative causes and institutions." Although trailing institutions like Ford, Carnegie, and Rockefeller in resources, conservative foundations targeted donations to the right and financed political action and not just problem-solving programs.[44]

Moreover, according to development scholar Robert Arnove, the traditional foundations that Reece had attacked in the 1950s for funding the left had morphed by the 1970s into agencies that protected the status quo from radical change. Progressive organizations that were dependent on foundations adopted what Karyn Strickler, former director of the National Endangered Species Coalition, named "the Do Nothing Strategy." In this view, militancy was discouraged in favor of compromise, pragmatism, and incremental reform. Instead of pushing for fundamental change, progressive groups competed for funds, endorsements, media coverage, and a "seat at the political table of insiders." Political sociologist G. William Domhoff similarly concluded that America's most important liberal policy groups "are funded by large foundations and are part of the moderate-conservative wing of the policy-planning network." This situation was precisely what J. Howard Pew had envisioned in the 1950s.[45]

In the near term, corporations responded less generously than conservative foundations to Powell's challenge. Irving Kristol wrote in 1977 that the "business community has never thought seriously about its philanthropy, and doesn't know how. . . . When you give away your stockholders' money, your philanthropy must serve the long-term interests of the corporation. Corporate philanthropy should not be, cannot be disinterested." Corporations needed to "shape or reshape the climate of public opinion." Nixon and Ford's treasury secretary William Simon, who became president of the Olin Foundation in 1977, agreed that corporate dollars needed to "rush by multimillions to the aid of liberty . . . to funnel desperately needed funds to scholars, social scientists, writers, and journalists who understand the relationship between political and economic liberty," and cease "the mindless subsidizing of colleges and universities whose department of economic, government, politics, and history are hostile to capitalism."[46]

Not until the 1990s would conservatives provide the explicit quid pro quos that opened the corporate floodgates. But Kristol and Simon made a start in 1978 by forming the Institute for Educational Affairs (IEA), with grants from the Scaife, Olin, JM, and Smith Richardson foundations and a few corporations. IEA sought to direct business philanthropy to the right. It guided business to sponsor professorships of private enterprise at universities and pledged to recruit and financially support promising students "and then find them jobs with activist groups, research projects, student publications, federal agencies or leading periodicals." IEA contributed $10,000 to the irreverently conservative *Dartmouth Review,* which launched such media stars as author Dinesh D'Souza and talk-show host Laura Ingraham. It established a Collegiate Network of conservative publications that covered seventy campuses, including Dartmouth, Harvard, Yale, Columbia, and Stanford.

Smaller contributions, solicited through techniques perfected by direct-mail wizard Richard Viguerie, proved no less important to the right than top-down donations. Viguerie became an indispensable resource for conservative candidates, PACs, think tanks, and lobbyists when his efforts to retire George Wallace's 1972 campaign debt added millions of names to his fund-raising lists. Fund-raising through the combination of direct-mail and foundations pushed conservative groups into uncharted fiscal territory as typical budgets rose tenfold from hundreds of thousands to millions of dollars.

By the late 1970s Viguerie's company was raising tens of millions of dollars annually while raking in healthy profits for itself. By reactivating "mail order government," conservatives circumvented the so-called liberal media and party bureaucracies to market their ideas, activate supporters, and promote candidates. Viguerie trolled not just for one-shot donors but for lifetime converts. In the 1977–78 election cycle, conservatives controlled the five best-funded independent Political Action Committees: Ronald Reagan's Citizens for the Republic, the National Conservative Political Action Committee (NCPAC), the Committee for the Survival of a Free Congress, the American Medical Political Action Committee, and Gun Owners of America. Only the American Medical PAC had existed five years earlier. In 1979–80 conservatives would control nine of the top ten independent PACs. Independent groups directly spent $10.6 million for Reagan in 1980, compared to just $28,000 for Carter.[47]

ANOTHER "NEW RIGHT"

Foundation, direct mail, and some corporate funding sustained a self-styled "new right" that revived campaigns for compelling virtue in a sinful society. Congressional staffers Paul Weyrich and Edward Feulner, former Nixon official Howard Phillips, magazine editor Emmett Tyrrell, youth organizer Morton Blackwell, gun rights lobbyist Lawrence Pratt, and Terry Dolan, who founded NCPAC—all under thirty-five in 1974—formed a new right vanguard with mentors Richard Viguerie and William Rusher. Allies included Pat Buchanan, M. Stanton Evans, Senator Jesse Helms, Representatives John Ashbrook and Phil Crane, and Phyllis Schlafly, the only consequential woman and the most gifted grassroots organizer on the right.

"This is not the first time there has been talk of a 'New Right' in American politics," Kevin Phillips wrote in 1975. In the 1940s, history professor Peter Viereck had discovered a new right in Richard Weaver's writings on traditional values. There quickly followed six more new right cohorts: Joseph McCarthy and his boosters, Buckley and the *NR* circle, the John Birch Society and the Liberty Lobby, Irving Kristol's neoconservatives, the libertarians, and finally the Weyrich-Viguerie crowd. The taxonomy became so tangled that a 1978 *Washington Post* profile described new right leaders as "the neo-conservatives." Rusher had to remind even Buckley "to use the word 'neo-conservatives,' with or without the hyphen, for the Kristol crowd, and to reserve 'New Right' with or without the initial capital letters, for Viguerie et al."[48]

This seventh "new right" in thirty years hoped to restore authority to traditional institutions and liberate working- and middle-class constituents from their attachment to liberal economic programs. Like neoconservatives, they decried the new class of parasitic professors, social workers, and bureaucrats as out-of-touch "liberal elites" who scorned traditional values and kept minorities and the poor dependent on government. "It is elitist denigration of tradition, habit and custom that has weakened the bonds of authority," Buchanan had warned in 1971. "It has been elitist assaults on traditional morality and traditional patriotism that have helped to weaken and destroy the ties between the young and the Church, and the young and the government. . . . To the central crisis—the crisis of authority—they offer less than nothing."[49]

This latest new right was new in style, personnel, and strategy but not in conservative core principles. Some new right leaders rebuked big business for putting profits ahead of morals, but it was bark with no bite because they backed business's agenda of low taxes, subsidies, reduced or friendly regulations, and opposition to unions. Like Wallace in 1968, they promised the middle and working classes relief from meddlesome bureau-

crats but not job training, public works, or federal health programs. Organizer Paul Weyrich said that the new right differed from the "old right"
not in ideology but in political strategy. Rather than public relations and
education, new right activists worked on developing the capacity for political action that conservatives had lacked. They aimed at "building a grass
roots base of activists and contributors who would constitute a participatory majority to achieve the election of conservative leaders and the implementation of conservative policy."[50]

Despite their grassroots pretensions, most new right leaders operated inside the Washington beltway. Like the *NR* crowd and the neocons,
the new conservatives hoped to rally the populist masses but they were
ill-suited to the task. Nearly all had emerged from Republican Party politics and *NR* spin-off groups. Instead of plowing the populist fields, they
hunkered down on Capitol Hill, compulsively organizing seminars, conferences, training sessions, and strategy meetings. "We have meetings every
15 or 20 minutes," cracked Terry Dolan of NCPAC. The new right elite
did not mingle with workers in union halls or veterans in their lodges. With
the exception of Schlafly, they did not rally farmers' groups or the citizens who joined PTAs, neighborhood associations, and civic groups. No
tillers of the soil or hardened blue-collar workers participated in the regular
conservative strategy meetings of the Kingston Group, the Stanton Group,
or the Library Court Group. Robert Whitaker, a theorist of "conservative
populism," and Robert Hoy, national field director of the Populist Forum,
tried in vain to meet with new right leaders at the 1976 CPAC conference.
Hoy said, "It was made clear to us through our experiences at CPAC and
at other times, that conservatives are genuinely NOT interested in these
kinds of people."[51]

Black conservatives gained new prominence in the 1970s, although
on a separate track from the new right. African-American economist
Thomas Sowell won a wide audience for his 1975 book *Race and Economics,* which challenged accounts of blacks as victims of racism and, like
journalist George Schuyler, trusted race progress to capitalism and not
civil rights programs. Three years later, J. A. "Jay" Parker, a black veteran of Young Americans for Freedom with ties to the World Anti-Communism League and the government of South Africa, established the
Lincoln Institute for Research and Education as America's preeminent
black conservative think tank. The institute published a newsletter and

a quarterly journal, the *Lincoln Review,* but failed to achieve a high profile among conservatives.

REBUILDING TOP DOWN

Led by the visionary Paul Weyrich, special assistant to conservative Republican senator Carl Curtis of Nebraska from 1973 to 1977, the new right rebuilt from the top down. It launched conservative caucuses within Congress, think tanks, and lobbying, training, and political action groups. Conservatives founded new journals, began training young recruits, and formed state legislative networks and legal advocacy groups. The first new right breakthrough came in 1973 when congressional staffers Weyrich and Feulner persuaded Representative Phil Crane and other conservatives to organize the House Steering Committee, later renamed the Republican Study Committee. This right-wing version of the liberal Wednesday Group quickly recruited some seventy members—nearly 40 percent of the House's GOP contingent, including thirty of forty-four Republicans first elected in 1972. It devised electoral strategy, analyzed bills and issues, and brainstormed ideas. It prepared speeches, strategy memos, and analyses of legislation. Conservative southern Democrats, losing clout to Republicans and liberal Democrats, formed a similar Dixie bloc, with about fifty members. In the Senate, Weyrich persuaded Carl Curtis to launch a Senate Steering Committee, which stagnated at about a dozen members. Still, "ideological polarization within the parties," Kevin Phillips noted at the time, could be "a prelude to a larger re-alignment" across the parties.[52]

To counter the liberal National Committee for an Effective Congress, Weyrich formed the Committee for the Survival of a Free Congress in 1974 (later the Free Congress Foundation), with financial assistance from Joseph Coors. The outgoing Coors emerged as a high-flying angel of the right in the 1970s, second in generosity only to the reclusive Scaife. MORE THAN COORS BEER MOVING EAST: OWNER PUMPING MILLIONS INTO RIGHT-WING GROUPS headlined the *Los Angeles Times* in 1975. Weyrich's committee trained candidates and their aides and provided staff assistance for conservatives in targeted races. By 1990 his budget would surpass $3 million.[53]

To complement Weyrich's group, Senator Jesse Helms and his political aide John Carbaugh launched the Conservative Caucus in 1974. The

Caucus's director, Howard Phillips, said that its goal was to "help create a conservative establishment in this country" by working in congressional districts to elect candidates of the right. The Caucus's founding statement highlighted social issues: the "right to life," the "right of parents to define the conditions and content of their children's education," the "freedom of individuals to pray to God," and the "rights of crime victims [above] those who commit crimes." It opposed "quotas as a basis of selection in education, employment, or conferring of benefits," as well as the use of government resources to "underwrite policy advocacy or political activity." It called for dismantling "the vast power of the Federal bureaucracy," placing a "ceiling on the proportion of income which government may take away in taxes," balancing the federal budget, and upholding American sovereignty. The statement contained not a word on communism, Russia, or China. By 1990 the Conservative Caucus would boast an annual budget of more than $3 million, a claimed 750,000 members, and twenty-five full-time employees.

Helms also played midwife to the first all-purpose Political Action Committee of the right: Terry Dolan's NCPAC, the National Conservative Political Action Committee. This self-styled "gut-cutting organization" followed the model of the American Medical Association in 1950, slamming liberal candidates for Congress and providing cover for conservative candidates. With backing from Reagan, NCPAC raised millions in the 1970s. Helms also organized his own PAC, the National Congressional Club, run by Tom Ellis, North Carolina's top political operative. The club worked with Viguerie to raise a record $7.7 million for Helms's reelection in 1978; he trounced his Democratic opponent in fund-raising by nearly thirty to one. The club backed conservative candidates nationwide, giving Helms a political machine that was unrivaled in Congress. With the exception of Political Action Committees, the new organizations mostly spent their money on their own operations; very little reached conservative candidates.[54]

With more hands than a Hindu god, Weyrich reached out to Joe Coors for seed money to launch the Heritage Foundation as a new kind of think tank to advance "individual liberty, free enterprise, limited government, a strong national defense, and traditional American values." It would be more daring and innovative, more openly political, and more attentive to anti-pluralist values than the American Enterprise Institute (AEI). The

Coors foundation pumped millions of dollars into Heritage through the 1980s. But Scaife's foundations gave more: $23 million through 1999. The Koch, Olin, and Bradley foundations wrote big checks to Heritage. General Motors, Ford, Procter and Gamble, Chase Manhattan Bank, Dow Chemical, Reader's Digest, and Mobil Oil chipped in lesser amounts.[55]

Heritage was more than a Corvette version of AEI's Chevrolet. Heritage pushed the envelope of its tax exemption to build a conservative movement. It was a forge for ideas and legislation, a PR shop, a talent agency, a speaker's bureau, and a political consulting and lobbying group. Rather than recruiting superstar scholars and swinging for home run ideas, Heritage hired journeymen staffers to shape day-to-day policy making and political debates. It sought to become indispensable to the media for a rightward slant on issues and to politicians for strategy, ideas, and analyses. Heritage aggressively marketed its products and collaborated with conservative leaders in Washington and state capitals. It published a quarterly journal, *Policy Review,* and a weekly newsletter. It churned out legislative analyses, background reports on issues, and papers on national security, education, and international affairs, all with a guaranteed conservative bent. It set up a Washington Semester Program for college students and a speaker's bureau. It published lists of thousands of conservative intellectuals and activists and hundreds of organizations available for media appearances and consultations. Heritage staffers wrote legislation, testified about it before Congress, and argued for it on television, radio, and the opinion pages of the nation's newspapers. It created access that the right had coveted for decades.

Unlike AEI, which touted balance and objectivity, Heritage lauded its contributions to conservative politics. A 1979 letter to donors said, "We uncovered and revealed Big Labor's shocking plans to force all Federal government workers into unions and line the pockets of Labor Bosses with untold millions in dues money." Heritage said that it "blew the whistle on President Carter's so-called $25 billion welfare 'reform' proposal and pegged it for what it was—a guaranteed prescription for flagrant abuse and waste of your tax dollars." It promised to oppose such "Big Labor/Liberal" proposals as "Ted Kennedy's socialized medicine scheme ... passage of the SALT II arms with the Soviet Union which would allow the Russians to gain clear military superiority," and "approval of government financing of political campaigns so liberals like George McGovern can use your tax dollars to pay for their TV ads." According to Edward Feulner, who became Heritage's president in 1977, "Many other think tanks have been overly cautious in deciding just how far they can opine and the result is that their impact has not been nearly as effective as it should be. We set out to change this."[56]

In pursuit of its anti-pluralist values, the Heritage Foundation took part in the culture war that in 1974–75 ripped through Kanawha County, West Virginia, which covered the city of Charleston and rural areas. White evangelical Protestant parents protested against school reading materials that were "destructive of social and cultural values, obscene, pornographic, unpatriotic, or in violation of individual and familial rights of privacy" in the words of school board member Alice Moore, who had earlier led a campaign against sex education in the public schools. The protesters objected to textbooks that they said contained selections by authors such as Mark Twain, Sherwood Anderson, Bernard Malamud, and Lawrence Ferlinghetti that mocked Christianity and patriotism and indoctrinated students in "secular humanism" and "moral relativity." Protesters decried the inclusion of excerpts by black authors such as Eldridge Cleaver and James Baldwin who used "filthy language," and "non-standard English," and presented a negative, "race-conscious" view of American life.[57]

The protesters consulted with America's leading authorities on offensive liberal texts, Mel and Norma Gabler of Longview, Texas. Since 1961 these conservative evangelical Protestants had run Educational Research Analysts. This mom-and-pop shop combed through texts slated for adoption in Texas schools. According to the Gablers, "acceptable textbooks should be based on high morality, fixed values, Christian concepts, and a proper portrayal of our nation's great heritage." Their rigorous reviews of textbooks prompted lengthy responses by publishers and condemnations by the National Education Association. Their work likely influenced textbook adoptions in Texas, where a state committee approved material for local schools. The couple gained national attention because a book killed in Texas' huge market could die elsewhere.[58]

As an astonished nation looked on, Kanawha County degenerated into mass protests, vandalism, shootings, arson, assaults, and bombings. Officials closed the public schools. Coal miners sympathetic to the protests launched a wildcat strike and one protester hurled a death curse against three school board members. The Ku Klux Klan, the John Birch

Society, the Populist Forum, conservative Republican Robert Dornan of the California group Citizens for Decency Through Law, the Reverend Carl McIntire, and local evangelical ministers rallied behind the protesters. The Heritage Foundation's lawyer, James McKenna, held legal seminars for protesters, conveyed their demands to the media, and defended them in court free of charge. The dissenters claimed to represent the everyday people of their community—the "Creekers"—against the county's highbrow elite—the "Hillers." But the dispute followed religious lines more closely than it did class lines. It pitted anti-pluralist Protestant evangelicals against mostly mainstream Protestants who believed that schools in a pluralist society should present a diversity of material. The Reverend Lewis Harrah of the evangelical Church of Jesus Christ in North Charleston said that protesters were upholding "the infallible Word of God. We do not intend to compromise our beliefs. . . . This is not a situation where opposing views can be reconciled." Local Episcopal minister James Lewis said, in contrast, "Our children are being sacrificed because of the fanatical zeal of our fundamentalist brothers who claim to be hearing the deep, resonant voice of God."[59]

A wary peace settled over Kanawha County after compromises that pleased neither side. Similar protests against pluralist culture erupted in hundreds of communities across America and continued to ebb and flow over the next three decades. But nothing quite matched the spectacle of the Kanawha County war, which cautioned school authorities nationwide about controversial book adoptions and prompted families to consider home schooling and private Christian schools as alternatives to public education. Don Marsh, an editor of the *Charleston Gazette*, wrote, "The books were only a symbol. . . . Many of the protesters are demonstrating against a changing world: short skirts, long hair, civil rights, nudity, dirty movies."[60]

Although Heritage's involvement in Kanawha County opened it to charges of extremism, the foundation survived and thrived under Feulner, who refocused Heritage on economic policy, national security, and foreign affairs. He upped the foundation's budget from $800,000 in 1977 to $5 million in 1980. The rise of Heritage did not lead to the fall of AEI. In the new era of foundation funding, AEI achieved Baroody's dream of rivaling the yearly spending of the Brookings Institution (although not its $60 million endowment) as his budget rose from $1 million in 1970 to $10 million in 1980. To showcase its star system, AEI recruited Gerald Ford as a distinguished fellow after he lost the presidency in 1976 and signed on his defense secretary Melvin Laird, his treasury secretary William Simon, and his Federal Reserve chair Arthur Burns. AEI recruited neoconservative Irving Kristol as a senior fellow in 1977, followed by Jeane Kirkpatrick, Ben Wattenberg, and Michael Novak. Other prominent neoconservatives gained preeminent positions within the cerebral right during the 1970s. They found homes not only at AEI but also at the Bradley and Olin foundations and at smaller conservative think tanks such as the Manhattan Institute, the Hudson Institute, and the pro-Israel Jewish Institute for National Security Affairs.[61]

Increasingly, conservatives recognized the value of cultivating young activists. M. Stanton Evans formed the National Journalism Center in 1977 to train aspiring conservative journalists in policy analysis, strategy, and technical skills. Notable graduates included conservative authors and media personalities Ann Coulter, John Fund, and Michael Johns. Two years later, in 1979, Morton Blackwell formed the broader Leadership Institute, which trained more than fifty thousand conservatives in journalism, policy making, and political strategy. Its graduates included Christian conservative leader Ralph Reed, Republican senator Mitch McConnell of Kentucky, and activist Grover Norquist.[62]

Other groups repackaged old issues. To circumvent a 1968 Supreme Court decision that banned the teaching of biblical creationism in public schools, proponents marketed creationism as a science, not a theology. In 1970 Dr. Henry Morris, a biblical literalist and a hydraulic engineer, founded the Institute for Creation Research (ICR) as an adjunct to evangelist Tim LaHaye's Christian Heritage College. Morris sought to establish "creation science" as an equal scientific competitor to evolution. He said, "While, as scientists, creationists must study as objectively as possible the actual data of geology, as Bible-believing Christians, we must also insist that these be correlated within the framework of Biblical revelation." For Morris, "Evolutionism is the basis of humanism, socialism, communism, fascism, racism, amoralism, and other such deadly philosophies." Biologists rejected creationism as religion dressed up as science, and creationism failed to penetrate peer-reviewed journals. But ICR put promotion above research. It established a graduate school, a publishing house, and a museum. Although ICR gained public support for teaching creation science in schools, new court decisions failed to accept its claim to be objective science rather than religious doctrine.[63]

After decades of subsisting on *National Review* and *Human Events*, conservatives enriched their diet. Viguerie launched *Conservative Digest* in 1975 to compile writings by conservatives and others. In 1977 editor Lee Edwards claimed that the *Digest* had become "the nation's largest political publication with 118,000 paid circulation." R. Emmett Tyrrell, a graduate student at Indiana University, founded what later became the first notable journal of conservative opinion since *National Review*. His magazine began life in 1967 as a student-run publication at Indiana University called *The Alternative: An American Spectator*. Like Buckley, Tyrrell had big dreams about reviving conservative politics through the power of his pen, and he too learned to finance the magazine through a tax-exempt foundation. In 1970 a $25,000 contribution from a Scaife foundation let Tyrrell extend his satiric journalism from campus radicals to national figures such as Jimmy Carter and Henry Kissinger. By the mid-1970s the *American Spectator* had a modest circulation of about twenty thousand, but articles by George Will, William Kristol, and Michael Novak kept it influential in conservative circles. Tyrrell bragged to Rusher in 1978 about the deep pocket that financed his magazine: "We must visit again, but this time on me—or rather on the CIA. They pay my bills these days."[64]

The right continued Spiro Agnew's tradition of battering the media through Accuracy in Media (AIM), which Federal Reserve economist Reed Irvine and retired communications professor Abraham Kalish set up in 1969. By jousting with media giants, the tax-exempt AIM expanded its budget from about $50,000 in 1970 to more than $200,000 in 1977. It charged the television networks, PBS, the *New York Times,* and the *Washington Post* with liberal bias, distortion, and inaccuracy. AIM purchased stock in media companies to rattle executives at stockholders meetings. Irvine wrote a syndicated column, and his group published a newsletter that reached thirty thousand readers and launched a radio show called *Media Monitor*. AIM generated some news coverage, a few factual corrections, and occasional testy responses from media executives.[65]

Conservatives followed Powell's advice to become legal advocates when former staffers for Governor Ronald Reagan launched the Pacific Legal Foundation in 1973. It was chaired by John Simon Fluor Jr., the former CEO of his family's Fluor Corporation. The foundation would represent not the public interest of Ralph Nader but "the public interest encompassed in the traditional value system held by the great majority of the American people." Two years later, conservatives established a National Legal Center for the Public Interest to help create a network of regional legal foundations. The founders recognized that "the courts, regulatory commissions and independent agencies play as important a role as our elected representatives in determining public policy issues on the widest possible range of social and economic issues." They would counter leftists who used the law for "restricting economic growth, blocking freedom of individual location, redistributing wealth from the productive to the unproductive, hindering national defense, and substituting government for individual decision making."[66]

The tax-exempt Legal Center began with about $500,000 from ten corporations, almost all of which were from the Midwest, the South, and the West, including Fluor, Coors, Sears, Halliburton, Dow Chemical, and Southern California Edison. The center coordinated regional "public interest law firms dedicated and committed to limited constitutional government, the competitive free enterprise system, and individual initiative and freedom with responsibility." By the 1990s affiliated groups would boast combined annual budgets of about $10 million. The U.S. Chamber of Commerce pitched in with its own legal foundation, the National Chamber Litigation Center, whose goal was "to enhance the private enterprise viewpoint before the courts and in the regulatory agencies of government." Other legal foundations followed, including the American Center for Law and Justice, which represented Christian conservative causes.[67]

Conservative foundations litigated or filed amicus briefs in cases to support the construction of dams and reservoirs, the use of DDT, grazing and timbering on public lands, restrictions on welfare payments, and the building of weapons systems opposed by environmentalists. They challenged affirmative action as reverse discrimination against whites, fought against enforcement of the Endangered Species Act, backed restrictions on abortion and tough criminal laws, and fought to balance economic costs against benefits in enforcing "post-material" regulations. They sought both to win cases and to dramatize their cause. By 1980 conservative groups were appearing regularly before the U.S. Supreme Court.

Overwhelmingly, conservatives defended business and property rights; backed restrictions on abortion, pornography, and criminal rights;

and opposed expansive applications of antidiscrimination laws. In contrast to the liberals' definition of the "the public interest," they offered the conservative vision of protecting private property, promoting entrepreneurship, respecting traditional values, and providing equality of opportunity, not results. "We're presenting the other side to counter-balance the extreme environmentalists who are trying to block the economic development of the West," said James Watt, president of the Mountain States Legal Foundation. "We believe in the free enterprise system. We believe in private property, we believe in individual liberties."[68]

The right attended to state government through the American Legislative Exchange Council, which began as a project of the American Conservative Union and became an independent tax-exempt organization in 1975. Weyrich, Feulner, *Human Events* editor Thomas Winter, and the Republican representative Robert Bauman of Maryland served on its board. Mostly Republican state legislators—and a few conservative Democrats—joined the ostensibly nonpartisan ALEC to benefit from its staff work, research, strategic advice, and model legislation. ALEC's membership soared after it teamed with the Gun Owners of America in 1978 to defeat a constitutional amendment on voting rights for the District of Columbia. It then allied with corporate interests to craft pro-business legislation on pollution, property rights, taxes, utility regulation, tort liability, and labor relations. By 2000 the Legislative Council would have an annual budget of $6 million and the participation of some twenty-four hundred state delegates and senators, nearly a third of all state legislators in America.

After his Watergate revelations, Reverend Moon entered conservative American politics, spending many tens of millions of dollars in the 1970s. His Unification Church opposed communism, abortion, birth control, sex outside of marriage, and homosexual relations. It backed anticommunist insurgencies and authoritarian pro-Western regimes across the world. The church created such political front groups as the Freedom Leadership Foundation, the Korean Cultural and Freedom Foundation, and the Confederation of the Associations for Unity of the Societies of the Americas.

The Unification Church helped financially sustain the World Anti-Communist League, which the rulers of South Korea and Taiwan had founded in 1967. In 1973 the church funded a U.S. sponsor for the World Anti-Communist League, the American Council for World Freedom.

Principal organizer Lee Edwards amassed impressive conservative fire-power for this leadership council: Walter Judd, Eleanor Schlafly, David Keene, Edgar Bundy, John Fisher, Fred Schwarz, Richard Viguerie, Reed Irvine, and a host of conservative scholars. Neil A. Salonen, American president of the Unification Church, represented Reverend Moon on the council. However, by the 1970s, the World Anti-Communist League had became a haven for neofascists and anti-Semites, including the Romanian Iron Guard, the Ukrainian OUN, and the Croatian Ustashe; the Tecos movement in Mexico; and anti-Israeli Arabs. The American Council for World Freedom, which anticipated hosting the World Anti-Communist League's 1974 conference, responded to charges of anti-Semitism by condemning prejudice against Jews only in communist nations, rejecting a proposal to "condemn anti-Semitism in any place, not only in communist states." Geoffrey Stewart-Smith, head of the World Anti-Communist League's British affiliate, advised the Americans to cancel the 1974 meeting, warning that "anti-Semitism and political extremism" ruled the British chapter and "member organizations and delegations" from outside western Europe were controlled by "extreme right wing, anti-Semitic, and fanatical separatists." He said that "any idea of reforming WACL from within is an illusion." Undaunted, the American Council for World Freedom brought the league to Washington, D.C., where featured speakers included Nicaraguan dictator Anastasio Somoza, Senator Sergio Onofre Jarpa of Augusto Pinochet's military government in Chile, former OUN head Yaroslav Stetsko, and William F. Buckley Jr.[69]

The American Council for World Freedom disbanded soon after the conference, with many members moving into an American Chilean Council that Marvin Liebman organized with Spruille Braden, a founding director of the John Birch Society. The new group sought to counter the left-wing "war" on Pinochet, who had seized power in a 1973 coup backed by the Nixon administration against the elected government of socialist Salvador Allende. The new council lauded Pinochet's cultivation of private enterprise and denied his responsibility for the murder of thousands of political opponents. It publicized Pinochet's self-serving claim that such charges reflected the communists' "capacity for invention" and "that whenever there has been an abuse of human rights, we [the Pinochet government] have recognized it, and proceeded to investigate and punish severely the person responsible."[70]

THE "PRO-FAMILY" RIGHT

The new right put a positive spin on anti-pluralist morality. They weren't just against sinners and feminists; they were the "pro-family" and "pro-life" champions of wholesome "family values." Still, defense of the family meant battling the Equal Rights Amendment (ERA), abortion, pornography, gay rights, and gun control. After Congress sent the ERA to the states in 1972, Schlafly organized a STOP ERA group to oppose ratification. The ERA, she said, dissolved men's obligation to support their wives and children, forced women into the workplace, and relegated their children to day-care centers. It made women share bathrooms and foxholes with men, deprived them of protections secured by age-of-consent and antirape laws, and created unworkable unisex marriages that jeopardized women's alimony, child support, and custody over children. It legalized homosexual marriage and required government to pay for abortions.

In concert with local opposition groups, Schlafly helped revive grassroots conservativism and won right-wing acclaim as the unmovable object that stopped the seemingly irresistible momentum of the ERA three states short of ratification. A study of ERA voting by state legislators showed a powerful association between opposition and membership in evangelical Protestant denominations and the Mormon church. Although claiming to represent ordinary folk who were opposed to liberal elites, Schlafly had mobilized an anti-pluralist minority to block an amendment favored by Congress, state legislatures representing three-quarters of Americans, and two-thirds or more of survey respondents nationwide.[71]

In 1975 Schlafly founded her pro-family Eagle Forum as a membership organization with an agenda broader than stopping the ERA. Her group would strive to preserve "the family as the basic unit of society, with certain rights and responsibilities, including the right to insist that the schools permit voluntary prayer and teach the 'fourth R' (right and wrong) according to the precepts of the Holy Scriptures." The group published an *Eagle Forum Newsletter,* with an informal and personal style crafted for a female audience. Two years later Schlafly founded the Pro-Family Coalition, published *The Power of the Positive Woman,* and organized a well-attended Pro-Family Rally that upstaged the feminist International Year of the Woman gathering in Houston, Texas, and inspired other women activists. She warned that feminists were "going to drive the homemaker out of the home. . . . They want to relieve mothers of the menial task of taking care of their babies. They want to put them in the coal mines and have them digging ditches." The ERA would "only benefit homosexuals. . . . The American women do not want ERA, abortion, lesbian rights, and they do not want child care in the hands of government."[72]

The threat to family life posed by the "homosexual lifestyle" loomed large for the right in the 1970s. Gays and lesbians were pressing for the same rights as racial minorities. But it took pop singer, Florida orange juice spokesperson, and evangelical Protestant Anita Bryant to put the right's vision of a gay menace on America's conceptual map when she formed Save Our Children in 1977 to oppose a Dade County gay rights ordinance. Bryant charged gay and lesbian activists with mounting a "disguised attack on God" and "recruiting children" to their immoral way of life. "What's happening is that, in the name of human rights, vice is becoming virtuous." She complained of reverse discrimination against straight parents and defended "the civil rights of parents to save their children from homosexual influence." With anti-pluralist conservatives from across America rallying to her aid, Bryant secured the signatures needed to submit the ordinance to a referendum of voters, the first of its kind in the nation. Voters rejected the ordinance two to one, but the battle over gay and lesbian rights had just begun.[73]

Protection of marriage, children, and the family from the gay lifestyle drove recruitment and fund-raising on the right. According to the Reverend Robert Billings, an advocate for private Christian schools who became Reagan's "religious coordinator" for the 1980 campaign, "We need an emotionally charged issue to stir up people and get them mad enough to get them up from watching TV and do something. I believe that the homosexual issue is the issue we should use." Even the National Conservative Political Action Committee, headed by closeted homosexual Terry Dolan, warned in a fund-raising letter, "Our nation's moral fiber is being weakened by the growing homosexual movement and the fanatical ERA pushers (many of whom publicly brag they are lesbians)." A few conservatives with libertarian bents such as David Brudnoy, a Boston-based talk-show host, questioned a campaign that said things like "Kill a Queer for Christ" and charged that "the drought in California is God's punishment because of liberalized sex laws there. . . . Good Lord!" He wondered how the right could "forget all the conservative great men and women of our time who are, or were, homosexuals." Most conservatives, however, including editors of the *National Review* and *Human Events*, fell in line.[74]

For many on the right the protection of families at a time of rampant crime required both broad police powers and the stout defense of citizens' Second Amendment right to own and bear arms. The National Rifle Association (NRA) took its first big step into electoral politics in 1976 when it spent more than $100,000 on direct mail for the Ford-Dole ticket and pro-gun candidates for Congress. The following year, at the organization's annual meeting in Cincinnati, hard-liners engineered the "revolt in Cincinnati." They voted out the NRA's patrician leadership that had enshrined sports and conservation over politics and pledged to lobby against gun control and punish enemies of "gun owners' rights" at the polls. From 1977 to 1980 the NRA grew from 1.2 million to 1.8 million members and its spending on elections climbed to $2 million. "Every member of Congress tells the same story," said Democratic House Majority Leader Jim Wright of Texas in 1981. "There are hundreds of people, in some cases literally thousands, who never write to them on any other subject but become irate and paranoid and very frightened at any suggestion of gun control." Beyond gun owners' rights, the NRA upheld traditional moral values, manly patriotism, self-reliance, and religious faith. These were virtues that the NRA's leadership viewed as threatened by the effete, bohemian "adversary culture" of gun controllers.[75]

The upstart Gun Owners of America topped the NRA with its absolutist approach to gun rights. For executive director Larry Pratt, self-defense through firearms ownership was as firmly pro-life as saving unborn children. Firearms, he said, "are very much part of the administration of justice in God's economy of protecting life," not only "at the corporate level through the state" but also "at the individual level, which Christ spoke to." Gun restrictions were an "implicit, illegal changing of the Second Amendment" and violated biblical strictures for self-defense. "To say that weapons are inherently antilife is to misunderstand the nature of man and what God has ordained that we do in this fallen world."[76]

After the Supreme Court established abortion rights for women in its 1973 *Roe v. Wade* decision, the body count of aborted babies became the most immediate and palpable evil for the anti-pluralist right. At first, the Catholic-dominated "pro-life" movement fit uneasily within the pro-family coalition. The National Conference of Catholic Bishops founded the National Right to Life Committee, which became independent in 1973 but still relied on church funding and Catholic recruits. Nellie J. Gray's March for Life Committee rallied mostly Catholics for its Capitol Hill demonstrations each year. The right began absorbing the movement in 1976 when the Republican platform praised the "efforts of those who seek enactment of a constitutional amendment to restore protection of the right to life for unborn children." Schlafly integrated opposition to abortion into her coalition and evangelical Protestants formed such single-issue pro-life groups as the National Pro-Life Political Action Committee and the American Life Lobby. In New York State, a Right to Life Party challenged the Conservative Party for ballot position.

Conservatives used their family values agenda to seize the moral high ground from liberals who were slow to respond. Eventually, liberals counterattacked by charging that conservatives did not protect families but forced Americans to conform to their falsely imagined traditions of family life and sex roles. Liberals pointed to the historical malleability of family life and the forging of new emotional bonds, customs, rituals, and parenting styles. They stressed that family planning, enlightened sex education, and safe and legal abortion contributed to family health and stability. They lauded the security and opportunity provided families by minimum wages, welfare safety nets, aid for housing and medical care, affordable child care, and civil rights protections. Liberals pointed to polls showing increasing tolerance in a centrist society of alternative lifestyles and gender parity. Still, the liberal agenda lacked the black-and-white certainty and moral outrage of the anti-pluralist message on families.[77]

SEARCHING FOR AN ALTERNATIVE

In his first full year as president, Ford faced daunting domestic and foreign challenges. When the federal government was forced to bail out financially strapped New York City during the 1975 recession, it seemed that America's postwar affluence had come to an end. Fighting continued to rage in Vietnam and Congress declined to commit renewed resources to the government of South Vietnam. By the end of April 1975, South Vietnam had surrendered, President Thieu had fled the country, and remaining American personnel had conducted a humiliating evacuation. Simultaneously, Cambodia fell to a brutal communist guerrilla force, the Khmer Rouge. With the exceptions of Hong Kong, Thailand, and South Korea, the Americans and Europeans had been driven out of mainland Asia, the goal the Japanese had sought to achieve in World War II.

In 1976 a host of Democrats competed to take on the beleaguered President Ford. Senator Henry Jackson, a founder of the Coalition for a Democratic Majority, campaigned as both a socially conservative and economically liberal candidate. Jackson melded liberal positions on economic and labor issues with a rousing defense of traditional culture, rocklike support for Israel, opposition to forced busing, and a hard line on the Cold War. His voting record earned him an 82 percent score from the AFL-CIO and a 90 percent score from the American Security Council. Jackson suggested that the United States use "food power" to starve the Russians into submission. "We've had enough of being kicked around," he said. "We've been a soft touch too long." He urged Americans to honor their country. "Our greatest foreign policy problem is our divisions at home. . . . America seems bent on eroding its influence and destroying its achievements in world affairs through an orgy of recrimination." But keepers of the conservative flame weren't buying Jackson's half-a-loaf conservatism. The GOP representative (later senator) Steven D. Symms of Idaho said, "When I see Scoop Jackson, when he carried the Massachusetts primary, labeled as a conservative, I have to throw up." Jackson faded from the Democratic race after losing a make-or-break primary in New York, leaving neoconservatives with shrinking options among Democratic contenders. But Jackson's foreign policies endured through neoconservative aides and advisers who went on to serve Republican presidents, among them Elliot Abrams, Douglas Feith, Richard Perle, and Paul Wolfowitz.[78]

The strongest Democratic candidate proved to be one of the least known, Jimmy Carter, the former governor of Georgia. With public trust of government at its lowest ebb since the advent of scientific polling, this born-again evangelical Christian campaigned skillfully as a competent, moral, and deeply religious outsider able to clean up the mess in Washington. Carter had the nomination in hand before the Democrats' July convention where he chose liberal Senator Walter Mondale of Minnesota as his running mate.

Conservative activists searched for an alternative to Ford. "In 1972 Republicans ridiculed McGovern as the Triple A candidate—amnesty, abortion, and acid," Paul Weyrich wrote. "Now in just one month, between President Ford, his wife [the outspoken, socially liberal Betty Ford], and Vice President-designate Nelson Rockefeller we have the new Triple A team. . . . I for one would gladly trade the just ended nightmare of Watergate for the current nightmare of liberalism revived in Republican clothing." For Howard Phillips, M. Stanton Evans, William Rusher, and Richard Viguerie, the quest for a new candidate led to the creation of a Committee for a New Majority, which explored the formation of a new party to integrate conservative Democrats and Republicans. Advocates of a new party attempted to woo Reagan with a letter from Evans, who said that as a candidate for the Republican nomination Reagan would be "playing in Ford's ball park," where the president's "organizational, patronage, and ceremonial strengths are maximized." Even if nominated, Reagan would inherit "Watergate, the Vietnam disaster, unemployment, inflation, and problems with the economy," which "the new party approach" avoided. Although Reagan wasn't buying, the committee sought to link up with the American Independent Party, a remnant of Wallace's 1968 campaign, which had access to ballot slots in some twenty states.[79]

Rusher believed that a new party would complement the *National Review*'s effort to rescue Christianity from enlightenment heresy. "For the metaphysical base of my proposed new party I have in mind the Western Christian tradition," Rusher wrote, although he kept it quiet "to make acceptance a little easier for those (and they are not few) who fear any tendency to the sort of theological state." But William S. Lind, a young conservative thinker, warned Rusher that awakening the ignorant and bigoted "Yahoo" masses "could easily lead to an unbearable tyranny of the majority, and the loss of republican liberties to populist forces." Moreover, "the Wallace bloc *is* isolationist" and "will not support the long-term foreign policy commitments you believe necessary. They will support jingoistic adventures such as attempts to seize oil-producing states; but it is precisely rapid vacillations between isolationism and adventurism—the only two ideas of which your social conservatives are capable . . . which have brought this century to disaster."[80]

RONALD REAGAN'S RUN

In 1976 the sixty-five-year-old Reagan made his first serious run for the Republican nomination, leading a Pickett's Charge against the high ground held by an incumbent president. Ford's turn to the right—he deftly pushed Rockefeller out of contention for the vice presidential nomination—did not slow the Reagan campaign, but Barry Goldwater did, saying Ford was as conservative as Reagan and "I don't know why he should be denied the nomination." He defended Ford's efforts to negotiate a treaty with Panama that would relinquish American control over the Panama Canal even though most conservatives scathed Ford for trying to give away the canal and undercutting U.S. pride, sovereignty, and property rights. To the dismay of conservative admirers, Goldwater endorsed Ford six weeks before the convention. "I have been accused of every left-wing situation known to man, from supporting women's lib on through the whole gamut," Goldwater said. Such accusations included charges of alcoholism. "I've been through that Old Crow bit, the whiskey bit, the gin bit," Goldwater admitted, "but I have cut down my drinking drastically this whole year." He questioned whether "the Republican Party will cease to exist as a Party . . . because of the disastrous attitude of the so-called conservatives who say you either do it my way, old boy, or we don't do it all, and that's not my way of living."[81]

Guided by Reagan's former strategist Stuart Spencer, Ford swept the early primaries. Reagan rallied, however, by blasting Ford for tossing away the Panama Canal, failing in his stewardship of the economy, and sleeping while America slipped behind the Soviets in military might. Reagan decried sexual permissiveness, crime, and abortion rights. He said America was "hungry for a spiritual renewal" and that if elected he would "take advantage of every opportunity to stress moral values." Reagan recovered in North Carolina with help from Senator Helms and Tom Ellis, and he then wounded Ford with a string of primary victories. Ford struck back with a Nixon-style attack strategy. "Its purpose, pure and simple, is to present Ronald Reagan as a dangerous warmonger on the Panama Canal and other international issues," Spencer wrote of his former client. "Barry Goldwater has given us an opening a mile wide to exploit the canal issue" while keeping the president "above the negative aspects of this issue." With Goldwater appearing in an ad chastising Reagan on Panama, the president won a crucial primary on home turf in Michigan, and the still-loyal Rockefeller delivered most of the New York delegation. Ford's ads for the California primary warned, "When you vote Tuesday, remember Governor Ronald Reagan couldn't start a war. President Reagan could."[82]

Reagan crushed Ford in California but the president held the lead among convention delegates nationally. With the clock running out, Reagan tried a Hail Mary pass, proposing liberal Republican senator Richard Schweiker of Pennsylvania as his vice presidential nominee. *National Review* effused: "The very boldness of the move constitutes another plus. Reagan showed himself capable of the kind of surprise and imaginative decision not associated with the more plodding Ford." But the play failed and Reagan lost narrowly on the first ballot to Ford.[83]

Delegates pleased the right with a conservative platform, and Ford chose for his running mate a mainstream conservative, Senator Robert Dole of Kansas. Still, Rusher's committee pressed on with plans to capture the presidential nomination of the American Independent Party (AIP), with its guaranteed ballot positions. The ultimate prize, contingent on winning 5 percent of the national vote, was $2 million in federal funds for 1980—a sturdy foundation for the new conservative party. But the American Independent Party repelled the new right raiders. After its keynote speaker condemned "atheistic political Zionism" as "the most insidious, far-reaching murderous force the world has ever known," the AIP nominated eccentric segregationist Lester Maddox, a former governor of Georgia.[84]

A downcast Rusher told the press that the AIP had "turned inward, backward, and downward" with the nomination of Maddox. AIP chairman William K. Shearer, a former leader of the California Citizens Council, responded by turning the new right's populist rhetoric against them. Rusher and Viguerie, he said, represented "the super-educated, highly affluent, country-club people" who thought they were they were "too good to commune with the just-average George Wallace people." Maddox's nomination "dashes our hopes of using this party to build a new conservative coalition," Viguerie admitted. M. Stanton Evans agreed. "For those who affirm the 'new majority' thesis, it's back to the drawing board." More prophetically, James Kilpatrick wrote in his syndicated column, "Bill Rusher's brave band is not yet large in numbers, but its potential for political service is great. They ought to be dwelling in the Republican house, which could yet, with the passage of time, be remodeled to their taste."[85]

The failure of either Maddox or John Birch candidate Tom Anderson to win more than token support in 1976 dashed the far right's hope to reshape politics from within. But its brand survived in the John Birch Society, the Liberty Lobby, the Klan, militias, survivalists, skinheads, and the National Association for the Advancement of White People, formed in 1980 by David Duke, the blow-dried, buttoned-down former grand wizard who urged the Klan to "get out of the cow pasture and into hotel meeting rooms." The Liberty Lobby also expanded during the 1970s when its publication, *Spotlight,* reached a record circulation on the right of some two hundred thousand. In 1978 the lobby promoted Holocaust denial through its publishing house Noontide Press and the Institute for Historical Review, which reiterated earlier far-right claims that Zionists fabricated Hitler's extermination camps to win sympathy for Israel after the war. Some small far-right militia and survivalist groups—such as the Posse Comitatus, Aryan Nations, and The Order—were influenced by the "Christian Identity" movement, which taught that blue-eyed Anglo-Saxons were descendents of Old Testament Israelites and contemporary Jews were imposters who descended from Eve's copulation with Satan or from Asiatic Khazars who converted to Judaism a thousand years after Christ. They anticipated a race war with the Khazar or Satanic Jews leading their black and brown minions against the Anglo-Saxons, a prelude to Christ's return.[86]

The Libertarians in 1976 refused to seek their destiny with the GOP. According to party chair Ed Crane, "For 25 years Conservatives have been competing with their Liberal brethren to harness the power of the state to serve their particular brand of intervention into voluntary human action." The Libertarian candidate for president, Roger MacBride, won only 175,000 votes.[87]

With few achievements, a shaky economy, and the burdens of Watergate, Ford struggled against the born-again Carter. "No one is going to co-opt Carter on God," admitted Ford adviser Mike Duval. Postconvention polls showed Ford ten to twelve points behind Carter, but the race tightened when the economy perked up in 1976 and Carter kept his ideology vague and put little pressure on Ford. In a televised debate on foreign policy, Ford stumbled. Perhaps thinking about recent accords with the Russians, he said, "There is no Soviet domination of Eastern Europe." Still, Gallup's final poll had Ford a point ahead. Carter won the election by two points in the popular vote and fifty-seven Electoral College votes. Otherwise the election registered little change in Congress or state governments.[88]

Carter swept the South with the exception of Virginia. "Blood was thicker than philosophy," Reagan reflected. But despite Carter's born-again appeal, Republicans still owned the white Protestant vote, with 60 percent, compared to 45 percent of Catholics, 29 percent of Jews, and 38 percent of others, according to the National Election Study. As compared to Nixon in 1972, Ford dropped ten to twelve points equally among liberal, moderate, and conservative voters. "Ford almost won it without any southern states except Virginia," Reagan said as he prepared for 1980. "Forgive the South its emotional binge and you have the new majority."[89]

THE REAGAN REVOLUTION, 1977–1984

In June 1980 the Heritage Foundation gambled that conservative Republican Ronald Reagan would defeat President Jimmy Carter in the November election. In anticipation of a Reagan victory, the foundation devoted its resources and personnel to a "Mandate for Leadership" project that prepared a "comprehensive game plan for implementing conservative policy goals under vigorous White House leadership." The gamble paid off. When Reagan won the presidency Heritage delivered to him three thousand pages of the most thorough blueprint in U.S. history for governing from the right. Heritage urged increased military and decreased domestic spending, diminished regulations, and major tax cuts. It called for rewriting the environmental laws, scrapping the Environmental Protection Agency and the Department of Energy, ending affirmative action, restricting the rights of accused criminals, tightening standards for proving civil rights violations, and imposing strong measures to quash domestic dissent. "It is axiomatic that individual liberties are secondary to the requirement of national security and internal civil order," Heritage said. The Heritage report became required reading in the Reagan administration, which adopted many of its recommendations. The report raised the public profile of the Heritage Foundation, created the impression that it guided policy making in the administration, and aided a fund-raising drive that increased its annual budget from $5 million in 1980 to $18 million in 1990.

THE HARD-LINERS ATTACK

The Carter presidency began optimistically. Carter's pollster and big political thinker Pat Caddell wrote that the president would have "new opportunities to shift the partisan balance and take advantage of the 1960s and 1970s" with innovative thinking that "both holds the older parts of the party and captures the growing segments of the overall electorate—the young and the middle class." Surveys from Carter's first four months showed that the public overwhelmingly backed national health insurance, rebuilding programs for the cities, more federal spending on mass transit, stringent environment laws, and government jobs programs over tax cuts.[1]

Still, as a procedural rather than a substantive liberal, Carter declined to resume the reform missions of Franklin Roosevelt and Lyndon Johnson. Domestically, Carter viewed the presidency as a clean-up operation to reorganize and upgrade the bureaucracy, make welfare more efficient, reform the tax system, and restore honesty to government. His loftiest aspiration was energy independence, but his means fell short of the dream. Despite his evangelical faith, Carter for the most part followed a conventional Democratic Party line on social issues and did not forge relationships with politically conservative evangelicals. But in a break from Cold War orthodoxy, Carter's faith reinforced a commitment to human rights and democracy worldwide, even in American-backed regimes such as Chile, Nicaragua, Taiwan, and South Korea. He sought to make America after the Vietnam War years a moral exemplar again for the world. Carter also intended to contain Soviet expansion while continuing to pursue arms control, détente, and economic relationships with the Soviets. It was policy that left the president open to attack from hard-liners who dismissed Carter's "soft" policies and remained convinced that only conservatives could guide the United States to victory in the Cold War.

During the Carter years, the right relentlessly critiqued the administration for allegedly capitulating to communists, mismanaging the economy, and degrading the culture. In the months between the 1976 election and Carter's inauguration, conservatives laid a foundation for challenging the president-elect's approach to national security. The CIA's director George H. W. Bush led the way by assembling a so-called Team B late in the Ford term to reevaluate CIA estimates of Soviet military capabilities and intentions. Even as other analysts told of an inefficient, collapsing Soviet system, Team B, working deductively from their view of Soviet history and intentions, uncovered a communist Goliath, more fearsome and aggressive than anything that even an alarmist CIA had contemplated.

Few analysts believed that the gray old men of the Kremlin would consider high-stakes nuclear blackmail or a suicidal first strike against the

United States. Even so, as Senator Arthur Vandenberg had told President Truman in 1947, we had to "scare them to death." Team B member General George Keegan, former head of the Defense Intelligence Agency, leaked his interpretation of the group's grim findings ten days before inauguration day. "I am unaware of a single important [strategic] category in which the Soviets have not established a significant lead over the United States." The Soviets believed "they could survive a nuclear war and win it." The outgoing secretary of defense Donald H. Rumsfeld added that the Soviet Union was "engaged in a serious, steady, and sustained effort which, in the absence of a U.S. response, could make it the dominant military power in the world." Critics, however, noted the several false alarms about Soviet superiority since the bogus "missile gap" of the 1950s. Former deputy director of the CIA Herbert Scoville Jr. still remembered "when Maj.—not then Maj. Gen.—Keegan was giving the briefings that by 1960 we would be second-rate to the Soviet Union."[2]

At the final meeting of President Ford's National Security Council in mid-January 1977, Bush said, "The [Team B] competitive analysis idea seemed good at the time and I certainly did not think it would go public. But now I feel I have been had. A former general officer has gone public, even before the experiment is finished. I have to recommend that the approach not be institutionalized." Ford responded, "The most discouraging aspect is the character of the people who leaked. Unforgivable." Kissinger gave voice to the dirty little secret of ideologically driven analysis: "I could find a board of Nobel Prize winners to construct any alternative analysis conceivable."[3]

Still, Team B members pressed on through the Committee on the Present Danger (CPD), which was a revived version of a group that eastern internationalists had initially founded in 1950 to support the anticommunist program of NSC-68. The new CPD united labor, multinational industry and finance, and domestically oriented firms and entrepreneurs. It brought together neoconservatives and hawkish Democrats from the Committee for a Democratic Majority with Republican conservatives such as W. Glen Campbell, Richard Mellon Scaife, and former Nixon official William J. Casey. The CPD's founding directors represented the AFL-CIO, affiliated unions, and major corporations such as Citibank, Time Inc., Olin Corporation, Caterpillar Tractor, Allied Chemical, Goldman, Sachs & Co., Hewlett-Packard, and Paraffin Oil. Armed with Team B findings, the CPD led the chorus against Carter's flaccid approach to the Cold War, which it said was epitomized by his nomination of the dovish Paul Warnke as America's negotiator on arms control.[4]

In 1977, however, the major conservative attack against the Carter administration struck closer to home when critics on the right charged that he undercut American security and sovereignty by negotiating treaties with Panamanian strongman Omar Torrijos that would cede the canal to Panama in 2000. "We plan something [on the canal] which is larger than anything that's been done before outside the major two parties," Richard Viguerie said. The American Conservative Union organized an Emergency Coalition to Save the Canal, which aired an antitreaty film on more than two hundred regional television stations and sent out two million letters under Senator Thurmond's signature. The Conservative Caucus also mailed out millions of letters and organized "Keep Our Canal" days and "Day of Infamy" marches.[5]

Patriotic and veterans' groups denounced the treaty, and a Republican "truth squad" on the canal shadowed administration officials. "We are going to look after American interests first," promised Republican senator Jake Garn of Utah. If other nations "don't like it, that's just too damn bad." Some on the right found the hidden hand of international financiers in the treaties. Phil Nicolaides, the campaign manager for Conservative Party Senate candidate James Buckley in 1970, wrote, "These are 'Establishment Treaties' par excellence. Big Government. Big Banks. Big Labor." Phyllis Schlafly pointed to "the power and prestige of the hidden backers of the treaties, namely, the giant international banks," which knew that their loans were "uncollectible unless Torrijos takes control of the U.S. Canal." Overall, opponents of the canal treaties outspent proponents by about five to one, energized the right, and persuaded most Americans to oppose the accords. Still, the treaties squeaked through the Senate by a single vote in the spring of 1978.[6]

Reagan reentered the Panama Canal debate but shunned the invective he had leveled against Ford. The toned-down Reagan led some conservatives to worry that this flexible politician, with his mixed conservative record as governor of California, was "soft" or "squishy" on the issues. In a 1978 article in the *Right Report,* conservative youth leader Morton Blackwell accurately took the measure of Reagan and the politics of the times. He predicted that Reagan would "sweep the nomination" and could even "be favored to win election. [He] would not, however, be what many conservative expect and liberals fear." Blackwell continued:

> Even for a consummate organizer, the job of totally reversing the course of the Federal government, even from the presidency, would take many years. And Reagan is not the consummate organizer. He's the best spokesman conservatives have, but no one is given all talents. Judged on the basis of his two terms as governor, President Reagan should not be expected to purge all the liberals from the bureaucracy. His programs would not zip through the Democrat-controlled Congress. He would not build the GOP into a mighty, permanently dominant power.[7]

The president's support for the SALT II treaty to equalize and reduce nuclear missiles and bombers opened another line of attack for conservatives. Paul Nitze, CPD spokesman and author of NSC-68, charged in 1977 that SALT II left America "locked into inferiority." A year later the CPD warned of a dire "window of vulnerability" because "Soviet strategic superiority will soon become a visible and unacceptable reality unless we move promptly to increase the survivability and effectiveness of our strategic forces." It said that America must respond by rejecting SALT II, massively expanding and upgrading its military, and plunging into a crash program of civil defense. To discredit a popular treaty, critics of SALT II outspent proponents fifteen to one. The funding was led by the Scaife foundations, which funneled more than $300,000 into the CPD. Carter withdrew the treaty from ratification when the Soviets invaded Afghanistan in late 1979.[8]

The CPD was a member of the Coalition for Peace Through Strength, which the American Security Council (ASC) organized in 1978. Other coalition members included the American Conservative Union, the American Legion, and Young Americans for Freedom, as well as about 140 members of Congress. ASC formed the coalition to combat America's "unilateral disarmament trend" and use "positive non-military means to rollback the growth of Communism." The council had been analyzing the international strategic balance since the early 1960s with results that closely tracked domestic politics. In 1962, ASC had assured Americans, "*The most significant development in the cold war is the unexpected weakness of Russia's strategic striking force.* The missile gap has been found to exist, but overwhelmingly in favor of the United States." America needed to "use our present advantage to *win* the cold war." In 1964, it issued guidelines for victory. In 1967, with the American military under pressure from critics of the Vietnam War, ASC abruptly reversed course, saying that "the preponderance of evidence points to the conclusion that the Soviet Union is succeeding in its massive drive toward strategic military superiority." It argued that "1967 falls in a crossover period" when a "megaton gap" was opening in favor of the Soviets—a decade before the CPD warned of a "window of vulnerability" for the United States.[9]

Another elite group, the Trilateral Commission, took a different approach to the world by working to integrate the three power centers of North America, Europe, and Japan. David Rockefeller, Nelson's banker brother, broached the idea for the commission at a meeting of the American Steering Committee of the secretive Bilderberg Group of international businessmen. The Trilateralists sought cooperation among industrialized nations, the upgrading of third-world economies, and not the conquest of communists but their seduction into the capitalist world system through arms control, trade, investments, and cultural exchange.

Willis Carto's Liberty Lobby scorned the Trilateral Commission as part of the cabal for a new world order. Carter, in this view, was a new Holy Roman emperor, a figurehead for the Trilateralists, who included Vice President Walter Mondale, Secretary of State Cyrus Vance, Defense Secretary Harold Brown, Treasury Secretary W. Michael Blumenthal, Federal Reserve chair Paul Volcker, and National Security Adviser Zbigniew Brzezinski—the new Kissinger. The mainstream right also viewed the conciliatory commission suspiciously as another effort to promote a form of "one-world government." But the Trilateralists' cooperative approach could not prevail against Paul Reveres crying that the Russians were coming.

AN ADMINISTRATION UNDER SIEGE

President Carter scored modest achievements in his first two years. He won the creation of a Department of Energy and legislation to keep Social Security solvent. He brokered the Camp David Accords, which provided for Israeli withdrawal from Egyptian territory captured in the 1967 war, established diplomatic relations between Egypt and Israel, and opened negotiations on Palestinian rights. He presided over an improved economy that followed the mid-decade recession and suffered only modest midterm losses of eleven House seats, three Senate seats, and six governorships in 1978. Democrats continued to control both houses of Congress. Following the midterms, Republicans began an early "vote Republican—for a change" advertising blitz as well as new programs to recruit and train congressional candidates for the 1980 elections. The Republican National Committee, which raked in far more money than its Democratic counterpart, reserved $5 million for state legislative races, which the national Democrats ignored. Robert Bauman, chair of the American Conservative Union, waged guerrilla warfare in the House by raising parliamentary points of order, forcing floor votes, and making after-hours speeches to political junkies watching on C-SPAN. Created by the cable industry in 1979 as a nonprofit corporation for public affairs programming, C-SPAN provided gavel-to-gavel coverage of the House. Bauman's rise up the House ladder, however, ended abruptly in 1980 when he was arrested for soliciting sex from a sixteen-year-old boy.[10]

A troubled final two years for the president began with the return of stagflation in 1979; economic growth slowed and inflation and unemployment rose. Fundamental changes were ripping through the American economy and workplace. In the new era, flexible work systems and collaborative team efforts began to replace repetitive mass production. New information technologies guided production and service, and finance supplanted manufacturing in the economy, which led to declining demand for unskilled workers and to a loss of stable, long-term jobs in industries such as steel and automobiles. After rising for decades, average real wages began a fifteen-year decline in 1979. Unions faced new pressures from hard-pressed employers and the gap between the rich and everyone else began to expand for the first time since the 1920s. With families needing two paychecks, the percentage of married women in the labor force passed 50 percent. Debt to foreign corporations and central banks began piling up and federal budget deficits climbed to peacetime records. Once the world's mighty creditor, America was on its way to becoming its most burdened debtor.

In the new economy, huge multinational companies operated seamlessly on several continents. Trade expanded and American finance capital flowed worldwide through private and public investment houses, hedge and pension funds, mutual funds, and savings and loan institutions. U.S. exports rose from $66 billion in 1970 to $1.1 trillion in 2000 and imports from $60 billion to $1.4 trillion, reversing the trade balance from slightly positive to decisively negative. The mean world *daily* turnover in foreign exchange trading exploded from under $15 billion in 1980 to $1.2 trillion in 2000.

Conservatives in the new era challenged the Keynesian idea of managing the economy by adjusting consumer demand for goods and services. Instead, they looked to increase the incentive to invest, work, and save by easing taxes and regulations. If free to innovate without penalty or control, entrepreneurs would create a new era of American abundance. They would produce enough goods and services to cure inflation, accelerate the growth of government revenue, and reduce the deficit.

These chamber of commerce notions from the 1930s sounded fresh after forty years of economic direction by liberals. Conservatives put a positive spin on their old ideas by labeling them "supply-side economics," an idea popularized by charismatic economist Arthur Laffer's famous Laffer curve, which purported to show a positive relationship between tax cuts and revenue. As the rich became richer, supply-side advocates said, their bonanza would flow down—or "trickle down," as critics charged—to the lower strata because employment and wages would grow. Like the televangelists, Laffer promised painless salvation. Americans could have it all: low taxes, balanced budgets, and a healthy growing economy. Promoters of supply-side economics included the *Wall Street Journal,* the *Public Interest,* and journalist Jude Wanniski who wrote a best-selling book on the topic (*The Way the World Works*), and proposed the "Two Santa Claus Theory," which states that Republicans must become the tax-cutting Santa Claus to counter Democrats' big-spending Santa Claus. Conservatives in the 1970s also drew upon a burgeoning scholarly literature to craft a more detailed economic critique of taxes and regulation than in earlier years. Economist Milton Friedman reached a large popular audience with his 1980 book and television series, *Free to Choose.*[11]

In 1975 Opinion Research Corporation had told its clients that "business and other institutions have dropped remarkably in public esteem in recent years." Corporations and business associations responded by expanding their political activities. This new activism was undertaken by many of the nation's leading publicly trading corporations, not just entrepreneurs and heads of family firms. Contributions to congressional candidates by corporate Political Action Committees rose from less than $5 million in 1974 to $19 million in 1980. Corporate PACs backed incumbents of both parties. But when corporations looked to decide elections rather than win favor with officeholders, their PAC contributions decidedly favored Republicans. Contributions by individual executives and so-called soft money contributions for party building and get-out-the-vote campaigns complemented PAC spending.[12]

Direct advocacy and lobbying by business also expanded in the mid-to late 1970s. Corporations spent $140 million on image and advocacy ads in 1976. Some five hundred corporations had Washington offices by 1978, quadrupling their representation from a decade earlier. Industry groups increased their contributions to trade associations and business elites dominated the boards of conservative think tanks. The National Association of Manufacturers moved its headquarters from New York to Washington in 1973 and established a major lobbying operation. In 1972, for the first time, CEOs of large enterprises formed their own lobbying group, the Business Roundtable. By 1975 the Roundtable had signed up more than 150 major corporate CEOs, including the heads of sixty-three of America's top one hundred industrial firms; these executives lobbied personally, mobilized company resources, and provided expert testimony to Congress. The Roundtable spent $1.2 million on ads in *Reader's Digest* to polish the image of business. It united behind issues of common interest to enterprise and avoided internal conflict. According to chair Irving Shapiro, also the chair of Du Pont, the Roundtable followed the strategy of opinion engineering to "make our case in terms of the public interest and resist the temptation to focus on a narrower concept labeled 'business interests.'"[13]

Small businesses lobbied aggressively as well. By the late 1970s the feisty National Federation of Independent Business (NFIB), which began modestly in 1943, had expanded to claim some half a million members. Its lobbyist John Motley bragged that the NFIB could activate "local auto dealers, local accountants and dry cleaners, hardware dealers, dairymen—Kiwanians, Lions, church people." It could "tell a Congressman, 'we've got 600 members in your district.'" A revived U.S. Chamber of Commerce represented twenty-five hundred local affiliates, thirteen hundred professional and trade associations, and sixty-eight thousand member companies. Its publications reached several million readers, including its

Washington Report weekly newsletter and its bimonthly report on opportunities for small businesses. President Richard Lesher, a tireless advocate, worked through six regional offices and a Washington headquarters to target "key resource people" with ties to policy makers. In 1975 the National Right to Work Committee led the campaign that had persuaded President Ford to veto legislation that authorized workers to picket an entire construction site in a dispute with a single employer. The committee spent some $800,000 to generate more than seven hundred thousand letters and postcards to the White House. In 1975 the committee had three hundred thousand dues-paying members and spent $4.5 million. Large and small business lobbies rose again in the early Carter years to block legislation for a Consumer Protection Agency and a package of pro-union reforms, and to secure reductions in the capital gains tax and an investment tax credit. Lawyers for corporate managers and major financial institutions also lobbied for the 1978 bankruptcy reforms that shielded corporations from financial losses and gave large creditors leverage over small holders of debt.[14]

There was little trace of liberalism in the new business activism of the 1970s. Rather, leaders of enterprise pushed American politics to the right. Big and small business usually united in backing subsidies and deregulation; restrictions on labor organizing and liability lawsuits; and business tax breaks. They opposed most welfare spending; consumer protection laws; environmental, health and safety regulations; conservation requirements; expanded federal health care benefits; tightened public control over private pension and benefit plans; and federal regulations on the membership of corporate boards. Rarely did business interests compete against one another in their backing for candidates.[15]

Business mobilization reached state governments, which assumed increased responsibility for economic development in the late twentieth century. Top-level business associations and lobbies and Republican officials united behind state programs to coinvest in private enterprise and promote economic development through subsidies and tax breaks. The movement for tax reduction first gained momentum in the states. An anti-tax movement led by the National Tax Limitation Committee and the National Taxpayer's Union stunned America in 1978 when 65 percent of voters in California ratified Proposition 13, which slashed property taxes and limited future rate hikes. Proposition 13 made celebrities of its elderly sponsors, Howard Jarvis, age seventy-five, and Paul Gann, age sixty-five.

Jarvis heralded "a new revolution," saying, "The people is [sic] going to run the government and the government is not going to run the people." Although antitax sentiment did not sweep the nation, about a dozen states enacted some variant of tax or spending limits. The 1970s tax revolt underscored the intensely local and personal impact of the decade's high inflation and sluggish growth. During the Great Depression, home assessments fell less rapidly than income, raising the real costs of property taxes. During the stagflation of the 1970s, home assessments rose more rapidly than income, with the same net effect on taxpayers.[16]

Conservatives offering to lighten tax burdens, not liberals proposing progressive tax reforms or burden shifting to business, set the course for policy debates. In Congress, two Republicans, Representative Jack Kemp of New York and Senator William Roth of Delaware, sponsored once unthinkable legislation to slash federal income taxes by 30 percent. Reagan, who backed Proposition 13 and supply-side economics, called the Kemp-Roth act a "replica of the Kennedy tax cut of 1964." Conservative think tanks and business lobbies backed income tax cuts, with sweeteners like increased depreciation for capital investments. The Democratic Party derided Kemp-Roth as "the Guaranteed Inflation and Increased Budget Deficits Act," but offered no compelling alternative.[17]

Under pressure from economic distress, foreign setbacks, and conservative critics, Carter shifted to the right in his last two years. Although the president secured new energy initiatives and environmental laws, a Department of Education, and limited reorganization of the civil service, he failed to reform taxes or welfare, revise labor laws, reshape the bureaucracy, or achieve energy independence for the United States. However, he began the deregulation of such industries as trucking, airlines, railroads, and banking. In a reprise of action taken by prior Republican administrations to rescue Lockheed Corporation and New York City, the Carter administration bailed out the troubled Chrysler Corporation, partly in return for concessions by the United Auto Workers union. In 1979 Carter's new Federal Reserve chair Paul Volcker, with cheers from much of business, put the economy into a cold bath by raising interest rates to fight inflation, increase the value of the dollar, and break the linkage between rising debt and inflation. "I have yet to meet a businessman who is not supportive of these moves," said Reginald H. Jones, chairman of General Electric and a member of the Business Council's executive committee, which unanimously endorsed Volcker's initiatives. Tight money policies, however, won no plaudits from labor, which preferred wage and price controls to what it saw as job-killing monetary policy.[18]

In 1979 America experienced an eerie replay of the foreign setbacks that hardened Cold War policy thirty years before. Under Carter, the challenges came from an Islamic revolution in Iran, the triumph of left-wing Sandinistas in Nicaragua, the fall of the Caribbean island of Grenada to a pro-Cuban insurgency, and the Soviet invasion of Afghanistan. In response, the president expanded defense spending by nearly a third in the second half of his presidency and warned against attempts by foreign powers to control the oil-rich Persian Gulf region. He authorized development of a new missile system, called the MX, which had multiple warheads and the capacity to destroy hardened Soviet missile sites. He shelved SALT II and sanctioned the Soviets by embargoing grain and boycotting the 1980 Moscow Olympics. The president also put aside his human rights scruples to forestall a Marxist revolution in El Salvador by aiding a repressive government tied to military death squads that had killed thousands of civilians, including four American churchwomen.

In foreign as in domestic policy, Carter's initiatives seemed inadequate to the challenges he faced. In November 1979 Iranian radicals seized the American embassy in Tehran and took sixty-six Americans hostage. Neither the breaking of diplomatic relations with Iran nor the imposition of economic sanctions moved the Iranian government to release the hostages; fifty-two Americans remained in Iranian custody in 1980. After a botched rescue effort in April, America seemed to be a hapless Gulliver, tied and tethered by Lilliputians of the less developed world.

THE NEWEST CHRISTIAN RIGHT

Evangelical political action boomed under the first born-again Christian elected to the presidency. Carter openly professed his piety and set a precedent for statements of personal faith by Ronald Reagan, Bill Clinton, and George W. Bush. But piety is not policy and Carter repulsed politically conservative evangelicals by strictly separating church and state and following a standard Democratic line on abortion, pornography, the ERA, and gay rights. And his IRS toughened regulations that denied tax exemptions to allegedly racially discriminatory private schools, many of them

Christian academies. These transgressions inspired the revival of evangelical political action pioneered by numerous organizations in earlier decades. The Christian right of the 1970s, however, differed from its ancestors in its overt partisanship on behalf of the Republican Party and its candidates.

The newest Christian right emerged from preexisting groups. After Abraham Vereide's death in 1969, his deputy Douglas Coe assumed control of Vereide's International Christian Leadership, which sponsored the National Prayer Breakfast and prayer groups worldwide. Coe reorganized the group as the secretive Fellowship Foundation, informally known as "the Family," expanded its branches worldwide, and tapped wealthy businessmen, the Lilly Foundation, and the Pew Charitable Trusts for the funds that raised its yearly budget from about $400,000 in 1971 to $1.3 million in 1977. The Family sponsored prayer groups in business trade associations, civic organizations, and colleges and universities. But its most significant presence was within government itself. The Family established private prayer groups in the judiciary, the military, Congress, state legislatures, and the agencies and departments of the federal, state, and local governments. It cosponsored prayer breakfasts with the president of the United States, members of the U.S. House and Senate, governors, mayors, and state legislators. And it conducted informal diplomacy through contacts with high officials abroad and travel by members of Congress associated with the Family. Coe led a growing movement through the first decade of the twenty-first century, when its annual budget reached $10 million. Over the course of eight decades the Fellowship Foundation created a male-dominated insider's world of power and influence open exclusively to those who professed their dedication to Christ. Without either fanfare or controversy, the Fellowship had come closer than any other movement in modern U.S. history to establishing Christianity as an official American religion.[19]

In 1974 John Conlan, GOP Representative from Arizona and a member of Coe's Family, persuaded Southern Baptist Edward McAteer, a board member of the evangelical Wycliffe Bible Translators and the marketing manager for the Colgate-Palmolive Company, to assume the leadership of the Christian Freedom Foundation's Washington office. The goal of McAteer and other new right leaders was to activate white evangelical Protestants, who represented perhaps 25 percent of voters. "The next real major area of growth for the conservative ideology and philosophy is among evangelical people," Richard Viguerie said in 1976.[20]

In 1979 McAteer and several new right leaders persuaded the Reverend Jerry Falwell to launch a new group, the Moral Majority, to unite "the vast majority of Americans against 'humanism.'" Falwell led the Thomas Road Baptist Church in Lynchburg, Virginia, founded Lynchburg Baptist College (later Liberty University), and gained national fame by hosting the television ministry *Old Time Gospel Hour*. Falwell, Jimmy Swaggart, James Robison, Rex Humbard, Oral Roberts, Jim Bakker, Pat Robertson, and other evangelical pastors built nationwide followings through TV ministries that delivered simple gospel messages and fund-raising appeals. Robertson quipped that of some 1.4 million calls to his *700 Club*, "not one caller asked about the theology of Karl Barth, Reinhold Niebuhr or Paul Tillich."[21]

Many of the televangelists, notably Falwell, Robertson, and Robison, mixed revivalism with conservative messages on communism, abortion, homosexuality, apartheid, feminism, and national defense. Four networks with national distribution—Robertson's Christian Broadcasting Network (CBN), Bakker's Praise the Lord (PTL), Trinity Broadcasting in California, and the National Christian Network in Florida—led the boom in religious broadcasting. Membership in the National Religious Broadcasters soared from about a hundred in 1965 to some nine hundred in 1979. Religious programs that year accounted for approximately 10 percent of all TV broadcasting, and televangelists raised hundreds of millions of dollars annually.

Falwell and the Moral Majority's executive director Robert Billings—who joined the Reagan campaign in 1980—raised about $1.5 million in start-up funds and claimed two million members across the nation during the 1980 campaign. Although Falwell professed to have raised an eclectic army of "cobelligerents" including Catholics and Jews, studies showed that 90 percent of his state leaders were Baptist ministers, mostly recruited through the Baptist Bible Fellowship, a fundamentalist group formed in 1950. Like Billy Graham and J. Howard Pew, Falwell grasped the symbiosis between conservatism in religion and politics. Although his Moral Majority was not a political action committee authorized to endorse candidates, Falwell broke new ground by pushing ministers to register voters, turn them out at the polls, and steer them to the right party and candidates. "What can you do from the pulpit?" Falwell asked. "You can register people to vote. You can explain the issues to them. And you can endorse candidates, right there in the church on Sunday morning." Individual pastors as opposed to tax-exempt churches, he said, could make such endorsements. Falwell reiterated these points in his monthly *Moral Majority Report*, which instructed people of faith on how to influence politics.[22]

Other Christian right vessels sailed with the Moral Majority. The Christian Voice, founded a year before the Moral Majority, established a political action committee, headed by Gary Jarmin—formerly of the Unification Church—that rated members of Congress according to a sixteen-point "moral report card." The Christian Voice set up Christians for Reagan, which harried President Carter for "turning his back on God." The National Christian Action Coalition also formed a political action committee in 1979, which circulated a similar "Family Issues Voting Index." In 1979 Edward McAteer founded the Religious Roundtable, modeled on the Business Roundtable, with preacher James Robison as its public face and a fifty-six-member advisory board (equal to the number of patriots who signed the Declaration of Independence) that included representatives of the Campus Crusade for Christ, the National Religious Broadcasters Association, the National Association of Evangelicals, and several new right organizations. In August 1980 the Religious Roundtable sponsored a National Affairs Briefing in Reverend Robison's home city of Dallas that attracted some fifteen thousand participants, seven thousand of whom were ministers. Its star speaker, Republican presidential nominee Ronald Reagan, urged the teaching of creationism and told the cheering crowd, "I know you can't endorse me because this is a non-partisan meeting, but I endorse you." Robison said, "I am sick and tired of hearing about all the radicals and the perverts and the liberals and the leftists and the Communists coming out of the closet. It's time for God's people to come out of the closet, out of the churches and change America." Reagan agreed. "Religious America is awakening," he said, "perhaps just in time for our country's sake."[23]

The divorced and remarried Ronald Reagan, who rarely saw the inside of a church or spent time with his children, looked the Christian faithful in the eye, said the right lines, and became one of them. As former Nixon speechwriter and *New York Times* columnist William Safire later wrote: "Being *in* the right and being *on* the right may be satisfying, but only by being *of* the right can a Republican get ahead on the national scene." Was Reagan sincere in his pledges to the Christian right? Reagan had said in 1978, "One thing I learned as an actor: you can't come over on the camera unless you really believe the lines you're speaking."[24]

Two organizations created with little public attention in the 1970s had a more enduring impact than the heralded Christian right groups of the time. In 1974 D. James Kennedy, the pastor of the mammoth Coral Ridge Presbyterian "mega-church" church in Fort Lauderdale, Florida, founded his nationwide Coral Ridge Ministries, which included a weekly television program, *The Coral Ridge Hour,* which eventually gained an audience of three and a half million viewers, and a daily radio program, *Truths That Transform,* which came to be broadcast on four hundred stations. Kennedy was explicit in combining his spiritual message with conservative views on abortion, pornography, homosexuality, evolution, anticommunism, and the need to infuse Christianity into government. Focus on the Family, quietly founded in 1977 by James Dobson, would become more influential than the Coral Ridge Ministries. A PhD psychologist trained in child-rearing, Dobson formed his tax-exempt organization "to cooperate with the Holy Spirit in disseminating the Gospel of Jesus Christ to as many people as possible, and, specifically, to accomplish that objective by helping to preserve traditional values and the institution of the family." Dobson pledged fidelity to "the Creator Himself, who ordained the family and gave it His blessing." Focus gathered its flock through dispensing advice on love, marriage, addiction, child-rearing, adoption, education, careers, and spiritual health. Not until the 1980s would Dobson turn explicitly to politics.[25]

With women's activism among conservatives still largely confined to single-sex groups, the Christian right group Concerned Women for America (CWA), founded in 1979 by Beverly LaHaye, Tim's spouse, overtook the Eagle Forum as the leading membership organization for conservative women. LaHaye organized CWA to offset the National Organization for Women, which she said represented "radical women." CWA recruited white evangelical Protestant women "to protect and promote Biblical values among all citizens—first through prayer, then education, and finally by influencing our society—thereby reversing the decline in moral values in our nation." Like the Minute Women of the 1940s, CWA relied on small, loosely organized groups of women, in this case spiritually engaged "prayer circles" of women that met "around the kitchen table." LaHaye also activated her network through top-down messages and instructions for political action, which ranged from letters and calls to congressmen to boycotts against smut in libraries.

Scholars have pointed to the formation of Christian right groups in the late 1970s as the political awakening of evangelicals after half a century of slumber. This interpretation is true only if we erase all memory of Spiritual Mobilization, the Church League of America, the American Council of Christian Churches, the Christian Freedom Foundation, the Christian Business Men's Association, the National Association of Evangelicals, the National Religious Broadcasters, Youth for Christ, the Campus Crusade for Christ, the Christian Crusade, Wycliffe Bible Translators, International Christian Leadership, and the Christian Anti-Communism Crusade. It is true only if we ignore such figures as James Fifield, Abraham Vereide, J. Howard Pew, Howard Kershner, John R. Rice, R. G. LeTourneau, Carl McIntire, Gerald L. K. Smith, Harold John Ockenga, Carl F. H. Henry, Billy Graham, William Cameron Townsend, Edgar Bundy, George Benson, Billy James Hargis, Fred Schwarz, and Douglas Coe.

America's Catholic hierarchy continued to shun partisan politics in the 1970s. The U.S. Catholic Conference warned against forming "a religious voting bloc" in the name of the church or "endorsing candidates." However, in 1980, Archbishop Cardinal Humberto Medeiros of Boston urged voters to "save our children, born and unborn," and reject politicians "who make abortions possible by law." The cardinal was implicitly targeting Barney Frank and James Shannon, pro-choice Democratic primary candidates facing antiabortion rivals in heavily Catholic congressional districts in the Boston area. "Cardinal Medeiros has joined the Moral Majority," Howard Phillips exulted. The cardinal "gives legitimacy to the whole process," Richard Viguerie added. But both Frank and Shannon won their primaries.[26]

In the 1970s, as in earlier years, some evangelical Protestants, despite their conservative political views, continued to fret over mixing religion and politics. In 1980 Pat Robertson resigned from the Religious Roundtable, citing "confusion in the public mind as to my role in political matters." He said, "No politician or group of politicians have the ability to solve the problems of the world." Jimmy Swaggart warned, "Legislation and new faces in office won't solve our real problems. From the beginning of time, changing the heart of man has been the only answer." Weyrich responded that good Christians had to counter the influence of humanist politicians who were "attempting to prevent souls from reaching eternal salvation."[27]

Like earlier Christian conservative groups, such organizations of the 1970s extended their moral vision to a broad range of issues, including economics, defense, and foreign policy. "The free enterprise system is clearly outlined in the Book of Proverbs of the Bible," Falwell said, echoing Carl McIntire of the American Council of Christian Churches. Candidates scored points on the Christian right's moral score cards by opposing SALT II, busing for integrating schools, "forced unionization" of teachers, and sanctions against the white settler government of Rhodesia. They scored points by supporting a federal balanced budget amendment, tax cuts, aid to Taiwan, and Jewish control of Israel. Support for Israel among evangelicals striving to win the world for Christ was grounded in a premillennial theology in which Jewish control over Israel was a precondition for the final clash between good and evil and the final judgment of Christ. Ironically, Jews who failed to convert to Christianity would be among those cast into hell.[28]

The teachings of theologian Francis Schaeffer, a former protégé of Carl McIntire, inspired Christian activists. Schaeffer's books and charismatic lectures decried the tragedy of modern "man-centered" life that turned the world into a machine and man into an interchangeable part, without meaning or grace. Christians must refute the humanists who "have polluted all aspects of morality, making standards completely hedonistic and relativistic." Schaeffer made old-time religion intellectually vibrant by offering biblically based critiques of the films of Ingmar Bergman, the art of Salvador Dalí, the science of Einstein, and the music of the Beatles. In 1979 Schaeffer and pediatric surgeon C. Everett Koop, later President Reagan's surgeon general, conducted antiabortion seminars in twenty cities and cowrote a companion book and film, *Whatever Happened to the Human Race*. Abortion, they said, devalued human life and sent mankind down a slippery slope to infanticide and euthanasia. If doctrinally rigid, Schaeffer was tactically flexible, introducing Falwell to the idea of cobelligerence among people of different faiths but common morals. In 1980 the Reverend Tim LaHaye wrote a popular version of the theologian's thought, *The Battle for the Mind*. LaHaye became a mentor of the Christian right and coauthored the "Left Behind" series about the end times on earth that sold in the tens of millions. In 2001 the *Evangelical Studies Bulletin* named LaHaye the most influential Christian leader of the last quarter of the twentieth century.[29]

A movement known as Christian Reconstruction or Dominion Theology, led by Rousas John Rushdoony of the Chalcedon Foundation, Gary North of the Institute for Christian Economics, and John Whitehead of the Rutherford Institute, extended Schaeffer's absolutist thinking. Dominion leaders aimed to make America a Christian nation. They desired to "take back government from the state and put it in the hands of Christians." This meant replacing secular "self-law" with "God's law," which meted out harsh punishments, including the death penalty for adulterers and homosexuals. Eventually, Dominion Theology would "occupy the whole world," subjecting all humanity to theocratic authority. Although the Christian Reconstruction movement clung to the outer margins of politics, it was richly funded by billionaire California banker Howard F. Ahmanson Jr. and its ideas influenced key figures on the Christian right.[30]

Analysts struggled to gauge the scope of an amorphous movement like the Christian right, with 1980s estimates ranging from 5 percent to 30 percent of voters. Studies showed that the Christian right consisted mainly of white evangelical Protestants and secondarily of devout white Catholics. Its followers were not downwardly mobile or notably less affluent than other Americans, despite lower educational levels.[31]

In 1979 the Republican senator Paul Laxalt of Nevada distilled a conservative Christian agenda into a "Family Protection Act," drafted mainly by Connaught "Connie" Marshner of the Free Congress Foundation. The bill proposed using federal funds as a lever for compelling states to adopt policies that supported traditional moral standards. A national Conference on the Family that President Carter called in 1980 to make recommendations on strengthening the family offered a different vision that outraged anti-pluralist Christians. The conference, which conservatives said Carter had stacked with liberals, refused to privilege heterosexual families and endorsed abortion rights, the ERA, and national health insurance. Conservative delegates walked out in protest. President Carter, who backed his party's social agenda, put a low priority on reconciliation with the Christian right. "The evangelicals had not been welcomed into the Carter administration as they had hoped," Pat Robertson said. Tim LaHaye called Carter either a "Christian who is naive about humanism [or] a humanist who masqueraded as a Christian to get elected and then showed his contempt for the 60 million 'born agains' by excluding them from his government."[32]

Critics charged the Christian right with violating the norms that held a pluralist society together: toleration of contrary views and disparate cultures and restraint in imposing personal morality on others. But anti-pluralist dynamism came precisely from insisting upon a single eternal truth that led people through earthly life and guided them to heaven. Liberal evangelicals such as Jimmy Carter and the editors of the journal *Sojourner* drew other lessons from scripture, but the din of marching Christian soldiers drowned out their voices.

REAGAN RETURNS

Despite misgivings about his age and conciliatory tendencies, the right sprinted to the finish in 1980 behind the sixty-nine-year-old Reagan, who started a furlong ahead of his competitors, with backing from 45 percent of Republicans, according to a New York Times/CBS poll in January. Reagan's pursuers included Senator Howard Baker of Tennessee with 11 percent, John Connally with 10 percent, George Bush with 6 percent, and Senator Dole with 5 percent. Illinois Representative John Anderson, who waved the tattered banner of Rockefeller Republicanism, stood at 2 percent. Reagan's strongest rival, former president Gerald Ford, chose not to run in 1980. Although Bush won the Iowa caucuses, Reagan took the New Hampshire primary and swept most of the remaining contests. All of Reagan's opponents withdrew, though Anderson ran as an independent, prompting a worried Carter team to attack his allegedly right-wing voting record.[33]

A *Washington Post* survey showed that Republican Convention delegates in 1980 formed a cohesive conservative bloc, with only 17 percent identifying as moderate to liberal. The convention adopted a conservative platform that dropped the party's long-standing endorsement of the Equal Rights Amendment and unequivocally backed a constitutional amendment to outlaw abortion, overriding the rights of states to set their own policies. Unlike Goldwater, Reagan pursued party unity by negotiating with Ford for second place on the ticket. But the former president asked for authority as vice president that no president could accept. Reagan then turned to his primary foe, George Bush—a member of the Trilateral

Commission who backed the ERA, ridiculed Reagan's budget proposals as "voodoo economics," and opposed banning abortions. The adaptable Bush, however, pledged full support for Reagan's agenda. Reagan also ingratiated himself to both the pro-family movement and the corporate establishment. He formed a Family Policy Advisory Committee that Connie Marshner of the Free Congress Foundation headed and a panel of forty top-tier executives that helped to shape his economic program. Unlike in 1964, big business lined up behind the conservative Republican in 1980.[34]

Reagan faced an opposition weakened by internal strife. Senator Edward Kennedy sought to rally liberals against President Carter in the Democratic primaries and the charismatic but erratic Jerry Brown, the former governor of California, also challenged Carter with a hybrid program of social liberalism, new age environmentalism, and fiscal responsibility. Carter staved off these threats and an effort by Kennedy backers to "open" the Democratic Convention by releasing delegates from first-ballot pledges. He then shifted focus to maligning Reagan as a right-wing extremist who threatened Social Security, civil rights, and world peace. An internal campaign recommended discrediting Reagan through such invidious comparisons as "Safe & Sound vs. Untested," "Vigorous vs. Old," "Smart vs. Dumb," "Engineer vs. Actor," and "Moderate vs. Rightwing." But it noted that "California politicians who know him well emphatically make the point that Reagan is a master at slipping punches, or in their words, 'sliding.'" The Carter campaign struggled to find a compelling theme to define Carter's presidency or set goals for a second term. Campaign chair Robert S. Strauss handwrote in the margins of a campaign memo: "The press has been pushing me for interviews of what J. C.'s 2nd term would mean—what kind of Pres. would he be—I have no answers." A memo on themes for the campaign had a conspicuous blank in the space reserved for "general encompassing theme."[35]

Reagan built a mandate for change from the right. He pledged to get government out of peoples' pockets and off their backs by cutting taxes, needless domestic spending, and burdensome regulations. He would uphold "traditional values" and let America "stand tall" again in the world by strengthening defense, confronting the reds, and putting third-world upstarts in their place. He called the Carter administration's failure to win release of the hostages held by Iran "a humiliation and a disgrace to this country" and said that if elected he would not "stand by and do nothing." He promised higher defense spending and smoothly adopted the line from the Committee on the Present Danger that Carter's "budget proposals do not begin to correct the dangerous shifts in the world balance of power achieved by the Soviet Union." He invoked supply-side magic, saying that government could balance its budget while slashing taxes and hiking military spending—a theory that George Bush had derided during the primaries as voodoo economics. Still, unlike Goldwater, the "sliding" Reagan couldn't be baited, avoided gaffes, and disarmingly murmured "there you go again" whenever Carter turned on him during their one televised debate.[36]

Carter could not overcome the failings of his first term. The Iranian hostage crisis persisted through Election Day and the Soviets remained in Afghanistan. The wounds of the nomination struggle did not readily heal and the economy hit a new low in the summer of 1980. Reagan pointedly asked Americans, "Are you better off than you were four years ago?" He cited a "misery index" of inflation and unemployment that topped 20 percent for the first time since the Great Depression. "Democratic liberalism by the end of the 1970s," wrote journalists Thomas and Mary Edsall, "was judged by many voters to have failed to live up to a basic obligation: that of rewarding and protecting its own constituents." Reagan proved that a conservative candidate could win the presidency decisively. He won 51 percent of the popular vote to 41 percent for Carter and 7 percent for Anderson. The challenger took forty-four states and, with the exception of Georgia, swept the South. Unlike the Republican landslides of 1956 and 1972, Reagan's success reverberated down the ticket. The GOP regained control of the Senate for the first time since 1954 and secured an ideological edge in the House. It gained in state offices and elected five new senators from the South, while voters dismissed such liberal icons as Senators George McGovern of South Dakota and Frank Church of Idaho.[37]

Reagan's victory had a thousand fathers—every conservative group from the Moral Majority to NCPAC claimed parentage. But the National Election Study showed that rising turnout among evangelical Protestants barely exceeded the national average and their votes did not decide the election; as compared to Ford in 1976, Reagan picked up nine points in the two-party vote among white Protestant evangelicals, compared to ten points among moderate white Protestants and three points among liberals. Neither did conservatives power Reagan to victory; relative to Ford, Reagan's two-party vote dropped by a percentage point among self-identified conservatives but soared by thirteen points among moderates—many of them so-called Reagan Democrats, the northern, blue-collar, Catholic voters conservatives had long coveted. Carter narrowly lost the Catholic vote nationwide, while losing heavily among white Protestants across the nation, including the South. Analysts debated at the time whether a true political realignment had begun in 1980. Democrats still controlled the House of Representatives and most state and local offices. The GOP, however, had gained near parity in party affiliation, suggesting that the balance of party power could soon change.

The right cared little about parsing election results. After fifty years in the liberal wilderness, conservatives had reached the promised land. Or so they thought. Between the dream and the reality fell the shadow of practical politics. "Reagan is a thoroughly sincere man and as close as a politician can ever get to being a 'movement conservative,'" *National Review* publisher William Rusher wrote to fellow conservative Michael Djordjevich the day before the new president's inauguration. But he would not be "the Ideal Mechanical Man which we could program to our heart's content to behave, in all cases whatsoever, in conservative ways." The problem was "how late it is" to cure the afflictions of liberal government. "Clif White and I agreed years ago that 1968 was, in our judgment, the last time when America could have been taken in hand and turned around. Now it may be too late."[38]

Reagan offered a kind of leadership unknown in America for decades. To borrow Sir Isaiah Berlin's illuminating metaphor, most modern American presidents are foxes that know a little about everything, poke their noses everywhere, and revel in detail. Reagan, however, like Calvin Coolidge, one of his favorite presidents, was a hedgehog that knew a few things but knew them very well. The hedgehog president knew for sure that he had to cure the ailing economy. If he didn't, he could forget reelection or a marquee role in history. Other issues, however precious to the right, would have to wait in line.

The administration's prescription for the economy, backed by business groups and conservative think tanks, called for cutting taxes and domestic spending, deregulating business, and continuing a tight money policy to stanch inflation and attract foreign capital into the United States. Budget director David Stockman prepared a "Rosy Scenario," which showed that these policies would restore balanced budgets by 1984, even with increased military spending. In a series of startling legislative triumphs during his first year—the period of the "Reagan Revolution"—the president put his stamp on national life. After surviving a near-fatal assassination attempt in March, Reagan achieved an historic victory in the summer of 1981 when Congress took a "riverboat gamble," in the words of Republican Senate leader Howard Baker, and passed deep cuts in federal income taxes. The Economic Recovery and Tax Act of 1981, which Reagan compared to the Kennedy/Johnson tax cuts of the 1960s, reduced personal income taxes by 5 percent in 1981 and 10 percent in each of the next two years, with the top rate tumbling from 70 percent to 50 percent. It increased tax breaks for depreciation and reduced estate, capital gains, and windfall profits taxes. It added new credits for investment and research, IRAs for all working taxpayers, and indexed tax brackets for inflation. This legislation was not just a prod to the economy. It was a foundational change in tax philosophy that eased liabilities on the rich, reduced tax costs for many businesses, insulated taxpayers from inflation, and further shifted burdens from progressive income taxes to regressive payroll taxes paid mostly by the middle class. From 1981 to 1991 the share of federal revenue from personal income taxes dropped from 48 percent to 44 percent and the share from payroll taxes rose from 31 percent to 38 percent.

The conservative coalition of Republicans and southern Democrats, the latter dubbed "boll weevils," backed Reagan's tax program in the Democratic House. The champagne flowed on the evening of the final vote as Reagan and his staff celebrated the greatest legislative triumph for conservatives since Taft-Hartley in 1947. The president fielded congratulatory calls from leaders of both parties, including Democratic Speaker of the House Tip O'Neill, who said, "Decisions have been made, you're now in charge of fiscal policy." Aides recounted that the president "met with 58 Congressmen in person and called another 25 [that week]. . . . Pretty good for a lazy president." The president's last words: "It was a rather nice day." Not until winning reelection in 1984 would the president again have such a day.[39]

The administration hit stiffer resistance to cutting domestic spending; Congress was reluctant to challenge special interests or reduce the benefits that ordinary Americans had come to expect from Uncle Sam. The administration gained increased military spending and cutbacks in revenue sharing with the states, aid to education, food stamps, mass transit, and housing aid. But Congress spared the massive entitlement programs of Social Security, Medicare, and Medicaid. Supply-siders in the administration derided the caution of deficit hawks who insisted that tax reductions needed to be offset by budget cuts. "We are not cutting the budget because of our tax rate decreases," wrote deputy presidential counsel James Jenkins. "The thrust of the President's Budget policy is merely to slow the growth in the Budget and in so doing reduce its burden on the country. Keynes is dead, and so are his ideas." Although domestic spending fell during Reagan's first term, military spending rose and the federal government's share of the economy remained unchanged at about 22 percent of GDP.[40]

Reagan deregulated business, not only to spur competition but also to alleviate the costs of post-material health, safety, energy, environmental, and civil rights regulations. Administration officials would hold government accountable to the same accounting standards as private business by requiring that the benefits of regulation justify its costs. Most change came through implementation, not legislation. Reagan appointees shifted policy toward privatization, voluntarism, localism, and equality of opportunity, not outcomes. The number of pages in the federal register, a rough gauge of regulation, fell by a third during Reagan's first two years after rising by more than 50 percent during Carter's term. Legislatively, the most notable change occurred in 1982, when the Garn–St. Germain Act completed deregulation of the savings and loan industry. "This bill is the most important legislation for financial institutions in the last 50 years," President Reagan said. "It provides a long-term solution for troubled thrift institutions." By late 1983, however, the push for regulatory reform had abated. According to an Opinion Research Corporation survey in December 1983, two-thirds of the public agreed that "federal government regulators have been influenced too much by business' arguments against regulations."

Reagan asserted his supremacy over unions in August 1981 when he fired federal air traffic controllers who were engaged in an illegal strike that had been called by the Professional Air Traffic Controllers Organization (PATCO). Like his 1950s mentor Lemuel Boulware, Reagan held fast to a position that he believed was right. The Federal Labor Authority then decertified PATCO, ironically one of the few national unions that had endorsed Reagan in 1980. Reagan won his battle with PATCO and the big unions that never rode to its rescue. He demonstrated to union chiefs, American voters, and foreign leaders the toughness and determination that many believed Carter had lacked. Nearly 70 percent of Americans agreed that Reagan was right to fire the strikers. The PATCO dispute reflected and contributed to declining union membership, which ravaged the grass roots of the Democratic Party. From a third of wage and salary workers in the mid-1950s, American union membership had steadily declined over twenty-five years to about 23 percent in 1980. Union membership fell at a faster pace under Reagan, plummeting to just 16 percent—12 percent in the private sector—when he left office in 1989. Reagan made pro-business appointments to the national labor board, opposed labor law reforms, and gave business a green light to pursue antiunion tactics developed during the hard times of the 1970s.[41]

By the fall of 1981 the new president had completed what observers at the time called the Reagan Revolution in taxes, spending, and regulation. Neoconservative analyst Benjamin Wattenberg saw the handwriting on the wall. In 1982 he wrote that the New Deal and the Great Society would survive the Reagan Revolution, with their big-ticket entitlement programs largely unscathed, but the hated "new politics" with its dour "McGovern mentality" would not. For Wattenberg the Reagan Revolution had put an end to the ideas that "law and order is a codeword for racism," that America is threatened by a "bloated military-industrial complex," that Americans had to reorder their priorities to protect the environment, that they had to adjust to an era of slow economic growth, and that their culture was corrupt and dangerous.[42]

This halfway revolution was too mild for some movement conservatives. The Heritage Foundation rated the president's first year as "pass but try harder" and a contingent of thirty-five prominent conservatives agreed with this assessment. They applauded President Reagan's "magnificent effort to articulate the case for limited government on the homefront, and firm defense of free world interests abroad." They commended "his attempts to control the rate of Federal spending, achieve tax rate reduction, and lift the stifling burden of unnecessary regulation from our economy." Still, undoing "the damage wrought by decades of liberal dominance" was so arduous a task as to elicit "deep concern." The critics fretted over appointments of "pragmatists," most notably Chief of Staff James A. Baker III. They worried that the administration would "undo its central feature—the Reagan tax rate reductions—by capitulating to demands for a series of Republican-sponsored tax increases allegedly needed to eliminate huge deficits." They complained that entitlement programs escaped budget cuts. They fretted about chasing "the illusions of détente" while neglecting social issues such as abortion, women's rights, pornography, and school prayer. They lamented Reagan's failure to "defund the left" by cutting funding for the Legal Services Corporation and grants to liberal groups.[43]

Reagan's racial policies also generated a mixed response from conservatives. The administration drew upon rhetoric fashioned in the 1960s to uphold the ideal of a colorblind society. It assailed affirmative action quota systems. It criticized welfare for creating dependence and touted economic programs that opened opportunities for minorities to find jobs, buy homes, and start businesses ("black capitalism") instead of idling on the dole or depending on civil rights programs. Yet the president refused to burn capital on striving to end affirmative action and signed a twenty-five-year extension of a strengthened Voting Rights Act. In 1982 the administration expanded the program that set aside a share of federal contracts for minority-owned firms. These policies reflected qualified support for affirmative action from corporate America and the administration's secure position with white southern voters. Reagan's advisers sought to avoid a damaging rift with moderate Republicans on civil rights; they still coveted a share of the black vote and backing from moderate white women. Whereas white men had surged to support the Reagan-Bush ticket in 1980 women had lagged seven percentage points behind, reversing women's onetime pro-Republican gender gap.[44]

The administration boosted black conservatives with the appointments of Clarence Thomas as director of the Equal Employment Opportunity Commission, Clarence Pendleton III as chair of the U.S. Commission on Civil Rights, and Alan Keyes as ambassador to the UN Economic and Social Council. Important black conservative thinkers such as Thomas Sowell, Robert Woodson, Walter Williams, Shelby Steele, and Glenn Loury gave intellectual ballast to the administration's economic program and critique of welfare. In 1981 Woodson, a fellow at the American Enterprise Institute, founded the National Center for Neighborhood Enterprise to conduct research on minority issues and develop demonstration projects for empowering neighborhood groups devoted to market-based, self-help strategies. The center received grants of more than $8 million from the Sarah Scaife and Bradley foundations in its first quarter century. It sought to solve inner-city problems through market solutions, religious values, personal initiatives, and faith-based programs. In a 1987 speech to the Heritage Foundation, Clarence Thomas exposed the still racially tinged vision of supposedly colorblind white conservatives. "It often seemed that to be accepted within the conservative ranks and to be treated with some degree of acceptance, a black was required to become a caricature of sorts, providing side shows of anti-black quips and attacks."[45]

Like professional mourners at a funeral, conservatives wept over Reagan's failings for effect. "A certain amount of percussion on the right simply helps Reagan to ignore the constant percussion on his left," Rusher told Buckley. "Remember how Tom Huston used to phone us, when he was in the Nixon White House, and beg us to pound on his boss."[46]

The Reagan Revolution had profoundly changed American politics. It had fundamentally altered American tax policies, shifted federal priorities from social programs to defense, eased regulations, and revived the engaged nationalist agenda to defeat the Soviet empire. It had undercut liberalism and effectively changed the national conversation about politics. Despite the administration's pragmatic tilt, conservatives had a major presence at the top through counselor to the president Ed Meese and a surprisingly conservative defense secretary, Caspar Weinberger. Morton Blackwell served as a liaison to the right and neoconservatives held key defense and foreign policy posts. Jeane Kirkpatrick served as UN ambassador, Richard Perle as assistant secretary of defense, and Elliot Abrams as assistant secretary of state. Max Kampelman and later Kenneth Adelman directed the Office of Arms Control and Richard Pipes joined the NSC. The pragmatists were also represented by Chief of Staff Baker and Special Assistant Michael Deaver's team of political strategists: former Nixon aide David Gergen; Lyn Nofziger from Reagan's California days; and the political prodigy Lee Atwater, who was just twenty-eight years old on inauguration day.

CONSERVATIVE INFRASTRUCTURE

In 1981 conservatives quietly hatched the Council for National Policy (CNP), the first successful umbrella organization on the right. The CNP emerged from a meeting convened by eight conservative Republican senators who were concerned that "major conservative leaders did not sit down regularly to plan the conservative agenda for the next week, month, or year." Speakers at the closed-door gathering included Dolan, Weyrich, Viguerie, Pratt, Blackwell, Dick Marable of the NAM, Henry Walther of the National Right to Work Committee, and leaders and members of the Senate Steering Committee and the Republican Study Committee. Participants considered how to advance their unending "war" with the left as they explored such matters as "Competition With the Enemy" and "Expanding the Political Offensive." Afterward, Tim LaHaye and H. L. Hunt's son Nelson Bunker Hunt took the lead in forming the CNP.[47]

CNP closed its membership lists and meetings, but directories leaked out to journalists. LaHaye served as the group's first president in 1981–82. He was followed by Jesse Helms's political operative Tom Ellis, Nelson Bunker Hunt, publishing executive Sam Moore, Pat Robertson, and Amway cofounder Richard DeVos. From thirty-five founders, the CNP's membership ballooned to about four hundred by 1985. All members were listed as sitting on a board of directors and were officially required to raise or pay an annual tax-deductible contribution of $5,000.

An analysis of 377 CNP members from the 1984–85 directory shows that this white (99 percent), male (96 percent), and Christian (99 percent) organization brought together business owners and executives, a few prominent officeholders, and movement conservatives of the Christian right and the new right, but not a single prominent neoconservative or representative of a Catholic organization. Despite big business's engagement with conservative politics, executives of publicly traded corporations still tried to avoid association with new right and Christian conservative groups. The business community accounted for 44 percent of CNP members, but nearly all were entrepreneurs or heads of family firms—none represented a Fortune 100 company. Eight-four percent of business members hailed from south of the Mason-Dixon Line or west of the Mississippi, and a staggering 26 percent hailed from Texas. About 21 percent had interests in oil and gas, 19 percent in real estate and development, and 16 percent in publishing and media.[48]

Every Christian right leader with big footprints joined the CNP: Dobson, Robertson, Bright, Falwell, Billings, McAteer, Robison, Jarmin, North, Rushdoony, Henry Morris, D. James Kennedy, and both LaHayes. So did lesser-known but influential figures. Robert T. Weiner headed Maranatha Campus Ministries, which recruited college students for close supervision of their lives by the group's so-called shepherd pastors. Donald

R. Howard founded Accelerated Christian Education, which assisted pastors in forming Christian schools and entering politics. Bob Dugan led the Washington Office of the National Association of Evangelicals. The Reverend Donald Wildmon, head of the National Federation for Decency, was the nation's leading monitor of obscenity in the media. Henry Morris directed the Institute for Creation Research. Jim Groen was president of Youth for Christ International, the Reverend Melvin Hodges of the Foundation for Black Christian Education, and Jay Parker of the Lincoln Institute. Jack Abramoff headed the College Republicans and H. Edward Rowe the Church League of America.

Every new right pacesetter joined the CNP—Rusher, Schalfly, Pratt, Phillips, Weyrich, Dolan, and Viguerie. So did Bill Ceverha, national chairman of the American Legislative Exchange Council; Reed Irvine, founder of Accuracy in Media; Reed Larson, president of the National Right to Work Committee; Lewis Lehrman, chairman of Citizens for America; Daniel J. Popeo, founder of the Washington Legal Foundation; John A. Howard, president of the Rockford Institute; and Thomas S. Winter, editor of *Human Events*. The mix included two dozen elected officials, nearly all Republicans, and several military men, among them General Daniel Graham, General John Singlaub, and Lieutenant Colonel Oliver North of Reagan's National Security Council. The John Birch Society had broad representation: Chairman A. Clifford Barker; speakers' bureau members W. W. Caruth III and W. Cleon Skousen; and board members William Cies, Nelson Bunker Hunt, and Meldrim Thomson. Prior John Birch Society chair Larry McDonald served on the CNP until his death in 1983, when his widow replaced him.

The CNP was not the secret command structure of the right. Its main function was to introduce donors to hungry organization heads and to serve as a meeting ground for bell ringers on the right. "A lot of side business is done in the corridors, etc.," Rusher wrote. "This is probably the most important thing that happens or that could happen." Meetings probed topics such as "high frontier missile defense," "humanism invading public education," "return to the gold standard," and the "election of conservatives." The CNP conducted briefings on current affairs and encouraged business members to acquire media properties. It maintained talent banks for future government appointments, gave out journalism awards, and published an insider's newsletter. It also spurred opposition to Reagan's first appointee to the High Court, the moderate Sandra Day O'Connor. "It is critical that a strong fight be waged" on O'Connor, explained executive director Woody Jenkins. "It is essential that the President realize that he *must* keep his conservative base and cannot 'broaden his base' by violating the principles that elected him."[49]

The group operated with a small staff and a relatively modest budget of about $500,000 in the mid-1980s. It relied on member contributions and grants from foundations controlled by members Richard DeVos, Joseph Coors, and Thomas K. Armstrong. It promoted such causes as missile defense, privatization of government, and opposition to abortion, welfare, taxes, civil rights laws, arms control, the United Nations, and business regulations. "It is not our intention to tinker with existing policy or to put band-aids on bad policy," wrote new executive director Jack G. Wilson in 1986. "Our goal is to develop policy as though we were in control and governing today."[50]

Conservative youth politics realigned during the Reagan years. Young Americans for Freedom had grown to prominence as a counterweight to left-wing agitation on campus, but it declined in the 1970s when campus demonstrations tapered off and internal strife escalated. "YAF has lost all meaningful political clout," godfather Marvin Liebman wrote in 1983. "It is neither a factor in national politics, youth politics, nor on campus." YAF did not officially disband but it faded away in the 1980s. Conservative newspapers took up the slack on campus and the College Republicans emerged as America's largest conservative student group. The Young Republicans and the Intercollegiate Society of Individualists (blandly renamed the Intercollegiate Studies Institute) lived on but with diminished vigor, and new groups came and went.[51]

Under new president Jack Abramoff, a graduate of liberal Brandeis University, the College Republicans lined up with the right. "It is and has been our sacred duty to wage the ideological struggle on campus," Abramoff wrote in 1983. Two other gifted organizers joined Abramoff: antitax activist Grover Norquist and Ralph Reed, an undergraduate at the University of Georgia. The College Republicans, Abramoff reported, sought to "defund the Left at the federal and university levels" and fight "Ralph Nader's PIRG groups and the radical United States Student Association." It would "start conservative newspapers on campus" and "support Reagan administration initiatives." The group initiated a "Poland Will

Be Free" campaign and "a peace through strength alternative to the U.S. 'nuclear freeze,'" which it denounced as a communist front. Its activists worked with House members, notably veteran conservatives Philip Crane of Illinois and Jack Kemp of New York, and relative newcomer Newt Gingrich of Georgia. This ambitious young politician with a PhD in history was first elected in 1978, but he inspired the young leaders with his big ideas about conservativism as the next great wave of human progress. Abramoff, Norquist, and Reed spent lavishly, convinced that destiny had called them. They drained the College Republicans' funds in anticipation of a big payoff when Gingrich became Speaker of the House and Kemp president of the United States.[52]

Conservatives increased their influence on the legal profession through the Federalist Society. Law students alienated from liberal faculty and students—Steven G. Calabresi at Yale and Lee Liberman and David McIntosh at the University of Chicago—began the society modestly in 1982. Professors Robert Bork at Yale and Antonin Scalia at Chicago mentored the group before Reagan appointed both of these academics to the federal bench. The Institute for Educational Affairs and William Simon's Olin Foundation gave seed money to the society, followed by six-figure grants from the Sarah Scaife and Bradley foundations. The group won some support beyond conservative foundations, with a $73,000 grant from the National Endowment for the Humanities to sponsor symposia on the two hundredth anniversary of the U.S. Constitution. The society aimed at forming "a conservative network that extends to all levels of the legal community" and reordering "priorities within the legal system to place a premium on individual liberty, traditional values and the rule of law." Most prominent Federalist Society members and associates, like Bork and Scalia, favored "strict construction" of the "original meaning" of the Constitution. In practice, this doctrine meant skepticism about regulatory laws, affirmative action, and rigid separation of church and state. It meant support for property rights and opposition to individual rights such as privacy that were not enumerated in the Constitution.

The media discovered the growing society in 1986 when Reagan placed Scalia on the Supreme Court. For years, however, his administration had been elevating Federalist Society members and supporters to the lower federal bench and slots in the White House and Justice Department. By 1986 the society had an annual budget of $400,000, two thousand members, chapters at seventy law schools, and lawyers' divisions in major cities across the nation. Bork and Orrin Hatch, chairman of the Senate Judiciary Committee, cochaired the society's board of trustees. By 2000, under the guidance of executive director Eugene B. Meyer (Frank Meyer's equally brilliant son), the Federalist Society would be the most active, influential, and richly financed legal association of the right or left, with a yearly budget of about $3 million, some twenty-five thousand members, chapters at some three-quarters of the nation's 182 accredited law schools, and lawyers' divisions in some sixty cities.

The Federalist Society filed no briefs, took no cases, and issued no official positions on legal or political issues. Yet it profoundly shaped American jurisprudence. It became a matchmaker for conservatives who attended its monthly lunches in the capital and its events at law schools and law firms across the country. Its network of members and associates served as the recruitment base for conservative public officials, judges, law clerks, and members of powerful private firms. The society published books and pamphlets and sponsored symposia where conservatives tested their ideas against liberal critics. It transformed ideas into practice by distributing lists of expert analysts and by organizing fifteen unofficial "practice groups," which scouted for pathbreaking cases, formulated theories and strategies for litigation, and encouraged lawyers to file suits, get funding and publicity, write briefs, and argue cases. Attorneys associated with the Federalist Society worked on cases to limit affirmative action and antidiscrimination law, protect property owners from eminent domain claims by the government, challenge the strict separation between church and state, and rein in the Endangered Species Act. Lawyers who sought to protect private property and enterprise commingled in the society with those focused on upholding traditional values.[53]

As a complement to the Federalist Society, conservative scholars backed by the resources of the Olin Foundation also began law and economics programs. Their objective was to instruct law professors and judges on how to include considerations of economic costs and efficiency in their academic studies and judicial rulings. New conservative public interest legal groups also established close relationships with the Federalist Society. These included the Center for Individual Rights, which focused on expanding free speech rights for religious groups and eliminating race- and gender-based social programs and the Institute for Justice, which focused on promoting school choice, private property rights, and freedom from economic regulations. Both groups gained backing from conservative foundations and took a more aggressive approach than the 1970s foundations to finding plaintiffs and controlling cases from start to finish. As a result of this strategy and a more conservative judiciary the two groups were more successful than their 1970s predecessors in establishing important legal preferences that expanded school choice and religious free speech and restricted affirmative action, enforcement of the Voting Rights Act, and the scope of government regulations.[54]

In Congress, the brash strategic thinker Newt Gingrich expressed the frustrations of movement conservatives with compromising Republicans. In 1982 he blasted Chief of Staff James Baker for a lack of conservative élan that "hurt the Republican party; aroused new candidates, money and energy for the Democrats; and sent precisely the wrong signals to the Party and the country." Gingrich urged his party to give "the country a clear choice between the values it favors and Republicans are fighting for [and] the Democratic Party's denial of those values." The following year, Gingrich and several kindred House Republicans—Vin Weber of Minnesota, Robert Walker of Pennsylvania, Duncan Hunter of California, and Connie Mack of Florida—organized a new internal House organization that they called the Conservative Opportunity Society. The founders aimed to reform the House, establish the GOP as an issue-oriented party, and develop winning political strategies. Gingrich echoed the ACU's decade-old call for Republicans to seize the policy agenda and not just chip away at liberal programs, even if it meant defying his party's leaders. "There is clearly a welfare-state wing of the Republican Party that sees itself as running essentially a cheaper and narrower version of the Democratic welfare state," Gingrich said in 1984. Its leader was Senate Majority Leader Dole, who Gingrich called the "tax collector for the welfare state." The pragmatic Dole responded, "While we're passing the legislation, they're looking around for new ideas." House Minority Leader Bob Michel agreed: "We have a responsibility to govern. . . . It's great to be out there talking, but we have to deliver."[55]

Gingrich rejected the dicta that "all politics is local" and called for nationalizing congressional elections as battles of competing principles, following the party-driven model of European politics and the notion of "responsible" ideologically coherent parties formulated by political scientists in the United States. Gingrich worked with the Heritage Foundation to fashion strategy for creating "a stable, right-of-center governing majority for the next half century" to counter the "left-of-center majority" that had "dominated the political debate." Gingrich's vision extended "beyond Ronald Reagan" and "beyond Washington to the state legislators, to the state houses, to the county commissions." He would "reach down into the colleges" and "into the newspaper business" to achieve "conservative-idea headlines based on conservative education based on a new understanding of the world."[56]

Gingrich combined the right's fidelity to traditional values with its affinity for new technologies. He would bring conservative politics into the modern world, as Francis Schaeffer had done with conservative theology. He implored Republicans to catch what futurist Alvin Toffler called the "next great wave of world civilization:" the information age that would succeed the industrial age and supplant bureaucratic, centralized institutions. Gingrich advocated a "shift in paradigms"—a scientific revolution in politics that would decentralize government, dismantle welfare bureaucracies, and replace regulations with private initiative. His new paradigm would arm individuals with the technological skills they needed to complete in the new era. Only the most gravely handicapped would need handouts from government. The Gingrich paradigm would recognize that "foreign nations are dangerous, the U.S. is good" and "reaffirm our belief in the importance of national survival both in military strength and in our moral and cultural strengths." Gingrich used the House ethics rules to engineer the resignation of Democratic House Speaker Jim Wright of Texas and followed Robert Bauman's lead in speaking after hours to the C-SPAN faithful. Membership in his Conservative Opportunity Society soared to fifty-three U.S. House members by the end of the Reagan years (about a third of House Republicans).[57]

Although the Heritage Foundation and the American Enterprise Institute remained the premier think tanks on the right, smaller groups flourished during the 1980s. The Manhattan Institute captured the ethos of the early 1980s by providing financial support for the writing of bestselling books by freelance author George Gilder and political scientist Charles Murray. Gilder's 1981 book *Wealth and Poverty* was a paean to the entrepreneurial spirit unleashed by Ronald Reagan. Three years later Murray's grim work, *Losing Ground: American Social Policy, 1950–1980*, damned welfare programs for creating perverse incentives to shun work and have children out of wedlock. The welfare system, Murray charged, fostered a culture that privileged handouts over self-help, perpetuated rather than cured poverty, undermined the family, and spawned crime, addiction, and other social pathologies. Ending welfare, not mending it, was Murray's solution. The Cato Institute, boosted by Reagan's call for less government, contributed to national debates with ideas such as converting Social Security contributions to private accounts. Unlike Heritage, Cato eschewed involvement in legislative battles. "We're trying to stand back from the congressional fray and take a broader view," said Cato founder Ed Crane. The Hudson Institute, following the 1983 death of longtime chairman Herman Kahn, secured $1.5 million from the Lilly Foundation to explore how America could reduce "the social and economic burdens that have been imposed by the expansion of government power . . . promote the growth and efficiency of private institutions," and reassume "the mantle of world leadership."[58]

The Rockford Institute, sponsored by Rockford University with financial assistance from Bradley and other foundations, represented what some called "paleoconservatism." This version of anti-pluralist nationalism upheld the superiority of the West's Christian tradition, backed state-enforced morality, and opposed free trade for dragging down living conditions and immigration for polluting American culture. Paleo-conservatives were fiercely anticommunist but suspicious of foreign interventions, aid to Israel, and involvements with multilateral projects. In a prelude to controversy stirred by paleoconservative Pat Buchanan's candidacy for president in 1992, Rockford's president Allan Carlson fired the Reverend Richard John Neuhaus as director of the institute's Center on Religion and Society in 1989. Neuhaus's offense was that he had called the Rockford Institute's *Chronicles* magazine "insensitive to the classic language of anti-Semitism."[59]

Other groups focused on conserving private enterprise. In 1984 Fred L. Smith, former economist for the Association of American Railroads, founded the Competitive Enterprise Institute (CEI) to promote freedom from regulations for business. The CEI made a splash in the late 1980s with its campaign against "death by regulation." It challenged in court the federal government's automobile mileage standards, which the group said sacrificed thousands of lives per year by forcing motorists to buy smaller, lighter vehicles. Amy Moritz—later Ridenour—who had lost to Jack Abramoff in an election for president of the College Republicans, launched the National Center for Public Policy Research in 1982. Her center backed a strong defense, American sovereignty, private enterprise, and market solutions to national problems. By the 1990s both groups had annual budgets in the low seven figures.

The John Birch Society experienced a renaissance in the Reagan era through the patronage of Larry McDonald, a conservative Democratic member of Congress from Georgia. In 1979 McDonald founded the Western Goals Foundation, which he closely affiliated with the JBS. Western Goals followed the tradition of gathering data on alleged subversives— "fill[ing] the critical gap caused by the crippling of the FBI, the disabling of the House UnAmerican Activities Committee (HUAC) and the destruction of crucial government files." The new group proposed to "rebuild and strengthen the political, economic, and social structure of the U.S. and Western Civilization so as to make any merger with the totalitarian world impossible." For its board, Western Goals recruited Birch Society members Dan Smoot, John Rees, and Sherman Unkefer. But McDonald also gained support from the respectable right, which was once unthinkable for a Birch-affiliated group. Sponsors included Republican representatives John Ashbrook and Phil Crane of Illinois, H-bomb scientist Edward Teller, retired admiral Thomas Moorer, and retired generals John Singlaub, Daniel Graham, George S. Patton III, and Lewis Walt. After a modest start, Western Goals' budget grew to $417,000 by 1982 when it signed up M. Stanton Evans for a weekly radio broadcast. In March 1983, after Robert Welch's retirement, McDonald became chairman of the John Birch Society, serving briefly until his death in September.

Western Goals took on the project of rehabilitating the reputation of Salvadoran leader Roberto D'Aubuisson, who was accused by the former ambassador to El Salvador and other U.S. officials of leading death squads and murdering prominent Catholic archbishop Oscar Romero. Support for authoritarian, sometimes murderous, leaders in Latin America was a politically sensitive issue for the right, but Western Goals gained top-flight conservative backing for D'Aubuisson. "You don't have perfect choices in trying to prevent a communist takeover of this world," Senator Jesse Helms said. After McDonald's death, a glitterati of the right honored D'Aubuisson at a 1984 dinner; sponsors included Young Americans for Freedom, Gun

Owners of America, the Moral Majority, the Conservative Caucus, the *Washington Times* newspaper, the Washington Legal Foundation, the Free Congress Foundation, the National Right to Work Committee, and the National Pro-Life Political Action Committee. A year later, D'Aubuisson was deemed such an unsavory character that the Reagan administration intervened in El Salvador's presidential election to deny him the office.[60]

The power of the Unification Church grew after Reagan's election, despite Reverend Moon's 1984 conviction and thirteen-month imprisonment for income tax invasion, which religious figures and civil libertarians said violated religious freedom. The church continued to satisfy cravings on the right for funds, volunteers, and a bully pulpit. Conservatives could speak at expenses-paid conventions and symposiums—sometimes with generous honorariums—sponsored by church front groups such as the Confederation of Associations for the Unification of the Societies of the Americas. (CAUSA), the World Media Conference, the International Conference of the Unity of Sciences, and the Professors World Peace Academy. They could publish articles in church journals, write opinion pieces for church newspapers, and hobnob with dignitaries at church-paid trips to Taiwan, Korea, South Africa, or Brazil. Through the mid-1980s, some five thousand scholars, including two dozen Nobel laureates, journeyed to conferences worldwide held by the church's front groups; thousands more attended the church's World Media Conferences. The Unification Church spent many hundreds of millions of dollars, beginning in 1982, to finance a new conservative newspaper in the nation's capital, the *Washington Times,* which President Reagan pumped as his favorite paper. It poured money into conservative causes, contributing, for example, $100,000 through the *Washington Times* to a fund for the Contras and $500,000 to a lobbying group that Terry Dolan formed. It rescued Viguerie's direct-mail company from bankruptcy by purchasing the firm's office building.[61]

The Unification Church made no secret that these initiatives sustained the holy war that divine avatar Reverend Moon waged against godless communism, the main obstacle to his quest for worldwide spiritual dominion. Moon's chief aide, Colonel Bo Hi Pak, a former South Korean intelligence agent, said, "So in this war, the entire things will be mobilized: political means, social means, economical means and propagandistic means." Although the Unification Church deified its leader, broke familial ties, denied the divinity of Christ, and veered into collectivism by absorbing members into church enterprises, conservatives largely spared it from rebuke. According to William Rusher, who received free trips from the Church and a $5,000 honorarium to chair the 1982 World Media Conference in Seoul, "It is as unfair to call them 'anti-Christian' as it would be to call the Mormons anti-Christian. Nor are the Moonies 'anti-family.' It does of course happen that youngsters who join the Unification Church thereby offend parents of other faiths—just as beloved daughters occasionally offend devout Baptist parents by running away and entering a Roman Catholic convent." Emmett Tyrrell, a lonely conservative critic, published in 1987 a biting critique of the right's involvement with the Unification Church by one of his *American Spectator* editors, Andrew Ferguson. Ferguson wrote that "for many conservatives a close association with the Unification Church is no longer considered distasteful." He asked, "Is a methodically deceptive, anti-family, socialistic, utopian, theocratic one-worlder who thinks he's God, a plausible ally, a reliable ally in the conservative cause?" But, he explained, "Moon gave conservatives many reasons to ignore the unpleasantness . . . millions and millions of reasons."[62]

From 1971 through the fall of the Berlin Wall in 1989, the Unification Church built by far the most expansive and expensive conservative anticommunist network in the history of the Cold War. The church likely spent more than a billion dollars on its political and related enterprises during these years. The decline of the red menace in the 1990s, however, diminished the appeal of Moon's political activities in the United States.

A STALLED REVOLUTION

In the late summer of 1981, before the tax cuts kicked in, the Federal Reserve Board's restrictive, anti-inflation policies plunged the economy into a deep recession, abruptly ending the Reagan Revolution. Falling revenues combined with booming defense spending widened the federal budget deficit from $79 billion in 1981 to $208 billion in 1983, or 6 percent of GDP—both peacetime records. Supply-siders dismissed deficits as inconsequential for the economy. "The more the administration focuses on deficits per se," warned Treasury official Paul Craig Roberts, "the greater the likelihood that monetarism or supply-side economics, or both, will be abandoned." But the true believers failed to move Congress, the business community, or the administration, from which leading supply-siders Norman Ture and Roberts at Treasury and Martin Anderson at the White House fled in 1982, landing softly at Heritage, the Center for Strategic and International Studies, and the Hoover Institution.[63]

Traditionalists worried that deficits "crowded out" private investment and drove up interest rates. Conservative Democrat James Jones of Oklahoma, chair of the House Budget Committee, called upon members to "save our Nation from ever-larger deficits, stagnant growth, and ruinous interest rates." Howard Phillips of the Conservative Caucus and Terry Dolan of the National Conservative Political Action Committee proposed to cut domestic spending by 30 percent, increase military spending by 20 percent, accelerate scheduled tax cuts, expand the deregulation of industry, and resurrect the gold standard. To show their impartiality, they proposed to pare down agencies that subsidized business, including the Export-Import Bank, the Agency for International Development, and the federal highway construction program. Led by Lewis Uhler of the National Tax Limitation Committee, some conservatives pushed for two-thirds of the states to call a constitutional convention to pass a balanced budget amendment. Other conservatives, however, feared that liberals could capture a convention and opposed the move, which fell two states short of its goal.[64]

The administration rejected both the right's austerity budget and its plea for action on postponed social issues like abortion and school prayer. In May 1982, when five of the president's top political advisers, including David Gergen and Lee Atwater, rated the administration's top twenty-nine political priorities, "moral and social issues" finished in eighteenth place. They gave their highest ratings to courting "populist/blue collar voters," backing "our Economic Recovery Program," and "showing support for the poor/needy in the U.S." Atwater explained, "Moral and social issues are very important to this Administration, but we must distinguish between the various 'social issues.' Abortion, ERA and gun control are controversial and have strong negatives, while school prayer, busing and affirmative action are 'winners.'" Another losing issue with most voters was restoring tax exemptions for private religious schools that discriminated on the basis of race. The administration abandoned efforts to protect these schools from what the 1980 platform had called a "regulatory vendetta." Although few Christian leaders challenged the president publicly, Gary Jarmin of the conservative political action group Christian Voice warned

Reagan's strategists, "The spark that set off the Christian powder keg leading to evangelical political involvement was the private schools issues. The
White House has managed to bungle this issue tactically and strategically.
Should this issue continue to deteriorate, then RR can kiss the evangelical vote goodbye." Even on school prayer, however, Reagan's advisers
concluded that too much "Presidential or party focus . . . would be, overall counterproductive," serving "only to stir up the opposition."[65]

Throughout the recession Reagan retained his optimism, even though
his advisers turned gloomy. Gergen warned, "All the small flaws and chinks
in the armor that we knew were there last year have suddenly become
magnified. And because we placed so many chips on the economy last year,
we've been thrown on the defensive as we await the recovery." Republicans, he wrote, again seemed to be the party of wealth, with Americans
thinking that "RR doesn't give a damn about people on the lower end of
the ladder, about blacks and women, about our schools, about the environment, etc." Atwater agreed.

> The "fairness issue" is haunting us, not among minority groups that
> wouldn't support us in any case, but among whites who are sensitive
> to this issue. A conservative administration will never be able to com-
> pete with the Democrats in terms of policy and substance because we
> will never be willing to spend as much money. However, we must be
> compassionate.[66]

Only about a quarter of Americans surveyed in early 1982 thought
Reagan's economic policies helped "people like me." So the president
changed course. As inflation fell, the administration persuaded monetary
authorities to expand the money supply and lower interest rates. Reagan
advisers joined congressional leaders in the so-called Gang of 17 negotiations to achieve bipartisan agreement on deficit-controlling tax hikes and
spending restraints. Although negotiation stalled on spending, Reagan
agreed to a tax increase of nearly $100 billion over three years. Kemp and
Gingrich futilely opposed the tax hike in the House, which pragmatic GOP
senators Bob Dole and Pete Dominici of New Mexico pushed through the
Senate.

The recession undercut Republican hopes for a political realignment.
"Our goal in 1982 is to get control of the House and to retain control of
the Senate," Lyn Nofziger wrote. "Only if we attain these two goals will

we be able to get the President's programs through with any degree of consistency." But with only 36 percent of Americans rating the president's economic program a success in an election-eve poll, the GOP lost twenty-six House seats. Republicans held even in the Senate and dropped seven governorships, retaining only sixteen. The election disappointed conservative political action groups. The National Conservative Political Action Committee spent a midterm record $5 million in 1982 but failed to bring down targeted liberal senators. Still, Reagan's cultivation of business paid off. The GOP enjoyed a stunning five-to-one fund-raising advantage, which kept the party's losses from becoming a rout. As a sidelight to the election, the national Republican Party agreed in federal court to cease and desist from so-called ballot-security programs that discouraged voter turnout in the guise of preventing voter fraud.[67]

Rather than reviving Keynesian economics, these midterm setbacks revived the political strength of debt hawks in the tradition of Eisenhower and Goldwater. By early 1983 the business coalition that backed Reagan's economic program had unravelled. In January a bipartisan coalition of four hundred former government officials and CEOs of major corporations warned that the budget was "out of control" and that "immense deficits . . . threaten to lock the economy in stagnation for the remainder of this century." The coalition prescribed stern measures for the economy: new taxes, cutbacks in Social Security, and deflation of the defense boom. "The potential damage being done to the future health of the economy by the current and projected budget deficits is so great," concluded the Committee for Economic Development in 1983, "that *deficit reduction is a first priority.*" Deficit reductions came on the revenue, not the spending, side of the budget. In his last two years, the president choked down three more tax hikes. Still, the net effect of the 1981 cuts accounted for nearly $200 billion in tax relief through 1984, tilted toward affluent taxpayers.[68]

In foreign affairs, the president detested both communism and nuclear weapons and wanted to rid the world of both evils. At times he frustrated both hard-liners who fixated on winning a potential nuclear war and moderates who preached peaceful coexistence. Through much of his first term, Reagan's tough side was most evident. He rejected détente, abandoned the SALT II treaty, and linked progress in arms control with better Soviet behavior. He pledged to spread democracy and freedom around the globe but also promulgated a Reagan doctrine to support anticommunist forces, with no requirement that they respect democracy or human rights. Reagan thus put to rest Jimmy Carter's emphasis on human rights and put into practice the thinking of his UN ambassador Jeane Kirkpatrick, who had written, "Rightest authoritarian regimes can be transformed peacefully into democracies, but totalitarian Marxist ones cannot.... They can be changed only by aiding armed opponents of communism."[69]

Rather than pursuing détente to dampen the threat of war and enticing the Soviets into the capitalist world, Reagan revived the conservatives' dream of rolling back communism through expensive military competition, economic sanctions, propaganda, and covert operations. A secret national security directive in January 1983 called for expanding and upgrading U.S. forces and preventing "the transfer of technology and equipment that would make a substantial contribution directly or indirectly to Soviet military power." The United States had to win the propaganda war by developing an "ideological thrust" that "clearly affirms the superiority of U.S. and western values." It needed to "support effectively those third world states that are willing to resist Soviet pressures, or oppose Soviet initiatives hostile to the U.S." And it should "loosen Moscow's hold" on eastern Europe, "keep maximum pressure on Moscow for withdrawal" from Afghanistan, and "ensure that the Soviet's political, military, and other costs" of occupation remained high.[70]

Fears that Reagan's hard line risked nuclear war inspired a "nuclear freeze" movement that swept across the United States and Europe. A New York Times/CBS News poll in May 1982 found that 72 percent of respondents nationwide favored freezing nuclear arsenals at their current levels provided it did not leave the United States at a military disadvantage. The following month, some 750,000 peace marchers rallied in New York City to protest the nuclear arms race, the largest political demonstration to that point in American history. By the fall a Gallup Poll found that 51 percent of Americans thought it "very or somewhat likely" that Cold War conflict would escalate into world war. It was a fear apparently shared by Soviet citizens, who were prodded by their leaders to fear American intentions under Reagan.

To deal with the Soviets from a position of strength, Reagan postponed strategic arms talks, rejected a nuclear freeze, and expanded and modernized strategic forces. He proposed negotiating with the Soviets on reducing strategic arsenals and eliminating intermediate-range nuclear weapons in

Europe. In early 1983, however, a Harris Poll found that only 39 percent of Americans gave a positive rating on foreign affairs to a president under fire from liberals for mongering war and from conservatives for waging peace. "Arms negotiations with the Soviet Union is a lie and a fraud and a deceit to the nation," neoconservative Norman Podhoretz said. But the president pleased the right when he told the National Association of Evangelicals in March 1983, "There is sin and evil in the world and we're enjoined by Scripture and the Lord Jesus to oppose it with all our might." He decried the temptation "to label both sides equally at fault, to ignore the facts of history and the aggressive impulses of an evil empire"—the Soviet Union. Lost amid the furor over what the press labeled his "evil empire" speech was Reagan's pledge to "negotiate real and verifiable reductions in the world's nuclear arsenals and one day, with God's help, their total elimination."[71]

Two weeks later Reagan called for America to develop a system for defending the nation from a ballistic missile attack. In 1981 retired general, Team B member, and Reagan campaign adviser Daniel Graham had founded the High Frontier group to lobby for a high-tech missile defense shield. Reagan endorsed Graham's proposal for a Strategic Defense Initiative, dubbed Star Wars after the popular movie, and his critique of traditional deterrence through mutually assured destruction. Reagan agreed with Graham that this approach to keeping the peace was another liberal mistake that left America at the mercy of the Soviets and excused the failure to roll back communism. The president denounced Russia for "accumulating enormous military might" beyond "all requirements of a legitimate defensive capability," including "weapons that can strike directly at the United States." Despite technological challenges, Reagan said, isn't a missile defense program "worth every investment necessary to free the world from the threat of nuclear war? We know it is."[72]

It was a typically brilliant Reagan performance in which his optimistic images and hopeful emotions helped to sell his policies to the public and the Congress. In the words of social critic Bob Greene, Reagan "manages to make you feel good about your country, and about the times in which you are living. . . . All those corny feelings that hid inside of you for so long are waved right out in public by Reagan for everyone to see—and even while you're listing all the reasons that you shouldn't fall for it, you're glad you're falling. If you're a sucker for the act, that's okay." Democrats and moderate Republicans in Congress worried about a program that could ignite a new arms race and drain the treasury without practical results. They noted that even under wildly optimistic projections of a 90 percent effective missile defense system, the Russians could still rain enough nuclear warheads on America to annihilate it. Still, suckers or not, Congress could not resist replacing the nightmare of mutual annihilation with the dream of junking nuclear weapons altogether. Rather than kill the dream, the congressional empire gave way and granted Reagan about three-quarters of the funds he requested for Star Wars.[73]

In the fall of 1983 Reagan invaded the tiny Caribbean nation of Grenada and dispatched its pro-Soviet government. Conservatives cheered that Reagan had rolled back the red frontier and refuted the Soviets' claim that they would never surrender an inch of communist territory—although it was questionable whether the Kremlin considered Grenada part of its domain. Nonetheless, Reagan had trumped Carter and Kennedy by averting both a potential hostage crisis and another Cuba. Despite the obscure theater of war and logistical blunders, America's first clear-cut military victory since World War II won rave public reviews.

Elsewhere Reagan, like Eisenhower, trod carefully, unwilling to wield the big stick of American power with the abandon urged by hawkish conservatives. He worked with compatible leaders around the world to promote his vision of an integrated world economy of private markets, free trade, open investment, and limited social intervention by government. He orchestrated an international bailout of Mexico's economy when the Mexican government announced in 1982 that it could not service its foreign debts. However, he also made concessions to industries such as textiles, steel, and machine tools seeking protection from foreign competition.

In April of 1983 terrorists blew up much of the American embassy in Beirut, and in October a terrorist truck bomb exploded at the U.S. Marines headquarters in Beirut, killing 241 Americans. Reagan responded cautiously by pulling American troops out of Lebanon. He displayed similar caution when in September 1983 the Soviets shot down a Korean passenger airliner (KAL 007) that had flown into Russian airspace, killing John Birch chair Larry McDonald and other Americans on board. Although Reagan condemned the Soviets, he resisted demands by conservatives for serious reprisals. The right sanctified McDonald as an anticommunist martyr. If John Birch was the first victim of the Cold War, McDonald, said a Western Goals aide, was "the first victim of World War III."

RETAKING THE MORAL HIGH GROUND

At the midpoint of Reagan's first term, his liaison to conservatives Morton Blackwell worried that "both the Administration and the liberal Democratic leadership chose deliberately to concentrate on economic battles," which dismayed conservatives who expected Reagan to deliver on moral reform. Blackwell argued that conservatives needed to break the addiction of the "have-nots" to the Democratic Party by raising "non-economic issues." Through January 1983, he lamented, the administration had failed to push Congress to hold votes on gun control, pornography, the death penalty, tuition tax credits, or busing, abortion, and school prayer. "Thus most of the conservative issues on which millions of people had been identified and activated were virtually absent from the headlines and absent from the TV news programs." So rather than "attacking liberal Democrats as in the past, the conservative groups concentrated their attention far too much on the Reagan Administration." After riding America's moral indignation to victory, Reagan had ceded "a monopoly to our opposition on the use of moral outrage." Like Atwater and Gergen, Blackwell said that liberals and their media allies, who understood "the use of moral outrage," had hurt the administration by charging that conservatives were "raping the environment for private greed," that "the rich are getting richer and the poor are getting poorer," and that "they want to make your home ground zero in an insane nuclear exchange with the Soviets."

Blackwell proposed retaking the moral high ground by confronting "those who say they want to help the poor but really want to take children away from home and neighborhood by forced busing." Liberals would put children "into the clutches of counterculture teachers who would fill their heads with pornography, abortion, and gun control, and prevent them from praying." Reagan should throw "the whole weight of the administration" into amending the Constitution to balance the budget, legalize prayer in schools, and prohibit abortion. He should strive to ease gun controls, stop unions from using dues for politics, abolish the Legal Services Corporation, tighten antipornography laws, establish tuition tax credits, and fund a new wish list of weapons systems. Reagan should bond with conservative activists and "discipline anyone in the Administration who sends out contrary signals." Otherwise, "the conservative organizations will more and more separate their fortunes from those of the President."[74]

Reagan's senior advisers rejected this call to war. Blackwell resigned from his White House post in early 1983 and returned to his Leadership Institute to place the next generation of conservatives into the training ground of the Reagan administration. But the administration mollified the Christian right in Nixonian style by pushing Congress to hold symbolic votes on bills without draining capital by pushing for their enactment. Blackwell's replacement in the Reagan administration, special assistant Faith Ryan Whittlesey, noted in memos on October 11, 1983, that "little organizational work has been done yet for the 1984 election period" by "fundamentalist and evangelical groups. . . . To maintain our credibility *the tuition tax credit bill must come up for Senate floor action this fall.*" As for school prayer, "this situation is not unlike the tuition tax credit issue. *Politically we win if we get votes on the Senate floor.*" The administration delivered on its promises to get Congress to hold votes on social issues, but no more. The Senate killed tuition tax credits and rejected amendments to ban abortion and authorize school prayer.[75]

The administration achieved one victory for the Christian right with legislation prohibiting public high schools from barring religious or philosophical groups from meeting during nonschool hours, although some worried that the law might open schools to cults and homosexual groups. President Reagan also began dedicating his bully pulpit to moral issues. In a January 1984 speech to the National Religious Broadcasters that launched his reelection campaign, Reagan said that the Bible contained "all the answers to all the problems that face us today—if we'd only read and believe." He added, "If we could get God and discipline back in our schools, maybe we could get drugs and violence out" and that "this nation cannot continue turning a blind eye and a deaf ear to the taking of some 4,000 unborn children's lives every day." No prior president had given such eloquent voice to the right's moral concerns, making anyone but Reagan unthinkable for Christian conservative voters.

MORNING IN AMERICA

For Republicans, the economy rebounded in time to save the 1984 elections. Economists debated whether supply-side incentives or rising aggregate demand from tax cuts and deficits prompted the recovery. No matter. What counted for voters was that unemployment fell from 9.6 percent in

1983 to 7.5 percent in 1984, the economy created more than four million new jobs, and real GDP shot up by 7 percent. In the summer of 1984 Reagan's approval rating topped 55 percent for the first time since 1981. By double-digit margins, survey respondents finally agreed that his economic policies helped "people like me." The president complemented the sunny economy by lightening his relationship with the Soviets, beginning with a January 1984 speech in which he called for "a working relationship" with Moscow. He said that "1984 is a year of opportunity for peace. . . . My dream is to see the day when nuclear weapons will be banished from the face of the earth." Reagan built a big lead in the polls over his Democratic rival Walter Mondale on who would best handle foreign affairs.

Still, the president's conservative speechwriter Anthony Dolan— Terry Dolan's brother—followed Blackwell by warning that the campaign was adopting "exactly the wrong strategy" by "running on the record of the Reagan-Bush Administration." This strategy "at best will certainly lead to an extremely limited . . . painfully hollow victory." Dolan urged the president to show "moral fervor" and prepare for a second term by running on "*ideas and intensity, coherence and consistency*." The campaign should expose the Democratic Party as "*America's version of Britain's Labor Party . . . the party of the left—the party of the glitter set, the special interests, the social welfare complex and the anti-defense lobby*."[76]

Reagan's technicians rejected an ideological campaign that catered to already converted conservatives. In a memo approved by campaign director Ed Rollins, adviser Jim Lake wrote that the campaign must capture "the center ground" on which elections were decided and avoid "focusing so much on the issues that are dear to the Christian Right. No one is going to know that he has delivered on his promises if, rather than focusing on the amount of new jobs . . . we focus instead on the amount of fetuses aborted." This was sound politics, given that voters had never dismissed an incumbent president in prosperous times, with no disaster abroad, disabling scandal, or turmoil at home. But as long-term strategy it lacked the thematic focus of 1980 and built little foundation for second-term policy or a strengthened conservative movement.[77]

Although Carter's former vice president, Walter Mondale, seemed a sure bet to win the Democratic nomination for president, he had to overcome opposition from Colorado's charismatic senator Gary Hart. Mondale's rival espoused a "neoliberalism" in vogue among some Democrats, including

Senator Paul Tsongas of Massachusetts, who famously said, "You cannot love jobs and hate employers." Conservatives had coined the term "neoliberalism" in the 1940s to describe the migration of traditional liberalism from free markets to the welfare state. However, its 1980s version accommodated liberalism to capital. Neoliberals would sustain social justice programs while attracting entrepreneurial voters with plans for cheaper and smarter weapons, renewable energy, and entitlement reforms. They would adopt programs that provided lifelong education for workers who frequently changed jobs in the postindustrial economy. They favored free trade and incentives for productive enterprise and federal grants to support innovative anticrime measures by local police forces. Yet neoliberalism, like Eisenhower's modern Republicanism, lacked the wallop of undiluted liberal or conservative ideas. When Mondale ran commercials asking "Where's the beef?" Hart faltered in explaining what was new in his hybrid ideas.

Mondale defeated not only Hart but also Jesse Jackson—the first competitive African-American candidate for president—who pledged to expand social programs, rebuild the cities, and disengage abroad. Mondale had benefited when the AFL-CIO, seeking to strengthen its hold over Democratic politics, broke precedent by endorsing him before the primaries began. The endorsement, however, seemed to certify that Mondale presided over a diminished Democratic Party, held together by "special interests." Mondale hoped to exploit interest-group politics by choosing the New York representative Geraldine A. Ferraro as the first woman candidate for vice president on a major-party ticket. But allegations of corruption against her husband, real estate mogul John Zaccaro, preoccupied Ferraro. And Mondale's politically bold—many said foolhardy—plan to raise taxes was aimed at cutting deficits, not building popular benefit programs.

Reagan won every state but Minnesota, 60 percent of the popular vote, and three-quarters of the votes cast by evangelical white Protestants. Still, the GOP had not completed the realignment of 1980 and become America's majority party. The Republicans picked up only seventeen seats in Congress, giving it 42 percent of the House, less than in 1981. The GOP lost two Senate seats, leaving it clinging to a 53 percent majority. The Democrats still held the bulk of state and local offices and narrowly maintained their once big lead in party loyalties.[78]

9

RESTORING THE CONSERVATIVE CONSENSUS, 1985–2000

As President Ronald Reagan prepared to leave office in 1988, conservatives debated his legacy. Heritage president Edwin J. Feulner said that Reagan stood with Franklin Roosevelt as the most important president since Lincoln. Although the "Reagan Revolution" was far from complete, the president had "changed the terms of the debate" in America so that even liberals were talking about conservative priorities. He had launched "the longest peacetime economic expansion in history," taken "major steps to deregulate the private sector," and moved America "from mere containment of totalitarian expansion to putting democratic capitalism on the offensive." Richard Viguerie, however, asked, "What revolution?" The president "never struck at the heart of the opposition" and gave only "lip service" to religious conservatives, while staffing his administration "largely with country-clubbers, Nixon-Ford retreads, and just plain accidents." He "picked supporters of detente for the Cabinet . . . bailed out Soviet agriculture . . . bailed out international banks that lent money to anti-American countries . . . and approved some of the biggest tax hikes in history."[1]

The jarring notes soon turned into Beethoven's final symphony, an ode to joy and triumph. Conservatives put aside all other differences to claim as their iconic leader a president who had had restored America's faith in itself and revived patriotism, wholesome values, and personal responsibility. Reagan had rescued a nation sinking under the weight of taxes, regulation, and spending. He had countered activist liberal judges with "strict constructionist" appointments and brought on prosperous times. Even arms control negotiations, which the right had opposed at the time, became a virtue for revisionist conservatives who praised Reagan for hard bargaining with Gorbachev and for anticommunist policies that won the Cold War.[2]

LOSING THE EDGE

With the Reagan administration short of new ideas, Congress wrote a second-term script on domestic policy, including the bipartisan Gramm-Rudman-Hollings Act of 1985 that put an obese government on a forced diet. Democratic backing for such drastic deficit cutting showed just how far the rudderless party had drifted from Lyndon Johnson's liberal vision of a Great Society. Although the Supreme Court struck down the law's mandatory budget cuts and Congress balked at raising taxes or slashing spending, a rapidly growing economy cut the deficit by about a third from 1985 to 1989. The landmark Tax Reform Act of 1986 also drew on bipartisan proposals. It reduced the top individual rate from 50 percent to 28 percent, increased the bottom rate from 11 percent to 15 percent, taxed income and capital gains equally, and eliminated many loopholes. For the first time in twenty-five years, some tax burdens shifted significantly from individuals to business. The act also lopped several million low-income Americans off the tax rolls and increased the Earned Income Tax Credit. Only lobbying by the president overcame conservative Republican opposition to the Tax Reform Act in the House. "Reagan put us in a box," said House Minority Whip Trent Lott of Mississippi. "The Democrats had hollered for years for fairness and the Republicans had to prove we were not the captives of special interests. So we resisted; we argued; we gnashed our teeth; we fought. And then we did it." One unintended consequence of tax reform was a decline in the value of real estate investments, which contributed to the failure of deregulated savings and loan institutions and led to a government bailout of troubled thrift institutions at an estimated cost of $150 billion.[3]

While Republicans struggled against their perceived subservience to the rich, Democrats sought to dispel their image as tax-and-spend, countercultural liberals. In 1985 party moderates formed the Democratic Leadership Council (DLC), which by 1986 claimed nineteen senators and seventy House members. Like the Committee for a Democratic Majority, the DLC backed the robust internationalism of Roosevelt, Truman, and Kennedy. It spurned radical chic diversions like the nuclear freeze and backed new missile programs, Star Wars, and a smarter military. The DLC followed the model of Gary Hart's neoliberalism in reconciling with corporate interests and embracing some socially conservative positions. It supported abortion rights, the ERA, and civil rights but also fiscal responsibility, free trade, anticrime measures, and accountability for teachers. It opposed racial quotas and supported work over welfare and faith and family over countercultural indulgence. It worked with business to expand the economic pie, not redistribute slices. With corporate dollars pouring in, the DLC hoped to rebuild its party in exile, like Republicans under Carter. However, the GOP had rebuilt its base on established conservative doctrine, not hybrid ideology. "Ronald Reagan got where he is today not by me-tooing the opposition when it was in power but by insisting on his beliefs," wrote Arthur Schlesinger Jr., cofounder of Americans for Democratic Action. "If American voters are in a conservative mood, they will surely choose the real thing and not a Democratic imitation."[4]

The 1986 midterm elections found voters in a less than conservative mood. Despite a growing economy that held GOP House losses to five seats, the party forfeited control of the Senate. Conservative strategist Paul Weyrich of the Free Congress Foundation argued that the GOP had lost its way by snubbing movement conservatives. "The winners in the closely contested elections," he wrote, "had an active association with movement conservative activists—the losers did not. . . . If the Republicans are smart they will learn how to work with coalition groups the way the Democrats and the unions do." Midterm losses mattered. Reagan's first-term Republican Senate had confirmed conservatives William Rehnquist as chief justice of the Supreme Court and Antonin Scalia as associate justice. But in 1987 the Democratic Senate rejected conservative Robert Bork, Richard Nixon's loyal solicitor who had fired the Watergate special prosecutor after the attorney general and his deputy had declined to do so. Liberals campaigned so relentlessly against him that "to Bork" became a verb meaning to assassinate the character of a political opponent. Many on the right, not mollified by Reagan's appointment of moderate conservative Anthony Kennedy, vowed to avenge Bork in every face-off with the left.[5]

ANTICOMMUNISM REVIVED

The Heritage Foundation hailed the anticommunist Reagan doctrine as a "new, positive policy of containing, confronting, and ultimately reversing the tide of Soviet imperialism on a global scale." Conservatives cheered the administration in its overtures to rebel leader Jonas Savimbi in Cuban-backed Angola and its support for the "Contra" insurgency that battled the left-wing Sandinista government of Nicaragua. They backed the president's unsuccessful veto of legislation that Congress passed in 1986 to impose economic sanctions against the apartheid government of South Africa, which they viewed as a bulwark against the advance of communism in Africa. The right also supported the administration's shift from the Carter-era strategy of harassing Soviets in Afghanistan to a policy of liberation. The CIA armed the mujahideen resistance with Stinger antiaircraft missiles, sniper rifles, and plastic explosives with timed detonators. Militants from across the Arab world, including Osama bin Laden, fought the Soviets in Afghanistan, aided by America's allies Saudi Arabia and Pakistan, while Pakistan came to back as well the Taliban, a extremist group within Afghanistan. Reagan also bombed Libya in retaliation for terrorist attacks and continued aiding Saddam Hussein to make sure that Iraq survived its war against Iran. He backed repressive governments in El Salvador and Guatemala against left-wing insurgent movements.

Still, Nicaragua was ground zero for the Reagan administration, which waged "low-intensity conflict" against the Sandinistas through propaganda, economic and diplomatic pressure, and covert action. Administration officials financed a proxy war by the Contras through subterranean channels after Congress prohibited them from spending funds directly or indirectly on military operations in Nicaragua. The administration's covert support for the Contras opened a channel for collaboration with the conservative organizations, which had the effect of privatizing U.S. foreign policy in Central America. Spitz Channell, former finance director of NCPAC, the National Conservative Political Action Committee, dedicated his tax-exempt National Endowment for the Preservation of Liberty to aiding the Contras. In 1985 Channell became part of Project Democracy, developed by the CIA director William Casey—a Knight of Malta—as an operation buried within government to aid the Contras, influence American opinion, and conduct covert missions without oversight or accountability. The point man for the project in Nicaragua, Lieutenant Colonel Oliver North of the National Security Council, said that Casey had conceived the project as an "off-the-shelf, self-sustaining, stand-alone entity that could perform certain [covert] activities on behalf of the United States."[6]

Channell raised some $10 million for his nonpartisan organization, aided by Colonel North's inspirational pleas to patriotic donors and the lure of meetings with administration officials or photo ops with a president who had told subordinates to keep the Contras alive "body and soul." Two wealthy widows—Council for National Policy member Ellen Garwood and the equally conservative Barbara Newington—donated some $5 million after the dashing colonel fired their passion for the Contras. Council for National Policy president and John Birch Society leader Nelson Bunker Hunt chipped in nearly $500,000 and Joseph Coors $65,000. Channell diverted several million dollars in donated funds for commissions, salaries, consulting, and personal use. In 1985–86 he pocketed $345,000 and paid $1.7 million to a public relations firm run by Richard Miller, formerly on the staff of Republican senator Dan Quayle of Indiana. Miller's firm also received a secret grant without competitive bidding from the Office for Public Diplomacy in Latin America and the Caribbean, set up under State Department adviser Otto J. Reich to implement the Reagan doctrine. Reich worked closely with neoconservative Elliot Abrams, assistant secretary of state for inter-American affairs. Reich's office intervened in domestic politics by planting stories in the media and selectively leaking classified information to win public support for the Contras.[7]

Channell solicited contributions to his National Endowment for the Preservation of Liberty for an ad campaign against liberal Democrats in Congress, although his group's tax status barred such political activity. "This is an incredible political benefit to every single Republican running for political office," he said. "It is essentially a $30,000 contribution to these challengers' campaign with the finest issue that President Reagan has in the country today." Channell secretly purchased arms for the Contras through a $2 million account labeled "toys." He said with a straight face that he had bought "Christmas gifts for the children of Contra rebels." In 1987 Channell and Miller pleaded guilty to conspiring to defraud the government and named North as a coconspirator.[8]

Neoconservatives backed the Contras through Friends of the Democratic Center in Central America (PRODEMCA) and the Institute on Religion and Democracy, both of which were formed in 1981 and shared members. Penn Kemble, former director of the Committee for a Democratic Majority, headed PRODEMCA. He was one of several hard-line Democratic operatives who supported Reagan's foreign policies. PRODEMCA received grants from Channel's National Endowment for the Preservation of Liberty and the National Endowment for Democracy, a government-funded agency that worked through the Republican and Democratic parties to finance pro-American, democratic forces worldwide. Knight of Malta William Simon and the group's American leader J. Peter Grace served on the board of PRODEMCA, which conducted orchestrated tours of Contra base camps in Honduras for American opinion makers. The Knights of Malta used its Central American membership and diplomatic privileges to funnel aid to Contra camps. The Knights also helped the military in El Salvador and Guatemala relocate Indian villagers to army-controlled camps as part of an anti-insurgency campaign.

The Institute on Religion and Democracy criticized liberals in both the Protestant and Catholic churches. It denounced the National and World Councils of Churches for "engaging in projects that undermine democratic values and strengthen causes of the revolutionary Marxist left." And it assailed the "liberation theology" of Catholic clergy in Latin America, which emphasized the Christian mission to uplift the poor and the oppressed through political action against the rich and powerful. The institute charged that liberation theology led to violent revolution, the destruction of private property, and the rise of oppressive left-wing governments. "This theology is to Marxist analysis what 'popular fronts' have typically been to Marxist movements elsewhere," wrote board member Michael Novak, who advocated Western-style democracy and capitalism as exemplified by the Contras.[9]

Other groups joined the campaign for the Contras and the Reagan doctrine, including Citizens for America, founded in 1983 with Reagan's encouragement by Republican Lewis Lehrman, the founder of the Rite Aid drugstore chain, who had narrowly lost to Democratic star Mario Cuomo for governor of New York in 1982. Lehrman recruited former College Republicans Jack Abramoff as director and Grover Norquist as his deputy. The group raised about $3.5 million in its first two years and developed a special relationship with Reich's office, which aided its lobbying on Central America. In 1985 Lehrman and Norquist journeyed to Angola rebel leader Jonas Savimbi's jungle base camp to host a conference of anticommunist "freedom fighters." When Lehrman returned, however, he learned that Abramoff had mismanaged and overspent the group's funds and fired both Abramoff and Norquist.[10]

Abramoff reemerged as a leader of the International Freedom Foundation, funded by the South African apartheid government to polish its image, avoid American sanctions, and denigrate Nelson Mandela's African National Congress as a communist front. The foundation worked with Senator Helms, several Republican House members, and Alan Keyes. Abramoff and his backers denied knowledge of the South African connection. Abramoff left the limelight to become an insider lobbyist and Norquist took over Americans for Tax Reform, where he made waves by tirelessly signing up members of Congress to an antitax pledge. By the early 1990s Norquist would rival Paul Weyrich as a ringmaster of the right, holding well-attended Wednesday morning meetings to share news, gossip, and strategy. Although Norquist labeled his group the "Leave Us Alone Coalition," it boasted a full complement of defense hawks and conservatives dedicated to moral reform.[11]

A revamped World Anti-Communist League also became part of an international Contra support system. American Roger Pearson, an advocate of racial science who had edited Willis Carto's *Western Destiny* magazine, held the league's presidency from 1978 until being ousted in 1980. Pearson's league berated President Carter for appeasing communists and questioned whether democratic societies had enough fortitude to defeat the reds. After Pearson, the league drifted until 1984, when U.S. Army General John Singlaub turned it into a front for the Contras. He claimed to have raised $10 million in private funds worldwide. But Singlaub had secured only $500,000 in private money and fabricated his story to divert attention from $44 million flowing in from Saudi Arabia, Brunei, and Taiwan—and $16 million to $25 million from profits of arms sales to Iran, although much of this bounty never reached the Contras.[12]

Illicit aid to the Contras ignited the worst presidential scandal since Watergate. In early November 1986, the press reported that the Reagan administration had sold arms to the terrorist state of Iran, ostensibly to gain influence with Iranian "moderates" but also as part of an arms-for-hostages deal that the president had approved. Then, on Thanksgiving Day, Attorney General Edwin Meese announced that Colonel North, with the approval of his boss, NSC director John Poindexter, had illegally diverted profits from the Iranian arms sales to the Contras through the Project Democracy network of secret bank accounts, financial intermediaries, and arms dealers. Like Dorian Gray, Ronald Reagan kept his bright face as the scandal turned ugly. In a televised address in March 1987, Reagan slid by the hard issues but persuaded Americans of his good intentions, raising his wilted approval rating above the 50 percent mark.[13]

The Iran-Contra investigators in Congress, trapped in the Watergate model of trying to learn "what the president knew and when he knew it," largely missed the big political, ethical, and constitutional questions of Iran-Contra. How did inside officials and outside conservatives manage to set up an illegal, self-financed, unaccountable network for manipulating domestic politics and foreign policy? Why did Congress, the IRS, the FBI, the State Department, and the Justice Department flub their oversight responsibilities? Let sleeping questions lie, Richard Nixon advised the president in August 1987. "Don't *ever* comment on the Iran-Contra matter again. Have instructions issued to all White House staffers and Administration spokesman that they must *never* answer any question on or off the record about that issue in the future."[14]

In the first major American scandal motivated not by personal or political gain but rather by ideology, conservatives transformed Colonel North from conspirator to patriot and hero. Although a special prosecutor indicted North in 1988, his trial came after the election. The arms sale and the diversion of profits to the Contras had failed to free most hostages held by militants, make America influential in Iran, or substantially aid the Contras. But the scandal faded by 1988, when the Sandinistas and Contras reached a cease-fire, the Soviet Union began withdrawing from Afghanistan, and Iran and Iraq ended their long bloody war.

CULTURAL FERMENT ON THE RIGHT

Conservative power waned during Reagan's final two years in office. The National Conservative Political Action Committee never recovered from Terry Dolan's death in 1986, hard times hit Viguerie's enterprises, and the Iran-Contra scandal cut short the administration's partnership with the right on foreign policy. Beset by financial woes and public indifference, most Christian right groups of the late 1970s shriveled or died. A 1988 memo from Paul Weyrich's Free Congress Foundation explained, "During the late 1970s the primary focus of the conservative movement was building a grass-roots base of activists and contributors who would constitute a participatory majority to achieve the election of conservative leaders and the implementation of conservative policies." However, "with Ronald Reagan's election and the concurrent capture of the U.S. Senate by professed conservatives, conservative leaders and grass-roots activists cut short their focus on the building of a locally based movement and began to focus on staffing and running an administration."[15]

The demise of the Moral Majority headlined conservative obituaries. As early as 1983 Reagan's political advisers wondered "what we can do to recapture enthusiasm in the fundamentalist and evangelical community. Clearly their political activism declined between 1980 and 1982." They had no answers. Although Falwell claimed millions of followers in the 1980s, his Moral Majority endured mainly as a fund-raising front, a newsletter, and names on a letterhead. Falwell appeared on *Nightline*, debated liberals, led rallies, and delivered sermons. He met with the president and steadfastly supported the administration. Readers of *Good Housekeeping* magazine rated him second only to Reagan as America's "most admired man." For nearly a decade, this Great Oz of the right had pulled the levers on a publicity machine from behind the curtain of his Moral Majority. He masterfully spun narratives and anecdotes that imparted his religious and political principles to the media and the public. But the curtain had frayed by 1986, when Falwell announced that the Moral Majority would be subsumed within a new Liberty Federation. A year later Falwell resigned his presidency after failing in a new mission to rescue the PTL (Praise the Lord) empire of scandal-plagued televangelists Jim and Tammy Bakker. The Moral Majority ended with a whimper in 1989, when Falwell blessed James Dobson, the founder of Focus on the Family, as his successor on the Christian right. Dobson had become politically active in the 1980s by founding the independent Family Research Council to lobby for traditional family values and joining a presidential advisory group on juvenile justice and delinquency.[16]

By 1987 conservatives were losing faith in politicians, as J. Howard Pew had in earlier times. With Reagan faltering, Weyrich advised conservatives to go "back to basics in framing the issues." His objective was to repackage the right's anti-pluralist ideology as "cultural conservatism." Weyrich proposed that the right combat cultural decline by toughening divorce laws, banning abortion and pornography, restoring God to public life, and teaching "traditional Western culture" in schools. But he also proposed an innovative new "compassionate conservatism" that would reject "a politics which says that it really doesn't matter what happens to the community as long as those who survive get theirs." Compassionate conservatives would follow "a conservative doctrine of service" by reaching out to help the needy help themselves. They would instill sound values and the ethic of personal responsibility in the poor by having faith-based organizations deliver social services. They would offer employers incentives for employee stock-ownership plans and provide tax breaks for businesses to locate in economically depressed communities.[17]

Yet cultural change resisted the usual methods of the right. Conservatives could commission studies and organize conferences and be confident of the results. But they could not by formula churn out compelling films and plays, hit television shows, best-selling books, or inspiring art and music. They seemed baffled by a time when visual and acoustic imagery supplanted the written word, fragmented images replaced linear narratives, and electronic media provided sex, violence, and other instant gratifications.

Some conservatives turned inward. They enrolled children in private Christian academies or schooled them at home. From 1989 to 1999 enrollment in schools affiliated with conservative Christian school associations soared by 46 percent and accounted for three-quarters of all new private school admissions. Christian conservatives started to create their own pop culture through music, books, films, broadcasting, and such religious kitsch as bobblehead Jesus and Mary dolls, rapture T-shirts, Bible comics, and "scripture" candy such as Atonemints and Forbidden Fruit sour apples. "You'll be keeping all your money in the kingdom now," conservative troubadour Steve Taylor sang with mild irony. "And you'll only drink milk from a Christian cow." Christian music hit the pop charts and the Campus Crusade for Christ's Jesus film project drew millions of viewers. Evangelical Christians even sought to co-opt the sexual revolution through advice books, classes, videos, and lectures. Evangelicals issued biblically guided sex manuals for married couples that described in anatomical detail sexual techniques for heterosexual intercourse. The manuals upheld male authority but also taught wives how to achieve happiness and material rewards by sexually flattering, exciting, and fulfilling their husbands.[18]

Conservatives influenced mainstream culture by preaching, talking, and singing on television and the radio. After suffering sex and money scandals in the mid-1980s, television preachers consolidated their enterprises, exploited new broadcast technologies and the Internet, developed niche markets, and purveyed Christian entertainment. They polished their salesmanship, tightened ethical standards, and updated formats without sacrificing content. Pat Robertson's cable Family Channel showed how to deliver a Christian pro-family message mixed with wholesome entertainment. Robertson sold the Family Channel in 1997 to conservative media baron Rupert Murdoch but continued hosting his religious talk show the *700 Club*.[19]

On the air, conservatives didn't just dominate talk radio, they *owned* it. In 1985 James C. Roberts, formerly of the American Conservative Union, began Radio America to air quality programs with a "commitment to traditional American values, limited government and the free market." Radio America quickly gained an audience, advertisers, and backing from the Bradley and Olin foundations and corporate sponsors. By 1987, when Reagan's Federal Communications Commission repealed the Fairness Doctrine that had required equal time for opposing viewpoints, Radio America claimed network status because it was broadcasting to some four hundred affiliate stations.

Then an unknown named Rush Limbaugh turned talk radio into a cultural phenomenon. In the late 1980s listeners and radio executives discovered in Sacramento the relentless conservative patter and antiliberal invective of this college dropout with a well-trained voice, a sense of humor, and, in his words, "talent on loan from God." By 1992 Limbaugh was hosting a syndicated program that reached an estimated thirteen and a half million listeners per week and won Reagan's blessing as "the number one voice for conservatism in our country." Rush did it alone, with scarcely any on-air guests—just the host and either setup critics or friendly callers who reveled in skewering liberals, Democrats, UN officials, civil rights advocates, "femi-Nazis," and "wacko" environmentalists. Limbaugh's callers began just saying "ditto" rather than repeating adulatory comments about his show. They created a virtual community of loyal "dittohead" listeners that basked in a culture of certainty, fellowship, and familiar innuendo and inside jokes. Limbaugh said in 1994, "Liberals are terrified of me. As well they should be. . . . I represent middle America's growing rejection of the elites." Limbaugh's audience rose to some twenty million per week by the mid-1990s, and other conservative talkers caught fire as well:

Oliver North, the young and brash Sean Hannity, convicted Watergate conspirator G. Gordon Liddy, and presidential son Michael Reagan. Studies showed that Limbaugh's most frequently repeated messages, especially his negative views, influenced audience opinion.[20]

In the 1990s, anyone who drove a car with the radio on heard country music and conservative talk. According to Christopher Manion, a religion professor, Heritage Foundation lecturer, and the son of conservative talk show pioneer Pat Manion, they delivered the same message. Rock and roll, he said, split up families and "celebrated the excesses of the passions of the sixties, every political, sexual, and hallucinogenic cause." Country music, however, taught the virtues of sin and retribution: "If you cheat on your spouse it's wrong and you suffer; if you hang out in bars, you're gonna get in trouble; and if you're a drunk, you'll go to jail." And country music was "usually intergenerational; it is often played by families. . . . Every bluegrass festival I go to features families singing and playing together. I've never seen that at a rock concert."[21]

PASSING ON THE LEGACY

Late in his second term, Reagan achieved an historic breakthrough in foreign policy that went against the grain of the right. In 1985 the new Soviet leader Mikhail Gorbachev introduced a modicum of democracy, civil liberties, economic freedom, and a more conciliatory approach to the West. Reagan's opposition to Soviet tyranny and nuclear weapons worked synchronously in the Gorbachev era. "Your hard liners and my hard liners are going to swallow very hard seeing us up here shaking hands and smiling," Gorbachev said at a 1985 summit meeting. A year later, at another summit in Reykjavik, Iceland, the two leaders came close to reducing drastically or even scrapping their nuclear arsenals. But Gorbachev insisted that the United States abandon its missile defense program to avoid upsetting the nuclear balance and igniting an arms race in space. Reagan refused to do so and Gorbachev rejected his offer to share American technology as insincere. Neither side had formed the "exceptional level of trust" necessary for agreement, said Gyorgy Arbatov, the Russians' leading "Americanologist." In December 1987, however, the two leaders agreed to an Intermediate Nuclear Forces treaty, the first treaty to eliminate a class of nuclear weapons. Afterward, Reagan said that the "evil empire" was from "another time, another era" and that Gorbachev was "a serious man committed to serious change."[22]

Conservative opinion makers, however, still opposed accords with treacherous reds. Conventional thinkers on the right and left failed to understand how Reagan could comfortably weave together what seemed to be contradictory ideas. He was a warrior against evil and a man of peace. He was a leader of principle and a pragmatist who understood better than his right-wing critics how the world had changed since 1980. In Reagan's deal making with Gorbachev, most leaders of the right saw betrayal and weakness, not hope and opportunity. "Seven years after Ronald Reagan's arrival in Washington, the U.S. government and its allies are still dominated by the culture of appeasement," wrote Michael Johns, an editor of the Heritage Foundation's journal *Policy Review*. Jesse Helms's political operative Tom Ellis formed the Leadership Coalition for Freedom Through Truth in 1987 to "delegitimize the Soviet Union." Ellis urged President Reagan to "re-focus the nation's attention on the central issue of Freedom vs. Communism; Christianity vs. Atheistic Humanism" and to recognize that Gorbachev was not "a new kind of Soviet leader." Richard Viguerie and Howard Phillips forged an Anti-Appeasement Coalition that compared Reagan to Hitler's notorious appeaser British prime minister Neville Chamberlain.[23]

Leading Republicans joined this chorus of protest. Conservative senator James A. McClure of Idaho said, "We still have a lot of faith in Reagan but there is a lot of distrust of the negotiating process, a feeling that it leads to concessions that are unwise." Four of six contenders for the 1988 GOP presidential nomination opposed the INF treaty: Pat Robertson, Representative Jack Kemp, former secretary of state Alexander Haig, and Delaware governor Pierre S. "Pete" Du Pont IV. Only Vice President Bush and Senator Bob Dole backed ratification, Dole reluctantly.[24]

Reagan did not relent. As Richard Nixon had earlier advised, "The trick here is to capture the conservative *voters* without being captured by the conservative *leaders*. . . . When they're wrong don't try to appease them. It won't work. They will still want more." In words reminiscent of Eisenhower, Reagan scorned conservatives who "have accepted that war is inevitable." With Reagan selling the treaty to the public, the Senate rejected amendments from conservatives that would have made the accord unacceptable to the Soviets and voted for ratification with only five dissenting votes in May 1988.[25]

Conservatives were also frustrated by their lack of a consensus choice to succeed Ronald Reagan. Vice President Bush and Senate Leader Dole failed to win the heart of the right. Kemp's campaign fizzled. Robertson, who had reconsidered his earlier aversion to mixing religion and politics, hoped to inspire an army of the faithful. He finished second to Dole and ahead of Bush in the Iowa caucuses but the preacher candidate made little impression elsewhere. Bush rebounded from Iowa to win the New Hampshire primary and then won the so-called front-loaded primaries that had been moved up to early March by sweeping all twenty of the mostly southern and border state contests held on Super Tuesday, March 8. Bush endorsed a conservative's dream platform: it backed Star Wars, a human life amendment to halt abortion, tort reform to quell lawsuits against business, and lower capital gains taxes. He picked young conservative senator Dan Quayle of Indiana as his running mate. To the conservative faithful Bush pledged: "Read my lips. No new taxes." His Democratic opponent, liberal Massachusetts governor Michael Dukakis, had weathered a stiff primary challenge from Jesse Jackson, who shook off the allegations of extremism and anti-Semitism that had plagued him four years earlier. In the hope of re-creating the Kennedy-Johnson magic, Dukakis ran with Senator Lloyd Bentsen of Texas.[26]

Dukakis left the Democratic convention with a seventeen-point lead in the polls and a resolve to back into the presidency with a Dewey-style campaign of "competence not ideology." But Dukakis's lead was illusory in an election that turned not on Bush's campaign skills but on Reagan's unbeatable record of economic expansion, progress in the Cold War, and domestic tranquillity. GOP strategist Lee Atwater believed that Bush would win the election in the white South and advance the Republican realignment there. "If George Bush wins the South . . . I am convinced that the South will go Republican for the rest of this century," Atwater said.[27]

Following Atwater's guidance, Bush campaigned on what he was against. He branded Dukakis with the "L word"—*liberal*—that Dukakis danced around but never fully embraced or rejected. An ad run by the obscure National Security Political Action Committee made Willie Horton—a convicted black felon who had raped a white Maryland woman and beat her husband while on furlough from a Massachusetts prison—a familiar face of the campaign. Bush, however, had surpassed Dukakis in the polls well before this vilification began. The vice president benefited little from an attack strategy that forfeited his chance to test ideas for governing after Reagan. Bush won forty states and 53.4 percent of the popular vote, although the GOP lost a Senate seat and three in the House. Bush won every southern state but the rest of his party stalled in the South.

In the aftermath of the Reagan administration, some liberals challenged conservatives by staking a claim to the Reagan legacy. Like neoconservative intellectual Ben Wattenberg they argued that Reagan had legitimized New Deal and Great Society programs, compromised on taxes, and turned from cold warrior to negotiator. Other liberals anointed Jimmy Carter the godfather of the Reagan Revolution for deregulating industry, expanding the military, imposing sanctions on the Soviets, and arming Afghan resisters. But liberals also blamed Reagan for a "me decade" of greed that helped the rich, shortchanged women and minorities, and squeezed average Americans. They charged him with piling up debt, neglecting the environment, sabotaging civil rights, and running a scandal-ridden administration. Perhaps worst of all, he had widened the gap between the rich and all other Americans. After declining or holding steady for many years, income inequality widened in the 1980s; the share collected by the top 1 percent rose from 8 percent to 13 percent. Critics said that Reagan had not pared down government but only shifted priorities from social programs to defense, law enforcement, and intelligence. They insisted that flaws in the communist system doomed the Soviet empire and Reagan had wasted hundreds of billions of dollars on a defense boom that impeded negotiations, strengthened hard-liners in the Soviet Union, and prolonged the Cold War. Liberals further claimed that Reagan had protected apartheid in South Africa and death squads in Latin America and actively aided Saddam Hussein and Islamic militants.[28]

No retrospective analysis of Reagan's political impact hit closer to the mark than Morton Blackwell's prediction back in 1978. "A Reagan presidency would give the country a breathing spell," he wrote. "A new generation of conservative recruits would get . . . the opportunity to build for the future. And liberals would find that they could survive four or even eight years of him." In 1988 the Heritage Foundation began grooming a "third generation" of conservatives to succeed Buckley's "first generation" and Paul Weyrich's "second generation," never mind the generations of Calvin Coolidge, Charles Hilles, Elizabeth Dilling, and J. Howard Pew or of Joseph McCarthy, George Benson, and Robert Taft.

THE LEGACY BETRAYED

For conservatives, the post-Reagan future looked bleak under a president who lacked eloquence, passion, and, in his own words, "the vision thing." With Bush drawing mainly on mainstream Republicans for his cabinet, only the nomination of former senator John Tower as secretary of defense cheered conservatives, however briefly. Liberals, energized by their victory over Bork, defeated Tower's nomination by harping on his drinking and womanizing. They were aided by a conflicted Weyrich, who declined "to overlook or conceal the immorality of public figures." Most conservative leaders disagreed, and they huddled with administration officials to salvage the nomination. Two *Washington Times* editors, managing editor Wesley Pruden and editorial editor Tony Snow, participated in their strategy session.[29]

President Bush took office with no guarantees that communism would collapse without bloodshed. Bush seemed shy and awkward, but not overmatched, at least in foreign affairs. His skeptical, steady-hand diplomacy prodded events forward without provoking a Soviet backlash. Just after the Berlin Wall fell in November 1989, Bush said that conservatives had urged him to "climb the Berlin Wall and make high-sounding pronouncements. . . . The administration, however, is not going to resort to such steps and is trying to conduct itself with restraint." Bush negotiated with Gorbachev and America's hesitant European allies for a unified Germany to remain in NATO. As the Iron Curtain lifted from Soviet satellite states, the United States quietly warned the Soviets against intervening in these nations and assured Moscow that it would not attempt to exploit the transition for its own ends. Not a single Soviet soldier fired a shot to preserve communism in eastern Europe. Death came rather in China, where the United States had little sway. Deng Xiaoping, Mao's successor, liberalized the Chinese economy but refused to grant political liberty. In June 1989 Chinese troops had massacred several hundred political protesters at Tiananmen Square in Beijing.[30]

By the end of 1990 Germany had unified and the Soviets had withdrawn from Afghanistan. In August 1991, after a failed coup against the Gorbachev government by communist reactionaries seeking to restore the old order, the Soviet Union crumbled. It was replaced by independent republics, which refuted the thesis that communist states could not peacefully change. The Cold War and its corollary arms race had ended. In its victory drama, the right gave star billing to Reagan, hard-line British prime minister Margaret Thatcher, and charismatic Pope John Paul II, who had inspired religious faith and anticommunism across the Soviet empire. Bush had to settle for a bit part as the mop-up man.[31]

In 1990 an economic slump led to declining federal revenue and a rising budget deficit. In response, Bush struck a deal with the Democratic majority in Congress to reduce deficits by raising taxes and restraining spending, forsaking his "read my lips" election pledge. Daniel J. Mitchell, Olin fellow at the Heritage Foundation, said, "If George Bush had pardoned Willie Horton, or burned Old Glory on the lawn of the White House, it would hardly have rivaled the flip-flop he has committed on taxes." Yet the deal was a consequence of Reagan-era policies that cut taxes but not spending. President Bush had to choose between letting deficits spin out of control or dealing with the devil. Bush said, "And every once in a while in one's Presidency, I think it dawns on the incumbent of the Oval Office that you're not going to get it exactly your own way.... But as I look at the ever-increasing deficits, I think it is time we do something and do something serious." Bush also broke with the right to sign the Americans with Disabilities Act and amendments that strengthened the Clean Air Act. He vetoed a civil rights bill that he said would establish quotas in attempting to reverse Supreme Court decisions that had weakened protections against employment discrimination. But he later signed similar legislation. He angered Christian conservatives by inviting representatives of gay rights groups to bill signings, leading to the resignation of special assistant Doug Wead, Bush's liaison to the right.[32]

Not every Bush initiative nettled conservatives. After the Supreme Court protected flag burning as a form of free speech, Bush supported a constitutional amendment that would ban it. With the red menace receding, Bush declared a new war on drugs. He anointed tub-thumping conservative William Bennett, formerly Reagan's secretary of education, as "drug czar." Bennett would fight drugs through policing—not rehabilitation or education—aimed at the inner cities and foreign suppliers, which exempted the GOP's suburban and small-town constituents and financial interests involved in drug-money laundering. Bush put Vice President Quayle in charge of a Competitiveness Council that quietly intervened in regulatory decisions to ease burdens on industry. Beyond the deficit deal, the president took no decisive action to reverse the sliding economy in 1990, confident that the business cycle would turn upward before 1992. "There's not another single piece of legislation that needs to be passed in the next two years for this president," said Chief of Staff John Sununu in 1990.[33]

Republicans fared better than pundits had expected in the 1990 midterm elections; the party lost seven seats in the House and one in the Senate. Conservatives cheered Senator Helms in North Carolina for defining affirmative action as "racial quotas" to exploit white voter fears of losing their jobs to blacks in his narrow victory over African-American Democrat Harvey Gantt. But the right complained that Bush had failed to defend conservatives or build a Republican majority. Viguerie said that the president was "heading into a civil war with GOP conservatives that will leave the political fields covered with blood." As an "agent" of "the establishment," Bush had "sent our sons to die in no-win wars . . . bused children across town to schools where prayer was almost the only activity not allowed," and "raised our taxes to pay for an already bloated budget. . . . Bush has done more harm to the GOP than any Democrat in a decade." Representative Gingrich said, "We're just sitting here, with half the party in despair because the White House is saying that governing means raising taxes and compromising with the Democratic Congress."[34]

After the election, Bush cheered the right by appointing conservative African American Clarence Thomas to the Supreme Court seat vacated by liberal hero Thurgood Marshall. Thomas survived "Borking" by liberals who charged him with extremism and sexual harassment to win confirmation votes from fifty-two senators, including eleven Democrats. Conservative columnist George Will said that Thomas represented "Blacks who will not let white liberals define permissible black beliefs [and] a judiciary that will not deliver by fiat the agenda that liberals cannot advance by democratic persuasion."[35]

An undaunted president continued to work magic abroad. In response to Iraq's invasion of oil-rich Kuwait—the only attempt by a UN member to annex forcibly another member—Bush assembled an international coalition that included Arab states and Russia. He gained United Nations approval to expel Iraqi armies from Kuwait, as well as congressional support. With the United States amassing overwhelming military force, its troops rapidly defeated Iraq's armies and liberated Kuwait with limited American casualties.

After agonized appraisals and reappraisals, the administration decided not to take Baghdad and topple Saddam. It believed that the Iraqi military would likely depose Saddam and that an American effort to topple him by force would be followed by chaos in Iraq and the rise of Iran as the dominant power in the Middle East. The administration encouraged local uprisings against Saddam which he brutally and bloodily suppressed, while President Bush steadfastly refused to let America become embroiled in what he called a "civil war" in Iraq and to assume the task of rebuilding the nation. Although some conservatives faulted Bush for failing to move against Saddam, on its own terms the war succeeded. The president validated collective security and achieved the first decisive triumph of American arms since World War II. "By God, we've kicked the Vietnam syndrome once and for all," he said.[36]

With his approval rating zooming to an uncharted 91 percent, Bush alarmed conservatives by speaking confidently of leading a "new world order." But he failed to deliver more than bold words. "We must plead guilty to the charge that our approach was often ad hoc," wrote Lawrence Eagleburger, secretary of state during Bush's last six months. "A certain degree of 'ad hocery' is a virtue, not a vice, when you are dealing with a world in crisis and in chaos." Neoconservatives, however, would not settle for ad hocery and did not envision the United Nations or collective security as the focal point of a new world order. In their grand version of engaged nationalism, American power should unilaterally rule the post-Soviet world. The United States should aggressively advance its global interests and democratic capitalism while keeping all rivals in check. Paul Wolfowitz, a former Team B member and undersecretary of defense for policy, prepared for Defense Secretary Dick Cheney a 1992 draft planning paper that called for "a new order that holds the promise of convincing potential competitors that they need not aspire to a greater role or pursue a more aggressive posture to protect their legitimate interests." It said that "the world order is ultimately backed by the U.S." and that "the United States should be postured to act independently when collective action cannot be orchestrated." The nation had to be prepared to act unilaterally to protect such vital interests as maintaining access to Persian Gulf oil, preventing the proliferation of weapons of mass destruction, and meeting "threats to U.S. citizens from terrorism." Secretary Cheney and the chairman of the Joint Chiefs of Staff Colin Powell rewrote the draft after it leaked to the *New York Times.* The key premises of the draft lived on, although the final version used more diplomatic language, more narrowly defined threats to U.S. security, and gave greater emphasis to multilateral cooperation.[37]

THE CHRISTIAN RIGHT REBORN

The Christian right rebounded in 1989 when Pat Robertson consolidated the "invisible army" of his presidential campaign into a Christian Coalition. Like the American Conservative Union, practical politicians ran the coalition, led by executive director Ralph Reed. The Moral Majority had extended Christian conservative politics beyond Spiritual Mobilization. The Christian Coalition moved the Christian right beyond the Moral Majority.

First, the coalition realized the long-deferred dream of William Anderson and his Christian Alliance to rally thousands of evangelical churches behind the Republican Party. Here was the missing piece on the right—the army of iron men to fight for candidates and issues. In 1992 the coalition claimed 250,000 members and spent $10 million on politics. It helped shape the Republican platform and distributed many millions of "Family Values Voter Guides." In 1994 Newt Gingrich's spokesman Tony Blankley said, "The organized Christian vote is roughly to the Republican Party today what organized labor was to the Democrats. It brings similar resources: people, money and ideological conviction."[38]

Although self-identified evangelical Christians comprised a vast and diverse group of Americans, by the first Reagan administration they were predominantly conservative in their political views. A 1983 survey divided evangelicals into non-fundamentalists and fundamentalists who regularly attended church and were most concerned about maintaining doctrinal purity. Results showed that 85 percent of evangelicals who identified themselves as fundamentalists and 69 percent of nonfundamentalist evangelicals classified themselves as political conservatives. By the 1990s evangelicals had become predominantly Republican as well. In 1972, according to the National Election Study, 42 percent of white Protestant evangelicals with a major party preference had identified as Republicans. In 1996, 57 percent identified as Republicans, pulling even with mainstream white Protestants who historically had led evangelicals, many of them southern Democrats, in Republican loyalty. Among regular churchgoing white evangelicals, this tide became a tsunami; Republican affiliation rose from 44 percent to 74 percent between 1972 and 1996.[39]

Second, the Christian Coalition did not just back the Republican Party. In collaboration with other conservative Christian groups, it *became* the Republican Party. The coalition recruited and trained Christian conservatives to run for state and local party positions, even at the risk of losing its official nonpartisan, tax-exempt status. The coalition's fifty-seven-page "county action plan" instructed leaders of state chapters to control county Republican organizations by recruiting candidates to compete for open seats or seats "held by people who are not conservative and pro-family." But local organizations should "never mention the name 'Christian Coalition' in Republican circles." From county-level positions, activists moved into state Republican committees and became national convention delegations, thereby influencing national party platforms, rules, and nominees. The Christian Coalition and allied groups also intervened in 138 U.S. House races in 1998 and slightly more than a hundred in 2000.[40]

As early as 1994, according to a study by *Campaigns and Elections* magazine, Christian conservatives had a "strong" influence on eighteen Republican state parties, with at least 50 percent of state GOP central committee members either backing "the issue agenda of Christian conservatives" or affiliated with Christian right organizations. Christian conservatives had a "moderate" influence on thirteen other state parties. Although the Christian Coalition declined after Ralph Reed resigned in 1997 and it lost its tax exemption after a long struggle with the IRS, Christian conservatives had come to stay within the GOP. An updated study for 2000 again found eighteen state parties with a strong Christian right influence, but the number with a moderate influence had doubled to twenty-six. The remaining seven state parties with weak influences were all in the Northeast.[41]

Third, the Christian Coalition relied on less threatening language and themes than had the 1970s groups. The coalition worked with Newt Gingrich and William Bennett to tutor candidates in rhetoric that resonated with a Christian conservative base without outraging the centrist majority. Yet the coalition and kindred groups conveyed a strikingly different message in direct-mail appeals for members, mobilization, and funds. A study of the Christian Coalition and Concerned Women of America found that their direct mail pilloried opponents as "abortionists," "militant homosexuals," and "ultra-feminists" intent upon "destroying marriage," "harvesting babies," and achieving "the wholesale destruction of parental authority." Still, one common theme linked public and private messages. Conservatives borrowed from civil rights rhetoric to defend Christians as victims of discrimination in a culture that grants freedom to all speech except religious speech, tolerates obscenity but not Christian imagery, and protects gays but not Christians from defamation. "Those who are working for the dissolution of our society," Pat Robertson said, "also want to destroy Christianity and Bible-based religion."[42]

Fourth, the Christian Coalition worked on state and local and not just national politics, and it addressed a broad range of issues. Echoing the Minute Women of the 1950s, Ralph Reed said, "The real battles of concern to Christians are in neighborhoods, school boards, city councils and state legislatures." The coalition taught local followers how to form political action committees, make speeches, write letters, and turn out voters. "I want to be invisible," Reed said to his later regret. "I paint my face and travel at night. You don't know it's over until you're in a body bag." The Christian right made some gains in elections for local positions, but the coalition never followed through on its promise of aiding candidates across the nation and fell far short of its goal of winning substantial control over America's local governments and school boards. Evangelical Christians also gained some state judicial posts, where they voted more conservatively than mainstream Protestants, Jews, and Catholics on issues such as women's rights, obscenity, and the death penalty.[43]

The coalition exemplified the synergy between conservative positions on moral and economic issues. It endorsed corporate priorities on taxes and budgets, health care, regulations, and foreign policy. "The pro-family movement has limited its effectiveness by concentrating disproportionately on issues such as abortion and homosexuality," Reed wrote. "To win at the ballot box and in the court of public opinion, however, the pro-family movement must speak to the concerns of average voters in the areas of taxes, crime, government waste, health care, and financial security." The coalition backed its words with $1 million to oppose Clinton's health care reform and $150,000 to challenge his budget. In 1995 the coalition released a Contract with the American Family that did not call for cracking down on homosexuals or enacting constitutional amendments to ban abortion or legalize school prayer.[44]

The Christian Coalition was the crown jewel of the "big three" Christian right groups, along with Focus on the Family and Concerned Women of America. In 1988 James Dobson's Focus on the Family had plunged into the political thicket when it absorbed the Family Research Council and hired former Reagan administration official Gary Bauer as its CEO. Dobson raised his public profile by opposing the Civil Rights Act of 1988 for violating the religious liberties of churches. He urged a boycott of Universal Studios for its supposedly sacrilegious film *The Last Temptation of Christ* and resigned from the Reagan administration's Panel on Teen Pregnancy Prevention to protest its sanctioning of sex education. In 1989 he conducted a videotaped interview with convicted serial killer Ted Bundy on the eve of Bundy's execution. In the video, which Dobson released to the media after Bundy's death, the killer blamed pornography for his depravity.[45]

When President George H. W. Bush granted Dobson an exclusive interview during the 1992 campaign, Focus on the Family had a staff of seven hundred and an annual budget of $60 million. That year Dobson led a referendum campaign in Colorado that banned gay rights laws (later overturned by the Supreme Court). Focus produced a weekly radio news program, organized lobbying coalitions, and published six magazines, including a monthly political publication, *Citizen Magazine*, with 130,000 subscribers. Dr. Dobson reached many millions with a syndicated daily radio program and newspaper column. Each month, more than two hundred thousand listeners sent him letters and thirty-five thousand dialed Focus on the Family's toll-free number. Politicians had to reckon seriously with Dobson's ability to activate millions of followers behind moral causes, although he usually avoided economic issues. Dobson's message was simple: "God is or God isn't. He has a standard or he doesn't. There is right and wrong or there isn't. . . . You've got to make a choice. It's one or the other." By the early twenty-first century Dobson's staff had increased to thirteen hundred and his budget to more than $100 million. Unlike Falwell and Robertson, however, Dobson stayed above the partisan fray, remaining a Father Knows Best for conservatives.[46]

In 1990 the president of Concerned Women for America Beverly LaHaye began a daily radio broadcast followed by a monthly magazine, *Family Voice*. By 1992 CWA's claimed membership of 573,000 and its $10 million budget swamped the $2 million budget and 80,000 membership of the Eagle Forum and also surpassed the liberal National Organization for Women. Unlike Phyllis Schlafly, LaHaye avoided clashing with liberals on op-ed pages or talk shows. She rallied women through Christian networks to lobby policy makers directly from home. She also mobilized experts for pro-family legal action, developed a Web site, circulated material to the media, and established a think tank in 1999. The CWA supported American military intervention abroad and an extensive missile defense system to protect the American family. It objected to UN declarations on the rights of gays, women, and children that it said undermined Christianity, traditional families, and U.S. sovereignty. CWA presumed that God worked through women and that women worked through men. "I think women are the key to turning this nation around," said Maxine Sielman, head of CWA's Iowa chapter. "A good woman can make a bad man good, but a bad woman can make a good man bad."[47]

In the 1980s politically and theologically conservative Christians gained command of the Southern Baptist Convention, whose fifteen million members made it America's largest Protestant denomination. The new leadership opposed civil rights laws, legal abortions, homosexual rights, and the distribution of birth control information and devices in schools. They hoped to convert Jews through the Messianic movement in which ethnic Jews embraced Christ as savior. Eighty-one percent of the Southern Baptist clergy said they voted for George Bush in 1988. Among all church members, 69 percent said they voted for Bush, up from the 49 percent who had backed Ford in 1976. The party identification of white Southern Baptists rose from 31 percent Republican in 1976 to 52 percent in 1988. A 1985 survey found that lay Southern Baptist deacons (all male) and presidents of Woman's Missionary Unions overwhelmingly opposed the ERA, abortion, and civil rights for gays and lesbians, with conservative politics and theology correlated closely. In 1998 the Republican Convention amended its statement of beliefs to state that "a wife is to submit herself graciously to the servant leadership of her husband." Two years later it banned women from the ministry.[48]

The Mormon Church, which has a unique ability in America to mobilize its membership behind issues, also became a mainstay of conservative politics after it played a major role in defeating the Equal Rights Amendment in the 1970s. Later in the century the Church became deeply involved in efforts to oppose gay and lesbian rights. Church leaders, for example, urged members not just to support a 2000 California ballot proposition banning gay marriages but also to join the opposition campaign. Survey data showed that Mormons were among the most socially conservative groups. Although the leadership rarely expressed opinions on economic matters, the surveys showed that Mormons usually embraced conservative positions on economic issues as well. The Church does not officially endorse candidates but the Mormon vote has been overwhelmingly Republican since the 1970s.[49]

Douglas Coe continued to expand the secretive enterprises of his Family in the late twentieth century. By 2000 his group had an annual budget of $10 million and close relationships with Republican senators Don Nickles of Oklahoma, Pete Domenici of New Mexico, Charles Grassley of Iowa, John Ensign of Nevada, James Inhofe of Oklahoma and Republican representatives James DeMint of South Carolina, Frank Wolfe of Virginia, and Zach Wamp of Tennessee. Also included in Coe's inner circle were Democratic senator Bill Nelson of Florida and Democratic representatives Bart Stupak of Michigan and Michael Doyle of Pennsylvania. The organization also prospered through its sponsorship of Chuck Colson's Prison Fellowship Ministries, which by 2000 had an annual budget that surpassed $40 million. Colson's group had branches in some one hundred nations and its seminars and Bible study programs had reached some 150,000 prisoners in the United States with its exclusively Christian message of conversion and redemption. The Prison Fellowship powerfully advocated for privately run prisons and the delivery of all social services by faith-based groups. Colson brought together politically conservative Catholics and Protestants for a statement of common beliefs, advised conservative politicians including Texas governor George W. Bush, and worked with Christian right leaders Pat Robertson and James Dobson on the development of political strategy. He disseminated conservative messages on sex roles, abortion, homosexuality, pornography, gay rights, and separation of church and state in his radio broadcasts and columns, reaching millions of Americans.[50]

Other para-church organizations expanded the reach of conservative Christians in the late twentieth century. Most notable was the Promise Keepers, founded in 1990 by University of Colorado football coach Bill McCartney as a men's only Christian revitalization movement. Like Bill Bright's Youth for Christ, the Promise Keepers did not advance a specific political agenda, but inculcated a conservative ideology. Its leadership called upon men to reassert their role as the heads of the family in a loving way and to restore the traditional sex roles that the feminist movement had attacked and undermined. They denounced the evils of abortion, homosexuality, pornography, divorce, and feminism. McCartney played a lead role in backing Colorado's 1992 anti–gay rights referendum and Thomas Fortson, who succeeded McCartney as president of the Promise Keepers in 2003, campaigned against gay marriage and abortion. The Promise Keepers advocated reconciliation of the races but only through common fellowship in Christ. Like earlier Christian conservative movements, the Promise Keepers believed that only a spiritual revival, not structural reform, could redeem a troubled nation. The group reached its peak in 1997 when it brought some one million men to Washington, DC, to pledge their loyalty to a "DC Covenant" of commitment to godly living and Christian faith.[51]

CAMPAIGNING WITHOUT VISION

Win or lose, George Bush worried the right in 1992. "Conservatives supported George Bush and they got Michael Dukakis," said Edwin Feulner, president of the Heritage Foundation. Or perhaps they got Richard Nixon. Feulner added, "By frequently talking conservative, and calling itself conservative—while pursuing or acquiescing to damaging policies that are anything but conservative—the administration has given the conservative cause a black eye [and] has all but invited challenge from the Right." The conservative challenge to Bush's nomination came from conservative media commentator Pat Buchanan, formerly a special assistant to Richard Nixon and communications director for Ronald Reagan. Buchanan adapted conservative core values for a time when America had vanquished evil abroad but succumbed to moral turpitude at home. Buchanan inspired conservatism's anti-pluralist mainstream by promising to outlaw abortion, restore

God to public life, and scotch affirmative action. He proposed to freeze federal spending and lower taxes. But Buchanan's opposition to immigration, free trade, and adventures abroad repulsed neoconservatives and establishment Republicans. He pledged to close the borders to inassimilable immigrants and end free trade agreements that undercut American sovereignty and let "predatory traders of Europe and Asia" target "American industry for dumping and destruction." He resurrected the disengaged nationalism of Charles Lindbergh and Robert Taft by pledging to bring U.S. troops home from abroad, halt aid to ungrateful foreign regimes, and avoid involvement in local conflicts. Buchanan said that Bush was "a globalist, and we are nationalists. . . . He would put America's wealth and power at the service of some vague new world order. We will put America first."[52]

Like George Wallace, Buchanan sought to gain media attention and inspire the conservative masses by firing his rhetorical buckshot without fear of collateral damage. He proposed to build the "Buchanan fence" across the Mexican border, called African immigrants "Zulus," and promised not to dump "our Western heritage onto some landfill called multiculturalism." Like Lindbergh in 1941, Buchanan opened himself to charges of anti-Semitism. He claimed that Jews acting as "Israel's amen corner" pushed the United States into the Gulf War, and he called Capitol Hill "Israeli-occupied territory." Like the southern agrarians of the 1930s he evoked nostalgia for the pre–Civil War South and its traditions of noblesse oblige, heroism, and faithful Christianity.

Buchanan tapped into a rich vein of neoconfederate culture, transmitted through conferences, newsletters, magazines, monuments, museums, music, and Civil War reenactments. Buchanan served as an adviser to the pro-Confederate magazine *Southern Partisan*. He said the Civil War was about "self-determination," not slavery, and visited a Confederate memorial at Stone Mountain in Georgia—the birthplace of the 1920s-era Klan. He said the Voting Rights Act discriminated against the South and cheered the Confederate battle flags that still flew in some southern capitals. Neoconfederate advocacy resonated with southern Republicans such as senators Jesse Helms and Trent Lott of Mississippi, both of whom had ties to the Council of Conservative Citizens, a diehard white supremacist group formed in 1988 by veterans of the White Citizens Councils. Lott keynoted the council's 1992 convention, saying that its members stood for "the right principles and the right philosophy." A decade later Lott lost his position as Senate Republican leader when he said that if America had elected Strom Thurmond president in 1948, "we wouldn't have had all these [racial] problems over all these years."[53]

Although William Buckley chided Buchanan for "a creeping cultural political insensibility to anti-Semitism," responsible conservatives never put Buchanan in the same deep freeze as they had Wallace. *Human Events* and Rush Limbaugh endorsed Buchanan for president and the *National Review* advised readers to cast a protest vote for him in the New Hampshire primary. But Newt Gingrich and William Bennett journeyed to New Hampshire and implored Republicans to uphold engaged nationalism and avert another Goldwater debacle. Although Buchanan won 37 percent of the primary vote in recession-chilled New Hampshire, he lacked the resources, political base, and strategic acumen to seriously challenge the incumbent president. Bush won a near unanimous nomination, while moving to the right. He sacked his director of the National Endowment for the Arts, John Frohnmayer, who Buchanan had charged with funding "obscene" and "blasphemous" work. He let conservatives write the party platform and speak at the convention, where Buchanan said, "There is a religious war going on in our country for the soul of America. It is a cultural war, as critical to the kind of nation we will one day be as was the Cold War itself." Analysts derided this divisive message, but Bush enjoyed a respectable, if short-lived postconvention bounce in the polls. An ABC News poll taken the day after the convention showed that Bush had cut Clinton's pre-convention lead from twelve percentage points to just one point.[54]

With Bush melting few conservative hearts, some turned to brash billionaire H. Ross Perot, a reincarnation of Texas John Slaughter, the legendary pint-size lawman. After launching his campaign on Larry King's TV show, Perot pledged to subdue the deficit and clean up corruption in Washington. In June 1992 he became the first insurgent candidate to top the major party candidates in a presidential preference poll. Burton Yale Pines, former vice president of the Heritage Foundation, lauded Perot's candidacy. "While I can quibble with Ross Perot on some issues, what overpowers everything is that the guy wants to come in with a blowtorch and level Washington." He said that Perot let conservatives "oppose Bush without supporting a Democrat." What *Talkers* magazine called Perot-mania swept conservative talk radio, including Rush Limbaugh's show.[55]

After peaking in June, however, Perot began tumbling in the polls. He was hurt by negative media scrutiny of his business practices and personality, a lack of clear positions on issues, and rookie mistakes on the campaign trail, such as calling African Americans "you people" at the convention of the NAACP. On July 16, the last day of the Democratic Convention, Perot withdrew from the race. The Democratic Party, he said, had "revitalized itself, and I have concluded that we cannot win in November." Perot reappeared in the fall as mysteriously as Martin Guerre and walked into the presidential debates, where his folksy style played well with television viewers. But he defied prudence when he said that he had initially withdrawn from the race because Republicans were plotting to embarrass him by disrupting his daughter's wedding. The headline of a *Houston Chronicle* editorial, PLAIN BIZARRE, typified America's baffled response to this strange story. Perot ignored the criticism and ended his campaign by dancing with his wife, Margot, at a hotel ballroom to their theme song, Patsy Cline's "Crazy."

Prominent Democrats afflicted by the mass illusion that President Bush was a sure winner in 1992 shunned the presidential race. Absent first-tier candidates, Arkansas governor Bill Clinton, chair of the Democratic Leadership Council, dominated the field after shaking off charges of marital infidelity. Clinton positioned himself as a "new kind of Democrat" armed, like Eisenhower, with a "third-way philosophy" that purported to transcend left and right. He promised to work cooperatively with business and to cut the deficit, reduce middle-class taxes, and build a strong military. He would put more police on the streets, uphold the death penalty, and "end welfare as we know it." He rebuked black militancy and distanced himself from his party's "special interests." But for Democratic base voters, Clinton pledged to expand health care coverage and invest in education and infrastructure. Bush implored voters to choose between "a liberal activist government that seeks to impose solutions on individuals, families and the private sector, and a conservative activist government that gives individuals, businesses and families the means to make their own choices." But the liberal flypaper that had snared Dukakis didn't stick on the agile Clinton, and the effort didn't convince conservative leaders that Bush had become a convert to their cause.[56]

Conservatives, however, applauded the Republicans who proposed a "Manifesto for Change in the House of Representatives," which was introduced by born-again reformer Bob Michel. Michel promised to "lead the first comprehensive reform of the House of Representatives in modern times" and achieve "a truly conservative revolution in the House." His manifesto listed ten domestic proposals, most of which were long familiar to conservatives. If given a chance to control the House, the GOP leadership pledged to schedule votes on "stiffer criminal laws, tax cuts, health reform, choice in education, welfare-to-workfare proposals, full disclosure of congressional activities, congressional term limits, balanced budget amendment, line item veto, and school prayer." They backed a strong defense and an aggressive foreign policy. They promised to make Congress "abide by all the rules and regulations and laws that we impose upon the American people" and enact nine institutional reforms. The Republicans introduced the manifesto into the *Congressional Record* but made little effort to sell its ideas to voters.[57]

Bill Clinton won a decisive Electoral College majority but only 43 percent of the popular vote. Perot won 19 percent, second among insurgent candidates to Theodore Roosevelt in 1912. He won votes across the ideological spectrum, with a slight edge among moderates, according to the National Election Study. Although Democrats lost ten House seats and held steady in the Senate, they regained unified control over the federal government for the first time since 1980. Moderate and conservative Republicans blamed each other. Peter Smith, head of the Ripon Society, the most liberal of Republican organizations, said, "The record shows the country finally got a look at them [right-wing extremists] in the Republican convention and the country turned its back on them." According to conservative strategist Burton Pines, however, Bush refused "to re-embrace the 'Reaganaut' policies and populism that won three presidential elections. By refusing to do this, George Bush and his White House aides broke faith with America's conservative majority." Disillusioned conservatives had not defeated Bush. According to the National Election Study, he won 73 percent of the conservative two-party vote, down just four percentage points from 1988, but he tumbled ten percentage points among both moderates and liberals, winning just 8 percent of the two-party liberal vote. During the late twentieth century, voting fell along class, racial, and religious lines. Bush won 53 percent of the most affluent 5 percent of voters, 59 percent of white Protestants, and 65 percent of white evangelical Protestants. He won 40 percent of Catholics, 26 percent of others, 10 percent of Jews, and 6 percent of blacks. "If everybody else had delivered their votes the way we delivered ours," Christian Coalition leader Ralph Reed said, "George Bush would be getting measured for a tuxedo right now."[58]

A FALSE DAWN FOR DEMOCRATS

In a book published shortly before the 1992 elections, conservative editor Emmett Tyrrell reflected on the "almost complete reversal of positions once held to be conservative." The "conservative believes that the economy prospers best not with the high tariffs his forbears swore by but with low tariffs or none at all." Conservatives who once "denounced the all-powerful presidency" now "fight to preserve presidential power from congressional Liberals." The conservative had "renounced his reverence for the balanced budget" and "states' rights." In academia, he called "for tolerance, diversity, and free speech," not "the inculcation of proper values on campus." Tyrrell speculated that such changes might make it easier for conservatives to work with liberals.[59]

Although the election of third-way Democrat Bill Clinton seemed to hold out the promise of such reconciliation, bitter partisan strife marked the Clinton years. Conservatives had not changed their core principles. Their commitment to traditional values clashed with Clinton's social liberalism and personal lifestyle. Their opposition to policies that redistributed resources, created dependent welfare clients, and imposed costs and restrictions on business clashed with his plans for universal health care.

"What a relief to be on the attack again," satirist P. J. O'Rourke said. "No more gentle sparring with the Administration.... We have game in our sights. Clinton may be a disaster for the rest of the nation, but he is meat on our table." For conservatives, Bill Clinton was a philandering, pot-smoking, draft-dodging hippie with an expensive haircut. Clinton seemed to perform on cue. Within two weeks of his inauguration, the president embraced permissive liberalism by proposing to lift the ban on gays in the military. "The issue of gays in the military is the frontline of a cultural battle," said Richard Cizik, spokesperson for the National Association of Evangelicals. "For us to accept homosexual practice as the moral equivalent of heterosexuality is to ask us to deny our Lord himself. You can't root out 4,000 years of religious history and tradition with the stroke of an executive order."[60]

The true battle royal between America's conservative and liberal traditions erupted over Clinton's health care plan, which for the right represented the liberal dream of making every American dependent on Uncle Sam. On November 1, 1993, Dick Armey, chair of the House Republican Conference, charted the conservative battle plan in a memo entitled "The Moral Equivalent of War: How Republicans Can Win the Health Debate and Enact True Health Reform." The United States, he wrote, had entered "the most important domestic policy debate of the past half-century—a debate that is, in effect, the Battle of the Bulge of big-government liberalism." Clinton and the Democrats were "launching a final desperate gambit to win the permanent loyalty of the great middle class through dependency on a massive new government entitlement. On the outcome of this gambit hangs the future, not only of the Republican party, but of every American citizen." Republicans had decisively beaten back Carter's "infamous energy security plan" rather than "merely tinkering at the margins," which had enabled the GOP "to make congressional gains in 1978 and recapture the Senate and White House in 1980. . . . It is often necessary to defeat, and not just modify, a bad policy, so as to take the debate in a completely new direction."[61]

The health care debate would decide whether America moved left or right in the new millennium. It would decide whether the Republicans could retake Congress and become America's majority party once again. Armey wrote:

> The failure of the Clinton plan will radically alter the political and policy landscapes. It will leave the President's agenda weakened, his plan's supporters demoralized, and the opposition emboldened. Our market-oriented ideas will suddenly become thinkable, not just on health care, but on a host of issues. . . . Criticisms of bad Democratic ideas will become louder and clearer. Historians may mark it as the end of the Clinton ascendancy and the start of the Republican renaissance.

A month later Bill Kristol, a second-generation neoconservative who had run Vice President Quayle's staff and now headed his own think tank, Project for the Republican Future, urged Republicans to reject both the idea of a health care crisis and Clinton's plan, "sight unseen."[62]

As the National Association of Manufacturers had advised in 1934, any specific proposal was vulnerable to attack, even when its objectives

commanded wide support. The president's third-way plan to cover uninsured Americans through employer mandates and federal cost controls
pleased neither liberals, who favored a single-payer system, nor conservatives, who preferred market-based policies. The administration had
hoped to win over major corporations burdened with employee health care
benefits. However, as in virtually every legislative battle since Nixon left
office, big business disappointed liberals. The Business Roundtable, the
National Association of Manufacturers, and the U.S. Chamber of Commerce came to reject Clinton's proposal as another entitlement, financed
with higher taxes and enforced by intrusive bureaucrats. The National
Conference of Catholic Bishops, which backed universal coverage, balked
at legislation that would cover abortion.[63]

The health care struggle showcased the maturity of a conservative
movement in developing and delivering a message and activating both elite
and grassroots support. In 1993 small business and health insurance groups
joined with the Christian Coalition, the American Conservative Union,
and other conservative groups to form the Coalition for Health Insurance
Choices and Citizens Against Rationing Health Care. The pharmaceutical industry launched a grassroots network, Rx Partners, to generate calls
and letters to targeted members of Congress, and the insurance industry
marshaled 140,000 local agents to lobby their senators and representatives.
The American Medical Association paid for television ads that featured
doctors criticizing the health care proposal. Contributions to members of
Congress by the medical and insurance industries doubled in 1993–94 compared to the previous midterm cycle of 1989–1990.[64]

Clinton's adversaries poured a record $50 million into advertising,
swamping the president's allies. They ran TV ads featuring a homey middle-
class couple, Harry and Louise, who worried that under Clinton's plan the
government would limit their coverage, choose their doctors, and raise
their costs. His conservative opponents rushed damning tracts into print,
including a widely cited critique that Elizabeth McCaughey of the Manhattan Institute, a conservative think tank, published in the traditionally
left-leaning *New Republic*. Radio talk show hosts, led by Rush Limbaugh, ridiculed Bill and Hillary's plan, and health insurers advertised on Limbaugh's
show. According to *Forbes* magazine, "Rush Limbaugh et al. deserve a Nobel
award for their Paul Revere–like sounding of the alarm [on] this massive,
politically motivated assault on the world's finest health care system."

Conservative columnists had their fattest target in years. George Will of the *Washington Post* warned of "a radical program" and syndicated columnist Cal Thomas of "socialized medicine," with the government deciding "who lives and who dies." William Safire of the *New York Times* derided Hillary Clinton for "working in secret, to concoct a Government takeover of a seventh of the American economy."[65]

Clinton failed even to get the Democratic Congress to hold a floor vote on his deflated health care plan. He failed to deliver a middle-class tax cut or reform welfare. Clinton withdrew his nomination of civil rights lawyer Lani Guinier as assistant attorney general for civil rights after Clint Bolick of the Institute for Justice had labeled her a "quota queen" for suggesting that minorities might benefit from alternatives to winner-take-all elections for legislative positions. Charges of foul play and cover-up swirled around the president after the suicide of White House aide Vince Foster in July 1993. More sober critics alleged fraud in connection with Clinton's investment in the Whitewater Development Corporation in Arkansas during the late 1970s. In 1994 a three-judge federal court appointed Republican Kenneth Starr, solicitor general under George Bush, as special counsel on Whitewater and other alleged transgressions by the administration.

THE GINGRICH REVOLUTION

For the 1994 elections Gingrich, Armey, and other House conservatives repackaged the manifesto of 1992 as a Contract with America, which likewise pledged to reform Congress and national policy, with a focus on domestic issues. The contract's ten-point program dropped health care and school prayer and added tort reform to limit citizens' lawsuits against business and opposition to the imposition of federal mandates on the states without funding assistance. House leaders drafted the contract during an eighteen-month planning process coordinated with the Republican National Committee, which was headed by the shrewd southern operative Haley Barbour. The planners would oppose Clinton's agenda, formulate alternative policies, recruit and train promising candidates, and get senior Republicans to raise money for fledgling candidates. Gingrich and his allies gave old ideas evocative new names. Tax cuts were the "American Dream Restoration Act," term limits were the "Citizen Legislature Act," welfare reform was the "Personal Responsibility Act," and tougher criminal laws were the "Taking Back Our Streets Act." House Republicans skillfully marketed the contract, which unlike a top-down "manifesto" implied mutual obligations between legislators and voters. They published the contract in *TV Guide*, the nation's most widely circulated magazine, and assembled more than three hundred candidates to introduce it on the U.S. Capitol steps. "If we break this contract, throw us out," the signers pledged.[66]

The results of the midterm elections exceeded Gingrich's fondest dreams. His Republican party won control of both chambers of Congress for the first time in forty years. The party picked up more than fifty House seats as well as ten Senate seats after Richard Shelby of Alabama and Ben "Nighthorse" Campbell of Colorado switched parties. Voters dismissed thirty-four Democratic House members but no Republican incumbents. The GOP won 52.4 percent of the nationwide congressional vote, adding nine million voters over 1990, while the Democrats lost one million. Republicans won 70 percent of white evangelical Protestants, and 68 percent of the most affluent 5 percent of voters. The GOP picked up nearly five hundred state legislative seats in addition to eleven governorships. In Texas the former president's son George W. Bush upset Governor Ann Richards and in New York George Pataki beat Mario Cuomo. The Contract with America advanced Gingrich's dream of converting the GOP into an issue-based party with a national agenda. But postelection polls indicated that only about 25 to 30 percent of the public had heard or read about the contract and that, as Armey had predicted, voters said their main disappointment with President Clinton was that he pursed a liberal agenda and proposed big government programs such as health care reform.[67]

The Gingrich revolution of 1994 advanced late-century conservatism no less than Reagan's revolution of 1980. It completed the right's dream of uniting white Protestant America, North and South. It entrenched the nation's conservative base within the GOP, heightened polarization between the parties, and united business leaders with Christian moralists. It ended President Clinton's flirtation with major liberal reform, inspired conservative activists, shattered the New Deal entitlement to welfare for the poor, and gave Senate Republicans the votes they needed to hold up Clinton's judicial nominations.

In 1994, for the first time in U.S. history, a majority of southern white Protestants joined their northern counterparts in voting for Republican congressional candidates. Perhaps more important, these southern white

Protestants also became Republican loyalists; 57 percent with a major-party preference would identify as Republicans in 2000, compared to 38 percent in 1982. The rise of southern Republicanism reflected class as well as race. Economic growth in the South and migration from the North expanded the region's white middle and upper classes. These well-off southerners did not live near or socialize with the less affluent or share common interests. In 2000 the National Election Study found that 74 percent of white Protestant southerners in the top one-third of earners identified as Republicans, compared to 43 percent in the bottom one-third. From 1994 to 2006 race, religion, and income all had strong independent influences nationwide on the decision to vote Republican or identify with the GOP. Gender and marital status also shaped voter decisions. Republicans did better among men than women and among married persons than single persons.[68]

In 1994 the GOP achieved its first ever majority of southern House and Senate seats when it added twenty-one House members and seven Senators. Between 1955 and 1995 the GOP had gained sixty southern House seats, while losing seats in all other regions. The party gained twelve southern Senate seats, compared to eight seats elsewhere. Thus Republican gains in the South accounted entirely for Republican control of the House and primarily for its control of the Senate. Gains in the South paid extra dividends because migration from the Frost Belt to the Sun Belt increased southern House seats from 122 in 1950 to 142 after the 2000 reapportionment, and increased Electoral College votes in the South from 148 to 168.

Realignment in the South increased political polarization by pushing Democrats to the left and Republicans to the right. Moderate southern Democrats were replaced in the Senate by conservative Republicans and in the House by either conservative Republicans or liberal black and Hispanic Democrats. Only nine House Democrats voted more conservatively than the most liberal Republican in 1995–96, compared to ninety-two Democrats who voted to the right of the most liberal Republican in 1971–72, a low point for polarization. Only one Senate Democrat voted more conservatively than the most liberal Republican, compared to twenty-six Democrats in 1971–72. As political scientists have cautioned, however, polarization of the political class did not necessarily reflect polarization within the electorate. But as ideological differences decreased within the parties and increased between the parties, the political system came to amplify, not dampen, conflicts within society.[69]

Southern legislators, who had lost influence within the Democratic Party, regained power as Republicans. Gingrich of Georgia, who had raised $1.5 million for GOP candidates in 1994, became Speaker of the House. Tom DeLay of Texas, who had raised $780,000, became majority whip. Dick Armey of Texas became majority leader, completing a southern sweep. In the Senate, Bob Dole served as majority leader for less than two years, yielding to Mississippi's Trent Lott when he ran for president in 1996. Majority Whip Don Nickles of Oklahoma, Republican Conference chairman Connie Mack of Florida, and National Republican Senatorial Committee chair Mitch McConnell of Kentucky completed the Senate's all-southern leadership. Every Republican southern House and Senate leader had voting records to the right of their party's center and, on average, all southern Republicans were more conservative than their northern counterparts.

The control of Congress bonded Republicans tightly with business. Republicans proposed tax cuts, deregulation, and limitations on civil lawsuits. But their larger agenda contemplated moving the functions and spending of government to the private sector. Republican plans for welfare reform would free recipients from their dependence on government checks and make them rely instead on wages from private business. Republican proposals for greater military spending would increase the flow of federal dollars to defense contractors. Tax cuts would send the money saved on diminished welfare programs back to individuals and business firms. Education vouchers and the privatization of government functions would transfer more tax dollars to the private sector. Strict criminal laws, minimum mandatory sentences, and tough sentencing guidelines that expanded the prison population benefited operators of for-profit prisons such as the Correctional Corporation of America and Wackenhut Corrections Corporation and industries that built and served prisons. Prison economies sustained depressed rural areas, and prison guards usually held more conservative values than other government workers. Personal Social Security accounts invested in private markets would bring millions of new customers to Wall Street and tie the financial well-being of retirees to corporate profits. What was good for General Motors would become good for senior citizens in Palm Beach and Tucson, and good for a Republican Party that guarded the interests of business.

Pro-business policies and control of Congress enhanced fund-raising by Republicans. In the 1992 and 1994 election cycles most business sectors evenly divided their contributions between the major parties, with Democrats benefiting from their control of Congress. In 1996 business contributions shifted decisively toward the GOP. More than 60 percent of contributions by the agribusiness, construction, energy and natural resources, finance and real estate, health, defense, and transportation sectors flowed to Republicans. Democrats shared equally in contributions from the communications and electronics industries and led only among lawyers and lobbyists. In all sectors, Republicans reaped $105 million more than Democrats.

Only America's increasing diversity kept the GOP from becoming the nation's majority party after 1994. Unlike in the 1950s, when J. Harvie Williams wrote his realignment memos, white Protestants no longer dominated the American electorate. From 1950 to 2000 the white Protestant share of the electorate fell from more than 60 percent to under 50 percent. Consequently, the GOP's recruitment of white Protestant voters did not reverse the New Deal realignment but brought Republicans into near parity with Democrats.

Republicans had to secure new voter blocs, with devout Catholics the most promising target of opportunity. In 1993 the Christian Coalition joined with Catholic leaders to elect social conservatives to New York City's school board. A year later, thirty-nine prominent conservative Catholics and evangelical Protestants published "Evangelicals and Catholics Together: The Christian Mission in the Third Millennium." This unofficial statement concluded that conservative Catholics and Protestants shared common political ground. Both groups supported school choice, chastity education, and market economies. Both groups opposed abortion, pornography, antireligious bigotry, and "misguided statist policies" that made people "virtual wards of the government." Journalist and author Richard John Neuhaus, a 1990 convert to Catholicism, and former Watergate felon Chuck Colson, who founded the Prison Fellowship, formulated the joint statement and recruited its signers, who included Pat Robertson, Bill Bright, Cardinal John O'Connor of New York, Archbishop Francis Stafford of Denver, and prominent Catholic theologian Avery Dulles. John White of the National Association of Evangelicals signed the statement four decades after his organization's founder, Harold John Ockenga, had denounced the Catholic Church in his presidential address.[70]

The Christian Coalition pursued a formal alliance with Catholics through a new Catholic Alliance. But it failed to resolve differences with

Catholic teachings and provoked a sharp rebuke from several American bishops in 1996, who said, "While the Catholic Church and the Christian Coalition (or other similar organizations) find agreement on issues such as abortion, euthanasia and pornography, we sharply disagree on issues such as welfare reform, capital punishment and health care reform." Still, a 2000 survey of Catholic priests found that 60 percent voted for pro-life candidate George W. Bush.[71]

Protestants and Catholics did unite behind a common strategy on abortion. To strike at abortion rights without offending moderates, they proposed to ban so-called partial-birth abortions, which purportedly differed from other abortions by partially withdrawing the fetus from the womb, puncturing the base of the skull, and suctioning out the contents of the fetal head. This shrewdly coined term evoked infanticide, not abortion—"the barbaric slaying of children as they are being born," according to Cardinal James Hickey of Washington, D.C. All eight American cardinals and some eighty bishops joined the Christian Coalition, Focus on the Family, and Concerned Women of America to lobby Congress and state governments to ban partial-birth abortions. Conservatives dangled partial-birth abortion as bait for the pro-choice movement, which generally bit hard. Most pro-choice leaders debated the need for partial-birth abortions on the terms defined by their opposition rather than arguing that proposed legislation was vaguely worded and could broadly deter doctors from performing abortions. Although Congress failed to enact partial-birth abortion bans over Clinton's vetoes in April 1996 and October 1997, the pro-choice movement lost credibility. In a 1995 Gallup Poll 56 percent of respondents identified as pro-choice and 34 percent as pro-life. By 1998, 48 percent identified as pro-choice and 45 percent as pro-life in an identically worded survey.[72]

Militant activists, led by a group called Operation Rescue, took direct action to halt abortions. Evangelical Protestant Randall Terry founded the organization in 1986 to save "unborn babies from death at the hands of the abortionists." It conducted "rescue missions" that placed volunteers between abortion clinics and women seeking their services. Terry hoped to provoke a political revolution that established God's rule over America and ended abortions and other evils. Terry recruited volunteers through churches and sponsored or inspired some 250 rescues across in the country in the late 1980s. Falwell, Robertson, and some Catholic leaders blessed his efforts. Terry shut down his national office in 1990 after a federal judge fined Operation Rescue $50,000 for violating injunctions against blocking women's access to abortion clinics. But Terry's example continued to influence efforts by other activists to limit access to legal abortions.[73]

EXPANDING THE MOVEMENT

Conservatives thrived in their opposition to President Bill Clinton. The *National Review,* the *American Spectator, Human Events,* and *Commentary* all reached peak audiences in the mid-1990s. In 1995 Bill Kristol, with financing from right-wing media mogul Rupert Murdoch, launched the *Weekly Standard.* Its circulation stalled at about sixty thousand but, like the early *National Review,* it had influence beyond its numbers. Murdoch bankrolled the Fox Cable News Network, which was run by Roger Ailes, the advertising genius behind Bush's 1988 campaign. With its pledge of "fair and balanced" coverage, Fox offered an alternative to what its founders saw as liberally biased television news. Conservatives could count on backing from the opinion pages of the *Wall Street Journal,* the *Washington Times,* Murdoch's *New York Post,* and state and regional papers across America. Compatible material appeared in such mass-circulation magazines as *Forbes, Reader's Digest,* and *U.S. News & World Report,* and conservative columnists had more of a presence than liberals on newspaper opinion pages, including the *Washington Post.*

Conservative leaders continued pursuing a "culture war," led by William Bennett, who founded the think tank Empower America in 1993. Bennett hit on the ingenious device of "quantifying America's decline." He contrived an "index of leading cultural indicators" to do for values what the index of leading economic indicators did for the economy. Before 1960 Americans worried about boys hitting baseballs through windows, girls gossiping too much, or dads working too hard. By 1993, according to Bennett's indicators, soaring rates of violent crime, teenage pregnancy and suicide, births out of wedlock, divorce, and other social pathologies revealed a nation in cultural decline. "What Bill has done is demonstrate in a kind of an irrefutable, evidentiary way the cultural and moral decline in family breakup in America," said Ralph Reed. To redeem the culture, Bennett said government must first "heed the old injunction, 'Do no harm'" by dismantling programs with "destructive incentives" like the "welfare

system." Government should embrace "morally defensible social legislation" including tougher criminal laws, more prisons, school vouchers,
measures to help women collect child support, tighter divorce laws, and
"radical welfare reform." America's vital "social and civic institutions" must
once again teach "self-control, compassion, tolerance, civility, honesty, and
respect for authority." In 1996 Bennett published his best-selling work *The
Book of Virtues,* yet the virtue of tolerance did not make it into the book.[74]

Conservatives also renewed their challenge to liberal bias in academia.
Companies and foundations pumped money into higher education to influence research priorities and faculty time. In addition, the National Association of Scholars (NAS), founded in 1987, gained a presence on campus
and in the media. The group included professors, graduate students, ad-
ministrators, and outside scholars. It claimed four thousand members by
2000 and recruited a board studded with neoconservative stars such as
Jeane Kirkpatrick, Irving Kristol, James Q. Wilson, Seymour Martin Lipset,
and Gertrude Himmelfarb. Unlike J. Howard Pew and William F. Buckley
Jr., the NAS upheld academic freedom as the best defense against so-called
political correctness, which it defined as mindless conformity to orthodoxy
of the left, usually at the expense of whites, males, Christians, and the
Western canon. Through tireless repetition, NAS and other conservative
groups helped make "political correctness" a hot topic of the 1990s. The
term had generated fewer than 50 Lexis-Nexis print and broadcast citations in 1990 compared to nearly one thousand two years later.[75]

Conservatives eclipsed liberals in carving out a protected space for
research, analysis, and advocacy that was insulated from the checks and
balances of professional scholarship. The right inundated the nation with
background papers, issue briefs, opinion pieces, and legislative analyses.
It established its own world of scholarly journals and conferences that
lacked the academic safeguards of open submissions and anonymous peer
reviews. Heritage, the Unification Church, the American Enterprise Institution, and other groups sponsored conservative scholarship by selected
contributors whose findings could usually be counted on to please conservatives. The right could rely on such journals as the *National Interest,
Regulation, Public Interest, Modern Age, Policy Review, American Enterprise, the
Salisbury Review,* and numerous other specialized publications.

Conservatives marketed work emerging from this protected space
to a media seeking "balanced" presentations and hyped-up "controversies"

that did not exist within peer-reviewed scholarship. The Discovery Institute, founded in 1990 by former Reagan official Bruce Chapman, extended the right's war against Darwinism and scientific materialism through its Center for the Renewal of Science and Culture, set up in 1996. Founding donors included Christian Reconstructionist Howard Ahmanson and the MacLellan Foundation, which financed groups "committed to furthering the Kingdom of Christ." The center renamed creation science as "intelligent design" to circumvent the 1987 Supreme Court ruling in *Edwards v. Aguillard* that prohibited the teaching of creation science in public schools. It promoted intelligent design as a nonreligious alternative to evolutionary theory, which posited that the complexity of life on earth required intervention by a higher intelligence. A 1999 internal memo entitled "The Wedge Project" cited intelligent design as the "wedge" for "nothing less than the overthrow of materialism and its damning cultural legacies" in favor of a "broadly theistic understanding of nature." The memo proposed to split the tree of nonreligious materialism through "a 'wedge' that, while relatively small, can split the trunk when applied at its weakest points. . . . Design theory promises to reverse the stifling dominance of the materialist worldview, and to replace it with a science consonant with Christian and theistic convictions."[76]

For the scientific community, intelligent design, like traditional creationism, represented theology masquerading as science with no testable hypotheses or predictions about the natural world. No empirical body of work to support intelligent design made it into peer-reviewed scientific journals. Nonetheless, the well-funded Center for the Renewal of Science and Culture skillfully created the appearance of scientific debate by financing sympathetic scholars and creating a self-contained network of journals, conferences, seminars, and books (many published by religious presses) that were marketed in the media and used by conservative politicians. The right said that schools should "teach the controversy" and let students hear "both sides." By 2005, eighty years after the Scopes trial, this position had won considerable popular support and the endorsement of President George W. Bush.

As in the 1920s, conservatives rejected evolution while also sustaining racial science. The Pioneer Fund, after founder Wickliffe Preston Draper's death in 1972, lived on to sustain the scientific racism it claimed the media and academy had suppressed. The fund dispensed some

$13 million to preselected recipients without formal proposals, public notice, peer review, or reporting requirements. J. Philippe Rushton of the University of Western Ontario, who became fund president in 2002, used Pioneer's funds in 1999 to send thirty thousand social scientists an edition of his book *Race, Evolution, and Behavior*. The book argued that genetics doomed black people to life with smaller brains, larger genitals, and less mental capacity and parenting ability. Genetics also accounted for a racial proclivity to crime, promiscuity, and sexually transmitted diseases.[77]

The most controversial defense of racial science came not, however, from a pioneer scholar but from political scientist Charles Murray, who had become a fellow of the American Enterprise Institute in 1990. A decade after skewering welfare, Murray struck another exposed nerve with his 1994 book *The Bell Curve* (coauthored with Richard J. Hernnstein). The book amassed mountains of empirical evidence, some of it based on research supported by the Pioneer Fund, on the relationship between heredity and intelligence. Attention, however, focused on the authors' claim that IQ tests proved the genetic inferiority of blacks to whites and Asians. *The Bell Curve* had profound political implications because of its extraordinary media coverage. It resurrected the idea that white stereotyping of blacks was scientifically justified and that social programs were self-defeating because they encouraged inferior racial stocks to breed and seek roles in society for which they were unfit. Responses fell tightly along political lines, with conservatives mostly defending the work and liberals blasting its methods, data, and assumptions. "*The Bell Curve*'s liberal critics," wrote Dan Seligman in a *National Review* symposium, "want its ideas suppressed. . . . They want the authors depicted as kooks and extremists. The case made by the book is just too threatening to their own egalitarian ideologies."[78]

In 1992 conservative psychiatrists and therapists founded the National Association for Research and Therapy of Homosexuality (NARTH), which challenged the scientific consensus by contending that homosexuality was a sexual disorder, preventable in childhood and curable in adulthood through "reparative therapy." NARTH, like other independent conservative groups, blamed contrary scientific findings on a code of silence imposed by politically correct associations and journals. NARTH held an annual meeting at the same venue as the American Psychological Association, published a newsletter, the *NARTH Bulletin*, three times a year, and placed its work in friendly journals such as the law review sponsored by Pat Robertson's Regent University. NARTH self-published a study, "Retrospective Self-Reports of Changes in Homosexual Orientation: A Consumer Survey on Conversion Therapy Clients"—cited as reliable scholarship by Christian right leaders but debunked by independent reviewers—which claimed success in curing homosexuals. Activist groups formed to propagate NARTH's philosophy, including Parents and Friends of ex-Gays (PFOX), which was launched in 1996 as an offshoot of James Dobson's Family Research Council. PFOX claimed to provide "support for families and public awareness for the community at large regarding the decision to leave homosexuality." In this view, the only healthy living arrangement for adults and children was in stable, monogamous, two-parent, heterosexual families with sex roles clearly defined.[79]

The Independent Women's Forum (IWF), founded in 1992 with grants from leading conservative foundations, promoted conservative visions of family and society with a post-feminist gloss. With a white, professional founding membership of a few hundred women, the forum provided media commentary and expert testimony while disclaiming political goals. Through its newsletter *The Women's Quarterly*—an "intellectual antidote" to the feminist *Ms.*—the IWF argued that civil rights laws had cured discrimination in the 1960s and '70s. Feminist leaders, IWF spokeswomen said, sought to keep women thinking of themselves as victims to prop up intellectually bankrupt women's studies programs and self-defeating affirmative action programs. The IWF defended the right of the Virginia Military Institute to reject women, backed Clarence Thomas's appointment to the Supreme Court, supported caps for welfare mothers who kept producing children, and in 2000 joined with other conservative groups to push the GOP platform to the right.[80]

IWF women, including its most shimmering personality, Laura Ingraham, were younger, sleeker, and sexier than Phyllis Schlafly or Beverly LaHaye. They projected a hip, fashionable image for the typically dowdy conservative movement. Like Abramoff, Reed, Kristol, and Norquist, Ingraham was a "third generation" conservative who came of age during the Reagan years. She edited the *Dartmouth Review,* earned a law degree from the University of Virginia, wrote speeches for Ronald Reagan, clerked for Clarence Thomas, and joined a prestigious law firm. She was briefly engaged to fellow third- generation conservative Dinesh D'Souza and graced the cover of the *New York Times Magazine* in a leopard-print miniskirt for a 1995 article about the new "opinion elite" of young conservatives. Ingraham's sex appeal, intelligence, and politically incorrect commentary earned her regular appearances on CBS and MSNBC and eventually her own radio talk show. Another alluring blonde media personality, author and attorney Ann Coulter, who described herself as "Christian first and a mean-spirited, bigoted conservative second," became an even more audacious conservative diva. By the late 1990s Coulter was ubiquitous on talk shows, and her book-length philippics against the left hit the top of the *New York Times* best-seller list (with help from bulk purchases by conservatives). In 2005 Coulter made the cover of *Time* magazine pictured in a little black dress and a pose that showcased her long thin legs.[81]

THINK TANKS AND LOBBY SHOPS

By the mid-1990s conservative think tanks had surpassed the liberal competition in numbers, funding, and visibility. According to a study of 165 ideological think tanks in 1996, 65 percent were conservative. The top five conservative think tanks in 1995 outspent their top five liberal competitors by about four to one and generated nearly four times as many Lexis-Nexis print and broadcast citations. News shows called upon conservative guests much more often than they did liberals and featured corporate executives over labor leaders. After 1994 congressional committees heard more testimony from representatives of conservative causes than was heard from their liberal counterparts.[82]

A new client and server relationship between business and right-wing organizations matured in the 1990s. Corporate donors came to expect value returned for value contributed, not defense of principle in the tradition of the Liberty League or the American Conservative Union. Right-wing organizations offered profit-making companies the cover of independent advocacy that used conservative themes such as free markets to frame client interests as public interests. Citizens for a Sound Economy (CSE), for example, served corporations that kicked in for an annual budget of $10 million in the 1990s. David Koch founded CSE in 1984 to promote limited government, low taxes, and free markets. CSE's president, Professor Richard Fink of George Mason University, provided academic credibility, while board chairman C. Boyden Gray, formerly Ronald Reagan's White House counsel, monitored its projects.

The CSE custom-tailored its research, advocacy, and lobbying to fit corporate priorities. According to records obtained by the *Washington Post,* CSE worked with donors from the oil, gas, and coal industries in 1994 to kill Bill Clinton's proposed energy tax. CSE opposed a multibillion-dollar federal project to restore the Everglades—it threatened Florida sugar-cane interests—and received $700,000 from Florida sugar companies. CSE gained $175,000 from Exxon after it derided theories of global warming as "junk science" and it spent $75,000 from the Florida auto rental industry to back legislation to limit renters' liability from lawsuits. CSE received more than $1 million in contributions from Philip Morris and, worked with company lobbyists to block increased excise taxes on cigarettes and the federal regulation of tobacco.[83]

Scores of kindred groups followed the CSE model nationally, region-ally, and locally, some with broad missions, others with a specialized focus. Extractive industries, for example, helped fund grassroots "wise use" groups during the late 1980s to challenge the environmental movement and pro-mote private access to public lands for development, mining, drilling, graz-ing, and logging. The groups also sought to shield property owners from environmental or endangered species regulations that undercut property values. Wise use groups also gained funding from the Unification Church and forged alliances with Christian conservatives who believed that the Bible ordained productive human use of the earth's resources. By funding groups with names like the Alliance for America or People for the West, corporations created the impression that such groups were mouthpieces for ordinary citizens. Wise use advocates claimed to be the true environ-mentalists who loved the land and its people far more than the Sierra Club with its anti-jobs "lock-it-up-and-keep-'em-out" agenda. "Give them [wise use groups] the money," Ron Arnold, a founder of the wise use movement, advised corporations. "You stop defending yourselves, let them do it, and you get the hell out of the way. Because citizens' groups have credibility and industries don't." The iron men of the wise use movement, however, proved too unruly for corporate executives, who shifted most of their dollars to slicker, more predictable outfits like CSE by the late 1990s.[84]

The marriage between business and conservative advocates in the 1990s produced a new breed of lobbyist who were different than the Tom Corcoran–style operatives who sold inside connections and exper-tise in government. The new lobbyists functioned as money managers, orchestrating complex, covert movements of funds among wealthy clients, conservative organizations, political action committees, candidates, officeholders, and the lobbyist's own enterprises. Just as J. Howard Pew used the Park Avenue Church as a conduit for money he contributed to *Christianity Today*, lobbyists funneled client money to conservative organizations. These groups in turn dispensed travel and other lavish perks to journalists, intellectuals, judges, legislators, and congressional aides that the clients could not legally provide. The intermediary conservative groups promoted client interests and kicked back contributions to the lobbyists and the campaigns of favored officeholders and candidates.

Jack Abramoff, late of the College Republicans, Citizens for America, and South Africa's International Freedom Forum, became the archetype of the new era. He generated huge financial transactions that enriched himself, his friends and associates, and his political allies. Abramoff cultivated a wealthy and generous client base in American Indian and Internet gambling interests and textile moguls in the American territory of the northern Mariana Islands. He developed special relationships with Texas representative Tom DeLay, old associate Grover Norquist, and his former competitor for the presidency of the College Republicans Amy Ridenour, who ran the National Center for Public Policy Research. Abramoff's clients poured millions of dollars into Ridenour's center, which used some of the money to fund luxury travel for policy and opinion makers. The center kicked back more than $2 million to public relations firms and foundations controlled by Abramoff and his business partner Michael Scanlon, formerly DeLay's press secretary. Ridenour pumped out articles and press releases in support of Abramoff's clients. Abramoff contributed to political action committees that DeLay controlled, hired the congressman's former aides, and included DeLay in foreign travel. In the late 1990s Abramoff contracted with former Christian Coalition director Ralph Reed to lobby for one Indian gaming client against another. To protect Reed from the appearance of profiting from gambling, Abramoff laundered his payments through the Norquist's Americans for Tax Reform Foundation. Abramoff prospered for a decade, raking in as much as $85 million in fees and becoming a fixture in conservative Washington. His empire collapsed amid revelations of unethical and illegal dealings in 2005. In early 2006 Abramoff was sentenced to nearly six years in prison.

In 1993 Heritage president Edwin Feulner, not usually one to bite the hand that fed him, warned that the right could lose its soul to business.

"The same rap that applies to George [H. W.] Bush—that he didn't stand for anything—applies to too many corporate executives," he said in his annual "State of Conservatism" message. Business leaders were looking "to turn a quick profit, or to undermine the competition, even if it costs them and the country in the long run." They saw "government as the engine driving the economy and politics as the golden key to a better profit-and-loss statement." The bargain between business and the right, however, proved to be sealed with too many payoffs to be undone even by the president of the Heritage Foundation.[85]

DEMOCRATS SURVIVE

The conservative revolution of 1994 stalled soon after its moment of triumph. As in 1946, Republicans had won a key battle but not the presidency nor a mandate to govern from the right. Gingrich pushed the House to vote on his Contract with America proposals, but most died in the more centrist Senate; others perished with President Clinton's veto. Still, Congress enacted a modest package of conservative reforms, including a landmark telecommunications bill that was designed to deregulate the telephone and cable television industries. In 1996 Republicans backed President Clinton's proposals to increase the minimum wage and make health care plans more portable when changing jobs. In return, Republicans gained a welfare reform bill that rewrote a major New Deal program—Aid to Families with Dependent Children—and for the first time erased a federal entitlement.

Although conservatives limited welfare dependency, they expanded prison dependency, shifting the purposes and beneficiaries of government spending and implementing their vision of personal responsibility. As the government stepped up the "war on drugs," adopted mandatory minimum sentences, and tightened sentencing guidelines, America's prison population soared from about half a million in 1980 to some two million in 2000. The 6.5 million persons in prison or under parole and probation accounted for about one out of every thirty-two adult Americans. In 2000 about 45 percent of America's prison and jail population was black and another 15 percent was Hispanic; one of every three African-America males aged twenty to twenty-nine was under custodial supervision of some kind; and privately owned prisons held nearly ninety-thousand prisoners in 2000, compared to two thousand in 1990.[86]

The GOP also failed to deliver a more open and less partisan Congress. Led by majority whip and later majority leader Tom DeLay, dubbed "the Hammer" for his effective pressure tactics, the GOP majority adopted closed rules that barred amendments to bills and held votes open for many hours to put the squeeze on undecided voters. Republican leaders exercised tight discipline over committee chairs and controlled what measures reached the House floor. They limited debate, added riders to appropriation bills, and shut Democrats out of conference committees that resolved differences between House and Senate versions of a particular bill.

Conservatives also faced stiff competition outside of Congress. The diminished union movement remained a powerful lobby and a fount of donations and volunteers for liberals. Liberal public interest groups dominated such issues as environmental protection, clean government, civil and women's rights, education, worker safety, and consumer protection. The NAACP, for example, had more Lexis-Nexus citations in the 1990s than the top five conservative think tanks combined. Many of these groups, however, because of their dependence on foundation and corporate funding, lacked the zeal of competing conservative organizations. Conservatives were also especially effective in mobilizing mass membership organizations. Voluntary organizations that enrolled more than 1 percent of the adult population in the 1990s included the National Rifle Association and the National Right to Life Committee.[87]

The Republican majority in Congress barely survived the 1996 election. The right's "angry white men" seemed to spin out of control, with no one replacing William Buckley as the responsible cop on the conservative beat. Gingrich branded Democrats as the "enemies of normal Americans" and the Clintons as "counter-culture McGovernicks" presiding over a White House of "left-wing elitists." Senator Helms warned that the president "better have a bodyguard" if he visited military bases in North Carolina. G. Gordon Liddy advised his listeners on how to shoot to kill intrusive federal agents: "head shots, head shots." Rush Limbaugh warned of an imminent "second violent American revolution" because "people are sick and tired of a bunch of bureaucrats in Washington driving into town and telling them what they can and can't do with their land."

In April 1995, Timothy McVeigh, who was reportedly associated with ultra-right, racist, and anti-Semitic militia groups, bombed the Federal Building in Oklahoma City and killed 168 of its occupants. In response,

Congress passed an antiterrorism bill that expanded federal death penalty crimes, made it easier to deport alien terrorists, put new controls on fundraising for terrorism, and limited habeas corpus appeals by prisoners. President Clinton decried "loud and angry voices" that "spread hate" and "leave the impression that, by their very words, violence is acceptable." After presidential vetoes led to two partial government shutdowns in late 1995, far more Americans blamed the fiasco on Republicans in Congress than on the president. In his 1996 State of the Union speech, Clinton said, "The era of big government is over." However, to accommodate the left, he added, "We cannot go back to the time when our citizens were left to fend for themselves." An ABC News poll found that, by 59 percent to 25 percent, Americans favored the direction set by Clinton rather than that by congressional Republicans.[88]

With the communist threat receding, foreign policy disputes stayed muted under Clinton, who surveyed the world from a position of greater strength than any previous American president. The United States accounted for about a quarter of the world economy and spent more on defense than any five nations combined. Ethnic conflict and economic policy, not threats of nuclear confrontation, preoccupied the administration. Clinton backed economic policies initially pushed by Republicans, international financiers, and increasingly large, diversified multinational corporations for keeping the world open to trade and investment. Clinton supported the North American Free Trade Agreement, the Uruguay Round of the General Agreement on Trade and Tariffs, and a World Trade Organization with independent powers to mediate trade disputes. Opposition to free trade initiatives came primarily from labor, which feared foreign pressure on jobs, wages, and working conditions, and from human rights and environmental activists concerned with degraded standards.

Even the World Trade Organization, however, failed to achieve central control of the global economy. Policies set by nations and regional blocs remained important, especially given competition to keep jobs and investment at home and gain advantages in foreign trade. European nations formed the European Union in the early 1990s and India, China, and other East Asian nations joined the ranks of major economic players, as did some Latin America nations. Still, international financial pressure could force nations into currency devaluations and interest rate hikes that undercut the domestic economy. The new economy also left much of the world behind. Grinding poverty beset subsaharan Africa and much of the Muslim world. In 2000, according to the first comprehensive study of the world's distribution of wealth, the wealthiest 2 percent of adults owned more than half the planet's wealth and the bottom 50 percent owned barely 1 percent.[89]

With communism dead in Europe, the newest and also one of the oldest threats to Christian civilization, militant Islam, began to worry conservatives. In 1994, a year after Islamic terrorists bombed the World Trade Center in New York, conservative scholar Daniel Pipes, whose father had headed Team B in 1976, laid down the gauntlet for a new crusade against sin, writing, "The Western confrontation with fundamentalist Islam has in some ways come to resemble the great ideological battle of the twentieth century, that between Marxist-Leninism and liberal democracy." Americans "differ among themselves on the question of fundamentalist Islam roughly along the same lines as they did on the Cold War. Liberals say: Co-opt the radicals. Conservatives say: Confront them. As usual, the conservatives are right."[90]

Conservatives entered the election of 1996 without a consensus candidate or much hope of defeating the front-runner for the Republican nomination, party warhorse Bob Dole, the seventy-three-year-old majority leader of the Senate. Two long-shot candidates from the right—Pat Buchanan and wealthy publisher Steve Forbes, with his signature flat tax plan—challenged Dole in the Republican primaries. Buchanan stunned the front-runner and the pundits by winning the New Hampshire primary. Buchanan pledged to defend "the right to life of the innocent unborn" and back those "whose jobs have been sacrificed on the altars of trade deals done for the benefit of transnational corporations who have no loyalty to our country." A Buchanan administration, he said, "will only be obedient to one sovereign America, and that is the sovereign of God himself and his laws."

With backing from the pragmatic Ralph Reed, Dole cut into Buchanan's base of white evangelical Protestants, won a do-or-die primary in South Carolina, and swept on to victory. Reed expected payoff, telling Dole, "You cannot, you should not, and you must not retreat from the pro-life and pro-family stand that . . . won you that majority in the first place." Dole obliged by abandoning his moderate stance on abortion and backing a conservative platform that endorsed a right-to-life constitutional amendment for the unborn. For his running mate, Dole picked conservative Jack Kemp, the former congressman from Buffalo and Ronald Reagan's secretary of housing and urban development.[91]

Dole quickly ditched the platform and ran a moderate campaign. But he needed more against an incumbent president in prosperous and peaceful times. The culture wars seemed to be losing their urgency; polls showed that most Americans held moderate positions on social issues and even William Bennett's cultural indicators registered improvement during the Clinton years. Dole resurrected Reaganomics by proposing to cut taxes by 15 percent across the board. But few still believed in supply-side magic. Like Bush in 1992, Dole tried but failed to paint Clinton as an elite liberal who was out of touch with ordinary Americans. On foreign policy, Dole mirrored Thomas Dewey in failing to challenge the substance of Clinton policy. Instead, he weakly charged the administration with "indecision, vacillation and weakness" and "a foreign policy of neglect, posturing, concessions and false triumphs." Dismayed neoconservatives Bill Kristol and Robert Kagan wrote in a coauthored article, "In foreign policy, conservatives are adrift." Conservatives disdained "Wilsonian multilateralism" but also resisted "the "neoisolationism of Patrick Buchanan." The authors thumped for the bold policies of Theodore Roosevelt and Ronald Reagan. They advocated massive increases in military spending to ensure that America would exert "preponderant influence and authority" over other nations.[92]

Ross Perot launched a second presidential campaign in 1996, this time as the nominee of a new Reform Party. Although Perot hit 20 percent in early preference polls, a falling budget deficit robbed him of a signature issue and the major parties shut him out of the presidential debates. Perot won only 8.4 percent of the popular vote. Clinton finished with 49 percent to 41 percent for Dole. It was not a big enough win to enable his party to recapture either chamber of Congress. Republicans also continued marching through the South, where they gained two southern Senate seats and four House seats. Elsewhere, Republicans lost a dozen House seats and held even in the Senate.

BAGGING THE PRESIDENT

With the Clinton administration advancing no bold agenda for its second term, politics became fiercely personal, leading to the first impeachment of a president since 1868. The impeachment crisis of 1998–99 was the culmination of a concerted effort by some on the right to discredit the president personally. From 1994 to 1997, Richard Mellon Scaife poured $2.4 million into the *American Spectator* magazine, which had embarked on an "Arkansas project" to uncover misdeeds in the president's past. Articles on Clinton's purported sexual escapades and corrupt dealings pushed up the *Spectator*'s circulation from thirty thousand in 1992 to three hundred thousand in 1995, although a backlash would eventually doom the magazine. Reverend Falwell, who returned to politics in 1991 as head of a new Liberty Alliance, aired and sold videos that insinuated Clinton's complicity in suicides and murders to cover-up alleged cocaine smuggling and money laundering in Arkansas. One video, *The Clinton Chronicles*, concluded with former Republican representative William Dannemeyer urging Congress to impeach the president. Conservatives gave former Arkansas state employee Paula Jones a forum to allege sexual harassment against Clinton and backed her lawsuit against the president, despite the right's usual distaste for such litigation.

The search for dirt on the president led down back roads of southern history to Jim Johnson, the former head of the Little Rock Citizens Council, and others who mourned the passing of Jim Crow and despised Bill Clinton as the smug face of a new South. Johnson spread rumors of scandal, crime, and infidelity, published his accusations in the *Washington Times*, and appeared in *The Clinton Chronicles*. Stories about Clinton's alleged transgressions circulated through alternative media of the right— Internet Web sites, newsletters, religious broadcasts, and talk radio shows. Limbaugh spread rumors that Vince Foster was killed in an apartment owned by Hillary Clinton. The Free Congress Foundation and the Western Journalism Center—both funded by Scaife and Joe Coors—disseminated scurrilous material that also appeared in the *Washington Times*, Murdoch's *New York Post*, the Scaife-owned *Pittsburgh Tribune-Review*, and the editorial pages of the *Wall Street Journal*. The Council for National Policy distributed *The Clinton Chronicles* to its membership. But some of the extravagant allegations against the president circulated in the mainstream media, including the *New York Times*, the *Washington Post*, and television networks.[93]

Clinton's own folly, however, led to the impeachment crisis that engulfed his presidency. In January 1998, Special Prosecutor Starr began probing allegations that the president had committed perjury and obstructed justice to conceal an affair with White House intern Monica Lewinsky. On September 11, 1998, Congress released Starr's report, replete with salacious details of the affair and allegations of numerous impeachable offenses. Leading newspapers called for the president's resignation and pundits expected Democrats to suffer in the midterm elections of 1998. Yet some two-thirds of Americans still approved of Clinton's presidency, opposed both impeachment and resignation, regarded the Lewinsky affair as a private matter, and attributed attacks on the president to politics not patriotism. For the first time since 1934, the party controlling the White House won House seats in a midterm contest, although the GOP narrowly held its majority. Speaker Gingrich did not survive the elections. In the wake of an incipient rebellion among Republicans unhappy with his negative image, credible rumors of an extramarital affair, reprimands from the House Ethics Committee, and failed electoral strategy, Gingrich resigned his seat in Congress. When his designated successor, Bob Livingston of Louisiana, stepped down after admitting to extramarital affairs, a party in search of consensus chose Dennis Hastert of Illinois as the new Speaker, with Majority Leader DeLay as the power behind the throne.

In a nearly straight party vote a month after the elections, the House backed two articles of impeachment on perjury and obstruction of justice. The Senate acquitted the president in March 1999, after a one-month trial. Five moderate Republicans from the Northeast—the remnant of Rockefeller Republicans—joined all forty-five Democratic senators in voting not guilty on both charges. These senators agreed with the Democrats that the president's actions were morally reprehensible but did not meet the constitutional standard of high crimes and misdemeanors. Public reaction against an impeachment crisis that seemed to weaken the presidency gave a green light for the assertion of strong presidential authority in the next administration.

DEFUNDING THE LEFT

After the 1998 midterm elections, a Republican Party memo on "defunding the left" explained the party's investment strategy for the new millennium. Through a continuation of the K Street Project, begun after Republicans recaptured Congress in 1994, and named after the capital's strip mall for lobbyists, the GOP would pressure corporations and lobbying firms "to hire more Republicans; Republican leadership refuses to meet with Dems; make Fortune 500 firms aware of whom they are hiring to represent them in Washington." Through its control of Congress, Republicans combined the carrot of policies to enhance business profits and stick of refusing to do business with firms that lagged in the hiring of Republican lobbyists. Ultimately, GOP leaders hoped to construct a shadow political machine of lawyers, lobbyists, and public relations specialists with access to hundreds of millions of dollars in campaign cash and the power to shape policy debates, influence legislation, and guide public opinion. DeLay initially led the K Street Project, while Grover Norquist hosted strategy sessions and compiled lists of lobbyists' party affiliations and contributions.[94]

The memo outlined strategy for defunding the left by eliminating "sources of hard currency for the Democratic Party" and by using Reagan's "model for cutting off the flow of hard currency to the Soviet Union." To further weaken the unions, Republicans would promote free trade and repeal the Davis Bacon Act that required prevailing wages on federally funded or assisted projects and the Jones Act that limited trade between U.S. ports to American vessels. The party would strive to restrict the use of compulsory union dues for political purposes. It would push for liability limitations on lawsuits to stanch the flow of funds from trial lawyers to liberals. The GOP would weaken the National Education Association by promoting "school choice." It would work to abolish the Legal Services Corporation and the Public Broadcasting System and kill incentives for tax-deductible donations to "liberal foundations" by repealing estate taxes.[95]

SHOWDOWN IN FLORIDA

The impeachment scandal darkened otherwise bright election prospects for Democrats in the 2000 presidential elections. A strong economy wiped out the budget deficit and produced surpluses in President Clinton's last three years. Although peace remained elusive in unsettled regions of the world and the Republican Senate blocked multilateral accords, no serious foreign threat faced the United States in 2000. Vice President Albert Gore achieved a consensus nomination after trouncing former New Jersey senator Bill Bradley in the primaries. For his running mate, Gore chose centrist senator Joseph Lieberman of Connecticut, the first Jewish nominee on a major party ticket. Among Republicans, a crowded field narrowed to Texas governor George W. Bush and the independent-minded Arizona senator John McCain. Bush undercut the system for controlling campaign finance by becoming the only candidate since John Connally in 1980 to reject public funding, which imposed a maximum spending cap on candidates. By the New Hampshire primary Bush had already raised a record $70 million, compared to $21 million for McCain. Much of Bush's money came from corporate executives and lobbyists who bundled together $1,000 contributions from individuals. Bush's take eventually surged to a record $100 million.

Still, thanks to backing from independents and crossover Democrats, McCain stunned Bush with an eighteen-point win in New Hampshire. Governor Bush, like Senator Dole in 1996, then called upon the Christian right for rescue in South Carolina's primary. Bush won South Carolina by carrying two-thirds of voters identifying as Christian conservatives and swept the remaining primaries. Buchanan reemerged as the Reform Party nominee. Buchanan had $12.6 million in federal funds to spend in the general election, because Ross Perot, the Reform Party candidate in 1996, had won more than 5 percent of the national popular vote. Although Buchanan might have taken some votes from Bush, he failed to wage a credible campaign. Insurgent candidate Ralph Nader, who threatened Gore's base, topped 5 percent in some polls.

Bush tilted right with a conservative platform and Dick Cheney as his running mate, but he campaigned as a moderate. He embraced the "compassionate conservativism" that Paul Weyrich had proposed in the 1980s and which was further elaborated in two influential books—*The Tragedy of American Compassion* (1992) and *Compassionate Conservatism: What it Is, What it Does, and How it can Transform America* (2000)—by University of Texas journalism professor and Bush adviser Marvin Olasky. Bush also defended "strategic humility," saying, "I'm not so sure the role of the United States is to go around the world and say, 'This is the way it's got to be.'" Gore won the popular vote by half a percent, but the Electoral College vote turned on disputed votes in Florida. Nader's vote faded to 2.7 percent nationally but he won 97,000 votes in Florida, costing Gore a clear victory. With Bush barely ahead, Gore called for a recall in selected Florida counties rather than statewide. An order by Florida's Supreme Court for a statewide recount came too late. On December 12, the U.S. Supreme

Court stopped the recount with Bush ahead by 537 votes out of six million cast. Bush won a bare majority 271 Electoral College votes, including all the South and about one-third in all other regions. Bush won the backing of 70 percent of voters in the top 5 percent of earners. He swept the vote of three-fifths of white Protestants, including two-thirds from white, evangelical Protestants. He won 55 percent of the vote cast by churchgoing white Catholics, compared to 45 percent from Catholics who rarely or never attended church. Bush won 19 percent of Jews, 8 percent of African Americans, 35 percent of Hispanics, and 30 percent of others and those with no religious affiliation.

Controversy over the Florida count lingered on. Studies showed that election officials had eliminated allegedly disenfranchised felons from the voter rolls with a flawed list that overcounted African Americans, who voted overwhelmingly Democratic, and undercounted Hispanics, who usually voted Republican in Florida. Florida officials had also rejected as invalid some 180,000 ballots either because a presidential vote could not be discerned or because the ballot appeared to register more than one vote. Analysis showed that election officials discarded as invalid more than one out of every ten ballots cast by African Americans, who voted 95 percent for Gore, compared to fewer than one out of every fifty ballots cast by whites, who voted 40 percent for Gore. If ballots cast by blacks had been rejected at the same rate as ballots cast by whites, more than 50,000 additional black votes would have been counted in Florida.[96]

On January 6, 2001, the president of the Senate, Al Gore, counted the Electoral College votes that elected George W. Bush president of the United States. The GOP clung to its narrow House lead but lost four Senate seats, creating a fifty–fifty tie, with Vice President Cheney holding the deciding vote. For the first time since 1953, a Republican president entered the White House with control of Congress. Republicans held more governorships and state legislatures than Democrats. Republicans had appointed seven of nine Supreme Court justices, including the Court's five conservatives. Not since the 1920s had the GOP held such power.

EPILOGUE
A CONSERVATIVE IMPLOSION?

THE CONSERVATIVE LEGACY AND CHALLENGE

In January 2001, the newly inaugurated president George W. Bush could survey the history of American conservatism with some satisfaction. Conservatives had set the terms of political debate in the 1920s and largely in the last quarter of the century. They had put in place Prohibition, immigration restriction, antisedition measures, and religious observances in public schools. They had rallied the nation against communism, won the Cold War, and turned back the tide of union organizing. They had slashed taxes, deregulated business, and rewritten the welfare laws and America's criminal statutes. The right had damned up the liberal state since the Nixon years. It had blocked the Equal Rights Amendment, turned civil rights measures into quota laws, and sounded the alarm against deviance and cultural decay. Conservatives had exposed liberalism's program of social engineering that ignored the moral teachings of religion. The right had achieved its goal of uniting white Protestant America behind Republican candidates and issues, made inroads among Catholics, and transformed the solidly Democratic South into a citadel of conservative Republican power. Conservatives had turned the words *liberal* and *feminist* into epithets and pushed a Democratic president into abandoning health care reform and rewriting a New Deal entitlement. They had created protected venues for the generation of conservative ideas. As Bush learned in the battle for Florida, conservatives had more passion for power than liberals and could count on the resources of business and a coordinated movement of intellectuals, publicists, lobbyists, educators, business leaders, journalists, preachers, talk show hosts, and grassroots activists.

Still, daunting challenges and choices lay ahead for the president-elect. The Reagan and Gingrich revolutions had brought the GOP to near parity with Democrats but had not matched the shattering realignment of the New Deal. Although many more Americans identified as conservatives than as liberals, a week after the 2000 election Democrats still led Republicans by 9 percentage points in party identification, according to a Gallup Poll. Republicans had only a nine-seat edge in the House and their control of the Senate depended on Vice President Cheney's tie-breaking vote. The main props of the New Deal, the Great Society, and Richard Nixon's liberal initiatives stood in place. Although conservatives held a narrow majority on the Supreme Court, *Roe v. Wade* still stood. Religion remained excluded from the schools, faith-based providers had not secured a place in government programs, and despite a relentless pounding from conservatives gays and lesbians had not returned to the closet. Liberals still dominated the academy, public education and Social Security had not been privatized, and the courts had blocked the teaching of creationism, or intelligent design as forms of science. Business remained burdened with liability lawsuits, pollution controls, health and safety edicts, and other unwanted regulations. The end of the Cold War took the edge off the right's defense of American civilization and sapped the nation's defenses. Since 1989 the defense budget had sagged from 27 percent to 17 percent of federal outlays and social spending had soared from 50 percent to 62 percent.

American culture appeared to be no less decadent than in the 1960s. In 1999 Paul Weyrich had written an open letter to fellow conservatives saying that "politics itself has failed. And politics has failed because of the collapse of the culture. The culture we are living in becomes an ever-wider sewer. In truth, I think we are caught up in a cultural collapse of historic proportions, a collapse so great that it simply overwhelms politics." Conservatives, he said, had "lost the culture war. . . . We need to drop out of this culture and find places, even if it is where we physically are right now, where we can live godly, righteous and sober lives."[1]

Bush's challenge was to consolidate his political power and advance a conservative policy agenda. He had to reconcile Christian right demands for moral regeneration with business expectations of payoffs in the billions for the millions they invested in Republican campaigns. He had to uphold conservatism's crusading spirit in the absence of a credible threat to U.S. security. He had to satisfy his anti-pluralist base without alienating centrist voters. He had to reconcile the right's distrust of redistributive government with public expectations for prosperity and benefits from Uncle Sam. He had to represent a party devoted both to personal morality and to bitter warfare against its opponents in a polarized political system.

The turning point of George W. Bush's presidency came with the September 11, 2001, terrorist attacks by al-Qaeda. In a carefully coordinated operation, al-Qaeda operatives crashed hijacked airplanes into both towers of New York City's World Trade Center and the Pentagon in Arlington, Virginia. Hijackers also took over United Airlines Flight 93, which crashed in rural Pennsylvania after passengers stormed the cockpit. Like Woodrow Wilson when he entered the Great War against Germany, President Bush justified a war on terrorism after 9/11 by articulating a grand vision for America and the world. With al-Qaeda shattering the myth of an invulnerable America, the president vowed to protect the nation from attack while battling evildoers and advancing democracy and freedom worldwide. Like Wilson at the end of World War I, Bush possessed vast military and economic power, prestige, and international goodwill. Two million French men and women had cheered President Wilson as he entered Paris in December 1918, armed with plans to remake the world at the Versailles peace conference. Six months later, with his global vision shattered, Wilson slipped quietly away under cover of night. What the British economist John Maynard Keynes said of Wilson might also apply to George W. Bush. "When it came to practice his ideas were nebulous and incomplete. He had no plan, no scheme, no constructive ideas for clothing with the flesh of life the commandments which he had thundered from the White House."[2]

Wilson and Bush both failed to give life to their commandments because of deep contradictions within their respective political traditions. Just as Wilson's second term effectively ended the Progressive era, Bush's second term might well be the end of America's dominant conservative era. Contrary to many critics on the right, George W. Bush was not a counterfeit or apostate conservative but the heir to a troubled tradition. For nearly a century, American conservatives had protected private enterprise and traditional values through adjustments and readjustments of dispensable ideas on states' rights, balanced budgets, free markets, individual liberties, public education, foreign relations, and the size, scope, and intrusiveness of government. In the early twenty-first century, however, these revisions threatened conservatism's survival as a viable political movement. By Bush's second term numerous critics on the right argued that Bush had betrayed the conservative tradition. In fact, Bush represented the culmination of twentieth-century American conservative politics, buoyed by its strengths and burdened by its contradictions.

COMING OUT CONSERVATIVE

Bush's conservative backers in 2000 brushed aside suggestions from media commentators that the president-elect fulfill his promise to be "a uniter not a divider" and emulate Rutherford B. Hayes who governed from the center after the disputed election of 1876. "You're going to think I'm crazy, but I didn't see this as a tie election," Representative DeLay said. "We have the House, we have the Senate, we have the White House, which means we have the agenda." Phyllis Schlafly called bipartisanship "a terrible model." Dick Cheney, who was poised to become the most influential vice president in American history, added, "The suggestion that somehow, because this was a close election, we should fundamentally change our beliefs I just think is silly."[3]

Within his first hundred days, the president faithfully assembled a conservative administration and implemented conservative policies. BUSH TEAM HAS "RIGHT" CREDENTIALS; CONSERVATIVE PICKS SEEN ECLIPSING EVEN REAGAN'S, reported a front-page *Washington Post* headline in March 2001. Conservative appointments included former Republican senator John Ashcroft as attorney general, Donald Rumsfeld as secretary of defense, and movement conservatives in second-tier jobs, including a host of neoconservatives. Paul Wolfowitz served as deputy secretary of defense and Douglas Feith as undersecretary of defense for policy. Richard Perle served as chairman of the Defense Policy Board Advisory Committee and Elliot Abrams as a special assistant to the president.

In his foreign policy the president left behind the humble rhetoric of his campaign. Well before 9/11, he revived the right's engaged nationalism, based on the unilateral use of American power to advance its interests and values worldwide. Bush rejected the international Kyoto Accords on greenhouse gas emissions and an agreement to curb chemical and biological weapons. He resurrected Ronald Reagan's dream of a nuclear shield by repudiating the 1972 Anti-Ballistic Missile Treaty and deciding to ramp up missile defense. He backed off from negotiations with North Korea and involvement in the Middle East peace process, and he ordered the bombing of missile sites in Iraq. His administration's first budget submission in March 2001 proposed expanded military spending. The Bush administration "has generated anxiety among foreign policy specialists about a doctrine variously dubbed 'unilateralism' or 'exceptionalism'," wrote *Los Angeles Times* reporter Robin Wright seven months before September 11. "The premise of the new doctrine is that the United States can do pretty much what it wants because its sophisticated democracy makes it politically and morally superior to the rest of the world—and sometimes even exempts it from international norms and treaties."[4]

RALLYING AMERICA TO WAR

The 9/11 attacks marked for conservatives the advent of a new enemy. Christian civilization had confronted implacable enemies for two thousand years. Why should the third millennium be any different? The attack seemed to confirm the West's dangerous confrontation with militant Islam that Professor Richard Pipes had envisaged in 1994 and to underscore Pipes's call for conservatives to confront the enemy. In October 2001, with overwhelming public and congressional support, Bush invaded Afghanistan to dethrone the Taliban regime, which harbored al-Qaeda terrorists. On June 1, 2002, the president enunciated a Bush doctrine that called for "military strength beyond challenge." The doctrine was formalized in the administration's *National Security Strategy*, promulgated in September 2002. It committed the United States to promoting democracy, free trade, and free markets across the world. It advocated unilateral American military action if international consensus could not be achieved and reserved for the United States the right to wage preemptive war against "emerging threats" from abroad, not just in cases of immediate peril to America's security.

Six months later President Bush put this doctrine into practice by invading Iraq. The U.S. had been pressuring and hoping to topple Saddam Hussein since President George H.W. Bush's decision to stop short of Baghdad during the Gulf War of 1991. The war on Iraq presented an opportunity to reshape the Middle East, reinforce America's global authority, and send a message to enemies around the world. It would settle old scores against Saddam Hussein and revive the military-industrial complex. It would secure control over Iraq's immense oil reserves and provide access to the oil and mineral riches of Central Asia. It would justify expanded presidential powers and awaken conservative patriotism at home. If a war against communist sin could save Harry Truman, a war against radical Muslim sin could save Bush's presidency as well. Bush's approval rating had soared from 51 percent in a poll completed on September 10 to 86 percent three days later.

None of these justifications, however, could rally America behind a preemptive war against Iraq. To stir up support for invading Iraq, administration officials warned of a dangerous rogue regime that nurtured al-Qaeda terrorists. They said that Saddam had stockpiled horrific biological and chemical weapons and was acquiring nuclear weapons to slip to terrorists or hurl against the United States. Intelligence reports provided circumstantial evidence on Iraq's weapons of mass destruction but no conclusive proof. Still, when President Bush questioned the CIA's case against Saddam on December 14, 2002, director George Tenet told him, "Don't worry, it's a slam dunk." But the administration had not waited for such assurance. On August 26, 2002, Vice President Cheney had said, "Simply stated, there is no doubt that Saddam now has weapons of mass destruction; there is no doubt that he is amassing them to use against our friends, against our allies and against us." On October 7, 2002, President Bush said that Iraq "possesses and produces chemical and biological weapons. It is seeking nuclear weapons. . . . Facing clear evidence of peril, we cannot wait for the final proof—the smoking gun—that could come in the form of a mushroom cloud."[5]

The administration made an even more problematic claim that Saddam had harbored and supported al-Qaeda terrorists. In this instance, the administration could not turn to the CIA or other established intelligence agencies, which had failed to uncover any substantial connection between Saddam and Osama bin Laden. Rather, the administration reconstituted another independent "Team B" under the direction of Douglas Feith, undersecretary of defense for policy, to reevaluate intelligence findings. Feith's team predictably concluded that al-Qaeda and Iraq had a "mature symbiotic relationship" that involved "cooperation in all categories" of terrorist activities. A 2007 report by the inspector general of the Defense Department noted, "Both the DIA [Defense Intelligence Agency] and the CIA published reports that disavowed any 'mature, symbiotic' cooperation between Iraq and al-Qaeda." Team B had thus provided misleading information to decision makers, including members of the administration and Congress. President Bush's 9/11 Commission likewise found no "collaborative relationship" between Iraq and al-Qaeda.[6]

Some analysts have suggested that neoconservatives such as Wolfowitz, Perle, and Feith hijacked the foreign policies of the Bush administration and pushed it into invading Iraq. But Bush's top policy makers were not neoconservatives but engaged nationalists in the model of William Knowland and Barry Goldwater, who largely shared the neoconservatives' unilateral, aggressive approach to foreign affairs. In 1991, as secretary of defense, Dick Cheney had opposed taking Baghdad. In 1992, however, he authored the revised Defense Policy Draft that became a model for neoconservative foreign policy. In 1997 both Cheney and Rumsfeld had joined Wolfowitz as signatories of the founding statement of the Project for the New America Century (PNAC), a think tank on foreign policy cofounded by neoconservatives William Kristol and Robert Kagan. The statement echoed Cheney's 1992 statement in urging the United States to "challenge regimes hostile to our interests and values" and "accept responsibility for America's unique role in preserving and extending an international order friendly to our security, our prosperity, and our principles." In 1998 PNAC wrote to President Clinton in support of a strategy that "eliminates the possibility that Iraq will be able to use or threaten to use weapons of mass destruction. In the near term, this means a willingness to undertake military action as diplomacy is clearly failing. In the long term, it means removing Saddam Hussein and his regime from power." In 2000 PNAC mapped out a military program for "a global *Pax Americana*," forgetting perhaps Tacitus's admonition to Rome: "They make a desert and call it peace."[7]

Major Christian right leaders also backed military action against Iraq. In October 2002 Richard Land, a leader of the Southern Baptist Convention, drafted a letter to George W. Bush that outlined a theological justification for preemptive war. Bush's proposal for using military force if necessary to disarm Saddam Hussein, the letter said, fell "well within the time-honored criteria of just war theory as developed by Christian theologians in the late fourth and early fifth centuries A.D." In addition to Land, the letter was signed by Bill Bright, founder of the Campus Crusade for Christ; Chuck Colson, the chair of Prison Fellowship Ministries; D. James

Kennedy, head of the Coral Ridge Ministries; and Carl D. Herbster, president of the American Association of Christian Schools.[8]

In the midterm elections of 2002, amid the flagwaving run-up to the Iraq war, Republicans regained control of the Senate, which it had lost in 2001 when Senator Jim Jeffords of Vermont turned away from the Republican Party and became an independent. The GOP also became only the second presidential party since 1934 to gain House seats in a midterm contest.

A CONSERVATIVE LEVIATHAN

With the war in Iraq, a conservative administration that disdained social engineering to fight poverty or revamp health care in the United States assumed perhaps the most daunting social engineering project in American history: to pacify, rebuild, and democratize a land with alien culture and traditions, no history of democratic practice, and deep sectarian divisions. The Bush administration neither planned nor prepared for this vast undertaking. Instead, it convinced itself that Iraqis would quickly establish a stable government once the United States disposed of Saddam Hussein. The U.S. military Central Command's war plan for Iraq assumed that Phase IV of the war—the period after military victory—would last only a matter of months and that nearly all U.S. forces would depart Iraq by the end of 2006. Its "key planning assumptions" were that the military phase of the war "will be the main national effort." It expected that "opposition groups will work with us," that "co-opted Iraqi units will occupy garrisons and not fight either U.S. forces or other Iraqi units," and that "DoS [Department of State] will promote creation of a broad-based, credible provisional government—prior to D-day." Although the president rejected the idea that the United States should establish a provisional government for Iraq in advance of the invasion, his advisers still accepted the notion of a quick war and a relatively brief occupation. On May 1, 2003, Bush landed on the aircraft carrier U.S.S. *Abraham Lincoln* to declare in front of a large sign that read MISSION ACCOMPLISHED that "in the battle of Iraq, the United States and our allies have prevailed."[9]

Other contradictions burdened the administration. Business interests had poured a record $50 million into Bush's 2000 campaign, more than triple their largesse to Gore, while more than two-thirds of white evangelical

Protestants had voted for Bush. Both business and Christian right leaders expected payback. The president delivered handsomely to business and gave Christian conservatives what politics and religion scholar John C. Green called during Bush's first year "the three S's—symbolism, sympathy, and selective concessions." Bush distracted the American people with one hand while dispensing benefits to his corporate benefactors with the other. The distraction came through the flash and bombast of explosive social issues such as abortion, gay rights, public displays of religion, end-of-life decisions, and creationism, while benefits flowed to Bush's business backers.[10]

The result was a conservative big government that contradicted the right's rhetorical defense of limited government, states' rights, fiscal responsibility, and individual freedom. Conservative big government differed from the liberal project of using government to reform society from the bottom up, funding welfare benefits, regulating business, empowering labor and minorities. The Bush administration began from the top down, subsidizing business and expanding its global reach, shielding corporations, and backing robust military, intelligence, and police forces. For decades, Republicans had complained of Democrats who created cadres of dependent voters: recipients of welfare and Social Security, members of federal employee unions, and beneficiaries of affirmative action programs. Liberals, libertarians, and some conservatives charged that President Bush's big government created corporate dependents instead.[11]

SERVING MAMMON AND GOD

The president unrolled his pro-business agenda at the onset of his term. He reversed a campaign promise to restrict carbon emissions by industry. He signed a law that repealed regulations on repetitive motion injuries suffered in the workplace. He responded to business demands on environmental and energy issues by proposing to drill for oil and gas in Alaska's Artic National Wildlife Refuge and to reduce arsenic standards in water and cleanup requirements for mining firms. He resurrected the push for privatization by advocating personal Social Security accounts to be invested in the securities market. He ended the American Bar Association's half-century advisory role in the nomination of federal judges. This shift, plus a disciplined ideological vetting of nominees, eased the way for the appointment of judges favorable to business, Christian conservative causes, and strong presidential authority.

President Bush surprised most pundits in his first year by steering a $1.3 billion tax cut through Congress. Although the reductions heavily benefited the rich and did not extend to the payroll taxes paid mainly by Americans of modest and limited means, twenty-eight conservative Democrats in the House and twelve in the Senate voted with the administration. Unlike Reagan, who signed multiple tax hikes after his first year, Bush gained two additional tax cuts from Congress in 2002 and 2003, despite rising budget deficits and vanishing Democratic support. The president also won broad bipartisan support for his No Child Left Behind Act, which was designed to improve the performance of public elementary and secondary schools nationwide. The right's historic opposition to federal control over education and increased spending levels led some conservatives to oppose the legislation. Most conservatives in Congress, however, backed legislation that held public schools accountable for student achievement, provided alternatives for parents in low-performing schools (although only within the public school system), and cultivated the reading, math, and science skills needed for a productive workforce. The arts, music, civics, history, and social studies did not receive equal attention. The law also benefited companies that marketed standardized tests, educational software, and for-profit educational centers. During the war in Iraq, the administration awarded lucrative contracts worth many billions of dollars to politically connected companies such as Bechtel and Halliburton, which Vice President Cheney had headed before joining the Bush ticket. In 2004 the administration narrowly pushed through Congress an expensive plan to subsidize prescription drug purchases by seniors that failed to restrain prices, giving drug companies large windfall profits.

Tax cuts without spending reductions turned a $128 billion budget surplus in 2001 into a $413 billion deficit in 2004. During Bush's first term, federal spending grew by 17 percent in constant dollars, compared to 11 percent during Bill Clinton's two terms. Discretionary domestic spending under Bush increased even more rapidly than total spending, "exactly the opposite of what was promised by Republican leaders when they first came to power in the 1990s," wrote conservative fiscal analyst Stephen Moore. The federal government's share of GDP rose to 19.9 percent in 2005, after declining from 22.1 percent to 18.4 percent during the Clinton years. Conservative big government opened fissures between the wealthy and other Americans. Income inequality shot ahead at a record rate between 2002 and 2005, reaching levels unknown in America since the eve of the Great Depression. In 2005 the top 10 percent of earners collected 44.3 percent of income, compared to 32.6 percent in 1975 and about equal to the 43.8 percent in 1929. The top 1 percent collected 17.4 percent compared to 8.0 percent in 1975 and 18.4 percent in 1929.[12]

Bush's concessions to the Christian right came primarily through executive actions. On January 22, 2001, the twenty-eighth anniversary of *Roe v. Wade*, the president signed an executive order that banned federal funds to international family planning groups that provided abortion services, counseling, or advocacy. The order reinstated a Reagan-era policy that President George H. W. Bush had let stand and President Bill Clinton had overturned. The administration also withheld a long-standing congressional appropriation for the United Nation's Population Fund and pressured other nations to reject abortion rights and contraceptive programs. In his first year, the president banned the use of federal money for research on human embryonic stem cells, which scientists said had the potential to help treat genetic diseases, cancer, juvenile diabetes, and spinal cord injuries. Pro-life activists charged that research on human embryos required the destruction of life, equivalent to abortion. In 2003 Bush signed a third version of the congressional ban on "partial-birth abortions" that Clinton had twice vetoed. The president set up a White House Office of Faith-Based and Community Initiatives and signed an executive order designed to assist churches and religious groups in competing for federal grants.

Like Reagan, however, Bush did not drain political capital on fights for Christian right priorities such as tax credits for private school tuition, antipornography laws, a constitutional amendment banning gay marriage, or richly funded faith-based programs. David Kuo, former deputy director of the White House Office of Faith-Based and Community Initiatives, said rather than fulfilling promises to the Christian right his "understaffed and underfunded" office became a "sad charade, to provide political cover to a White House that needed compassion and religion as political tools." In 2002, he added, the White House used funds for faith-based initiatives to hold twenty conferences that mobilized voters in targeted U.S. Senate and House races.

Bush's political team "knew that the 'nuts' [Christian conservatives] were politically invaluable, but that was the extent of their usefulness," Kuo said. "We had used people of faith to further our political agenda and hadn't given them anything in return." Earlier, John DiIulio, who resigned in 2001 as the first director of the president's faith-based program, had said, "What you have is everything—and I mean everything—being run by the political arm. It's the reign of the Mayberry Machiavellis."[13]

THE POLITICAL USE OF POWER

The political use of religion showed the administration's dedication to controlling a cutthroat, polarized political system. Although the president's political "architect" Karl Rove had learned politics from Richard Nixon, Bush's approach to political control was calculated and systematic, not driven by Nixonian paranoia. The administration tightened secrecy and information control, politicized government service, and aggressively deployed executive power for political ends.[14]

Well before 9/11, the administration discouraged oversight by Congress, and brawled with the General Accounting Office (GAO) over access to records of Vice President Cheney's energy task force that set policy behind closed doors with industry. After 9/11, the administration stepped up the classification and reclassification of information and encouraged federal agencies to reject Freedom of Information Act requests. It restricted access to presidential records and authorized White House staff members to use private e-mail accounts to evade legal requirements for preserving and disclosing federal records. Larry Klayman, director of the conservative group Judicial Watch, said in 2002, "We see an unprecedented secrecy in this White House that . . . we find very troubling. . . . True conservatives don't act this way."[15]

The administration used information control proactively as well. In February 2002 the president pushed the USA PATRIOT Act through Congress. It loosened restrictions on domestic surveillance and gave federal agents greater latitude to use "national security letters" to gain secret access to people's financial, travel, e-mail, and phone records without a court order or a grand jury's finding of probable cause. It imposed a gag order that forbade recipients of such letters from disclosing the demand for records. In a reprise of Vietnam-era events, the Justice Department's inspector general found that the FBI failed to follow legal guidelines in issuing more than 143,000 national security letter requests from 2003 to 2005, compared to 8,500 in the year before passage of the Patriot Act. "Do we have so many potential terrorists running around the country?" asked conservative Republican congressman James Sensenbrenner Jr. of Wisconsin. "The FBI has had a gross overreach." The administration also asserted its authority to hold and try so-called enemy combatants in secret. It covertly transferred aliens representing "special interest cases" to foreign prisons and authorized harsh interrogation methods for suspected terrorists. Through an expanded application of "signing statements"—presidential statements that interpret the legislation they sign—Bush implicitly reserved the right to override provisions of many hundreds of federal laws. In his first five years Bush issued some seven hundred signing statements, compared to seventy-one by Reagan and a hundred and five by Clinton in their full two terms in office.[16]

The political use of government extended into the traditionally off-limits precincts of science, law enforcement, and national security. The administration extended to government the model of private organizations like the Discovery Institute by creating a protected space for ideologically compatible science. It applied political criteria to scientific appointments, rewrote scientific findings to fit political priorities, and overrode the recommendations of scientific panels. Richard H. Carmona, surgeon general of the United States from 2002 to 2006, testified before Congress that the administration made decisions about critical public health issues—including teen pregnancy prevention, smoking, and stem cell research—based on politics and ideology, not science. "Anything that doesn't fit into the political appointees' ideological, theological, or political agenda is ignored, marginalized, or simply buried," he said. Press reports disclosed that on several occasions White House officials without scientific expertise had substantially revised scientific reports and testimony to downplay the dangers of global climate change. A report by the Interior Department's inspector general found that Julie MacDonald, a political appointee in Fish, Wildlife, and Parks with no training in natural science, had similarly revised scientific reports to minimize the threats posed to endangered species by industry and development. In December 2007, Stephen L. Johnson, the head of the Environmental Protection Agency, overruled the recommendations of his technical advisers and blocked efforts by California and other states to stringently regulate greenhouse gas emissions from automobiles.[17]

Within the Department of Justice, congressional testimony by high officials and information provided by attorneys who had served under both Republican and Democratic presidents indicated that the Bush administration had applied political criteria to the hiring and firing of career personnel. Within the department's Civil Rights Division, career attorneys said that politics guided not only personnel matters but also substantive decisions on litigation priorities, the approval of redistricting plans for Congress and state legislatures, and voter fraud prosecutions. The results of these practices, said Joseph D. Rich, who had served for thirty years in the Department of Justice, was that "the damage done to one of the federal government's most important law enforcement agencies is deep and will take time to overcome."[18]

In 2003 administration officials used their access to classified national security information to leak the identity of undercover CIA agent Valerie Plame to the media in an effort to discredit her husband, former ambassador Joseph Wilson, whose on-site investigations cast doubt on presidential claims that Iraq had purchased yellowcake uranium in Africa for the purpose of manufacturing nuclear weapons. Federal prosecutors did not charge any officials for leaking Plame's identity, but they convicted Vice President Cheney's chief of staff I. Lewis "Scooter" Libby on four counts of lying and obstructing justice in his testimony on the leak investigation. President Bush later commuted his thirty-month prison sentence.

A TROUBLED NEW TERM

Despite relatively low approval ratings for the president, the country was faring well enough in 2004 to reelect the incumbent president. Overconfident Democrats misread the political situation and their nominee, Massachusetts senator John Kerry, expected to back into office by emulating Michael Dukakis's politics of competence. President Bush, who shattered his own record by raising nearly $275 million in campaign contributions, won both the popular and Electoral College vote. Voters in eleven states overwhelmingly enacted referenda that prohibited gay marriage within their jurisdictions. These positive results stood in marked contrast to the right's failed effort to pass right-to-work referenda in 1958. The GOP expanded its Senate majority from fifty-one to fifty-five seats and picked up three House seats, which padded the majority to thirty seats. It gained

six House seats in Texas through an unprecedented redrawing of previously established congressional district lines led by Tom DeLay. Political
appointees in the Department of Justice overruled a unanimous finding
by career attorneys that the DeLay plan violated the Voting Rights Act.[19]

In 2005 conservative consultant Craig Shirley wrote that, after
Reagan, "It is unconscionable to think that any modern Republican would
aggressively or gleefully embrace the growth of government or oppose the
decentralization of power in Washington." By that year, however, Bush
had broken both of these commandments. A revealing moment came in
March 2005. In another symbolic concession to social conservatives, President Bush and Representative DeLay pushed Congress to intervene in the
case of Terri Schiavo, a brain-damaged patient in Florida who had existed
in a vegetative state for fifteen years. State courts had sanctioned a decision by Schiavo's husband to remove her feeding tube and stop prolong-
ing her life, but right-to-life conservatives had made her plight a national
issue that they hoped would put a human face on their movement. To
prevent the imminent removal of the feeding tube, Congress passed an
emergency bill requiring federal courts to review the case. This federal in-
trusion into a state and family matter contradicted the right's self-professed
principles, including judicial restraint, the sanctity of the family, the sacred bond between husband and wife, private decision making without
government meddling, and deference to states and localities. Prominent
conservatives criticized the intervention and three-quarters of American
registered their disapproval in opinion polls. The conservative movement
seemed to be fragmenting in full public view. A few months later the administration compounded its troubles with a botched response to Hurri-
cane Katrina in New Orleans. Afterward, the president again spurned
conservative principle to promise a massive government rebuilding program for New Orleans, although critics later charged that the results fell
far short of the promise.[20]

New elements of conservative big government emerged in the second term. The administration confirmed in late 2005 that the president
authorized the National Security Agency to wiretap Americans without
warrants, bypassing requirements of the Foreign Intelligence Surveillance
Act of 1978. In July 2005 the administration won passage of an energy bill
that subsidized big energy companies. Even the bill's proponents cautioned
that it would do little to reduce energy prices or America's dependence

on foreign oil. Members of Congress, both Republicans and Democrats, seized their own opportunities to benefit from big government through the record $286 billion transportation bill of 2005 that earmarked more than six thousand special projects for nearly every member's state or district. Among the earmarked projects was $2.3 million for landscaping on the Ronald Reagan Freeway in California. "I wonder what Ronald Reagan would say," asked Senator John McCain of Arizona, one of only four senators to vote against the bill.

The administration gained a renewed Patriot Act and the Military Commissions Act of 2006 that gave the executive branch authority to define persons, possibly including U.S. citizens, as "unlawful enemy combatants" who potentially could be detained indefinitely. Aliens, including legal residents of the United States who the government defined as unlawful enemy combatants and were tried by military tribunals, could be denied protections of the Geneva Convention against torture, habeas corpus rights to challenge their imprisonment, and constitutional safeguards against the use of coerced and secret testimony. "Have Republicans become the party of torture, secret prisons, and indefinite detention?" asked libertarian author James Bovard in *American Conservative* magazine, which Pat Buchanan had founded in 2002. "The new law—far more dangerous than the more controversial Patriot Act—is perhaps the biggest disgrace Congress has enacted since the Fugitive Slave Act of 1850."[21]

Still, the war in Iraq weighed most heavily on President Bush and his party. By the midterm election year of 2006, social engineering in Iraq had gone badly awry. Iraq appeared to be descending into civil war and a leaked National Intelligence Estimate concluded, "The Iraq war has made the overall terrorism problem worse." On the eve of the 2006 elections, the American death toll in Iraq approached three thousand, Iraqi deaths numbered in the scores to hundreds of thousands, and America's prestige had crumbled across the world. A consensus of polls released in early November showed that Bush's approval ratings had fallen below 40 percent and that only a third of Americans approved his handling of the Iraq war. Democrats cut in half the Republicans' fund-raising lead of 2002 and won control over Congress by picking up six Senate and thirty-one House seats. Democrats became the first party since the 1850s to not lose a single seat in either chamber. In the aftermath of the election, the Democratic lead in party loyalties jumped to 15 percent in some polls. However, in its first year the Democratic Congress disappointed liberals by failing to change policy on the Iraq War and adopting an energy bill that increased fuel economy standards for automobiles and did not include alternative fuel mandates for utilities or repeal tax breaks for big oil companies.

In October 2005, editor Fred Barnes of the *Weekly Standard* had accurately foreseen an emerging "conservative revolt" against President Bush. In 2006 Richard Viguerie said that "George W. Bush and other big government Republicans hijacked the conservative cause." Bruce Bartlett, a White House aide to Ronald Reagan, called Bush a "pretend conservative" who "betrayed the Reagan Legacy." In the unkindest cut of all, patriarch William F. Buckley Jr. said, "If you had a European prime minister who experienced what we've experienced it would be expected that he would retire or resign." Veteran conservative columnist Robert Novak wrote in March 2007, "In half a century, I have not seen a president so isolated from his own party in Congress—not Jimmy Carter, not even Richard Nixon as he faced impeachment."[22]

Business executives mostly counted their money and held their tongues. So did established Christian right leaders who had their eyes on the U.S. Supreme Court. On April 18, 2007, both of Bush's appointees to the Supreme Court—the chief justice John Roberts and Samuel Alito—voted in a 5 to 4 majority to uphold the federal ban on partial-birth abortions. These Bush appointees, joined by Antonin Scalia, Clarence Thomas, and Anthony Kennedy, also backed a pro-business agenda, for example, by weakening antitrust laws and making it more difficult for plaintiffs to sue companies for fraud or discrimination in pay. In the new courts, the core social and economic principles of conservative politics meshed without grinding gears.

Not just conservative activists and intellectuals but Republican candidates for the 2008 presidential nomination deserted their president. In the primary debates, the candidates ignored President Bush and instead invoked Ronald Reagan as their conservative role model. In Congress, Republicans failed to rally behind embattled Attorney General Alberto Gonzalez, who resigned in September 2007 amid allegations that he had fired nine United States attorneys for political reasons. Many Republicans in Congress opposed Bush's policies on immigration and stem cell research and endorsed gutting No Child Left Behind by letting states bypass testing requirements.

In October 2007 David Brooks, a conservative columnist for the *New York Times,* offered another provocative critique of the Bush administration. He said that the president and his allies were "creedal conservatives" who were zealously pursuing an unbending ideological agenda. They had made the mistake of ignoring what Brooks called the roots of conservativism in the ideas of eighteenth-century British statesman Edmund Burke, who advocated skepticism about all ideological creeds and "a reverence for tradition, a suspicion of radical change." The Bush administration, Brooks wrote, had abandoned the "temperamental conservativism" that imposes prudent limitations on political action. Yet throughout the modern history of American conservatism, leaders inclined temperamentally to distrust ideological zeal and rapid social change have not been conservatives but rather moderate Republicans, such as Thomas Dewey, Dwight Eisenhower, or Bob Dole. Their caution stands in contrast to the boldness of the right's major leaders, for example, J. Howard Pew, Frank Gannett, Carl McIntire, Robert Taft, Joseph McCarthy, William F. Buckley Jr., Barry Goldwater, Jerry Falwell, Pat Robertson, Paul Weyrich, Phyllis Schlafly, Ronald Reagan, and Newt Gingrich. President Bush stands firmly within an American conservative tradition that since the 1930s has had the revolutionary objective of overturning the liberal order and challenging America's pluralist civilization.[23]

Recent pathbreaking research by behavioral scientists John Alford, Carolyn Funk, and John R. Hibbing has shown that individuals attracted to right-wing politics had strongly genetic and to a lesser extent socially conditioned attitudes that inclined them to creedal, not temperamental, conservatism. According to their work, the conservative disposition was "absolutist." Conservatives were "characterized by a relatively strong suspicion of out-groups (e.g., immigrants), a yearning for in-group unity and strong leadership . . . a desire for clear, unbending moral and behavior codes (strict constructionists), a fondness for swift and severe punishment for violations of this code (the death penalty), a fondness for systematization (procedural due process), a willingness to tolerate inequality (opposition to redistributive policies), and an inherently pessimistic view of human nature." Consistent with the thesis of this book the researchers also argued that the attitudes held by today's conservatives were "remarkably similar" to those held by conservatives "at earlier times in American history." From the perspective of a scholar of linguistics, George Lakoff came to the similar conclusion that conservatives are attracted to a hierarchical "strict father" model of life, marked by clear moral authority, exacting rules of behavior, and rigorous enforcement through certain punishment for transgressions.[24]

WHITHER CONSERVATISM?

In 2008, as in 1952, the right sought a conservative prince to rescue their movement. Yet any conservative president would face the same pressures and contradictions that plagued the Bush administration. Like his predecessors, a new conservative leader would depend on campaign contributions and other forms of political support from corporate interests that would demand large paybacks from government. Such pressures would pose once again the contradiction between the right's defense of free markets and its backing for corporate loans, subsidies, tax breaks, no-bid contracts, and other forms of special treatment from government. He would be entwined in the dilemma of how to advance the conservative goals of protecting national security and upholding morality and decency in society without a large and meddlesome state that contradicted the right's defense of personal freedom and small government. As illustrated by the Terri Schiavo case, conservatives' historic opposition to federal interference in private decisions and state issues would remain juxtaposed against demands from the Christian right for federal prohibitions on abortion, gay marriage, pornography, stem cell research, and doctor-assisted suicide.

A new conservative president would have to cope with the trade-off between low taxes and large budget deficits. He would have to reconcile the business community's need for immigrant labor with the fears of anti-pluralist conservatives that immigrants were debasing the culture, increasing poverty and crime, and overwhelming public services. He would have to mediate between firms seeking opportunities in the global economy and those seeking protection from foreign competition. He would have to consider how to limit the size and scope of the state and still meet people's demands for benefits they have come to expect from government. A new conservative president would have to ponder ways of avoiding social engineering projects abroad without returning to the disengaged nationalism of Lindbergh and Taft. He would have to consider whether to call off the war on the left and work for political consensus, to open the executive branch to greater public scrutiny and congressional supervision, and to back off from politicizing the departments and agencies of government.

Additionally, he would be faced with the contradiction between conservatives' public morality and their private vices. Although conservatives had weathered sex scandals before, they had never before faced a situation comparable to the seven sex scandals that erupted in a twelve-month period beginning in the fall of 2006. In September 2006, conservative Republican representative Mark Foley of Florida resigned after the press revealed that he had been sending sexually explicit e-mails to teenage boys who had served as congressional pages. The scandal extended to members of the Republican leadership who had known about and ignored Foley's transgressions. In November 2006, the Reverend Ted Haggard, an informal adviser to the Bush administration on family issues, resigned as president of the National Association of Evangelicals after admitting to having sex with a male prostitute. In July 2007 the phone number of Republican senator David Vitter of Louisiana, who had made his reputation as a family values crusader, was included in the client records of an escort service that federal prosecutors said was a front for prostitution. In August 2007 *Roll Call* newspaper revealed that Republican senator Larry Craig of Idaho, another Christian conservative, had been arrested for making sexual advances to an undercover police officer in a public restroom and had pleaded guilty to a lesser offense of disorderly conduct. Also in August 2007, Glenn Murphy Jr. resigned as president of the Young Republican National Federation after a twenty-two-year-old man accused of him of an attempted sexual assault. Two other scandals in the summer of 2007 implicated local figures. Coy Privette, president of the North Carolina Christian Action League and former head of the State Baptist Convention, pleaded guilty to patronizing a female prostitute, and conservative Republican state senator Bob Allen of Florida was arrested for soliciting oral sex from an undercover police officer in a public restroom.

Conservative leaders after Bush may also have to confront a major changeover in America's evangelical Protestant leadership. Ralph Reed, the Christian right's shrewdest political strategist, was tainted by his association with corrupt lobbyist Jack Abramoff and in 2006 lost the Republican nomination for lieutenant governor in his home state of Georgia. That year, the Southern Baptist Convention elected a moderate minister, the fifty-three-year-old Frank Page, as its new president. Bill Bright of the

Campus Crusade for Christ died in 2003. Jerry Falwell died in May 2007 and D. James Kennedy of the Coral Ridge Ministries died in September. In 2007 Pat Robertson turned seventy-seven years of age, Douglas Coe and Beverly LaHaye turned seventy-eight, and James Dobson turned seventy-one. Tim LaHaye, who turned eighty-one in 2007, had been preoccupied since 1995 with coauthoring his novels about the end times on earth. New evangelical stars such as Bill Hybels and Rick Warren, who have built associations of many thousands of churches, are less politically active than Falwell and Robertson. They are also more open to liberal ideas about civil rights, the environment, and social justice and less inclined to back moral crusades by government, either at home or abroad. Surveys of young evangelical Protestants also showed that they held conservative social views but had less of an attachment to the Republican Party than their elders.[25]

Conservatives vying for leadership of the Republican Party in 2008 have shunned George W. Bush, much as liberals had shunned Lyndon Johnson in 1968. Yet none have explained how to resolve contradictions within the conservative tradition or advanced a new vision for the right. Conservatism is far too entrenched in American life to disappear as a viable political force. But it remains an open question whether the right faces a temporary decline in fortune or an internal implosion with lasting effects. Rather than rejoicing, however, liberals might heed Brent Bozell's warning from 1969 that, although liberalism had fallen, conservatives had not stepped into the breech of history with their own, distinctive program for the nation.

ACKNOWLEDGMENTS

Since the inception of this book in the late 1990s, many people have generously contributed to its formulation, research, and final production. I am especially grateful to Leonard Moore for suggesting the idea of a sweeping, synthetic study of the modern American conservative movement and to Robert Griffith and Richard Breitman for their meticulous reading and commentary on early drafts. I also thank Karyn Strickler, Kara Lichtman, and Peter Kuznick for their insightful commentary on manuscript drafts.

I had the pleasure of working with many student assistants who helped with research and production, especially John Schmitz, Clifford Schecter, Devin Maroney, Dan Ballentyne, and Lisa Sherman. My work has been enriched greatly by the research papers and dissertations produced by my students over many decades, notably the work of Holly Werner-Thomas on the National Association of Manufacturers and the John Birch Society. I would also like to thank the helpful archivists at the many repositories I visited, and those who generously agreed to grant interviews for the book.

I am indebted to the outstanding professionals at Grove/Atlantic Press, especially my extraordinary editor Jofie Ferrari-Adler. His work greatly improved both the substance and the style of the book.

All errors, of course, I claim for myself.

APPENDIX

REPUBLICAN PERCENTAGE:
U.S. HOUSE AND SENATE, 1919–2007

This chart demonstrates trends in Republican strength in the U.S. House and Senate. With the exception of 1947–48 and 1953–54, Democrats controlled the House until 1994. With the exception of these two congresses, plus the congresses of 1981–1986, Democrats also controlled the Senate until 1994.

Years	% Rep Senate	% Rep House
1919–1920	51%	55%
1921–1922	61%	69%
1923–1924	53%	52%
1925–1926	58%	57%
1927–1928	51%	55%
1929–1930	58%	61%
1931–1932	50%	51%
1933–1934	36%	27%
1935–1936	26%	24%
1937–1938	17%	21%
1939–1940	24%	38%
1941–1942	29%	38%
1943–1944	39%	48%
1945–1946	40%	44%
1947–1948	53%	57%
1949–1950	44%	39%
1951–1952	49%	46%
1953–1954	50%	51%
1955–1956	49%	47%

Years	% Rep Senate	% Rep House
1957–1958	49%	46%
1959–1960	35%	35%
1961–1962	35%	40%
1963–1964	33%	41%
1965–1966	32%	32%
1967–1968	36%	43%
1969–1970	43%	43%
1971–1972	44%	41%
1973–1974	42%	44%
1975–1976	37%	33%
1977–1978	38%	33%
1979–1980	41%	36%
1981–1982	53%	44%
1983–1984	54%	38%
1985–1986	53%	42%
1987–1988	45%	41%
1989–1990	45%	40%
1991–1992	44%	38%
1993–1994	43%	41%
1995–1996	53%	53%
1997–1998	55%	52%
1999–2000	54%	51%
2001–2002	50%	51%
2003–2004	51%	53%
2005–2006	55%	53%
2007-	49%	47%

Source: U.S. Department of Commerce, *Historical Statistics of the United States*, Congressional Quarterly, *Congress and the Nation*.

This table reports the Republican percentage after the midterm elections and the resolution of changes in party affiliation and disputed elections. All percentages are approximate, however, given that the composition of the two houses frequently changes through vacancies, appointments, special elections, and changes in the party affiliation of legislators. In 1931–32, such changes eventually gave Democrats control over the House.

NOTES

Introduction

1. Arabella Kenealy, *Feminism and Sex-Extinction* (London: T. Fisher Unwin, 1922), 96.

Chapter 1

1. "The Nomination of Harding," *New York Times,* 13 June 1920, 1. Historians have debunked the notion that a few party bosses nominated Harding in a "smoke-filled room." Wesley M. Bagby, "The 'Smoke-Filled Room' and the Nomination of Warren G. Harding," *Mississippi Valley Historical Review* 41 (March 1955), 657–74. On Harding and the 1920 election see Robert K. Murray, *Harding Era: Warren G. Harding and His Administration* (Minneapolis: University of Minnesota Press, 1969); John W. Dean, *Warren G. Harding* (New York: Times Books, 2004); John A. Morello, *Selling The President, 1920: Albert D. Lasker, Advertising, And The Election Of Warren G. Harding* (Westport, CT: Praeger, 2001).

2. "Harding Proposes Immigration Curb," *New York Times,* 15 September 1920, 3.

3. "Preachers Urged to Fight for Drys on Primary Day," *Chicago Tribune,* 4 September 1918, 12; Joe L. Coker, "Liquor in the land of the Lost Cause: Southern White Evangelicals and the Prohibition Movement, 1880–1915," Ph.D. dissertation, Princeton Theological Seminary, 2005, 194–275; Catherine Gilbert Murdock, *Domesticating Drink: Women, Men, and Alcohol in America, 1870–1940* (Baltimore: Johns Hopkins University Press, 1998); Thomas R. Pegram, *Battling Demon Rum: The Struggle for a Dry America, 1800–1933* (Chicago: Ivan R. Dee, 1998).

4. A. F. Pollard, *Factors in American History* (New York: Macmillan, 1925), 83.

5. Jay A. Gertzman, *Bookleggers and Smuthounds: The Trade in Erotica, 1920–1940* (Philadelphia: University of Pennsylvania Press, 1999); Will Durant, "The New Morality," *Forum* 81 (May 1929), 309–12.

6. Frank R. Kent, "Filth on Main Street," *The Independent,* 20 June 1925, 686–88; Nellie B. Miller, "Fighting Filth on Main Street," *The Independent,* 10 October 1925, 411–13.

7. Paul S. Boyer, *Purity in Print: The Vice Society Movement and Censorship in America* (New York: Scribner's, 1968), 67; John S. Sumner, "Are American Morals Disintegrating?" *Current Opinion* 70 (May, 1921), 608–12; Andrea Friedman, *Prurient Interests: Gender, Democracy, and Obscenity In New York City, 1909–1945* (New York: Columbia University Press, 2000); Alison M Parker, *Purifying America: Women, Cultural Reform, and Pro-Censorship Activism, 1873–1933* (Urbana: University of Illinois Press, 1997).

8. Allan M. Brandt, *No Magic Bullet: A Social History of Venereal Disease in the United States Since 1880* (New York: Oxford University Press, 1987), 12–125; Harvey J. Locke, "Changing Attitudes Toward Venereal Disease," *American Sociological Review* 4 (December 1939), 836–43.

9. W. A. Warn, "Smith Approves Theatre Padlocks," *New York Times,* 8 April 1927, 1; Paul S. Boyer, "Boston Book Censorship in the Twenties," *American Quarterly,* 15 (Spring 1963), 3–24; "Prosecutor Assails Boston Book Sellers," *New York Times,* 16 April 1927, 16.

10. "Letter of Pope Explains Evils Following the War," *Chicago Tribune,* 2 August 1920, 1; "Full Text of Rules by Pope on Dress," *New York Times,* 17 February 1930, 5.

11. Francis C. Couvares, "Hollywood, Main Street, and the Church: Trying to Censor the Movies Before the Production Code," *American Quarterly* 44 (1992), 589; Gaines M. Foster, "Conservative Social Christianity, the Law, and Personal Morality: Wilbur F. Crafts in Washington," *Church History* 71 (December 2002), 799–819.

12. Thomas Doherty, *Pre-Code Hollywood: Sex, Immorality, and Insurrection in American Cinema, 1930–1934* (New York: Columbia University Press, 1999), the code on 347–67. Daniel A. Lord, *Played by Ear: The Autobiography of Daniel A. Lord* (Chicago: Loyola University Press, 1956), 298.

13. "Says that Drug Addicts Become AntiSocial," *Los Angeles Times,* 2 October 1923, I18; "Snatched by Dealers in Human Souls!," *Washington Post,* 22 June 1924, SM1; David F. Musto, *The American Disease: Origins of Narcotic Control* (New Haven, CT: Yale University Press, 1973), 91–229; Joseph F. Spillane, "Building a Drug Control Regime, 1919–1930," in Jonathon Erlen and Joseph F. Spillane, eds., *Federal Drug Control: The Evolution of Policy and Practice* (Binghamton, NY: Pharmaceutical Products, 2004), 25–59.

14. David Kyvig, *Repealing National Prohibition* (Chicago: University of Chicago Press, 1979); Harrison E. Spangler to Robert H. Lucas, 14 November 1930, Robert H. Lucas Papers, box 8, Herbert Hoover Presidential Library, West Branch, Iowa.

15. On anticommunism and Hoover see Richard Gid Powers, *Not Without Honor: The History of American Anticommunism* (New York: Free Press, 1995); Ted Morgan, *Reds: McCarthyism in Twentieth Century America* (New York: Random House, 2003); Athan G. Theoharis and John Stuart Cox, *The Boss: J. Edgar Hoover and the Great American Inquisition* (Philadelphia: Temple University Press, 1988).

16. Kenneth Ackerman, *Young J. Edgar Hoover: Hoover, the Red Scare, and the Assault on Civil Liberties* (New York: Carroll & Graf, 2007).

17. *Gitlow v. New York,* 268 U.S. 652 (1925).

18. William Pencak, *For God and Country: The American Legion, 1919–1941* (Boston: Northeastern University Press, 1989); American Legion, *Summary of Proceedings,*

1921 and 1925 National Conventions, American Legion Archives, Indianapolis, Indiana.

19. Cecilia O'Leary, *To Die For: The Paradox of American Patriotism* (Princeton, NJ: Princeton University Press, 1999); David W. Blight, *Race and Reunion: The Civil War and American Memory* (Cambridge, MA: Harvard University Press, 2001).

20. Harry Jung, "The Fifth Column," Address, 4 June 1940, *National Republic* Collection, reel 670, Hoover Institution on War, Revolution, and Peace, Palo Alto, California.

21. "Tells of Red Drive in Public Schools," *New York Times,* 2 December 1920, 17; "A New Menace?" *Current Opinion* (April 1921), 509; Patrick J. McNamara, "Edmund A. Walsh, S, J., and Catholic Anticommunism in the United States, 1917–1952," Ph.D. dissertation, The Catholic University of America, 2003, 76.

22. William Whitford, "The Story of the Sentinels of the Republic," undated, Sentinels, Executive Committee Minutes, 27 January 1925, 8 May 1925 and "20 Reasons for Rejection of the so-called 'Child Labor' Amendment," undated, Papers of Alexander Lincoln, boxes 2, 5, Arthur and Elizabeth Schlesinger Library, Cambridge, Massachusetts; Lynn Dumenil, "'The Insatiable Maw of Bureaucracy': Anti-statism and Education Reform in the 1920s," *Journal of American History* 77 (September 1990), 499–524.

23. Bruce Watson, *Sacco and Vanzetti: The Men, the Murders, and the Judgment of Mankind* (New York: Viking, 2007); "White Terror and Red Terror," *Outlook,* 2 November 1921, 334.

24. Kirsten Marie Delegard, "Women Patriots: Female Activism and the Politics of American Anti-Radicalism, 1919–1935," Ph.D. dissertation, Duke University, 1999, 125; "Pacifists and Reds Assailed Bitterly by Women Patriots," *Washington Post,* 11 February 1927, 5.

25. Elna C. Green, "From Anti-Suffragism to Anti-Communism: The Conservative Career of Ida M. Darden," *Journal of Southern History* 65 (May 1999), 287–316; Christine Kimberly Erickson, "Conservative Women and Patriotic Maternalism: The Beginnings of a Gendered Conservative Tradition in the 1920s and 1930s," Ph.D. dissertation, University of California, Santa Barbara, 1999.

26. By the 1920s, the media employed "conservative" and "liberal" in ways that are recognizable today, with the term "progressive" applied mainly to Republicans in the tradition of Theodore Roosevelt. Anna Shaw Faulkner, "Does Jazz Put the Sin in Syncopation," *Ladies Home Journal* (August 1921), 16.

27. Putnam to Harding 16 August 1921, Papers of Elizabeth Putnam, box 33, Schlesinger Library; Katherine T. Balch, "To Readers of The Woman Patriot," *The Woman Patriot,* 15 November 1921, 4. This and other important documents are available digitally from Alexander Street Press, "Women and Social Movements in the United States, 1600–2000," Kathryn Sklar and Thomas Dublin, eds.

28. Delegard, "Women Patriots," 127–29; "Lack of National Defense Criminal, Women are Told," *Washington Post,* 23 February 1925, 2; "Patriotic Women Take Stand for Adequate National Defense," *Daughters of the American Revolution Magazine* (March 1928), 147; Christy Jo Snider, "Patriots and Pacifists: The Rhetorical Debate

about Peace, Patriotism, and Internationalism, 1914–1930," *Rhetoric & Public Affairs* *8.1 (2005)*, 72.

29. Kim E. Nielson, *Un-American Womanhood: Antiradicalism, Antifeminism, and the First Red Scare* (Columbus: Ohio State University Press, 2001), 75–79; Carrie Chapman Catt, "The Lie Factory," *The Woman Citizen,* 20 September 1924, 24.

30. Glenda Gilmore, *Gender and Jim Crow: Women and the Politics of White Supremacy in North Carolina, 1896–1920* (Chapel Hill: University of North Carolina Press, 1996); Marjorie Spruill Wheeler, *New Women of the New South: The Leaders of the Woman Suffrage Movement in the Southern States* (New York: Oxford University Press, 1993); Rosalyn Terborg-Penn, *African-American Women in the Struggle for the Vote, 1850–1920* (Bloomington: Indiana University Press, 1998); Allan J. Lichtman, *Prejudice and the Old Politics: The Presidential Election of 1928* (Lanham, MD: Lexington Books, 2000), 77–92. Additional statistical results based on the same methodology are available from the author.

31. National League of Women Voters, Minutes, National Convention, 29 April 1924, National League of Women Voters Papers, Microfilm, Part II, reel 4; Minutes, Jubilee Convention of the National American Woman Suffrage Association, 24–29 March 1919, League Papers, Part II, reel 1; Barbara Stuhler and Robert H. Walker, *For the Public Record: A Documentary History of the League of Women Voters* (Westport, CT: Greenwood, 2000), 41.

32. NLWV, Meeting of the Executive Committee, 9–11 July 1924, League Papers, Part I, reel 2; National Convention, 14–20 April 1926, Part II, reel 3.

33. "Strident Sex in Politics," *Chicago Tribune,* 12 July 1925, 8; "The Blanket Equality Bill Proposed by the National Woman's Party for State Legislators: Why It Should not Pass," pamphlet, (New York: National Consumers League, May 1922).

34. Stuhler and Walker, *For the Public Record,* 52, 110; NLWV, "Statements of Policy, January 1923–November 1925," League Papers, Part II, reel 5.

35. "Women in Politics," *Youth's Home Companion,* 27 November 1924, 786.

36. Allan J. Lichtman, "The First Gender Gap," *Christian Science Monitor,* 16 August 1983, 23; Emily Newell Blair, "Are Women a Failure in Politics?" *Harper's* (October 1925), 514; Report of Managing Director, *The Woman Citizen,* NLWV, Proceedings, National Convention, 9–14 April 1923, League Papers, Part II, reel 5; The pro-Republican gender gap for women is documented statistically in Lichtman, *Prejudice,* 159–65 and in "Men's and Women's Vote, September 26, 1932," Emil Hurja Papers, box 69, Franklin D. Roosevelt Presidential Library, Hyde Park, New York. Hurja's analysis of straw polls from 15 states partitioned by sex showed women leading men by a mean 13.3 percentage points in support for Republicans.

37. Nielsen, *Un-American Womanhood,* 124–57; Francesca Constance Morgan, "'Home and Country': Women, Nation, and the Daughters of the American Revolution, 1890–1939," Ph.D. dissertation, Columbia University, 1998, 423–79, 570–85; "Pamphlet Attacks D.A.R. Leadership," *New York Times,* 9 April 1928, 1.

38. Helen Bailie, "Our Threatened Heritage: A Letter to the Daughters of the American Revolution," 5 April 1928, Jane Addams Papers, Series 1, reel 19, Swarthmore College Peace Collection, Swarthmore, Pennsylvania; "Woman Is Defeated in D.A.R. Libel Suit," *New York Times,* 11 October 1928, 19.

39. Debate Notes on Evolution, undated, Papers of Aimee Semple McPherson, Billy Graham Center Archives, Wheaton College, Wheaton, Illinois, reel 1; for recent overviews of fundamentalism see George M. Marsden, *Fundamentalism and American Culture,* 2nd ed. (New York: Oxford University Press, 2006), Mark A. Noll, *American Evangelical Christianity: An Introduction* (Malden, MA: Blackwell, 2001), and for comparative perspectives, the epochal collection, *The Fundamentalism Project,* vols. 1–5, Martin E. Marty and R. Scott Appleby, eds., (Chicago: University of Chicago Press, 1991–1993).

40. "Bishop J. F. Berry Praises Sunday," *The Billy Sunday Campaign in New York,* 19 February 1917, Billy Sunday, "Draft Article," undated 1921, "Sermon," 1 November 1925, Billy Sunday Papers, box 2 and reel 16, Graham Archives; William Trollinger, *God's Empire: William Bell Riley and Midwestern Fundamentalism* (Madison: University of Wisconsin Press, 1990); Robert F. Martin, *Hero of the Heartland: Billy Sunday and the Transformation of American Society* (Bloomington: Indiana University Press, 2002).

41. Jeffrey P. Moran, "The Scopes Trial and Southern Fundamentalism in Black and White: Race, Region, and Religion," *Journal of Southern History* 70 (February 2004), 95–120.

42. Rolin Lynde Hartt "Deep Conflict Divides Protestantism," *New York Times,* 16 December 1923, XX5; J. Gresham Machen, *Christianity and Liberalism* (New York: Macmillan, 1923), 7; "Church Storm Spreading to Other Faiths," *Chicago Tribune,* 19 December 1923, 1.

43. Anonymous, "The Modernist's Quest for God," *Atlantic Monthly* (February 1926), 231-32.

44. Robert T. Handy, *The American Religious Depression, 1925–1935* (Philadelphia: Fortress Press, 1968); Tona J. Hangen, *Redeeming the Dial: Radio, Religion, and Popular Culture in American History* (Chapel Hill: University of North Carolina Press, 2002).

45. Shailer Mathews, "Ten Years of American Protestantism," *The North American Review,* May 1923, 592; Marsden, *Fundamentalism and American Culture,* 92, 193–95.

46. Markku Ruotsila, "Conservative American Protestantism in the League of Nations Controversy," *Church History* 72 (September 2003), 593-616; Michael S. Hamilton, "Women, Public Ministry, and American Fundamentalism," *Religion and American Culture* 3 (Summer 1993), 171–96; Vivian Deno, "God, Authority, and the Home: Gender, Race, and U. S. Pentecostals, 1906-1926," *Journal of Women's History* 16 (Fall 2004), 83–106.

47. Alvin W. Johnson and Frank H. Yost, *Separation of Church and State in the United States* (Minneapolis: University of Minnesota Press, 1948), 33; Jerome K. Jackson and Constantine F. Malmberg, *Religious Education and the State* (Garden City, NY: Doubleday, 1928), 1–80; Edward J. Larson, *Summer for the Gods: The Scopes Trial and America's Continuing Debate Over Science and Religion* (New York: Basic Books, 1997), 230–31.

48. E. Y. Mullins to Billy Sunday, 1 February 1927, Sunday to Mullins, 5 February 1927, Sunday Papers, box 2.

49. A. B. Kendall, "Our Duty as Christian Citizens," *Herald of Gospel Liberty,* 10 February 1927, 133; Rolf Lundén, *Business and Religion in the American 1920s* (Westport, CT: Greenwood, 1988), Bok on pages 15–16.

50. Coolidge Greeting Read to Cardinals," *New York Times*, 19 June 1926, 1; "Christians Rule Trade Says Bible Teacher," *Los Angeles Times*, 14 June 1930, 2; Richard M. Fried, *The Man Everybody Knew: Bruce Barton and the Making of Modern America* (Chicago: Ivan R. Dee, 2005), 84–113; Leo P. Ribuffo, "Jesus Christ as Business Statesman: Bruce Barton and the Selling of Corporate Capitalism," *American Quarterly* 33 (Summer 1981), 206-31.

51. "Corruption in High Places," *Atlanta Constitution*, 10 January 1885, 4; Speers, "Hoover Turns the Light on the Lobbies," *New York Times*, 15 September 1929, XX1.

52. Stuart D. Brandes, *American Welfare Capitalism, 1880–1940* (Chicago: University of Chicago Press, 1976); Sanford M. Jacoby, *Modern Manors: Welfare Capitalism Since the New Deal* (Princeton, NJ: Princeton University Press, 1997), 11–34.

53. Oliver McKee Jr., "The Poor Man in Politics," *North American Review* (August 1929), 185–92.

54. "Finds Big Business no Longer Feared," *New York Times*, 9 June 1927, 18; Lichtman, *Prejudice*, 166–98; Lundén, *Business and Religion*, 31–56; Sharon Murphy, "The Advertising of Installment Credit in the 1920s," *Essays in History* 37 (1995).

55. Rinehart John Swenson, *The National Government and Business* (New York: Century Company, 1924), 3–4. For quotations, emphasis is always in the original, never added by the author.

56. Ellis W. Hawley, *The Great War and the Search for a Modern Order: A History of the American People and Their Institutions, 1917–1933* (New York: St. Martin's, 1979), 80–117; Ruth O'Brien, *Workers' Paradox: The Republican Origins of New Deal Labor Policy, 1886–1935* (Chapel Hill: University of North Carolina Press, 1998), 120–47; Andrew Gibson and Arthur Donovan, *The Abandoned Ocean: A History of United States Maritime Policy* (Columbia: University of South Carolina Press, 2000), 121–24; Thomas W. Hazlett, "The Rationality of U. S. Regulation of the Broadcast Spectrum," *Journal of Law and Economics* 33 (1990), 133–75.

57. "Peace at a Considerable Price," *The Independent*, 26 December 1925, 722.

58. Warren I. Cohen, *Empire Without Tears: American Foreign Relations 1921–1933* (Philadelphia: Temple University Press, 1987), 18–44; Jeffrey W. Legro, "Whence American Internationalism," *International Organization* 54 (April 2000), 253–89.

59. Twelve Southerners, *I'll Take My Stand: The South and the Agrarian Tradition* (New York: Harper & Brothers, 1930); "Texas Is Feeling its Cultural Oats," *New York Times*, 1 February 1931, 57; Paul V. Murphy, *The Rebuke of History: The Southern Agrarians and American Conservative Thought* (Chapel Hill: University of North Carolina Press, 2001).

60. David A. Horowitz, *Beyond Left and Right: Insurgency and the Establishment* (Urbana: University of Illinois Press, 1997), 1–90.

61. Daniel Kevles, *In the Name of Eugenics: Genetics and the Uses of Human Heredity* (New York: Knopf, 1985); Christina Cogdell, *Eugenic Design: Streamlining America in the 1930s* (Philadelphia: University of Pennsylvania Press, 2004); Ann Gibson Winfield, *Eugenics and Education in America: Institutionalized Racism and the Implications of History, Ideology, and Memory* (New York: Peter Lang, 2007).

62. "Race Suicide Menace," *Chicago Tribune*, 24 October 1924, 23.

63. "Build More Prisons if Needed," *New York Times,* 9 January 1927, 1; "Justice Unsheathes Blade," *Los Angeles Times,* 18 June 1927, 4; "Kuhne Would Kill All Drug Addicts," *New York Times,* 6 July 1926, 44.

64. Philip R. Reilly, *The Surgical Solution: A History of Involuntary Sterilization in the United States* (Baltimore: Johns Hopkins University Press, 1991); *Buck v. Bell* 172 U.S. 200 (1927).

65. Desmond King, *Making Americans: Immigration, Race, and the Origins of the Diverse Democracy* (Cambridge. MA: Harvard University Press, 2000), 173; Mae M. Ngai, "The Architecture of Race in American Immigration Law: A Reexamination of the Immigration Act of 1924," *Journal of American History,* 86 (June 1999), 67–92; Roger Daniels, *Guarding the Golden Door: American Immigration Policy and Immigrants Since 1882* (New York: Hill and Wang, 2004), 47–58.

66. "Alien Law Defended in Biological Study," *Washington Post,* 2 January 1925, 3; John Trevor, "The Immigration Act," *New York Times,* 1 February 1927, 26; Louis Marshall, et al., to Coolidge, 22 May 1924, Papers of Calvin Coolidge, reel 78, Library of Congress, Washington, D. C.

67. *U.S. v. Thind* 261 U.S. 204 (1923); *Gong Lum v. Rice* 275 U.S. 78 (1927); Gary Gerstle, *American Crucible: Race and Nation in the Twentieth Century* (Princeton, NJ: Princeton University Press, 2001), 128-374.

68. James N. Gregory, *The Southern Diaspora: How the Great Migrations of Black and White Southerners Transformed America* (Chapel Hill: University of North Carolina Press, 2005); James R. Grossman, *Land of Hope: Chicago, Black Southerners and the Great Migration* (Chicago: University of Chicago Press, 1989); Milton C. Sernett, *Bound for the Promised Land: African American Religion and the Great Migration* (Durham, NC: Duke University Press, 1997).

69. Mark Robert Schneider, *We Return Fighting: The Civil Rights Movement in the Jazz Age* (Boston: Northeastern University Press, 2002); Theodore Kornweibel Jr., *Seeing Red: Federal Campaigns Against Black Militancy, 1919–1925* (Bloomington: Indiana University Press, 1998); E. David Cronon, *Black Moses: The Story of Marcus Garvey and the Universal Negro Improvement Association* (Madison: University of Wisconsin Press, 1969).

70. National Colored Republican Conference, "Memorandum of Conference," March 1924, Coolidge Papers, reel 93.

71. Grossman, *Land of Hope,* 161–258; Kevin Boyle, *Arc of Justice: A Saga of Race, Civil Rights, and Murder in the Jazz Age* (New York: Henry Holt, 2004), 102–32; Desmond S. King and Rogers M. Smith, "Racial Orders in American Political Development," *American Political Science Review* 99 (February 2005), 75–92; Michael Jones-Correa, "The Origins and Diffusion of Racial Restrictive Covenants," *Political Science Quarterly* 115 (Winter 2000/2001), 541–68.

72. "A White Man's Holiday," *New York Times,* 15 March 1929, 18.

73. Roger Daniels, *Asian America: Chinese and Japanese in the United States Since 1850* (Seattle: University of Washington Press, 1988), 67–185; Alexandra Minna Stern, "STERILIZED in the Name of Public Health: Race, Immigration, and Reproductive Control in Modern California," *American Journal of Public Health,* 95 (July 2005), 1135;

Neil Foley, *White Scourge: Mexicans, Blacks, and Poor Whites in Texas Cotton Culture* (Berkeley: University of California Press, 1997); David Gutiérrez, *Walls and Mirrors: Mexican Americans, Mexican Immigrants, and the Politics of Ethnicity* (Berkley: University of California Press, 1995).

74. Charles Wollenberg, *All Deliberate Speed: Segregation and Exclusion in California Schools, 1855–1975* (Berkeley: University of California Press, 1976).

75. For examples of recent work on the Klan, see Leonard Moore, *Citizen Klansmen: The Ku Klux Klan in Indiana, 1921–1928* (Chapel Hill: University of North Carolina Press, 1991); Nancy MacLean, *Behind the Mask of Chivalry: The Making of the Second Ku Klux Klan* (New York: Oxford University Press, 1994); Shawn Lay, *Hooded Knights on the Niagara: The Ku Klux Klan in Buffalo, New York* (New York: New York University Press, 1995); Michael Newton, *The Invisible Empire: The Ku Klux Klan in Florida* (Gainesville: University Press of Florida, 2001); Rory McVeigh, "Structural Incentives for Conservative Mobilization: Power Devaluation and the Rise of the Ku Klux Klan 1915–1925," *Social Forces* 77 (June 1999), 1461–96; Philip Jenkins, *Hoods and Shirts: The Extreme Right in Pennsylvania, 1925–1940* (Chapel Hill: University of North Carolina Press, 1997).

76. Kathleen N. Blee, "Women of the 1920s Ku Klux Klan Movement," *Feminist Studies* 17 (Spring 1991), 67; Blee, *Women of the Klan: Racism and Gender in the 1920s* (Berkeley: University of California Press, 1991).

77. Hiram Wesley Evans, "The Klan's Fight for Americanism," *North American Review,* 1 March 1926, 33–63.

78. Joseph Newton Pew to David Lawrence, 8 November 1937, David Lawrence Papers, box 91, Seeley G. Mudd Manuscript Library, Princeton University, Princeton, New Jersey.

79. Victoria Saker Woeste, "Insecure Equality: Louis Marshall, Henry Ford, and the Problem of Defamatory Anti-Semitism," *Journal of American History* 91 (December 2004), 877–905; Martha F. Lee, "Nesta Webster: The Voice of Conspiracy," *Journal of Women's History* 17 (Fall 2005), 81–105; Chip Bertlet and Matthew N. Lyons, *Right-Wing Populism in America: Too Close for Comfort* (New York: Guilford, 2000), 104–20; Gertrude Margaret Coogan, *The Money Creators. Who Creates Money? Who Should Create it?* (Chicago: Sound Money, 1935).

80. Burl Noggle, *Teapot Dome: Oil and Politics in the 1920s* (Baton Rouge: Louisiana State University Press, 1962).

81. Samuel McCoy, "Coolidge Making a 'Silent' Campaign," *New York Times,* 14 September 1924, XX1; Thomas Hardwick, "Democratic Party's Crushing Defeat Due to the Worship of False Gods," *Atlanta Constitution,* 8 November 1924, 6.

82. Liette Gidlow, *The Big Vote: Gender, Consumer Culture, and the Politics of Exclusion, 1890s–1920s* (Baltimore: Johns Hopkins University Press, 2004).

83. Bernard Baruch to Winston Churchill, 12 November 1928, Papers of Bernard Baruch, unit # 6, volume 20, Mudd Library.

84. *Chicago Tribune,* 24 September 1928, 4; Lichtman, *Prejudice,* 144–59.

85. Lichtman, *Prejudice,* 166–98.

86. The states are California, New York, Pennsylvania, Oregon, and West Virginia. The cities are Buffalo, Los Angeles, New York, Oakland, Philadelphia, Pittsburgh, Portland (OR), Rochester, and San Francisco. For responses to Roosevelt's survey see, Before Convention, Democratic National Campaign Committee Correspondence, 1928–33 Roosevelt Library; Lichtman, *Prejudice,* 199–246, and "Critical Election Theory and the Reality of American Presidential Politics, 1916–1940," *American Historical Review* 8 (April 1976), 317–51.

87. Borah to Charles Hilles, 7 November 1928, Papers of Charles D. Hilles, box 194, Davis to Edward Brannon, 14 November 1928, Papers of John W. Davis, box 23, both at Sterling Library, Yale University, New Haven, Connecticut; Allan J. Lichtman, "They Endured: Democrats Between World War I and the Depression," in Peter Kovler, ed., *Democrats and the American Idea: A Bicentennial Appraisal* (Washington, DC: Center for National Policy, 1992), 229–46.

Chapter 2

1. Minutes, Republican National Committee Meeting, 5 June 1934, *Meetings of the Republican National Committee, 1911–1980,* microfilm, reel 4, Library of Congress.

2. "Minutes, Board of Directors Meeting, April 28, 29, and 30, 1930," Papers of the Chamber of Commerce of the United States, box 1, Hagley Museum and Library, Wilmington, Delaware; William S. Myers, *The State Papers and Other Public Writings of Hebert Hoover,* vol. 1 (New York: Doubleday, 1934), Address, 1 May 1930, 289.

3. William J. Barber, *From New Era to New Deal: Herbert Hoover, the Economists, and American Economic Policy, 1921–1933* (New York: Cambridge University Press, 1985), 92.

4. Thomas S. Barclay, "The Publicity Division of the Democratic Party, 1929–30," *American Political Science Review* 25 (February, 1931), 68–72; Meeting of Presidential Appointees in Washington, 24 September 1930, Remarks of Secretary Hurley, Lucas Papers, box 6; "They Say," *New York Times,* 19 October 1930, 134.

5. Trevor Parry-Giles, "Property Rights, Human Rights, and American Jurisprudence: The Rejection of John J. Parker's Nomination to the Supreme Court," *Southern Communication Journal* 60 (Fall 1994), 57–73.

6. Scott Lucas to Nathan William MacChesney, 22 December 1930, Papers of Nathan William MacChesney, box 12, Hoover Library; Loyal Republican Club, "A Complete, Accurate RECORD of all that Geo. W. Norris has EVER DONE for The People of Nebraska," 1930, George W. Norris to Edward Jeffries, 23 March 1931, Papers of George W. Norris, boxes 8, 38, Library of Congress.

7. James H. MacLafferty Diary, 24 December 1930, Papers of James H. MacLafferty, box 2, Hoover Library.

8. Charles A. Beard, "Conservatism Hits Bottom," *New Republic,* 19 August 1931, 7–11.

9. David T. Beito, *Taxpayers in Revolt: Tax Resistance During the Great Depression* (Chapel Hill: University of North Carolina Press, 1989); New York *Daily News* editorial in *Literary Digest,* 18 July 1931, 16.

10. Myers, *State Papers,* vol. 1, Address, 7 October 1930, 395–401.

11. Myers, *State Papers,* vol. 2, 11 July 1932, 232.

12. John H. Bartlett to Walter Newton, 26 January 1932, Presidential Subject file, New Hampshire 1930–32, box 264, Hoover Library. Similar warnings from Republicans are found throughout the state files.

13. Clyde P. Weed, *The Nemesis of Reform: The Republican Party During the New Deal* (New York: Columbia University Press, 1994), 26.

14. Douglas Craig, *After Wilson: the struggle for the Democratic Party, 1920–1934* (Chapel Hill: University of North Carolina Press, 1992); Myers, *State Papers,* vol. 2, 31 October 1932, 418, 5 November 1932, 452.

15. Louise Overacker, "Campaign Funds in a Depression Year," *American Political Science Review* 27 (October 1933), 769–83; Simeon Fess to John Taggart, 31 October 1932, Papers of Simeon D. Fess, box 32, Edward Tracey Clark to Coolidge, 16 September 1932, Papers of Edward Tracey Clark, box 3, both at Library of Congress.

16. "Men's and Women's Vote," 26 September 1932, Hurja Papers, box 69; Ted Joslin to Henry J. Allen, 14 November 1932, Papers of Theodore G. Joslin, box 1, Hoover Library.

17. J. L. Matthews, "Political Trends in California," 30 October 1933, PostPresidential Subject file, box 254, Hoover Library.

18. MacLafferty Diary, 30 November 1932, MacLafferty Papers, box 2.

19. Ibid., 9 December 1932; *Literary Digest,* 23 June 1934, 13.

20. Charles Hilles to Mrs. Paul Fitzsimmons, 13 November 1934, Hilles Papers, box 122.

21. Charles Hilles to John T. Adams, 12 June, 1934, Hilles Papers, box 121; James Beck to Frank Buxton, 5 December 1933, Papers of James M. Beck, box 1, Mudd Library.

22. Unless otherwise cited, poll data come from the collection of the Roper Center for Public Opinion Research available through Lexis-Nexis. Kenneth Finegold and Theda Skocpol, *State and Party in America's New Deal* (Madison: University of Wisconsin Press, 1995).

23. Simeon Fess to Lowell Fess, 29 May 1933, Fess Papers, box 33; Hubert Work to Ogden L. Mills, 23 April 1933, Papers of Ogden L. Mills, box 46, Library of Congress; Gary Dean Best, *Herbert Hoover: The Postpresidential Years, 1933–1964* vol. 1 (Stanford: Hoover Institution Press, 1983), 14.

24. Meeting of the Republican National Committee, 5 June 1934, *Meetings of the Republican National Committee, 1911–1980,* reel 4, Library of Congress; David Sherman Beach to William E. Borah, 4 December 1934, Papers of William E. Borah, box 751, Library of Congress.

25. Thomas R. Dye and John W. Pickering, "Governmental and Corporate Elites: Convergence and Differentiation," *Journal of Politics* 36 (November 1974), 900–25, document the demographic composition of American business leaders; Robert F. Burk, *The Corporate State and the Broker State: The Du Ponts and American National Politics,*

1925–1940 (Cambridge: Harvard University Press, 1990), 105–42; Bernard Bellush, *The Failure of the NRA* (New York: Norton, 1975).

26. Robertson, Address, U.S. Chamber of Commerce, *Twenty-second Annual Meeting, May 1934*, Chamber of Commerce Papers, box 7; Burk, *Corporate State*, 130; Frank Buxton to Bainbridge Colby, 17 June 1934, Papers of Bainbridge Colby, box 30, Library of Congress.

27. Frederick Rudolph, "The American Liberty League, 1934–1940," *American Historical Review* 56 (October 1950), 19–33; George Wolfskill, *The Revolt of the Conservatives: A History of the American Liberty League* (Boston: Houghton Mifflin, 1962); Burk, *Corporate State*, 143–298. Sheldon Richman, "A Matter of Degree, Not Principle: The Founding of the American Liberty League," *Journal of Libertarian Studies* 6 (Spring 1982), 145–67, presents a contrary view.

28. Donaldson Brown's warnings were based on an analysis prepared by S. M. Dubrul of General Motors. Donaldson Brown to John J. Raskob, 23 July 1934, 3 August 1934, S. M. Dubrul to Brown, 19 June 1934, Papers of John J. Raskob, files 61B, 61C, Hagley Library; Elisabeth S. Clemens, *The People's Lobby: Organizational Innovation and the Rise of Interest Group Politics in the United States, 1890–1925* (Chicago: University of Chicago Press, 1997).

29. All citations are from Memorandum on Labor Trouble and Publicity (A) and (B), Employment Relations Committee, National Association of Manufacturers (NAM), 1 November 1934, NAM Papers, series V, box 1, Hagley Library.

30. NAM, "A 1943 Platform for the National Industrial Information Committee," NIIC, "Analysis of Basic Public Relations Problems Facing NAM," 13 January 1945, NAM Papers, Series III, box 842; NAM, "Minutes of the Committee on Public Relations," 18 March 1935, NAM Papers, series V, box 1; Richard S. Tedlow, *Keeping the Corporate Image: Public Relations and Business, 1900–1950* (Greenwich, CT: JAI Press, 1979), 59–79; Elizabeth FonesWolf, "Creating a Favorable Business Climate: Corporations and Radio Broadcasting, 1934 to 1954," *Business History Review* 73 (Summer 1999), 221–55.

31. Jacob S. Hacker and Paul Pierson, "Business Power and Social Policy: Employers and the Formation of the American Welfare State," *Politics and Society* 30 (June 2002), 300–301; Jacob S. Hacker, "Privatizing Risk Without Privatizing the Welfare State: The Hidden Politics of Social Policy Retrenchment in the United States," *American Political Science Review* 98 (May 2004), 243–60, demonstrates that "strategies of stealth, obstruction, and indirection" (p. 243) endured through the late twentieth century.

32. "Labor Law Scored by Manufacturers," *New York Times*, 22 April 1937, 10; George Gallup, "South Leads Demand for U. S. Supervision," *Washington Post*, 16 May 1937, B1.

33. "Industrial Policing and Espionage," *Harvard Law Review* (March 1939), 792–804; Jerold S. Auerbach, *Labor and Liberty: The La Follette Committee and the New Deal* (Indianapolis, IN: Bobbs-Merrill, 1966), 97–130; Pencak, *For God & Country*, 208–34.

34. Raymond Clapper, "G.O.P. to Continue Drive on New Deal," *Washington Post*, 15 September 1934, 9; Bertrand Snell, Radio Address, 5 November 1934, Papers

of Bertrand H. Snell, box C1.1, Crumb Library, State University of New York, Potsdam, New York.

35. Walter Edge to Henry Fletcher, 13 November 1934; Fletcher to Edge, 16 November 1934, Henry Prather Fletcher Correspondence in the Charles Dewey Hilles, James Rockwell Sheffield, and Edward M. House Papers, microfilm, 1 reel.

36. James Wadsworth to Dennis T. Flynn, 15 May 1935, Papers of James W. Wadsworth, Library of Congress, box 28; M. L. Requa, Memo: Political Organization and Activities for the Upcoming Campaign, April 1936, Hilles Papers, box 125.

37. Chase Mellen to Henry Fletcher, 21 December 1934, Borah Papers, box 398; Charles Hilles to Mrs. Paul FitzSimons, 15 June 1935, Hilles Papers, box 123.

38. For a summary and analysis of the scholarly debate over business and Social Security, see Hacker and Pierson, "Business Power and Social Policy," 277–325. For a different perspective, see Peter Swenson, *Capitalists Against Markets: The Making of Labor Markets and Welfare States in the United States and Sweden* (New York: Oxford University Press, 2002), 191–244.

39. Robert E. Lane, "Government Regulation and the Business Mind," *American Sociological Review* 16 (April 1951), 165; "Summary of Preliminary Conclusions Reached at Meeting of N.A.M. Special Committee on Industrial Economics," 16 September 1936, NAM Papers, series V, box 1; "Labor Bill is Opposed," *New York Times,* 16 April 1935, 19; *Dow Theory Comment,* "Supplement to Mailing 121," 16 January 1936, Hurja Papers, box 81; Herman E. Krooss, *Executive Opinion: What Business Leaders Said and Thought on Economic Issues, 1920s–1960s* (Garden City, NY.: Doubleday, 1970), 183–86.

40. Business Advisory and Planning Council, "Confidential Memo on Wagner Labor Relations Bill," 10 April 1935, "Report of the Committee on Amendments to the A.A.A.," 21 February 21, 1935, "Report of the Committee on the Public Utility Holding Company Bill," 30 April 30, 1935, "Report on the Tax Bill," 13 August 13, 1935, Records of the Department of Commerce, Business Advisory Council, RG 40, box 2, National Archives and Records Administration, College Park, Maryland; "Report of Special Committee on the Proposed Banking Act of 1935," RG 40, box 1; "A Letter to Secretary of Commerce Daniel C. Roper," 6 March 1934, RG 40, box 785; W. Averell Harriman to Daniel Roper, 3 December 1937, Papers of W. Averell Harriman, box 152, Library of Congress; Kim McQuaid and Edward Berkowitz, *Creating the Welfare State: The Political Economy of Twentieth-Century Reform,* 2nd edition (New York: Praeger, 1988), 100–101.

41. Contribution Records March 1936; E. F. Hutton, "Will America Go Radical?" *Magazine of Wall Street,* 20 July 1935, Liberty League Reprint; W. H. Stayton, "Memorandum Concerning Certain Signers of the A.L.L. Loan Agreements," undated 1936; John J. Raskob to Alfred P. Sloan, 24 April 1936, Raskob Papers, files 61M, 61I, 61N.

42. Wolfskill, *Revolt of the Conservatives,* 85–98; Burk, *Corporate State,* 159–63.

43. American Liberty League, "The Platform of the American Liberty League," undated pamphlet, Rightwing Collection of the University of Iowa Libraries, microfilm, reel 12; John J. Raskob, Address, 24 October 1935, Raskob Papers, File 61N; Craig, *After Wilson,* 289–90; Burk, *Corporate State,* 155–68, 223–24.

44. Ogden Mills to Walter Frew, 10 May 1934; Robert A. Taft to Mills, 20 August 1934; Mills to Taft, 27 August 1934, Mills Papers, box 80A.

45. Crusaders, "Which Way America?" undated, Mills Papers, box 80A.

46. National Economic Council, "What it Is, What it Does," undated, Papers of J. Howard Pew, box 18, Hagley Library.

47. Sentinels, "Pink Slip Repeal … A Beginning!" *Bulletin No. 1,* June 1935, Lincoln Papers, box 2.

48. Sentinels, Comments and Interpretations, undated, 1935; "Unique in Public Affairs," *Bulletin No. 4,* January 1936, Lincoln Papers, boxes 2, 7.

49. Marian D. Irish, "Political Thought and Political Behavior in the South," *Western Political Quarterly* 13 (June, 1960), 408–409; Donald T. Critchlow, *The Brookings Institution, 1916–1952: Expertise and the Public Interest in a Democratic Society* (DeKalb: Northern Illinois University Press, 1985).

50. Joseph Pew to Charles A. Halleck, 2 February 1943 and Joseph Pew to Charlton McVeigh, 17 May 1943, Papers of Joseph Newton Pew Jr., box 34 and 35, Hagley Library.

51. J. Howard Pew to James Fifield, 27 October 1953, Pew Papers, box 36.

52. Joseph Pew to Graham Patterson, 16 September 1935; Patterson to Joseph Pew, 9 February 1937, 11 February 1937, 23 August 1946, 27 December 1946, Joseph Pew Papers, box 32.

53. J. Howard Pew to Henry S. Brown, 30 April 1945; J. Howard Pew to Robert Lund, 31 January 1950; J. Howard Pew to James I. Wendell, 27 October 1950, J. Howard Pew Papers, box 8 and box 26.

54. Bainbridge Colby to William Pattangall, 8 August 1934, to William Randolph Hearst, 21 September 1935, Colby Papers, box 30.

55. Leo P. Ribuffo, *The Old Christian Right: The Protestant Far Right From the Great Depression to the Cold War* (Philadelphia: Temple University Press, 1983); Jenkins, *Hoods and Shirts.*

56. Sander A. Diamond, *The Nazi Movement in the United States, 1924–1941* (Ithaca, NY: Cornell University Press, 1974), 128–207; Leland V. Bell, *In Hitler's Shadow: The Anatomy of American Nazism* (Port Washington, NY: Kennikat, 1973), 753; "Trouble," *Time,* 4 December 1939, 18.

57. Jenkins, *Hoods and Shirts,* 89–113, 212–14; John P. Diggins, *Mussolini and Fascism: The View From America* (Princeton, NJ: Princeton University Press, 1972), 77–110; Wilson D. Miscamble, "The Limits of American Catholic Antifascism: The Case of John A. Ryan, *Church History,* 59 (December 1990), 523–38; Harold Lord Varney to Henry P. Fletcher, 30 October 1933, Fletcher Papers, box 15.

58. Joel A. Carpenter, ed., *Biblical Prophecy in an Apocalyptical Age: Selected Writing of Louis S. Bauman* (New York: Garland, 1988), 6; "Is Man Bound to Win," *Sunday School Times,* 26 March 1933, 208; *The Teacher,* August 1935, 27, 39; James Edward Congdon, "Christian Patriotism," *Moody Monthly* (November 1936), 112. See generally, Joel Carpenter, *Revive Us Again: The Reawakening of American Fundamentalism* (New York: Oxford University Press, 1997).

59. *The Teacher,* September 1934, 51 and July, 1935, 57, in Kent L. Johnson, *War, Depression, Prohibition and Racism: The Response of the Sunday School To An Era of Crisis, 1933–1941* (Lanham, MD: University Press of America, 1992), 26; *Christian Advocate,* 2 January 1936, 21; Elzoe Prindle Stead, "Consummating Programs," typescript, 1933, Papers of Gerald L. K. Smith, box 1, Bentley Historical Library, University of Michigan, Ann Arbor, Michigan; "Faith Alone Seen as Light of World," *New York Times,* 25 November 1935, 10.

60. Warren L. Vinz, "*Sword of the Lord,*" Thomas J. Ferris, "*Christian Beacon,*" in Ronald Lora and William Henry Longton, eds., *The Conservative Press in Twentieth Century America* (Westport, CT: Greenwood, 1999), 131–51; David Keith Bates, Jr., "Moving Fundamentalism Toward The Mainstream: John R. Rice And The Reengagement Of America's Religious And Political Cultures," Ph.D. Dissertation, Kansas State University, 2006.

61. ACCC, "A Brief History," undated, Carl McIntire Papers, box 2, Bentley Library.

62. R. G. LeTourneau, *Mover of Men and Mountains* (Englewood Cliffs, NJ: Prentice-Hall, 1960).

63. "Spiritual Mobilization: Early History," *Truth in Action,* 15 January 1943, Iowa Collection, reel 133.

64. James W. Fifield, "What is S.M.?," October 1948; J. Howard Pew to Jasper Crane, 21 June 1948, Pew Papers, boxes 6 and 19; Fifield, "A Principle and a Personality," *Los Angeles Times,* 3 November 1940, B4.

65. Raymond A. Eve and Francis B. Harrold, *The Creationist Movement in Modern America* (Boston: Twayne Publishers, 1991), 26–27.

66. Joseph Breen to Joseph Wilfrid Parsons, 20 October 1932, Papers of Joseph Wilfred Parsons, box 3, Georgetown University Library, Washington, DC; Gregory D. Black, *Hollywood Censored: Morality Codes, Catholics, and the Movies* (Cambridge: Cambridge University Press, 1994), 198–291.

67. Carpenter, *Revive Us Again.*

68. "Petition," National Association of Women Lawyers, 7 September 1934; "Partial List Of Talks Given on 'Women and Money,'" and "Radio Talk on Wall Street" by Cathrine Curtis, Raskob Papers, File 61C; June Melby Benowitz, *Days of Discontent: American Women and Right-Wing Politics, 1933–1945* (DeKalb: Northern Illinois University Press, 2002), 18–20; "Crusaders Seek Women's Aid in Patriotic Drive," *Chicago Tribune,* 28 August 1934, 4.

69. The Paul Reveres, Lesson Number One, undated, *National Republic* Collection, reel 669, Hoover Institution on War, Revolution, and Peace, Stanford, California; "Author of Soviet Critique Calls Upon Women of California to Resist Communism," *Los Angeles Times,* 1 December 1934, 6.

70. Erickson, "Conservative Women and Patriotic Maternalism," 86–101; Mildred Diane Gleason, "In Defense of God and Country: Elizabeth Dilling, A Link Between the Red Scares," Ph.D. dissertation, University of Arkansas, 1997, 58–87.

71. Morgan, "'Home and Country,'" 481–82, 494; Gleason, "In Defense of God and Country, 86–7; Erickson, "Conservative Women," 109–19.

72. Frank A. Warren, *Liberals and Communism: The "Red Decade" Revisited* (Bloomington: Indiana University Press, 1966); Michael Denning, *The Cultural Front: The Laboring of American Culture in the Twentieth Century* (New York: Verso, 1996), 31–59.

73. Benowitz, *Days of Discontent,* 125; American Women Against Communism, "Communists Incite Racial Uprising," undated 1936, *National Republic* Collection, reel 91.

74. Alexander Lincoln to Abraham Kraditor, 15 May 1936; Thomas Cadwalader to H.G. Torbert, 22 April 1936; Henry Joy to Joseph Brainin, 6 May 1936, Lincoln Papers, box 7.

75. Wolfskill, *The Revolt,* 212–13; James W. Wadsworth to William E. Stayton, 19 June 1936, Wadsworth Papers, box 26.

76. Frank Gannett to William Borah, 6 January 1936, 7 March 1936, Papers of Frank E. Gannett, box 1, Cornell University Library, Ithaca, New York; Hamilton Fish to Henry S. McKee, 15 February 1936, E. W. Campbell to P. F. O'Neill, 15 February 1936, Borah Papers, box 869; Borah to Gannett, 18 March 1936, Gannett Papers, box 1; David A. Horowitz, "Senator Borah's Crusade to Save Small Business From the New Deal," *Historian* 55 (Summer 1993), 693–708.

77. *New York Herald Tribune,* 16 August 1936, 1; Charles E. Coughlin, *A Series of Lectures on Social Justice* (Royal Oak, MI: Radio League of the Little Flower, 1936).

78. Wolfskill, *The Revolt,* 196–98; "Quit Roosevelt, Form Party," *Chicago Tribune,* 9 August 1936, 1.

79. Michael Patrick Allen, "Capitalist Response to State Intervention: Theories of the State and Political Finance in the New Deal," *American Sociological Review* 56 (October 1991), 679–89; Michael J. Webber, *New Deal Fat Cats: Business, Labor, and Campaign Finance in the 1936 Presidential Election* (New York: Fordham University Press, 2000). For a different view see Thomas Ferguson, "From Normalcy to New Deal: Industrial Structure, Party Competition, and American Public Policy in the Great Depression," *Industrial Organization* 38 (Winter 1984), 41–94.

80. "A Report by the Industrial Division of the Republican National Committee, 1936 Campaign," Papers of Sterling Morton, box 4, Chicago Historical Society, Chicago, Illinois; Morton to William F. Buckley Jr., 2 November 1959, Papers of William F. Buckley Jr., Part 1, box 8, Yale University Library, New Haven, Connecticut. All Buckley citations are from Part 1, the private papers.

81. Alf Landon to Raymond Clapper, 16 November 1936, Papers of Alfred M. Landon, box 10.78, Kansas State Historical Society, Topeka, Kansas; James Reed to Bainbridge Colby, 28 December 1936, Colby Papers, box 42.

82. Will Alexander to Rexford Tugwell, "Negroes in the Next Election," 12 July 1935, OFC300, Colored Folder, Roosevelt Library.

83. John Brueggermann, "Racial Considerations and Social Policy in the 1930s," *Social Science History* 26 (Spring 2002), 139–77; Robert C. Lieberman, *Shifting the Color Line: Race and the American Welfare State* (Cambridge, MA: Harvard University Press, 1998); Ira Katznelson, *When Affirmative Action Was White: An Untold History of Racial Inequality in Twentieth Century America* (New York: Norton, 2005), 25–79.

84. Virginia Sapiro, "The Gender Basis of American Social Policy," *Political Science Quarterly* 101 (1986), 221–38; Suzanne Mettler, *Dividing Citizens: Gender and Federalism in New Deal Public Policy* (Ithaca, NY: Cornell University Press, 1998).

85. Elazar Barkan, *The Retreat of Scientific Racism: Changing Concepts of Race in Britain and the United States Between the World Wars* (New York: Cambridge University Press, 1992), 310; Reilly, *The Surgical Solution*, 97; Keith Fitzgerald, *The Face of the Nation: Immigration, the State, and the National Identity* (Stanford, CA: Stanford University Press, 1996), 162–74.

86. "Primary Election Vote, 1928–1936," Hurja Papers, box 69.

Chapter 3

1. Papers of the Republican Party, Minutes, Meeting of the RNC, 17 December 1936, reel 5.

2. Fireside Chat, 9 March 1937, PPA, 1937, 122–23; Samuel Pettengill to Tricks, 15 February 1937, Papers of Samuel Pettengill, box 12, University of Oregon Library, Eugene, Oregon; Marian C. McKenna, *Franklin Roosevelt and the Great Constitutional War: The Court-Packing Crisis of 1937* (New York: Fordham University Press, 2002).

3. Frank Gannett to Josephus Daniels, 5 May 1937; Committee for Constitutional Government, "Organized Leadership: The Story of the Committee for Constitutional Government," 27 April 1944, Gannett Papers, boxes 2, 4; Richard Polenberg, "The National Committee to Uphold Constitutional Government, 1937–1941," *Journal of American History* 52 (December 1965), 591; Gannett to Douglas Johnson, 30 April 1937; "Financial Report to Contributors," 22 May 1937, Papers of Amos Pinchot, box 60, Library of Congress.

4. Edmund P. Grice to James Byrnes, 23 February 1937, in William E. Leuchtenburg, *The Supreme Court Reborn: The Constitutional Revolution in the Age of Roosevelt* (Oxford: Oxford University Press, 1995), 136–37; Ralph Nollner to Amos Pinchot, 12 October 1937, Pinchot Papers, box 69; Joseph Alsop and Turner Catledge, *The 168 Days* (Garden City, NY: Doubleday, 1938), 180.

5. Ray Tucker, "The National Whirligig," typescript, 1937, Pinchot Papers, box 60.

6. George Benson to Joseph Pew, 22 March 1937, Pew Papers, box 32.

7. Richard O. Davies, *Defender of the Old Guard: John Bricker and American Politics* (Columbus: Ohio State University Press, 1993), 47.

8. Polenberg, "The National Committee," 589; Committee to Uphold Constitutional Government, "1946 Report," Iowa Collection, reel 29; Church League of America, "A Statement of Premise and Program," undated, *National Republic* Collection, reel 76; "'Snoop Census' Fight Grows," *Chicago Tribune*, 6 March 1940, 1.

9. Constitutional Educational League, "A Record of Achievement," and "Memorandum," undated, 1939, *National Republic* Collection, reel 670.

10. Jenkins, *Hoods and Shirts,* 18; Patrick Scanlon to Wilfrid Parsons, 2 August 1938, Parsons Papers, box 5; Richard Gribble, "The Other Radio Priest: James Gillis's Opposition to Franklin Delano Roosevelt's Foreign Policy," *Journal of Church and State* 44 (Summer 2002), 501–19.

11. Joseph Moreau, *Schoolbook Nation: Conflicts over American History Textbooks from the Civil War to the Present* (Ann Arbor: University of Michigan Press, 2003), 219–63.

12. Frank Knox to Neil Carothers, 18 July 1937, Papers of William Franklin Knox, box 4, Library of Congress; Arthur Vandenberg to Alf Landon, 19 October 1937 and Landon to C. P. Dorsey, 29 November 1937, in James T. Patterson, *Congressional Conservatism and the New Deal* (Lexington: University of Kentucky Press, 1967), 258–59.

13. *America's Future,* I (Mid-Spring 1939), 32, Polenberg, "The National Committee," 592; Edward Rumely to Samuel Pettengill, 9 November 1938, Pettengill to Rumely, 23 November 1938, Pettengill Papers, box 2.

14. To measure congressional ideology this work relies on measures of liberal and conservative voting developed in Keith T. Poole and Howard Rosenthal, *Congress: A Political-Economic History of Roll Call Voting* (New York: Oxford University Press, 1997). Their measurements are valid within and between congresses and coincide for the later twentieth century with ratings by liberal and conservative interest groups. For an introduction to their path-breaking work see Lichtman, "History, Examples of Social Science Methods Used in," in Kimberly Kempf-Leonard, ed., *Encyclopedia of Social Measurement* (New York: Academic Press—Elsevier, 2004).

15. *New York Times,* 17 December 1937, 1; John Robert Moore, "Senator Josiah W. Bailey and the 'Conservative Manifesto' of 1937," *Journal of Southern History* 31 (February 1965), 21–39.

16. Ernest Cuneo, "Tommy the Cork: A Secret Chapter of American History," typescript, undated, Papers of Ernest Cuneo, box 110, Roosevelt Library; Sean J. Savage, *Roosevelt the Party Leader, 1932–1945* (Lexington: University of Kentucky Press, 1991); "Primaries," *Time,* 26 September 1938, 13.

17. Frank Knox to Samuel Pettengill, 27 May 1938, Pettengill Papers, box 13; Minutes of the 26th Annual Meeting of the United States Chamber of Commerce, Chamber of Commerce Papers, box 8; Chamber of Commerce, "What Business Needs, *Washington Review,* 9 May 1938, 21; Clarence Francis to George Sloan, 3 November 1937, Harriman Papers, box 143; NAM, "Report of the Meeting of the Committee of Economists," 27 May 1937, NAM Papers, series V, box 2.

18. Editorial opinions in "Papers Call Vote Roosevelt Defeat," *New York Times,* 9 April 1938, 2; "Press Comment on Defeat of 'Dictator' Bill," *Chicago Tribune,* 10 April 1938, 13.

19. Richard Polenberg, *Reorganizing Roosevelt's Government: The Controversy Over Executive Reorganization* (Cambridge, MA: Harvard University Press, 1966); John W. Jeffries, "A 'Third New Deal'? Liberal Policy and the American State, 1937–1945," *Journal of Policy History* 8 (1996), 387–409; Patrick D. Reagan, *Designing a New America:*

The Origins of New Deal Planning, 1890–1943 (Amherst: University of Massachusetts Press, 1999), 196–223; Alan Brinkley, *The End of Reform: New Deal in Recession and War* (New York: Alfred A. Knopf, 1995), 86–136.

20. "Minutes of The Sun Valley Conference," April 1938, Harriman Papers, box 150.

21. Frederick Steiwer to Charles Hilles, 22 November 1937, Hilles Papers, box 128; Karl A. Lamb, "Program Committees and the Nationalization of Republican Policy," undated manuscript, Hamilton Papers, box 1; Herbert Hoover in *Time*, 16 May 1938, 13.

22. Catherine E. Rymph, *Republican Women: Feminism and Conservatism from Suffrage Through the Rise of the New Right* (Chapel Hill: University of North Carolina Press, 2006), 65–97.

23. "Analysis of Determining Forces 1940 Presidential Campaign," unsigned memo, 3 June, 1939, Pettengill Papers, box 25; Robert F. Burroughs to Joseph Martin, 18 July 1939, Papers of Joseph Martin, box 10, Stonehill College Archives, Easton, Massachusetts.

24. John O'Laughlin to Charles Hilles, 23 November 1938, Hilles Papers, box 129; "Vandenberg Asks Neutrality Stand," *New York Times*, 7 May 1939, 39.

25. *New York Times*, 16 September 1939, 9, 14 October 14, 1939, 10; Johnpeter Horst Grill and Robert L. Jenkins, "The Nazis and the American South in the 1930s: A Mirror Image?" *Journal of Southern History* 58 (November 1992), 675; Daniel W. Aldridge, III, "A War for the Colored Races: Anti-Interventionism and the African American Intelligentsia, 1939–1941," *Diplomatic History* 28 (June 2004), 321–52; Justus D. Doenecke, *In Danger Undaunted: The Anti-Interventionist Movement of 1940–1941 as Revealed in the Papers of the America First Committee* (Stanford, CA: Hoover Institution, 1990), 30.

26. "Get Ready for the New Order," undated 1941; Papers of Philip C. Jessup, box A207, Library of Congress.

27. Edgar Queeny to Edward Stettinius, 12 August 1940, in Richard E. Holl, "The Corporate Liberals and the Roosevelt Administration Preparedness Program, 1939–1941," Ph. D. dissertation, University of Kentucky, 1996, 254; Wayne S. Cole, *America First: The Battle Against Intervention, 1940–1941* (Madison: University of Wisconsin Press, 1953), 17–34; Roland N. Stromberg, "American Business and the Approach of War, 1935–1941," *Journal of Economic History* 13 (Winter 1953), 58–78.

28. Edwin Black, *IBM and the Holocaust: The Strategic Alliance Between Nazi Germany and America's Most Powerful Corporation* (New York: Crown Publishers, 2001); Reinhold Billstein et al., *Working for the Enemy: Ford, General Motors, and Forced Labor in Germany During the Second World War* (New York: Berghahn Books, 2000); Gabriel Kolko, "American Business and Germany, 1930–1941" *Western Political Quarterly* 15 (December 1962), 725.

29. Joseph Martin to Alf Landon, 4 November 1939, Charles Plumley to Martin, 22 September, 1941, Martin Papers, boxes 10, 14.

30. Gerald L. K. Smith to George Hamilton Combs, 21 March 1942, Smith Papers, box 1; Glen Jeansonne, *Gerald L. K. Smith: Minister of Hate* (New Haven: Yale University Press, 1988), 64–100.

31. American Legion, "Subversive Activities in America First Committee in California," undated 1941, *National Republic* Collection, reel 3; Earl Southard, Secretary, Citizens Keep America Out Of War Committee, to Gerald L. K. Smith, 30 September 1941, Smith Papers, box 1; Francis MacDonnell, *Insidious Foes: The Axis Fifth Column and the American Home Front* (New York: Oxford University Press, 1995).

32. Crane to Carpenter, 16 January 1940, Papers of Jasper E. Crane, box 33, Hagley Library.

33. Kenneth O'Reilly, *Hoover and the Un-Americans: The FBI, HUAC, and the Red Menace* (Philadelphia: Temple University Press, 1983), 37–74; Powers, *Not With Honor,* 124–29; MacDonnell, *Insidious Foes,* 174–77; Athan Theoharis, "FBI Wiretapping: A Case Study of Bureaucratic Autonomy," *Political Science Quarterly* 107 (Spring, 1992), 101–22; M. J. Heale, *McCarthy's Americans: Red Scare Politics in State and Nation, 1935–1965* (Athens: University of Georgia Press, 1998), 83–103.

34. Glen Jeansonne, *Women of the Far Right: The Mother's Movement and World War II* (Chicago: University of Chicago Press, 1996); Kari Frederickson, "Cathrine Curtis and Conservative Isolationist Women, 1939–1941," *Historian* 58 (Summer 1996), 825–39; Laura McEnaney, "He-Men and Christian Mothers: The America First Movement and the Gendered Meanings of Patriotism and Isolationism," *Diplomatic History* 18 (Winter 1994), 47–57.

35. Clarence Manion to Hamilton Fish, 22 September 1941, Papers of Clarence Manion, box 1, Chicago Historical Society; Amos Pinchot in *The Herald,* 31 October 1941, 3, Iowa Collection, reel 60.

36. Charles Hilles to Henry W. Marsh, 22 October 1940, box 130, Hilles Papers.

37. George Ellis to Nicholas Butler, 17 October 1940, Hilles Papers, box 129; Charles Peters, *Five Days in Philadelphia: The Amazing 'We Want Willkie' Convention and How it Freed FDR to Save the Western World* (Washington, DC: Public Affairs, 2005).

38. Frank Kent to Martha Taft, 6 July 1940, Taft Papers, box 1440; Elizabeth Dilling, "Round Table Letter," 22 October 1940, *National Republic* Collection, reel 144; "Kennedy Backs FDR: Denies Any War Promises," *Chicago Tribune,* 30 October 1940, 4.

39. Rev. John Evans, "Baptist Journal Sees Religion a Campaign Issue," and "Clerics Charge Dictator Plot," *Chicago Tribune,* 2 April 1940, 10, 28 May 1940, 12.

40. Louise Overacker, "Campaign Finance in the Presidential Election of 1940," *American Political Science Review* 35 (August 1941), 705.

41. Ibid.; Political Gifts Made by John D. Rockefeller Jr., 1 January 1940 to 31 December 1940, Rockefeller Family Papers, "Civic Interests," box 27, Rockefeller Archive Center, Sleepy Hollow, New York.

42. Walter White to Roosevelt, 27 November 1939; Rowe, "Memorandum for the President: Negroes," 31 October 1940, Papers of James Rowe, Jr., box 23, Roosevelt Library; Henry Patterson to Glenn Frank, 29 February 1940, Taft Papers, box 146; James J. Kenneally, "Black Republicans During the New Deal: The Role of Joseph W. Martin, Jr.," *Review of Politics* 55 (Winter 1993), 117–34.

43. James Wadsworth to J.R. Shoemaker, 18 November 1940, Wadsworth Papers, box 28.

44. Alfred L. Castle, *Diplomatic Realism: William R. Castle, Jr., and American Foreign Policy, 1919–1953* (Honolulu: Samuel and Mary Castle Foundation, 1998), 106–18.

45. Page Hufty to Ethyle Stevenson, 19 September 1941, America First Committee Records, box 1, Hoover Institution; America First Committee, "Press Release, 25 September 1941," Jessup Papers, box A207; Doenecke, *In Danger Undaunted,* 400.

46. Doenecke, *In Danger Undaunted,* 469; "Lindbergh to Members of the America First Committee," 14 December 1941, Papers of Robert E. Wood, box 9, Hoover Library; Herbert Hoover to Robert Taft, 8 December 1941, Taft Papers, box 286; R. Douglas Stuart, Jr., "TO ALL CHAPTER CHAIRMEN," 8 December 1941, Sterling Morton to Stuart, 12 December 1941, Morton Papers, box 6.

47. James A. Hagerty, "Willkie Wins Republicans to his Anti-Isolationist Stance," *New York Times,* 21 April 1942, 1.

48. Bruce R. Bartlett, *Cover-Up: The Politics of Pearl Harbor, 1941–1946* (New Rochelle, NY: Arlington House, 1978); Thomas Fleming, *The New Dealers' War: Franklin D. Roosevelt and the War Within World War II* (New York: Basic Books, 2001).

49. Elizabeth Fones-Wolf, *Selling Free Enterprise: The Business Assault on Labor and Liberalism, 1945–1960* (Urbana: University of Illinois Press, 1994), 26–29; Daniel Lee Lykins, "Total War to Total Diplomacy: The Advertising Council, Domestic Propaganda and Cold War Consensus," Ph.D. dissertation, University of Kentucky, 1998; Mark H. Leff, "The Politics of Sacrifice on the American Home Front in World War II," *Journal of American History* 78 (March 1991), 1296–318; Robert Griffith, "The Selling of America: The Advertising Council and American Politics, 1942–1960," *Business History Review* (Autumn 1983), 388–412.

50. Henry Elmer Barnes to Roger Baldwin, 8 April 1944, Wood Papers, box 3.

51. John T. Flynn, "The Smear Offensive: A Report," 23 March 1944, Flynn to Robert E. Wood, 7 April 1944, Robert Wood to Flynn, 25 May 1944, Wood Papers, box 5.

52. Arthur Vandenberg to Samuel Pettengill, 24 August 1943, Pettengill Papers, box 2.

53. Laurence H. Shoup and William Minter, "Shaping a New World Order: The Council on Foreign Relations' Blueprint For World Hegemony," in Holly Sklar, ed., *Trilateralism: The Trilateral Commission and Elite Planning for World Management* (Boston: South End Press, 1980), 135–51.

54. Suzanne Mettler, "The Creation of the G.I. Bill of Rights of 1944: Melding Social and Participatory Citizenship Ideals," *Journal of Policy History* 17 (October 2005), 345–74; Ira Katznelson, *When Affirmative Action Was White,* 80–141; Margot Canady, "Building a Straight State: Sexuality and Social Citizenship under the 1944 G. I. Bill," *Journal of American History* 90 (December 2003), 935–57.

55. *Time,* 20 December 1943, 13–15. Also, see Patterson, *Congressional Conservatism and the New Deal,* and Ira Katznelson, Jim Geiger, and Daniel Kryder, Limiting

Liberalism: The Southern Veto in Congress, 1933-1950," *Political Science Quarterly* 108 (Summer 1993), 283-306.

56. Carl McIntire, "The American Council of Christian Churches-Its Purpose and Testimony," sermon preached on 28 September 1941, "What Is the American Council of Christian Churches?" 1943, *National Republic* Collection, reel 76; W.O.H. Garman to Carl McIntire, 5 April 1946, Papers of Merwin K. Hart, box 3, University of Oregon, Eugene, Oregon.

57. "National Association of Evangelicals: What Is It and How Does It Function?" 1943, "Report of the NAE Field Secretary," 21 September 1943, Papers of the National Association of Evangelicals, box 65, Billy Graham Center Archives, Wheaton, Illinois.

58. NAE, "Resolutions Adopted by the 8th Annual Convention," 21 April 1950, Papers of Herbert John Taylor, box 67, Graham Archives; Bernard Kruse, "An Organization Which Stands Fast," *Chicago Tribune*, 14 May 1950, 14.

59. "National Association of Evangelicals, Press Release," May 1 and 2, 1945, National Association of Evangelicals Papers, box 65; NAE, "Your Church and NAE," undated 1970, Iowa Collection, reel 98. The NAE's self-critique gained attention with Carl F. H. Henry's *The Uneasy Conscience of Modern Fundamentalism* (Grand Rapids, MI: Eerdmans, 1947).

60. NAE, "Press Release, 3 May 1945," National Association of Evangelicals Papers, box 65, "Resolutions passed by American Council of Christian Churches," 6–9 May 1948, Papers of J. Strom Thurmond, box 143, Robert Muldrow Cooper Library, Clemson University, Clemson, South Carolina.

61. Thomas E. Bergler, "Winning America: Christian Youth Groups and the Middle-Class Culture of Crisis, 1930–1965," Ph.D. dissertation, University of Notre Dame, 2000, 110; Joel Carpenter, *Revive Us Again*, 161–76; International Council Report in *The Christian Beacon*, 4 April 1946, *National Republic* Collection, reel 76.

62. L. Edward Hicks, "*Sometimes in the Wrong, but Never in Doubt," George S. Benson and the Education of the New Religious Right* (Knoxville: University of Tennessee Press, 1994).

63. Norman Vincent Peale to J. Howard Pew, 8 December 1944, Eddie Rickenbacker to Pew, 25 June 1944, Pew to Lowell Thomas, 13 December 1944, J. Howard Pew Papers, box 7.

64. Samuel Pettengill, Press Release, 2 October 1940, Pettengill Papers, box 14; "The Christian American Movement," 1 July 1942, *National Republic* Collection, reel 71; Victor Riesel, "The Technique of the 'Christian Americans': How to Choke Unions," *The Nation*, 31 July 1943, 126.

65. American Economic Foundation, "What Is the American Economic Foundation," 1959, Crane Papers, box 2.

66. Graham Patterson to Joseph N. Pew, 23 August 1946 and 27 December 1946, Pew Papers, box 32.

67. Morley and Hanighen, "Human Events," undated, Joseph Pew Papers, box 14.

68. Morley to Joseph Pew, 10 April 1944, Ibid; Morley to Henry Regnery, 30 December 1946, "Vice President's Report to Human Events, Inc.," 12 September 1949, Papers of Henry Regnery, box 31, Hoover Institution.

69. William S. Knudson to Irenee Du Pont, 28 September 1937, Raskob Papers, file 61R.

70. Edmund P. Russell, "'Speaking of Annihilation': Mobilizing for War against Human and Insect Enemies, 1914–1945," *Journal of American History* 82 (March 1996), 1505–1529; John Dower, *War Without Mercy: Race and Power in the Pacific War* (New York: Pantheon, 1986); Arthur Goodfriend to Chief, Special and Information Services, 7 December 1944, Papers of James F. Byrnes, box 8, Cooper Library; Michael J. Curley to Wilfred Parsons, 5 December 1944, Parsons Papers, box 7.

71. Carl O. Smith and Stephen B. Sarasohn, "Hate Propaganda in Detroit," *Public Opinion Quarterly* 10 (Spring 1946), 24–52; Anthony S. Chen, "'The Hitlerian Rule of Quotas': Racial Conservatism and the Politics of Fair Employment Legislation in New York State, 1941–1945," *Journal of American History* 92 (March 2006), 1238–264; Thomas J. Sugrue, "Crabgrass-Roots Politics: Race, Rights, and the Reaction Against Liberalism," *Journal of American History* 82 (September 1995), 551–78; Kenneth Durr, *Behind the Backlash: White Working Class Politics in Baltimore, 1940–1980* (Chapel Hill: University of North Carolina Press, 2003); Arnold R. Hirsch, *Making the Second Ghetto: Race and Housing in Chicago, 1940–1960* (New York: Cambridge University Press, 1983); Kevin M. Kruse, *White Flight: Atlanta and the Making of Modern Conservatism* (Princeton, NJ: Princeton University Press, 2005); Eric Avila, *Popular Culture in the Age of White Flight: Fear and Fantasy in Suburban Los Angeles* (Berkeley: University of California Press, 2004).

72. Elmo Roper to Russell Davenport, 26 July 1943, Papers of Russell Wheeler Davenport, box 23, Library of Congress.

73. Papers of the Republican Party, Minutes, Meeting of the RNC, 6 December 1942, microfilm, reel 5; Lawrence Dennis to Robert Wood, 19 November 1942, "Memorandum on Grand Strategy for the Party Until 1944," Wood Papers, box 3.

74. Robert Wood to Joseph N. Pew, 6 January 1944, Wood Papers, box 12; Arthur Vandenberg to Samuel Pettengill, 24 August 1943, Pettengill Papers, box 2; Clare Boothe Luce to Douglas MacArthur, 3 May 1943, Vandenberg to Luce, undated, Papers of Clare Boothe Luce, boxes 380, 396, Library of Congress.

75. Clare Booth Luce, Ibid.; Robert Wood to Karl Mundt, 1 November 1943, Wood Papers, box 10; Arthur Vandenberg to Wood, 5 August 1943, 15 September 1943, and 1 May 1944; Wood Papers, box 17; John D. M. Hamilton, "MacArthur and the 1944 Nomination," undated typescript, Hamilton Papers, box 14.

76. Clare Boothe Luce to Douglas MacArthur, 3 May 1943, Luce Papers, box 380.

77. Robert Lucas to Arthur Geissler, 15 December 1944, Lucas Papers, box 6.

78. Sterling Morton to J. Howard Pew, Pew Papers, box 5; John Hamilton to Clare Boothe Luce, 13 February 1945, Luce Papers, box 497.

Chapter 4

1. "The National Education Program," 1957 brochure, George Benson, "A Statement to 'Set The Record Straight' in Regard to Harding College," 1962, Papers of Herbert A. Philbrick, box 110, Library of Congress; Hicks, *Sometimes in the Wrong, but Never in Doubt*," 51–94.

2. NIIC, "Program Recommendations for 1945," NAM Papers, Series III, box 847.

3. NAM, "Program Recommendations for 1945," "A New Public Relations Policy for NAM," 13 November 1944, "Report of Special NAM-NIIC Committee," undated, "Analysis of Basic Public Relations Problem Facing NAM," 13 January 1945, Walter Weisenberger to Cloud Wampler, 21 February 1945, NAM Papers, Series III, boxes 842, 847; "Public Relations Program of the NAM for 1946," J. Howard Pew Papers, box 10; Andrew A. Workman, "Manufacturing Power: The Organizational Revival of the National Association of Manufacturers 1941–1945," *Business History Review* 72 (Summer 1998), 279–317.

4. NAM, "Analysis of Basic Public Relations Problem Facing NAM, NAM Papers."

5. "Labor Parlays Adjourn Without Any Agreement," *Los Angeles Times,* 1 December 1945, 1.

6. Barbara S. Griffith, *The Crisis of American Labor: Operation Dixie and the Defeat of the CIO* (Philadelphia: Temple University Press, 1988); Stephen Kemp Bailey, *Congress Makes a Law: The Story Behind the Employment Act of 1946* (New York: Columbia University Press, 1950); Nelson Lichtenstein, "From Corporatism to Collective Bargaining: Organized Labor and the Eclipse of Social Democracy in the Postwar Era," in Gary Gerstle and Steve Fraser, eds., *The Rise and Fall of the New Deal Order* (Princeton, NJ: Princeton University Press, 1989), 122-52; David H. Rosenbloom, "'Whose Bureaucracy Is This Anyway?' Congress' 1946 Answer," *PS: Political Science and Politics* 34 (December 2001), 773–77.

7. "Industrial Outlook," *Business Week,* 8 December 1945, 111.

8. Jacob Viner, "The Place of the United States in the World Economy," 8 October 1946, Papers of H. Alexander Smith, box 91, Mudd Library.

9. J. Howard Pew to James W. Fifield, 10 November 1944, Pew Papers, box 6.

10. Michael J. Hogan, *A Cross of Iron: Harry S. Truman and the Origins of the National Security State, 1945–1954* (New York: Cambridge University Press, 1998), 1–118.

11. Stephen W. Hartman, "The Impact of Defense Spending on the Domestic American Economy, 1946–1972," *Public Administration Review* 33 (July, 1973), 382; Harold G. Vatter and John F. Walker, *The Inevitability of Government Growth* (New York: Columbia University Press, 1990); Kim McQuaid, *Uneasy Partners: Big Business in American Politics, 1945–1990* (Baltimore: Johns Hopkins University Press, 1994), 1–21.

12. Allan J. Lichtman, "Tommy the Cork: The Secret World of Washington's First Modern Lobbyist," *Washington Monthly* (February 1987), 41– 49; David McKean, *Tommy the Cork: Washington's Ultimate Insider from Roosevelt to Reagan* (South Royalton, VT: Steerforth, 2004).

13. Earle R. Muir, "Bankers Going Socialist, Too?" *Changing Times* (June 1950), 25–26; Frank Chodorov, "For Want of a Radical Rich," *National Review,* 28 December 1957, 590.

14. Republican Party Papers, Minutes, Meeting of the RNC, 5 December 1946, reel 8.

15. Erwin S. Mayer, "Union Security and the Taft-Hartley Act," *Duke Law Journal* 4 (Autumn 1961), 505–24.

16. Clark M. Clifford, "Memorandum for the President," 19 November 1947, Clark Clifford Political File, box 20, Harry S. Truman Presidential Library, Independence, Missouri; Walker and Vatter, *The Rise of Big Government,* 154–55.

17. Robert Taft, "The Trends of Post-War Legislation," *Executives' Club News,* 27 September 1946, 3, 10; Taft to Claude O. Vardaman, 8 April 1947, Taft Papers, box 890; Richard O. Davies, "'Mr. Republican' Turns 'Socialist,'" *Ohio History* (Summer 1964), 135–43.

18. Ralph Gwinn to J. Howard Pew, 9 June 1948, Pew Papers, box 20.

19. Sterling Morton to J. Calvin Callaghan, 25 January 1947, Morton Papers, box 9; John Vorys to Bruce Barton, 2 April 1947, Papers of John Vorys, box 15, Ohio Historical Society, Cincinnati, Ohio.

20. Lawrence Dennis, "Truman Doctrine: Opening Gun of World War III," *The Appeal to Reason,* 15 March 1947.

21. William Knowland to George Marshall, 26 September 1947, H. Alexander Smith Papers, box 91; Republican Party Papers, Minutes, Meeting of the RNC, 21 April 1947, reel 8; Frank Gannett, "form letter," 5 March 1948, Gannett Papers, box 5.

22. Sterling Morton to Alfred Landon, 14 March 1947, Morton Papers, box 40; John Vorys, op cit.; Ralph Gwinn to Hugh Scott, 3 January 1949, Joseph Pew Papers, box 34; James Burnham, *The Struggle for the World* (New York: John Day, 1947), 243.

23. Frances Stonor Saunder, *The Cultural Cold War: The CIA and the World of Arts and Letters* (New York: New Press, 1999); Stacey Cone, "Presuming a Right to Deceive: Radio Free Europe, Radio Liberty, the CIA and the News Media," *Journalism History* 24 (Winter 1998/1999), 151; Martin J. Medhurst, "Eisenhower and the Crusade for Freedom: the Rhetorical Origins of a Cold War Campaign," *Presidential Studies Quarterly* 27 (Fall 1997), 646–61.

24. Peter Grose, *Operation Rollback: America's Secret War Behind the Iron Curtain* (Boston: Houghton Mifflin, 2000), 188; C. D. Jackson to Henry Luce, 3 February 1956, Papers of C. D. Jackson, box 56, Dwight David Eisenhower Presidential Library, Abilene, Kansas.

25. Athan Theoharis, "The FBI and the American Legion Contact Program, 1940–1966," *Political Science Quarterly* 100 (Summer 1985), 271–86; Alexander Charns, *Cloak and Gavel: FBI Wiretaps, Bugs, Informers, and the Supreme Court* (Urbana: University of Illinois Press, 1992).

26. Heale, *McCarthy's Americans,* 1–78; Frank Donner, *Protectors of Privilege: Red Squads and Police Repression in Urban America* (Berkeley: University of California Press, 1990).

27. U.S. House of Representatives, Committee on Un-American Activities, *Menace of Communism: Statement of J. Edgar Hoover*, March 26, 1947, 80th Congress, 1st Session, 11.

28. Gerald Horne, *Class Struggle in Hollywood, 1930–1950: Moguls, Mobsters, Stars, Reds, and Trade Unionists* (Austin: University of Texas Press: 2001); Stephen Vaughn, *Ronald Reagan in Hollywood: Movies and Politics* (New York: Cambridge University Press, 1994).

29. AWARE, Inc., "An Organization to Combat the Communist Conspiracy in the Entertainment World," 16 February 1953, Philbrick Papers, box 50.

30. American Council of Christian Laymen, "How Red Is the Federal Council of Churches," 1949, J. Howard Pew Papers, box 21; John T. Flynn, *The Road Ahead: America's Creeping Revolution* (New York: Devin-Adair, 1949), 106–119; Rick Nutt, "For Truth and Liberty: Presbyterians and McCarthyism," *Journal of Presbyterian History* 78 (Spring, 2000), 51–66; Harry Overstreet, *The Strange Tactics of Extremism* (New York: Norton, 1964), 157–169; Circuit Riders, news release, 30 July 1956, *National Republic* Collection, reel 75.

31. World Council of Churches, "Press Release No. 53," 2 September 1948, Papers of Charles P. Taft, box 131, Library of Congress; "George Dugan, "Church Council Eases Criticism of Capitalism in Final Session," *New York Times*, 5 September 1948, 1.

32. "Subversive Teachers Are Greatest Threat to Americanism," *Southern Conservative*, November–December 1951, 2, Iowa Collection, reel 114; Benjamin Fine, "Attack on Schools Declared Gaining," *New York Times*, 4 July 1951, 19.

33. Lucille Crain to John T. Flynn, 18 July 1950, "Excerpt from a Statement by Mrs. Lucille Crain," undated, 1951, Crain to William F. Buckley Jr. 27 February 1951, Crain to editor, *Lakeville Journal*, 18 October 1951, Papers of Lucille Cardin Crain, University of Oregon Library, boxes 34, 6, 27, 26,.

34. Advances by William F. Buckley, October 15, 1948–January 16, 1950, Buckley to Lucille Crain, 17 March 1950, Crain Papers, box 26; John T. Flynn to David Johnston, 31 July 1952, Leonard Read to Trustees of FEE, 9 July 1952, "Goodbye," *Educational Reviewer* (October 1953), Crain Papers, boxes 26, 34, 35, 61.

35. Minute Women, *Newsletter*, November–December 1960, Iowa Collection, reel 76.

36. Abby Scher, "Cold War on the Home Front: Middle Class Women's Politics in the 1950s," unpublished Ph.D. dissertation, New School for Social Research, 1995, 169–218; Minute Women, *Newsletter*, December 1954, Iowa Collection, reel 76; "Who Shall Control Houston Schools?" *Southern Conservative*, February 1955, 3.

37. J. Howard Pew to Jasper Crane, 27 March 1953, Crane Papers, box 68, and to High P. King, 15 February 1953, Pew Papers, box 33; J. P. Seiberling to Crane, 15 November 1948, Crane Papers, box 69.

38. William F. Buckley Jr., "A Prospectus for a New Magazine," undated 1955, Regnery Papers, box 10.

39. Matthew J. Flynn, "Reconsidering the China Lobby: Senator William F. Knowland and US-China Policy, 1945–1958," Ph. D. dissertation, Ohio University, 2004; Stanley D. Bachrack, *The Committee of One Million: "China Lobby" Politics, 1953–1971* (New York: Columbia University Press, 1976), 20–178; Joseph Keely, *China Lobby Man: The Story of Alfred Kohlberg* (New Rochelle, NY: Arlington House, 1969); Simei Qing, *From Allies to Enemies: Visions of Modernity, Identity, and U.S.-China Diplomacy, 1945–1960* (Cambridge: Harvard University Press, 2007).

40. David Everitt, *A Shadow of Red: Communism and the Blacklist in Radio and Television* (Chicago: Ivan R. Dee, 2007); American Jewish League Against Communism, "What Is the American Jewish League Against Communism," *National Republic* Collection, undated, 1948; George Sokolsky to William F. Buckley Jr., 24 August 1960 and 22 June 1961, Buckley Papers, boxes 12 and 13.

41. John T. Donovan, *Crusader in the Cold War: A Biography of Fr. John S. Cronin* (New York: Peter Lang, 2005).

42. Jasper Crane to J. Howard Pew, 23 December 1949, Crane Papers, box 68; NAE, "Resolutions Adopted by the 8th Annual Convention," 21 April 1950, Herbert John Taylor Papers, box 67.

43. Facts Forum, "New Release," 10 February 1955, Papers of Albert C. Wedemeyer, box 112, Hoover Institution; Dan Smoot, *People Along the Way: The Autobiography of Dan Smoot* (Tyler, TX: Tyler Press, 1996), 187–224; "This Is My Side," *Dan Smoot Report,* 29 June 1955, Iowa Collection, reel 37.

44. "Freedom Train to Start September 17," *New York Times,* 17 May 1947, 5, and "Fete at Freedom Train," *New York Times,* 18 October 1948, 1.

45. ADA, "Notes on ADA," June 1962, Papers of Karl E. Mundt, microfilm, reel 184; Steven M. Gillon, *Politics and Vision: The ADA and American Liberalism, 1947–1985* (New York: Oxford University Press, 1987).

46. David Lawrence to John Bennett, 9 January 1953 and 10 March 1953, Lawrence Papers, box 22.

47. Republican Party Papers, Minutes, Republican National Strategy Committee, 13 December 1949, reel 10; John T. Flynn, *The Road Ahead,* 9–11, 60; John Edgerton, Secretary, Southern States Industrial Council, to J. Howard Pew, 1 April 1950, Pew Papers, box 26; Robert Taft to Albert W. Hawkes,18 March 1949, Taft Papers, box 910; John E. Moser, *Right Turn: John T. Flynn and the Transformation of American Liberalism* (New York: New York University Press, 2005), 177–179; Cecil Palmer, "Press Statement," 3 February 1949, J. Howard Pew Papers, box 23.

48. Mathilde Ernestine, "Henry Regnery—Publisher With a Purpose—Patriotism!" undated, Buckley Papers, box 9; Henry Regnery to J. Howard Pew, 5 July 1956, Pew Papers, box 51; Sterling Morton to Jasper Crane, 3 October 1957, Crane Papers, box 52. The classic study of conservative intellectuals remains George H. Nash, *The Conservative Intellectual Movement in America, Since 1945,* 30th anniversary edition (Wilmington, DL: ISI, 2006).

49. B. E. Hutchinson to J. Howard Pew, 13 April 1954, Pew Papers, box 38.

50. Leonard Read, "Memo to Members," Board of Trustees, 17 December 1946, FEE, Donors of $500 and Over, Fiscal Year Ending March 31, 1949, Officers

and Trustees, 1951–52, Jasper Crane to F. A. Hayek, 28 December 1948, Read, "Wealth Can Have A Spiritual Role," typescript, 22 March 1960, Crane Papers, boxes 34, 52, 35; Edmund Opitz to J. Howard Pew, 10 September 1953, Pew Papers, box 36.

51. "The Mont Pelerin Society," 1 January 1961, Fredrich Hayek to Jasper Crane, 31 January 1949, Crane Papers, boxes 54, 52.

52. Lionel Trilling, *The Liberal Imagination* (New York: Viking Press, 1950); For an analysis of the scholarly response to post–World War II conservatism, see William B. Hixson Jr., *Search for the American Right Wing: An Analysis of the Social Science Record, 1955–1987* (Princeton, NJ: Princeton University Press, 1992).

53. Robert Wood to Merwin K Hart, 22 October 1945, Wood Papers, box 7; Wood, fund-raising letter, undated 1946, Wood Papers, box 14; "American Action Spent $114,828," *New York Times,* 5 November 1946, 22.

54. William Anderson to Robert Taft, 31 July 1946, Taft Papers, box 879; ACA, Post-Election Memorandum, December 1948, B. Carrol Reece to Issac Miller Hamilton, 12 October 1946, J. Howard Pew Papers, boxes 20 and 11.

55. Alfred P. Haake, "Spiritual Mobilization Report," 24 December 1945, J. Howard Pew Papers, box 8; Eckard V. Toy Jr., "Spiritual Mobilization: The Failure of an Ultraconservative Ideal in the 1950s," *Pacific Northwest Quarterly* 61 (April 1970), 77–86.

56. Don Mitchell to J. Howard Pew, 26 May 1948, B. E. Hutchinson to Pew, 16 July 1948, Pew Papers, box 19.

57. "Proposed letter to be sent over the signature of Captain Eddie Rickenbacker, 1947," Papers of Edward V. Rickenbacker, box 15, Library of Congress.

58. John Hamilton to Clare Boothe Luce, 13 February 1945, Luce Papers, box 497; *President Harry S. Truman's 1947 Diary Book,* transcribed by Raymond H. Geselbracht, 25 July 1947, Truman Library; Douglas MacArthur to Luce, 14 November 1945, Luce Papers, box 497; MacArthur to Robert Wood, 16 November 1947, Wood Papers, box 10.

59. Clark Clifford, "Memorandum for the President"; Kari Frederickson, *The Dixiecrat Revolt and the End of The Solid South, 1932–1968* (Chapel Hill: University of North Carolina Press, 2001).

60. Richard Russell to Strom Thurmond, 2 February 1948, Thurmond Papers, box 146.

61. Strom Thurmond, radio address, 17 March 1948, Thurmond Papers, box 148; "Enough of This States' Rights Double-Talk," *Winnsboro News and Herald,* 2 September 1948, 18.

62. E. F. Hutton to Herbert W. Brownell, 30 September 1948, J. Howard Pew Papers, box 17.

63. Frederickson, *The Dixiecrat Revolt,* 183–238; Ernest B. Ferguson, *Hard Right: The Rise of Jesse Helms* (New York: Norton, 1986), 41–55; "Dixiemania," *Washington Post,* 12 November 1951, 8; Strom Thurmond to *Bedford Democrat,* 10 December 1951, Thurmond Papers, box 161.

64. Merwin Hart to Reverend John LaFarge, 23 April 1948, Hart Papers, box 3; George Washington Robnett, "Four Horsemen of 1951," undated, Papers of George

W. Robnett, box 3, University of Oregon Library; Henry Regnery to J. K. Breedin, 11 May 1948, Thurmond Papers, box 143; Sterling Morton to Scerial Thompson, 5 November 1947, Morton Papers, box 10.

65. George Schuyler, "The Negro Question Without Propaganda," in Jeffrey B. Leak, ed., *Rac[e]ing to the Right: Selected Essays of George S. Schuyler* (Knoxville: University of Tennessee Press, 2001), 60.

66. Karl Mundt, "Speech Notes," undated 1949, Mundt Papers, reel 179; George Hansen reporting for the Subcommittee on Civil Rights, Republican Party Papers, Meeting of the RNC, 4 August 1949, reel 9; Robert Taft to Stanley M. Rowe, 31 December 1946, 30 September 1946, Taft Papers, box 879; Chen, "The Party of Lincoln and the Politics of State Fair Employment Practices in the North, 1945–1964."

67. Robert Taft to Charles Paul, 22 January 1949, Taft Papers, box 910; "'Blackout' Is Seen in Economics Field," *New York Times*, 24 November 1948, 25; "Business Is Scored for 'Propaganda,'" *New York Times*, 6 December 1950, 61; E. F. Hutton to Wallace F. Bennett, 29 March 1950, Robert Lund to Pew, 27 January 1950; J. Howard Pew Papers, box 26.

68. Clarence Kelland to Joseph Pew, 5 November 1948, Pew Papers, box 33; Marrs McLean to Hugh Scott, undated, 1949, Tom Curtis to Robert Taft, 12 November 1949, Taft Papers, box 910.

69. J. Harvie Williams, "The Republican Dilemma: A Conservative's Appraisal of the 1950 Political Scene," 30 November 1950, Papers of Oscar Ewing, Truman Library; "A Political Program for Conservatives," 27 August 1954, Joseph Pew Papers, box 34.

70. Samuel Pettengill to Karl Mundt, 9 March 1951, Pettengill Papers, box 25.

71. Dan Moody to Edward R. Burke, 26 December 1951, Papers of Donald Richberg, box 42, Library of Congress; Committee to Explore Political Realignment, "Summary of Findings and Conclusions," 10 December 1951, Crane Papers, box 6; Frank Hanighen to Joseph Pew, 21 August 1952, Pew Papers, box 34.

72. Irving Ives, "Meet the Press Interview Transcript," 7 January 1949, Taft Papers, box 911; Russell Davenport to Senator John Sherman Cooper, 8 August 1951, Henry Luce to Davenport, 7 January 1949; Davenport to Dwight D. Eisenhower, 22 August 1952, Davenport Papers, boxes 24, 25, 27.

73. Jasper Crane, form letter, undated 1948, Herbert Hoover to Crane, 6 November 1948, Crane Papers, box 69; "The Faith of the Freeman," 2 October 1950, *National Republic* Collection, reel 669; "Memorandum on *The Freeman*," 23 November 1950, Crane Papers, box 39; Charles H. Hamilton, "*The Freeman*," in Lora and Longton, *The Conservative Press*, 321–29.

74. International Society of Individualists, "Resume of Activities 1952–1954," J. Howard Pew Papers, box 38; E. Victor Milione to Jasper Crane, 7 October 1959, Crane to J. Howard Pew, 31 August 1959, Crane to Eugene C. Pulliam, 4 September 1959, Crane Papers, box 45.

75. "Group Prayer Helps Build Good Athletes," *Washington Post*, 15 May 1957, D2.

76. "A Condensed History and Proposed Future of the F.C.A.," 15 January 1956, Papers of Branch Rickey, box 58, Library of Congress.

77. E. F. Hutton to J. Howard Pew, 7 April 1950, Pew Papers, box 26; Hutton to Ramon Castroviejo, 2 March 1956, Buckley Papers, box 2; Ken Wells to Herbert Hoover, 2 February 1949 and 18 August 1949, Post-Presidential Subject File, box 165, Hoover Library.

78. J. Howard Pew to Robert Wood, 28 November 1949, to Ralph Robey, 1 April 1948, "Contributions to America's Future," undated 1949, Pew Papers, boxes 24, 21, 33; Paul F. Heard, "A Protestant Looks at Films," *Film and Radio Guide* (December 1946), 37; "Discussion of Statement in Re Possibility of Writing a Book," Conference Board, 8 February 1946, Crane Papers, box 48.

79. J. Howard Pew to Verne Kaub, 12 June 1950, Pew Papers, box 26; Pew to John Mackay, 7 January 1952, Crane Papers, box 68; "Economic Mastery Linked to Freedom," *New York Times,* 22 October 1951, 18.

80. "U.S. Tolerance of Reds Blamed for Atom Gains," *Chicago Tribune,* 26 September 1949, 12; Greg Mitchell, *Tricky Dick and the Pink Lady: Richard Nixon vs. Helen Gahagan Douglas—Sexual Politics and the Red Scare, 1950* (New York: Random House, 1998); Sam Tanenhaus, *Whittaker Chambers: A Biography* (New York: Modern Library, 1998), 153–439.

81. Robert Griffith, *The Politics of Fear: Joseph R. McCarthy and the Senate* (Amherst, MA: University of Massachusetts Press, 1970); Ellen Schrecker, *Many Are the Crimes: McCarthyism in America* (Boston: Little, Brown, 1998); John Earl Haynes and Harvey Klehr, *In Denial: Historians, Communism and Espionage* (San Francisco: Encounter, 2003).

82. Griffith, *The Politics of Fear,* 73; David W. Reinhard, *The Republican Right Since 1945* (Lexington: University Press of Kentucky, 1983), 63; Peter L. Steinberg, *The Great "Red Menace": United States Prosecution of American Communists, 1947–1952* (Westport, CT: Greenwood, 1984), 210.

83. Michael Ybarra, *Washington Gone Crazy: Senator Pat McCarran and the Great American Communist Hunt* (Hanover, NH: Steerforth, 2004).

84. NSC-68 at http://www.fas.org/irp/offdocs/nsc-hst/nsc-68.htm; Hamilton Fish Armstrong et al. to President Truman, 12 December 1950, Papers of Philip D. Reed, box 17, Hagley Library.

85. Rymph, *Republican Women,* 118; "A.M.A. Says It Spent Millions in Election," *New York Times,* 26 November 1950, 56; Jonathan Bell, *The Liberal State on Trial: The Cold War and American Politics in the Truman Years* (New York: Columbia University Press, 2004), 198–276; "Congressional Voting, Summary Tables," undated, 1952, President's Secretary's Files, boxes 113 and 232, Truman Library.

86. William S. White, "McCarthy's Influence Is Greater in the 82nd," *New York Times,* 7 January 1951, 129.

87. Richard Lowitt, ed., *The Truman-MacArthur Controversy* (Chicago: Rand McNally, 1967), 30–46.

88. Douglas MacArthur to Everett Martin, 20 March 1951, Harry Cain to Constituents, 5 September 1952, H. Alexander Smith Papers, boxes 106, 221; Everett

Dirksen to Nathan William MacChesney, 28 April 1951, MacChesney Papers, box 13; NAE, "Resolution," 11 April 1951, Iowa Collection, reel 98.

89. Lawrence Dennis to Sterling Morton, 18 July 1951, Morton Papers, box 13; Norman Thomas to H. Alexander Smith, 20 November 1951, Smith Papers, box 104.

90. "Interview with General Eisenhower," July 1951, Papers of Henry Cabot Lodge II, reel 28, Massachusetts Historical Society, Boston, Massachusetts; "Demolish the Enemy," unsigned, undated campaign memorandum 1952, Papers of Thomas E. Stephens, box 7, Eisenhower Library; Eisenhower to Edward J. Bermingham, 8 February 1951, Wood Papers, box 43.

91. George Smith, Memorandum, 23 April 1952, Taft Papers box 422; Homer Capehart to Joseph Pew, 28 May 1952, Pew Papers, box 33; Taft, handwritten notes, undated, 1952, Taft Papers, box 285.

92. Ralph Gwinn to J. Howard Pew, 22 June 1950, Pew Papers, box 26; Robert Taft to John Temple Graves, 1 June 1949, Taft Papers, box 910; Robert Wood to Melvin Osterman, 12 June 1952, Wood Papers, box 43.

93. Walter Judd to Betty Lindley, 30 June 1952, Papers of Walter H. Judd, box 212, Hoover Institution; D Clayton James, *The Years of MacArthur Volume III: Triumph and Disaster 1945–1964* (Boston: Houghton Mifflin, 1985), 649–650.

94. "Statement by Carroll Reece," undated, 1952, Taft Papers, box 285.

95. Robert Taft, "Memorandum on General Eisenhower," "Analysis of the 1952 Convention," undated 1952, Taft Papers, box 1286.

96. "Eisenhower Addresses April – November 1952," Republican National Committee News Clippings and Publications, vol. 1, boxes 28, 29, Eisenhower Library; Nathan B. Blumberg, *One-Party Press? Coverage of the 1952 Presidential Coverage in 35 Daily Newspapers* (Lincoln: University of Nebraska Press, 1954), 14–16.

97. Lizabeth Cohen, *A Consumer's Republic: The Politics of Mass Consumption in Postwar America* (New York: Knopf, 2003), 333; Robert Bendiner, "How Much Has TV Changed Campaigning?" *New York Times,* 2 November 1952, SM13.

Chapter 5

1. U.S. Senate, *Executive Sessions of the Senate Permanent Subcommittee on Investigations of the Committee on Government Operations, Made Public 2003,* Vol. 2, 83rd Congress, 2nd Session, 1954, 1374–76; *Mesarosh v. U.S.,* 352 U.S. 808 (1956).

2. Dwight D. Eisenhower to B. G. Chynoweth, 13 July 1954, to Lucy Eisenhower, 6 May 1960, to Edgar Eisenhower, 8 November 1954, DDE Diaries, boxes 7, 49, 8; Eisenhower to Herbert Brownell, 4 November 1953, Whitman Papers, Administration, box 8.

3. Norman A. Graebner, *The New Isolationism: A Study in Politics and Foreign Policy Since 1950* (New York: Ronald Press, 1956), 122; Karl Mundt to Elton Walth, 3 February 1960, Mundt Papers, reel 190. See also, Gary W. Reichard, *The Reaffirmation of Republicanism: Eisenhower and the Eighty-Third Congress* (Knoxville: University of Ten-

nessee Press, 1975); Robert Griffith, "Dwight D. Eisenhower and the Corporate Commonwealth," *American Historical Review* 87 (February 1982), 87–122.

4. "Time Chart of Relative Gross Capabilities to Deliver a Decisive Nuclear Attack," unsigned memo, November 1954, with Eisenhower's handwritten comments, Whitman Diary; Robert R. Bowie and Richard H. Immerman, *Waging Peace: How Eisenhower Shaped an Enduring Cold War Strategy* (New York: Oxford University Press, 1998).

5. Dwight D. Eisenhower to E. L. Hering, 29 May 1959 and Eisenhower to Swede Hazlett, 23 October 1954, DDE Diaries, boxes 41 and 8; Seth Jacobs, "'Our System Demands the Supreme Being,': The U. S. Religious Revival and the 'Diem Experiment,' 1954–55," *Diplomatic History* 25 (Fall 2001), 589–624.

6. B. E. Hutchinson to Homer Ferguson, 26 March 1954, J. Howard Pew Papers, box 37.

7. Henry Cabot Lodge to Dwight D. Eisenhower, 19 February 1954, Lodge Papers, II, reel 28; "One Worlders' Route Drawn by Sen. Bricker," *Chicago Tribune*, 5 Jun. 1954, 7.

8. Duane Tananbaum, *The Bricker Amendment Controversy: A Test of Eisenhower's Political Leadership* (Ithaca, NY: Cornell University Press, 1988), 113–32 "'Vigilant Women' Endorse Bricker," *New York Times* 26 January 1954, 14; Scher, "Cold War on the Home Front," 225; *Manion Forum*, "Fourth Anniversary," October 1958, Herbert Hoover Post-Presidential Papers, box 218.

9. Austin Mosher to D. B. Lewis, 5 March 1957, Stone, "To All Members," undated 1957, Papers of Willis E. Stone, box 19, University of Oregon Library.

10. D. B. Lewis, fund-raising letter, 7 December 1956, Stone Papers, box 19; "Mississippi Scores!" *Freedom Magazine*, Mary –June 1964, 1, Iowa Collection, reel 54.

11. R. B. Snowden, Memo to the Trustees, 9 December 1955, "1956 Plan," 1 July 1956, Crane Papers, box 9; Snowden to J. Howard Pew, 17 July 1958, Pew to Snowden, 26 August 1958, Pew Papers, box 57.

12. U.S. House of Representatives, *Report of the Special Committee to Investigate Tax-Exempt Foundations and Comparable Organizations*, 83rd Congress, 1st Session, 1953, 18–19.

13. Rockefeller Foundation, "Confidential Monthly Report: 1 March 1950," *Trustees Bulletin, 1950*, 22–23.

14. J. Howard Pew to Guy M. Rush, 24 December 1952, to B.E. Hutchinson, 7 December 1953, Pew Papers, boxes 32, 34.

15. Dwight D. Eisenhower to William Robinson, 12 March 1954, Robinson Papers, box 2; Henry Cabot Lodge to Eisenhower 23 February 1954, Lodge Papers, II, reel 28.

16. The plan is closely paraphrased from Marvin Liebman, *Coming Out Conservative: An Autobiography* (San Francisco: Chronicle Books, 1992), 89–90.

17. Advertising Council, "Religion in American Life," 1–24 November 1949 and "The 1950 Religion in American Life Program," Charles P. Taft Papers, box 84.

18. L. Nelson Bell to J. Howard Pew, 13 September 1961, Christianity Today Papers, Billy Graham Archives, box 2; David Stoll, *Fishers of Men or Founders of Empire?*

The Wycliff Bible Translators in Latin America (Cambridge, MA: Cultural Survival, 1982). See also Gerard Colby and Charlotte Dennett's controversial *Thy Will Be Done: The Conquest of the Amazon; Nelson Rockefeller and Evangelism in the Age of Oil* (New York: HarperCollins, 1995).

19. White House Branch Liaison Office, "The Principles that Guide the Eisenhower Administration," 2 December 1953, Rockefeller Family Papers, Series J–1, box 7

20. Craig Lee Keller, "The Intellectuals and Eisenhower: Civil Religion, Religious Publicity, and the Search for Moral and Religious Communities," Ph.D. dissertation, George Washington University, 2002; "Eisenhower Says U.S. Needs Religious Faith," *Christian Science Monitor*, 5 February 1953, 7; William H. Stringer, "President Hails Spiritual Aims," *Christian Science Monitor*, 2 February 1956, 2.

21. Sterling Morton to J. Howard Pew, 10 October 1951, Morton Papers, box 14; Pew to C. Gilbert, 3 April 1950, Pew Papers, box 26; Pew to Morton, 8 November 1951, Morton Papers, box 14; Pew to Johnston M. Hart, 16 June 1953, to Walter M. Haushalter, 14 December 1953, Pew Papers, box 34; National Lay Committee, "Affirmation," undated, 1954, Charles Taft Papers, box 102; Eckard V. Toy, Jr., "The National Lay Committee and the National Council of Churches: A Case Study of Protestants in Conflict," *American Quarterly* 21 (Summer 1969), 190–209; Fones-Wolf, *Selling Free Enterprise*, 236-45

22. National Lay Committee, "Basic Principles," undated, Pew Papers, box 34; Charles Taft, Remarks at the General Board, NCC, 20 January 1954, to J. Howard Pew, 2 July 1954, Taft Papers, boxes 98, 99; Pew to B. E. Hutchinson, 30 August 1955, Papers of B. E. Hutchinson, box 38, Hoover Institution; William Mullendore to Jasper Crane, 20 February 1956, Crane Papers, box 62.

23. NAM, "Building a Better America," 28 November 1952, NAM Papers, Series I, box 6.

24. Jacoby, *Modern Manors*, 35–262; Fones-Wolfe, *Selling Free Enterprise*, 32–107, 158–217; National Industrial Conference Board, "The Place in Corporate Philanthropy of 'American Way' and Economic Oganizations," 9 May 1960, Baroody Papers, box 96; Howell John Harris, *The Right to Manage: Industrial Relations Policies of American Business in the 1940s* (Madison: University of Wisconsin Press, 1982).

25. Jack Barbash, "Ideology and the Kohler Strike," *Wisconsin Law Review* (Spring 1967), 468–473; Walter H. Uphoff, *Kohler on Strike* (Boston: Beacon, 1966).

26. Heather Hendershot, "God's Angriest Man: Carl McIntire, Cold War Fundamentalism, and Right-Wing Broadcasting," *American Quarterly* 59 (June 2007), 373–396.

27. "Bible-Balloons Help Hungarian Revolt," *Christian Crusade Magazine* (December 1956), Iowa Collection, reel 21; Janice M. Irvine, "On Lies, Secrets, and Right-Wing Sexual Politics: Reflections on Laud Humphreys' 'Breastplate of Righteousness,'" *International Journal of Sociology and Social Policy* 24 (Iss. 3–5, 2004), 95 –111; Overstreet, *The Strange Tactics*, 189–203.

28. Christian Anti-Communism Crusade, "The Christian Answer to Communism," undated, Radical Right Papers, box 35, Hoover Institution; Fred Schwarz,

"Will the Kremlin Conquer America by 1973?" undated 1959, Philbrick Papers, box 65.

29. Francis Schaeffer, "A Revolutionary Christianity," American Council of Christian Churches pamphlet, undated, Papers of Carl McIntire, box 2, Bentley Library.

30. Church League of America, "What Is the Church League of America?" undated 1966, Papers of Marvin Liebman, box 9, Hoover Institution; "The Church League of America Presents Ronald Reagan on the Welfare State," undated 1963, Philbrick Papers, box 69; "A Detective Agency Defends Using Data on Political Opinion," *New York Times,* 27 January 1977, 41.

31. H. L. Hunt to Albert Wedemeyer, 6 October 1958, Wedemeyer Papers, box 116; "The LIFE LINE Story," *Life Lines,* 3 May 1961, "LIFE LINE Fights Loss of Liberty," undated 1966, Iowa Collection, reels 71, 74; William Rusher to James Wick, 22 November 1957, Rusher Papers, reel 2.

32. Frank Buchman, radio address, 27 November 1938, David Lawrence Papers, box 81; "Buchman's Kampf," *Time,* 18 January 1943, 65; "An Idea to Win the World: World Assembly for Moral Rearmament," reprinted from *Congressional Record,* 6–17 January 1955, Charles Taft Papers, box 95.

33. "The Breakfast Group," June 1942, Lawrence Papers, box 16; Dan L. Thrapp, "ICL Works to Lift World Leadership," *Los Angeles Times,* 23 November 1952, 13.

34. Abraham Vereide, "Report to the 1955 Annual Conference of the ICL," 5 February 1955, "Annual Christian Action Conference 3–5 February 1955," Papers of the Fellowship Foundation, box 495, Graham Archives.

35. "Records of the Fellowship Foundation, Historical Background," Graham Archives, and online at www.wheaton.edu/bgc/archives/GUIDES/459.htm; "Church Group Votes, Elects 17 From Congress," *Washington Post,* 17 January 1946, 8; "Christian Leadership Group Told of Meetings at The Hague," *Washington Post* 5 July 1952, 12.

36. Dwight D. Eisenhower to Thomas Dewey, 8 October 1954; Gabriel Hauge to Eisenhower, 27 September 1954, DDE Diaries, box 8.

37. Bryce Harlow to Sherman Adams, 21 March 1955, Howard Pyle files, box 46, Eisenhower Library; Republican National Committee, "Analysis of 1954 Election," Papers of Robert Humphreys, box 12, Eisenhower Library; *Pennsylvania v. Nelson,* 350 U.S. 497 (1956).

38. Allen Weinstein and Alexander Vassiliev, *The Haunted Wood: Soviet Espionage in America, the Stalin Era* (New York: Random House, 1999).

39. M. J. Heale, *McCarthy's Americans,* 7–78; David K. Johnson, *The Lavender Scare: The Cold War Persecution of Gays and Lesbians in the Federal Government* (Chicago: University of Chicago Press, 2004).

40. Theoharis, *The Boss,* 312–314.

41. Dwight D. Eisenhower to William Robinson, 12 March 1954, Robinson Papers, box 2; C. D. Jackson to J. K. Jessup, 9 November 1956, Jackson Papers, box 56; Henry Cabot Lodge, *Confidential Journal,* 21 January 1954, Lodge Papers, II, reel 17.

42. William F. Buckley Jr., "A Young Republican View," *Commonweal*, 25 January 1952, 392–93; Buckley to *Freeman*, 1 December 1954, Buckley Papers, box 2, published, *Freeman*, (January 1955), 244.

43. "Coexistence Red Victory, Knowland Says," *Los Angeles Times*, 16 November 1954, 8; William S. White, "Knowland Pressure Shapes Battle Over Foreign Policy," *New York Times*, 25 November 1954, 1; Graebner, *The New Isolationism*, 226–30.

44. Dwight D. Eisenhower, "Memorandum for the Secretary of State," 15 November 1954, DDE Diaries, box 8; Chester Bowles to Dean Acheson, October 9, 1956, Papers of Dean G. Acheson, box 96, Truman Library; Jonathan Soffer, "The National Association of Manufacturers and the Militarization of American Conservatism," *Business History Review*, 75 (Winter 2001), 775–806.

45. Samuel Pettengill to Francis Casey, 16 December 1957, Pettingill Papers, box 3; William F. Buckley Jr. to William Brady, 7 February 1961, Buckley Papers, box 14; David Franke, "The Student Loyalty Oath," *Individualist* (December 1959), 1–4.

46. James Burnham, "Litmus Propositions for Liberal-Conservative Test," undated, Papers of James Burnham, box 3, Hoover Institution.

47. Styles Bridges, "Remarks on the Fund For the Republic," April 1956, Buckley Papers, box 4.

48. Jasper Crane to Lois B. Hunter, 19 March 1954, Leonard Read, "Flight from Integrity," typescript, 25 June 1959, Crane Papers, boxes 60, 35; Read, Address, "Big Government: Threat to Our Free Market," 10 February 1960, Rusher Papers, reel 8; Edmund Opitz, *Religion and the Social Problem* (Philadelphia: The Intercollegiate Society of Individualists, 1956), 13; Russell Kirk to B. E. Hutchinson, 14 July 1955, Hutchinson Papers, box 39.

49. J. Howard Pew to Leonard Read, 8 October 1954, Pew Papers, box 37; Douglas K. Stewart and Ted C. Smith, "Celebrity Structure of the Far Right," *The Western Political Quarterly* 17 (June 1964), 349–55; Ayn Rand to Jasper Crane, 21 February 1950, Crane Papers, box 69.

50. William J. Baroody to H. W. Prentis Jr., 21 February 1956, Papers of William J. Baroody, box 40, Library of Congress.

51. William J. Baroody to Harvey Peters, 17 July 1959, Baroody Papers, box 40.

52. William L. McGrath to Harry P. Jeffrey, 2 July 1964, Baroody Papers, box 39.

53. "Strategic Study Center Opens September 1," *Washington Post*, 3 June 1962, 31; W. Glenn Campbell to William J. Baroody, 13 April 1964, Baroody Papers, box 90.

54. For America, "The Story of For America," 25 June 1954, Hamilton Fish to Robert Wood, 21 September 1954, Manion Papers, box 2.

55. Harry T. Everingham, "Blueprint for Victory," undated 1955; We, The People!, financial statement, January 21, 1955 to October 31, 1955, Willis Stone to Ernest Anthony, 25 January 1956; Stone Papers, box 16; We, The People! "Program for Patriots," 18 September 1955, Iowa Collection, reel 54; "'We, The People,' Political Group, Opens Sessions," *Washington Post*, 18 September 1955, 14.

56. William F. Buckley Sr. to Lucille Cardin Crain, 18 July 1950, Crain Papers, box 26; William F. Buckley Jr. to Robert Donner, 5 January 1955, Buckley Papers, box 2.

57. Frank Chodorov to William F. Buckley Jr., 11 April 1955, Buckley to E. Victor Milione, 31 October 1955, Buckley to William Mullendore, 22 March 1955, Buckley Papers, boxes 1, 2, 3; Buckley to William Rusher, undated, 1959, Buckley to Marvin Liebman, 7 April 1961, Liebman to staff, undated, January 1961, Rusher Papers, reels 12, 4, 9.

58. William F. Buckley Jr. to Donner, 5 January 1955; William Rusher to Ferdinand Lathrop Mayor, 4 February 1960, Rusher Papers, reel 10. On the founding of *National Review* see John B. Judis, *William F. Buckley, Jr.: Patron Saint of the Conservatives* (New York: Simon & Schuster, 1988), 113–61; Linda Bridges and John R. Coyne, Jr., *Strictly Right: William F. Buckley, Jr. and the American Conservative Movement* (Hoboken, NJ: John Wiley, 2007), 32–44.

59. Anthony Harrigan, "Notes on Some American Conservatives," *U.S.A.*, 26 April 1957, Iowa Collection, reel 135.

60. For debates among Catholic intellectuals see Patrick Allitt, *Catholic Intellectuals and Conservative Politics in America, 1950–1985* (Ithaca, NY: Cornell University Press, 1993).

61. Tom Bower, *The Paperclip Conspiracy: The Hunt for Nazi Scientists* (Boston: Little, Brown, 1987); Peter C. Kent, *The Lonely Cold War of Pope Pius XII: The Roman Catholic Church and the Division of Europe, 1943–1950* (Montreal, Canada: McGill-Queen's University Press, 2002), 87–100, 257–61.

62. John L. Allen Jr., *Opus Dei: An Objective Look Behind The Myths And Reality of the Most Controversial Force In the Catholic Church* (New York: Doubleday, 2005), 284, 298. See also Robert Hutchinson, *Their Kingdom Come: Inside the Secret World of Opus Dei* (New York: St. Martin's Press, 1999).

63. William F. Buckley Jr., "fund-raising letter," 17 November 1955, Buckley to Rev. Richard Ginder, 13 April 1959, Adolfo Echevarria to Buckley, 2 July 1959, Buckley to Jose Maria de Areilza, 23 June 1959 and 6 July 1959, Buckley Papers, boxes 1, 7, 17, 4.

64. William Rusher to Judith Walter, 19 October 1962, Rusher Papers, reel 14; J. Howard Pew to Stewart Robinson, 15 September 1953, Pew Papers, box 42; "Anti-Defamation League of B'Nai B'rith Press Release," 14 June 1962, Philbrick Papers, box 62.

65. David L. O'Connor, "Defenders of the Faith: American Catholic Lay Organizations and Anticommunism, 1917–1975," Ph.D. dissertation, State University of New York at Stony Brook, 2000, 177, 185; L. David O'Connor, "The Cardinal Mindszenty Foundation: American Catholic Anti-Communism and its Limits," *American Communist History* 5 (June 2006), 37–66; "The Four Freedoms," *The Mindszenty Report*, 15 December 1962, Philbrick Papers, box 62.

66. J. Howard Pew to B. E. Hutchinson, 25 February 1955, box 43; Pew to L. Nelson Bell, 17 January 1955, Pew Papers, box 41; Billy Graham, "My Answer," undated, Pew Papers, box 55; Billy Graham to J. Howard Pew, 27 September 1956, Pew Papers, box 48.

67. Billy Graham to J. Howard Pew, 26 March 1955, Pew Papers, box 42.

68. L. Nelson Bell to J. Howard Pew, 20 April 1955, Pew to Billy Graham, 7 April 1955, Pew to Bell, 24 May, 1956, Pew Papers, boxes 52, 42, 47.

69. Barrie Foster, Opinion Research Corporation, to J. Howard Pew, 10 April 1958, "Minutes," Board of Directors, 6 January 1958, Pew Papers, boxes 53, 48; "Why Christianity Today," *Christianity Today* 29 October 1956, 20–23; "Conservatism Today," *Time,* 13 July 1962, 81.

70. J. Howard Pew to John Young, 18 June 1957, Pew to Billy Graham, 1 October 1956, Graham to Pew, 27 September 1956, Carl Henry to L. Nelson Bell, 12 July 1957, Pew Papers, boxes 48, 53; Minutes, Board of Directors, 6 January 1959, *Christianity Today* Papers, box 1.

71. "Diary, 9 February 1956," Ann Whitman Diary, box 8 "Andrews Blasts Income Tax and Federal Aid," *Free Men Speak* (November 1956), Iowa Collection, reel 62.

72. Christopher J. Tudda, "'Reenacting the Story of Tantalus,' Eisenhower, Dulles, and the Failed Rhetoric of Liberation," *Journal of Cold War Studies* 7 (Fall 2005), 3–35; Charles Gati, *Failed Illusions: Moscow, Washington, Budapest, and the 1956 Hungarian Revolt* (Stanford, CA: Stanford University Press, 2006); Johanna Granville, "'Caught with Jam on Our Fingers': Radio Free Europe and the Hungarian Revolution of 1956," *Diplomatic History* 29 (November 2005), 811–39; Dwight D. Eisenhower to E. E. "Swede" Hazlett, 2 November 1956, Whitman Papers, box 20.

73. David L. Stebenne, *Modern Republican: Arthur Larson and the Eisenhower Years* (Bloomington: Indiana University Press, 2006), 151–254.

74. Republican Party Papers, Minutes, Meeting of the RNC, Executive Committee, 30 January 1958, reel 16.

75. Security Resources Panel of the Science Advisory Committee, "Deterrence and Survival in the Nuclear Age," 7 November 1957, National Security Archive, George Washington University. This document was called the Gaither Report after H. Rowan Gaither, the head of the study group, although Paul Nitze, the author of NSC-68, was the primary drafter.

76. "Ike Gets Poor Labor Advice, Hartley Says," *The Washington Post,* 4 September 1956, 2; James J. Kilpatrick to William F. Buckley Jr., 26 November 1958, Buckley Papers, box 6.

77. Thomas W. Evans, *The Education of Ronald Reagan: The General Election Years and the Untold Story of His Conversion to Conservatism* (New York: Columbia University Press, 2006); Kimberly Phillips-Fein, "American Counterrevolutionary: Lemuel Ricketts Boulware and General Electric, 1950–1960," in Nelson Lichtenstein, ed., *American Capitalism: Social Thought and Political Economy in the Twentieth Century* (Philadelphia: University of Pennsylvania Press, 2006), 249–70.

78. Richard E. Mooney, "Business Widens Drive in Politics; 'Work' Act a Key," *New York Times,* 5 October 1958, 1; Andrew Hacker and Joel D. Auerbach, "Businessmen in Politics," *Law and Contemporary Problems* 27 (Spring 1962), 266–79; Fones-Wolfe, *Selling Free Enterprise,* 271.

79. R. Alton Lee, *Eisenhower and Landrum-Griffin: A Study in Labor-Management Politics* (Lexington, KY: University of Kentucky Press, 1990).

80. Owen Brewster to Joseph Pew, 24 November 1958, Pew Papers, box 33; ACA, "Executive Director's Report," July 1959, Iowa Collection, reel 13; ACA, "Annual Report, 1965," Crane Papers, box 2; Ben Moreell, "Religion in American Life," *Ideas on Liberty,* (May 1955), 62.

81. Ben A. Franklin, "Passman Seeking Outside Help in His Fight on Foreign Aid," *New York Times,* 15 January 1965, 12; "The Truth About Liberty Lobby," *Liberty Letter,* March 1965, "Happy Birthday to Liberty Lobby," *Liberty Letter,* July 1965, Iowa Collection, reel 69.

82. "The Issue," *Right,* 6 March 1956, 1. See also Frank P. Mintz, *The Liberty Lobby and the American Right: Race, Conspiracy, and Culture* (Westport, CT: Greenwood, 1985).

83. American Security Council, "Services," undated, C. W. Hooper Jr. to Philbrick, undated, Philbrick Papers, box 38; "U. S. Group Exposes Red Propaganda," *Cleveland Press,* 20 August 1964, F1.

84. Robert Welch to B. E. Hutchinson, 24 November 1958, Hutchinson Papers, box 13; *The Blue Book of the John Birch Society* (Belmont, MA: Western Islands, 1961); Albert Wedemeyer to Welch, 5 September 1961, Wedemeyer Papers, box 115.

85. Jonathan M. Schoenwald, "We Are an Action Group: The John Birch Society and the Conservative Movement of the 1960s," and Jeff Roche, "Cowboy Conservativism," in David Farber and Jeff Roche, *The Conservative Sixties* (New York: Peter Lang, 2003), 21–36, 79–92.

86. Massachusetts Women's Political Club, *Chronological History of the Fluoridation Hoax,* undated, 1956 Iowa Collection, reel 77; Ruth Alexander, "Siberia Scheme Uncovered in USA," *Los Angeles Examiner,* 4 March 1956, X; Jo Hindman, "Terrible 1313," *American Mercury* (January 1959), S75; "Art in U.S.," *Newsletter, The Minute Women of the U. S. A.* (November–December 1960), 1, Iowa Collection, reel 76.

87. Thomas Brady, "Address," 28 October 1954, Iowa Collection, reel 9; Neil R. McMillen, *The Citizens' Council: Organized Resistance to the Second Reconstruction, 1954–1964* (Urbana: University of Illinois Press, 1971), 139; FBI, "Racial Tensions and Civil Rights," 1 March 1956, Whitman Papers, Cabinet, box 6, Eisenhower Library. See also, Numan V. Bartley, *The Rise of Massive Resistance: Race and Politics in the South During the 1950s* (Baton Rouge: Louisiana State University Press, 1969); Francis M. Wilhoit, *The Politics of Massive Resistance* (New York: George Braziller, 1973).

88. Andrew S. Winston, "Science in the Service of the Far Right: Henry E. Garrett, the IAAEE, and the Liberty Lobby," *Journal of Social Issues* 54 (Spring 1998), 179–210; William H. Tucker, *The Science and Politics of Racial Research* (Urbana, IL: University of Illinois Press, 1994), 158; *Stell v. Savannah-Chatham Board of Education* 333 F. 2nd 55 (1964), *Evers v. Jackson School District* 232 F. Supp 241 (1964).

89. William H. Tucker, *The Funding of Scientific Racism: Wickliffe Draper and the Pioneer Fund* (Urbana and Chicago: University of Illinois Press, 2002); Douglas A. Blackmon, "Silent Partner: How the South's Fight to Uphold Segregation Was Funded Up North," *Wall Street Journal,* 11 June 1999, 1.

90. Reverend G. T. Gillespie, "A Christian View of Segregation," 4 November 1954, Iowa Collection, reel 9; Association of Citizens' Councils, "A Jewish View on Segregation," undated 1956, David Lawrence Papers, box 123.

91. Jeff Woods, *Black Struggle, Red Scare: Segregation and Anti-Communism in the South, 1948–1968* (Baton Rouge: Louisiana State University Press, 2004).

92. "The Real Issue in the South and North," *American Way,* 16 October 1957, We, The People!, "Conferences Reports," 17–18 September 1955, Iowa Collection, reels 8, 54.

93. E. Earle Ellis, "Segregation and the Kingdom of God," and "The Church and the Race Problem," *Christianity Today* 18 March 1957, 6–9, 20–21.

94. "Segregation and Democracy," *National Review* 25 January 1956, 5; "Why the South Must Prevail," *National Review,* 24 August 1957, 149; Richard Weaver, "The Regime of the South," *National Review,* 14 March 1959, 587–89; Weaver to William F. Buckley Jr., 9 March 1961, Buckley Papers, box 17.

95. William F. Buckley Jr. to Nemesio Garcia-Naranjo, 21 April 1961, and to Douglas Stewart, 10 October 1961, Buckley Papers, boxes 14, 17; American Afro-Asian Educational Exchange, "South Africa and the United Nations," 30 November 1962, Rusher Papers, reel 16; Buckley, "South African Fortnight," *National Review,* 15 January 1963, 23.

96. Robert Alan Goldberg, *Barry Goldwater* (New Haven, CT: Yale University Press, 1995) 92–125; William Jenner to Clarence Manion, 16 April 1957, Manion Papers, box 3; "Goldwater's Eisenhower-Support Record," Rockefeller Family Papers, Record Group 4, Series J1, Politics, box 18.

97. "How a Conservative Wins: Goldwater Sets Example," *Indianapolis Star,* 12 November 1958, 1; "Human Events Played a Part," *Human Events,* 25 July 1964, 9.

98. Goldberg, *Goldwater,* 138–48.

99. "Rally in Chicago," *Independent American* (November 1959), 1; Austin C. Wehrwein, "Third Party Move Begins in Chicago," *New York Times,* 24 October 1959, 12.

100. Frank S. Meyer, "Principles and Heresies," *National Review* 19 December 1959, 555; James Burnham to William F. Buckley Jr., 9 October 1960, William Rusher to Buckley, 10 October 1960, Buckley Papers, box 10. On Meyer and Burnham from conservative perspectives, see Kevin J. Smant, *Principles and Heresies: Frank Meyer and the Shaping of the American Conservative Movement* (Wilmington, DE: ISI, 2002) and Daniel Kelly, *James Burnham and the Struggle for the World: A Life* (Wilmington, DE: ISI, 2002).

101. L. Nelson Bell to J. Howard Pew, 29 October 1960, Papers of L. Nelson Bell, box 41, Billy Graham Archives; Bell to Board of Directors, 18 August 1960, *Christianity Today* Papers, box 1; Charles Morrison, "Open Letter to Senator Kennedy," *Christianity Today,* 12 September 1960, 18, 32–33; "Transcript of Kennedy Talk to Ministers and Questions and Answers," *New York Times,* 13 September 1960, 22.

102. Dwight D. Eisenhower, 27 November 1959, quoted in Don Paarlberg, Oral History Transcript, 36–39, Eisenhower Library.

103. Walter Judd to Thomas Sauner, 10 February 1961, Judd Papers, box 43.

Chapter 6

1. "Left-Wing Extremists Weight Administration," *Student Statesman* (April 1962), 1; American Flag Committee, *Newsletter* (May 1963), Iowa Collection, reels 119, 6.

2. Herbert Goldhamer, "Political Implications of Posture Choices," Rand Corporation, 1 December 1960, President's Office Files, box 64, John F. Kennedy Presidential Library, Boston, Massachusetts; Meeting Transcripts, "President Kennedy and Senior Civilian and Military Advisors," 2–5 October 1963, Presidential Recordings Program, Miller Center of Public Affairs, University of Virginia, Charlottesville, Virginia.

3. Walter W. Heller, Memorandum for the President, 2 August 1961, Papers of Walter W. Heller, box 5, Theodore C. Sorenson, "The Kennedy Administration and Business," 2 June 1962, Papers of Theodore C. Sorenson, Kennedy Library.

4. Wilson Wright, "The Economic Situation," typescript, 21 November 1963, Baroody Papers, box 39.

5. CED, "Reaction to CED Proposals," undated, unsigned 1961, Reed Papers, box 16.

6. Laurence Chang and Peter Kornbluh, *The Cuban Missile Crisis, 1962: A National Security Archives Documents Reader,* 2nd ed. (New York: The New Press, 1998).

7. Eddie Rickenbacker to Louis Ruthenberg, 20 August 1963, and Address, undated, 1964, Rickenbacker Papers, boxes 32, 36; Marvin Liebman to William F. Buckley Jr., 1 October 1963, Liebman Papers, box 9.

8. Hedrick Smith, "G.O.P in South Sees Hope for '64 Vote Gains," *New York Times,* 9 November 1962, 39.

9. Thomas M. Storke, "How Some Birchers Were Birched," *New York Times,* 10 December 1961, SM 9; Rick Perlstein, *Before the Storm: Barry Goldwater and the Unmaking of the American Consensus* (New York: Hill and Wang, 2001), 118. Perlstein brings the Goldwater campaign to life with his novelistic style.

10. Attorney General Stanley Mosk to Governor Edmund G. Brown, 7 July 1961, Manion Papers, box 56; Barbara S. Stone, "The John Birch Society: A Profile," *Journal of Politics* 36 (February 1974), 184–97.

11. Marvin Liebman, "Memorandum to All Concerned," 16 January 1962, Liebman Papers, box 89; "Goldwater Impressed by Birch Membership," *Washington Post,* 30 March 1961, B5; Perlstein, *Before the Storm,* 261.

12. John Birch Society, "Accountants' Report, 1964," Manion Papers, box 60.

13. Clarence Manion to Robert Welch, 27 September 1961, Manion Papers, box 61; Barry Goldwater to William F. Buckley Jr., 14 January 1962, Buckley Papers, box 20.

14. "Justice for Gen. Walker," *Chicago Tribune,* 5 September 1961, 16

15. Waldemar A. Nielsen, "Huge, Hidden Impact of the Pentagon," *New York Times,* 25 June 1961, SM9; Ole R. Holsti, "A Widening Gap Between the U.S. Military and Civilian Society? Some Evidence, 1976–96," *International Security* 23 (Winter 1998), 5–42.

16. Lisa McGirr, *Suburban Warriors: The Origins of the New American Right* (Princeton, NJ: Princeton University Press, 2001), 8.

17. The Minutemen, "A Short History of the Minutemen," undated, Philbrick Papers, box 139; J. Harry Jones Jr., *The Minutemen* (Garden City: Doubleday, 1968), 6, 12, 38, 53, 92, 127; Gladwin Hill, "Minutemen Guerilla Unit Found To Be Small and Loosely Knit," *New York Times,* 12 November 1961, 1.

18. William Rusher to William F. Buckley Jr., 23 February 1961, Rusher Papers, reel 3.

19. Frank Meyer, memos, 5 September 1961, 17 January 1962, 4 February 1962, Rusher Papers, reel 9; William Rusher to L. Brent Bozell, 28 September 1961, Buckley Papers, box 14.

20. William F. Buckley Jr. to Charles Raddock, 16 January 1962, Buckley Papers, box 20; Jeffrey Hart, *The Making of the American Conservative Mind: National Review and Its Times* (Wilmington, DL: ISI, 2005), 161–68; "The Brown Decade," *National Review,* 21 June 1964, 434.

21. Gregory L. Schneider, *Cadres for Conservatism: Young Americans for Freedom and the Rise of the Contemporary Right* (New York: New York University Press, 1999); Sharon Statement, 183–84; John A. Andrew III, *The Other Side of the Sixties: Young Americans for Freedom and the Rise of Conservative Politics* (New Brunswick: Rutgers University Press, 1997).

22. Richard G. Braungart, "Family Status, Socialization, and Student Politics: A Multivariate Analysis," *American Journal of Sociology* 77 (July 1971), 108–30; Neils Bjerre-Poulsen, *Right Face: Organizing the American Conservative Movement, 1945–65* (Copenhagen, Denmark: Museum Tusculanum Press, 2002), 165-68.

23. Opinion Research Corporation, "Conservatism on the College Campus," January 1962, Papers of Ray C. Bliss, box 7, Ohio Historical Society, Columbus, Ohio.

24. William Rusher to William F. Buckley Jr., 5 September 1961 and to L. Brent Bozell, 28 September 1961, Buckley Papers, boxes 17, 14; Rusher, undated memo, Rusher Papers, reel 3.

25. "William F. Buckley Jr. to All Concerned," 22 January 1957, "The New York State Conservative Political Association: A Political Prospectus," 4 July 1961, Buckley Papers, boxes 1, 13; "A Brief History of the Conservative Party," undated, Mundt Papers, reel 184.

26. George J. Marlin, *Fighting the Good Fight: A History of the New York Conservative Party* (South Bend, IN: St. Augustine's Press, 2002), 66–9.

27. Edward T. Folliard, "Kennedy Lashes Out at Birchites, Other Rightist 'Fanatics,'" *Washington Post,* 19 November 1961, 1; Victor G. Reuther, *The Brothers Reuther and the Story of the UAW* (Boston: Houghton Mifflin, 1976), Reuther memo, 491–500.

28. John A. Andrew III, *The Power to Destroy: The Political Uses of the IRS from Kennedy to Nixon* (Chicago: Ivan R. Dee, 2002), 11–74; Hendershot, "God's Angriest Man," 378–84.

29. William Rusher to William F. Buckley Jr., 2 March 1962; Willmoore Kendall, "The Conservative Upsurge," undated, 1962, typescript, Buckley Papers, box 20.

30. Meyer Feldman, "Memorandum for the President," 15 August 1963, President's Office Files, box 106; Benjamin Moreell, Address, 11 January 1963, Iowa Collection, reel 13.

31. William Rusher to L. Brent Bozell, 28 September 1961, Buckley Papers, box 14; Rusher, "A Footnote to Republican History," undated typescript, Rusher Papers, reel 18.

32. Barry Goldwater to Frank S. Meyer, 29 February 1963, Papers of the Free Society Association, box 1, Hoover Institution; Goldwater to Willliam Rusher, 8 June 1984, Rusher Papers, box 35; B. E. Hutchinson to H. Frederick Hagemann Jr., 9 June 1960, Hutchinson Papers, box 29.

33. John McNeil Burns, Republican Congressional Campaign Committee, "Report from the Field," 3 May 1963, Papers of George L. Hinman, box 8, Rockefeller Archives.

34. George Hinman to Nelson Rockefeller, 11 December 1961 and 23 November 1962, Hinman Papers, box 93.

35. Republican State Party, "South Carolina Election Analysis," 1965, Thurmond Papers, box 17; Grant Reynolds to Senator Thruston Morton, 23 January 1963, Hinman Papers, box 51; Katherine Neuberger to Charlton Lyons, 4 January 1963, Rusher Papers, box 155.

36. Republican National Committee, *The Republican Southern Challenge*, 1962, 7; Laura Jan Gifford, "'Dixie is No Longer in the Bag,'" South Carolina Republicans and the Election of 1960," *Journal of Policy History* 19 (April 2007), 207–33.

37. George Hinman to Nelson Rockefeller, 11 December 1961, "The State of the Party," *Advance Magazine Newsletter*, January 1964, Hinman Papers, boxes 93, 1; John Sherman Cooper to George Garner, Papers of John Sherman Cooper, box 300, University of Kentucky Library, Lexington, Kentucky.

38. Cohen, *A Consumer's Republic*, 194–289.

39. Ronald P. Formisano, *Boston Against Busing: Race, Class, and Ethnicity in the 1960s and 1970s*, (Chapel Hill: University of North Carolina Press, 1991), 22–43; "Realtor Group Opposes Forced Sales to Negroes," *New York Times*, 14 June 1963, 32.

40. Rowland Evans and Robert Novak, "The White Man's Party," *Washington Post*, 25 June 1963, 6; Dan T. Carter, *The Politics of Rage: George Wallace, the Origins of the New Conservatism, and the Transformation of American Politics* (New York: Simon and Schuster, 1995), 202–16, Wallace on p. 215.

41. Barry Goldwater to Denison Kitchel, 19 June 1963, Papers of Denison Kitchel, box 2, Hoover Institution.

42. "Rockefeller Opens Fire on Goldwater," *Chicago Tribune*, 15 July 1963, 3; Karl Mundt to Roy Houck, 24 July 1963, Mundt Papers, reel 191; Robert Sprinkel to William Rusher, 11 July 1963, Rusher Papers, reel 18.

43. Robert Dallek, *Flawed Giant: Lyndon Johnson and His Times, 1961–1973* (New York: Oxford University Press, 1998), 54–121.

44. "Partial Text of Goldwater Speech," *Washington Post*, 12 September 1964, 6; Senate Minority Leader Everett Dirksen failed to gain votes on these amendments. Dirksen, "Press Release, 26 June 1964," Papers of Everett M. Dirksen, Campaigns and Politics, Folder 50, Dirksen Congressional Center, Pekin, Illinois.

45. William Rusher to William F. Buckley Jr., 27 February 1964, Rusher Papers, reel 18.

46. Barry Goldwater, stump speech, Omaha, Nebraska, 11 May 1964, Free Society Association Papers, box 4; Peter Kuznick, "Scientists on the Stump," *Bulletin of the Atomic Scientists* (November/December 2004), 31.

47. "Goldwater Poses New Asian Tactics," *New York Times,* 25 May 1964, 1; "The Man on the Bandwagon," *Time* 12 June 1964, 31–34.

48. Julius Duscha, "Gov. Scranton to Fight for GOP Nomination," *Washington Post,* 13 June 1964, 1.

49. Earl Mazo, "Extremism Cited," and "Disaster at San Francisco," *New York Times,* 18 July 1964, 1, 19 July 1964, E8; Barry Goldwater to Richard M. Nixon, 7 August 1964, Harry Jaffe, "Extremism and Moderation," 27 July 1964, Kitchel Papers, box 3; "Barry Gives Definition of Extremism," *Chicago Tribune,* 10 August 1964, 1.

50. Jerald Ter Horst, "The Grenier Plan for the G.O.P.," *Reporter,* 8 October 1964, 24–26; "Random Notes From All Over: Goldwater Aides Counter Right," *New York Times,* 16 September 1963, 30; W. Glenn Campbell to Harvey Peters, 13 April 1964, Baroody Papers, box 90.

51. "Democrats Charge G.O.P. Poll Watch Today Will Harass the Negroes and the Poor," *New York Times,* 3 November 1964, 22.

52. Michael William Flamm, "'Law and Order:' Street Crime, Civil Disorder, and the Crisis of Liberalism," Ph.D. dissertation, Columbia University, 1998, 101–102.

53. Charles Mohr, "Goldwater Hits U. S. Moral Rot," *New York Times,* 11 October 1964, 76; "Text of Goldwater Kickoff Talk," *Los Angeles Times,* 4 September 1964, 16.

54. John D. Pomfret, "Goldwater Sees Rights Act Flaw," 28 October, 26; Anthony Lewis, "Campaign Issues," 1 November, 79; Pomfret, "Senator Is Buoyed," 3 November, 21, all in *New York Times,* 1964; "Why a Democratic Senator Turned Republican," *U.S. News & World Report,* 28 September 1964, 83; Perlstein, *Before the Storm,* 494-496.

55. Charles Mohr, "Goldwater Calls Tax Cut 'Cynical,'" Mohr, "Humphrey Scores G.O.P. Fiscal Plan," *New York Times,* 9 September 1964, 27, 13 September 1964, 68.

56. "Executive Director Reports," *BIPAC Newsletter,* December 1964, Regnery Papers, box 48; "Political Action Backed by NAM," *New York Times,* 9 August 1963, 21; "Business and Politics," *Washington Post,* 8 August 1963, 14; Candice J. Nelson, "The Business-Industry PAC: Trying to Lead in an Uncertain Election Climate," in Robert Biersack et al., eds., *Risky Business? PAC Decisionmaking in Congressional Elections* (Armonk, NY: M. E. Sharpe, 1994), 29–38.

57. Kim McQuaid, *Uneasy Partners: Big Business in American Politics, 1945–1990* (Baltimore: Johns Hopkins University Press, 1994), 128–29; John W. Finney, "Miller Attacks 'Big' Government," *New York Times,* 28 October 1964, 24.

58. Barry Goldwater to Stephen Shadegg, 23 June 1965, Kitchel Papers, box 2.

59. Mary Brennan, *Turning Right in the Sixties: The Conservative Capture of the GOP* (Chapel Hill: University of North Carolina Press, 1995), 101.

60. Eddie Rickenbacker to Barry Goldwater, 10 November 1964, Rickenbacker Papers, box 42.

61. United Republicans of America, "Dear Fellow Conservative," 14 May 1965, Mundt Papers, reel 185; "Conservative Win Depends on Common Sense Plan," *California Statesman* (December 1964), 3, Iowa Collection, reel 19.

62. "Republicans: Beyond Ideology," *Time,* 22 January 1965, 20; George Romney to Barry Goldwater, 21 December 1964, Robert Taft, Jr., Remarks, 18 January 1965, Bliss Papers, box 3; Robert C. Albright, "GOP Governors All but Demand Ouster of Burch," *Washington Post,* 6 December 1964, 1.

63. Statistics in Byron E. Shafer and Richard Johnston, *The End of Southern Exceptionalism: Class, Race, and Partisan Change in the Postwar South* (Cambridge, MA: Harvard University Press, 2006), 13.

64. Sherman T. Rock to Thruston Morton, 18 April 1966, Papers of Thruston Morton, box 16, University of Kentucky Library; David Jacobs and Daniel Tope, "The Politics of Resentment in the Post-Civil Rights Era: Minority Threat, Homicide, and Ideological Voting in Congress," *American Journal of Sociology* 112 (March 2007), 1458–94.

65. Geoffrey Kabaservice, *The Guardians: Kingman Brewster, His Circle, and the Rise of the Liberal Establishment* (New York: Henry Holt, 2004), 333.

66. Barry Goldwater, "memo," 4 March1965, Charles Lichenstein to Dean Burch, 28 July 1965, Free Society Association Papers, boxes 2, 9.

67. Donald C. Bruce, "Confidential Memorandum, re: American Public Affairs Educational Fund, Inc.," 14 January 1965, Liebman Papers, box 8.

68. Minutes, Board of Directors Meeting, American Conservative Union, 19 December 1964, Rusher Papers, box 134; "Confidential Preliminary Report on the American Conservative Union," January 1965, Liebman Papers, box 7.

69. "Get on Target with the American Conservative Union," undated 1965, Free Society Association Papers, box 1; Marvin Liebman Associates, "fund-raising memo," 13 April 1966, Liebman Papers, box 57.

70. American Conservative Union "The DMV Report," June 1967, Liebman Papers, box 59; "The Financiers of Revolution," April 1969, Philbrick Papers, box 33; American Conservative Union, "The Ripon Society," undated 1966, Liebman Papers, box 11.

71. Richard C. Cornuelle quoted in T. George Harris, "A New Conservative Manifesto," *Look,* 29 December 1964, 20.

72. American Security Council, "Top-Level Civilian Committee Urges Adoption of Strategy for Victory in the Cold War," 12 August 1964, Philbrick Papers, box 38; "Ike to Inaugurate Security Council Radio Series," *Washington Post,* 28 September 1964, 10.

73. James L. Buckley, "To Fellow Conservatives," undated 1965, Liebman Papers, box 8.

74. "Buckley vs. Buckley, William F. Buckley, Jr. Interrogates Himself Before the National Press Club, Washington, D.C.," 4 August 1965; Edward C. Burks, "Buckley Assails Vietnam Protest," Sidney H. Schanberg, "Buckely Asserts a Vote for Him Will be 'Vision of a New Order,'" *New York Times,* 22 October 1965, 1, 1 November 1965, 1; Jonathan M. Schoenwald, *A Time for Choosing: The Rise of Modern American Conserva-*

tism (New York: Oxford University Press, 2001), 174; "Conservative Vote Sets Record Here," *New York Times*, 3 November 1965, 1. See also Jonathan Rieder, *Canarsie: The Jews and Italians of Brooklyn Against Liberalism* (Cambridge: Harvard University Press, 1985).

75. Schoenwald, *A Time for Choosing*, 122–202; Phyllis Schalfly, *A Choice Not an Echo* (Alton, IL: Pere Marquette Press, 1964); Donald T. Critchlow, *Phyllis Schlafly and Grassroots Conservatism: A Woman's Crusade* (Princeton, NJ: Princeton University Press, 2005), 109–62.

76. Cathie Jo Martin, *Stuck in Neutral: Business and the Politics of Human Capital Investment* (Princeton, NJ: Princeton University Press, 2000), 78–80.

77. McQuaid, *Uneasy Partners*, 133–39.

78. Ernest van den Haag, "More Immigration?" *National Review*, 21 September 1965, 821–22.

79. Jasper Crane to J. Howard Pew, 25 April 1967, Crane Papers, box 68.

80. Christian Heritage Center, "The Hippies and Anti-Christ," 29 January 1971, Philbrick Papers, box 68; "The Second Sexual Revolution," *Time*, 24 January 1964, 54; Lawrence B. Finer, "Trends in Premarital Sex in the United States, 1954–2003," *Public Health Reports* 122 (January–February 2007), 76.

81. Martha Rountree, "Speech Text," undated 1970, Papers of Rogers C. B. Morton, box 277, University of Kentucky Library.

82. Robert Salter to Don Lipsett, 15 May 1965, Liebman Papers, box 7; Christian Anti-Communism Crusade, "Janet Greene Sings," undated, Philbrick Papers, box 66; Woolsey Teller, "Young Patriots Are Not Without A Song," *Indianapolis Star*, 10 April 1966, 2.

83. John Steinbacher, "Secular Humanism—The Public School Cult," *Educator* (November 1969), Iowa Collection, reel 163; Janice M. Irvine, *Talk About Sex: The Battles Over Sex Education in the United States* (Berkeley: University of California Press, 2002), 17–62.

84. Kirk W. Ellison and C. Kirk Hadaway, "Prayer in Public Schools: When Church and State Collide," *Public Opinion Quarterly* 49 (Autumn 1985), 317–29; "The War Against Religion," *Wall Street Journal*, 6 May 1964, 12.

85. Maxwell Taylor to Lyndon Johnson, 6 January 1965, NSC History, "Deployment of U. S. Forces to Vietnam," box 40, Cabinet Minutes, 18 June, 1965, Cabinet Papers, box 3, Lyndon Johnson Presidential Library, Austin, Texas.

86. Albert S. Porter to Hubert Humphrey, 21 December 1966, White House Central Files, Ex Pl, box 1; Cabinet Minutes, 2 August 1967, Cabinet Papers, box 9, Johnson Library.

87. Jo Freeman, *At Berkeley in the Sixties: Education of an Activist, 1961–1965* (Indianapolis: Indiana University Press, 2004).

88. W. Marvin Matson, Memorandum for the President, 12 January 1967, and AFL-CIO, COPE, "1966 Elections," undated, White House Central Files, PL2, boxes 77 and 101, Johnson Library.

89. Matthew Dallek, *The Right Moment: Ronald Reagan's First Victory and the Decisive Turning Point in American Politics* (New York: Oxford University Press, 2004); Seth

Rosenfeld, "The Campus Files: The Governor's Race," *San Francisco Chronicle,* 9 June 2002, F6.

90. "Unsigned memorandum," 15 July 1967, White House Central Files, PL6, box 77, National Committee for an Effective Congress, "Underlying Cause of Democrats' Agony," 23 September 1968, Papers of Harry McPherson, box 30, Johnson Library.

91. United States Senate, *Hearings Before the Select Committee to Study Governmental Operations With Respect to Intelligence Activities,* 94th Congress, 1st Session, Vol. 6, 1975, 393.

92. Kathryn Olmstead, *Challenging the Secret Government: The Post-Watergate Investigation of the CIA and FBI* (Chapel Hill: University of North Carolina Press, 1996).

93. Notes, 12 September 1967, 22 March 1968, White House Central Files, Special Meeting Notes, box 2, Johnson Library.

94. Fred Panzer, "Memorandum to the President," 15 March 1968, White House Central Files, PL 2, box 77, Johnson Library.

95. "Political Degeneration," *National Council Letter,* 15 September 1968, Iowa Collection, reel 163.

96. William Baroody, "The Union of Thought and Power," typescript, 12 February 1967, Richard Ware to Baroody, 10 January 1967, Baroody Papers, box 96.

97. William F. Buckley Jr., "Say It Isn't So, Mr. President," *New York Times,* 1 August 1971, SM8.

98. Carter, *Politics of Rage,* 324–70; Michael Kazin, *The Populist Persuasion: An American History* (New York: Basic Books, 1995), 221–42; Thomas Bryne Edsall and Mary D. Edsall, *Chain Reaction: The Impact of Race, Rights, and Taxes on American Politics* (New York: Norton, 1991), 76–82.

99. "Where the Candidates Stand," *Statecraft* (October 1968), Judd Papers, box 213.

100. Neil McCaffrey to William Rusher, 2 October 1968, Rusher Papers, box 57; Kent Courtney, "National Review vs. Wallace," *The Independent American* (May–June 1967), 3, Iowa Collection, reel 62.

101. Eve Edstram, "Agnew Assails 'Spoiled Brats' Who Flout Law," *Washington Post,* 29 September 1968, 4; E. W. Kenworthy, "Nixon, in Texas, Sharpens His Attack," *New York Times,* 3 November 1968, 1; Larry Berman, *No Peace, No Honor: Nixon, Kissinger, and Betrayal in Vietnam* (New York: Free Press, 2002), 1.

Chapter 7

1. Gordon Brownell to Harry S. Dent, 29 October 1969; Dent, "Memorandum for the President: Report on Liberal GOP Leadership Conference," 23 March 1970, Papers of Harry S. Dent, boxes 3, 5, Cooper Library.

2. James J. Kilpatrick, "Needed: An Affirmative Conservatism," *Washington Star Syndicate,* 5 October 1969, F–2; "The Conservative Dilemma," *Battle Line* (August 1969), 4; Brent Bozell, "Letter to Yourselves," *Triumph* (March 1969), 11–12.

3. Pat Buchanan to Richard M. Nixon, undated 1969, White House Central Files, PL, box 47, Nixon Presidential Materials, National Archives and Records Administration, College Park, Maryland; Nicol C. Rae, *The Decline and Fall of the Liberal Republicans From 1952 to the Present* (New York: Oxford University Press, 1989), 163–218.

4. Elvis Presley to Richard M. Nixon, undated 1970, National Security Archives, George Washington University, Washington, DC; Jack Anderson, "Presley Gets Narcotics Bureau Badge," *Washington Post,* 27 January 1972, D23.

5. See notes, John D. Ehrlichman, 9 August 1970, 29 December 1969, 16 March 1970, 27 January 1972, 7 December 1972, Papers of John D. Ehrlichman, Hoover Institution, boxes 1, 3; Oval Office Conversation, 13 May 1971, Miller Center.

6. Peter Steinfels, *The Neoconservatives: The Men Who Are Changing America's Politics* (New York: Simon and Schuster, 1979); Gary J. Dorrien, *The Neoconservative Mind: Politics, Culture, and the War of Ideology* (Philadelphia: Temple University Press, 1993); Mark Gerson, *The Neoconservative Vision: From Cold War to the Culture Wars* (Lanham, MD: Madison Books, 1996); Murray Friedman, *The Neoconservative Revolution: Jewish Intellectuals and the Shaping of Public Policy* (New York: Cambridge University Press, 2005); Francis Fukuyama, *America at the Crossroads: Democracy, Power, and the Neoconservative Legacy* (New Haven: Yale University Press, 2006).

7. Irving Kristol, "What Is a Neo-Conservative," *Newsweek,* 19 January 1976, 17.

8. Leo Strauss, *What Is Political Philosophy? And Other Studies* (Glencoe, Illinois: Free Press, 1959), 55.

9. For debates on Strauss's thought, see Grant Havers, "Leo Strauss, Willmoore Kendall, and the Meaning of Conservatism," *Humanitas,* 18 (2005), 5–25.

10. Albert Wohlstetter and Henry Rowen, "Objectives of the United States Military Posture," *RM-273,* 1 May 1959.

11. Karl Hess, "Conservatism and Libertarianism," *Libertarian Outlook,* 4 June 1969, 2, Mundt Papers, reel 186; Murray Rothbard, *For a New Liberty: The Libertarian Manifesto* (New York: Macmillan, 1973); Ronald Reagan to David Keene, 8 October 1969; Keene to Reagan 30 October 1969, Rusher Papers, box 174.

12. James W. Harris, "Nolan: Innovator for Liberty," *The Liberator* (Summer 1996), 1.

13. William F. Buckley Jr., "The Conservative Reply," *New York Times,* 16 February 1971, 33; "Political Perspective," Ed Crane, "A Look at Conservatives' Plan," Donald Feder, "Conservatives Our Natural Allies?" *Libertarian Party News* September/October 1973, 5–6, May/June 1975, 2, January/February 1975, 2, 5, Iowa Collection, reel 67.

14. "Heroes and (Mainly) Villains in Congress," *Libertarian Party News* November/December 1973, 5, Iowa Collection, reel 67.

15. Americans for Constitutional Action, "Speech Kit," undated 1970, Papers of John N. "Happy" Camp, box 6, Carl Albert Center Archives, Norman, Oklahoma. Constituent letters are collected in Camp Papers, box 5 and Papers of Page H. Belcher, box 152, Albert Center.

16. H. R. Haldeman, "Confidential Memorandum," 25 July 1970, Dent Papers,

box 4; Dwight Chapin, "Memorandum for Mr. Ron Walker," 21 October 1970, White House Central Files, PL, box 46, Nixon Materials.

17. James H. Naughton, "Agnew Assails Protesters as 'Misfits' and Garbage," and "Agnew in Delaware," *New York Times,* 31 October 1970, 12, 15 October 1970, 52; Jules Witcover, "Agnew: The Step-by-Step Creation of a Conservative," *Los Angeles Times,* 10 May 1970, K1; Lyn Nofziger to H. R. Haldeman, 3 March 1970, Papers of Jeb Stuart Magruder, box 6, Hoover Institution; Robert Mason, *Richard Nixon and the Quest for a New Majority* (Chapel Hill: University of North Carolina Press, 2004), 86–112.

18. "'Southern Strategy' Fails to Brainwash Southern People," and "Agnew Sounds Like Wallace," *George C. Wallace Newsletter* (October 1970), Iowa Collection, reel 59.

19. John R. Brown to Harry Dent, 19 December 1969, Dent, "First Meeting of the Middle America Committee," 16 October 1969, Dent Papers, boxes 1, 2.

20. Tom Charles Huston to Harry Dent, 11 August 1970, Dent Papers, box 5; John Ehrlichman, "Memorandum for the President," 21 October 1970, Ehrlichman Papers, box 1.

21. "Key Issues of 1972," 31 July 1971, Charles Colson to John Mitchell, undated 1971, White House Central Files, PL, box 46; Richard Reeves, *President Nixon: Alone in the White House* (New York: Simon & Schuster, 2001), 467–68; John Ehrlichman to Richard M. Nixon, 21 October 1971, John Ehrlichman, notes, 16 November 1970, Nixon to Ehrlichman, 12 April 1972, Ehrlichman Papers, boxes 1, 2.

22. Reeves, *President Nixon,* 294, 637.

23. Nigel Bowles, *Nixon's Business: Authority and Power in Presidential Politics* (College Station: Texas A&M University Press, 2005), 117–250.

24. Oval Office Conversation, 8 June 1971, Miller Center; "Has the Economy Vindicated Meany?" *Chicago Tribune,* 28 May 1972, 5; U. S. Department of Treasury, *Report on Foreign Holdings of U. S. Long-Term Securities* (Washington, DC: Government Printing Office, 2002).

25. Oval Office Conversation, 3 August 1972, Miller Center.

26. "The Strategy of Collapse," *Battle Line* (July 1971), 1.

27. M. Stanton Evans, "Submerging The Republican Majority: The First 1,000 Days of Richard Nixon," undated, 1971, Rusher Papers, box 30.

28. Michael Djordjevich to William Rusher, 31 July 1971, Jerry Harkins, "Memorandum to William F. Buckley Jr. et al.," 4 November 1971, Rusher Papers, boxes 26, 167.

29. H. R. Haldeman, *The Haldeman Diaries: Inside the Nixon White House* (New York: G.P. Putnam's Sons, 1994), 332, 368.

30. David Greenberg in *Nixon's Shadow: The History of an Image* (New York: Norton, 2003), probes Nixon's multiple identities and the reluctance of liberals to claim his legacy.

31. Mason, *Richard Nixon,* 164–68.

32. Fred Malek to H. R. Haldeman, "Responsiveness Program," 17 March 1972 and "Responsiveness Program: Progress Report," 7 June 1972, Papers of Fred Malek, box 7, Hoover Library; Karl Rove, "Project Open Door," 25 March 1971, Camp Papers,

box 11; Stephen Green, "College GOP Directed to Win Mock Elections," *Washington Post*, 31 October 1972, 7; John Ehrlichman notes, 3 May 1971, Ehrlichman Papers, box 2.

33. George McGovern, "My Stand," Bill Kovach, "Wallace Calls McGovern Part of the Establishment," *New York Times*, 25 April 1972, 43, 34.

34. "One for the Books," *Libertarian Party News*, January/February 1973, 1, Iowa Collection, reel 67.

35. Coalition for a Democratic Majority, "Come Home, Democrats," undated 1973, Papers of Henry M. Jackson, box 35, University of Washington Library, Seattle, Washington.

36. Mason, *Richard Nixon*, 192–210; Edward Brooke to Thomas Shirley, 7 February 1974, Papers of Edward W. Brooke, box 640, Library of Congress.

37. Michael Djordjevich to William Rusher, 11 February 1974, Rusher Papers, box 25; Rusher to Djordjevich, 20 February 1974, Rusher Papers, box 25; Howard Phillips, "Conservatives Should Help Remove Nixon," Press Release, 30 July 1974, Magruder Papers, box 2.

38. Laurence Stern and William R. MacKaye, "Rev. Moon Called Messiah by Some, A Quack by Others," *Washington Post*, 15 February 1974, 1.

39. David R. Mayhew, "Divided Party Control: Does It Make a Difference?" *PS: Political Science and Politics* 24 (December 1991), 637–40.

40. Bill Brock, address, Young Republican Leadership Conference, 27 February 1975, Handwriting File, box 36, Gerald R. Ford Presidential Library, Ann Arbor, Michigan; Clare Boothe Luce, "An SOS for a 'Lost Constituency,'" *Wall Street Journal*, 9 June 1975, 12.

41. Julian E. Zelizer, *On Capitol Hill: The Struggle to Reform Congress and its Consequences, 1948–2000* (New York: Cambridge University Press, 2004), 156–205; Lee Atwater, undated memo, Lee Atwater Files, QA2904, Reagan Library.

42. Lewis Powell to Eugene B. Sydnor Jr., Chairman, Education Committee, U. S. Chamber of Commerce, 23 August 1971, Baroody Papers, box 60; Paul Pierson, "The Rise of Activist Government," in Paul Pierson and Theda Skocpol, *The Transformation of American Politics: Activist Government and the Rise of Conservatism* (Princeton, NJ: Princeton University Press, 2007), 19–38.

43. American Conservative Union, "A Conservative Agenda for Action," 1973, Rusher Papers, box 131.

44. Robert G. Kaiser and Ira Chinoy, "How Scaife's Money Powered a Movement," *Washington Post*, 2 May 1999, 1.

45. Robert Arnove, ed. *Philanthropy and Cultural Imperialism: The Foundations at Home and Abroad* (Boston: G. K. Hall, 1980), 1; Karyn Strickler, "The Do Nothing Strategy: An Expose of Progressive Politics," *Counterpunch*, 30 June 2003; Joan Roelofs, *Foundations and Public Policy: The Mask of Pluralism* (Albany: State University of New York Press, 2003); G. William Domhoff, *Who Rules America?: Power, Politics, and Social Change* (Boston: McGraw-Hill, 2006), 102.

46. Irving Kristol, "On Corporate Philanthropy," *Wall Street Journal*, 21 March 1977, 18; William E. Simon, *A Time for Truth* (New York: Reader's Digest Press, 1978), 230–31.

47. Nick Kotz, "King Midas of 'The New Right,'" *Atlantic* (November 1978), 52–61; Adam Clymer, "$10 Million Spent for Reagan in '80," *New York Times,* 29 November 1981, 33.

48. Kevin Phillips, "The 'New Right' in American Politics," King Features Syndicate, 7 July 1975; William Rusher to William F. Buckley Jr., 26 February 1979, Rusher Papers, boxes 141, 122; "For a Broader Constituency," *Washington Post,* 29 January 1978, 14. For a sociological analysis of the new right, see Jerome L. Himmelstein, *To the Right: The Transformation of American Conservatism* (Berkeley: University of California Press, 1990). In *The Rise of the Counter-establishment: From Conservative Ideology to Political Power* (New York: Times Books, 1986), journalist Sidney Blumenthal, later a member of president Bill Clinton's inner circle, traces the development of new right infrastructure.

49. Kevin Phillips, "The Economics of the New Conservative Populism," *American Political Report,* 4 April 1975; Pat Buchanan, Graduation Address, Rosemont College, 22 May 1971, Rusher Papers, box 13.

50. Howard Phillips to editor, *The Nation,* 26 January 1977, Rusher Papers, box 71; Paul Weyrich, "The Future of the Conservative Movement," undated 1988 memo, Charlotte DeMoss Files, Weyrich Folder, Ronald Reagan Presidential Library, Simi Valley, California.

51. Robert Hoy to William Rusher, 16 March 1977, Rusher Papers, box 41.

52. Edwin J. Feulner Jr., *Conservatives Stalk the House: The Republican Study Committee, 1970–1982* (Ottawa, IL: Green Hill Publishers, 1983); Kevin Phillips, "Special Survey: Ideological Stratification in the House of Representatives," *American Political Report,* 2 July 1973.

53. Dan Baum, *Citizen Coors: An American Dynasty* (New York: William Morrow, 2000), 102–105, 122–23.

54. "Conservative Political Action Committee Evokes Both Fear and Adoration," *New York Times,* 31 May 1981, 1; "Bigger Spenders Won 85 Pct. of Senate Contests," *Washington Post,* 16 November 1978, 11; "Helms Group Helps Conservative Cause," *New York Times,* 13 November 1979, B15; John S. Saloma III, *Ominous Politics: The New Conservative Labyrinth* (New York: Hill and Wang, 1984), 90.

55. Lee Edwards, *The Power of Ideas: The Heritage Foundation at 25 Years* (New York: Jameson, 1997), is a thorough, insider account. See also James Allen Smith, *The Idea Brokers: Think Tanks and the Rise of the New Policy Elite* (New York: Free Press, 1991), 200–203, 279–80.

56. "Dear Heritage Member," 14 February 1979, Rusher Papers, box 39; Smith, *The Idea Brokers,* 201.

57. Edward B. Jenkinson, *Censors in the Classroom: The Mind Benders* (Carbondale: Southern Illinois University Press, 1979), 17–27, 108–32, Alice Moore on page 18; Justin J. McHenry, "Silent, No More: The 1974 Kanawha County Textbook Controversy and the Rise of Conservatism in America," Ph.D. dissertation, West Virginia University, 2006.

58. Frank Edward Piasecki, "Norma and Mel Gabler: The Development and Causes of Their Involvement Concerning the Curricular Appropriateness of School Textbook Content (Texas)," Ph.D. Dissertation, North Texas State University, 1982;

Barbara Parker, "Your Schools May be the Battlefield in the Crusade Against 'Improper' Textbooks," *American School Board Journal* CLXVI (June 1979), 21–26.

59. George Hillocks Jr., "Books and Bombs: Ideological Conflict and the Schools—a Case Study of the Kanawha County Book Protest," *School Review* 86 (August 1978), 632–54; Jenkinson, *Censors in the Classroom,* 20.

60. Ben A. Franklin, "Textbook Dispute Has Many Causes," *New York Times,* 14 October 1974, 31.

61. Smith, *The Idea Brokers,* 176–84.

62. Richard Viguerie and David Franke, *America's Right Turn: How Conservatives Used New and Alternative Media to Take Power* (Chicago: Bonus Books, 2004), 167–71.

63. Gary E. Crawford, "Science as an Apologetic Tool for Biblical Literalists," *Science, Technology, and Human Values* 7 (Summer 1982), 90; Ronald L. Numbers, *The Creationists: The Evolution of Scientific Creationism* (New York: Knopf, 1992), 200–339; Henry Morris to William Rusher, 26 December 1981, Rusher Papers, box 148.

64. Lee Edwards to William Rusher, 18 February 1975, 8 February 1977, Rusher Papers, box 29; "Major Contributors to the Alternative Educational Foundation," 20 November 1980, R. Emmett Tyrrell to Rusher, 16 August 1978, Rusher Papers, boxes 69, 92.

65. Daniel Epstein, "The Anatomy of AIM," Freedom of Information Center Report No. 313, School of Journalism, University of Missouri at Columbia, Rusher Papers, box 6; "Media's Full-Time Watchdog," *Washington Post,* 21 October 1977, 19.

66. National Legal Center for the Public Interest, "A Proposal," undated 1975, Rusher Papers, box 92.

67. Leonard J. Theberge, president, National Legal Center, to William Rusher, 15 November 1975, Rusher Papers, box 92; Lee Edwards, *Bringing Justice to the People: The Story of the Freedom-Based Public Interest Law Movement* (Washington DC: Heritage Books, 2004); Jonathan Adler, "A Vast Right-Wing Conspiracy," *Legal Affairs* (May/June 2005), legalaffairs.org; "The Chamber's Public Interest Law Firm, *New York Times,* 31 March 1977, 75.

68. Karen O'Connor and Lee Epstein, "The Rise of Conservative Interest Group Litigation," *Journal of Politics* 45 (May 1983), 479–89; Pacific Legal Foundation, "Annual Report Winter 1974–75," Rusher Papers, box 92; Robert Lindsey, "Business Interests Fighting Back on Regulation," *New York Times,* 12 February 1978, 28.

69. "Minutes, Annual Meeting of American Council for World Freedom," 7 April 1973, Geoffrey Stewart-Smith to American Council for World Freedom, February 1974, Proposed Program, Seventh WACL Conference, Philbrick Papers, box 33.

70. "American Chilean Council Report," 28 March 1977, Philbrick Papers, box 64.

71. Critchlow, *Phyllis Schlafly,* 212–53; Ethel B. Jones, "ERA Voting: Labor Force Attachment, Marriage, and Religion," *Journal of Legal Studies* 12 (January 1983), 157–68.

72. Bill Curry, "15,000 Hold Opposition Rally," Sally Quinn, "The Pedestal Has Crashed," *Washington Post,* 20 November 1977, 1, 23 November 1977, B1.

73. "Singer Pledges Anti-Gay Drive Nationwide," *Washington Post,* 28 March

1977, D 12; Save Our Children, Inc., "The Civil Rights of Parents," Advertisement, *Miami Herald,* 21 March 1977, 3A.

74. Jim Peron, "The New Theocracy," *Libertarian Review* (September 1981), 30; David Brudnoy to William Rusher, 15 June 1977 and 20 August 1977, Rusher Papers, box 12.

75. Steven Roberts, "Rifle Group Viewed as Key to Gun Law," *New York Times,* 5 April 1981, 31; Joseph P. McGarrity and Daniel Sutter, "A Test of the Structure of PAC Contracts: An Analysis of House Gun Control Votes in the 1980s," *Southern Economic Journal* 67 (July 2000), 41–63; Emilie Raymond, *From My Cold, Dead Hands: Charlton Heston and American Politics* (Lexington, KY: University Press of Kentucky, 2006), 250–53.

76. "Guns: Should They Be in Christian Homes?," *Christianity Today,* 18 August 1989, 42–3.

77. James Davison Hunter, *Culture Wars: The Struggle to Define America* (New York: Basic Books, 1991), 176–96.

78. Anthony Lewis, "The Cold Warrior," *New York Times,* 8 March 1976, 24; James Reston, "Kissinger and Jackson," *New York Times* 12 March 1976, 32; Robert G. Kaufman, *Henry M. Jackson: A Life in Politics* (Seattle: University of Washington Press, 2000), 301–41, 407–408.

79. Paul Weyrich, "The New Triple A," *Washington Post,* 16 September 1974, 23; M. Stanton Evans to Ronald Reagan, undated, 1975, Rusher Papers, box 133.

80. William Rusher to Michael Djordjevich, 1 July 1975, William Lind to Rusher, 1 June 1975, Rusher Papers, boxes 26, 52.

81. Barry Goldwater to Gerald Ford, 7 May 1976, "Re: Sen. Barry Goldwater," 9 March 1976, President Ford Committee Records, Political Office, box C1, Ford Library; Goldwater to Ron Docksai, 30 June 1976, Goldwater to B.F. Harris, 18 June 1976, Rusher Papers, boxes 26, 35.

82. Stuart Spencer to Rogers C.B. Morton, 5 May 1976, Ford Committee Records, 1975–76, box B10.

83. "Schweiker!?" *National Review,* 20 August 1976, 880.

84. Stephen Issacs, "Newcomers' Hopes Are Scuttled at 3d-Party Session," *Washington Post,* 29 August 1976, 3.

85. Christopher Lydon, "American Party Completes Ticket," *New York Times,* 29 August 1976, 25; Neil Mehler, "Maddox Picks ex-Mayor for VP," *Chicago Tribune,* 29 August 1976; James J. Kilpatrick, "Conservative Orphans," *Washington Star Syndicate,* 4 September 1976, Rusher Papers, box 141.

86. Michael Barkun, *Religion and the Racist Right: The Origins of the Christian Identity Movement* (Chapel Hill: University of North Carolina Press, 1997); Catherine McNicol Stock, *Rural Radicals: Righteous Rage in the American Grain* (Ithaca, NY: Cornell University Press, 1996), 143–76; Gerald L. K. Smith, "What Is Christian Nationalism," undated pamphlet, Iowa Collection, reel 127.

87. Ed Crane, "A Look at Conservatives' Plan," *Libertarian Party News* (May–June 1975), 2, Iowa Collection, reel 67.

88. Michael Duval to Richard Cheney, 17 July 1976, Michael Raoul-Duval Files, box 27, Ford Library.

89. Jon Nordheimer, "Reagan Hints at Active Role in Shaping G.O.P. Future," *New York Times,* 5 November 1976, 16.

Chapter 8

1. Patrick Caddell, "Initial Working Paper on Political Strategy," 10 December 1976, Deputy Chief of Staff Landon Butler Collection, Jimmy Carter Presidential Library, Atlanta, Georgia.

2. Douglas F. Garthoff, "Estimating Soviet Military Intentions and Capabilities," in Gerald K. Haines and Robert E. Leggett, eds., *Watching the Bear: Essays on the CIA's Analysis of the Soviet Union* (Langley, VA: Center for the Study of Intelligence, 2003); Anne Hessing Cahn, *Killing Détente: The Right Attacks the CIA* (University Park: Pennsylvania State University Press, 1998); Milton R. Benjamin and Lloyd H. Norman, "Cassandra of the Cold War," *Newsweek,* 10 January 1977, 23; Norman Kempster, "Rumsfeld Gives Grim Assessment of Russ. Strength," *Los Angeles Times,* 19 January 1977, 20.

3. Minutes, National Security Council Meeting, 13 January 1977, NSC Meetings, Minutes, Ford Library; United States Senate, *Report of the Select Committee on Intelligence, Subcommittee on Collection, Production, and Quality, National Intelligence Estimates A-B Team Episode Concerning Soviet Strategic Capability and Objectives,* 95th Congress, 2nd Session, 1978.

4. Charles Tyroler II, ed., *Alerting America: The Papers of the Committee on the Present Danger* (Washington: Pergamon-Brassey's, 1984), 3; Jerry Sanders, *Peddlers of Crisis: The Committee on the Present Danger and the Politics of Containment* (Boston: South End Press, 1983); John L. Boies, *Buying for Armageddon: Business, Society, and Military Spending Since the Cuban Missile Crisis* (New Brunswick, NJ: Rutgers University Press, 1994), 45–74, 97–172.

5. "New Right: Many Times More Effective Now," *Congressional Quarterly,* 24 December 1977, 2649-53.

6. Phil Nicolaides, "The Selling of the Panama Canal Treaties," *Register,* 9 December 1977, 1; "Final Issues in the Panama Canal Giveaway," *Phyllis Schlafly Report* (April 1978), 1; "Anti-Treaty Groups," unsigned, undated Carter administration memo, George Moffett Collection, boxes 10, 11, Jimmy Carter Presidential Library, Atlanta, Georgia; Peter C. Stuart, "Panama Lobbying—$5 Against, $1 For," *Christian Science Monitor,* 10 March 1978, 1.

7. Morton Blackwell, "President Ronald Reagan," *Right Report,* 24 March 1978, Rusher Papers, box 11.

8. Susanna McBee, "Administration Rebuts Criticism of SALT," *Washington Post,* 6 November 1977, 2; Tyroler, *Alerting America,* 87; "Anti-Salt Lobbyists Outspend Pros 15 to 1," *Christian Science Monitor,* 23 March 1979, 1.

9. American Security Council, "The Balance of Strategic Forces," 25 June 1962, "Strategy for Victory in the Cold War," 12 August 1964, "Counter-Deterrence and the ABM," 21 August 1967, Philbrick Papers, box 38.

10. Morton Mintz, "Republicans Far Ahead in Harvesting Cash," *Washington Post,* 22 February 1981, 24; Andrew E. Busch, *Reagan's Victory: The Presidential Election of 1980 and the Rise of the Right* (Lawrence: Univrsity of Kansas Press, 2005), 22–134.

11. Mark A. Smith, *Right Talk: How Conservatives Transformed the Great Society into the Economic Society* (Princeton, NJ: Princeton University Press, 2007), 95–150.

12. Don Clawson and Alan Neustadtl, "Interlocks, PACS, and Corporate Conservatism," *American Journal of Sociology* 94 (January 1989), 749–73.

13. U. S. Chamber of Commerce, Minutes, Committee on Business Overview, 21 November 1975, Baroody Papers, box 86; Steven Rattner, "Big Industry Gun Aims at the Hill," *New York Times,* 7 March 1976, F3; Nick Paretsky, "Policy-Planning Organizations and Capitalist Support for Industrial Policy, 1970–1984," Ph.D. dissertation, University of Missouri-Columbia, 2003, 469–72; S. Prakash Sethi, *Advocacy Advertising and Large Corporations* (Lexington, MA: Lexington Books, 1977), 8, 115–78; David Vogel, *Fluctuating Fortunes: The Political Power of Business in America* (New York: Basic Books, 1989), 113-239; Shapiro, Address, 15 April 1977, Name Files, Carter Library.

14. "New Corporate Clout in the Capital," *Time,* 4 July 1977, 63; Eric Posner, "The Political Economy of the Bankruptcy Reform Act of 1978," *Michigan Law Review* 96 (October 1997), 47–126.

15. Mark S. Mizruchi, *The Structure of Corporate Political Action: Interfirm Relations and Their Consequences* (Cambridge, MA: Harvard University Press, 1992), 117–57; Thomas Byrne Edsall, *The New Politics of Inequality* (New York: Norton, 1984), 14, 107–40; Patrick J. Akard, "Corporate Mobilization and Political Power: The Transformation of U.S. Economic Policy in the 1970s," *American Sociological Review* 57 (October 1992), 597–615.

16. J. Craig Jenkins, Kevin T. Leicht, and Heather Wendt, "Class Forces, Political Institutions, and State Intervention: Subnational Economic Development Policy in the United States, 1971–1990," *American Journal of Sociology* 111 (January 2006), 1122–80; Tom Wicker, "A 'New Revolution,'" *New York Times,* 9 June 1978, 27; Robert O. Self, "Prelude to the Tax Revolt: The Politics of the 'Tax Dollar' in Postwar California," in Kevin Kruse and Thomas Sugrue, eds., *The New Suburban History* (Chicago: University of Chicago Press, 2006), 144–60.

17. Leonard Silk, "Economic Scene," *New York Times,* 29 February 1980, D2; John C. White, Chair, DNC, "Dear Congressman," 7 August 1978, White House Central Files, PL, box 1, Carter Library.

18. Merrill Brown, "Miller, Volcker Cheery About U.S. Outlook," *Washington Post,* 13 October 1979, D9; Clayton Fritchey, "Economic High Priest," *Washington Post,* 22 October 1979, 23.

19. "Fellowship Foundation Contributors," undated 1977, and "Leadership (Fellowship) Council Chart," undated, Fellowship Foundation Papers, boxes 574, 381.

20. Gary Wills, "'Born Again' Politics," *New York Times,* 1 August 1976, 159; Sara Diamond, *Roads to Dominion: Right-Wing Movements and Political Power in the United States* (New York: Guilford Press, 1995), 228–73; Andrew R. Flint and Joy Porter, "Jimmy Carter: The Re-emergence of Faith-Based Politics and the Abortion Rights

Issue," *Presidential Studies Quarterly* 35 (March 2005), 28–51. Retrospectively, Paul Weyrich and Richard Viguerie said that the attack on Christian schools led to the rise of the 1970s Christian right. See Robert Freedman, "The Religious Right and the Carter Administration," *Historical Journal* 48 (March 2005), 231–60. However, Carter's religious adviser said, "Two issues attract the most attention: abortion and prayer in the public schools." Bob Mattox to Jody Powell, "Religious Aspects of the Campaign," undated, Ray Jenkins Collection, box 3, Carter Library.

21. George Vecsey, "Militant Television Preachers," *New York Times,* 21 January 1980, 21.

22. Kenneth A. Briggs, "The Electronic Church," *New York Times,* 10 February 1980, E10; David Snowball, *Continuity and Change in the Rhetoric of the Moral Majority* (New York: Praeger, 1991), 67–71; Susan Friend Harding, *The Book of Jerry Falwell: Fundamentalist Language and Politics* (Princeton, NJ: Princeton University Press, 2000), 3–29.

23. Howell Raines, "Reagan Backs Evangelicals in Their Political Action," *New York Times,* 23 August 1980, 8; Anthony Lewis, "Political Religion," *New York Times,* 25 September 1980, 27; William Martin, *With God on Our Side: The Rise of the Religious Right in America* (New York: Broadway Books, 1996), 214–18. For other recent overviews on the Christian right from various perspectives, see Michael Lienesch, *Redeeming America: Piety and Politics in the New Christian Right* (Chapel Hill: University of North Carolina Press, 1993); Kenneth Heineman, *God is a Conservative: Religion, Politics, and Morality in Contemporary America,* new ed. (New York: New York University Press, 2005); John C. Green, *The Faith Factor: How Religion Influences American Elections* (Westport, CT: Praeger, 2007); Diamond, *Roads to Dominion;* Clyde Wilcox and Carin Larson, *Onward Christian Soldiers: The Religious Right in American Politics,* 3rd ed. (Boulder, CO: Westview, 2006).

24. William Safire, "The Ersatz Agnew," *New York Times,* 25 October 1984, 27; Tom Wicker, "Ronald Reagan's Magic," *New York Times,* 13 June 1978, 19.

25. Dan Gilgoff, *The Jesus Machine: How James Dobson, Focus on the Family, and Evangelical America Are Winning the Culture War* (New York: St. Martin's, 2007), 18–42.

26. George C. Higgins, Catholic University of America, "Statement at Press Conference on Religious Political Action," 6 October 1980, White House Central Files, PL2, Carter Library; Anthony Lewis, "Religion and Politics," *New York Times,* 17 September 1980, 31; George B. Merry, "Liberals Top Bay State Primaries," *Christian Science Monitor,* 18 September 1980, 6.

27. Michael Lienesch, "Right-Wing Religion: Christian Conservatism as a Political Movement," *Political Science Quarterly* 97 (Autumn 1982), 423–24; Karlyn Barker, "Christian Broadcaster Dedicates University in Va.," *Washington Post,* 2 October 1980, C20; Kenneth A. Briggs, "Evangelicals Hear Plea: Politics Now," *New York Times,* 24 August 1980, 33.

28. Frances FitzGerald, *Cities on a Hill: A Journey Through Contemporary American Cultures* (New York: Simon and Schuster, 1986), 121-201, Falwell on page 167.

29. Francis A. Schaeffer and Lane T. Dennis, *The Complete Works of Francis A. Schaeffer: A Christian World View,* 5 vols. (Westchester, IL: Crossway Books, 1982); Kerry

N. Jacoby, *Souls, Bodies, Spirits: The Drive to Abolish Abortion Since 1973* (Westport, CT: Praeger, 1998), 102–103; Michael Standaert, *Skipping Towards Armageddon: The Politics and Propaganda of the Left Behind Novels and the LaHaye Empire* (Brooklyn, NY: Soft Skull Press, 2006).

30. Gary North, "The Eschatological Crisis of the Moral Majority," *Christian Reconstruction* (January/February 1981), 1–2; J. Ligon Duncan III, "Moses' Law for Modern Government: The Intellectual and Sociological Origins of the Christian Reconstructionist Movement," paper presented at the annual convention of the Social Science History Association, October 1994, online at www.reformed.org/ethics/index.html?mainframe=/ethics/ligon_duncan_critique.html.

31. Joseph Tamney and Stephen Johnson, "Explaining Support for the Moral Majority," *Sociological Forum* 3 (Spring 1988), 234-55.

32. Spencer Rich, "Band of Conservatives Walks Out of Conference on Families," *Washington Post,* 7 June 1980, 5; *700 Club* transcript, 6 November 1980, "Robertson" folder, WHCF—Name Files, Carter Library; Freedman, "The Religious Right," 255.

33. Stuart Eizenstat, "The Anderson Record," 19 May 1980, White House Central Files, PL2, Carter Library.

34. Haynes Johnson, "Despite Delegates' Loyalty to Reagan, He Still Worries Them," *Washington Post,* 12 July 1980, 1; James W. Fuller/Peter D. Hanaford, "Establishment of a Business Advisory Panel," 20 May 1980, Fuller to Donald Regan, 28 July 1980, Papers of Donald T. Regan, box 222, Library of Congress.

35. Gerald L. Rafshoon, "1980 General Election Themes," 3 July 1980, Hamilton Jordan, "Planning Memorandum," undated 1980, with Robert S. Strauss handwritten marginal note, Susan Clough Collection, boxes 24 and 37; Pat Caddell, "Themes," undated, Hamilton Jordan Collection, box 80, Carter Library.

36. Douglas E. Kneeland, "Reagan and Carter Attack Each Other Over the Hostages," *New York Times,* 22 October 1980, 1.

37. Edsall and Edsall, *Chain Reaction,* 142.

38. William Rusher to Michael Djordjevich, 19 January 1981, Rusher Papers, box 26.

39. OMB, "Support for the President's Economic Program in the House of Representatives," March, 1982, "In the Oval Office after the tax cut vote," unsigned, undated typescript, David Gergen Files, OA10529, OA10523, Reagan Library.

40. James Jenkins to Edwin Meese, 19 November 1981, Gergen Files, OA10523.

41. Evans, *The Education of Ronald Reagan,* 204–205.

42. Benjamin Wattenberg, "The New Moment: How Ronald Reagan Ratified LBJ's Great Society and Moved on to Other Important Items," *Public Opinion* (December/January 1982), 5.

43. "Statement of Conservative Leaders," 21 January 1982; Rollins to James A. Baker III, undated 1982, Lee Atwater Files, OA2903.

44. Nicholas Laham, *The Reagan Presidency and the Politics of Race: In Pursuit of Colorblind Justice and Limited Government* (Westport, CT: Praeger, 1998) From 1960 to 1980, the male two-party vote for the Democratic presidential candidate plunged by 13 percentage points, whereas female support remained unchanged, according

to the National Election Study. On the Democrat Party's problem with men, see David Paul Kuhn, *The Neglected Voter: White Men and the Democratic Dilemma* (New York: Macmillan, 2007).

45. Frank Harold Wilson, "Neoconservatives, Black Conservatives, and the Retreat From Social Justice," in Gayle Tate and Lewis A. Patterson, eds., *Dimensions of Black Conservatism in the U.S.: Made in America* (New York: Palgrave, 2002), 179–96; Clarence Thomas, "No Room at the Inn," *Policy Review* (Fall 1991), 76.

46. William Rusher to William F. Buckley Jr., 28 July 1982, Rusher Papers, box 122.

47. Senator William Armstrong et al. to William Rusher, 9 April 1979, Rusher Papers, box 26.

48. CNP, *Directory, 1984–1985,* Rusher Papers, box 149. The directory includes member biographies.

49. William Rusher to Woody Jenkins, 12 September 1983; Tom Ellis to CNP members, undated 1983; Jenkins to CNP members, 8 July 1981, Rusher Papers, box 149.

50. "Grants to Council on National Policy," Media Transparency, www.media transparency.org/recipientgrants.php?recipientID=2119; Jack Wilson to William Rusher, 28 July 1986, Rusher Papers, boxes 148, 149.

51. Marvin Liebman to William F. Buckley Jr., 13 September 1983, Rusher Papers, box 174.

52. Amy Moritz to William F. Buckley Jr., 28 June 1984, Rusher Papers, box 174; Jack Abramoff to Willam Rusher, 9 February 1983, 31 May 1983, Rusher Papers, box 20.

53. "Judge Scalia's Cheerleaders," *New York Times,* 23 July 1986, B6; Jerry M. Landay, "The Conservative Cabal That's Transforming American Law," *Washington Monthly* (March 2000), 19–23; Terry Carter, "The In Crowd," *ABA Journal* 87 (Sept 2001), 46–51; Steven M. Teles, "Conservative Mobilization Against Entrenched Liberalism," in Pierson and Skocpol, *The Transformation of American Politics,* 181–83.

54. Steven Teles, "Conservative Mobilization," 183–86; David Friedman, *Law's Order: What Economics Has to Do With Law and Why It Matters* (Princeton, NJ: Princeton University Press, 2000).

55. Newt Gingrich to James A. Baker III, 25 February 1982, Rusher Papers, box 34; Helen Dewar, "Republicans Wage Verbal Civil War," *Washington Post,* 19 November 1984, 1.

56. Newt and Marianne Gingrich, "Key Steps in Developing a Survivable United States," undated typescript, 1982, Rusher Papers, box 34.

57. Newt Gingrich, "Conservative Opportunity Society Brings Old-Time Hope," *Atlanta Journal Constitution,* 25 April 1983, 13–A; William Raspberry, "'Inventing' Black Leaders," *Washington Post,* 21 December 1983, 27; Newt Gingrich, *Window of Opportunity: A Blueprint for the Future* (New York: Tom Doherty Associates, 1984).

58. Keith B. Richburg, "Washington Awash in Think Tanks," *Washington Post,* 7 December 1984, 25.

59. Richard Bernstein, "Magazine Dispute Reflects Rift on U. S. Right," *New York Times,* 16 May 1989, 1.

60. Joel Brinkley, "Helms and Rightists," *New York Times,* 1 August 1984, 20; Joanne Omang, "D'Aubuisson Honored by Conservatives at Capitol Hill Dinner," *Washington Post,* 5 December 1984, 25.

61. Michael Isikoff, "Moon Group Financing Anti-Communist Lobby," *Washington Post,* 14 September 1984, 1; Isikoff, "Church Spends Millions on Its Image," *Washington Post,* 17 September 1984, 1.

62. Isikoff, "Church Spends Millions;" William Rusher to David Michael Staton, 7 April 1982, Rusher Papers, box 172; Andrew Ferguson, "Can Buy Me Love: The Mooning of Conservative Washington," *American Spectator* (September 1987), 23.

63. Paul Craig Roberts, "Will Reaganomics Unravel?" typescript, 23 October 1981, Gergen Files, OA10533, Reagan Library.

64. James Jones, "Dear Bobbi," 17 March 1982, Gergen Files, OA 10533, Reagan Library; Paul Taylor, "Conservatives Offer Their Own Budget," *Washington Post,* 17 April 1982, 8.

65. Craig Fuller, "Scheduling Objectives and Priorities," 4 May 1982; Gary Bauer to Edwin L. Harper, 18 June 1982, President of the United States, FG001; Wirthlin to Edwin Messe III, 1 April 1982, Papers of Richard S. Williamson, A7318; Gary Jarmin to Lyn Nofziger and Ed Rollins, 20 September 1983; Don Shea to Frank Fahrenkopf, 26 April 1983, *Christian Voice* files, Reagan Library; Aaron Haberman, "Into the Wilderness: Ronald Reagan, Bob Jones University, and the Political Education of the Christian Right," *Historian* 67 (Summer 2005), 234–53.

66. David Gergen to Jim Baker, 8 March 1982; Lee Atwater to Craig Fuller, 6 May 1982, FG001, Reagan Library.

67. Lyn Nofziger to Cabinet Members, 31 December 1981, Regan Papers, box 186.

68. Robert C. Holland to Martin Feldstein, 6 January 1984, Council of Economic Advisers files, OA10514, Reagan Library.

69. Jeane J. Kirkpatrick, "Dictatorships and Double Standards," *Commentary* 68 (November 1979), 34–45.

70. *National Security Directives of the Reagan and Bush Administrations: The Declassified History of U.S. Political and Military Policy, 1981–1991* (Boulder, CO: Westview, 1995).

71. Paul Taylor, "Rightist Group Says Reagan Has Strayed," *Washington Post,* 20 January 1983, 8; Ronald Reagan Address, 8 March 1983, online at www.archives.gov/federal-register/publications/presidential-papers.html.

72. Ronald Reagan, Address, 23 March 1983, Ibid. Frances Fitzgerald, *Way Out There in the Blue: Reagan, Star Wars, and the End of the Cold War* (New York: Simon and Schuster, 2000), 114–264.

73. Bob Greene quoted in Lawrence Grossberg, "Rockin' with Reagan, or the Mainstreaming of Postmodernity," *Cultural Critique* 10 (Autumn 1988) 148–49.

74. Morton Blackwell, "Reviving the Winning Coalition: The Strategy for Conservatives," 17 January 1983, Rusher Papers, box 12.

75. Faith Whittlesey to James A. Baker III, et al., "The Fundamentalist and Evangelical Groups" and "Tuition Tax Credits, School Prayer, and Pornography," 11 October 1983, Faith Ryan Whittlesey Files, box 8F, Reagan Library.

76. Anthony Dolan, "Memorandum for Senator Paul Laxalt," 25 July 1984, Rusher Papers, box 26.

77. Jim Lake to James Baker, 8 March 1984, James A. Baker III Files, Series I, box 9, Reagan Library. The "Keys" prediction system predicted the Reagan victory in April of 1982. See Allan J. Lichtman, "How to Bet in '84," *Washingtonian Magazine*, April 1982, 147–49.

78. Reagan's rise to power followed a similar turn to the right in Great Britain under Margaret Thatcher. In an effort to establish cross-national commonalities, some scholars have tangled the terminology of politics by dubbing Reagan's program not as conservative but "neoliberal." This terminology locates conservatives within a nineteenth-century tradition that sharply differs from modern American conservatism in its fidelity to free markets rather than private enterprise and its indifference to cultural and religious values. See, for example, David Harvey, *A Brief History of Neoliberalism* (New York: Oxford University Press, 2005).

Chapter 9

1. Edwin J. Feulner, "Where the Reagan Revolution Should Go From Here," *Christian Science Monitor,* 29 September 1988, 11; Richard Viguerie, "What Reagan Revolution?" *Washington Post,* 21 August 1988, C2.

2. For positive narratives on the Reagan legacy from conservatives, see Dinesh D'Souza, *Ronald Reagan: How an Ordinary Man Became an Extraordinary Leader* (New York: Touchstone, 1997); Peter F. Schweiker, *Reagan's War: The Epic Story of His Forty-Year Struggle and Final Triumph Over Communism* (New York: Doubleday, 2003).

3. Larry Reynolds, "Tax Reform: Why Business Will For Over Another $120 Billion," *Management Review* (January 1987), 13.

4. Arthur Schlesinger Jr., "For Democrats, Me-Too Reaganism Will Spell Disaster," *New York Times,* 6 July 1986, E13.

5. "Paul Weyrich to Republican Officials," 13 November 1986, Rusher Papers, box 96.

6. U. S. Senate, Select Committee on Secret Military Assistance to Iran and the Nicaraguan Opposition, and U. S. House of Representatives, Select Committee to Investigate Covert Arms Transactions with Iran, *Joint Hearings: Testimony of Oliver L. North,* 100th Congress, 1st Session, 1987, 317–18.

7. *Report of the Congressional Committees Investigating the Iran-Contra Affair,* Ibid., 85–103; United States Department of State, Office of Inspector General, *Audit Report, No. 7PP–008, Special Inquiry into the Department's Contacts with International Business Communications and Its Principles,* July 1987, 2, Exhibit B, 12; Comptroller General of the United States to Jack Brooks and Dante B. Fascell, 30 September 1987, 7, National Security Archives; "1987 Tape Suggests Reagan Solicitation," *New York Times,* 10 October 1997, 21.

8. Democratic Congressional Campaign Committee, *Federal Election Commission*

Complaint, undated, 1987, Documentary Appendix, NEPL, Fund-raisers Meeting—May 23, 1986, National Security Archives.

9. Michael Novak, "The Case Against Liberation Theology," *New York Times Magazine,* 21 October 1984, SM51.

10. Comptroller General to Brooks and Fascell, 5–6; Sidney Blumenthal, "Staff Shakeup Hits Conservative Group," *Washington Post,* 27 July 1985, 10.

11. Dele Olojede and Timothy Phelps, "South Africa's Front for Apartheid," *Newsday,* 16 July 1995, 12; Nina J. Easton, *Gang of Five: Leaders at the Center of the Conservative Ascendancy* (New York: Simon and Schuster, 2000), 161–76, 259–82.

12. Richard Sobel, "Contra Aid Fundamentals: Exploring the Intricacies and the Issues," *Political Science Quarterly* 110 (Summer 1995), 287–306.

13. George Schultz, meeting notes, 24 November 1986, Regan Papers, box 208.

14. Richard M. Nixon to Ronald Reagan, 13 August 1987, White House Central Files, PR00502, Reagan Library.

15. The Free Congress Foundation, "Memorandum: Center for Conservative Governance," undated 1988, Mari Maseng Files, Weyrich Folder, OA19354, Reagan Library.

16. "Meeting With Dr. Jerry Falwell," Presidential Briefing Papers, Chronological File, 14 March 1983, Reagan Library; Adam Clymer, "Religiously-Oriented Right-Wing Group Plans Drive," *New York Times,* 12 April 1981, 26; Jeffrey K. Hadden, et al., *Why Jerry Falwell Killed the Moral Majority* (Bowling Green, OH: Bowling Green University Popular Press, 1987), 101–15; Frank Rich, "The Reverend Falwell's Heavenly Timing," *New York Times,* 20 May 2007, 13.

17. Institute for Cultural Conservativism, Free Congress Research and Education Foundation, *Cultural Conservatism: Toward a New National Agenda* (Lanham, MD: UPA, 1987); E. J. Dionne, Jr., "A Conservative Call for Compassion," *New York Times,* 30 November 1987, B12.

18. U.S. Department of Education, National Center for Education Statistics, *Private Schools Survey, 1989–1990,* 3, and *Private Schools Survey, 1999–2000,* 5, 6; Heather Hendershot, *Shaking the World for Jesus: Media and Conservative Evangelical Culture* (Chicago: University of Chicago Press, 2004), 17–86; Amy DeRogatis, "What Would Jesus Do? Sexuality and Salvation in Protestant Evangelical Sex Manuals, 1950s to the Present," *Church History* 74 (March 2005), 97–137.

19. Razelle Frankl, "Transformation of Televangelism: Repackaging Christian Family Values," in Linda Kintz and Julia Lesage, eds., *Media, Culture, and the Religious Right* (Minneapolis: University of Minnesota Press, 1998), 163–90.

20. Rush Limbaugh, "Voice of America," *Policy Review* 70 (Fall 1994), 4–10; Philip M. Seib, *Rush Hour: Talk Radio, Politics, and the Rise of Rush Limbaugh* (Fort Worth, TX: Summit, 1993); David C. Barker, "Rushed Decisions: Political Talk Radio and Vote Choice, 1994–1996," *Journal of Politics* 61 (May 1999), 527–39; David Barker and Kathleen Knight, "Political Talk Radio and Public Opinion," *Public Opinion Quarterly* 64 (Summer 2000), 149–70.

21. Christopher Manion, "Beyond Government: The Future of Christian Virtue," *The Heritage Lectures,* 388, 13 May 1992.

22. "Summit Notes," 20 November 1985, Regan Papers, box 215; Soviet-American Summit, Reykjavik, October 11–12, 1986, "RECORD of talks in the working group on military issues," Russian transcript, National Security Archive, George Washington University; Secretary of Defense, "Post-Reykjavik Activities," 5 December 1986, National Security Council Files, Reagan Library; Jim Hoagland, "Political Performances Outshine Humdrum Diplomacy," *Washington Post,* 2 June 1988, 23.

23. Michael Johns, untitled, *Washington Times,* 7 August 1987; "Memorandum: Leadership Coalition for Freedom Through Truth," 14 August 1987, Tom Ellis to Ronald Reagan, 25 March 1987, Rusher Papers, box 153.

24. Don Oberdorfer and Helen Dewar, "Conservative GOP Opposition Portends Hard Ratification Fight," David Hoffman, "Reagan Lashes Conservative Foes of Treaty," *Washington Post,* 25 November 1987, 1, 4 December 1987, 1.

25. Richard M. Nixon to Donald Regan, 28 January 1985, Regan Papers, box 215.

26. "A Survey of Conservative Leaders," *Conservative Digest* (October 1983), 7–8.

27. Thomas B. Edsall, "Why Bush Accentuates the Negative," *Washington Post,* 2 October 1988, C1.

28. For examples of liberal critiques see the essays in Kyle Longley et al., *Deconstructing Reagan: Conservative Mythology and America's Fortieth President* (Armonk, NY: M. E. Sharpe, 2007).

29. "Meeting with Conservative Leaders," and Doug Wead to John Sununu, 1 March 1989, White House Office of Public Liaison, GSOF82, George Bush Presidential Library, College Station, Texas.

30. John Robert Greene, *The Presidency of George Bush* (Lawrence: University Press of Kansas, 2000), 89–108; "Transcripts from the Malta Summit, 2–3 December 1989," Cold War International History Project, 891202.

31. John O'Sullivan, *The President, the Pope, and the Prime Minister: Three Who Changed the World* (Washington, DC: Regnery, 2006).

32. Daniel J. Mitchell, "Bush's Deplorable Flip-Flop on Taxes," Heritage Foundation, *Executive Memorandum,* 271, 28 June 1990, Papers of Mickey Edwards, box 93, Carl Albert Center; George H. W. Bush, "Remarks to Business Leaders on the Federal Budget Agreement," 2 October 1990, online at www.archives.gov/federal-register/publications/presidential-papers.html.

33. Michael Kranish, "Root of Bush Defeat," *Boston Globe,* 6 November 1990, 1.

34. Richard Viguerie and Steve Allen, "Bush Can Do Little to Stop Revolt of Conservatives," *St. Petersburg Times,* 19 December 1990, 19; David Broder, "Why Are Republicans Fighting Like Democrats?" *Washington Post,* 2 December 1990, C1.

35. George Will, "Liberals' Reliance on Courts Made Thomas a Threat," *St. Petersburg Times,* 17 October 1991, 18.

36. Charles Krauthammer, "Good Morning, Vietnam: The Syndrome Returns," *Washington Post,* 19 April 1991, 23; Christian Alfonsi, *Circle in the Sand: Why We Went Back to Iraq* (New York: Doubleday, 2006), an analysis of decision-making within the George H. W. Bush administration.

37. Lawrence Eagleburger, "Charting the Course: U. S. Foreign Policy in a Time of Transition," U. S. Department of State, *Dispatch,* 11 January 1993; Patrick E. Tyler, "U.S. Strategy Plan Calls For Insuring No Rivals Develop," *New York Times,* 8 March 1992, 1; David Armstrong, "Dick Cheney's Song of America," *Harper's* (October 2002), 76–83; Jim Mann, *The Rise of the Vulcans: The History of Bush's War Cabinet* (New York: Viking, 2004), 209–15; Tyler, "Pentagon Drops Goal of Blocking New Superpowers," *New York Times,* 24 May 1992, 1.

38. Robin Toner, "Thinkers on the Right," *New York Times,* 22 November 1994, B7.

39. Corwin Smidt, "Evangelicals Within Contemporary American Politics: Differentiating Between Fundamentalist and Non-Fundamentalist Evangelicals," *Western Political Quarterly* 41 (September 1988), 601–20.

40. John C. Green and Nathan S. Bigelow, "The Christian Right Goes to Washington: Social Movement Resources and the Legislative Process," in Paul S. Herrnson et al., eds., *The Interest Group Connection: Electioneering, Lobbying, and Policymaking in Washington* (Washington DC: CQ Press, 2005), 189–211; Douglas Usher, "Strategy, Rules and Participation: Issue Activists in Republican National Conventional Delegations, 1976–1996," *Political Research Quarterly* 53 (December 2000), 887–903.

41. Kimberly H. Conger and John C. Green, "Spreading Out and Digging in: Christian Conservatives and State Republican Parties," *Campaigns and Elections* (February 2002), 58–65.

42. Jon A. Shields, "Between Passion and Deliberation: The Christian Right and Democratic Ideals," *Political Science Quarterly* 122 (Spring 2007), 89–113; Ken Sidey, "Open Season for Christians?" *Christianity Today,* 23 April 1990, 34–36; Pat Robertson, *The Turning Tide: The Fall of Liberalism and the Rise of Common Sense* (Dallas: Word, 1993), 144–45.

43. Seth Mydans, "Evangelicals Gain with Covert Candidates," *New York Times* 27 October 1992, 1; James Carney, "The Rise and Fall of Ralph Reed, *Time,* 24 July 2006, 52–53; Melissa M. Deckman, *School Board Battles: The Christian Right in Local Politics* (Washington, DC: Georgetown University Press, 2004); Donald R. Songer and Susan J. Tabrizi, "The Religious Right in Court: The Decision-Making of Christian Evangelicals in State Supreme Courts," *Journal of Politics* 61 (May 1999), 507–26.

44. Ralph Reed, "Casting a Wider Net," *Policy Review* 65 (Summer 1993), 31.

45. "Bundy Interview Inspires Tape Burning," *Washington Post,* 27 January 1989, C7.

46. Peter Steinfels, "No Church, No Ministry, No Pulpit, He Is Called Religious Right's Star," *New York Times,* 5 June 1990, 22; Gilgoff, *The Jesus Machine,* xv, 27–29, 44–46.

47. Randall Balmer, *Mine Eyes Have Seen the Glory: A Journey into the Evangelical Subculture in America* (New York: Oxford University Press, 1989), 120–21.

48. Nancy T. Ammerman, "Southern Baptists and the New Christian Right," *Review of Religious Research* 32 (March, 1991); Hanna Rosin, "Southern Baptists Vote to Ban Female Pastors," *Washington Post,* 15 June 2000, 1.

49. David E. Campbell and J. Quin Monson, "Following the Leader: Mormon

Voting on Ballot Propositions," American Democracy Working Papers at Notre Dame University, 2002, online at http://americandemocracy.nd.edu/working_papers/files/following_the_leader.pdf.

50. Jeffrey Sharlet, "Jesus Plus Nothing: Undercover Among America's Secret Theocrats," *Harper's Magazine* (March 2003), 53–64.

51. David S. Gutterman, *Prophetic Politics: Christian Social Movements and American Democracy* (Ithaca, NY: Cornell University Press, 2005), 94–128.

52. "Key Conservative Plans Speech Critical of Bush," *Wall Street Journal,* 23 January 1992, 18.

53. Dan Goodgame and Karen Tumulty, "Tripped up by History," *Time,* 23 December 2002, 22.

54. David Broder, "Coherent Message Elusive; At Halftime GOP Hunts for Theme," *Washington Post,* 19 August 1992, 1.

55. Walter V. Robinson, "On the Right, Direction is Toward Perot," *Boston Globe,* 22 June 1992, 1; Laura Randall, "Talk Radio," *Christian Science Monitor,* 25 June 1992, 14.

56. E. J. Dionne Jr., "A Philosophical Bush Sets Second-Term Agenda," *Washington Post,* 27 October 1992, 14.

57. "Securing the Future: A Blueprint for Governing America," 14–16 March 1991, Edwards Papers, box 167; "A Manifesto for Change in the House of Representatives," 30 January 1992, Papers of Robert H. Michel, Dirksen Center, box 14.

58. Robin Toner, "The Transition: The Republicans; Looking to the Future, Party Sifts Through Past," *New York Times,* 11 November 1992, 22; John Dillin, "GOP Peers Into Post-Election Looking Glass," *Christian Science Monitor,* 12 November 1992, 1.

59. R. Emmett Tyrrell, *The Conservative Crack-up* (New York: Simon and Schuster, 1992), 293–94.

60. Byron York, "The Life and Death of the American Spectator," *Atlantic Monthly* (November, 2001), 99; "Christian Right Sees Clinton as Top Target," *National Catholic Reporter,* 4 March 1994, 6.

61. "Dick Armey to Republicans," 1 November 1993, Papers of Richard Armey, Albert Center, box 2.

62. Jeanne Cummings, "Strategist Urges Republicans to Kill Democrats' Efforts at Health Reform," 8 December 1993, *Atlanta Journal and Constitution,* B4.

63. Cathie Jo Martin, "Mandating Social Change: The Business Struggle Over National Health Reform," *Governance* 10 (October 1997), 397–428.

64. On the health care controversy and the opposition tactics see Theda Skocpol, *Boomerang: Clinton's Health Security Effort and the Turn Against Government* (New York: W. W. Norton., 1996); Jill Quadango, *One Nation Uninsured: Why the U.S. Has No National Health Insurance* (New York: Oxford University Press, 2005).

65. Robert E. Moffitt, "A Guide to the Clinton Health Plan," *Heritage Foundation Talking Points,* 19 November 1993; "Radio Truth-Tellers Tanking Clinton's Unhealthy Rx," *Forbes,* 20 June 1994, 23; George Will, "Most Americans May Support Health Care

Filibuster," *New Orleans Times-Picayune,* 15 August 1994, B5; Cal Thomas, "Does Universal Care Equal Socialized Medicine," *New Orleans Times-Picayune,* 10 August 1994, B7; William Safire, "Why the Rush," *New York Times,* 15 August 1994, 15.

66. Major Garrett, *The Enduring Revolution: How the Contract with America Continues to Shape the Nation* (New York: Crown Forum, 2005).

67. Dean McSweeney and John E. Owens, eds., *The Republican Takeover of Congress* (New York: St. Martin's, 1998).

68. Earl Black and Merle Black, *The Rise of Southern Republicans* (Cambridge, MA: Harvard University Press, 2002); Matthew D. Lassiter, *The Silent Majority: Suburban Politics in the Sunbelt South* (Princeton, NJ: Princeton University Press, 2006); Shafer and Johnson, *The End of Southern Exceptionalism.*

69. Morris P. Fiorina, Samuel J. Abrams, and Jeremy C. Pope, *Culture War? The Myth of a Polarized America* (New York: Pearson Longman, 2005); Paul DiMaggio, John Evans, and Bethany Bryson, "Have Americans' Social Attitudes Become More Polarized?" *American Journal of Sociology* 102 (November 1996), 690–755.

70. Charles Colson and Richard John Neuhaus, *Evangelicals and Christians Together Toward a Common Mission* (Dallas: Word, 1995).

71. "Bishops Speak Out Against Christian Coalition," *National Catholic Reporter,* 2 February 1996, 8; Mary E. Bendyna et al., "Uneasy Alliance: Conservative Catholics and the Christian Right," *Sociology of Religion* 62 (Spring 2001), 51–64.

72. William Saletan, *Bearing Right: How Conservatives Won the Abortion War* (Berkeley: University of California Press, 2003), 233–37.

73. Randall Terry, *Accessory to Murder: The Enemies, Allies, and Accomplices to the Death of Our Culture* (Brentwood, TN: Wolgemuth and Hyatt, 1990); Jacoby, *Souls, Bodies, Spirits,* 131–77.

74. William Bennett, "Quantifying America's Decline," *Wall Street Journal,* 15 March 1993, 12; Bennett, *The Book of Virtues* (New York: Simon and Schuster, 1993).

75. Barbara Vobejda, "'New Orthodoxy' on Campus Assailed," *Washington Post,* 14 November 1988, 3.

76. *Edwards v. Aguillard,* 482 U.S. 578 (1987); Barbara Forrest and Paul R. Gross, *Creationism's Trojan Horse: The Wedge of Intelligent Design* (New York: Oxford University Press, 2004), 15–34, 264–65. The Wedge memo is online at: http://www.public.asu.edu/~jmlynch/idt/wedge.html.

77. Tucker, *The Funding of Scientific Racism,* 131–96.

78. Richard J. Hernnstein and Charles Murray, *The Bell Curve: Intelligence and Class Structure in American Life* (New York: Free Press, 1994); Dan Seligman, "Trashing the Bell Curve," *National Review,* 5 December 1994, 60.

79. Christopher Miller-Coles, "A Perfect Storm: The Collision of Forbidden Sex and Conservative Politics," Ph.D. Dissertation, Wright Institute, 2004, 25–31; David W. Dunlap, "AIDS Quilt of Grief on Capital Mall," *New York Times,* 13 October 1996, 22; Judith Stacey, "Scents, Scholars, and Stigma: The Revisionist Campaign for Family Values," *Social Text* 40 (Autumn 1994), 51–75.

80. Paul M. Barrett, "A New Wave of Counterfeminists is Providing Conservatism with a Female Face," *Wall Street Journal,* 13 October 1995, A16; Barbara Spindel,

"Conservatism as 'Sensible Middle': The Independent Women's Forum, Politics, and the Media," *Social Text* 21 (Winter 2003), 99–125.

81. Jonathan Pitts, "She's the Hammer; Liberals Her Nail," *Baltimore Sun,* 30 July 2006, C3.

82. Andrew Rich, *Think Tanks, Public Policy, and the Politics of Expertise* (New York: Cambridge University Press, 2004).

83. Dan Morgan, "Think Tanks: Corporations' Quiet Weapon," *Washington Post,* 29 January 2000, 1; David Pedreira, "'Tort Reform' Spins Wildly," *Tampa Tribune,* 8 April 1998, 1.

84. David Helvarg, "Perception Is Reality," *E—The Environmental Magazine* 7 (November–December 1996), 38–41.

85. John Cunniff, "Conservative Lashes Out at Business Executives," *Journal Record,* 9 January 1993.

86. Data from the U. S. Department of Justice, Bureau of Justice Statistics, http://www.ojp.usdoj.gov/bjs/; Sean Nicholson-Crotty, "The Politics and Administration of Privatization: Contracting out for Corrections Management in the United States," *Policy Studies Journal* 32 (February 2004), 41–57.

87. Jeffrey M. Berry, *The New Liberalism: The Rising Power of Citizen Groups* (Washington: Brookings Institution, 1999); Theda Skocpol, "Government Activism and the Reorganization of American Civic Democracy," in Pierson and Skocpol, *The Transformation of American Politics,* 39–67.

88. Howard Kurtz and Dan Balz, "Clinton Assails Spread of Hate Through Media," *Washington Post,* 25 April 1995, 1.

89. Jeffrey A. Frieden, *Global Capitalism: Its Fall and Rise in the Twentieth Century* (New York: Norton, 2006), 392–456; James B. Davies et al., "The World Distribution of Household Wealth," World Institute for Development Economics Research of the United Nations University, 5 December 2006.

90. Jacobs, "'Our System,'" 589; Daniel Pipes, "Same Difference: The Struggle Against Fundamentalist Islam has Revived the Divisions of the Cold War," *National Review,* 7 November 1994, 61.

91. Kenneth J. Garcia and Susan Yoachum, "Dole Caught Between Sides on Abortion," *San Francisco Chronicle,* 1 April 1996, 1.

92. Eric Black, "What's the United States' Place in the World?" *Minneapolis Star Tribune,* 20 October 1996, 1; Irving Kristol and Robert Kagan, "Toward a Neo-Reaganite Foreign Policy," *Foreign Affairs* 75 (July-August 1996), 18–32.

93. Joe Conason, *The Hunting of the President: The Ten-Year Campaign to Destroy Bill and Hillary Clinton* (New York: St. Martin's, 2000); Lou Kilzer, "Coors Funds Take on Clinton," *Rocky Mountain News,* 23 August 1998, 5.

94. Matthew Continetti, *The K Street Gang: The Rise and Fall of the Republican Machine* (New York: Doubleday, 2006); Juliet Eilperin, "Ethics Panel Chastises DeLay," *Washington Post,* 14 May 1999, 1.

95. "Defund the Left," unsigned, undated memo, 1999, Armey Papers, box 12.

96. Allan J. Lichtman, "What Really Happened in Florida's 2000 Presidential Election," *Journal of Legal Studies* 32 (January 2003), 221–43.

Epilogue

1. Paul Weyrich, "Letter to Conservatives," 16 February 1999, online at www.nationalCenter.org./Weyrich299.html.

2. John Maynard Keynes, *The Economic Consequences of the Peace* (New York: Harcourt, Brace and Howe, 1920), 42–43.

3. Bill Walsh, "Conservatives Watching Bush's Moves," *New Orleans Times-Picayune,* 20 December 2000, 1; John Sawyer, "Bush's Conservative Backers Shun Talk of Conciliation," *St. Louis Post-Dispatch,* 17 December 2000, 10; Richard W. Stevenson, "The 43rd President: The Vice President-Elect," *New York Times,* 18 Dec, 2000, 21.

4. Robin Wright, "Powell Sees U.S. Leading the Way on Foreign Affairs," *Milwaukee Journal Sentinel,* 4 February 2001, 8.

5. "Eyes on Iraq," *New York Times,* 27 August 2002, 8; George W. Bush, "Address to the Nation on Iraq," 7 October 2002, online at www.archives.gov/federal-register/publications/presidential-papers.html.

6. Inspector General, United States Department of Defense, "Review of the Pre-Iraqi War Activities of the Office of the Undersecretary of Defense for Policy," *Report No. 07-INTEL-04,* 9 February 2007.

7. PNAC documents are online at www.newamericancentury.org.

8. The full text of the Land Letter is online at http://erlc.com/article/the-so-called-land-letter.

9. "U.S. Central Command Slide Compilation, ca. August 15, 2002," National Security Archive.

10. John C. Green, "Bush's Religious-Right Challenge," *Christian Science Monitor,* 23 January 2001, 9.

11. Allan J. Lichtman, "In Plain Sight: With the Public Distracted, George W. Bush Is Building a Big Government—of the Right," *Newsday,* 7 August 2005, 12.

12. Stephen Moore, "The Federal Budget Ten Years Later: The Triumph of Big Government," in Chris Edwards and John Samples, eds., *The Republican Revolution 10 Years Later: Smaller Government or Business as Usual?* (Washington, DC: Cato Institute, 2005), 64. See http:elsa.berkley.edu/~saez/TabFig2005prel.xls for income distribution data compiled by economists Thomas Piketty and Emmanuel Saez. These results do not count capital gains income, which flows mainly to the more affluent.

13. David Kuo, *Tempting Faith: An Inside Story of Political Seduction* (New York: Free Press, 2006), xii, 201, 229, 242–43; Ron Suskind, "Why Are These Men Laughing," *Esquire* (January 2003), 97.

14. For accounts by journalists of Bush's effort to build a political majority see Thomas B. Edsall, *Building Red America: The New Conservative Coalition and the Drive for Permanent Power* (New York: Basic Books, 2006), and John Micklethwait and Adrian Wooldridge, *Right Nation: Conservative Power in America* (New York: Penguin, 2004).

15. Larry Klayman in Laurence McQuillan, "For Bush, Secrecy is a Matter of Loyalty," *USA Today,* 14 March 2002, 1.

16. United States Department of Justice, Office of the Inspector General, *A Review of the Federal Bureau of Investigation's Use of National Security Letters,* March 2007; R. Jeffrey Smith, "FBI Violations May Number 3,000 Official Says," *Washington Post,* 21 March 2007, 7; Phillip J. Cooper, "George W. Bush, Edgar Allan Poe, and the Use and Abuse of Presidential Signing Statements," *Presidential Studies Quarterly* 12 (September 2005), 515–32.

17. Richard Alonso-Zaldivar, "Health Official Claims Censorship," *Los Angeles Times,* 11 July 2007, 10; U.S. Department of the Interior, Office of Inspector General, *Report of Investigation: Julie MacDonald, Deputy Assistant Secretary, Fish, Wildlife, and Parks,* March 2007, 2; Andrew C. Revkin, "Official Played Down Emissions' Links to Global Warming," *New York Times,* 7 June 2005, 1; Revkin, "Climate Change Testimony Was Edited by White House," *New York Times,* 25 October 2007, 16; Juliet Eilperin, "EPA Chief Denies Calif. Limit on Auto Emissions," *Washington Post,* 20 December 2007, 1.

18. Carol D. Leonning, "Political Hiring in Justice Division Probed," *Washington Post,* 21 June 2007, 1; Joseph D. Rich, "The Attack on Professionalism in the Civil Rights Division," in William L. Taylor, Dianne M. Piche, Crystal Rosario, and Joseph D. Rich, eds., *The Erosion of Rights: Declining Civil Rights Enforcement Under the Bush Administration* (Washington, DC: Citizens' Commission on Civil Rights, 2007), 17.

19. Allan J. Lichtman and Vladimir Keilis-Borok, "What Kerry Must Do," *CommonDreams.org,* 28 July 2004; Lichtman, "They're Fired: Memo to Kerry, Get Rid of the Hucksters and Start Acting Like a President," *American Prospect Online,* 22 October 2004.

20. Shirley, *Reagan's Revolution,* 83.

21. James Bovard, "Sins of Commission," *American Conservative,* 18 December 2006, 38.

22. Richard A. Viguerie, *Conservatives Betrayed: How George W. Bush and Other Big Government Republicans Hijacked the Conservative Cause* (Los Angeles: Bonus, 2006); Bruce Bartlett, *Impostor: How George W. Bush Bankrupted America and Betrayed the Reagan Legacy* (New York: Doubleday, 2006); Fred Barnes, "The Conservative Revolt," *Daily Standard,* 10 October 2005; Robert Novak, "Bush Isolated from GOP Lawmakers," *Chicago Sun-Times,* 26 March 2007, 37.

23. David Brooks, "The Republican Collapse," *New York Times,* 5 October 2007, 25.

24. John Alford, Carolyn Funk, and John R. Hibbing, "Are Political Orientations Genetically Transmitted?" *American Political Science Review* 99 (May 2005), 153–167; George Lakoff, *Moral Politics: How Liberals and Conservatives Think* (Chicago: University of Chicago Press, 2002).

25. David D. Kirkpatrick, "The Evangelical Crackup," *New York Times,* 28 October 2007, 6.

BIBLIOGRAPHY

Prior to the late 1980s, despite the publication of such classic works as George Nash's *The Conservative Intellectual Movement in the United States* (originally published in 1975) and Leo Ribuffo's *The Old Christian Right* (1983), scholarship on the modern American conservative movement was relatively sparse, especially when compared to work on liberalism. Since that time, there has been a wealth of scholarship on the conservative movement. Most recent work, however, focuses on the second half of the twentieth century. No synthetic study to date covers the years since World War I and places the conservative movement within the big picture of twentieth- and early-twenty-first-century history. Although this work draws extensively on the secondary literature, it is built upon the study of material from more than 150 manuscript collections and more than one hundred newspapers and magazines. It also draws upon work in political science and sociology, statistical analyses of election results, public opinion polls, and post-election surveys of voters. Although I have conducted numerous interviews of conservative figures, I have relied on oral histories only for leads and background information. The books documents events from contemporary sources rather than later recollections.

Books

Ackerman, Kenneth. 2007. *Young J. Edgar Hoover: Hoover, the Red Scare, and the Assault on Civil Liberties*. New York: Carroll & Graff.

Alfonsi, Christian. 2007. *Circle in the Sand: Why We Went Back to Iraq*. New York: Doubleday.

Allen Jr., John L. 2005. *Opus Dei: An Objective Look Behind the Myths and Reality of the Most Controversial Force in the Catholic Church.* New York: Doubleday.

Allitt, Patrick. 1993. *Catholic Intellectuals and Conservative Politics in America, 1950-1985.* Ithaca, NY: Cornell University Press.

Alsop, Joseph, and Turner Catledge. 1938. *The 138 Days.* Garden City, NY: Doubleday.

Andrew III, John A. 1997. *The Other Side of the Sixties: Young American for Freedom and the Rise of Conservative Politics.* New Brunswick, NJ: Rutgers University Press.

Andrew III, John A. 2002. *The Power to Destroy: The Political Uses of the IRS from Kennedy to Nixon.* Chicago: Ivan R. Dee.

Apple, Michael W. 2006. *Educating the "Right" Way: Markets, Standards, God, and Inequality.* New York: Routledge.

Arnove, Robert. ed. 1980. *Philanthropy and Cultural Imperialism: The Foundations at Home and Abroad.* Boston: G. K. Hall.

Auerbach, Jerold S. 1966. *Labor and Liberty: The La Follette Committee and the New Deal.* Indianapolis, IN: Bobbs-Merrill.

Avila, Eric. 2004. *Popular Culture in the Age of White Flight: Fear and Fantasy in Suburban Los Angeles.* Berkeley: University of California Press.

Bachrack, Stanley D. 1976. *The Committee of One Million: "China Lobby" Politics, 1953-1971.* New York: Columbia University Press.

Bailey, Stephen Kemp. 1950. *Congress Makes a Law: The Story Behind the Employment Act of 1946.* New York: Columbia University Press.

Balmer, Randall. 1989. *Mine Eyes Have Seen the Glory: A Journey into the Evangelical Subculture in America.* New York: Oxford University Press.

Balmer, Randall. 1999. *Blessed Assurance: A History of Evangelicalism in America.* Boston: Beacon Press.

Balz, Daniel J., and Ronald Brownstein. 1996. *Storming the Gates: Protest Politics and the Republican Revival.* Boston: Little, Brown.

Barber, William J. 1985. *From New Era to New Deal: Herbert Hoover, the Economists, and American Economic Policy, 1921-1933.* New York: Cambridge University Press.

Barkan, Elazar. 1992. *The Retreat of Scientific Racism: Changing Concepts of Race in Britain and the United States Between the World Wars.* New York: Cambridge University Press.

Barkun, Michael. 1997. *Religion and the Racist Right: The Origins of the Christian Identity Movement.* Chapel Hill: University of North Carolina Press.

Barkun, Michael. 2003. *A Culture of Conspiracy: Apocalyptic Visions in Contemporary America.* Berkeley: University of California.

Barron, Bruce. 1992. *Heaven on Earth? The Social and Political Agendas of Dominion Theology.* Grand Rapids, MI: Zondervan.

Bartlett, Bruce R. 1978. *Cover-Up: The Politics of Pearl Harbor, 1941-1946.* New Rochelle, NY: Arlington House.

Bartlett, Bruce. 2006. *Impostor: How George W. Bush Bankrupted America and Betrayed the Reagan Legacy.* New York: Doubleday.

Bartley, Numan. 1969. *The Rise of Massive Resistance: Race and Politics in the South During the 1950s.* Baton Rouge: Louisiana State University Press.

Baum, Dan. 2001. *Citizen Coors: An American Dynasty.* New York: William Morrow

Beito, David T. 1989. *Taxpayers in Revolt: Tax Resistance During the Great Depression.* Chapel Hill: University of North Carolina Press.

Bell, Jonathan. 2004. *The Liberal State on Trial: The Cold War and American Politics in the Truman Years.* New York: Columbia University Press.

Bell, Leland V. 1973. *In Hitler's Shadow: The Anatomy of American Nazism.* Port Washington, NY: Kennikat.

Bellant, Russ. 1989. *Old Nazis, the New Right, and the Republican Party.* 2nd ed. Boston, MA: South End.

Bellush, Bernard. 1975. *The Failure of the NRA.* New York: Norton.

Benowitz, June Melby. 2002. *Days of Discontent: American Women and Right-Wing Politics, 1933-1945.* DeKalb: Northern Illinois University Press.

Berman, Larry. 2002. *No Peace, No Honor: Nixon, Kissinger, and Betrayal in Vietnam.* New York: Free Press.

Berry, Jeffrey M. 1999. *The New Liberalism: The Rising Power of Citizen Groups.* Washington, DC: Brookings Institution.

Bertlet, Chip, and Matthew N. Lyons. 2000. *Right-Wing Populism in America: Too Close for Comfort.* New York: Guilford.

Biersack, Robert, et al., eds. 1994. *Risky Business? PAC Decisionmaking in Congressional Elections.* Armonk, NY: M. E. Sharpe.

Billstein, Reinhold, et al. 2000. *Working for the Enemy: Ford, General Motors, and Forced Labor in Germany During the Second World War.* New York: Berghahn.

Birnbaum, Jeffrey, and Alan Murray. 1987. *Showdown at Gucci Gulch: Lawmakers, Lobbyists, and the Unlikely Triumph of Tax Reform.* New York: Random House.

Bjerre-Poulsen, Niels. 2002. *Right Face: Organizing the American Conservative Movement, 1945-65.* Copenhagen: Museum Tusculum Press.

Black, Earl, and Merle Black. 2002. *The Rise of Southern Republicans.* New York: Harvard University Press.

Black, Edwin. 2001. *IBM and the Holocaust: The Strategic Alliance Between Nazi Germany and America's Most Powerful Corporation.* New York: Crown.

Blee, Kathleen N. *Women of the Klan: Racism and Gender in the 1920s.* Berkeley: University of California Press, 1991

Blight, David W. 2001. *Race and Reunion: The Civil War and American Memory.* Cambridge, MA: Harvard University Press.

Blumberg, Nathan B. *One-Party Press? Coverage of the 1952 Presidential Campaign in 35 Daily Newspapers.* Lincoln: University of Nebraska Press.

Boies, John L. 1994. *Buying for Armageddon: Business, Society, and Military Spending Since the Cuban Missile Crisis.* New Brunswick, NJ: Rutgers University Press.

Bower, Tom. 1987. *The Paperclip Conspiracy: The Hunt for Nazi Scientists.* Boston: Little, Brown.

Bowie, Robert R., and Richard H. Immerman. 1998. *Waging Peace: How Eisenhower Shaped an Enduring Cold War Strategy.* New York: Oxford University Press.

Bowles, Nigel. 2005. *Nixon's Business: Authority and Power in Presidential Politics.* College Station: Texas A&M University Press.

Boyer, Paul S. 1968. *Purity in Print: The Vice Society Movement and Censorship in America.* New York: Scribner's.

Boyle, Kevin. 2004. *Arc of Justice: A Saga of Race, Civil Rights, and Murder in the Jazz Age.* New York: Henry Holt.

Brandes, Stuart D. 1976. *American Welfare Capitalism, 1880-1940.* Chicago: University of Chicago Press.

Brandt, Allan M. 1987. *No Magic Bullet: A Social History of Venereal Disease in the United States Since 1880.* New York: Oxford University Press.

Brennan, Mary. 1995. *Turning Right in the Sixties: The Conservative Capture of the GOP.* Chapel Hill: University of North Carolina Press.

Bridges, Linda, and John R. Coyne Jr. 2007. *Strictly Right: William F. Buckley Jr. and the American Conservative Movement.* Hoboken, NJ: John Wiley.

Brinkley, Alan. 1995. *The End of Reform: New Deal in Recession and War.* New York: Knopf.

Burk., Robert F. 1990. *The Corporate State and the Broker State: The Du Ponts and American National Politics, 1925-1940.* Cambridge, MA: Harvard University Press.

Burkett, Elinor. 1998. *The Right Women: A Journey through the Heart of Conservative America.* New York: Scribner.

Busch, Andrew. 2005. *Reagan's Victory: The Presidential Election of 1980 and the Rise of the Right.* Lawrence: University of Kansas Press.

Cahn, Anne Hessing. 1998. *Killing Détente: The Right Attacks the CIA.* University Park: Pennsylvania State University Press.

Callahan, David. 1999. *$1 Billion for Ideas: Conservative Think Tanks in the 1990s.* Washington, DC: National Committee for Responsive Philanthropy.

Cannadine, David. 2006. *Mellon: An American Life.* New York: Knopf.

Carpenter, Joel A. ed. 1988. *Biblical Prophecy in an Apocalyptical Age: Selected Writing of Louis S. Bauman.* New York: Garland.

Carpenter, Joel. 1997. *Revive Us Again: The Reawakening of American Fundamentalism.* New York: Oxford University Press.

Carter, Dan T. 1995. *The Politics of Rage: George Wallace, the Origins of the New Conservatism, and the Transformation of American Politics.* New York: Simon and Schuster.

Castle, Alfred L. 1998. *Diplomatic Realism: William R. Castle, Jr. and American Foreign Policy, 1919-1953.* Honolulu, HI: Samuel and Mary Castle Foundation.

Chang, Laurence, and Peter Kornbluh. 1998. *The Cuban Missile Crisis, 1962: A National Security Archives Documents Reader.* 2nd ed. New York: The New Press.

Charns, Alexander. 1992. *Cloak and Gavel: FBI Wiretaps, Bugs, Informers, and the Supreme Court.* Urbana: University of Illinois Press.

Clemens, Elisabeth S. 1997. *The People's Lobby: Organizational Innovation and the Rise of Interest Group Politics in the United States, 1890-1925.* Chicago: University of Chicago Press.

Cogdell, Christina. 2004. *Eugenic Design: Streamlining America in the 1930s.* Philadelphia: University of Pennsylvania Press.

Cohen, Lizabeth. 2003. *A Consumer's Republic: The Politics of Mass Consumption in Postwar America.* New York: Knopf.

Cohen, Warren I. 1987. *Empire Without Tears: American Foreign Relations 1921-1933.* Philadelphia: Temple University Press.

Colby, Gerard and Charlotte Dennett. 1995. *Thy Will be Done: The Conquest of the Amazon; Nelson Rockefeller and Evangelism in the Age of Oil.* New York: Harper Collins.

Cole, Wayne S. 1953. *America First: The Battle Against Intervention, 1940-1941.* Madison: University of Wisconsin Press.

Colson, Charles, and Richard John Neuhaus. 1995. *Evangelicals and Christians Together Toward a Common Mission.* Dallas: Word.

Conason, Joe. 2000. *The Hunting of the President: The Ten-Year Campaign to Destroy Bill and Hillary Clinton.* New York: St. Martin's.

Continetti, Matthew. 2006. *The K Street Gang: The Rise and Fall of the Republican Machine.* New York: Doubleday.

Coogan, Gertrude Margaret. 1935. *Money Creators. Who Creates Money? Who Should Create it?.* Chicago: Sound Money.

Cornuelle, Richard C. 1965. *Reclaiming the American Dream.* New York: Random House.

Coughlin, Charles E. 1936. *A Series of Lectures on Social Justice.* Royal Oak, MI: Radio League of the Little Flower.

Covington, Sally. 1997. *Moving a Public Policy Agenda: The Strategic Philanthropy of Conservative Foundations.* Washington, DC: National Committee for Responsive Philanthropy.

Craig, Douglas. 1992. *After Wilson: The Struggle for the Democratic Party, 1920-1934.* Chapel Hill: University of North Carolina Press.

Critchlow, Donald T. 1985. *The Brookings Institution, 1916-1952: Expertise and the Public Interest in a Democratic Society.* DeKalb: Northern Illinois University Press.

Critchlow, Donald T. 2005. *Phyllis Schlafly and Grassroots Conservatism: A Woman's Crusade.* Princeton, NJ: Princeton University Press.

Critchlow, Donald T. 2007. *The Conservative Ascendancy: How the GOP Right Made Political History.* Cambridge, MA: Harvard University Press.

Cronon, E. David. 1969. *Black Moses: The Story of Marcus Garvey and the Universal Negro Improvement Association.* Madison: University of Wisconsin Press.

Cuneo, Michael W. 1997. *The Smoke of Satan: Conservative and Traditionalist Dissent in Contemporary American Catholicism.* New York: Oxford University Press.

Dallek, Matthew. 2004. *The Right Moment: Ronald Reagan's First Victory and the Decisive Turning Point in American Politics.* New York: Oxford University Press.

Dallek, Robert. 1998. *Flawed Giant: Lyndon Johnson and His Times, 1961-1973.* New York: Oxford University Press

Daniels, Roger. 1988. *Asian America: Chinese and Japanese in the United States Since 1850.* Seattle: University of Washington Press.

Daniels, Roger. 2004. *Guarding the Golden Door: American Immigration Policy and Immigrants Since 1882.* New York: Hill and Wang.

Davies, Richard O. 1993. *Defender of the Old Guard: John Bricker and American Politics.* Columbus: Ohio State University Press.

Dean, John W. *Warren G. Harding.* 2004. New York: Times Books.

Deckman, Melissa M. 2004. *School Board Battles: The Christian Right in Local Politics.* Washington, DC: Georgetown University Press.

Denning, Michael. 1996. *The Cultural Front: The Laboring of American Culture in the Twentieth Century.* New York: Verso.

Diamond, Sander A. 1974. *The Nazi Movement in the United States, 1924-1941.* Ithaca, NY: Cornell University Press.

Diamond, Sara. 1989. *Spiritual Warfare: The Politics of the Christian Right.* Boston: South End Press.

Diamond, Sara. 1995. *Roads to Dominion: Right-Wing Movements and Political Power in the United States.* New York: Guilford.

Diamond, Sara. 1998. *Not by Politics Alone: The Enduring Influence of the Christian Right.* New York: Guilford Press.

Diggins, John P. 1972. *Mussolini and Fascism: The View from America.* Princeton, NJ: Princeton University Press.

Doenecke, Justus D. 1990. *In Danger Undaunted: The Anti-Interventionist Movement of 1940-1941 as Revealed in the Papers of the America First Committee.* Stanford, CA: Hoover Institution.

Doherty, Thomas. 1999. *Pre-Code Hollywood: Sex, Immorality, and Insurrection in American Cinema, 1930-1934.* New York: Columbia University Press.

Domhoff, G. William. ed. 2006. *Who Rules America?: Power, Politics, and Social Change.* Boston: McGraw-Hill.

Donner, Frank. 1990. *Protectors of Privilege: Red Squads and Political Repression in America.* Berkeley: University of California Press.

Donovan, John T. 2005. *Crusader in the Cold War: A Biography of Fr. John S. Cronin.* New York: Lang.

Dorrien, Gary J. 1993. *The Neoconservative Mind: Politics, Culture, and the War of Ideology.* Philadelphia: Temple University Press.

Dower, John. 1986. *War Without Mercy: Race and Power in the Pacific War.* New York: Pantheon.

D'Souza, Dinesh. 1997. *Ronald Reagan: How an Ordinary Man Became an Extraordinary Leader.* New York: Free Press.

Durham, Martin. 2000. *The Christian Right, the Far Right and the Boundaries of American Conservatism.* Manchester: Manchester University Press.

Durr, Kenneth. 2003. *Behind the Backlash: White Working Class Politics in Baltimore, 1940-1980.* Chapel Hill: University of North Carolina Press.

Easton, Nina J. 2000. *Gang of Five: Leaders at the Center of the Conservative Ascendancy.* New York: Simon and Schuster.

Edsall, Thomas Byrne. 1984. *The New Politics of Inequality.* New York: Norton.

Edsall, Thomas Byrne. 2006. *Building Red America: The New Conservative Coalition and the Drive for Permanent Power.* New York: Basic Books.

Edsall, Thomas Bryne, and Mary D. Edsall. 1991. *Chain Reaction: The Impact of Race, Rights, and Taxes on American Politics.* New York: Norton.

Edwards, Chris, and John Samples, eds. 2005. *The Republican Revolution 10 Years Later: Smaller Government or Business as Usual?* Washington, DC: Cato Institute.

Edwards, Lee. 1997. *The Power of Ideas: The Heritage Foundation at 25 Years.* New York: Jameson.

Edwards, Lee. 2004. *Bringing Justice to the People: The Story of the Freedom-Based Public Interest Law Movement.* Washington DC: Heritage Books.

Erlen, Jonathon, and Joseph F. Spillane, eds. 2004. *Federal Drug Control: The Evolution of Policy and Practice.* New York: Pharmaceutical Products.

Evans, Thomas W. 2006. *The Education of Ronald Reagan: The General Election Years and the Untold Story of His Conversion to Conservatism.* New York: Columbia University Press.

Eve A. Raymond, and Francis B. Harrold. 1991. *The Creationist Movement in Modern America.* Boston: Twayne.

Everitt, David. 2007. *A Shadow of Red: Communism and the Blacklist in Radio and Television.* Chicago: Ivan R. Dee.

Farber, David, and Jeff Roche. eds. 2003. *The Conservative Sixties.* New York: Peter Lang.

Ferguson, Ernest B. 1986. *Hard Right: The Rise of Jesse Helms.* New York: Norton.

Feulner Jr., Edwin J. 1983. *Conservatives Stalk the House: The Republican Study Committee, 1970-1982.* Ottawa, IL: Green Hill.

Finegold, Kenneth, and Theda Skocpol. 1995. *State and Party in America's New Deal* Madison: University of Wisconsin Press.

Fiorina, Morris P., Samuel J. Abrams, and Jeremy C. Pope. 2005. *Culture War? The Myth of a Polarized America.* New York: Pearson Longman.

Fitzgerald, Frances. 1986. *Cities on a Hill: A Journal Through Contemporary American Cultures.* New York: Simon and Schuster.

Fitzgerald, Frances. 2000. *Way Out There in the Blue: Reagan, Star Wars, and the End of the Cold War.* New York: Simon and Schuster.

Fitzgerald, Keith. 1996. *The Face of the Nation: Immigration, the State, and the National Identity.* Stanford, CA: Stanford University Press.

Flamm, Michael W. 2005. *Law and Order: Street Crime, Civil Unrest, and the Crisis of Liberalism in the 1960s.* New York: Columbia University Press.

Fleming, Thomas. 2001. *The New Dealers' War: Franklin D. Roosevelt and the War Within World War II.* New York: Basic Books.

Flynn, John T. 1949. *The Road Ahead: America's Creeping Revolution.* New York: Devin-Adair.

Foley, Neil. 1997. *White Scourge: Mexicans, Blacks, and Poor Whites in Texas Cotton Culture.* Berkeley: University of California Press.

Fones-Wolf, Elizabeth. 1994. *Selling Free Enterprise: The Business Assault on Labor and Liberalism, 1945-1960.* Urbana: University of Illinois Press.

Formisano, Ronald P. 1991. *Boston Against Busing: Race, Class, and Ethnicity in the 1960s and 1970s.* Chapel Hill: University of North Carolina Press.

Forrest, Barbara, and Paul R. Gross. 2004. *Creationism's Trojan Horse: The Wedge of Intelligent Design.* New York: Oxford University Press.

Foster, Gaines. 2002. *Moral Reconstruction: Christian Lobbyists and the Federal Legislation of Morality, 1865-1920.* Chapel Hill: University of North Carolina Press.

Frank, Thomas. 2004. *What's the Matter with Kansas?: How Conservatives Won the Heart of America.* New York: Metropolitan.

Frederickson, Kari. 2001. *The Dixiecrat Revolt and the End of the Solid South, 1932-1968.* Chapel Hill: University of North Carolina Press.

Freeman, Jo. 2004. *At Berkeley in the Sixties: Education of an Activist, 1961-1965.* Indianapolis: Indiana University Press.

Fried, Richard M. 2005. *The Man Everybody Knew: Bruce Barton and the Making of Modern America.* Chicago: Ivan R. Dee.

Frieden, Jeffrey A. 2006. *Global Capitalism: Its Fall and Rise in the Twentieth Century.* New York: Norton.

Friedman, Andrea. 2000. *Prurient Interests: Gender, Democracy, and Obscenity in New York City, 1909-1945.* New York: Columbia University Press.

Friedman, Murray. 2005. *The Neoconservative Revolution: Jewish Intellectuals and the Shaping of Public Policy.* New York: Cambridge University Press.

Fukuyama, Francis. 2006. *America at the Crossroads: Democracy, Power, and the Neoconservative Legacy.* New Haven: Yale University Press.

Gati, Charles. 2006. *Failed Illusions: Washington, Budapest, and the 1956 Hungarian Revolt.* Stanford, CA: Stanford University Press.

Gaustad, Edwin, and Leigh Eric Schmidt. 2004. *The Religious History of America.* New York: Harpers.

Gerson, Mark. 1996. *The Neoconservative Vision: From Cold War to the Culture Wars.* Lanham, MD: Madison.

Gerstle, Gary, and Steve Fraser, eds. 1989. *The Rise and Fall of the New Deal Order.* Princeton, NJ: Princeton University Press.

Gerstle, Gary. 2001. *American Crucible: Race and Nation in the Twentieth Century.* Princeton, NJ: Princeton University Press.

Gertzman, Jay A. 1999. *Bookleggers and Smuthounds: The Trade in Erotica, 1920-1940.* Philadelphia: University of Pennsylvania Press.

Gibson, Andrew, and Arthur Donovan. 2000. *The Abandoned Ocean: A History of United States Maritime Policy.* Columbia: University of South Carolina Press.

Gidlow, Liette. 2004. *The Big Vote: Gender, Consumer Culture, and the Politics of Exclusion, 1890s-1920s.* Baltimore: Johns Hopkins University Press

Gilgoff, Dan. 2007. *The Jesus Machine: How James Dobson, Focus on the Family, and Evangelical America Are Winning the Culture War.* New York: St. Martin's.

Gillon, Steven M. 1987. *Politics and Vision: The ADA and American Liberalism, 1947-1985.* New York: Oxford University Press.

Gilmore, Glenda. 1996. *Gender and Jim Crow: Women and the Politics of White Supremacy in North Carolina, 1896-1920.* Chapel Hill: University of North Carolina Press.

Gingrich, Newt. 1984. *Window of Opportunity: A Blueprint for the Future.* New York: Tom Doherty Associates.

Goldberg, Robert Alan. 1995. *Barry Goldwater.* New Haven, CT: Yale University Press.

Goossen, Rachel Waltner. 1997. *Women Against the Good War: Conscientious Objection and Gender on the American Home Front, 1941-1947.* Chapel Hill: University of North Carolina Press.

Gottfried, Paul. 2007. *Conservatism in America: Making Sense of the American Right.* New York: Palgrave.

Graebner, Norman A.. 1956. *The New Isolationism: A Study in Politics and Foreign Policy Since 1950*. New York: Ronald.

Green, John C. 2007. *The Faith Factor: How Religion Influences American Elections*. Westport, CT: Praeger.

Greenberg, David. 2003. *Nixon's Shadow: The History of an Image*. New York: Norton.

Greene, John Robert. 2000. *The Presidency of George Bush*. Lawrence: University Press of Kansas.

Gregory, James N. 2005. *The Southern Diaspora: How the Great Migrations of Black and White Southerners Transformed America*. Chapel Hill: University of North Carolina Press.

Griffith, Barbara S. 1988. *The Crisis of American Labor: Operation Dixie and the Defeat of the CIO*. Philadelphia: Temple University Press.

Griffith, Robert. 1970. *The Politics of Fear: Joseph R. McCarthy and the Senate*. Amherst: University of Massachusetts Press.

Grose, Peter. 2000. *Operation Rollback: America's Secret War Behind the Iron Curtain*. Boston: Houghton Mifflin.

Grossman, James R. 1989. *Land of Hope: Chicago, Black Southerners and the Great Migration*. Chicago: University of Chicago Press.

Gutiérrez, David. 1995. *Walls and Mirrors: Mexicans Americans, Mexican Immigrants, and the Politics of Ethnicity*. Berkley: University of California Press.

Gutterman, David S. 2005. *Prophetic Politics: Christian Social Movements and American Democracy*. Ithaca, NY: Cornell University Press.

Hadden, Jeffrey K., et al. 1987. *Why Jerry Falwell Killed the Moral Majority*. Bowling Green, OH: Bowling Green University Popular Press.

Haines, Gerald K., and Robert E. Leggett. 2003. *Watching the Bear: Essays on the CIA's Analysis of the Soviet Union*. Langley, VA: Center for the Study of Intelligence.

Haldeman, H. R. 1994. *The Haldeman Diaries: Inside the Nixon White House*. New York: G.P. Putnam's Sons.

Halper, Stefan, and Jonathan Clarke. 2004. *America Alone: The Neo-conservatives and the Global Order*. New York: Cambridge University Press.

Handy, Robert T. 1968. *The American Religious Depression, 1925-1935*. Philadelphia: Fortress.

Hangen, Tona. 2002. *Redeeming the Dial: Radio, Religion, and Popular Culture in America*. Chapel Hill: University of North Carolina Press.

Harding, Susan. 2000. *The Book of Jerry Falwell: Fundamentalist Language and Politics*. Princeton, NJ: Princeton University Press.

Hardisty, Jean V. 1999. *Mobilizing Resentment: Conservative Resurgence from the John Birch Society to the Promise Keepers*. Boston: Beacon.

Harris, Howell John. 1982. *The Right to Manage: Industrial Relations Policies of American Business in the 1940s*. Madison: University of Wisconsin Press.

Hart, Jeffrey. 2005. *The Making of the American Conservative Mind: National Review and Its Times*. Wilmington, DL: ISI.

Herman, Didi. 1997. *The Antigay Agenda: Orthodox Vision and the Christian Right*. Chicago: University of Chicago Press.

Hernnstein, Richard J., and Charles Murray. 1994. *The Bell Curve: Intelligence and Class Structure in American Life.* New York: Free Press.

Herrnson, Paul S., et al. eds. 2005. *The Interest Group Connection: Electioneering, Lobbying, and Policymaking in Washington.* Washington D.C.: CQ Press.

Harvey, David. 2005. *A Brief History of Neoliberalism.* New York: Oxford University Press.

Hawley, Ellis W. 1979. *The Great War and the Search for a Modern Order: A History of the American People and Their Institutions, 1917-1933.* New York: St. Martin's.

Haynes, John Earl, and Harvey Klehr. 2003. *In Denial: Historians, Communism and Espionage.* San Francisco: Encounter.

Heale, M. J. 1998. *McCarthy's Americans: Red Scare Politics in State and Nation, 1935-1965.* Athens: University of Georgia Press.

Heineman, Kenneth. 2005. *God Is a Conservative: Religion, Politics, and Morality in Contemporary America.* new ed. New York: New York University Press.

Hendershot, Heather. 2004. *Shaking the World for Jesus: Media and Conservative Evangelical Culture.* Chicago: University of Chicago Press.

Henry, Carl F. H. 1947. *The Uneasy Conscience of Modern Fundamentalism.* Grand Rapids, MI: William B. Eerdmans.

Hicks, L. Edward. 1994. *"Sometimes in the Wrong, but Never in Doubt": George S. Benson and the Education of the New Religious Right.* Knoxville: University of Tennessee Press.

Himmelstein, Jerome L. 1990. *To the Right: The Transformation of American Conservativism.* Berkeley: University of California Press.

Hirsch, Arnold R. 1983. *Making the Second Ghetto: Race and Housing in Chicago, 1940-1960.* New York: Cambridge University Press.

Hixson, Jr., William B. 1992. *Search for the American Right Wing: An Analysis of the Social Science Record, 1955-1987.* Princeton, NJ: Princeton University Press.

Hodgson, Godfrey. 1996. *The World Turned Right Side Up: A History of the Conservative Ascendancy in America.* Boston: Houghton Mifflin.

Hoeveler, J. David. 1991. *Watch on the Right: Conservative Intellectuals in the Reagan Era.* Madison: University of Wisconsin Press.

Hogan, Michael J. 1998. *A Cross of Iron: Harry S. Truman and the Origins of the National Security State, 1945-1954.* New York: Cambridge University Press.

Horne, Gerald. 2001. *Class Struggle in Hollywood, 1930-1950: Moguls, Mobsters, Stars, Reds, and Trade Unionists.* Austin: University of Texas Press.

Horowitz, David A. 1997. *Beyond Left and Right: Insurgency and the Establishment.* Urbana: University of Illinois Press.

Hunter, James Davison. 1991. *Culture Wars: The Struggle to Define America.* New York: Basic Books.

Hutchinson, Robert. 1999. *Their Kingdom Come: Inside the Secret World of Opus Dei.* New York: St. Martin's.

Institute for Cultural Conservativism, Free Congress Research and Education Foundation. 1987. *Cultural Conservatism: Toward a New National Agenda.* Lanham, MD: University Press of America.

Irvine, Janice M. 2002. *Talk About Sex: The Battles Over Sex Education in the United States.* Berkeley: University of California Press.

Jackson, Jerome K., and Constantine F. Malmberg. 1928. *Religious Education and the State.* Garden City, NY: Doubleday.

Jacoby, Kerry N. 1998. *Souls, Bodies, Spirits: The Drive to Abolish Abortion Since 1973.* Westport, CT: Praeger

Jacoby, Sanford M. 1997. *Modern Manors: Welfare Capitalism Since The New Deal.* Princeton, NJ: Princeton University Press.

James, D Clayton. 1985. *The Years of MacArthur, Volume III: Triumph and Disaster, 1945-1964.* Boston: Houghton Mifflin.

Jeansonne, Glen. 1988. *Gerald L.K. Smith: Minister of Hate.* New Haven, CT: Yale University Press.

Jeansonne, Glen. 1996. *Women of the Far Right: The Mother's Movement and World War II.* Chicago: University of Chicago Press.

Jenkins, Philip. 1997. *Hoods and Shirts: The Extreme Right in Pennsylvania, 1925-1940.* Chapel Hill: University of North Carolina Press.

Jenkinson, Edward B. 1979. *Censors in the Classroom: The Mind Benders.* Carbondale: Southern Illinois University Press.

The John Birch Society. 1961. *The Blue Book of the John Birch Society.* Belmont, MA: Western Islands.

Johnson, Alvin W., and Frank H. Yost. 1948. *Separation of Church and State in the United States* Minneapolis: University of Minnesota Press.

Johnson, David K. 2004. *The Lavender Scare: The Cold War Persecution of Gays and Lesbians in the Federal Government.* Chicago: University of Chicago Press.

Johnson, Kent L. 1992. *War, Depression, Prohibition, and Racism: The Response of the Sunday School to an Era of Crisis, 1933-1941.* Lanham, MD: University Press of America.

Jones Jr., J. Harry. 1968. *The Minutemen.* Garden City, NY: Doubleday.

Judis, John B. 1988. *William F. Buckley Jr.: Patron Saint of the Conservatives.* New York: Simon and Schuster.

Kabaservice, Geoffrey. 2004. *The Guardians: Kingman Brewster, His Circle, and the Rise of the Liberal Establishment.* New York: Henry Holt.

Katagiri, Yasuhiro. 2001. *The Mississippi State Sovereignty Commission: Civil Rights and States' Rights.* Jackson: University Press of Mississippi.

Katznelson, Ira. 2005. *When Affirmative Action Was White: An Untold History of Racial Inequality in Twentieth-Century America.* New York: Norton.

Kaufman, Robert G. 2000. *Henry M. Jackson: A Life in Politics.* Seattle: University of Washington Press.

Kazin, Michael. 1995. *The Populist Persuasion: An American History.* New York: Basic Books.

Keely, Joseph. 1969. *China Lobby Man: The Story of Alfred Kohlberg.* New Rochelle, NY: Arlington House.

Kelly, Daniel. 2002. *James Burnham and the Struggle for the World: A Life.* Wilmington, DE: ISI.

Kent, Peter C. 2002. *The Lonely Cold War of Pope Pius XII: The Roman Catholic Church and the Division of Europe, 1943-1950.* Montreal, Canada: McGill-Queen's University Press.

Kevles, Daniel. 1985. *In the Name of Eugenics: Genetics and the Uses of Human Heredity.* New York: Knopf.

Keynes, John Maynard. 1920. *The Economic Consequences of the Peace.* New York: Harcourt, Brace and Howe.

King, Desmond. 2000. *Making Americans: Immigration, Race, and the Origins of the Diverse Democracy.* Cambridge, MA: Harvard University Press.

Kintz, Linda. 1997. *Between Jesus and the Market: The Emotions that Matter in Right-Wing America.* Durham, NC: Duke University Press.

Kintz, Linda, and Julia Lesage. eds. 1998. *Media, Culture, and the Religious Right.* Minneapolis: University of Minnesota Press.

Klatch, Rebecca. 1987. *Women of the New Right.* Philadelphia: Temple University Press

Klatch, Rebecca. 1999. *A Generation Divided: The New Left, the New Right and the 1960s.* Berkeley, CA: University of California Press.

Kornweibel, Theodore, Jr. 1998. *Seeing Red: Federal Campaigns Against Black Militancy, 1919-1925.* Bloomington: Indiana University Press.

Kovler, Peter, ed. 1992. *Democrats and the American Idea: A Bicentennial Appraisal.* Washington D.C.: Center for National Policy.

Krehely, Jeff, Meaghan House, and Emily Kernan. 2004. *Axis of Ideology: Conservative Foundations and Public Policy.* Washington, DC: National Committee for Responsive Philanthropy.

Krooss, Herman E. 1970. *Executive Opinion: What Business Leaders Said and Thought on Economic Issues, 1920s-1960s.* Garden City, N.Y.: Doubleday.

Kruse, Kevin, and Thomas Sugrue, eds. 2006. *The New Suburban History.* Chicago: University of Chicago Press.

Kuo, David. 2006. *Tempting Faith: An Inside Story of Political Seduction.* New York: Free Press.

Kyvig, David. 1979. *Repealing National Prohibition.* Chicago: University of Chicago Press.

Laham, Nicholas. 1998. *The Reagan Presidency and the Politics of Race: In Pursuit of Colorblind Justice and Limited Government.* Westport, CT: Praeger.

Lakoff, George. 2002. *Moral Politics: How Liberals and Conservatives Think.* Chicago: University of Chicago Press

Larson, Edward J. 1997. *Summer for the Gods: The Scopes Trial and America's Continuing Debate Over Science and Religion.* New York: Basic Books.

Lassiter, Matthew D. 2006. *The Silent Majority: Suburban Politics in the Sunbelt South.* Princeton, NJ: Princeton University Press.

Lay, Shawn. 1995. *Hooded Knights on the Niagara: The Ku Klux Klan in Buffalo, New York.* New York: New York University Press.

Leak, Jeffrey B., ed. 2001. *Rac[e]ing to the Right: Selected Essays of George S. Schuyler.* Knoxville: University of Tennessee Press.

Lee, R. Alton. 1990. *Eisenhower and Landrum-Griffin: A Study in Labor-Management Politics.* Lexington: University of Kentucky Press.

LeTourneau, R. G. 1960. *Mover of Men and Mountains.* Englewood Cliffs, NJ: Prentice-Hall.

Leuchtenburg, William E. 1995. *The Supreme Court Reborn: The Constitutional Revolution in the Age of Roosevelt.* New York: Oxford University Press.

Lichtenstein, Nelson. ed. 2006. *American Capitalism: Social Thought and Political Economy in the Twentieth Century.* Philadelphia: University of Pennsylvania Press.

Lichtman, Allan J. 2000. *Prejudice and the Old Politics: The Presidential Election of 1928.* Lanham, MD: Lexington.

Lichtman, Allan J. 2008. *The Keys to the White House: 2008 Edition.* Lanham, MD: Rowman and Littlefield.

Lieberman, Robert C. 1998. *Shifting the Color Line: Race and the American Welfare State.* Cambridge, MA: Harvard University Press.

Liebman, Marvin. 1992. *Coming Out Conservative: An Autobiography.* San Francisco: Chronicle.

Longley, Kyle, et al. 2006. *Deconstructing Reagan: Conservative Mythology and America's Fortieth President.* Armonk, NY: M. E. Sharpe.

Lora, Ronald, and William Henry Longton. eds. 1999. *The Conservative Press in Twentieth-Century America.* Westport, CT: Greenwood.

Lord, Daniel A. 1956. *Played by Ear: The Autobiography of Daniel A. Lord.* Chicago: Loyola University Press.

Lowitt, Richard, ed. 1967. *The Truman-MacArthur Controversy.* Chicago: Rand McNally.

Lundén, Rolf. 1988. *Business and Religion in the American 1920s.* Westport, CT: Greenwood.

MacDonnell, Francis. 1995. *Insidious Foes: The Axis Fifth Column and the American Home Front.* New York: Oxford University Press.

MacLean, Nancy. 1994. *Behind the Mask of Chivalry: The Making of the Second Ku Klux Klan.* New York: Oxford University Press.

Mann, Jim. 2004. *The Rise of the Vulcans: The History of Bush's War Cabinet.* New York: Viking.

Marlin, George J. 2002. *Fighting the Good Fight: A History of the New York Conservative Party.* South Bend, IN: St. Augustine's Press.

Marsden, George M. 2006. *Fundamentalism and American Culture.* New York: Oxford University Press.

Martin, Cathie Jo. 2000. *Stuck in Neutral: Business and the Politics of Human Capital Investment.* Princeton, NJ: Princeton University Press.

Martin, Robert F. 2002. *Hero of the Heartland: Billy Sunday and the Transformation of American Society.* Bloomington: Indiana University Press.

Martin, William. 1996. *With God on Our Side: The Rise of the Religious Right in America.* New York: Broadway.

Marty, Martin E., and R. Scott Appleby, eds., 1991-1993. *The Fundamentalism Project,* vols. 1-5. Chicago: University of Chicago Press.

Mason, Robert. 2004. *Richard Nixon and the Quest for a New Majority.* Chapel Hill: University of North Carolina Press.

McDonald, W. Wesley. 2004. *Russell Kirk and the Age of Ideology.* Columbia: University of Missouri Press.

McGirr, Lisa. 2001. *Suburban Warriors: The Origins of the New American Right.* Princeton, NJ: Princeton University Press.

McGuinn, Patrick J. 2006. *No Child Left Behind and the Transformation of Federal Education Policy, 1965-2005.* Lawrence: University of Kansas Press.

McKean, David. 2004. *Tommy the Cork: Washington's Ultimate Insider from Roosevelt to Reagan.* South Royalton, VT: Steerforth.

McKenna, Marian C. 2002. *Franklin Roosevelt and the Great Constitutional War: The Court-Packing Crisis of 1937.* New York. Fordham University Press.

McMillen, Neil R. 1971. *The Citizens' Council: Organized Resistance to the Second Reconstruction, 1954-1964.* Urbana: University of Illinois Press.

McQuaid, Kim. 1994. *Uneasy Partners: Big Business in American Politics, 1945-1990.* Baltimore: Johns Hopkins University Press.

McQuaid, Kim, and Edward Berkowitz. 1988. *Creating the Welfare State: The Political Economy of Twentieth-Century Reform,* 2nd edition. New York: Praeger.

McSweeney, Dean, and John E. Owens, eds. 1998. *The Republican Takeover of Congress.* New York: St. Martin's.

Mettler, Suzanne. 1998. *Dividing Citizens: Gender and Federalism in New Deal Public Policy.* Ithaca, NY: Cornell University Press.

Micklethwait, John, and Adrian Woodridge. 2004. *The Right Nation: Conservative Power in America.* New York, Penguin Press.

Mintz, Frank P. 1985. *The Liberty Lobby and the American Right: Race, Conspiracy, and Culture.* Westport, CT: Greenwood.

Mitchell, Greg. 1998. *Tricky Dick and the Pink Lady: Richard Nixon vs. Helen Gahagan Douglas—Sexual Politics and the Red Scare, 1950.* New York: Random House.

Mizruchi, Mark S. 1992. *The Structure of Corporate Political Action: Interfirm Relations and Their Consequences.* Cambridge, MA: Harvard University Press.

Moore, Leonard Moore. 1991. *Citizen Klansmen: The Ku Klux Klan in Indiana, 1921-1928.* Chapel Hill: University of North Carolina Press.

Moreau, Joseph. 2003. *Schoolbook Nation: Conflicts over American History Textbooks from the Civil War to the Present.* Ann Arbor: University of Michigan Press.

Morello, John A. 2001. *Selling the President, 1920: Albert D. Lasker, Advertising, and the Election of Warren G. Harding.* Westport, CT: Praeger.

Morgan, Ted. 2003. *Reds: McCarthyism in Twentieth-Century America.* New York: Random House.

Moser, John E. 2005. *Right Turn: John T. Flynn and the Transformation of American Liberalism.* New York: New York University Press.

Murdock, Catherine Gilbert. 1998. *Domesticating Drink: Women, Men, and Alcohol in America, 1870-1940.* Baltimore: Johns Hopkins University Press

Murphy, Paul V. 2001. *The Rebuke of History: The Southern Agrarians and American Conservative Thought.* Chapel Hill: University of North Carolina Press.

Murray, Charles. 1984. *Losing Ground: American Social Policy, 1950-1980.* New York: Basic.

Murray, Robert K. 1969. *Harding Era: Warren G. Harding and His Administration.* Minneapolis: University of Minnesota Press.

Musto, David F. 1973. *The American Disease: Origins of Narcotic Control.* New Haven, CT: Yale University Press.

Nash, George H. 2006. *The Conservative Intellectual Movement in America, Since 1945.* 30th-anniversary edition. Wilmington, DL: ISI.

Newton, Michael. 2001. *The Invisible Empire: The Ku Klux Klan in Florida*. Gainesville: University Press of Florida.

Nielsen, Kim E. 2001. *Un-American Womanhood: Anti-Radicalism, Antifeminism, and the First Red Scare*. Columbus: Ohio State University Press.

Nisbet, Robert A. 1953. *The Quest for Community: A Study in the Ethics of Order and Freedom*. New York: Oxford University Press.

Noggle, Burl. 1962. *Teapot Dome: Oil and Politics in the 1920s*. Baton Rouge: Louisiana State University Press. 1962.

Noll, Mark A. 2001. *American Evangelical Christianity: An Introduction*. Malden, MA: Blackwell.

Numbers, Ronald L. 1992. *The Creationists: The Evolution of Scientific Creationism*. New York: Knopf.

O'Brien, Ruth. 1998. *Workers' Paradox: The Republican Origins of New Deal Labor Policy, 1886-1935*. Chapel Hill: University of North Carolina Press.

Olasky, Marvin. 1992. *The Tragedy of American Compassion*. Washington, D.C.: Regnery.

Olasky, Marvin. 2000. *Compassionate Conservatism: What It Is, What It Does, and How It Can Transform America*. New York: Free Press.

O'Leary, Cecilia. 1999. *To Die For: The Paradox of American Patriotism*. Princeton, NJ: Princeton University Press.

Olmstead, Kathryn. 1996. *Challenging the Secret Government: The Post-Watergate Investigation of the CIA and FBI*. Chapel Hill: University of North Carolina Press.

Opitz, Edmund A. 1956. *Religion and the Social Problem*. Philadelphia: Intercollegiate Society of Individualists.

O'Reilly, Kenneth. 1983. *Hoover and the Un-Americans: The FBI, HUAC, and the Red Menace*. Philadelphia: Temple University Press.

O'Sullivan, John. 2006. *The President, the Pope, and the Prime Minister: Three Who Changed the World*. Washington, D.C.: Regnery

Overstreet. Harry. 1964. *The Strange Tactics of Extremism*. New York: Norton.

Parker, Alison M. 1997. *Purifying America: Women, Cultural Reform, and Pro-Censorship Activism, 1873-1933*. Urbana: University of Illinois Press, 1997.

Patterson, James T. 1967. *Congressional Conservatism and the New Deal*. Lexington: University of Kentucky Press.

Patterson, James T. 1972. *Mr. Republican: A Biography of Robert A. Taft*. Boston: Houghton Mifflin.

Pegram, Thomas R. 1998. *Battling Demon Rum: The Struggle for a Dry America, 1800-1933*. Chicago: Ivan R. Dee.

Pencak, William. 1989. *For God and Country: The American Legion, 1919-1941*. Boston: Northeastern University Press.

Perlstein, Rick. 2001. *Before the Storm: Barry Goldwater and the Unmaking of the American Consensus*. New York: Hill and Wang.

Peters, Charles. 2005. *Five Days in Philadelphia: The Amazing "We Want Willkie" Convention and How It Freed FDR to Save the Western World*. Washington, D.C.: Public Affairs.

Phillips, Kevin P. 1969. *The Emerging Republican Majority*. New Rochelle, NY: Arlington House.

Pierard, Richard V., and Robert Dean Linder. 1988. *Civil Religion and the Presidency.* Grand Rapids, MI: Academie Books.

Pierson, Paul, and Theda Skocpol. 2007. *The Transformation of American Politics: Activist Government and the Rise of Conservatism.* Princeton, NJ: Princeton University Press.

Polenberg, Richard. 1966. *Reorganizing Roosevelt's Government: The Controversy Over Executive Reorganization.* Cambridge, MA: Harvard University Press.

Pollard, A. F. 1925. *Factors in American History.* New York: Macmillan.

Poole, Keith T., and Howard Rosenthal. 1997. *Congress: A Political-Economic History of Congressional Roll Call Voting.* New York: Oxford University Press.

Powers, Richard Gid. 1995. *Not Without Honor: The History of American Anticommunism.* New York: Free Press.

Qing, Simei. 2007. *From Allies to Enemies: Visions of Modernity, Identity, and U.S.-China Diplomacy, 1945-1960.* Cambridge, MA: Harvard University Press.

Quadango, Jill. 2005. *One Nation Uninsured: Why the U. S. Has No National Health Insurance.* New York: Oxford University Press.

Rae, Nicol C. 1989. *The Decline and Fall of the Liberal Republicans from 1952 to the Present.* New York: Oxford University Press.

Raymond, Emilie. 2006. *From My Cold, Dead Hands: Charlton Heston and American Politics.* Lexington: University of Kentucky Press.

Reagan, Patrick D. 1999. *Designing a New America: The Origins of New Deal Planning, 1890-1943.* Amherst: University of Massachusetts Press.

Reeves, Richard. 2001. *President Nixon: Alone in the White House.* New York: Simon and Schuster.

Reichard, Gary W. 1975. *The Reaffirmation of Republicanism: Eisenhower and the Eighty-Third Congress.* Knoxville: University of Tennessee Press.

Reilly, Philip R. 1991. *The Surgical Solution: A History of Involuntary Sterilization in the United States.* Baltimore: Johns Hopkins University Press.

Reinhard, David W. 1983. *The Republican Right Since 1945.* Lexington: University of Kentucky Press.

Reuther, Victor G. 1976. *The Brothers Reuther and the Story of the UAW.* Boston: Houghton Mifflin.

Ribuffo, Leo P. 1983. *The Old Christian Right: The Protestant Far Right from the Great Depression to the Cold War.* Philadelphia: Temple University Press.

Rich, Andrew. 2004. *Think Tanks, Public Policy, and the Politics of Expertise.* New York: Cambridge University Press.

Rieder, Jonathan. 1985. *Canarsie: The Jews and Italians of Brooklyn Against Liberalism.* Cambridge, MA: Harvard University Press.

Robertson, Pat. 1993. *The Turning Tide: The Fall of Liberalism and the Rise of Common Sense.* Dallas: Word.

Roelofs, Joan. 2003. *Foundations and Public Policy: The Mask of Pluralism.* Albany: State University of New York Press.

Rothbard, Murray. 1973. *For a New Liberty: The Libertarian Manifesto.* New York: MacMillan.

Rymph, Catherine E. 2006. *Republican Women: Feminism and Conservatism from Suffrage Through the Rise of the New Right*. Chapel Hill: University of North Carolina Press.

Saloma III, John S. 1984. *Ominous Politics: The New Conservative Labyrinth*. New York: Hill and Wang.

Saletan, William. 2003. *Bearing Right: How Conservatives Won the Abortion War*. Berkeley: University of California Press.

Sanders, Jerry. 1983. *Peddlers of Crisis: The Committee on the Present Danger and the Politics of Containment*. Boston: South End.

Saunder, Frances Stonor. 1999. *The Cultural Cold War: The CIA and the World of Arts and Letters*. New York: New Press.

Savage, Sean J. 1991. *Roosevelt the Party Leader, 1932-1945*. Lexington: University of Kentucky Press.

Scammon, Richard M., and Ben J. Wattenberg. 1970. *The Real Majority*. New York: Coward-McCann.

Schaeffer, Francis A., and Lane T. Dennis. 1982. *The Complete Works of Francis A. Schaeffer: A Christian World View*. 5 vols. Westchester, IL: Crossway.

Schlafly, Phyllis. 1964. *A Choice Not an Echo*. Alton, IL: Pere Marquette.

Schneider, Gregory L. 1999. *Cadres for Conservatism: Young Americans for Freedom and the Rise of the Contemporary Right*. New York: New York University Press.

Schneider, Mark Robert. 2002. *We Return Fighting: The Civil Rights Movement in the Jazz Age*. Boston: Northeastern University Press.

Schoenwald, Jonathan M. 2001. *A Time for Choosing: The Rise of Modern American Conservatism*. New York: Oxford University Press.

Schrecker, Ellen. 1998. *Many Are the Crimes: McCarthyism in America*. Boston: Little, Brown.

Schweiker, Peter F. 2003. *Reagan's War: The Epic Story of His Forty-Year Struggle and Final Triumph Over Communism*. New York: Doubleday.

Scotchie, Joseph. ed. 1999. *The Paleoconservatives: New Voices of the Old Right*. New Brunswick, NJ: Transaction Publishers.

Seib, Philip M. 1993. *Rush Hour: Talk Radio, Politics, and the Rise of Rush Limbaugh*. Fort Worth, TX: Summit.

Sernett, Milton C. 1997. *Bound for the Promised Land: African American Religion and the Great Migration*. Durham, NC: Duke University Press.

Sethi, S. Prakash. 1977. *Advocacy Advertising and Large Corporations*. Lexington, MA: Lexington.

Shafer, Byron E., and Richard Johnston. 2006. *The End of Southern Exceptionalism: Class, Race, and Partisan Change in the Postwar South*. Cambridge, MA: Harvard University Press.

Simon, William E. 1978. *A Time for Truth*. New York: Reader's Digest.

Sklar, Holly. ed. 1980. *Trilateralism: The Trilateral Commission and Elite Planning for World Management*. Boston: South End.

Skocpol, Theda. 1996. *Boomerang: Clinton's Health Security Effort and the Turn Against Government*. New York: Norton.

Smant, Kevin J. 2002. *Principles and Heresies: Frank Meyer and the Shaping of the American Conservative Movement.* Wilmington, DE: ISI.

Smidt, Corwin E. ed. 2004. *Pulpit and Politics: Clergy in American Politics at the Advent of the Millennium.* Waco, TX: Baylor University Press.

Smith, Daniel A. 1998. *Tax Crusades and the Politics of Direct Democracy.* New York: Routledge.

Smith, James Allen. 1991. *The Idea Brokers: Think Tanks and the Rise of the New Policy Elite.* New York: Free Press.

Smith, Mark A. 2007. *Right Talk: How Conservatives Transformed the Great Society Into the Economic Society.* Princeton, NJ: Princeton University Press.

Smoot, Dan. 1993. *People Along the Way: The Autobiography of Dan Smoot.* Tyler, TX: Tyler Press.

Snowball, David. 1991. *Continuity and Change in the Rhetoric of the Moral Majority.* New York: Praeger.

Standaert, Michael. 2006. *Skipping Towards Armageddon: The Politics and Propaganda of the Left Behind Novels and the LaHaye Empire.* Brooklyn, NY: Soft Skull Press.

Stebenne, David L. 2006. *Modern Republican: Arthur Larson and the Eisenhower Years.* Bloomington: Indiana University Press.

Steinberg, Peter L. 1984. *The Great "Red Menace": United States Prosecution of American Communists, 1947-1952.* Westport, CT: Greenwood.

Steinfels, Peter. 1979. *The Neoconservatives: The Men Who Are Changing America's Politics.* New York: Simon and Schuster.

Stock, Catherine McNicol. 1996. *Rural Radicals: Righteous Rage in the American Grain.* Ithaca, NY: Cornell University Press.

Stoll, David. 1982. *Fishers of Men or Founders of Empire? The Wycliff Bible Translators in Latin America.* Cambridge, MA: Cultural Survival.

Strauss, Leo. 1959. *What Is Political Philosophy? And Other Studies.* Glencoe, IL: Free Press.

Stuhler, Barbara, and Robert H. Walker. 2000. *For the Public Record: A Documentary History of the League of Women Voters.* Westport, CT: Greenwood.

Swenson, Peter. 2002. *Capitalists Against Markets: The Making of Labor Markets and Welfare States in the United States and Sweden.* New York: Oxford University Press.

Swenson, Rinehart John. 1924. *The National Government and Business.* New York: Century Company.

Tananbaum, Duane. 1988. *The Bricker Amendment Controversy: A Test of Eisenhower's Political Leadership.* Ithaca, NY: Cornell University Press.

Tanenhaus, Sam. 1998. *Whittaker Chambers: A Biography.* New York: Modern Library.

Tate, Gayle, and Lewis A. Patterson. eds. 2002. *Dimensions of Black Conservatism in the U.S.: Made in America.* New York: Palgrave.

Tedlow, Richard S. 1979. *Keeping the Corporate Image: Public Relations and Business, 1900-1950.* Greenwich, CT: JAI.

Terborg-Penn, Rosalyn. 1998. *African-American Women in the Struggle for the Vote, 1850-1920.* Bloomington: Indiana University Press.

Terry, Randall. 1990. *Accessory to Murder: The Enemies, Allies, and Accomplices to the Death of Our Culture.* Brentwood, TN: Wolgemuth and Hyatt.

Theoharis, Athan G., and John Stuart Cox. 1988. *The Boss: J. Edgar Hoover and the Great American Inquisition.* Philadelphia: Temple University Press.

Thompson, Michael J. ed. 2007. *Confronting the New Conservatism: The Rise of the Right in America.* New York: New York University Press.

Trilling, Lionel. 1950. *The Liberal Imagination.* New York: Viking.

Trollinger, William. 1990. *God's Empire, William Bell Riley and Midwestern Fundamentalism.* Madison: University of Wisconsin Press.

Tucker, William H. 1994. *The Science and Politics of Racial Research.* Urbana: University of Illinois Press.

Tucker, William H. 2002. *The Funding of Scientific Racism: Wickliffe Draper and the Pioneer Fund.* Urbana: University of Illinois Press.

Twelve Southerners. 1930. *I'll Take My Stand: The South and the Agrarian Tradition.* New York: Harper and Brothers.

Tyroler, II, Charles, ed. 1984. *Alerting America: The Papers of the Committee on the Present Danger.* Washington: Pergamon Brassey's.

Tyrrell, R. Emmett. 1992. *The Conservative Crack-Up.* New York: Simon and Schuster.

Uphoff, Walter H. 1966. *Kohler on Strike.* Boston: Beacon.

Vatter, Harold G., and John F. Walker. 1990. *The Inevitability of Government Growth.* New York: Columbia University Press.

Vaughn, Stephen. 1994. *Ronald Reagan in Hollywood: Movies and Politics.* New York: Cambridge University Press.

Viguerie, Richard A. 2006. *Conservatives Betrayed: How George W. Bush and Other Big Government Republicans Hijacked the Conservative Cause.* Los Angeles: Bonus.

Viguerie, Richard, and David Franke. 2004. *America's Right Turn: How Conservatives Used New and Alternative Media to Take Power.* Chicago: Bonus.

Voegelin, Eric. 1952 *The New Science of Politics: An Introduction.* Chicago: University of Chicago Press.

Vogel, David. 1989. *Fluctuating Fortunes: The Political Power of Business in America.* New York: Basic.

Warren, Frank A. 1966. *Liberals and Communism: The "Red Decade" Revisited.* Bloomington: Indiana University Press.

Watson, Bruce. 2007. *Sacco and Vanzetti: The Men, the Murders, and the Judgment of Mankind* New York: Viking.

Webber, Michael J. 2000. *New Deal Fat Cats: Business, Labor, and Campaign Finance in the 1936 Presidential Election.* New York: Fordham University Press.

Weed, Clyde P. 1994. *The Nemesis of Reform: The Republican Party During the New Deal.* New York: Columbia University Press.

Weinstein, Allen, and Alexander Vassiliev. 1999. *The Haunted Wood: Soviet Espionage in America-The Stalin Era.* New York: Random House.

Wheeler, Marjorie Spruill. 1993. *New Women of the New South: The Leaders of the Woman Suffrage Movement in the Southern States.* New York: Oxford University Press.

Wilcox, Clyde, and Carin Larson. 2006. *Onward Christian Soldiers: The Religious Right in American Politics.* 3rd ed. Boulder, CO: Westview.

Wilhoit, Francis M. 1973. *The Politics of Massive Resistance.* New York: George Braziller.

Winfield, Ann Gibson. 2007. *Eugenics and Education in America: Institutionalized Racism and the Implications of History, Ideology, and Memory.* New York: Lang.

Wolfskill, George. 1962. *The Revolt of the Conservatives: A History of the American Liberty League.* Boston: Houghton Mifflin.

Wollenberg, Charles. 1976. *All Deliberate Speed: Segregation and Exclusion in California Schools, 1855-1975.* Berkeley: University of California Press.

Woods, Jeff. 2004. *Black Struggle, Red Scare: Segregation and Anti-Communism in the South, 1948-1968.* Baton Rouge: Louisiana State University Press.

Ybarra, Michael. 2004. *Washington Gone Crazy: Senator Pat McCarran and the Great American Communist Hunt.* Hanover, NH: Steerforth.

Zelizer, Julian E. 2004. *On Capitol Hill: The Struggle to Reform Congress and its Consequences, 1948-2000.* New York: Cambridge University Press.

Articles

Adler, Jonathan. "A Vast Right-Wing Conspiracy." *Legal Affairs* (May/June 2005), legalaffairs.org.

Aldridge, Daniel W. "A War for the Colored Races: Anti-Interventionism and the African American Intelligentsia, 1939-1941." *Diplomatic History* 28 (June 2004): 321-52.

Allen, Michael Patrick. "Capitalist Response to State Intervention: Theories of the State and Political Finance in the New Deal." *American Sociological Review* 56 (October 1991): 679-89.

Armstrong, David. "Dick Cheney's Song of America." *Harper's Magazine* (October 2002): 76-83.

Bagby, Wesley M. "The 'Smoke Filled Room' and the Nomination of Warren G. Harding." *Mississippi Valley Historical Review* 41 (March 1955): 657-74.

Barclay, Thomas S. "The Publicity Division of the Democratic Party, 1929-30." *American Political Science Review* 25 (February, 1931): 68-72.

Barker, David C., and Kathleen Knight. "Political Talk Radio and Public Opinion." *Public Opinion Quarterly* 64 (Summer 2000): 149-70.

Barker, David C. "Rushed Decisions: Political Talk Radio and Vote Choice, 1994-1996." *Journal of Politics* 61 (May 1999), 527-39.

Blee, Kathleen N. "Women of the 1920s Ku Klux Klan Movement." *Feminist Studies* 17 (Spring 1991): 57-77.

Boyer, Paul S. "Boston Book Censorship in the Twenties." *American Quarterly*, 15 (Spring 1963): 3-24.

Braungart, Richard G. "Family Status, Socialization, and Student Politics: A Multivariate Analysis," *American Journal of Sociology* 77 (July 1971): 108-30.

Brinkley, Alan. "The Problem of American Conservatism," *American Historical Review* 99 (April 1994), 409-29.

Brueggermann, John. "Racial Considerations and Social Policy in the 1930s." *Social Science History* 26 (Spring 2002): 139-77.

Canady, Margot. "Building a Straight State: Sexuality and Social Citizenship under the 1944 G. I. Bill." *Journal of American History* 90 (December 2003): 935-57.

Chen, Anthony S. "'The Hitlerian Rule of Quotas': Racial Conservatism and the Politics of Fair Employment Legislation in New York State, 1941-1945." *Journal of American History* 92 (March 2006): 1238-64.

Clawson, Don., and Alan Neustadtl. "Interlocks, PACS, and Corporate Conservatism." *American Journal of Sociology* 94 (January 1989): 749-73.

Cone, Stacey. "Presuming a Right to Deceive: Radio Free Europe, Radio Liberty, the CIA and the News Media." *Journalism History* 24 (Winter 1998/1999): 148-57.

Couvares, Francis C. "Hollywood, Main Street, and the Church: Trying to Censor the Movies Before the Production Code." *American Quarterly* 44 (1992): 584-616.

Crawford, Gary E. "Science as an Apologetic Tool for Biblical Literalists." *Science, Technology, & Human Values.* 7 (Summer 1982): 88-93.

Davies, Richard O. "'Mr. Republican' Turns 'Socialist.'" *Ohio History* (Summer 1964): 135-43.

Deno, Vivian. "God, Authority, and the Home: Gender, Race, and U. S. Pentecostals, 1906-1926." *Journal of Women's History* 16 (Fall 2004): 83-106.

DeRogatis, Amy. "What Would Jesus Do? Sexuality and Salvation in Protestant Evangelical Sex Manuals, 1950s to the Present." *Church History* 74 (March 2005): 97-137.

Dumenil, Lynn. "'The Insatiable Maw of Bureaucracy': Antistatism and Education Reform in the 1920s." *Journal of American History* 77 (September 1990): 499-524.

Dye, Thomas R., and John W. Pickering. "Governmental and Corporate Elites: Convergence and Differentiation." *Journal of Politics* 36 (November 1974): 900-25.

Ellison, Kirk W., and C. Kirk Hadaway. "Prayer in Public Schools: When Church and State Collide." *Public Opinion Quarterly* 49 (Autumn 1985): 317-29.

Ferguson, Thomas. "From Normalcy to New Deal: Industrial Structure, Party Competition, and American Public Policy in the Great Depression." *Industrial Organization* 38 (Winter 1984): 41-94.

Finer, Lawrence B. "Trends in Premarital Sex in the United States, 1954-2003." *Public Health Reports* 122 (January-February 2007): 73-78.

Flint, Andrew R., and Joy Porter. "Jimmy Carter: The Re-emergence of Faith-Based Politics and the Abortion Rights Issue." *Presidential Studies Quarterly* 35 (March 2005): 28-51.

Fones-Wolf, Elizabeth. "Creating a Favorable Business Climate: Corporations and Radio Broadcasting, 1934 to 1954." *Business History Review* 73 (Summer 1999): 221-55.

Foster, Gaines M. "Conservative Social Christianity, the Law, and Personal Morality: Wilbur F. Crafts in Washington." *Church History* 71 (December 2002): 799-819.

Frederickson, Kari. "Cathrine Curtis and Conservative Isolationist Women, 1939-1941." *Historian* 58 (Summer 1996): 825-39.

Freedman, Robert. "The Religious Right and the Carter Administration." *The Historical Journal* 48 (March 2005): 231-60.

Gifford, Laura Jan. "'Dixie Is No Longer in the Bag,' South Carolina Republicans and the Election of 1960." *Journal of Policy History* 19 (April 2007): 207-33.

Granville, Johanna. "'Caught with Jam on Our Fingers': Radio Free Europe and the Hungarian Revolution of 1956." *Diplomatic History* 29 (November 2005): 811-39.

Green, Elna C. "From Anti-Suffragism to Anti-Communism: The Conservative Career of Ida M. Darden." *Journal of Southern History* 65 (May 1999): 287-316.

Gribble, Richard. "The Other Radio Priest: James Gillis's Opposition to Franklin Delano Roosevelt's Foreign Policy." *Journal of Church and State* 44 (Summer 2002): 501-19.

Griffith, Robert. "Dwight D. Eisenhower and the Corporate Commonwealth." *American Historical Review* 87 (February 1982): 87-122.

Griffith, Robert. "The Selling of America: The Advertising Council and American Politics, 1942-1960." *Business History Review* (Autumn 1983): 388-412.

Grill, Johnpeter Horst, and Robert L. Jenkins. "The Nazis and the American South in the 1930s: A Mirror Image?" *Journal of Southern History* 58 (November 1992): 667-94.

Grossberg, Lawrence. "Rockin' with Reagan, or the Mainstreaming of Postmodernity." *Cultural Critique* 10 (Autumn, 1988): 123-49.

Hacker, Andrew, and Joel D. Auerbach. "Businessmen in Politics." *Law and Contemporary Problems* 27 (Spring 1962): 266-79.

Hacker, Jacob S. "Privatizing Risk Without Privatizing the Welfare State: The Hidden Politics of Social Policy Retrenchment in the United States." *American Political Science Review* 98 (May 2004): 243-60.

Hacker, Jacob S., and Paul Pierson, "Business Power and Social Policy: Employers and the Formation of the American Welfare State." *Politics and Society* 30 (June 2002): 277-301.

Hamilton, Michael S. "Women, Public Ministry, and American Fundamentalism." *Religion and American Culture* 3 (Summer 1993): 171-96.

Havers, Grant. "Leo Strauss, Willmoore Kendall, and the Meaning of Conservatism." *Humanitas* 18 (2005): 5-25.

Hazlett, Thomas W. "The Rationality of U. S. Regulation of the Broadcast Spectrum." *Journal of Law and Economics* 33 (1990): 133-75.

Hillocks Jr., George. "Books and Bombs: Ideological Conflict and the Schools – A Case Study of the Kanawha County Book Protest." *The School Review* 86 (August 1978): 632-54.

Holsti, Ole R. "A Widening Gap Between the U. S. Military and Civilian Society? Some Evidence, 1976-96." *International Security* 23 (Winter 1998): 5-42.

Horowitz, David A. "Senator Borah's Crusade to Save Small Business from the New Deal." *Historian* 55 (Summer 1993): 693-708.

"Industrial Policing and Espionage." *Harvard Law Review* (March 1939): 792-804.

Irish, Marian D. "Political Thought and Political Behavior in the South." *Western Political Quarterly* 13 (June 1960): 406-20.

Irvine, Janice M. "On Lies, Secrets, and Right-Wing Sexual Politics: Reflections on Laud Humphreys' 'Breastplate of Righteousness.'" *International Journal of Sociology and Social Policy* 24 (Iss. 3-5, 2004): 95-111.

Jacobs, David, and Daniel Tope. "The Politics of Resentment in the Post–Civil Rights Era: Minority Threat, Homicide, and Ideological Voting in Congress,." *American Journal of Sociology* 112 (March 2007): 1458-94.

Jacobs, Seth. "'Our System Demands the Supreme Being': The U. S. Religious Revival and the 'Diem Experiment,' 1954-55." *Diplomatic History* 25 (Fall 2001): 589-624.

Jeffries, John W. "A 'Third New Deal'? Liberal Policy and the American State, 1937-1945." *Journal of Policy History* 8 (1996): 387-409

Jelen, Ted G. "Political Christianity: A Contextual Analysis." *American Journal of Political Science* 36 (August 1992): 672-714.

Jenkins, J. Craig., Kevin T. Leicht, and Heather Wendt. "Class Forces, Political Institutions, and State Intervention: Subnational Economic Development Policy in the United States, 1971-1990." *American Journal of Sociology* 111 (January 2006): 1122-80.

Jones, Ethel B. "ERA Voting: Labor Force Attachment, Marriage, and Religion." *Journal of Legal Studies* 12 (January 1983): 157-68.

Jones-Correa, Michael. "The Origins and Diffusion of Racial Restrictive Covenants." *Political Science Quarterly* 115 (Winter 2000/2001): 541-68.

Katznelson, Ira, Jim Geiger, and Daniel Kryder. "Limiting Liberalism: The Southern Veto in Congress, 1933-1950." *Political Science Quarterly* 108 (Summer 1993): 283-306.

Kenneally, James J. "Black Republicans During the New Deal: The Role of Joseph W. Martin, Jr." *Review of Politics* 55 (Winter 1993): 117-34.

King, Desmond S., and Rogers M. Smith, "Racial Orders in American Political Development." *American Political Science Review* 99 (February 2005): 75-92.

Kirkpatrick, Jeane J. "Dictatorships and Double Standards." *Commentary* 68 (November 1979): 34-45.

Kolko, Gabriel. "American Business and Germany, 1930-1941." *Western Political Quarterly* 15 (December 1962): 713-28.

Kotz, Nick. "King Midas of 'The New Right.'" *Atlantic* (November 1978): 52-61.

Kuznick, Peter. "Scientists on the Stump." *Bulletin of the Atomic Scientists* (November/December 2004): 28-35.

Landay, Jerry M. "The Conservative Cabal That's Transforming American Law." *Washington Monthly* (March 2000): 19-23.

Lane, Robert E. "Government Regulation and the Business Mind." *American Sociological Review* 16 (April 1951): 163-73.

Lee, Martha F. "Nesta Webster: The Voice of Conspiracy." *Journal of Women's History* 17 (Fall 2005): 81-105.

Leff, Mark H. "The Politics of Sacrifice on the American Home Front in World War II." *Journal of American History* 78 (March 1991): 1296-1318.

Legro, Jeffrey W. "Whence American Internationalism." *International Organization* 54 (April 2000): 253-89

Lichtman, Allan J. "Critical Election Theory and the Reality of American Presidential Politics, 1916-1940." *American Historical Review* 8 (April 1976): 317-51.

Lichtman, Allan J. "Tommy the Cork: The Secret World of Washington's First Modern Lobbyist." *Washington Monthly* (February 1987): 41- 49.

Lienesch, Michael. "Right-Wing Religion: Christian Conservatism as a Political Movement." *Political Science Quarterly* 97 (Autumn 1982), 403-24.

Limbaugh, Rush. "Voice of America." *Policy Review.* 70 (Fall 1994): 4-10.

Locke, Harvey J. "Changing Attitudes Toward Venereal Disease." *American Sociological Review* 4 (December 1939): 836-43.

Mayor, Erwin S. "Union Security and the Taft-Hartley Act." *Duke Law Journal* 4 (Autumn 1961): 505-24.

McEnaney, Laura. "He-Men and Christian Mothers: The America First Movement and the Gendered Meanings of Patriotism and Isolationism." *Diplomatic History* 18 (Winter 1994): 47-57.

McGarrity, Joseph P., and Daniel Sutter. "A Test of the Structure of PAC Contracts: An Analysis of House Gun Control Votes in the 1980s." *Southern Economic Journal* 67 (July 2000): 41-63.

McVeigh, Rory. "Structural Incentives for Conservative Mobilization: Power Devaluation and the Rise of the Ku Klux Klan 1915-1925." *Social Forces* 77 (June 1999): 1461-96.

Medhurst, Martin J. "Eisenhower and the Crusade for Freedom: the Rhetorical Origins of a Cold War Campaign." *Presidential Studies Quarterly* 27 (Fall 1997): 646-61.

Mettler, Suzanne. "The Creation of the G. I. Bill of Rights of 1944: Melding Social and Participatory Citizenship Ideals." *Journal of Policy History* 17 (October 2005): 345-74.

Moore, John Robert. "Senator Josiah W. Bailey and the 'Conservative Manifesto' of 1937." *Journal of Southern History* 31 (February 1965): 21-39.

Moran, Jeffrey P. "The Scopes Trial and Southern Fundamentalism in Black and White: Race, Region, and Religion." *Journal of Southern History* 70 (February 2004): 95-120.

Murphy, Sharon. "The Advertising of Installment Credit in the 1920s." *Essays in History* 37 (1995).

Newton, Leon. "The Role of Black Neo-Conservatives During President Reagan's Administration." *House Studies Compendium* 6 (Winter 2006).

Ngai, Mae M. "The Architecture of Race in American Immigration Law: A Reexamination of the Immigration Act of 1924." *Journal of American History,* 86 (June 1999): 67-92.

Nutt, Rick. "For Truth and Liberty: Presbyterians and McCarthyism," *Journal of Presbyterian History* 78 (Spring 2000): 51-66.

O'Connor, Karen, and Lee Epstein. "The Rise of Conservative Interest Group Litigation." *Journal of Politics* 45 (May 1983): 479-89.

O'Connor, L. David. "The Cardinal Mindszenty Foundation: American Catholic Anti-Communism and Its Limits." *American Communist History* 5 (June 2006): 37-66.

Parker, Barbara. "Your Schools May be the Battlefield in the Crusade Against 'Improper' Textbooks." *American School Board Journal* CLXVI (June 1979): 21-26.

Parry-Giles, Trevor. "Property Rights, Human Rights, and American Jurisprudence: The Rejection of John J. Parker's Nomination to the Supreme Court." *Southern Communication Journal* 60 (Fall 1994): 57-73.

Polenberg, Richard. "The National Committee to Uphold Constitutional Government, 1937-1941." *Journal of American History* 52 (December 1965): 582-98.

Posner, Eric. "The Political Economy of the Bankruptcy Reform Act of 1978." *Michigan Law Review* 96 (October 1997): 47-126.

Reynolds, Larry. "Tax Reform: Why Business Will Fork Over Another $120 Billion." *Management Review* (January 1987): 10-13.

Ribuffo, Leo P. "Jesus Christ as Business Statesman: Bruce Barton and the Selling of Corporate Capitalism." *American Quarterly* 33 (Summer 1981): 206-31.

Ribuffo, Leo P. "Why Is There so Much Conservatism in the United States and Why do so Few Historian Know Anything About It?" *American Historical Review* 99 (April 1994): 438-49.

Richman, Sheldon. "A Matter of Degree, Not Principle: The Founding of the American Liberty League." *Journal of Libertarian Studies* 6 (Spring 1982): 145-67.

Rosenbloom, David H. "'Whose Bureaucracy Is This Anyway?' Congress' 1946 Answer." *PS: Political Science and Politics* 34 (December 2001): 773-77.

Rudolph, Frederick. "The American Liberty League, 1934-1940." *American Historical Review* 56 (October 1950): 19-33.

Ruotsila, Markku. "Conservative American Protestantism in the League of Nations Controversy." *Church History* 72 (September 2003): 593-616.

Russell, Edmund P. "'Speaking of Annihilation': Mobilizing for War against Human and Insect Enemies, 1914-1945." *Journal of American History* 82 (March 1996): 1505-29.

Sapiro, Virginia. "The Gender Basis of American Social Policy." *Political Science Quarterly* 101 (1986): 221-38.

Smidt, Corwin. "Evangelicals Within Contemporary American Politics: Differentiating Between Fundamentalist and Non-Fundamentalist Evangelicals." *Western Political Quarterly* 41 (September 1988): 601-20.

Smith Carl O, and Stephen B. Sarasohn. "Hate Propaganda in Detroit." *Public Opinion Quarterly* 10 (Spring 1946): 24-52.

Snider, Christy Jo. "Patriots and Pacifists: The Rhetorical Debate about Peace, Patriotism, and Internationalism, 1914–1930." *Rhetoric & Public Affairs 8.1 (2005)*: 59-83.

Sobel, Richard. "Contra Aid Fundamentals: Exploring the Intricacies and the Issues." *Political Science Quarterly* 110 (Summer 1995): 287-306.

Soffer, Jonathan. "The National Association of Manufacturers and the Militarization of American Conservatism." *Business History Review*, 75 (Winter 2001): 775-806.

Stern, Alexandra Minna. "STERILIZED in the Name of Public Health: Race, Immigration, and Reproductive Control in Modern California." *American Journal of Public Health* 95 (July 2005): 1128- 38.

Stewart, Douglas K., and Ted C. Smith. "Celebrity Structure of the Far Right." *The Western Political Quarterly* 17 (June 1964): 349-55.

Stone, Barbara S. "The John Birch Society: A Profile." *Journal of Politics* 36 (February 1974): 184-197.

Strickler, Karyn. "The Do Nothing Strategy: An Exposé of Progressive Politics." *Counterpunch*, 30 June 2003.

Stromberg, Roland N. "American Business and the Approach of War, 1935-1941." *Journal of Economic History* 13 (Winter 1953): 58-78.

Sugrue. Thomas J. "Crabgrass-Roots Politics: Race, Rights, and the Reaction Against Liberalism." *Journal of American History* 82 (September 1995): 551-78.

Theoharis, Athan. "The FBI and the American Legion Contact Program, 1940-1966." *Political Science Quarterly* 100 (Summer 1985): 271-86.

Theoharis, Athan. "FBI Wiretapping: A Case Study of Bureaucratic Autonomy." *Political Science Quarterly* 107 (Spring, 1992): 101-22.

Thomas, Clarence. "No Room at the Inn." *Policy Review* (Fall 1991): 72-78.

Toy Jr., Eckard V. "The National Lay Committee and the National Council of Churches: A Case Study of Protestants in Conflict." American Quarterly 21 (Summer 1969): 190-209.

Toy Jr., Eckard V. "Spiritual Mobilization: The Failure of an Ultraconservative Ideal in the 1950s." *Pacific Northwest Quarterly* 61 (April 1970): 77-86.

Tudda, Christopher J. "'Reenacting the Story of Tantalus,' Eisenhower, Dulles, and the Failed Rhetoric of Liberation." *Journal of Cold War Studies* 7 (Fall 2005): 3-35.

Usher, Douglas. "Strategy, Rules and Participation: Issue Activists in Republican National Conventional Delegations, 1976-1996." *Political Research Quarterly* 53 (December 2000): 887-903.

Wattenberg, Benjamin. "The New Moment: How Ronald Reagan Ratified LBJ's Great Society and Moved on to Other Important Items." *Public Opinion* (December/January 1982): 2-6, 59-60.

Winston, Andrew S. "Science in the Service of the Far Right: Henry E. Garrett, the IAAEE, and the Liberty Lobby." *Journal of Social Issues*, 54 (Spring 1998): 179-210.

Woeste, Victoria Saker. "Insecure Equality: Louis Marshall, Henry Ford, and the Problem of Defamatory Anti-Semitism." *Journal of American History*, 91 (December 2004): 877-905.

Workman, Andrew A. "Manufacturing Power: The Organizational Revival of the National Association of Manufacturers 1941-1945." *Business History Review* 72 (Summer 1998): 279-317.

Dissertations

Bates, David Keith, Jr. "Moving Fundamentalism Toward the Mainstream: John R. Rice and the Reengagement of America's Religious and Political Cultures." Kansas State University, 2006.

Bergler, Thomas E. "Winning America: Christian Youth Groups and the Middle-Class Culture of Crisis, 1930-1965." University of Notre Dame, 2001.

Coker, Joe L. "Liquor in the land of the Lost Cause: Southern White Evangelicals and the Prohibition Movement, 1880-1915," Princeton Theological Seminary, 2005.

Delegard, Kirsten Marie. "Women Patriots: Female Activism and the Politics of American Anti-Radicalism, 1919-1935." Duke University, 1999.

Erickson, Christine Kimberly. "Conservative Women and Patriotic Maternalism: The Beginnings of a Gendered Conservative Tradition in the 1920s and 1930s." University of California, Santa Barbara, 1999.

Flamm, Michael William. "'Law and Order': Street Crime, Civil Disorder, and the Crisis of Liberalism." Columbia University, 1998.

Flynn, Matthew J. "Reconsidering the China Lobby: Senator William F. Knowland and US-China Policy, 1945-1958." Ohio University, 2004.

Gleason, Mildred Diane. "In Defense of God and Country: Elizabeth Dilling, A Link Between the Red Scares." University of Arkansas, 1997.

Holl, Richard E. "The Corporate Liberals and the Roosevelt Administration Preparedness Program, 1939-1941." University of Kentucky, 1996.

Keller, Craig Lee. "The Intellectuals and Eisenhower: Civil Religion, Religious Publicity, and the Search for Moral and Religious Communities." George Washington University, 2002.

Lykins, Daniel Lee. "Total War to Total Diplomacy: The Advertising Council, Domestic Propaganda and Cold War Consensus." University of Kentucky, 1998.

McHenry, Justin J. 2006. "Silent, No More: The 1974 Kanawha County Textbook Controversy and the Rise of Conservatism in America." West Virginia University, 2006.

McNamara, Patrick J. "Edmund A. Walsh, S, J., and Catholic Anticommunism in the United States, 1917-1952," The Catholic University of America, 2003.

Miller-Coles, Christopher. "A Perfect Storm: The Collision of Forbidden Sex and Conservative Politics," Ph.D. Dissertation, Wright Institute, 2004.

Morgan, Francesca Constance. "'Home and Country': Women, Nation, and the Daughters of the American Revolution, 1890-1939." Columbia University, 1998.

O'Connor, David L. "Defenders of the Faith: American Catholic Lay Organizations and Anticommunism, 1917-1975." State University of New York at Stony Brook, 2000.

Paretsky, Nick. "Policy-Planning Organizations and Capitalist Support for Industrial Policy, 1970-1984." University of Missouri-Columbia, 2003.

Phillips-Fein, Kimberly. "Top-down Revolution: Businessmen, Intellectuals and Politicians Against the New Deal." Columbia University, 2005.

Piasecki, Frank Edward. "Norma and Mel Gabler: The Development and Causes of Their Involvement Concerning the Curricular Appropriateness of School Textbook Content (Texas)." North Texas State University, 1982.

Scher, Abby. "Cold War on the Home Front: Middle Class Women's Politics in the 1950's." New School for Social Research, 1995.

Government Documents

U.S. Department of Education, National Center for Education Statistics. *Private Schools Survey, 1989-1990* and *1999-2000*.

U.S. Department of the Interior, Office of Inspector General. *Report of Investigation: Julie MacDonald, Deputy Assistant Secretary, Fish, Wildlife, and Parks*. March 2007.

U.S. Department of Justice, Office of the Inspector General. *A Review of the Federal Bureau of Investigations Use of National Security Letters*. March 2007.

U.S. Department of State, Office of Inspector General. *Audit Report, No. 7PP-008, Special Inquiry Into the Department's Contacts with International Business Communications and Its Principles*. July 1987.

U.S. Department of Treasury, *Report on Foreign Holdings of U. S. Long-Term Securities* (Washington, DC: Government Printing Office, 2002).

U.S. House of Representatives, Committee on Un-American Activities. Investigation of Un-American Propaganda Activities in the U.S. Part 2: Testimony of J. Edgar Hoover. March 26, 1947, 80th Congress, 1st Session.

U.S. House of Representatives, Select Committee to Investigate Covert Arms Transactions with Iran and U. S. Senate, Select Committee On Secret Military Assistance to Iran and the Nicaraguan Opposition. *Report of the Congressional Committees Investigating the Iran-Contra Affair*. 100th Congress, 1st Session. 1987.

U.S. Senate. *Executive Sessions of the Senate Permanent Subcommittee on Investigations of the Committee on Government Operations, Made Public 2003*. Vol. 2. 83thd Congress, 2nd Session. 1954.

U.S. Senate. Hearings Before the Select Committee to Study Governmental Operations With Respect to Intelligence Activities. 94th Congress, 1st Session. Vol. 6. 1975.

U.S. Senate. Select Committee on Secret Military Assistance to Iran and the Nicaraguan Opposition and U. S. House of Representatives, Select Committee to Investigate Covert Arms Transactions with Iran. Joint Hearings: Testimony of Oliver L. North. 100th Congress, 1st Session. 1987.

Manuscript Sources

Abilene, Kansas—Dwight David Eisenhower Presidential Library
     Eisenhower Diaries
     Robert Humphreys Papers
     C. D. Jackson Papers
     Howard Pyle Files
     William Robinson Papers
     Thomas E. Stephens Papers
     Ann Whitman Files
Ann Arbor, Michigan—Gerald R. Ford Presidential Library
     Handwriting File

National Security Council Meetings, Minutes
President Ford Committee Records
Michael Raoul-Duval Files
Ann Arbor, Michigan—Bentley Historical Library, University of Michigan
Henry B. Joy Papers
Carl McIntire Papers
Gerald L.K. Smith Papers
Atlanta, Georgia—Jimmy Carter Presidential Library
Susan Clough Collection
Ray Jenkins Collection
Hamilton Jordan Collection
George Moffett Collection
Name Files
White House Central Files
Austin, Texas—Lyndon Johnson Presidential Library
Cabinet Minutes
Harry McPherson Papers
White House Central Files
Boston, Massachusetts—John F. Kennedy Presidential Library
Walter W. Heller Papers
President's Office Files
Theodore C. Sorenson Papers
White House Central Files
Boston, Massachusetts—Massachusetts Historical Society
Henry Cabot Lodge Papers
Cambridge, Massachusetts—Arthur and Elizabeth Schlesinger Library
Alexander Lincoln Papers
Elizabeth Putnam Papers
Charlottesville, Virginia—Alderman Library, University of Virginia
Carter Glass Papers
James Jackson Kilpatrick Papers
Hugh Scott Papers
Howard W. Smith Papers
Chicago, Illinois—Chicago Historical Society
Clarence E. Manion Papers
Sterling Morton Papers
Clemson, South Carolina—Robert Muldrow Cooper Library, Clemson University
James F. Byrnes Papers
Harry S. Dent Papers
J. Strom Thurmond Papers
College Park, Maryland—National Archives and Records Administration
Business Advisory Council Papers
Nixon Presidential Materials
White House Central Files

College Station, Texas—George Bush Presidential Library
    White House Office of Public Liaison
Columbus, Ohio—Ohio Historical Society
        Ray C. Bliss Papers
        John W. Bricker Papers
        John Vorys Papers
Easton, Massachusetts—Stonehill College Archives
        Joseph Martin Papers
Eugene, Oregon—University of Oregon Library
        Lucille Cardin Crain Papers
        Merwin K. Hart Papers
        Samuel Pettingill Papers
        George W. Robnett Papers
        Willis E. Stone Papers
Hyde Park, New York—Franklin D. Roosevelt Presidential Library
        Ernest Cuneo Papers
        Democratic National Campaign Committee
        Emil Hurja Papers
        President's Official File
        James Rowe Jr. Papers
Independence, Missouri—Harry S. Truman Presidential Library
        Dean G. Acheson Papers
        Clark Clifford Political File
        President's Secretary's Files
        Truman's 1947 Diary Book
Indianapolis, Indiana—American Legion Archives
        American Legion Papers
Lexington, Kentucky—University of Kentucky Library
        Rogers C. B. Morton Papers
        Thruston Morton Papers
        John Sherman Cooper Papers
New Haven, Connecticut— Sterling Library, Yale University
        William F. Buckley, Jr. Papers
        John W. Davis Papers
        Charles D. Hilles Papers
Norman, Oklahoma—Carl Albert Center Archives
        Richard Armey Papers
        Page H. Belcher Papers
        John N. "Happy" Camp Papers
        Mickey Edwards Papers
        J. C. Watts Papers
Palo Alto, California—Hoover Institution Library and Archives
        America First Committee Papers
        James Burnham Papers

John D. Ehrlichman Papers
Free Society Association Papers
B. E. Hutchinson Papers
Walter Judd Papers
Denison Kitchel Papers
Marvin Liebman Papers
Jeb Stuart Magruder Papers
Fred Malek Papers
National Republic Magazine Collection
Radical Right Papers
Henry Regnery Papers
Albert C. Wedemeyer Papers
Pekin, Illinois—Dirksen Congressional Center
Everett M. Dirksen Papers
Robert H. Michel Papers
Princeton, New Jersey—Seeley G. Mudd Manuscript Library, Princeton University
Bernard Baruch Papers
James M. Beck Papers
David Lawrence Papers
H. Alexander Smith Papers
Seattle, Washington—University of Washington Library
Henry M. Jackson Papers
Simi Valley, California—Ronald Reagan Presidential Library
Lee Atwater Files
James A. Baker III Files
Council of Economic Advisers Files
Charlotte DeMoss Files
David Gergen Files
Mari Maseng Files
National Security Council Files
White House Central Files
Faith Ryan Whittlesey Files
Richard S. Williamson Files
Sleepy Hollow, New York—Rockefeller Archive Center
George L. Hinman Papers
Rockefeller Family Papers
Topeka, Kansas—Kansas State Historical Society
Alfred M. Landon Papers
Washington, D.C. —Library of Congress
William E. Baroody Papers
William H. Borah Papers
Edward W. Brooke Papers
Edward Tracey Clark Papers
Bainbridge Colby Papers

Russell Wheeler Davenport Papers
Simeon D. Fess Papers
Henry P. Fletcher Papers
W. Averell Harriman Papers
Philip C. Jessup Papers
William Franklin Knox Papers
Clare Booth Luce Papers
Charles McNary Papers
Ogden L. Mills Papers
George W. Norris Papers
Herbert Philbrick Papers
Amos Pinchot Papers
Donald T. Regan Papers
Edward V. Rickenbacker Papers
Branch Rickey Papers
William A. Rusher Papers
Charles P. Taft Papers
Robert A. Taft Papers
James Wadsworth Papers
Washington, D.C.—Georgetown University Library
Anna M. Brady Papers
Daniel Lord, S. J. Papers
Joseph Wilfred Parsons Papers
Carroll Quigley Papers
West Branch, Iowa—Herbert Hoover Presidential Library
Theodore G. Joslin Papers
Robert H. Lucas Papers
Nathan William MacChesney Papers
James H. MacLafferty Papers
Post-Presidential Subject File
Presidential Subject File
Lewis Strauss Papers
Robert E. Wood Papers
Wheaton, Illinois—Billy Graham Center Archives
L. Nelson Bell Papers
Christianity Today Papers
Fellowship Foundation Papers
Billy Graham Press Conferences
Aimee Semple McPherson Papers
National Association of Evangelicals Papers
Billy Sunday Papers
Herbert John Taylor Papers
Wilmington, Deleware—Hagley Museum and Library
Chamber of Commerce of the United States Papers

Jasper Crane Papers
Du Pont Family Papers
National Association of Manufacturers Papers
J. Howard Pew Papers
Joseph Newton Pew Papers
John Jacob Raskob Papers
Philip D. Reed Papers

Microfilm Manuscript Collections

Calvin Coolidge Papers
Henry Prather Fletcher Correspondence in the Charles Dewey Hilles, James Rockwell
    Sheffield, and Edward M. House Papers
League of Women Voters Papers
Meetings of the Republican National Committee
Karl E. Mundt Papers
Rightwing Collection of the University of Iowa Libraries

Online Documents

International Cold War History Project, Woodrow Wilson International Center for
    Scholars, Washington, D.C.
National Security Archives, George Washington University, Washington, D.C.
Presidential Recordings Program, Miller Center of Public Affairs, University of Vir-
    ginia, Charlottesville, Virginia.
"Women and Social Movements in the United States, 1600–2000," Kathryn Sklar and
    Thomas Dublin, eds., Alexander Street Press.

INDEX